Modern Arabic Literature

Modern Arabic Literature

A Theoretical Framework

Reuven Snir

EDINBURGH
University Press

Edinburgh University Press is one of the leading university presses in the UK. We publish academic books and journals in our selected subject areas across the humanities and social sciences, combining cutting-edge scholarship with high editorial and production values to produce academic works of lasting importance. For more information visit our website: edinburghuniversitypress.com

Edinburgh University Press Ltd
The Tun – Holyrood Road
12 (2f) Jackson's Entry
Edinburgh EH8 8PJ

Typeset in 10.5/13 pt Adobe Text by
Servis Filmsetting Ltd, Stockport, Cheshire

A CIP record for this book is available from the British Library

ISBN 978 1 4744 2051 8 (hardback)
ISBN 978 1 4744 2052 5 (webready PDF)
ISBN 978 1 4744 2053 2 (epub)

For Mariana

Contents

	Preface	ix
	Notes on Transliteration	xii
	Introduction	**1**
1.	**The Modern Arabic Literary System**	**8**
	The Scope of the Research Subject	9
	Popular Literature and Legitimation	14
	Assumptions behind the Operative Model	19
2.	**Literary Dynamics in Synchronic Cross-section**	**35**
	Canonical Literature	35
	Texts for Adults	35
	Texts for Children	55
	Translated Texts	62
	Non-canonical Literature	65
	Texts for Adults	67
	Texts for Children	84
	Translated Texts	87
	Internal and External Interrelationships	89
3.	**Outlines of Diachronic Intersystemic Development**	**100**
	Literature / Religion	116
	Literature / Territory	150
	Literature / Language	155
	Literature / State Nationalism	160
4.	**Literary Dynamics in Generic and Diachronic Cross-section**	**175**
	Periodization	176

Classical vis-à-vis Modern Literature 182
The Development of the Genres 193
  Poetry 194
  Fiction 206
  Theater 218
Generic Interrelationships 222

Conclusion **228**

References 279
Index 369

Preface

No scholar or historian of literature can systematically study literary phenomena without relating them, implicitly or explicitly, to some framework of facts or ideas. The very choice of a framework could, however, have a determining influence upon the kinds of results that can be achieved. The present study outlines a theoretical dynamic operative framework, in which the historical development of modern Arabic literary texts can be studied, and, at the same time, it offers flexible, transparent, and (as much as possible) unbiased tools to understand their relevant contexts in the literary system. This system is autonomous in that it forms a network of the relations that obtain between texts (including potential texts) and ensures that they "belong to" and "constitute" a single, unified whole. I hope that the framework offered here for the systematic study of modern Arabic literature will enhance our understanding of this literature, throw light on areas of literary production that traditionally have been neglected, and stimulate others to take up the fascinating challenge of mapping them out and exploring them.

During the periods in which the data for this study was being collected and the pages of this study were being written, the scholarship on Arabic literature witnessed two major unprecedented developments. The first development was the significant increase in scholarly publications in Arabic and other languages. *Index Islamicus*, which contains material published in European languages on all matters related to Islam and the Muslim World, clearly reflects this development: When I began writing this preface, there were only 4,503 publications on Arabic literature listed as having been published before 1985; now, that is, at the time of completion of the entire manuscript of this book, the number is 20,279.[1]

The second development was the rapid growth and proliferation of sophisticated forms of media, particularly Internet-related technologies:

[1] Checked on 1 September 2016.

blogging, techno-writing, and interactive literature. New possibilities for literary voices have been opened for Arab writers to imagine new realities, and these possibilities provided additional forums and stages for literary and critical texts to be presented and discussed side by side with the traditional ones.[2] Revolutionizing virtually every aspect of how our lives function now, including our literary lives, the Internet has catapulted us into an immediate, collaborative, and interconnected existence that is characterized, as Cathy Davidson suggests, by the sudden breakdown of barriers such as those between private and public, work and play, domestic and foreign, and office and home: "With the Internet, we have seen dramatic rearrangements in the most basic aspects of how we communicate, interact, gather knowledge of the world, develop and recognize our social networks and our communities, do business and exchange goods, understand what is true, and know what counts and is worthy of attention."[3]

Translations from Arabic in this book are my own unless otherwise indicated. Original texts in Arabic and other foreign languages are only cited when they are necessary for the presentation of an argument. Original texts in Arabic are generally translated when they appear in the main text and the footnotes with the exception of some cases where they are only quoted for their linguistic features.

A project such as this is not done in isolation, and it is my pleasure to thank the many friends and colleagues who have helped me throughout its research and production stages. First and foremost, I would like to thank both the undergraduate and graduate students (especially those who participated in my seminars) at the Department of Arabic Language and Literature at the University of Haifa. During the last three decades, they have taken an active interest in and realized the importance of developing a viable historical model in the field of Arabic literature, and our discussions have helped me crystallize and polish my arguments, some of which have already appeared

[2] See Kirchner 2001, pp. 137–58; Anderson 2005, pp. 252–63; al-Buraykī 2008; Abdel-Messih 2009, pp. 515–23; El-Ariss 2010, pp. 533–48; El Sadda 2010, pp. 312–32; Raven 2010, pp. 201–17; Sabra 2010, pp. 32–5; Daoudi 2011, pp. 146–63; Armbrust 2012, pp. 155–74; El-Ariss 2012, pp. 510–31; El Sadda 2012; Pepe 2012, pp. 547–62; Dūs and Davies 2013, pp. 365–9; El-Ariss 2013, pp. 145–71; and Pepe 2015, pp. 73–91. On the role of Internet technologies in the development of Arab liberal discourse, see Hatina 2011, pp. 8–9. On interactive Arabic literature, see al-Buraykī 2008, pp. 123–56. One of the literary expressions of the new horizons opened up by Internet technologies is the cultural magazine *Bi-Dūn/Bidoun* (*Without*) (<http://bidoun.org/> [last accessed 7 October 2016]). Lisa Farjam, the magazine's founding editor, had this to say about its creation: "When I came up with the name, I was struggling. I felt like I was without a place. I belong to many places and none. That was when I found that word. It meant a lot to me" (*New York Times*, 26 December 2015).

[3] Davidson 2011, p. 11.

in print elsewhere, generally in more tentative forms. Next, I would like to thank the editors and publishers of my previous books and articles for granting me permission to reproduce these arguments here, and Professor Roger Allen for reading the first draft of the completed manuscript and for providing me with numerous suggestions and references to improve the study. Finally, a special word of thanks and appreciation is due to the editor Michael Helfield for his excellent work on the manuscript and for his significant contribution to the final shaping of the book. My interest in the systematic study of Arabic literature began in the early 1980s, and the research on which the present book is based was conducted during the course of more than thirty years. In the summer of 1984 I made my first study trip to Egypt, where I enjoyed the resources and facilities of the Israeli Academic Center in Cairo. My research was supported as well by grants and fellowships which I had obtained from the Israel Science Foundation (1992–5); the Memorial Foundation for Jewish Culture (1993 and 1998); the Oxford Centre for Hebrew and Jewish Studies (2000 and 2008); the Seminar für Sprachen und Kulturen des Vorderen Orients and Hochschule für Jüdische Studien, Heidelberg University (2002), Wissenschaftskolleg zu Berlin—Institute for Advanced Study; Seminar für Semitistik und Arabistik (2004–5), Freie Universität Berlin (2005); the Radcliffe Institute for Advanced Study, Harvard University (2009–10); and the Simon Dubnow Institute for Jewish History and Culture at Leipzig University (2015).

Notes on Transliteration

أ؛ ؤ؛ ئ	'i; 'u; 'a	ز	z		ق	q
ب	b	س	s		ك	k
ت	t	ش	sh		ل	l
ث	th	ص	ṣ		م	m
ج	j	ض	ḍ		هـ	h
ح	ḥ	ط	ṭ		و	w
خ	kh	ظ	ẓ		و (long)	ū
د	d	ع	'		ي	y
ذ	dh	غ	gh		ي (long)	ī
ر	r	ف	f		ِ ; َ ; ُ (short)	i; a; u

1. The definite article *al* is used before solar and lunar letters. The *waṣla* over silent *alif* is systematically ignored.
2. ' (أ) is not indicated when it is at the beginning of a word or after the definite article *al.*
3. ة at the end of words and names is not transliterated (i.e. *ḥikāya* for حكاية). When ة occurs in the first word of an *iḍāfa* (construction), it is transcribed as *t.*
4. ا or آ or ى are transcribed as *ā.*
5. A *shadda* (ّ) is represented by doubling the relevant letter.
6. Final *nisba* is transcribed as *ī* (masculine, i.e. *'Arabī* for عربي) and *iyya* (feminine, i.e. *'Arabiyya* for عربية).
7. Anglicized spellings of commonly used names and locations have been retained, and foreign names in transliterated passages generally appear in their English form. In English quotations, transliterated Arabic words appear as is, even if they differ from our preferred system.
8. Ellipses in English quotations are indicated by [...], and ellipses in Arabic quotations are indicated by (...).

Introduction

Without fear of exaggeration, one could say that the changes that Arabic literature has seen since the mid-nineteenth century are as momentous or even radical as the ways in which Arabic literature had been transformed following the rise of Islam in the seventh century. Since the mid-twentieth century, the writing and publishing of contemporary Arabic literature has taken flight all over the world, as has the concomitant increase in literary consumption by Arab and foreign reading publics. Modern Arabic literature has become such a huge field; the number of Arabic literary texts produced in recent decades is so enormous that they cannot be covered in any meaningful way by traditional scholarly studies. In fact, dealing with this output in its entirety is now a task well beyond the combined efforts of all scholars working in the field, let alone the efforts of only one of them. Also, there is our duty as students of this literature to constantly revise the way we approach our material, which has not only grown quantitatively, but qualitatively as well. Referring to the need to rewrite the literary history of the Arabic novel, Roger Allen, the most experienced contemporary scholar in the literary history of modern Arabic literature, proclaims—in the words of Oscar Wilde—that "the one duty that we owe to history is to rewrite it" and then adds the following:

> I wish to challenge many of the premises and organizing principles that have governed research and publication that I have done previously, not so much in order to suggest that they were not relevant or even useful for their time, but rather that the changing nature of Arabic fiction—a primary facet of its very essence, of course—requires a continuingly [sic] changing perspective in order to reflect both the creativity of Arab littérateurs and the kind of studies now being devoted to it.[1]

1 Allen 2007, p. 248. On the need to challenge premises and organizing principles of Arabic literary history, see also Sacks 2015 and the review of the book by Terri DeYoung in *Journal of Arabic Literature* 47.1–2 (2016), pp. 222–6.

Given the recent expansion of Arabic literary texts and the need, as Allen argues, to change our perspective on their study, I would like to propose a shift in approach, that is, a new theoretical framework or model that would make possible the comprehensive study of the diverse and multifarious texts that make up modern Arabic literature. In my preliminary studies,[2] I attempted to show that the highly prolific and diverse production of contemporary literary texts makes scholarly research on modern Arabic literature, as a historical phenomenon, almost impossible without a proper, comprehensive theoretical framework in which the research can be done. Based on further study and some changes to my theoretical hypothesis, the present study is an attempt to increase the scope of my previous conceptions on the matter and further develop my preliminary model. Its main outlines are based on the theoretical achievements of historical poetics, in particular those of Russian Formalism and its theoretical legacy.[3]

It was Formalist historical poetics that first made scholars pay attention to so-called "trivial" and "popular" literature (*culture populaire*, *Volkskultur*) and subject it to literary analysis.[4] Accordingly, I am basing my model on the assumption that all Arabic literary texts (including foreign texts translated into Arabic), whether written for adults or children, are to be seen as forming one dynamic, autonomous literary system. This system is autonomous in that it forms a network of the relations that obtain between texts (including potential texts) and ensures that they "belong to" and "constitute" a single, unified whole. Sociocultural distinctions of text production in this system are conceptualized, following Victor Shklovsky, in terms of literary stratification: canonized (canonical) versus non-canonized (non-canonical) texts. By canonized texts, I mean literary works that have been accepted by dominant circles within Arab culture that have become part of a community's historical heritage and that have entered into its collective memory. Conversely, non-canonized texts are those literary works that have been rejected by the same circles as illegitimate and that often in the long run are forgotten by the community. This means that canonicity is not seen as an inherent feature of textual activities on any level and that the canonized/non-canonized classification is by no means intended to isolate original can-

2 Especially Snir 1994, pp. 61–85; Snir 1994c, pp. 49–80; Snir 1998, pp. 87–121; and Snir 2001.

3 On Russian formalism, see Erlich 1969; Steiner 1984; and Sebeok 1986, II, pp. 841–5. A major theoretical basis for the present book can be found in the work of Itamar Even-Zohar, especially Even-Zohar 1990 and his various contributions in Sebeok 1986. In this regard, see also Guillen 2015.

4 For more on the terms "popular" and "trivial" and their various connotations, see Sheffy 1996, pp. 225–6.

onized texts for adults—still the main field of scholarly research on modern Arabic literature—from other components of the literary system. On the contrary, the study of non-canonized texts and their relationships with canonized texts becomes absolutely essential if we want to arrive at an adequate understanding of the historical development of Arabic literature.

One of the main functions of literature, according to the Russian formalists, is to de-automatize the preconceived notions, imagination, and worldview of the reader. Shklovsky postulated that literary devices wear out as a result of repetitious usage and that they undergo automatization, a process in which they start functioning as "automatic stock."[5] In other words, with time literary devices are no longer efficient with regard to their assumed poetic function. In order to revitalize the literary discourse and to overcome stereotyping and loss of contact with the real world, the de-automatization (or defamiliarization) process calls for innovation and it posits change. As Shklovsky puts it, a "work of art is perceived against the background of and through association with other works of art. Its form is determined by its relation to other forms that existed prior to it." A new form appears not to express new content but to replace an old form that has lost its artistic quality.[6] This automatization/de-automatization dialectic has been adopted by historical poetics, where it is seen as the major law governing systemic shift.[7] Consequently, the history of literature can be described as a sequence of changes in literary systems (styles, techniques, genres) caused by loss of effect and significance when literary expressions become too familiar and commonplace.[8]

The Formalists argue that the study of literature should be confined to the *differentia specifica* of literature, that is, to that which is specific to literary and poetic uses of language: "The subject of literary scholarship," writes Roman Jakobson, "is not literature in its totality but literariness (*literaturnost*), that is, that which makes of a given work a work of literature."[9] At the same time, since it has an addresser and an addressee, a literary text must also be seen in a pragmatic, communicative, and sociocultural context. Hence, while Arabic literature should be viewed as an autonomous system not subject to external forces, it does interact, as all literatures do, with external literary systems and forms a social force that acts amidst and interacts with other social, non-literary systems. It is these various interactions that form the substance of the

5 Sebeok 1986, I, pp. 66–7. Cf. Shklovsky 1965, pp. 3–24; and Erlich 1969, pp. 171–91.

6 Steiner 1984, p. 56.

7 "Systemic" in the sense of "relating to a system" (Steiner 1984, p. 99).

8 On issues and methods related to literary history, see also Allen 2006, pp. 3–6; and al-Bagdadi 2008, pp. 437–61.

9 Erlich 1969, p. 172.

historical development of Arabic literature from the start of the nineteenth century.

Current scholarly research on contemporary Arabic literature is very limited. Research carried out over several decades by literary critics and academics has generally been confined, rather unsurprisingly, to canonized literature for adults. One of the principal aims of the historical model suggested here is to claim the whole of Arabic literary production as one potential field of research. In other words, it calls for the aesthetic legitimation of popular literature generally discarded by scholars of Arabic literature and typically vilified as mindless, tasteless trash.[10] Building on the concepts of canonicity and canonization, this model suggests that we analyze the literary inventories and historical development of the Arabic literary system on the principle that every textual element, literary text, and literary subsystem has a non-static function in a wider framework. In other words, it requires that we assume a dynamic, functional correlation between all components of the literary system on every level.

Notwithstanding a more detailed discussion in Chapter One of the modern Arabic literary system and the new theoretical framework for its study that I am proposing, this book contains three principal components. The first, explored in Chapter Two, looks at literary dynamics in synchronic cross-section. Inventories of canonized and non-canonized literary texts are presented separately in three sections or subsystems: texts for adults, texts for children, and translated texts for adults and children. The resulting six subsystems—three canonized and three non-canonized—are seen as autonomous networks of relationships and as interacting literary networks on various levels. The internal and external interrelationships and interactions between the various subsystems need to be studied if we want to arrive at a comprehensive understanding of the modern Arabic literary system.

The second component, explored in Chapter Three, presents some outlines of the diachronic intersystemic development of the modern Arabic literary system. Semiotically, a literary text is an utterance made by someone to someone else in a pre-existing language at a certain time and within a certain social and cultural context.[11] The space between the text, its author, and the reader is understood as constituting both an economic environment (for example, literary markets, publishing) and a sociocommunicative system that passes the meaning potential of the text through various filters (for example, criticism, literary circles, groups, salons, public opinion) in order to concretize and realize it. All the other spaces related to literary production

[10] For exceptions, see Shusterman 1992, p. 290, n. 1.

[11] Based on Sebeok 1986, I, pp. 453–9.

and consumption, including the linguistic, spiritual, social, national, and economic spaces, are also considered. Therefore, even if Arabic literature is regarded as an autonomous system for the purpose of its study as *literature*, we must also consider the various ways it interacts with other external literary and non-literary systems. Literary works are never fully intelligible in themselves. According to Terry Eagleton, "you have to see them as belonging to a global literary space, which has a basis in the world's political landscape, but which also cuts across its regions and borders to form a distinctive republic of its own."[12] For example, in order to determine the general characteristics of the historical development of Arabic literature from the start of the nineteenth century, we should look at the interaction of literature with, for example, religion, territory, state nationalism, language, politics, economy, gender, electronic media, and philosophy, as well as foreign literatures and cultures. Here I will discuss in some detail only some of these intersystemic interactions because of space considerations and because of a lack of scholarly studies on many of these interactions.

Finally, the third component, explored in Chapter Four, concentrates on the historical, diachronic development that each genre underwent and the relationships that exist between them. As with any scholarly treatment of genre, it will refer to the developing innovations and discussions of genre theory and the question, "What is genre?" Crucial in this regard is the concept of periodization, that is, how one is to delimit and define "literary periods." Since literary genres do not emerge in a vacuum, the issue of generic development cannot be confined to certain time spans, and emphasis will be placed on the relationship between modern literature, on the one hand, and classical and medieval[13] literature, on the other. The complete study of the historical, diachronic development of literary dynamics requires an analysis of every genre and subgenre, of the interrelationships and interactions between the genres, as well as of the interactions and interrelationships between the genres and the subgenres. For reasons of practicality, this component will only look at three main genres: poetry, fiction, and theater.

If the historical model that I set out to explain in the following pages proves capable of providing a framework for the systematic study of modern Arabic literature as a whole, this study will have achieved its principal aim. Thus, this model may enhance our understanding of all the elements that

12 *New Statesman*, 11 April 2005. For more on the concept of the "republic of letters," see below, the Conclusion.

13 The terms "classical" and "medieval" are used here and throughout the present study to refer to periods of literary creation prior to the nineteenth century. As for the demarcation between classical, medieval, post-classical, and pre-modern periods, see al-Musawi 2015b, p. 323, n. 1. See also Bauer 2007, pp. 137–8.

together make up modern Arabic literature, and it may throw light on traditionally neglected aspects of literary production. At the same time, I am well aware that we lack sufficient information on most sectors of this literary system and that the current paucity of relevant studies on this topic means that some of the theses introduced here are preliminary. In this sense, I hope this study will succeed in stimulating others to take up the fascinating challenge of mapping out all those areas of modern Arabic literature that are as yet unexplored.

While I was preparing the manuscript of the present book for publication, I read *The Medieval Islamic Republic of Letters: Arabic Knowledge Construction* (2015) by Muhsin Jassim al-Musawi as well as his articles on the topic of Arab modernity in *The Cambridge Journal of Postcolonial Literary Inquiry.*[14] These contributions are very important not only for the scholarship of premodern Arabic literature, but also for the study of modern Arabic literature (in the current volume, I will explain the significance of the continuity of literary writing in Arabic since ancient times until the present day). Al-Musawi opens the introduction (*Khuṭbat al-Kitāb,* lit. "Preliminary Discourse") to his book as follows:

> This book argues that the large-scale and diverse cultural production in Arabic in the post-classical era (approximately the twelfth through the eighteenth centuries) was the outcome of an active sphere of discussion and disputation spanning the entire medieval Muslim world. I explore this production over a long temporal stretch and across a vast swathe of Islamic territories. My focus is on the thematic and genealogical constructions that were of greatest significance to the accumulation of cultural capital, which, I argue, constitutes a medieval Islamic "republic of letters."[15]

In his conclusion, al-Musawi explains that his medieval Islamic republic of letters "implies an umbrella term that subsumes within its frame of reference multiple coexisting and/or successive communities of literary world-systems that existed across Asia and Africa."[16]

At first, I could hardly resist the temptation to change the title of my present study to *The Modern Arabic Republic of Letters,* but I was soon to become aware of the differences between al-Musawi's project and my own. His thoughtful and impressive book deserves to be treated in a separate study. And I intend to write such a study, one that will pay special attention

[14] Al-Musawi 2014; al-Musawi 2015; al-Musawi 2015a; al-Musawi 2015b (for a review essays of the book, see *Journal of the Society for Contemporary Thought and the Islamicate World,* 19 November 2015, pp. 1–6 [by Mohammad Salama]; and *Journal of Arabic Literature* 47.1–2 [2016], pp. 209–13 [by Kristina Richardson]).

[15] Al-Musawi 2015b, p. 1.

[16] Al-Musawi 2015b, p. 305.

to the book's theoretical foundations and the inspiration that it drew from Dena Goodman's *The Republic of Letters: A Cultural History of the French Enlightenment* (1994) and Pascale Casanova's *The World Republic of Letters* (2004). However, as al-Musawi's study and my own both aspire to present new frameworks for the study of Arabic texts over different spans of time, and because there are some points of interface between both studies,[17] I will make some comments on *The Modern Arabic Republic of Letters* in the Conclusion of this book.

17 Only *literary* texts in my study as I have defined them (see above, pp. 3–6). Al-Musawi does not clarify the character of the corpus of texts which he investigated besides their having been written in Arabic.

Chapter 1

The Modern Arabic Literary System

A literary text may be defined as any text that in a given community has been imbued with cultural value and that allows for high levels of complexity and significance in the way it is constructed. At the same time, the designation "literary text" points not to an inherent property of certain kinds of objects, but rather to a quality assigned by people involved in producing, reading, and analyzing those objects. Texts perceived as literary by one culture or community are seen as non-literary by another, and one and the same text may also change from the former category to the latter and vice versa.[1] Additionally, in certain periods non-literary genres may serve a function which in other periods was served by literary genres (and vice versa).[2] For the purpose of the present study, I will define the Arabic literary system as the network of relationships that exist at any period of time between *all texts* written or uttered in Arabic and that were considered to be *literary texts* as of this study's creation.[3] That is, I will consider any text, as soon as it is perceived to be literary by any community either within or outside the Arab world, to be part of the system regardless of how one may evaluate it.[4]

[1] Based on Sebeok 1986, II, pp. 1080–8. Cf. Giffen 1972, pp. xiii–xiv (Arabic translation: Giffen 1996, pp. 14–15); Blachère 1952, pp. viii–ix (Arabic translation: Blachère 1984, pp. 11–12); and Pettersson 1990, pp. 219–29.

[2] See, for example, the poetic *marthiya* (elegy) compared to the non-literary obituaries. On the latter as a genre, see Eid 2002.

[3] My definition of the literary system differs from other definitions, such as that of William Marx. Marx argues that the writing of the history of literature presupposes "the prior establishment of a corpus whose greater or lesser extension is itself determined by an implicit valuation of the works it includes, with a perverse return effect: the corpus under consideration eventually strengthens the unformulated aesthetic criteria that were used to define it. Therefore, it is always an epistemological necessity to deconstruct the corpuses that are at our disposal" <http://www.wiko-berlin.de/en/fellows/fellowfinder/detail/2014-marx-william/> (last accessed 7 October 2016).

[4] In her study of the "Nineties' Poets" in Egypt, Clarissa Burt suggests that "the disdainful attitude that Western academia has to precanonical literature is denial of responsibility.

Viewed as a dynamic, literary, and autonomous system, this network of relationships encompasses not only all original literary texts written in Arabic, but also texts translated into Arabic and even potential texts, all of which thus simultaneously "belong to" and "constitute" a single whole. And this is for a purely practical reason: For the reader, this network may include all literary texts existing at the moment he or she is perusing these pages.[5]

Before I set out the theoretical framework that underlies this literary system, which will be our main concern in this study, I will first outline the scope of our research subject and look at the question of how popular literature or—if you wish—popular art in general can be given aesthetic legitimation.

THE SCOPE OF THE RESEARCH SUBJECT

In Chapter Ten of his *An Overview of Modern Arabic Literature* (1990), Pierre Cachia deals with "unwritten Arabic fiction and drama."[6] Based on research that he carried out with editions of the *New York Times Book Review* published from November 1988 to May 1989, Cachia demonstrates the dizzying range of fictional literature that was available to the American reader at the time. The topics included in his discussion, to mention only the most absurd and bizarre, were the impact of alcoholism on a child; carnivorous toads; love dolls that give sexual satisfaction; the tensions in an easily recognizable wealthy political family when its patriarch dies in the arms of a mistress; a gay community decimated by AIDS; the conflict between man's need of a god to worship and his urge to indulge his appetites; a golfer's

For, as in other systems of knowledge in the twentieth century, it is becoming increasingly hard to maintain an attitude of removed objectivity when we discuss historical processes. I suggest then, that, as in other disciplines, observation necessarily affects and interacts with the objects of study. By delaying our consideration until after canonical processes have filtered literary material, we in effect accept the judgments of the filter, without regard for the intrinsic value of the material in question. Only by being conscious of the raw material from which a literary edifice is constructed can we appreciate the nature of the edifice and the aesthetic, legitimizing, sociopolitical values which inform it. By comparing precanonical and canonical materials, we begin to acknowledge the contribution of our own values to our relationship with evaluation of literary products and the canonical edifice" (Burt 1997, p. 147).

5 Roger Allen suggests that the historical frameworks which have been used for the development of Arabic literature are in need of some radical rethinking and that Arabic literature needs now to be explored with regard to an analysis of the *khuṣūṣiyyāt* (particularities) of literary writings at the national and regional level (Allen 2007, pp. 249–50). Allen's suggestion reinforces the need to view literary writing in Arabic according to models and frameworks which traverse temporal and spatial considerations and which will be able to stand the test of time (i.e. changing circumstances).

6 Cachia 1990, pp. 171–8.

career; attempts by individuals to escape provincialism, impending death, or guilt; a growing boy's discovery of his homosexuality; the discovery of a galaxy that destroys the concept of near and far as opposites; the efforts of a German Jewish refugee to adjust to life in India; the appearance in our time of a Christ-like figure; a family destroyed by incest; the minds of abused children; and a family of "freak" children. All this in addition to the usual fare of love stories, detective and spy thrillers, monster and science fiction novels, and historical romances. Turning to the literature available to the American reader's Arab counterpart, Cachia says:

> Needless to say, this [American] literary wealth belongs to a populous country with a very high level of literacy, where more than 50,000 books and hundreds of journals are published every year. With this, the resources of Arab writers are in no way comparable. It is instructive nevertheless to search for gaps in Arab fiction and drama, especially since these genres reached maturity.[7]

Concluding that modern Arabic literature is virtually all about Arabs, Cachia alludes to the paucity of a literature of mere entertainment, "unless love stories and historical novels be reckoned as such." And he underlines the fact that no Arab writer has made a name for him or herself as a writer of detective, spy, Gothic, or science fiction novels, or of sport and adventure stories. The same, he says, is true of works of humor: "No Arab novelist, however, has established himself mainly as a humorous writer—there is no P. G. Wodehouse in the Arab world." Cachia indicates that "the comparative disinterest of Arab writers in genres that might have been expected to attract a wide readership and financial reward is particularly impressive." Furthermore, he finds in Arabic fiction "a marked reticence to strike themes that may cast doubt on national unity" or more controversial themes such as homosexuality:

> The programme which Arab intellectuals have been proclaiming for about a hundred years is modernity, broadly understood as the realization of the values of Western civilization, and these values are most powerfully cemented together by nationalism. More recently, socialism has become an almost integral part of it. By some unspoken consensus, writers eschew those aspects of reality that may cast doubt not only on the validity of their idealizations, but even on the extent to which they have been actualized. It is between these self-set limits that they allow themselves to probe the depths.[8]

[7] Cachia 1990, p. 172.
[8] Cachia 1990, pp. 177–8.

Notwithstanding the fact that it confuses Arab intellectuals' attitude to modernity with the "realization of the values of Western civilization,"[9] the view that Cachia presented more than twenty-five years ago seems to illustrate the traditionally narrow scholarly conception of contemporary Arabic literature during the past few decades on the part of Western critics and scholars, with only a few exceptions.[10] As we can see, reference is made almost exclusively to those literary types and genres which have been recognized by the literary and scholarly establishment as belonging to highbrow culture.[11] Another example is the *Cambridge History of Arabic Literature*'s volume on modern Arabic literature (1992): Of its fourteen chapters, only one is devoted to non-formal literature.[12] We find, however, that this attitude is by no means confined to Western scholarly circles; rather, it is widespread also within the Arabic literary world itself. For example, among literary magazines in the Arab world there is no parallel to the *Sunday Times Books*, which places canonical and popular literature side by side.[13] Yet, even a brief visit to any of the general book fairs held in the Arab world will reveal a totally different picture: Struggling to find room to move, we would find enormous quantities of books in various popular fields (for example, spy literature, science fiction, journalistic types, and semi-literary types), popular journals with literary texts for men and women, not to mention large

9 Since the second half of the nineteenth century, Arab intellectuals themselves have been careful to distinguish between modernization and Westernization: Modernization denotes what Arab intellectuals mean by *tamaddun dākhilī* (lit. "civilized from within")—a process by which traditional Arab society is reformed and advanced by the universally "good" valid ideas and values of modernity such as freedom, individual dignity, orderliness, equality, and tolerance. On the other hand, Westernization denotes what was meant at the time by *tamaddun khārijī* (lit. "superficially civilized")—adopting only the superficial mannerisms of Western culture (Halevi and Zachs 2007, pp. 416–30. Cf. Bawārdī 2008, pp. 190–4. On *Tamaddun* [Civilization] and *Taqaddum* [Progress], see Abu-ʿUksa 2016, pp. 50–83).

10 See, for example, the *Edebiyât* issue on oral narratives (II.1–2, 1988). The majority of the articles are revised versions of papers read at the conference "A Symposium of Middle Eastern Oral Narratives" that was held at Berkeley in May 1980.

11 I use the term "culture" here mainly to refer to "all those practices, like the arts of description, communication, and representation, that have relative autonomy from the economic, social, and political realms and that often exist in aesthetic forms, one of whose principal aims is pleasure" (Said 1994, p. xii. See also van Gelder 2013, pp. xiii–xiv).

12 Badawi 1992, pp. 463–82 ("Poetry in the Vernacular" by Marilyn Booth). The same concepts were employed by Badawi in his *A Short History of Modern Arabic Literature* (1993). For an analysis of these concepts, see Snir 1994, pp. 61–85.

13 For instance, if we take an example from the 1990s, the 17 September 1995 issue includes the following reviews side by side: in the biography section, a review of Jeffrey Meyers' *Edmund Wilson—A Biography*, which discusses the life of "America's greatest literary critic" (p. 10), and in the fiction section, a review of John Arden's *Jack Juggler and the Emperor's Whore*, which is "a rackety, roistering saga of sex, violence, intrigue and political skulduggery" (p. 13).

quantities of original and translated children's literature.[14] Moreover, even if one were to accept Cachia's narrow conception of Arabic literature, one would see that several of the gaps that he mentions are not gaps at all.

For example, although Islam guarantees male homosexuals a place in hell,[15] Arabic love poetry was just as often pederastic as it was heterosexual. By the eighteenth century "at least in the urban centres of Egypt, Syria and northern Iraq, love-poetry of women seems to have been exception rather than rule."[16] The prevalent attitude among literate Arabs toward homosexual love has changed radically—in the modern period, it has never been easy to be gay.[17] Yet, this does not mean that the topic is considered taboo in literary culture[18] or highbrow Arabic fiction.[19] And in addition to love poetry,

[14] See, for example, the sales report in the 1994 Beirut International Book Fair published in the newspaper *al-Quds* on 19 January 1994 (p. 15).

[15] Pellat 1992, p. 152. On homosexuality in Islam, see Farah 1984, pp. 37–9; Pellat 1986a, pp. 776–9 (see an enlarged version in Pellat 1992, pp. 151–67); and Schmitt 2001–2, pp. 49–110. On homosexuality, or rather effeminate types, in medieval Arabic literature, see Rowson 1991, pp. 50–79; and Rowson 1991a, pp. 671–93 and the bibliographical references mentioned in the notes. On the role of the *mukhannathūn* in semi-theatrical scenes in medieval times, see Moreh 1992, pp. 25–7. On the study of homosexuality in Arab/Islamic civilization, culture, and literature, see AbuKhalil 1993, pp. 32–4; Sadek 1994, p. 65; Lagrange 2000, pp. 169–98; El-Ariss 2013a, pp. 293–312; Hadeed 2013, pp. 271–91; and al-Musawi 2015b, pp. 272–7. On Western attitudes toward homosexuality in the Middle East, see Hopwood 1999, pp. 175–82.

[16] El-Rouayheb 2005, p. 17.

[17] See Brian Whitaker, "Homosexuality on Trial in Egypt," *The Guardian*, 19 November 2001. Compared to Egypt and most Arab countries, lesbian, gay, bisexual, and transgender (LGBT) rights in Jordan are considered to be relatively advanced. Same-sex sexual activity was legalized in 1951, and a gay magazine in English, *MY.Kali* (<https://mykalimag.com/> [last accessed 7 October 2016]), was established in 2007. The May/June 2016 double cover celebrates the magazine's sixtieth issue and its first Arabic dedicated cover. See the interview with Khalid Abdel-Hadi (nicknamed Kali) the founder, spokesman, and creative director of the magazine, at <http://www.egyptindependent.com/node/2454725> (last accessed 26 July 2015).

[18] Cf. Fedwa Malti-Douglas' introduction in El Saadawi 1994 (p. xxxii).

[19] One of the most pioneering Arabic literary works in this field is the short story "Abū al-Rijāl" by Yūsuf Idrīs (1927–91), which is an attempt to probe the mind and soul of a gay man. First published in the Cairene magazine *October* (1 November 1987, pp. 40–5), the story was also incorporated into *al-ʿAtab ʿalā al-Naẓar* (*Vision at Fault*) (Idrīs 1987, pp. 69–99. For an English translation, see Idris 1988. On the story, see Vatikiotis 1991, p. 182; and Elkhadem 2001, pp. 13–16). The title of the story literally means "The Father of Men," but it might also be understood ironically, since the protagonist is not a "man" in the traditional masculine sense. Originally, Idrīs called the story "al-Kumūn" ("Latency"), but because the same word could also be read as "al-Kammūn" (Cumin), the author was persuaded by Ṣalāḥ Muntaṣir (b. 1933), the editor of *October*, to give it a new title (Elkhadem 2001, p. 13). In line with the canonical nature of the art of the short story as well as with his own canonical status in the literary system, the author never used vulgar expressions and never depicted sexual episodes. For other attempts to deal with this subject, see the character of Kirsha in Najīb Maḥfūẓ's *Zuqāq al-Midaqq* (Maḥfūẓ n.d. [1947]); the homosexual love scene in al-Janābī

there are Arab writers who have made a name as writers of detective stories,[20] science fiction,[21] and humor (as opposed to what Cachia has argued),[22] and modern Arabic literature is not just about Arabs.[23] Still, in the face of this multifaceted contemporary output of literary production, critics and scholars continue to pay attention almost exclusively to the study of highbrow literary types and genres. Having accepted the challenge of writing on political humor in the Arab world, one scholar has complained that "there remained the other, no less daunting, challenge of finding the material. Political humor is a relatively recent subject of study, little acknowledged by the Arabs."[24] That is, the *habitus* of the intellectual's field tends implicitly to dismiss the importance and seriousness of what falls under the rubric of popular literature, a dismissive attitude that prevents serious aesthetic attention from being given to such literature. The result is that, even when such works have significant aesthetic quality, they tend to go unnoticed or tend to be minimized, which in turn reinforces the basic dismissive attitude toward popular literature and those who produce it.

John A. Haywood complains in his *Modern Arabic Literature 1800–1970*

1995, p. 61; and the prominence of homosexuality in *'Imārat Ya'qūbyān* (*The Yacoubian Building*) by the Egyptian 'Alā' al-Aswānī (b. 1957) (al-Aswānī 2002; English translation: Aswani 2005. See also Lindsey 2005, pp. 60–1; Guth and Ramsay 2011, II, pp. 95–107 [by Stephan Guth]; Allan 2013, pp. 253–69; Lewis 2013, pp. 101–26; and al-Samman and El-Ariss 2013, pp. 205–9). For homosexuality in Egyptian films, see Armbrust 1996, pp. 254–5, n. 44. Lesbianism (*siḥāq, musāḥaqa*) as a subject is rarely treated in modern Arabic literature, but the theme can be found in some literary works, for example in the novel *Jannāt wa-Iblīs* (*Jannāt wa-Iblīs* [the Arabic names of the two central characters]) by the feminist writer Nawāl al-Sa'dāwī (b. 1931) (al-Sa'dāwī 1992; English translation: El Saadawi 1994. Cf. Malti-Douglas 1995, pp. 132–3). On homoerotic desire in the stories of Muslim women writers, see Mitra 2010, pp. 311–29. On lesbianism in Muslim societies, see Juynboll 1997, pp. 565–7, including the detailed bibliography; and Guthrie 2001, pp. 196–9. For homosexual and lesbian love as one of the signs of the Day of Judgment (*ashrāṭ al-sā'a*), see al-Suyūṭī 1990, p. 70; and al-Jāḥiẓ 1991, I, p. 151. On the increase of homosexual and lesbian characters in contemporary Arabic fiction and its effects on the status of gay rights in the Arab world, see al-Samman 2008, pp. 270–310. On the general issue of Arab sexuality (*al-jinsāniyya al-'Arabiyya*) and its cultural contexts, see al-Nābulsī 2013; and al-Nābulsī 2013a.

20 See, for example, below, pp. 82–3, 87–8.

21 See, for example, below, pp. 81–2.

22 See, for example, Kishtainy 1985; 'Abd al-Fattāḥ 1993; and 'Abd al-Fattāḥ 1993a. On humor in Arabic literature until the modern period, see Sadān 1983.

23 See, for example, Arabic literary works by Iraqi Jews, especially those by Samīr Naqqāsh (1938–2004). About Iraqi-Jewish literature in Arabic and relevant references, see my publications listed in the References. Cachia (1990) mentions, among the "strange" subjects in American fiction, the efforts of a German-Jewish refugee to adjust to life in India, while one of Naqqāsh's stories, "Yawm Ḥabalat wa-Ajhaḍat al-Dunyā" ("The Day in which the World Has Been Conceived and Miscarried"), in fact deals with Iraqi Jews adjusting to life in India (Naqqāsh 1980, pp. 9–56).

24 Kishtainy 1985, p. ix.

(1971) that "modern Arabic literature has been largely neglected until the last few years." Though modern Arabic literature "is taken to mean the literature of the nineteenth and twentieth centuries," when speaking about popular literary works Haywood states that "not only have there been few attempts to write literary works wholly or largely in the colloquial, but even the dialogue of modern novels and plays is sparing in its use of colloquialisms, for fear of restricting the readership."[25] How this attitude was reflected in the scholarly research until the mid-1980s can be seen from a survey of doctoral dissertations submitted to North American universities on Arabic literature (classical, medieval, and modern) from 1938 to 1984: Of about fifty dissertations, only three deal with poetry in the vernacular and none were found to deal with other popular lowbrow types and genres.[26] The first English monograph on popular culture in Islamic society was only published in 1993.[27] For academic and professional scientific periodicals, the situation is much the same.[28] Suffice it to say that the forty-seven volumes of the English-language *Journal of Arabic Literature* (published by Brill), the thirty-six volumes of the Arabic-language *al-Karmil—Abḥāth fī al-Lugha wa-l-Adab* (published by the Department of Arabic Language and Literature at the University of Haifa), and the fifty-four volumes of *Banipal—Magazine of Modern Arab Literature* have mainly concentrated on the canonized genres.[29]

POPULAR LITERATURE AND LEGITIMATION

Anyone calling for the study and research of popular literature to be accepted as a legitimate subject immediately comes up against the general question of how this literature is to be given aesthetic legitimation. In the West, the debate has been going on for several decades,[30] but it has hardly begun in the Arab world.[31] Yet the charges leveled in contemporary Western studies on

25 Haywood 1971, p. 1.

26 *The Arab World: A Catalogue of Doctoral Dissertations, 1938–1984* (University Microfilms International, February 1985), pp. 33–4.

27 Shoshan 1993.

28 The only field of popular literature which has attracted the attention of scholars (mainly inside the Arab world) is vernacular poetry. A possible explanation is the local cultural activities of Arab nation-states and the need for these local cultures to emphasize their particular folkloristic heritage (see below, pp. 160–74).

29 The number of issues published for all three journals is as of the writing of this study.

30 See, for example, Shusterman 1992, particularly pp. 169–235. Shusterman's study refers to the major relevant contributions in the field. The following discussion is based on Shusterman 1992; Shusterman 1993, pp. 101–22; and Shusterman 1993a, pp. 215–24. For a summary of the various views about the aesthetics of popular art, see Novitz 2003, pp. 733–47.

31 For exceptions, see al-Wardī 1957, especially pp. 4–12, 287–308; and al-Wardī 2001 [1951],

the philosophy of art against popular art or mass culture,[32] from aesthetic and sociocultural points of view, seem to be much the same as those mentioned directly or alluded to indirectly in Arab culture. From the aesthetic point of view, it is being argued, for example, that popular literature gives only spurious and false satisfaction; evokes no activity or effort, but only a passive response; lacks aesthetic self-respect; is uncreative and standardized; is deficient in form; and is too superficial to engage the intellect.[33] Such "charges" sound even more formidable in light of the difficulties that generally arise where "meaning" is concerned in contemporary highbrow literature, especially as the obscurity and hermetic nature of much contemporary writing make such demands on our efforts to extract meaning.[34] Elitist poetry, for

pp. 70–4. On ʿAlī al-Wardī (1918–95), see Abdel-Malek 1965, pp. 145–8; Baṣrī 1994, II, pp. 550–2; and Baṣrī 1999, III, pp. 420–1. See also the introduction to *al-Ughniyya al-Shaʿbiyya* by Aḥmad ʿAlī Mursī (Mursī 1983, pp. 7–22) as well as the introduction of Fārūq Khūrshīd (1928–2005) and Maḥmūd Dhihnī to their book *Fann Kitābat al-Sīra al-Shaʿbiyya* (Khūrshīd and Dhihnī 1980, pp. 5–18). They dedicated the book to ʿAbd al-Ḥamīd Yūnus (1910–88), "the first explorer of popular studies in our Arabic literature." For Yūnus' views, see Yūnus 1973, especially pp. 3–19. For more on Yūnus, who won the Egyptian state prize for literature in 1980, see al-Saḥḥār 1999, pp. 252–3.

32 The debate over the proper term is significant and instructive: The term "popular" has much more positive connotations, whereas the term "mass" suggests an undifferentiated and typically inhuman aggregate. Walter Armbrust uses "popular culture" to refer to expressive culture presented in mass media, including the print media, television, cinema, and recorded music on cassette tapes (Armbrust 1996, p. 221, n. 1). For more on this terminological debate, see Gans 1974, p. 10. The discussion in the present book generally ignores the issue of "popular" as "extra-individual" or "officially invented" unless something else is indicated, such as in the use of popular culture as a factor in the process of nation-building in the Arab world (see below, pp. 160–74). On the general issue of that differentiation, see Jakobson and Bogatyrev 1971, pp. 91–3; and Shavit 1996, pp. 327–45. On mass culture in the Middle East, see Stauth and Zubaida 1987.

33 Cf. Mursī 1983, p. 8. Already in the thirteenth century, the Shīʿī poet and critic Ṣafī al-Dīn al-Ḥillī (1278–c.1349) refers to several of these arguments when describing popular genres of poetry in the opening of his book *al-Kitāb al-ʿĀṭil al-Ḥālī wa-l-Murakhkhaṣ al-Ghālī* (al-Ḥillī 1956, p. 6):

فهي الفنون التي إعرابها لحن، وفصاحتها لكن، وقوّة لفظها وهن؛ حلال الإعراب بها حرام، وصحّة اللفظ بها سقام؛ يتجدّد حسنها إذا زادت خلاعة، وتضعف صنعتها إذا أودعت من النحو صناعة؛ فهي السهل الممتنع، والأدنى المرتفع، طالما أعيت بها العوامّ الخواصّ، وأصبح سهلها على البلغاء يعتاص؛ فإن كلّف البليغ منها فنّا تراه يريغه، ويتجرّعه ولا يكاد يسيغه، فمعرفتها بالطبع السليم، وآفتها من الفهم السقيم.

The Egyptian poet Masʿūd Shūmān (b. 1966) argues that sometimes classical critical texts are much more progressive in their attitudes toward popular culture and in their concentration on the aesthetic merits of the texts, ignoring the canonical/non-canonical dichotomy and the exclusive control of the canonical circles over the evaluation of literature and art. One of the obstacles in the legitimation of Arabic popular literature is that, with the emergence of the Qur'ān, *fuṣḥā* acquired a divine status to the point that classical Arabic poetry such as the *Muʿallaqāt* was considered to be another holy Qur'ān (*al-Kitāba al-Ukhrā* 7 [February 1994], pp. 139–40).

34 See Preminger 1974, p. 345; and Cuddon 1986, pp. 304–5.

example, because of its highly subjective language and imagery, has become even more self-regarding, and poets are writing mainly for themselves or for small coteries. This may be explained by the way many poets imply a negative judgment on the complexities of modern life, by the relative inaccessibility of the exact sciences, and the way the arts have become separated from most people's everyday lived experience. Poets who have increasingly been playing down poetry-as-communication or poetry-as-message and who have instead been concentrating on exploiting poetry as a medium tend to write less about public matters and more about themselves, and they tend to write for others who share the same sensibilities.[35] No such complexities and obscurities are to be found in popular poetry, which, according to Ṣalāḥ 'Īsā (b. 1939) in his introduction to the memoirs of the Egyptian poet Aḥmad Fu'ād Najm (Nigm) (1929–2013), is:

> devoid of any "combative history," "Sisyphic agony" or "existentialist alienation." Only sweet, sad, and simple singing as well as a confident strong voice, and an irony that makes one burst out in laughter or tears, and a boldness that knows no fear, does not hesitate nor reconsider, since it does not have and does not strive to possess anything to be afraid of.[36]

From a sociocultural point of view, we often find the following arguments made against popular literature and art in general: they promote excessive commercialism; they make society more susceptible to totalitarianism; they ruin high culture by corrupting audiences; and they lower the cultural quality of society as a whole. Apart from these general charges, some are relevant only to popular Arabic literature. For example, some have argued that Western influence and the growth of secularism may undermine Arab unity and lead to a neglect of Arabic literature's Islamic heritage. Due to a lack of space, the counter-arguments that have been made against these and other charges will be discussed here only when they are relevant to Arabic literature.[37] Before broaching these specific counter-arguments, a short discussion of several general problems with the whole idea of the legitimation of popular literature may be instructive. For example, it has been argued that attempts at aesthetic legitimation will somehow destroy the character of popular literature by "expropriating" it from its popular audiences and modes of reception. Dismissing popular literature as beneath serious aes-

[35] Preminger 1974, pp. 582–3. See also the bibliographical list on pp. 583–4. Cf. Eliot 1950, p. 248. On obscurity in modern Arabic literature, see Snir 1992, p. 9, n. 4; and Abu-Deeb 1997, pp. 101–3.

[36] Nigm 1993, p. 19.

[37] For a detailed consideration of the other general indictments and charges, see Shusterman 1992, pp. 169–200; and Shusterman 1993, pp. 101–22.

thetic consideration would, however, mean leaving it to the marketplace and its mercenary criteria to decide what value it has and what future awaits it:

> Long denied philosophical attention and artistic recognition, popular art has been deprived of the criticism and aesthetic monitoring which could render it more aesthetically rewarding and refined. Thus, rather than excluding popular art from the domain of philosophical aesthetics, aesthetic inquiry should be directed to seeing whether popular art has the potential to meet the aesthetic requirements we demand of good art, and how it may overcome its obvious shortcomings to best realize its aesthetic potential.[38]

According to Richard Shusterman's melioristic view, popular art should be and can be improved because it can, and often does, achieve real aesthetic merit. It has also been argued that attacking the intellectual critique leveled against legitimating popular literature in effect means waging a campaign in enemy territory. Most popular literature enthusiasts feel no need at all to justify such literature by anything more than the satisfaction it gives them. The result is that many people who would be eminently qualified to justify popular literature are simply not interested in doing so over and above their own continued consumption of it.[39] However, aestheticians, especially when they themselves indulge in it, cannot ignore the question of the legitimation of popular literature, since it divides them against themselves.[40] As Shusterman has it, "we are made to disdain the things that give us pleasure and to feel ashamed of the pleasure they give."[41] Intellectual defenders of popular literature, rather than making a case for its aesthetic validity, also tend to be too apologetic about its aesthetic shortcomings by adducing social needs and democratic principles as extenuating circumstances. Popular literature, they argue, is good only for those who lack the education and culture to appreciate high culture. It is not to be celebrated but only tolerated until we can provide enough educational resources "to permit everyone to choose

38 Shusterman 1993a, p. 219. On art and pleasure, see Shusterman 2000.

39 Cf. Cohen and Cohen 1996, p. 14.

40 Cf. Mursī 1983, p. 63: "We find a lot of folklore with the common people, but it does not mean that we cannot find a lot of folklore with educated people."

41 Shusterman 1993a, p. 216. Academic attention in the West to popular culture has been steadily growing since the 1970s, especially in the United States. An obvious sign of this phenomenon is the emergence of specific academic journals for popular culture such as the *Journal of Popular Culture* and the *Journal of Popular Literature* published by Bowling Green State University. According to the editorial policy of the latter, which began publication in the mid 1980s, the journal is "dedicated to the study of popular fiction throughout the world" (as stated on the cover). (This journal stopped being published in 1991. See, for example, <https://searchworks.stanford.edu/view/493438> [last accessed 7 October 2016]).

from higher taste cultures."[42] Yet by perpetuating the myth of its aesthetic worthlessness, these apologists clearly play into the hands of its intellectualist critics and undermine efforts to build a genuine defense of popular literature.[43] Finally, while we tend to think of high literature almost exclusively in terms of its more celebrated works of genius, popular literature is typically identified with its most mediocre and standardized products. However, just as high literature is not an unblemished collection of masterpieces, so too popular literature is not an amorphous abyss of tastelessness in which no aesthetic criteria are displayed or exercised. In both these kinds of literature, "the distinction between them being flexible and historical rather than rigid and intrinsic, there is room and need for aesthetic discriminations of success and failure."[44]

A good illustration of the aforementioned argument is the appreciation of canonical writers to certain masterpieces of popular literature. For example, one cannot disagree about the canonical status of the writings of the Syrian poet Muḥammad al-Māghūṭ (1934–2006) and their high esteem in the contemporary Arabic literary system, but he himself does not hesitate to argue that the song entitled "Kīfak Inta?" ("How are You?") by the Lebanese singer Nuhād Ḥaddād, known as Fayrūz (b. 1935), "is equal for me to the entire poetry of [the 'Abbāsīd canonical poet] al-Buḥturī [821–97]."[45] Also, history clearly shows that the popular entertainment of a given culture can subsequently come to be regarded as "classic" (and vice versa).[46] The genre of the novel started in England as a popular cultural phenomenon and then became an elitist one,[47] while the subgenre of the popular detective novel started as a purely elitist phenomenon.[48] Even within the very same cultural period, a given work can function either as popular literature or as high literature depending on how it is interpreted and appropriated by its public. In nineteenth-century America, for example, Shakespeare was both vaudeville and high theater.[49] Recent developments have shown that old

42 See, for example, Gans 1974, p. 128.

43 Shusterman 1993a, p. 216. Cf. Fishelov 2007, pp. 24–6.

44 Shusterman 1993a, p. 217. Cf. Shapira et al. 2007, p. 12.

45 Al-Māghūṭ 2002, p. 73.

46 See the case of *Alf Layla wa-Layla* below on pp. 90–7, 263. See also Franco Moretti's new project at Wissenschaftskolleg zu Berlin about "Lost Bestsellers of 19th-Century Britain"—twenty novels that were enormously popular at the time of publication and are now almost completely forgotten (according to *Fellows' Projects 2016/2017* [2016], pp. 84–5).

47 Cohen and Cohen 1996, p. 22. See, for example, the case of *Robinson Crusoe* and the change in its status in England (Fishelov 2007, pp. 21–3).

48 On the elevated status of detective novels up to the 1930s, see Cohen and Cohen 1996, pp. 27–8.

49 See Levine 1988, pp. 13–81; and Shusterman 1992, p. 169.

categories of high and low art have been collapsing. For example, American singer-songwriter Bob Dylan (b. 1941) has won the 2016 Nobel Prize in Literature—in choosing a popular musician for the literary world's highest honor, the Swedish Academy, which awards the prize, redefined the boundaries of literature, setting off a debate about whether song lyrics have the same artistic value as poetry or novels.

As soon as we accept that it has aesthetic legitimacy, we make room for scholarly study of popular literature as an aesthetic historical phenomenon. However, as it is, the existing historical frameworks applied to contemporary Arabic literature do not allow for the inclusion of popular literature. Consequently, the systematic scholarly study of and systematic scientific research on the entirety of Arabic literary production has remained rather limited. The aforementioned Cambridge *Modern Arabic Literature* (1992) is only one example of the problems that the scholarly projects in this field are facing. Indeed, few of them rely on any solid theoretical framework and thus are merely eclectic. If we only look at the present Arabic literary reality and take into account the development of the general study of other literary systems and other cultural fields worldwide, we will realize that we need to widen the scope of scholarly research and to search for more adequate historical theoretical frameworks.

ASSUMPTIONS BEHIND THE OPERATIVE MODEL

In the present study, all literary texts for adults and children, including those that are translations, are seen as components of the dynamic, autonomous literary system[50] regardless of any evaluative judgments or hierarchies of value that may say otherwise.[51] If we take this to be our guiding principle, it is clear that our conception differs from most other conceptions that scholars have employed to describe Arabic literature or at least parts of it. For example, in the introduction to the encyclopedic dictionary of twentieth-century Arab poets entitled *Muʿjam al-Bābaṭīn li-l-Shuʿarāʾ al-ʿArab*

50 Cf. Sebeok 1986, I, pp. 463–6.

51 Cf. Anders Pettersson's observation: "[M]y distinction between serious literature and light literature is in itself, in spite of the value-laden terms, not evaluative but descriptive. It differentiates between presentational compositions designed to convey different kinds of values. Since it differentiates between presentational compositions governed by different *intentions* ('designed to'), it is moreover compatible with the fact that certain light literature may in reality be superior to not a little serious literature even from an artistic point of view" (Pettersson 1990, p. 231). Sometimes, an evaluative judgment is pronounced not only on literary texts but on entire literary periods, as for example in the following statement referring to the few hundred years before the nineteenth century: "Arabic literature [...] suffered from stagnation and triviality" (Somekh 1991, p. 4). On this issue, see the Conclusion.

al-Muʿāṣirīn (*The al-Bābaṭīn Dictionary of Contemporary Arab Poets*) (1995), we find the following statement:

> لما كان هدف المعجم رسم خريطة كاملة للشعر العربي، والتعريف بشعراء العالم مشرقه ومغربه، فإنه لم يحصر نفسه في كبار الشعراء وحدهم، وإنما فسح مكانا فيه لشباب الشعراء ولغير المشهورين الذين حققوا مستوى جيّدا يستحقّون به أن يسلّط الضوء عليهم، وأن ينالوا شيئا من عناية الساحة الأدبية.

> The purpose of the dictionary was to draw a complete map of Arabic poetry and introduce poets of the Arab world whether in the East or West. Thus, the dictionary does not limit itself to the great and famous poets, but also makes room for young and lesser-known poets—those who deserve to be singled out for their achievements and who deserve to be given attention in the literary arena.[52]

The dictionary's criteria, however, are principally evaluative: linguistic perfection (*salāma lughawiyya*), musical perfection (*salāma mūsīqiyya*), and aesthetic and artistic level (*al-mustawā al-jamālī wa-l-fannī*).[53] A similar conception lies behind Robert B. Campbell's two-volume *Aʿlām al-Adab al-ʿArabī al-Muʿāṣir: Siyar wa-Siyar Dhātiyya* (*Contemporary Arab Writers: Biographies and Autobiographies*) (1996).[54]

By contrast, my conception excludes any evaluative judgments, that is, it sees the Arabic literary system as a network of relations between all forms of literary texts, which are seen as constituting a single whole. I argue that Arabic literature can be more adequately analyzed as a historical phenomenon when conceived of as a system that replaces the search for data about material aspects of literary phenomena with the uncovering of the functions that these aspects have. Thus, as I. Even-Zohar states, "instead of a conglomerate of material phenomena, the functional elements hypothesized by the system approach are considered as interdependent and correlated. The spe-

52 *Muʿjam al-Bābaṭīn li-l-Shuʿarāʾ al-ʿArab al-Muʿāṣirīn* (1995), I, p. 43. The dictionary was published in Kuwait by Muʾassasat Jāʾizat ʿAbd al-ʿAzīz Saʿūd al-Bābaṭīn li-l-Ibdāʿ al-Shiʿrī (The Institute of ʿAbd al-ʿAzīz Saʿūd al-Bābaṭīn's Prize for Poetic Creation) and includes in its first edition 1,644 poets from all over the Arab world. In 2008 another dictionary was published, *Muʿjam al-Bābaṭīn li-Shuʿarāʾ al-ʿArabiyya fī al-Qarnayn al-Tāsiʿ ʿAshar wa-l-ʿIshrīn* (*The al-Bābaṭīn Dictionary of Poets in Arabic in the Nineteenth and Twentieth Centuries*), which includes about 8,000 poets. For the electronic edition of the dictionary, see <http://www.almoajam.org/main_page.html> (last accessed 7 October 2016).

53 *Muʿjam al-Bābaṭīn li-l-Shuʿarāʾ al-ʿArab al-Muʿāṣirīn* (1995), I, pp. 24, 42. A critical evaluative approach to this dictionary is found in Juḥā 1999, p. 6: "Is it reasonable that we have now in the Arab world more than 1,600 poets? The number of the great creative poets are no more than we can count on fingers!"

54 See, for example, Campbell 1996, p. 8. For critical notes, see Juḥā 1999, especially p. 7: "How a foreigner can dare to deal with all the writers and poets in all Arab countries [...] this is a deficient and distorted work."

cific role of each element is determined by its relational positions vis-à-vis all other (hypothesized) elements."[55]

As I have outlined above, sociocultural distinctions of text production in the Arabic literary system are conceptualized in the present study in terms of literary stratification, that is, canonized (canonical) versus non-canonized (non-canonical) texts.[56] Various Arabic terms are used for the description of this stratification, the most prominent among them for canonical literary activities being *al-adab al-rāqī, al-adab al-ʿālī, al-adab al-rasmī, al-adab al-rafīʿ, al-adab al-khāṣṣ, al-adab al-faṣīḥ, al-adab al-sāʾid, al-adab al-sulṭānī, adab al-qurrāʾ al-muthaqqafīn, adab al-khāṣṣa, adab al-markaz, adab al-nukhba, adab al-faqāqīʿ*, and *adab al-ṣafwa*. For non-canonical literary activities, the following terms are used: *al-adab al-ʿāmmī, adab al-ʿāmma, al-adab al-shaʿbī, al-adab al-jamāhīrī, al-adab ghayr al-rasmī, adab mā warāʾ al-rasmī, al-adab ghayr al-muʿtaraf bihi, al-adab al-shāʾiʿ, al-adab al-hāmishī, adab al-hāmish, al-adab al-rakhīṣ, adab al-aṭrāf, adab al-ummiyyīn, al-adab al-shādhdh ʿan al-mustawā al-maqbūl, adab al-fiʾāt al-dunyā*, and *kitāba ukhrā*.[57] As one can certainly see, some of the terms have negative connotations and are likely used by proponents of canonical or non-canonical literary activities against one another.

The term "canonized texts" refers to those highbrow literary works which are accepted in a given society and recognized as legitimate by the literary establishment and dominant cultural circles of that society. Although ordinary people share in the process of defining sociocultural distinctions, it is the literary and critical elite who have the decisive role in that process. That elite is a minority group of individuals, who, from a sociocultural point

55 Sebeok 1986, I, p. 463.

56 See Even-Zohar 1990, p. 15. From an anthropological point of view, we refer to the "great tradition/little tradition" dichotomy, which is based on terms coined by Robert Redfield and Milton Singer (Redfield and Singer 1969, pp. 206–33; and Singer 1972, especially pp. 46–7, 55–6, 67–8, 77–9, 184–6). In his translation of Lois Anita Giffen's *Theory of Profane Love among the Arabs: The Development of the Genre* (Giffen 1972), Najm ʿAbd Allāh Muṣṭafā rendered the term "classical literature" as *al-adab al-rafīʿ*, explaining that such a translation is preferable to *al-adab al-klāsīkī* (Giffen 1996, p. 7, n. 1). Unlike Muṣṭafā, who emphasizes that we should consider *al-adab al-rafīʿ* as a value-laden term, our conception of the term in this study is based on unloading all the denotative and connotative evaluative baggage that accompany it (and the aforementioned terms). On the term "classical" as "a stamp of the quality" and in the sense of "exemplary, providing the standards," see Bauer 2007, pp. 137–41.

57 The last term is used as a title for an Egyptian magazine—*al-Kitāba al-Ukhrā* (*The Other Writing*)—whose first issue appeared in May 1991. On the issue of terminology, see also Armbrust 1996, p. 37. Referring to the *adab* literature, Sadan suggests calling the Arabic medieval non-canonized literary texts "sub-*adab*" or "para-*adab*." At the same time, Sadan states that we can hardly find, in *adab* literature, texts wholly belonging to the non-canonized sector (Sadān 1983, p. 21). On the term *adab*, see al-Musawi 2015b, pp. 176–85 and the relevant references as well as below, the Conclusion.

of view, are acknowledged as superior in some sense and who influence or control some or all of the other segments of the population.[58] Canonical texts receive the attention of people engaged in literary production, consumption, and evaluation, including writers, critics, scholars, editors of literary periodicals, publishers, and educators, and are preserved by the collective memory of the community to become part of its historical heritage. Literary prizes are the most evident expression of canonicity in every literary system.[59] Any such authoritative choices—or, in other words, such institutional controls over interpretation—require the consensus of a relatively small number of people resisting not only those who are considered to be incompetent or unqualified, but also those who are seen as charismatic outsiders.[60]

On the other hand, the term "non-canonized texts" refers to those literary works which are rejected in a given society and seen as illegitimate by the dominant cultural circles of that society. Thus, unless their status changes, these texts do not receive the attention of the literary establishment and are, in the long run, often forgotten by the community. Still, canonicity is not an inherent feature of textual activities on any level, and it is by no means a euphemistic way of referring to a work as "good" or "bad." Therefore, the canonized/non-canonized classification used in this study is not intended to set the original canonized texts for adults apart from other, popular, components of the literary system. On the contrary, the study of non-canonized Arabic popular texts and their various relationships with canonized official texts is essential if we want to arrive at an adequate understanding of the historical development of Arabic literature. It is also essential for an adequate understanding of canonical texts.[61] There is nothing paradoxical about this

[58] Ghālī Shukrī (1935–98) considers the sociocultural stratification to be political as well (Shukrī 1994, p. 11). In his book on popular literature in Yemen, the Yemenite poet ʻAbd Allāh al-Baraddūnī (1929–99) alludes to a fierce struggle between the national or the people's scholars (*al-akādīmiyyūn al-shaʻbiyyūn*) and the official scholars (*al-rasmiyyūn al-akādīmiyyīn*) (al-Baraddūnī 1988, p. 9).

[59] From this perspective, even in the 1990s the Arabic literary system still faced difficulties in the process of freeing itself from the "chains" of the canonicity of the first half of the twentieth century. For instance, the 1995 King Fayṣal International Prize for Arabic Literature (given to studies dealing with prominent modern Arab writers) was jointly awarded to the Egyptian Ḥamdī Sayyid Aḥmad al-Sakkūt (b. 1930) for his two-volume work about ʻAbbās Maḥmūd al-ʻAqqād (1889–1964), to the Syrian Salmā Luṭfī al-Ḥaffār al-Kuzbarī (1923–2006) for her book about Mayy Ziyāda (1886–1941), and to the Egyptian Muḥammad Abū al-Anwār Muḥammad ʻAlī (1932–2009) for his three-volume work about Muṣṭafā Luṭfī al-Manfalūṭī (1876–1924). On the issue of literary prizes, see the anonymous essay entitled "al-Jawā'iz al-ʻArabiyya fī Qafaṣ al-Ittihām" published in *al-ʻĀlam*, 20 April 1991, p. 51.

[60] Cf. Kermode 1988, pp. 125–6.

[61] Cf. Malti-Douglas 2001a, p. x: "The marginal could inform us about the Arabo-Islamic textual world in ways that complemented and redefined the discourses that we might think of as dominant."

if we recall that popular Arabic literature was never only the product of inferior circles in Arab society.[62] Since, in "real" literary life, the boundaries between canonized and non-canonized texts are neither always fully obvious nor uncontested,[63] the elementary and rather general way we deal with them here inevitably betrays a great deal of abstraction and simplification. It is clear why this should be so. First, condemnation of popular literature is generally made in equally simplifying, binary terms;[64] and second, abstraction and simplification are theoretical necessities for the historical model we want to present, and they are a convenient shortcut when it comes to drawing up the schema of the research field.

Delimiting factors between canonized and non-canonized texts as well as between aesthetic and non-aesthetic objects are by no means static. As I have already mentioned, a text or an object referred to in a certain period by one community as non-canonized or non-aesthetic can be considered by the same community in a subsequent period as canonized and aesthetic.[65] The relationships between the subsystems of the literary system may be compared with the relationships between the various components of the basic unit of any literary system, that is, the text. As a "vehicle of function and meaning,"[66] the text may be considered as a synchronic reflection of the entire system, which is the sum of its texts. Again, "being" a literary text is not an inherent category; it is rather a context-dependent functional category which can be assigned to various texts. Likewise, "being" canonized/non-canonized or aesthetic/non-aesthetic is not an inherent category, but a context-dependent functional category of a given text or work of art. Just as many texts are perceived as literary by one culture or community and as non-literary by another—texts may shift categories[67]—so one and the same text

62 Cf. Caspi and Blessing 1993, p. 355. J. L. Kraemer's instructive remark on the culture bearers of humanism in Islam is very useful here: "The culture bearers were in many respects marginal people. And they performed the cultural role that marginal people often carry out within the framework of majority culture that differs from their own [...] [M]arginal people tend to undermine the politically dominant culture so as to escape from their own marginality. In doing so they often become innovators" (Kraemer 1984, pp. 17–18).

63 See Sadan 1998, pp. 7–22; and Bauer 2007, pp. 151–8.

64 Cf. Shusterman 1992, pp. 170–1. Shusterman's relevant observation is important: "If one were forced to define the high/popular art distinction, it would be better to do this not simply in terms of different objects but largely in terms of different modes of reception or use. 'Popular' usage is contrasted to 'high' usage in being closer to ordinary experience and less structured and regulated by schooling and standards inculcated by the system of formal education and dominant intellectual institutions. In France, popular art is accordingly contrasted with 'l'art savant', and the very idea, or category, of 'popular art' may be largely an intellectual invention of devalorizing distinction" (Shusterman 1992, p. 291, n. 4).

65 See above, p. 8.

66 Sebeok 1986, I, p. 163.

67 Based on Sebeok 1986, II, pp. 1080–8.

may "wander" from one sector of the literary system to another. This kind of historical relativism, that is, the notion that every generation reads the literary works of the past in its own way, is reminiscent of the idea that a work of art is something that grows, evolves, and changes with succeeding generations. As T. S. Eliot (1888–1965) put it, when a new work of art is created, something happens simultaneously to all the works of art which preceded it.[68]

Although it is autonomous, the Arabic literary system, like any other system, retains various relationships with other literary systems by means of interference. Arabic literature may become a source for direct or indirect loans to another literature and vice versa. Translated texts may constitute the initial channel for interference.[69] Moreover, together with historiography, anthologizing, and criticism, translation—the main medium through which one literature influences another—prepares works for inclusion in the canon of world literature.[70] Interference normally occurs when a target literature lacks a sufficient repertoire to absorb newly needed functions, and it tends to be stronger when a body of literature is either in a state of emergence, in a vacuum, or at a turning point in its history.[71] Thus, whenever it is in need of innovation and unable to use its own repertoire to that end, a literature tends to make use of whatever repertoire is within reach. Although availability may arise as a result of physical contacts, "it is nevertheless ultimately determined by the cultural promptness ('openness,' 'readiness') of the target literature to consider a potential source as 'available.'"[72] For example, although Arabic literature during the Abbasid period came under the strong influence of Greek culture, no major Greek literary models were

68 On this issue, see Preminger 1974, pp. 160–1. See the quotation from Eliot below, pp. 33–4.

69 Cf. Sebeok 1986, I, pp. 462–3.

70 Lefevere 1990, p. 27. On the concept of world literature, see Elster 1901, pp. 33–47; Elster 1986, pp. 7–13; Damrosch 2003; Schildgen et al. 2006; Damrosch 2009; Damrosch 2009a; Apter 2013; D'haen et al. 2013; and Ganguly 2015, pp. 272–81. One of the definitions of world literature is in agreement with the conception of the present study that excludes any evaluative judgments or hierarchies of value, namely, "all of the world's literature, without pronouncing on questions of quality and influence" (D'haen et al. 2013, p. xi). On Arabic fiction and world literature, see Rooke 2011, pp. 201–13. On extending the paradigm of world literature beyond hegemonic global centers and attending to the trajectories that shape "literature in the world," see Helgesson 2015, pp. 253–60. On world literature and the demise of national literatures, see Clüver 1986, pp. 14–24; Clüver 1988, pp. 134–9; Clüver 1988a, pp. 143–4; Konstantinovic 1988, pp. 141–2; and Steinmetz 1988, pp. 131–33. See also below (pp. 160–74) regarding the issue of national literatures.

71 Cf. Haddad 1970, p. 3; and al-ʿAẓm 1992, p. 159:

لا ينجح الغزو الثقافي في التأثير الفاعل والعميق على المجتمع المغزوّ إلا بمقدار الخواء الثقافي الذي يقع عليه الغزو. فحيثما توجد ثقافة حيّة نامية متحرّكة تتعامل مع مشكلات عصرها الكبرى وتحدّياته المصيرية بنجاح معقول وتتفاعل مع قضاياها الوطنية والفكرية والعلمية والتقنية والفنية بصورة خلاّقة ينكمش تأثير الغزو الثقافي ويميل فعله إلى التلاشي تلقائيا والعكس بالعكس.

72 Sebeok 1986, I, p. 462.

introduced into the Arabic literary system.[73] Indeed, works in other fields such as agriculture, astronomy, grammar, music, philosophy, medicine, and even poetics and some literary genres were translated from Greek into Arabic,[74] but Greek epic poetry, represented by such works as Homer's *Iliad* and *Odyssey*, although it was translated by other Eastern cultural groups such as the Indians, Persians, and Syrians into their own languages, was not translated into Arabic until the twentieth century.[75] Unaware of or outright ignoring the Greek models, the Arabs produced no epic poetry, unlike their Indian, Persian, (ancient) Egyptian, and Turkish counterparts.[76]

Sulaymān al-Bustānī (1856–1925), the first to translate the *Iliad* into Arabic at the beginning of the twentieth century,[77] suggested three main reasons why the Arabs had neglected Greek literature: first, there was the religion (*al-dīn*), that is, the strong pagan elements, depicted in the *Iliad*;

73 Rajā' ʻĪd's description of the great impact of Greek culture on Abbasid literature (ʻĪd 1993, pp. 285–90) is highly exaggerated—it does not distinguish between the Greek impact on literature and its impact on other aspects of Arab culture.

74 On translations from Greek into Arabic, see Gutas 1998, pp. 225–31 (for the various fields, see p. 229); Gutas 1999; and Mavroudi 2015, pp. 28–59. For a chronological bibliography of studies on the significance of the translation movement for Islamic civilization, see Gutas 1999, pp. 212–15. See also Gutas 2000. On the Greek impact on Arab culture, see Goodman 1983, pp. 460–82.

75 According to Gutas 1999, pp. 194–5, "high Greek literature was not translated into Arabic. It was reported that Ḥunayn [ibn Isḥāq, (809–73)] himself could recite Homer in Greek by heart, but none of this Homeric citation survives in either Syriac or Arabic translation [...] What was translated into Arabic from Greek literature was what may be loosely called 'popular' and 'paraenetic' literature." Cf. Kilito 2002, pp. 47–55, 110–14; and al-Musawi 2015b, pp. 205–19.

76 On views opposing such a statement, see Qabbish 1971, pp. 372–3; Gamal 1984, pp. 25–38; and Makdisi 1990, p. 134. The Egyptian literary critic Aḥmad Ḥasan al-Zayyāt (1885–1968) considered *Sīrat ʻAntara* to be the *Iliad* of the Arabs (al-Zayyāt n.d., p. 394. Cf. Elkhadem 1985, p. 55; and Reynolds 1995, pp. 1–20).

77 See al-Bustānī 1904; and al-Bustānī 1996. On the nature of his translation, see Hamori 1980, pp. 15–22. This translation is considered by some Arab scholars and intellectuals to be a great triumph for the Arabic language (e.g. al-Jundī 1963, p. 159). In 1925, the Lebanese poet Ilyās Abū Shabaka (1903–47) wrote an elegy on Sulaymān al-Bustānī (Abū Shabaka 1985, I, pp. 119–121), in which he alludes to the excellence of the *Iliad* translation. In another elegy on al-Bustānī, Abū Shabaka (1985, I, pp. 188–9) argues that the Arabic translation is more sublime than the original Greek, and that is why

وخفّ هومير بالإلياذ محرقـــــــــها   أمام عينيك بخورا وقربانـــــا
فصافحتك أثينا وهي باســــــــمة   حبّا وعانقت اليونان لبنـــــان

Homer hurried burning the *Iliad* before your eyes as incense and a thanks offering.
Athens is greeting you smiling with love, Greece embracing Lebanon.

On the main aspects of literary criticism presented in al-Bustānī's introduction to his translation of the *Iliad* and in the notes appended to it, as well as on al-Bustānī's general critical conceptions, see Ṣawāyā 1960; Fanous 1980, pp. 185–227; Fanus 1986, pp. 105–19; Fahd 1993, pp. 259–66; and Holmberg 2006, pp. 141–65. On al-Bustānī and his literary and critical work, see al-Hāshim 1960; Hourani 1991a, pp. 174–87; and Moreh 2000, pp. xlix–l.

second, the Arab poets did not know Greek (*ighlāq fahm al-Yūnāniyya ʿalā al-ʿArab*), that is, those Arab poets capable of translating the *Iliad* into Arabic never mastered Greek; and third, the translators were unable to compose Arabic poetry (*ʿajz al-naqala ʿan naẓm al-shiʿr al-ʿArabī*), that is, the mainly Christian translators of Greek science were unable to write gracefully in Arabic.[78] Ṭāhā Ḥusayn (1889–1973) rejected al-Bustānī's arguments, even describing the first of them regarding the pagan elements in the *Iliad* as "highly stupid and foolish," since the Arabs did translate Greek philosophical texts, which also contained elements of ancient Greek religion.[79] Other scholars[80] have tried to explain the phenomenon by quoting al-Jāḥiẓ's (776–886) words:

> الشعر لا يستطاع أن يترجم ولا يجوز عليه النقل ومتى حُوّل تقطّع نظمه وبطل وزنه وذهب حسنه وسقط موضع التعجّب لا كالكلام المنثور (...) لو حُوّلت حكمة العرب بطل ذلك المعجز الذي هو الوزن (...) إن الترجمان لا يؤدّي أبدا ما قال الحكيم.

> It is impossible to translate poetry and to convert it [to another language], since when it is translated the arrangement of words is disrupted and the meter is abolished and the beauty of poetry disappears and likewise its charm. Poetry is not like prose [...] If the wisdom of the Arabs is translated, this miracle which is the meter disappears [...] translation will never convey the meaning of what the wise man says.[81]

As a target literature, Arabic literature in the Abbasid period, far from being in a state of emergence, stuck in a vacuum, or at some turning point or crossroads in its history, was fully capable of performing the functions which Arab society needed it to fulfill. This means that, because Arabic literature at the time saw itself as self-sufficient and regarded the outsider with contempt, other repertoires, even when available,[82] were simply ignored or rejected. If the Arabic literary system in the Abbasid period had been in need of new

78 See al-Bustānī 1904, pp. 65–7; and al-Bustānī 1996, pp. 61–3. Cf. al-Labābīdī 1943, pp. 33–4; al-Badawī al-Mulaththam 1963, pp. 81–3; Semah 1974, pp. 115–16; and Moreh 1976, p. 129, n. 19.

79 Ḥusayn 1967 [1956], pp. 192–3.

80 Such as ʿAbd al-Ḥayy 1977, p. 15. On the attitude of the Arabs to Greek poetry, see also ʿAbbās 1977, pp. 23–38.

81 Cf. al-Jāḥiẓ 1938, I, pp. 75–6. On al-Jāḥiẓ's views and on whether Arabic poses unique problems that render it less translatable than other languages, see Kilito 2002; and Kilito 2008. See also "To Translate or Not to Translate Arabic: Michael Cooperson and Waïl S. Hassan on the Criticism of Abdelattah Kilito," *Comparative Literature Studies* 48.4 (2011), pp. 566–75. On Kilito's injunction "thou shalt not translate me," see Apter 2013, pp. 247–61.

82 The psychological explanation alluded to by Gustave E. von Grunebaum is also relevant here (von Grunebaum 1953, pp. 258–347; von Grunebaum 1967, pp. 1–14). On von Grunebaum's approach to literary criticism and the role of history and psychology within the Western Orientalist tradition, see Riedel 1998, pp. 111–22.

models, it had Greek literary models at hand and certainly would have found ways "to eliminate or neutralize any element endangering its religious foundation [...] to obscure the foreign character of important borrowings and to reject what could not be thus adjusted to its style of thinking and feeling."[83]

In contrast, interference from foreign cultures from the start of the nineteenth century onward has existed because most branches of Arab culture had found themselves during this period without a sufficient repertoire for newly needed functions.[84] This comes most clearly to the fore when we look at concepts current in languages of other societies with which Arabs were in contact and for which they sought equivalents. An illustration of this may be found in the following statement in 1858 by a Lebanese journalist in *Ḥadīqat al-Akhbār*, one of the first privately owned Arabic newspapers:

> If anybody should find [such a definition] presumptuous and insulting to the Arab intelligence, let him take the trouble of translating a speech by a British Parliament member or, better still, render into Arabic the proceedings of a session; an article on European theater; a political study; a commercial report, and the like. Surely, he would find himself facing an abyss with every single sentence. He might not transcend it without seriously complicating the language, leaving his readers in disconcertment and doubt.[85]

As the aforementioned examples show, translations into Arabic may tell us about the self-image of Arab culture at various periods in time and the changes which that self-image undergoes over time.[86]

Factors associated with changes in a given literature cannot be dealt with separately from those associated with changes in the culture and society in

83 Von Grunebaum 1953, p. 321. Cf. Abū Sa'ūd 1934, p. 968. L. E. Goodman states that "the processes by which Greek themes and modes of thought were made at home in the Islamic world of *Arabic literature*, not merely disguised, but adjusted to the Islamic experience and the Arabic idiom, is an even more fascinating and complex subject than the movement of translation itself" (Goodman 1983, pp. 481–2, my emphasis); however, as is evident from his study, he is not referring to belles-lettres.

84 The absence of a sufficient repertoire for newly needed functions is illustrated in Salāma Mūsā's statement in his article "al-Klasiyya Dā' al-Adab al-'Arabī" ("Classicism Is the Malady of Arabic Literature") (Mūsā 1945, p. 82). Cf. Tobi's (1995, pp. 39–42) argument concerning the development of the relationship between Hebrew poetry and Arabic poetry in the Middle Ages: During the first century of Islam, "thanks to the strength of Hebrew poetry and its distance from Arabic poetry, there was no need for defensive measures [...] Arab culture and Islam, which had not yet attained a high level of development, still did not constitute a threat to the integrity of Judaism." However, during the ninth and tenth centuries, "the turn to Arabic poetry came about as a result of the marked weakness of the paytanic school of Hebrew poetry, which had exhausted itself almost entirely after an active period of close to seven centuries."

85 *Ḥadīqat al-Akhbār*, 22 December 1858, p. 2 (quoted from Ayalon 1987, p. 5). Cf. Mansiyyah 1993.

86 Cf. Lefevere 1990, p. 27. On the self-image of Arab culture, see below, the Conclusion.

which that literature exists. However, unlike pre-functionalist doctrines, a literary system, like any literary text,[87] is not considered to be subject to external factors. The pre-functionalists assumed a unilateral and univalent subordination of literature to either social, spiritual, or economic forces in society. Modern theories of literature have hypothesized literature itself to be a social force and have suggested conceiving of it as both an autonomous and heteronomous system "among a series of (semiotically) correlated systems operating in the 'system-of-systems' of society."[88] Literature is just one system of institutionalized symbolic interactions among many others within society.[89] From this perspective, literature becomes part of a social and cultural system, and it should be analyzed with regard to other social and cultural systems.[90] Yet, while the need for and the rate and tempo of change may depend on the social and cultural norms adapted by the literary system, any change that is actualized is conditioned by the literary system and the specific poetic norms within it.[91]

At this point, a short reference should be made to the issue of canonicity and canonization in Arabic literature as well as to the standards and criteria for literary stratification. Unlike small literary systems, such as Hebrew literature,[92] the question of intentionality and responsibility—that is, who should be held accountable for any pattern of inclusion and exclusion—is irrelevant to such a huge literary system as Arabic literature. Beside the point as well for Arabic literature are any implications of intentional conspiracy alluded by the short-story-cum-essay "Canon Confidential: A Sam Slade Caper," by Henry Louis Gates (b. 1950), which opens his book *Loose Canons* (1992).[93] Ṭāhā Ḥusayn—one of the major representatives of the Arabic literary establishment during the 1940s and 1950s—claimed that

87 Although a literary text might be considered to be a microcosm of a literary system, one can by no means employ any textual component in the description of the literary system, especially when referring to several types of criticism, such as historical, biographical, sociological, and psychological criticism. These types have distinctive ways of defining the relations between the text and external factors, such as trying "to suggest what is in the poem by showing what lies behind it" (Preminger 1974, p. 167). In that sense, the characteristics of the literary system are similar to the characteristics of the text as seen by those critics who argue that there is no necessary connection between an idea or experience inside a text and the same idea or experience outside it. Moreover, an idea or experience inside a text is not considered to be subject to the same idea or experience outside it.

88 Sebeok 1986, I, p. 459.

89 With regard to literary theory, cf. Navarrete 1986, pp. 123–4.

90 See below, pp. 100–74.

91 Sebeok 1986, I, p. 460. It seems that Idwār al-Kharrāṭ (1926–2015) alludes to these specific intra-literary circumstances by what he described as *āliyyāt hādhā al-mujtama' al-aṣīla al-kāmina* ("the genuine inherited mechanics of this [Arab] society") (al-Kharrāṭ 2005, p. 94).

92 Cf. Gluzman 2003, pp. 181–5.

93 Gates 1992, pp. 3–15.

the basic criterion for canonical and non-canonical literature was the use of *fuṣḥā* and *ʿāmmiyya*—or, as he put it, the difference between "literature" and "non-literature."[94] Authors resorted to *ʿāmmiyya*, he said, mainly in order to increase their readership.[95] In fact, canonicity in Arabic literature until today generally depends on the language of production: *fuṣḥā* is the basic medium of canonized texts, whereas *ʿāmmiyya* is that of non-canonized texts. Nevertheless, in recent decades *ʿāmmiyya* has been increasingly employed in contemporary canonized literature, especially in drama where we can find entire texts written in dialect.[96] It is also being employed in novels, particularly in dialogue but also in narrative sections where one recognizes clear lexical, phraseological, and syntactical elements of *ʿāmmiyya*.[97] The latter are even found in contemporary canonized poetry, in which *fuṣḥā* is still dominant.[98]

At the same time, not every text written in *fuṣḥā* is regarded as canonized, as illustrated by the newborn genre of science fiction[99] and by Islamist literature (see below). We can see it even in the field of secular modernist poetry written in *fuṣḥā*. For example, in the introduction to the inaugural issue of the magazine *al-Kitāba al-Ukhrā* (*The Other Writing*), entitled "al-Ḥarāfish Yafʿalūna al-Kitāba" ("The Common People Make the Writing"),[100] the editor-in-chief Hishām Qishṭa presents the texts which the magazine plans to publish as literary marginalia, the aim of the magazine being to provide a forum for those whose work might otherwise remain unpublished.[101] Qishṭa

94 Ḥusayn 1945, p. 14; Ḥusayn n.d. [1958], p. 14. The terms *fuṣḥā* and *ʿāmmiyya* will be used in the following pages to denote the pan-Arab language as distinct from local dialects. On this issue and the other terms used to describe these types of language as well as other mixed types of language, see Somekh 1991, pp. 6–10; and Reynolds 1995, pp. 30–1. On the diglossia in the Arabic language in general (along with bibliographical references), see Versteegh et al. 2006, I, pp. 629–37. On diversity and stratification in medieval Arabic culture, see al-Musawi 2015b, pp. 130–1.

95 Ḥusayn 1945, pp. 26-27; Ḥusayn n.d. [1958], pp. 30–1.

96 Somekh 1991, pp. 37–45.

97 Somekh 1991, pp. 21–35.

98 Somekh 1991, pp. 58–64.

99 See Snir 2000, pp. 263–85; Snir 2002b, pp. 209–29.

100 *Al-Kitāba al-Ukhrā* 1 (May 1991), pp. 3–7. The first study in the magazine (pp. 11–37) is by ʿAlī Fahmī and deals with *Dīn al-Ḥarāfish* ("The Religion of the Common People"). On the Ḥarāfish and the attitude of the Mamluk elite to them, see Brinner 1963, pp. 190–215; and al-Musawi 2015b, pp. 286–7.

101 In 2001, the magazine *al-Kitāba al-Ukhrā* stopped its activities; it renewed regular publication in January 2010, when it released new issues, among them one about the Tunisian revolution entitled *Kitāb al-Thawra: al-Ishārāt al-Tunisiyya* (*The Book of the Revolution: The Tunisian Signs*) (<http://www.sampsoniaway.org/hamdy-elgazzar-arabic/2013/03/11/the-book-of-the-revolutiontunisian-signs-arabic-text/> [11 March 2013] [last accessed 7 October 2016]). On the magazine and its role in Egyptian cultural life since its first issue, see the words of its editor-in-chief, Hishām Qishṭa: "The margins from which *al-Kitāba*

contrasts *al-Ḥarāfīsh* writing in *fuṣḥā* with the canonical literary establishment (*al-mu'assasa al-thaqāfiyya al-rasmiyya*) and calls for adventurous and experimental poetic writing, but sometimes the usual political anti-Zionist agenda of Egyptian men of letters ended up overshadowing their purely poetical discourse.[102] The question, however, is whether the conception articulated by Qishṭa can be taken as evidence that there is an incipient change taking place in the concept of canonization within the Arabic literary system. The canonized social drama—whose entire text is written in dialect—would at first glance appear to be a major genre, in which such a change has actually transpired. However, upon taking a closer look at the function of language in such a drama, we find that the employment of *'āmmiyya* is by no means due to an aesthetic preference for the vernacular over *fuṣḥā*, but stems rather from a generic constraint, namely, the need to produce an "authentic" representation of reality. Where no such justification is needed, *'āmmiyya* is avoided even in this genre, as illustrated by the stage directions which are always in *fuṣḥā*. Even in collections of vernacular poetry (*zajal*), information regarding publishing houses, editions, covers, printing, and almost all the dedications written by the *zajal* poets themselves are given in *fuṣḥā*.[103] The same issue of canonicity is relevant also to such humoristic magazines as the Egyptian weekly *Kārīkātīr* (*Caricature*) that was published in the early 1990s by al-Majmū'a al-'Arabiyya li-l-Nashr wa-l-I'lān. Despite its popular humoristic character, the magazine does not leave the canonical status of *fuṣḥā* in doubt.[104]

However, the claim that an authentic representation of reality in literature must be achieved through the employment of *'āmmiyya*[105] is a groundless argument (in spite of what we just saw with the use of *'āmmiyya* in the can-

al-Ukhrā emerged were the real corpus of Egyptian culture, and they have made the canonical formal corpus marginal" (*al-'Arabī al-Jadīd*, 21 April 2015).

102 See, for example, the opening article Qishṭa wrote to issue 8 (1994).

103 See, for example, the dedications in two of the collections of 'Abd al-Raḥmān al-Abnūdī (1938–2015) (al-Abnūdī 1986 [1964], p. 3; and al-Abnūdī 1986 [1970], p. 3). Exceptions are very few, such as the dedication in *'āmmiyya* by Aḥmad Fu'ād Nigm (Najm) (1929–2013) in his memoirs written to his daughters (Nigm 1993, p. 3). However, even in this book the information given by the publisher and the introduction by Ṣalāḥ 'Īsā (pp. 9–28) are written in *fuṣḥā*.

104 For example, issue 77 (27 May–2 June 1992) includes caricatures with texts in *'āmmiyya* but also many items in *fuṣḥā*, such as the editorial which contains some passages of dialogue (p. 3); a letter by the Saudi prince Fayṣal ibn Fahd ibn 'Abd al-'Azīz (1944–99) following a preceding issue dealing with the problem of drugs (p. 5); an essay by the writer Anīs Manṣūr (1925–2011) (p. 9); humoristic anecdotes from around the world (p. 12); and a *maqāma* by the poet Kamāl 'Ammār (1932–2007) (p. 13).

105 See, for example, al-Baqlī 1962 (p. 31) about the poet in the vernacular: "He can describe the inclinations of society, its passions and moods much more than the canonical poet who stays in his ivory tower without being in touch with the people."

onized social drama). Composing a dialogue in *fuṣḥā* does not violate "one of the major norms of realism,"[106] and when it comes to literature as *literature*[107] it is irrelevant to claim that when written in *fuṣḥā* "a novel or drama becomes totally dissimilar to the situations which it attempts to depict."[108] Besides, even if we accept the kind of simplified and naïve meaning of "realism" which is implied here, it does not necessitate the use of *'āmmiyya*, since art is never a literal transposition of reality. As the Egyptian critic Muḥammad Mandūr (1907–65) has written, what must reflect reality is the description an author gives of situations and events rather than the linguistic means he or she uses to that end.[109] Everyday situations and events can be described even in *fuṣḥā*, and the transfer from the linguistic expression actually used to the speech of everyday life can easily be made by the readers themselves.[110] Ṭāhā Ḥusayn mentions that history has preserved realistic masterpieces composed in a literary idiom by the ancient Greeks, Romans, and Arabs as well as by the neoclassical writers of the West.[111]

The increase in the prominence of literary works in dialect in the second half of the twentieth century was considered by many writers at the time to

106 Sasson Somekh, "A Literature in Search of Language," Inaugural Lecture, The Irene Halmos Chair of Arabic Literature, Tel Aviv University, 23 October 1983, p. 5; Somekh 1991, p. 37; and Somekh 1993a, p. 176. Cf. Philip K. Hitti's introduction to his edition of *Kitāb al-I'tibār* by Usāma ibn Munqidh (1095–1188), in which he refers to the employment of *'āmmiyya*'s phrases as "a brilliantly realistic literary choice" (Ibn Munqidh 1930, p. *thth* [sic]).

107 "Since literature itself is a form of interpretation, it must be linked to the real world. Consequently, it cannot be abstracted from reality—the ideal of autonomous Art—and it cannot replace reality—the ideal of the Paris revolutionaries. Nor can it merely imitate reality, as was claimed by the concept of mimesis" (Iser 1989, p. 210).

108 Abdel-Malek 1972, p. 132. See also al-Qishṭīnī 2001, p. 12.

109 Cf. the argument of the Syrian poet and critic Adūnīs ('Alī Aḥmad Sa'īd) (b. 1930): "The problem of colloquial and literary standard Arabic is contrived. I have never used colloquial Arabic in my writings. I am not, however, against the use of spoken Arabic in writing. The distinction between the language of literary expression and the language of poetry will always be there in all languages" (Deeb 1983, p. 262).

110 See Mandūr 1984, pp. 75–6: "Realism is not in the language but in the internal description of characters and in the correspondence between this description and the reality of life, the external and invisible [...] The writer speaks in his own language and he is required to be honest in the expression of the life of his characters, and from this point of view, there is no difference writing in *fuṣḥā* or in *'āmmiyya* or in any other language." Cf. Abdel-Malek 1972, p. 133.

111 Ḥusayn 1966 [1958], pp. 21–9, 179–91. Cf. Semah 1974, p. 120; and Starkey 2006, p. 18. See also Qāsim 1980, pp. 391–7; Siddiq 1992, pp. 97–105; Armbrust 1996, p. 230, n. 21; and Siddiq 2007, pp. 11–12. On the general issue of relativism with regard to realism and the "authentic" representation of reality in art, see Jakobson 1971, pp. 38–46 (Russian original: Matejka and Pomorska 1971, pp. 30–6. Hebrew version: Jakobson 1986, pp. 226–32). See also Grant 1970.

be a "danger."[112] Some writers and critics have even argued that *'āmmiyya* is associated with ignorance and vulgarity and cannot be a means of precise expression, since it is the speech of culturally deprived illiterates whose experiences, desires, and emotions are relatively limited.[113] Nobel laureate Najīb Maḥfūẓ (1911–2006) and *al-Ādāb*'s editor Suhayl Idrīs (1925–2008), two prominent figures of the canonical core of Arabic literature, were at the center of the opposition to the use of any form of language other than *fuṣḥā* in literature.[114] In the early 1960s, Maḥfūẓ described *'āmmiyya* as a disease (*maraḍ*):

> إن اللغة العامّية من جملة الأمراض التي يعاني منها الشعب والتي سيتخلّص منها حتما حينما يرتقي،
> وأنا أعتبر العامّية من عيوب مجتمعنا مثل الجهل والفقر والمرض تماما.
>
> *'Āmmiyya* is one of the diseases the people are suffering from and which they are bound to rid themselves of as they progress. I consider *'āmmiyya* one of the failings of our society, exactly like ignorance, poverty, and disease.[115]

About forty years later, Maḥfūẓ considered the reception of his novels as proof that *fuṣḥā* must be the language of literature. The fact that many who

112 See Versteegh et al. 2006, I, pp. 601–2.

113 Apart from the attempt to increase their readership (see above), Ṭāhā Ḥusayn considers authors who employ *'āmmiyya* as lazy because of their failure to master *fuṣḥā* (Ḥusayn 1964, III, pp. 200–1. See also Mandūr 1984, p. 92).

114 See *al-Ādāb* 1.4 (1953), p. 38; Somekh 1973a, pp. 94–100, 151–5, 187–90; and Somekh 1993a, p. 179.

115 Duwāra 1963, pp. 19–20; Duwāra 1965, pp. 286–7. The translation is according to Cachia 1990, pp. 71–2. Cf. Somekh 1991, p. 27; Maḥfūẓ 1999, p. 10 (the introduction by the writer Muḥammad Jibrīl [b. 1938]); Holes 2004, p. 380; al-Naqqāsh 2006, pp. 171–6; and Starkey 2006, p. 18. See also Armbrust 1996, p. 43; and the argument of the *zajal* poet Wilyam Ṣa'b (1912–99): "The writer should direct the nation into sublime aims, in the direction of the public welfare, and that demands promoting *'āmmiyya* to the level of *fuṣḥā* in a way that will not leave differences harming the essence. In order to reach that aim, those who write in the language of the people should purify their writings of the local phrases and use only phrases from *fuṣḥā*" (*al-Adīb*, January 1943, p. 42). It is interesting that, more than forty years after the publication of Maḥfūẓ's aforementioned complaint about *'āmmiyya* as one of the failings of Arab society, the same arguments are frequently mentioned. For example, the Yemenite poet and critic 'Abd al-'Azīz al-Maqāliḥ (b. 1937) argues that "the enemies of Arabic are the Arabs themselves—the ignorant Arabs and the careless Arabs." 'Alī Ṣalāḥ Ahmad, Chairman of the Yemen TV and Radio Corporation, says that the decline we see in Arabic is a result of the weakness of the people and that the laziness that stops people from using correct *fuṣḥā* led to a decline in morals in general; people are lazy and that is why they like *'āmmiyya* and prefer it over *fuṣḥā*, ignoring and overlooking the consequences that this occurrence will grow and grow. His compatriot Jamīl 'Izz al-Dīn argues that writers and journalists are not only to blame for the decline and deterioration, but that the trend of globalization has had a major influence on this decline and deterioration: "The 'global culture' in the world today that comes from developed countries aims at the nullifying of Arabic and of Islamic identity in Arab and Islamic nations" (Al-Alaya'a 2006). On globalization, see below, pp. 265–71.

read his novels were not consciously aware of whether the characters were speaking *fuṣḥā* or *ʿāmmiyya* was for him absolute proof that he had overcome the problem of dialogue in fiction.[116] In his *Memories in Translation* (2006), the Canadian-born British writer and translator Denys Johnson-Davies (b. 1922),[117] who was the first to translate Maḥfūẓ's work into English, described how Maḥfūẓ eschewed the colloquial language and made even the least likely of his characters to do so express themselves in *fuṣḥā*. Maḥfūẓ himself put it thus:

> [B]y introducing colloquial language, for example in the dialog, one might estrange non-Egyptian readers. As for Egyptian readers, they would automatically in their minds render the dialog into suitable idiomatic colloquial language.[118]

Thus, what we find is that it is not the literary aspects and poetic aspects of a text that may work to undermine the equations *fuṣḥā* = canonized literature and *ʿāmmiyya* = non-canonized literature, but the non-literary aspects. I have in mind here, for example, texts that are part of the social engineering that comes with nation-building.[119]

Based on the aforementioned assumptions, the concepts of canonicity and canonization, and the *fuṣḥā*/*ʿāmmiyya* dichotomy, the chapters that follow present the literary inventories and historical development of the Arabic literary system as analyzed through the functional dynamic historical model. With the metaphor of the system serving as our primary frame of reference,[120] I hope to show that a dynamic functional correlation may be assumed on every literary level by revealing how every textual element, literary text, or literary subsystem plays a non-static function in this wider framework. This "idea of order" has been perhaps most compellingly described by T. S. Eliot:

> No poet, no artist of any art, has his complete meaning alone. His significance, his appreciation is the appreciation of his relation to the dead poets and artists. You cannot value him alone; you must set him, for contrast and comparison,

116 Mahfouz 2001, p. 87. Despite Maḥfūẓ's negative attitude toward *ʿāmmiyya*, he used in the dialogue in his fiction, from an early stage in his literary career, phrases in the dialect after "adapting" them to the structure of *fuṣḥā*: For example, in *Qaṣr al-Shawq* (1957) he used in the dialogue sentences like *nāwin taʿmalu ḥāditha?*, which is an adaptation of the dialectical Egyptian phrase *nāwī tiʿmal ḥāditha?* ("do you want to cause an incident?").

117 On his role in promoting Arabic literature in the English-speaking world, see Al-Halool 2013, pp. 39–53. On the occasion of Johnson-Davies' ninetieth birthday, *Banipal* published a special feature in its spring 2012 issue (43).

118 Johnson-Davies 2006, p. 30.

119 See below, pp. 160–74. It is obvious, regarding all periods of Arabic literature, that the language of a literary work is not enough to serve as a shibboleth between canonized and non-canonized literature (cf. Bauer 2007, pp. 151–8).

120 Steiner 1984, p. 99.

> among the dead. I mean this as a principle of aesthetic, not merely historical, criticism. The necessity that he shall conform, that he shall cohere, is not one-sided; what happens when a new work of art is created is something that happens simultaneously to all the works of art which preceded it. The existing monuments form an ideal order among themselves, which is modified by the introduction of the new (the really new) work of art among them. The existing order is complete before the new work arrives; for order to persist after the supervention of novelty, the whole existing order must be, if ever so slightly, altered; and so the relations, proportions, values of each work of art toward the whole art readjusted; and this is conformity between the old and the new. Whoever has approved this idea of order, of the form of European, of English literature will not find it preposterous that the past should be altered by the present as much as the present is directed by the past. And the poet who is aware of this will be aware of great difficulties and responsibilities.[121]

Referring to Eliot's conception, the mutual influence of one text on another is, as Frank Kermode argues, "intemporal in itself, appearing in time only by means of commentary." And "the idea of canon is used in the service of an order which can be discerned in history but actually transcends it, and makes everything timeless and modern."[122]

121 Eliot 1950, pp. 4–5.
122 Kermode 1988, p. 116.

Chapter 2

Literary Dynamics in Synchronic Cross-section

In presenting the literary dynamics of Arabic literature in the synchronic cross-section, I will treat both canonical and non-canonical literary texts in the following three subsystems: literature for adults; literature for children; and literary translations for adults and children. As I mentioned in the Introduction, the resulting six subsystems can be understood as networks of relationships interacting on various levels. And as we have seen, although *fuṣḥā* is occasionally used in non-canonical texts and although *ʿāmmiyya* appears in varying degrees in canonical texts, *fuṣḥā* remains the basic medium for canonical Arabic literature and *ʿāmmiyya* remains the basic medium for non-canonical literature.

CANONICAL LITERATURE

Texts for Adults

The inventory of texts in this canonical subsystem includes four main genres:

Poetry

The texts in this genre are written only in *fuṣḥā*, although dialectical elements are occasionally present.[1] A good illustration of this is the aforementioned encyclopedic dictionary *Muʿjam al-Bābaṭīn li-l-Shuʿarāʾ al-ʿArab al-Muʿāṣirīn* (1995), which includes 1,644 entries by twentieth-century Arab poets.[2] In their introduction, the editors outline three preconditions

[1] Cf. Somekh 1991, pp. 119–28. On the general phenomenon, see Adūnīs 1993, pp. 133–7, 185.

[2] On 6 January 2002 the cornerstone of the al-Bābaṭīn Central Library for Arabic Poetry was laid in Kuwait City, and the library was inaugurated on 9 April 2006. The library had at the time more than 27,000 books, and the aim was to make it "a centre of interaction between poets and to exchange information and ideas. It is expected to become a reference place for

for inclusion: linguistic perfection (*salāma lughawiyya*), musical perfection (*salāma mūsīqiyya*), and aesthetic and artistic level (*al-mustawā al-jamālī wa-l-fannī*).[3] Writing to the Palestinian poet Fārūq Mawāsī (b. 1941) about why they had decided not to include his work in the dictionary, the Institute of ʿAbd al-ʿAzīz Saʿūd al-Bābṭīn's Prize for Poetic Creation gave the following reasons: defects in meter; the use of dialectical words; and the employment of Hebrew words.[4] Another, more recent, illustration is the TV program *Amīr al-Shuʿarā'* (*Prince of Poets*), which attracts millions of viewers from across the Arab world. In 2008 the program received applications from 7,000 poets, all of whom had to "show their commitment to the old tradition." Those who did not conform to classical guidelines were rejected. The program has enormous appeal with the younger demographic, and the contestants themselves must be between the ages of eighteen and forty-five.[5]

The novel

Novels exist primarily in *fuṣḥā*, although there are novels which employ *ʿāmmiyya* in dialogues. In the few examples of whole novels written in the vernacular, the inferior status of *ʿāmmiyya* in the literary system is beyond any doubt.[6] When the Egyptian writer Yūsuf al-Qaʿīd (b. 1944) published

all Arabs and a place for the gathering of poets for seminars, exhibitions, and intellectual courses" (<http://www.kuwaittimes.net>, 10 April 2006 [last accessed 11 October 2016]). In an update, I found that the total number of all collections "is some 138,000 books, excluding periodicals and electronic resources" (<http://www.albabtainlibrary.org.kw/new/en/about.php> [last accessed 31 May 2016]).

3 *Muʿjam al-Bābaṭīn li-l-Shuʿarā' al-ʿArab al-Muʿāṣirīn* (1995), I, pp. 24, 42.

4 Letter from the institute to Fārūq Mawāsī, dated 14 January 1996. I am indebted to Dr Mawāsī for kindly giving me permission to quote from the letter.

5 See <http://www.thenational.ae/article/20080813/OPINION/924843602/1033&templat e=opinion> (13 August 2008. The link is no longer active). The program is a reality television poetry competition on the United Arab Emirates television network Abu Dhabi TV. It was created in April 2007 by the Abu Dhabi Authority for Culture and Heritage (<http://www.princeofpoets.com/ar/> [last accessed 23 May 2016]).

6 Two famous attempts to write novels in the vernacular were *al-Sayyid wa-Marātu fī Bārīs* (*The Gentleman and his Wife in Paris*) by Bayram al-Tūnisī (1893–1961), which is a humorous description of his life outside Egypt (al-Tūnisī 1986. Cf. Dūs and Davies 2013, pp. 85–9), and *Mudhakkirāt Ṭālib Baʿtha* (*Memoirs of an Overseas Mission Student*) by Lūwīs ʿAwaḍ (1915–90). ʿAwaḍ's novel, written in 1942 and recording the author's personal experiences in Cambridge, was only published for the first time in 1965 (on the book, see El-Enany 1998, pp. 61–71; and Oliverius 2000, pp. 16–23. Cf. Dūs and Davies 2013, pp. 115–17). ʿAwaḍ provides a very instructive description of his encounter in 1944 with the censor who banned the publication of the book since "[it] is written in *ʿāmmiyya* and books must be published only in *fuṣḥā*" (ʿAwaḍ 1991 [1965], pp. 16–18). In 1966 ʿAwaḍ published the novel *al-ʿAnqā' aw Ta'rīkh Ḥasan Muftāḥ* (*The Phoenix, or the History of Ḥasan Muftāḥ*) (ʿAwaḍ 1966). According to Denys Johnson-Davies, ʿAwaḍ originally wrote the novel in the 1940s in the

the novel *Laban al-ʿUṣfūr* (*The He-Sparrow's Milk*),[7] he gave it the subtitle *Riwāya bi-l-ʿĀmmiyya al-Miṣriyya* (*A Novel in the Egyptian Vernacular*). However, the publisher took some "defensive measures" to "justify" its publication and to point out the difference between the canonical status of *fuṣḥā* and the non-canonical status of *ʿāmmiyya*. For example, the opening pages of the book written by the publisher are all in *fuṣḥā*. And to the biographical note about the author at the end of the book, the publisher added the following:

> النصّ مكتوب بلغة الهوامش البشرية الذين لا يملكون سوى قاموس الحدّ الأدنى اللغوي. ربما كانت مغامرة أو نزوة ولكنها من حقّ المؤلّف خاصّة أننا نرحّب بالعامّيّة شعرا ولكننا نرفضها قصّا وحكاية، ويعتبرها البعض مؤامرة على وحدة الوطن العربي. من حقّ الروائي، بعد أن ينتهي من وضع أسس بناء عالمه الروائي أن يجرّب أحيانا وأن يحاول الخروج على ما هو سائد.

> The text is written in the language of human marginalia, who possess only a minimal vocabulary. This may be an adventure or whim on the part of the author, but it is his right, especially because we welcome the use of *ʿāmmiyya* in poetry. However, we reject the use of *ʿāmmiyya* in fiction and stories, and there are those who even regard it as a conspiracy against the unity of the Arab homeland. Still, having completed the building of his narrative world, the author may well be allowed to experiment once in a while and to attempt to revolt against the prevailing situation.[8]

vernacular and even then gave the manuscript to several of his friends to read. Among them was Johnson-Davies himself. However, ʿAwaḍ eventually published it in *fuṣḥā* (Johnson-Davies 2006, p. 52). In the introduction to the book, ʿAwaḍ did not mention that the novel was originally written in the vernacular, but he wrote that Tawfīq al-Ḥakīm (1898–1987) read it in the beginning of 1965 and remarked that "had the novel been published when it was written in the 1940s, it would have changed the course of the Arabic novel" (ʿAwaḍ 1966, p. 50). In his epilogue to the second edition of *Blūtūlānd wa-Qaṣāʾid Ukhrā min Shiʿr al-Khāṣṣa* (first edition was in 1947; the second was in 1988), which includes poems in *ʿāmmiyya* (alongside poems in *fuṣḥā*), ʿAwaḍ states that in those poems as well as in the novel he employed the same *ʿāmmiyya* in which the more well-known intellectuals of the Arab world expressed "their sublime ideas and feelings" (ʿAwaḍ 1988 [1947], p. 148. On ʿAwaḍ's poetic experiments, see Khouri 1970, pp. 137–44. On ʿAwaḍ as a standard-bearer for a secular Egyptian national culture, see Vatikiotis 1991, pp. 179–80). On the vernacular in fiction in general, see also Holes 2004, pp. 375–80. On the novel *Qanṭara al-Ladhī Kafara* (*Qanṭara Who Became an Infidel*), by Muṣṭafā Muṣṭafā Musharrafa (1902–66), entirely written in Egyptian dialect in the 1940s and published in the early 1960s, see De Angelis 2013, pp. 19–27.

7 See al-Qaʿīd 1994. Cf. Dūs and Davies 2013, pp. 137–40. Although the language of the novel seems to be the *ʿāmmiyya* of Cairo, it also contains elements from other dialects. For a description of the language of the novel—orthography, morphology, syntax, and lexicon—see Zack 2001, pp. 193–219. The title of the novel is a sort of "*adynata*" or "*adynaton*," that is, a stringing together of impossibilities (Zack 2001, p. 196, n. 11. Cf. Canter 1930, pp. 32–41; and Snir 1994a, p. 52. See also the title of the collection of short stories *Ḥalīb al-Thīrān* [*Bulls' Milk*] by the Iraqi writer Fātiḥ ʿAbd al-Salām [ʿAbd al-Salām 1999]).

8 Al-Qaʿīd 1994, p. 226. Cf. Holes 2004, p. 380.

This "revolt against the prevailing situation" may perhaps offer further aesthetic justification for the employment of *'āmmiyya* in this novel, as the whole text has no narrative sections at all. It consists, rather, of monologue in the first person by Tirtir, a poor woman from one of the slums of Cairo, who, bewailing her fate, tells of the events that led to her imprisonment. Only a few reviews of the novel were published in the Egyptian press—one reviewer, while expressing his admiration for the way in which the author depicted the lives of poor people, nevertheless criticized the use of *'āmmiyya.*[9] Al-Qa'īd, who had previously written stories and novels in *fuṣḥā*, published just before the appearance of the novel "an advocacy of the colloquial written in the standard Arabic." As a representative of the poor and the outcasts of society, he says, he had to express their feelings in their own language.[10]

Some circles of the literary establishment, however, consider novels which employ *'āmmiyya* to be only partially canonical because for them *'āmmiyya* has no room in literature. This is illustrated in the way the art of the Egyptian novelist Yūsuf al-Sibā'ī (1917–78) developed. Al-Sibā'ī went through three phases of linguistic expression:[11] First, he was held captive by the fact that *fuṣḥā* was *the* criterion for canonicity and therefore wrote his novels strictly in *fuṣḥā*. Later, he began occasionally to borrow from *'āmmiyya* for his narrative sections and for his dialogues. In the introduction to his novel *al-Saqqā Māt* (*The Water Carrier Died*) (1952), he tells the story of how Aḥmad 'Abbās, the chief inspector of Arabic language in the Egyptian Ministry of Education, had informed him that the ministry had wanted to include several of his books in the school curricula but that the relevant committee had been prevented from doing so by "several phrases in *'āmmiyya*" in these books.[12] In order to please the ministry, he had decided that he would write *al-Saqqā Māt* entirely in *fuṣḥā*:

> صمّمت على أن أقيم سياجا منيعا يحول دون تسرّب الألفاظ العاميّة التي تأبى إلا أن تفرض نفسها فرضا في سياق الحديث، وأخذت في الكتابة محاولا إجراء الحوار بين أبطال القصّة باللغة العربية، ولكني لم أكد أكتب بضع صفحات، ولم أكد «أحمى» في الكتابة حتى وجدت أبطال القصّة ينطقون على الرغم منّي في الحديث باللغة العامّية.

I resolved to erect an impregnable fence against the sneaking in of colloquial expressions that insisted on imposing themselves on the dialogue, and I proceeded to write, resolving to keep the conversation between the characters of

[9] *Al-Ahrām*, 17 July 1994, p. 20. Cf. Zack 2001, p. 197.

[10] *Akhbār al-Adab*, 15 May 1994, p. 31. Cf. Zack 2001, p. 197.

[11] According to Abdel-Malek 1972, pp. 132–41.

[12] The Egyptian novelist and short story writer Ibrāhīm Aṣlān (1935–2012) relates that, when he sent one of his first stories to be published in one of the journals, it was rejected because "the line of the journal, which is committed to *fuṣḥā*, makes it impossible" (Aṣlān 2003, p. 9).

> the novel in standard Arabic. But no sooner had "I warmed up" and written a few pages, than I found the characters of the novel conversing—in spite of me—in colloquial language.[13]

In his third phase, al-Sibāʿī used a style that seems to be a compromise between *fuṣḥā* and *ʿāmmiyya*, showing how canonical norms of the literary system have even had an impact on a writer whose internal and aesthetic preference favors the use of *ʿāmmiyya*.

The short story

The use of *ʿāmmiyya* in this genre is limited. As with the novel, on the rare occasion that an entire story is written in the vernacular, the writer or the publisher generally alludes in some way to the inferior status of *ʿāmmiyya*. The entire text of Yūsuf Idrīs' short story "Qiṣṣat Dhī al-Ṣawt al-Naḥīl" ("The Story of the Man with the Thin Voice"), published in his collection *Lughat al-Āy Āy* (*The Language of Ay-Ay*),[14] is written in *ʿāmmiyya* except for the first few lines, which are written in *fuṣḥā*. These lines, however, gradually move into *ʿāmmiyya*:

> في مثل هذا الآوان بصوت واهن كأنه الحفيف غير مبال باهت، محدود بدأ كلّ شيء، وكانت المشكلة دائما أن يبدأ كلّ شيء، مشكلتي ومشكلة زوجتي والآخرين وسأتحدّث بالتفصيل عنهم. كنت هناك وكانت الدنيا ليلا أسود يخيف، مليئا بالأشياء التي تخيف. هناك كلام لا بدّ أن أقوله لأي أحد، لا بدّ أن يعرف واحد على الأقلّ كلّ شيء المهمّ كلّ شيء. نفس العمارة، عمارتنا التي نسكنها الآن، قلت لسايس الجاراج والبوّابين عن كلّ شيء، ووعدوني هم أيضا ساعة يرونهم سيخبرونني بكلّ شيء، بالتفصيل كلّ شيء. السكّان القاطنون فوقنا كويسين وعرفنا نتفاهم بسهولة، إنما السكان اللي تحت (...)

The gradual transition into *ʿāmmiyya* is here justified by an aesthetic constraint, that is, the need to express realistically the inner thoughts of the paranoiac protagonist.[15] This also renders pointless Idrīs' declaration that "all that has been written in *fuṣḥā* is unimportant."[16]

13 Al-Sibāʿī 1952, p. 6. For an English translation of the story, see Fry and King 1974, pp. 113–16.

14 Idrīs n.d. [1965], pp. 29–32. On the story as a cover for "smuggling in some trenchant criticism on the régime's high-handed way of running the country," see Kurpershoek 1981, pp. 145–6.

15 Therefore, we cannot refer to the story as a "deviation" in the narrative art of Idrīs or as an attempt to imitate the language of "speakers and lecturers in contemporary Arab society" (Somekh 1984, p. 91).

16 Ibrāhīm 1965, p. 60:

> وفي رأيي أن كلّ ما كتب بالفصحى ليس فيه شيء وقد قرأت كلّ ما كتب بالفصحى قديما وحديثا فلم أجد فيه فنّا أو شيئا ذا قيمة حتى ليمكننا أن نلغي التراث العربي كلّه بجرّة قلم دون أن نفقد شيئا.

("In my opinion, all that has been written in *fuṣḥā* is unimportant; I read all that has been written in *fuṣḥā* in the past and in the present and I could not find something valuable; moreover, we can abolish the entire Arab heritage with one stroke of a pen without losing anything"). See also Idrīs' words in the early 1970s (Faraj 1971, p. 102) that what has been

Drama

In this genre, *'āmmiyya* is gradually starting to be accepted, especially in social dramas that are originally written for presentation on professional stages. Yet, it happens that the canonical center of Arabic literature refuses to consider these texts as an integral part of the Arabic literary heritage. As the Egyptian critic Muḥammad Mandūr (1907–65) has it:

وكلّ ما هو عاميّ أو ركيك اللغة لا يزال مجتمعنا كما قلنا يرفض أن يعتبره جزءا من تراثنا الأدبي ولو كانت تلك المسرحيات العاميّة متينة التأليف من الناحية الفنية البحتة.

> Everything written in the vernacular or that is weak from the point of view of the language is still considered by our society as not being worthy enough to be a part of our literary heritage, even if, from a purely artistic point of view, these plays in the vernacular are well composed.[17]

Plays in *'āmmiyya* presented on stage have gradually infiltrated the canonical center of Arabic literature. The commercial success that these plays have had among audiences, and, when televised, throughout the Arab world, has certainly helped to accelerate the process of their canonization. More and more canonical dramatists have begun writing in the vernacular in order to enjoy the success that these types of plays often ensure. Yet, while social dramas generally use *'āmmiyya,* historical plays and versified dramas always use *fuṣḥā.*[18] And stage directions, even for social dramas, are always written in *fuṣḥā.*

At this point, a few comments about two outstanding phenomena in the canonical literary sector for adults may be helpful. The first phenomenon is the structure of the canonical center of the Arabic literary system, and the second phenomenon is the almost willful exclusion of Islamist literature (see below) from said center. Two factors explain why those poets and writers who "controlled" the canonical center of the Arabic literary system since the late 1950s have been able to consolidate their elite status ever since: The first is the enormous spread of literary production in print, and the second is the more overt forms of territorial nationalism that have come to characterize the nation-state, at least until the late twentieth century.[19] In poetry, for example, those who were responsible for the breakthrough of the "new poetry," and who acquired canonical status[20] with the canonization of that

written in the past is no more than "a very ancient museum between which and my present feelings there is a great spiritual distance that it is impossible to cross." Cf. Kurpershoek 1981, p. 46; Somekh 1984, pp. 11–19; and David Semah's review of Somekh's book in *al-Karmil—Abḥāth fī al-Lugha wa-l-Adab* 5 (1984), pp. 103–4.

17 Mandūr 1984, p. 25.

18 Cf. Somekh 1991, pp. 37–9.

19 See below, pp. 160–74.

20 If we accept that "canonization" as applied to works of literature derives from the can-

poetry, are still at the canonical center. Canonical poets and writers have generally been able to retain their position[21] and rebuff attempts by other poets and writers, especially those who are young and/or have gained great popularity among the masses, to infiltrate the center.[22] Prominent among the latter are the Egyptian prose writer Iḥsān ʻAbd al-Quddūs (1919–90) and the Syrian poet Nizār Qabbānī (1923–98), who interwove non-canonical literary elements within the established matrix of canonical literary elements into their works by breaking down taboos concerning what can and what cannot be mentioned in canonical literature. Not surprisingly, they have both been accused of courting sensationalism and gratuitous titillation.[23] Both of them also had control over influential means of publishing.[24] ʻAbbās Maḥmūd al-ʻAqqād (1889–1964) used to refer to ʻAbd al-Quddūs' literary works as *adab al-firāsh* (bedroom literature).[25] Concerning ʻAbd al-Quddūs' literary work, Yūsuf Idrīs (1927–91) wrote the following:

> Iḥsān writes about sex for adolescents who read his works and who have yet to discover that there is prose that can actually be worthy of being called a work of art. His writings remind me of those restaurants that gain fame among their patrons not for any carefully prepared dish they may present them with, but simply for the way they stimulate the appetite and nothing more [...] Iḥsān is representative of a group of writers dispersed throughout many countries who aim to amuse readers without solving their problems or dealing with the problems of society.[26]

onization of Christian saints, the latter "does not imply a 'blanket' approval by the canonizing authority of all a saint's words and deeds, his or her opinions, policies, and politics" (Attwater 1985, p. 10). Likewise, the canonization of poets or writers does not imply the "blanket" canonization of all their literary works. See, for example, the case of the *zajal* poems by Aḥmad Shawqī (1868–1932) which were not canonical. They were therefore not included in his official *Dīwān* but in *al-Shawqiyyāt al-Majhūla* (Ṣabrī 1979. See also below, p. 79). For new approaches to canonization processes, see the various contributions in Finkelberg and Stroumsa 2003 and the introduction of the editors (pp. 1-8).

21 The Iraqi poet Fāḍil al-ʻAzzāwī (b. 1940) considers them as "the idols who are guarding the gate of the temple" (*al-aṣnām al-latī taḥrusu bāb al-maʻbad*) (al-ʻAzzāwī 1997, p. 8).

22 The Egyptian poet Muḥammad Sulaymān (b. 1946) from the group of *Aṣwāt* deplores the publishing situation: "We are the generation that was destined to carry what it has written to the critics. We have to make the material available, in person. [...] The poet Salah Abdul Saboor, for example, did not have this problem. His work was published when he was in his thirties. As for us, all our work remains in the drawers" (Mehrez 1994a, p. 182).

23 Cf. Badawi 1992, p. 146.

24 ʻAbd al-Quddūs is the son of Fāṭima (Rūz) al-Yūsuf (1898–1958), a well-known actress, singer, and journalist who founded *Rūz al-Yūsuf* in 1925. Qabbānī owned Manshūrāt Nizār Qabbānī in Beirut.

25 Fawzī 1988a, pp. 169–70.

26 Ibrāhīm 1965, pp. 59–60. See also Vial 1986, p. 190 about ʻAbd al-Quddūs who "flirts with scandal" and whose "gallery of pretty girls at once innocent and greedy for liberty has aroused many adolescent dreams." Muḥammad Ḥusayn Faḍl Allāh (1935–2010), the

Likewise, the Iraqi poet ʿAbd al-Wahhāb al-Bayyātī (1926–99) refused to consider Qabbānī a poet at all:

> He is not a poet in the revolutionary, humanitarian, and universal sense. He is not a poet of suffering, but he is rather like those singers who every day appear and then again disappear and die like flies in a cloudy winter. As I mentioned in my collection *al-Nār wa-l-Kalimāt*, in the poem "Abū Zayd al-Sarūjī,"[27] he reminds me of those eunuch poets in the *maqāmāt* of al-Ḥarīrī, but in a more sophisticated manner.[28]

Al-Bayyātī's poem runs as follows:

كان يغنّي
كان شحّاذا بلا حياء
يجترّ ما في كتب الأمواتِ،
أو يسطو على الأحياء
كان يغنّي
في المواخير،
وفي ولائم الملوك
في شهيّة، لأنه كان بلا حياء

كان يغنّي
كان في مدينتي يفعل ما يشاء
يغوي الصبيّات
ويستجدي

spiritual leader of the Shiʿa militant Lebanese group and political party Ḥizb Allāh (Party of God), says the following about ʿAbd al-Quddūs' employment of sex episodes in his writings: "Several writers, such as Iḥsān ʿAbd al-Quddūs, are dragging sex in their stories in every opportunity" (*al-ʿUnf al-Uṣūlī: Muwājahāt al-Sayf wa-l-Qalam* 1995, p. 212). The sex episodes were at the time part of the attraction of ʿAbd al-Quddūs' works, making producers and directors eager to adapt some of them for film and television. On the literary "value" of ʿAbd al-Quddūs' works and his "contribution" to the national cause, see also Shukrī 1972, pp. 176–9. A poll conducted in 1954 found ʿAbd al-Quddūs to be the most popular living Arabic writer (Meisami and Starkey 1998, I, p. 18).

27 Published in the collection *Kalimāt Lā Tamūtu* (1960) (al-Bayyātī 1979, I, pp. 567–9) (not *al-Nār wa-l-Kalimāt* [1964] as al-Bayyātī indicated in the aforementioned quotation).

28 Dāghir 1989, p. 41. See also al-Bayyātī's words in al-Sayyid 1999 (p. 14) that writers such as Qabbānī "have corrupted cultural life." In an interview with *al-Wasaṭ* (9 August 1999, p. 12) published after his death, al-Bayyātī accused Qabbānī of slandering him before Iraq's late president Ṣaddām Ḥusayn (1937–2006) while he [al-Bayyātī] still stayed in Baghdad. Cf. Makiya 1993, p. 45: "He [Qabbāni] thinks of himself as a revolutionary, for instance, when all that he is really doing is hurling abuse into the wind—being angry but providing no reasons, no rationalizations, no intellectual connections. In an age when the Arabs want their poets to be political and to avenge them against the outside world, Qabbani fitted the bill perfectly. He writes against the Saudis, but he gets published by their newspapers. In fact it no longer matters what he says because the subject is no longer actually Zionism, Imperialism, the Palestinian question, or the dissembling kings and presidents of the Arab world; it is the mindless permanent anger of the poet himself."

على قارعة الطريق في المساء
صنعتُه: تقبيل أيدي الناس - والغناء -
وشتمهم، لأنه حرباء
يعرف من أين تؤكل الأكتافُ
والأثداء.

كان بلا صوت يغنّي
كان في أسماله السوداء
يظهر في كلّ زمان، راكبا
بغلته البرصاء
تتبعه الغربان والوباء

كان يغنّي
عندما أغار هولاكو على بغداد
واستسلمت «طرواد»
وعُلقّت في قلب «مدريد» وفي أبوابها
الأعواد.
لأنه كان، بلا ميعاد
يظهر في كلّ زمان، راكبا
بغلته البرصاء
يتبعه الجراد والوباء.

He used to sing
He was a shameless beggar
Rehashing what's in the books of the dead
Or pouncing on living beings

He used to sing
In the brothels
And at the banquets of kings
With great appetite, because he was shameless.
He used to sing
In our city, he used to do whatever he wanted
Seduce girls
And beg
In the evening on the open road
His craft: kissing people's hands, singing
And cursing them, because he was a chameleon
He knew how to devour shoulders and breasts.[29]

He used to sing without voice
In his black worn garments
He appeared as ever riding

[29] The popular Arab proverb describes someone who knows how to handle things as *ya'lamu min ayna tu'kalu al-katifu*, since the shoulder of a chicken is more difficult to eat than other parts (Wehr 1976, p. 814; al-Bustānī 1977, p. 770).

His leprous female mule
And trailed by crows and plagues.

He used to sing
When Hulagu attacked Baghdad,
When Troy surrendered,
And when in the heart of Madrid and at its gates the *'ūds*
Were hung.[30]
Because he would suddenly
Appear as ever, riding
His leprous female mule
Trailed by locusts and diseases.[31]

Al-Bayyātī added a note to the effect that the Abū Zayd al-Sarūjī of his poem was not a historical figure but rather some sort of archetype of people he could find almost anywhere at any time:

> In this poem, I described Abū Zayd al-Sarūjī as [the harbinger of] disease and plague of periods of defeats in whose wake follow locusts and crows. He rides his leprous female mule and stops near the gates of cities that have been taken and violated. In the poem, I describe him, for example, when Troy fell and the plagues appeared. He is not one particular figure but the prototype of all artists and poets like him throughout history, and this type can appear anytime in a new figure.[32]

Asked how he could explain the enormous popularity of Qabbānī's poetry, al-Bayyātī said:

[30] The word *al-a'wād* (plural of *'ūd*) refers to the well-known string instrument, but can also mean "sticks," thus alluding to the gallows. In both cases, the allusion is to "that crime in Granada," according to the elegy by Antonio Machado (1875–1939) (Machado 1973, pp. 252–3. For an Arabic translation of the poem, see *al-Ṭalī'a*, August 1976, pp. 163–4), that is, the execution of the Spanish poet Federico García Lorca (1898–1936). Lorca has for many years enchanted and captivated the minds of poets throughout the Arab world (e.g. al-Sayyāb 1971, I, pp. 333–4, 355–8; 'Abd al-Ṣabūr 1972, pp. 228–30; al-Bayyātī 1979, I, pp. 605–9, II, pp. 225–7, 249–51, 258–61, 332–7, 344–54, III, pp. 221–42, 321–7, 331–40, 407–19. Cf. 'Abd al-Ṣabūr n.d., pp. 167–75; Badawi 1975, pp. 210, 224, 250, 262; Moreh 1976, p. 268; Jayyusi 1977, pp. 565, 577, 691–2, 749; Shukrī 1978 [1968], pp. 49, 149; Badīr 1982, pp. 129, 177; 'Abd al-'Azīz 1983, pp. 271–99; El-Enany 1989, pp. 252–64; Jihad 2000, pp. 110–13; Azouqa 2005, pp. 188–223; and al-Musawi 2006a, pp. 144–6). The connection between Lorca's musical instrument (the guitar) and his murder appears in a poem by the Palestinian poet Samīḥ al-Qāsim (1939–2014) entitled "Laylan, 'alā Bāb Federico" ("At Night, at Federico's Door") (al-Qāsim 1986, pp. 49–53) which contains the lines "The blood is screaming on the strings / And the guitar is burning." The French-American Palestinian poet Nathalie Handal (b. 1969) published *Poet in Andalucía* (Handal 2012), in which she recreated Lorca's *Poeta en Nueva York* (written 1930; published posthumously in 1940. See *Poet in New York* [trans. Pablo Medina and Mark Statman] [New York: Grove Press, 2008]).

[31] Al-Bayyātī 1979, I, pp. 567–9.

[32] In an interview with *al-Waṭan al-'Arabī*, al-Bayyātī said that Qabbānī was ready to write anything in order to please the readers and to gain money (al-Mizghannī 1999, pp. 434–5).

> You know, flies are used to landing on poisoned candy. Don't forget that we are living in the third world, which is full of paradoxes and miracles. There are no criteria for things here, and this is actually all the more proof that we are the third world. If this poisoned candy was not so popular, we could have left the third world and entered the second or the first.[33]

A similar approach was expressed by the literary critic Jihād Fāḍil, at the time editor of the cultural section of the Lebanese magazine *al-Ḥawādith,* who described Qabbānī as a poet who is willing to adapt himself to the popular taste and who provides his readers with whatever they want.[34] Muḥammad al-Māghūṭ (1934–2006) referred to Qabbānī's poetry as "not differing from any declaration of any governmental official in the Arab world [...] Here is a great poet dealing with minor issues."[35] In his *Mashrū' Zilzāl* (*Earthquake Project*), al-Māghūṭ wrote that Qabbānī was

> just a superficial wound in the forehead of Arabic poetry, but it was an awesome and charming wound [...] He does not see of the woman but her breasts [...] his great tragedy that he wrote about the Suez War and the tripartite aggression, and about the most important local, Arab, international, national, religious, tactical, and strategic issues, with lipstick![36]

The Iraqi poet Sarkūn Būluṣ (1944–2007) considered Qabbānī to be a poet who knew "how to benefit from the old ear" and therefore his rhythms are "mechanical."[37] Unlike his colleagues, *al-Ādāb*'s editor Suhayl Idrīs (1923–2008) considered the simplicity and the spontaneous nature of Qabbānī's poems to be among the main characteristics of true poetry. He compared these poems to the *fuṣḥā* poems of Sa'īd 'Aql (1911–2014), stating that the complexity of 'Aql's poetry in *fuṣḥā* was nothing but the other face of his campaign in favor of *'āmmiyya.*[38] It should be noted that Qabbānī himself was proud that his poetry was not elitist. Referring to himself in the third

33 Dāghir 1989, p. 41. See also al-Bayyātī's words in al-Muṣliḥ 1999, pp. 69–70. Cf. Ḥusām al-Khaṭīb's article in *al-'Arabī* (Kuwait), November 1982, about al-Nafzāwī's *al-Rawḍ al-'Āṭir fī Nuzhat al-Khāṭir* (al-Nafzāwī 1983, pp. 63–7), especially the following: "Books that deal with the intimate or social life of non-European societies enjoy great readership [among the Europeans], especially what related to women" (p. 66).

34 See Fāḍil 1989, p. 82: "Nizār Qabbānī is a poet of what the listeners want, a poet whose eyes are on the ticket box." However, Fāḍil's criticism of Qabbānī's poetry is not disconnected from what he describes as the *shu'ūbī* tendency of Qabbānī. On the *shu'ūbiyya* in modern Arabic literature, see al-Jundī 1977; see also below, p. 170. *Shu'ūbiyya* is an allusion to the movement within the early Islamic commonwealth of nations which refused to recognize the privileged position of the Arabs. For a bibliographical list on the *shu'ūbiyya* in Arabic and Western languages, see Sadān 1988, p. 19, n. 28.

35 Al-Māghūṭ 2002, p. 71.

36 Al-Māghūṭ 2005, pp. 596–600.

37 Al-Nu'aymī 2001, p. 224.

38 *Al-Ādāb* 22.3 (March 1975), pp. 2–4.

person in some autobiographical paragraphs published in his handwriting, he said that he

> invented for his own use a special language, close to the daily language of speaking, directing his poetry to all classes of Arab people, breaking into the hierarchy of culture and into those feudal and bourgeoise monopolies of poetry; poetry became in his hands daily bread and popular clothes for 150 million Arabs.[39]

The second important phenomenon we need to consider is the marginal status of traditional Islamist writing in the canonical Arabic literary system.[40] The variety of that category of literary production may be referred to as either belonging to the margins of canonical literature or as existing as an isolated system. Inasmuch as the Arabic literary system tends toward secularism,[41] we find that religious circles have retained their independence and continue to adhere to their traditional literary activities, prompted by the various local Islamic institutions as well as by general institutions active throughout the Muslim world.[42] Wherever demands are made for "reintroduction" of *sharīʿa* (Islamic law), one also finds articles and books proving that Islam and art do indeed go together, as there is no inherent contradiction between art and religion. This in itself is nothing new. Since the emergence of modern Arabic literature, authors defining themselves as committed Muslims have created a huge number of fictional works. Still, until the 1980s literature in the modern sense—with its division into the genres of novel, short story, and drama—has been marginal within religious circles. The main genre in these circles is still poetry. Often written in the traditional Arabic poetic form (*qaṣīda*) and published in anthologies,[43] or in collections published by religious notables,

39 Naṣr Allāh 2006, p. 11.

40 When pointing to the literary and cultural activities and theories of the religious circles since the 1970s, I will use the adjective *Islamist* and not *Muslim* or *Islamic*, which I apply to the traditional, cultural, and religious aspects of society more broadly defined. A similar distinction is found in the writings of some Arab scholars who use the adjective *Islāmānī* instead of *Islāmī* (e.g. al-ʿAẓm 1992). It goes without saying that this distinction cannot be found in the writings of the Islamist scholars and writers themselves.

41 The term "secularism" has been translated into Arabic either as *ʿilmāniyya* (derived from *ʿilm*, "science" or "knowledge") or as *ʿalmāniyya* (from *ʿālam*, "world"). For more on the Arabic terminology, see Polka 2000, pp. 60–5. On Islam and secularism and the origins of Arab secularism, see Esposito 2000, pp. 1–12; Tamimi 2000, pp. 13–28; Lewis 2003, pp. 96–116; and Abu-Rabiʿ 2004, pp. 93–125; 210–14, 310–12.

42 See, for example, Markaz Tawzīʿ al-Kitāb al-Islāmī (The Center for the Distribution of Islamist Book) within Rābiṭat al-ʿĀlam al-Islāmī (The Muslim World League) in Mecca (*Rābiṭat al-ʿĀlam al-Islāmī fī Khamsatin wa-ʿIshrīn ʿĀman*, 1987, pp. 29, 83–9; *Rābiṭat al-ʿĀlam al-Islāmī, al-Dalīl al-Iʿlāmī*, 1989, pp. 13–17. Cf. Snir 2006, pp. 21–2).

43 See, for example, al-Jadaʿ and Jarrār 1978–85. The nine-volume anthology includes poems of over fifty poets, none of whom is considered major figure in the contemporary Arabic literary system. The anthology is part of a wider project to collect poems of religious notables

poems include not only religious themes but also topics such as love, society, and politics.[44] One can find single poems on these topics in religious journals such as *Majallat al-Azhar*,[45] *Minbar al-Islām*,[46] *Majallat al-Taṣwwuf al-Islāmī*,[47] and *Liwā' al-Islām*.[48] This kind of poetry can also be found

so as "to save them from oblivion and make them an instrument to enrich the Muslim youth and guide them along the path of praying and the glory of God" (al-Qaraḍāwī 1985, p. 5). Yūsuf al-Qaraḍāwī (b. 1926) is one of these notables, and his own *Dīwān* (al-Qaraḍāwī 1985) contains twelve poems in the form of *qaṣīda* and six hymns. According to al-Qaraḍāwī, there can be no Arab culture without Islam: "Arab culture is composed of Islam, the Arabic language, and the values and conceptions which have been inherited and accumulated throughout history [...] There is no culture without religion, whatever that religion is" (al-Qaraḍāwī 1994, pp. 17–22. On al-Qaraḍāwī and his ideas, see Polka 2000; Winter 2000, pp. lxxi–lxxvi; and Baroudi 2016, pp. 94–114).

44 See, for example, Faḍl Allāh 1984; Faḍl Allāh 1985; and Faḍl Allāh 1990. On Faḍl Allāh, his outlooks on and attitudes toward poetry, see Suwayd 1995, pp. 93–121, especially pp. 94–5, where Faḍl Allāh argues that there is not a single Iraqi poet, not even Badr Shākir al-Sayyāb (1926–64), who has not been influenced by the intellectual activities in the Shiite center of Najaf. See also Faḍl Allāh 1994, pp. 45–6; Kramer 1997, pp. 85–91; and Kramer 1998, pp. 13–18.

45 See, for example, *Majallat al-Azhar* 57.2 (November 1984), pp. 238–41; 57.5 (February 1985), pp. 725–30; and 57.6 (March 1985), pp. 900–3. This volume also includes two critical essays about the poets ʿAbduh Ismāʿīl al-Ṭahṭāwī (1921–70) (pp. 904–12) and ʿAlī Aḥmad Bākathīr (1910–69) (pp. 913–18). See other examples in 66.2 (August 1993), pp. 238–46; 66.3 (September 1993), pp. 412–21; 66.5 (November 1993), pp. 706–14; and 68.3 (August 1995), pp. 357–61. The poems were published within a section entitled *al-Shiʿr wa-l-Shuʿarāʾ* ("Poetry and Poets"), which has been published since the mid-1980s. Preceding issues of the magazine also include similar poems, but not in any organized and systematic way. Still, a very limited number of poets published their poems in this section, and they deal with an equally limited range of subjects, such as *Mawlid al-Nabī* (The Birthday of the Prophet), *al-Ḥajj* (The Pilgrimage), and *al-Hijra* (The Flight [of the Prophet from Mecca to Medina in AD 622]). In the 1990s, the editor of this section—which generally included between three and five poems—was Rashād Yūsuf (b. 1933), who himself made frequent contributions to it. Another habitual contributor to this section was Muḥammad ʿAbd al-Raḥmān Ṣān al-Dīn (1923–2014). Later, *Majallat al-Azhar* changed its policy regarding the publication of literary works: For example, in 2004 the poems published in the journal were not included in any specific section and were in general previously published in other places by relatively well-known poets who expressed "Islamic" feelings. At the same time, a new regular section appeared, *Qiṣṣat al-ʿAdad* ("The Story of the Issue"), which included narratives based on some events from Islamic history.

46 See, for example, *Minbar al-Islām* 54.2 (July 1995), pp. 41, 53, 60–1, 77; and 54.3 (August 1995), pp. 9, 23, 29, 47, 77, 83. The journal includes a special supplement for children entitled *al-Firdaws, Majallat al-Ṭifl al-Muslim*. Its August 1995 issue was heavily imbued with religious messages and included stories from Muslim history, a traditional poem, and comics for children encouraging moral Muslim behavior. On Islamist literature for children, see Abū al-Riḍā 1993; and Badr 1993, pp. 25–8.

47 See, for example, *Majallat al-Taṣwwuf al-Islāmī*, September 1984, pp. 25, 39. The poems that are published in this journal (and others like it) differ from the popular songs performed by the Sufi *munshidūn* (singers) during the *dhikr* rituals (Waugh 1989).

48 See, for example, *Liwā' al-Islām*, May 1989, pp. 57–8 (one of the poems is not written in the form of a *qaṣīda*). The literary section of this issue also includes two short stories (pp. 50–9).

extensively in Shiite magazines such as *al-Mawsim*,[49] published by al-Markaz al-Wathā'iqī li-Turāth Ahl al-Bayt 'Alayhim al-Salām (The Documentary Center for the Heritage of the Prophet's Family Peace Be Upon Them) (Beijerland, Holland) and *al-Tawḥīd*, published by *Munaẓẓamat al-I'lām al-'Arabī* (The Organization of Arab Information) (Qumm, Iran).[50] Recent decades, however, have witnessed the emergence of other literary genres among religious circles, many of which have been inspired by the authors' experience of imprisonment.[51] The widespread nature of Islamist literary

[49] See, for example, *al-Mawsim* 17 (1994), a special issue dedicated to the memory of the Iranian Imām Abū al-Qāsim al-Khū'ī (1899–1992). The issue includes about one hundred elegies in the form of classical *rithā'* (see especially pp. 291–400).

[50] This magazine is exceptional among religious magazines in its commitment to regularly publish not only poetry in the form of *qaṣīda* but also *shi'r ḥurr* (free verse) and short stories. See, for example, *al-Tawḥīd*, December 1992–February 1993, pp. 61–4 (poem dedicated to the memory of 'Alī ibn Abī Ṭālib), pp. 116–20 (short story about the tragedy of Sarajevo); and March–April 1993, pp. 97–100 (*shi'r ḥurr*), pp. 161–4 (short story). This issue also includes a call to the readers encouraging them to write short stories for publication in the magazine, but they have "to employ the Islamic human committed methods" (p. 164). The magazine also published short stories translated from Persian (e.g. July–August 1993, pp. 120–3) and literary studies (e.g. July–August 1993, pp. 178–89, a study of the poems published in previous issues of the magazine). The magazine was also published (at least until 1988) in English under the title *al-Tawḥīd: A Quarterly Journal of Islamic Thought and Culture*, but without the literary items.

[51] Islamist prison memoirs are inspired in part by secular prison literature (*adab al-sujūn*), which emerged in the general literary system in the 1960s. Complaining that this genre is "almost absent, purposefully, from modern Arabic literature," in 1971 Ghālī Shukrī was one of the first Arab critics to turn the public's attention to its existence (*al-Ṭalī'a*, December 1972, pp. 166–73). At the same time, one should not necessarily consign a literary work dealing in its title or subject matter with prison and prisoners to the genre of prison literature; for example, in Maḥmūd Amīn al-'Ālim's (1922–2009) 1974 poetry collection *Qirā'a li-Judrān Zinzāna* (*A Reading of a Prison Cell's Walls*), the prison is merely a metaphor. On the genre, see Abū Niḍāl 1981; Tomiche 1982, pp. 255–71; Bannūra 1984, pp. 71–4; Booth 1987, pp. 35–41; al-Fayṣal 1994; Camera d'Afflitto 1998, pp. 148–56; Peled 1998, pp. 69–76; Abū Shamāla 2002; Elinson 2009, pp. 289–303; Orlando 2010, pp. 273–88; Cooke 2011, pp. 169–87; Elimelekh 2012, pp. 166–82; and Elimelekh 2014. See also the article published in *al-Quds* on 1 February 1995 on *al-Shamandūra* (*The Buoy*) by the Egyptian writer Muḥammad Khalīl Qāsim (1922–95) (Qāsim 1968). The jails in Egypt from the 1960s to the 1980s as well as in Israel and in the Occupied Territories "have provided literary fodder for men and women from all walks of political life" (Malti-Douglas 1995, pp. 160–1) as well as ideological fodder for the writings of Islamist leaders (Kepel 1984, pp. 31–3). On Palestinian poetry written in prisons, see Ḥananī 2016. On the phenomenon of theatrical presentations of prisoners inside prisons, see Slyomovics 1991, p. 34. On Moroccan prison narratives, human rights, and the politics of resistance, see Moukhlis 2008, pp. 347–76. On women's literary reconfiguration of the prison, see Sinno 2011, pp. 67–94. Several Muslim notables have also written poems describing their experiences in prison (e.g. Yūsuf al-Qaraḍāwī's poems in al-Qaraḍāwī 1985 [pp. 43–5, 47–53], in which he describes his experiences during his detention in Egypt's al-Ṭūr prison in 1949). By the term *adab al-sujūn*, I am referring to both branches of that literature: literature actually written *inside* prisons that describes the writer's own experiences, on the one hand (e.g. Tawfīq Zayyād's poems "14 Tammūz" and

production coincides with theoretical attempts to lay the foundations for an Islamist literature (*Adab Islāmī*) encompassing the various branches of production. In the introduction to the first bio-bibliographical reference for Islamist literature *Khuṭwa 'alā Ṭarīq al-Ta'ṣīl* (*A Step on the Road to Consolidation*), Ḥasan al-Amarānī (b. 1949) from Rābiṭat al-Adab al-Islāmī al-'Ālamiyya (The International Association of Islamist Literature) states:

> A quarter century ago, the term Islamist literature was strange to many persons, even denoting inferiority among some. What is Islamist literature? What are its basic traits and tenets? Is it a new heresy (*bid'a*)? And how can we distinguish between literature and ideology? And how can we refer to our long and varied literary history? [...] Within less than twenty years, Islamist literature has acquired its disciples, writers, and readers, and has found its way into their hearts, while in the eyes of its rivals it is at the very least a literary phenomenon that can no longer be ignored.[52]

Since the early 1970s, Islamist literature has undergone many changes.[53] It now has its own literary magazines, such as *al-Mishkāt* in Morocco, *al-Adab al-Islāmī* in India, and another *al-Adab al-Islāmī* in Turkey. Universities in the Islamic world have started to teach the subject, and on 8 January 1986 the first conference of Rābiṭat al-Adab al-Islāmī al-'Ālamiyya was held in Lucknow, India. All that before the development of the Internet technologies whose impact on Arabic culture, Islamist literature included, is significant, as we shall see below.

At the same time, we can discover several attempts to define the characteristics of the various genres Islamist literature now includes.[54] Most significant perhaps have been the attempts to outline the theoretical basis of

"Fahd" written in al-Dāmūn prison in Israel in July 1958 [Zayyād n.d., pp. 41–6, 77–82], or his poem "Min Warā' al-Quḍbān" written in al-Ramla prison in May 1958 [Zayyād n.d., pp. 102–12]. See also Ṣalāḥ 2006); and, on the other hand, literature written *outside* the prison that describes experiences from within the prison regardless of the question of whether those experiences are based on the writer's own personal experiences (e.g. Nawāl al-Sa'dāwī's *Mudhakkirāt fī Sijn al-Nisā'* [al-Sa'dāwī 1984; English translation: El-Sa'adawi 1986; El-Sa'adawi 1994a (with afterword by the author); on the memoirs, see Malti-Douglas 1995, pp. 159–76] and al-Sa'dāwī's play *al-Insān: Ithnay 'Ashara* [sic] *Imra'a fī Zinzāna Wāḥida* [al-Sa'dāwī 1982. French translation: El Saadaoui 1984]), or of others (e.g. Najīb Maḥfūẓ's *al-Karnak* [1974]. English translation in: El-Gabalawy 1979, pp. 67–132. On the novel, see Beard and Haydar 1993, pp. 69–71; al-Fayṣal 1994, pp. 95–8; and Elkhadem 2001, pp. 17–21. See also Geer 2009, pp. 653–69). On the general issue of prison literature, see Davis 1990.

52 Badr 1993, p. 5.

53 Cf. Malti-Douglas 2001, pp. 1–14 and the bibliographical references in the notes.

54 The Islamist novel is still making its first steps. One of the first novels which could be considered as such is 'Azīza al-Ibrāshī's *Iṣlāḥ* (al-Ibrāshī 1960), in which she describes her way to Islam.

Islamist theater (*Masraḥ Islāmī*)[55] and to define the fundamental elements of this kind of "Islamist art."[56] Authors sympathetic to Islamic concepts have turned to writing literary works to help popularize Islamic ideas. The genre of theater appeals mainly to them due to its "immediacy of action and the tangible form it gives to abstract concepts." Social action is exemplified by characters who serve as models of behavior: "Actors and audience alike experience a dramatic catharsis, mentally and emotionally, through identification with the characters portrayed."[57] The Egyptian writer Aḥmad Rā'if (1940–2011) preferred theatrical drama because it enabled the Islamic "cause to take root in the minds and souls of the audience."[58] Of course, dramatic art has been popular with all sorts of cultural circles wishing to disseminate their ideas, because of the direct impact it has on the masses and the way it can be used as an alternative means of mass communication—as we find in the case of nation-building.[59] Interestingly, for these same reasons, and because of its "utopian" nature, Islamist writers also write science fiction.[60] Like other

55 See, for example, Qāsim 1980 (Aḥmad); Ibn Zaydān 1987, pp. 416–17. The literary section of the May 1989 issue of *Liwā' al-Islām*, for example, includes a description of two "Islamist plays" staged in Saudi Arabia (pp. 56–7). See also Abū Ṣūfa 1993, p. 11. For an analysis of Aḥmad Rā'if's drama *al-Bu'd al-Khāmis* (*The Fifth Dimension*) (Rā'if 1987), see Szyska 1995, pp. 95–125; and Szyska 1997–8, pp. 115–42. On Aḥmad Rā'if and his works, see Szyska 1995, p. 96, n. 6. On Islamist theater, see also al-Kaylānī 1986a. For a list of Islamist plays, see Badr 1993, pp. 110–14. A distinction should be made between "Islamist theater" and Islamic elements in modern Arabic drama and theater (e.g. Chelkowsky 1984, pp. 45–69).

56 Qāsim 1980 (Aḥmad), pp. 407–9. In addition to Islamist theater, we find also Islamist cinema (*sīnamā Islāmiyya*). The First Islamist Conference of Cinema Producers and Directors was held in Tehran (5–11 February 1994) with the participation of more than fifty producers and directors from Arab and Muslim countries. A major aim of the conference was "to face the trend of Westernization and the tendencies which have been hostile to Muslim thought, to help young Islamist cinema, and to seek Muslim markets for it" (*al-Bilād*, 26 March 1994, p. 54). On Islamist cinema in Egypt, see Ṣalāḥ al-Dīn 1998.

57 Szyska 1995, p. 111.

58 Szyska 1995, p. 112.

59 See, for example, Snir 1995a, pp. 29–73.

60 See, for example, the aforementioned drama *al-Bu'd al-Khāmis* (Rā'if 1987) by Aḥmad Rā'if. The genre of science fiction for the propagation of Islamic ideas is also employed by non-Arabic Muslim writers (e.g. Turkish authors). See, for example, the novel *Uzay Çiftçileri* (*Space Farmers*) by the Turkish author Ali Nar (b. 1941). On these works, see Szyska 1995, pp. 95–125. Opposition to the genre in Muslim circles is by no means due to its essential features, but only to the ideas underlying specific works. The aforementioned Shi'a Islamist militant group Ḥizb Allāh, for example, criticized the Hollywood blockbuster *Independence Day* as Jewish propaganda, for "the so-called genius of the Jews and their concern for humanity [...] blended with the hegemonistic power of America [...] The movie clearly hints that the source of danger to mankind emanates from certain parts of the Third World, particularly from the Arab and Islamic world" (*al-Akhbār* list, Muslim World News, 5 November 1996 ["I. A. P." *iapinfo@IAP.ORG*]—*Independence Day*, a science fiction thriller, tells the story of aliens trying to destroy the Earth only to be thwarted by an American-Jewish scientist and computer genius backed by US military might. See <http://

genres of Islamist literature, the basis for Islamist theater and science fiction is the notion that Islamist art is not confined to Qur'ānic themes; rather, "it may use all kinds of themes, subjects and modes. But one constraint remains: it must spring from the Islamic concept of the great existence, or at least it must not contradict or reject Islamic concepts of the universe, life and the human being."[61]

The first to try and define the relationship between art and Islam were members of Egypt's al-Ikhwān al-Muslimūn, the Muslim Brotherhood, especially their leader Sayyid Quṭb (1906–66). Influenced by the idea of *iltizām* (commitment) first introduced by the Lebanese literary magazine *al-Ādāb*, Quṭb called for an Islamist art that was to serve the spread of the Islamic mission.[62] Quṭb developed this concept of a committed Islamist literature in *Khaṣā'iṣ al-Taṣawwur al-Islāmī wa-Muqawwimātuhu* (*Characteristics of the Islamic World View and its Basic Constituents*) (1965), which still serves as a model for the subject to this day.[63] One of the first books on the relationship between art and Islam is *Minhaj al-Fann al-Islāmī* (*The Method of Islamic Art*) (1960) by Muḥammad Quṭb (1919–2014), Sayyid Quṭb's brother, which defines Islamist art as artistic expression in accordance with Islamic concepts. Although it discusses all of the fine arts, the book's main focus is on literature. To this end, the author includes the work of non-Muslim writers even if other critics insist that Islamist literature can only be written by sincere Muslims. The book includes theoretical sections dealing with the nature of artistic sense;[64] realism;[65] samples of Islamist literature; non-Arabic literary texts whose nature corresponds to Islamist art, such as poems by Muḥammad Iqbāl (1877–1938)[66] and Rabindranath Tagore (1861–1941) translated into Arabic;[67] a short story by the Egyptian writer 'Abd al-Ḥamīd Jawda al-Saḥḥār (1913–74);[68] and even a translation

www.imdb.com/title/tt0116629/> [last accessed 12 October 2016]). On Ḥizb Allāh's cultural sphere, see Alagha 2011, pp. 149–75.

61 Qāsim 1980 (Aḥmad), p. 408. Cf. Quṭb 1963? [1960], pp. 6, 177–203; and 'Imāra 1991, pp. 197–247.

62 On *iltizām* in modern Arabic literature, see Snir 1992, pp. 7–54; Snir 1993c, pp. 49–93; Snir 1997–8, pp. 199–230; and Snir 2002.

63 See Quṭb 1965. On the Islamic concept of *iltizām* in general, see Szyska 1999a, pp. 33–62. For a study of Islamic commitment as reflected in the works of 'Alī Aḥmad Bākathīr (1910–69), see Tawfiq 1980. Before engaging in Islamist literature, Sayyid Quṭb participated in the scholarly discourse about secular Arabic literature. On Quṭb and Najīb Maḥfūẓ, for example, see Colla 2007, pp. 234–72.

64 Quṭb 1963? [1960], pp. 15–21.

65 Quṭb 1963? [1960], pp. 66–94.

66 Quṭb 1963? [1960], pp. 268–81.

67 Quṭb 1963? [1960], pp. 292–6.

68 Quṭb 1963? [1960], pp. 301–25.

of the one-act play *Riders to the Sea* (1904) by the Irish writer J. M. Synge (1871–1909).[69]

Muḥammad Quṭb further elaborated on his conception of Islamic literature and culture in a popular textbook which he wrote together with Muḥammad al-Mubārak and Muṣṭafā Kāmil entitled *al-Thaqāfa al-Islāmiyya* (*Islamic Culture*), which, since it was first published in 1976, has gone through no less than eleven printings. As the authors see it, one of the aims of modern Islamist culture is to prevent a foreign "intellectual invasion" from "undermining" Islamist culture, art, and electronic media in order to steer them away from Islam.[70]

Another contribution to the theoretical definition of Islamist literature is *al-Islāmiyya wa-l-Madhāhib al-Adabiyya* (*Islamism and Literary Trends*) by the Egyptian novelist Najīb al-Kaylānī (al-Kīlānī) (1931–95), who analyzes the differences between Western and Islamist literatures.[71] Taking his cue from Muḥammad Quṭb, al-Kaylānī develops the concept of Islamist realism (*wāqiʿiyya Islāmiyya*) and defines it over and against socialist realism. Al-Kaylānī sharply criticizes the latter as an atheist mode of writing which emphasizes the sleazy sides of life.[72] All Islamist writers share the idea that Islamist literature should help bring about an Islamic society.[73] That this attempt to create a modern Islamist cultural and artistic discourse is not confined to the Arab world, but is also found in other Muslim societies such as those of Turkey and Iran, is especially interesting if we recall that, unlike the premodern Arab culture, and what is described by Muhsin J. al-Musawi as the "Medieval Islamic Republic of Letters,"[74] Arabs, Turks, and Persians, as the three major peoples of the Middle East, have become intellectually isolated from one another in the course of the twentieth century. While Cairo, Tehran, and Istanbul have grown apart from the perspective

69 Quṭb 1963? [1960], pp. 239–351.

70 Quṭb et al. 1988 [1976], p. 8. On the Islamic conception of literature, see Khalis 1990, pp. 54–7.

71 Al-Kaylānī 1963 (= al-Kaylānī 1981). See also al-Kaylānī 1985; al-Kaylānī 1985a; al-Kaylānī 1986; al-Kaylānī 1986a; and al-ʿArīnī 1989. On al-Kaylānī, his autobiographical and theoretical writings, and the concept of Islamist *littérature engagée*, see Christian Szyska, "Najīb al-Kaylānī on his Career or How to Become the Ideal Muslim Author," paper presented at the symposium "Poets'/Authors' Mission as Seen by Themselves" held at the Institut für Islamwissenschaften, Bern, 13–16 July 1997. I am indebted to Christian Szyska, who sent me a copy of the text of his paper immediately after the symposium. An article based on the paper was published two years later (Szyska 1999, pp. 221–35). See also Khan 1995, pp. 178–9.

72 On Islamist realism in al-Kaylānī's novels, see al-Qāʿūd 1996.

73 On the principle of Islamist realism, see also Sāʿī 1985 as well as Szyska 1995, p. 112.

74 Al-Musawi 2015b. On the book, see below, the Conclusion.

of modern secularist discourse, modern Islamist discourse is bringing them closer together again.[75]

The modern Arabic literary establishment has totally overlooked literary works by Islamist writers, despite their widespread popularity among the masses. As illustrated by Muḥammad Hādī Amīnī's book about the intellectual and literary figures in al-Najaf, Iraq, there is a whole body of work by

[75] One of the common traits on which the Islamist discourse in the Middle East is built is the struggle against Western cultural symbols and the need to produce alternative symbols which conform to Islamic thought. For example, in October 1996 Iran launched a drive to produce its own style of computer games and toys to protect children from the "catastrophic" effects of "Barbie culture" and the violence of American video games. The state-owned Children Cultural Promotion Center (CCPC) began designing a series of dolls whose appearance was in tune with the country's national and Islamic identity. The main character, Sara, had darker skin, black hair and eyes, and was dressed in accordance with the Islamic dress code. According to CCPC official Majid Ghaderi, "Barbie dictates to our little girls what they should look like when they grow up. From an aesthetic point of view, they will find a woman who looks like Barbie beautiful [...] This will remove them from their own cultural identity. We have our own models to emulate and reject Western prototypes." The CCPC also started designing "benign and refined" computer games based on traditional children's games like hide-and-seek and hopscotch as alternatives to the violent foreign video games that were smuggled into the country. Ghaderi said that some video games produced in the United States were "blatantly opposed to Iran and its revolution." One such game, F-117, depicted a US pilot taking off on a mission to destroy so-called "terrorist" camps in several countries, including Iran (according to details published on 23 October 1996 in *AKHBAR* <akhbar@yorku.ca> sponsored by the Islamic Association for Palestine [IAP]). See also the *New York Times* of 25 October 1996, which carried a photo of the Iranian dolls with the caption: "Babes in Islamic Toyland." Twenty years later, the same drive went on and the national Iranian TV news program broadcasted a clip of a ceremony which took place at a school near Tehran in which schoolgirls burn Barbie dolls in a declared goal to counter Western symbols, which "promote moral laxity." As a reward, they were given dolls with covered hair, Sara and Dara (<https://en.iranwire.com/features/6998/>[6 January 2016] [last accessed 6 January 2016]). The Iranian drive against symbols of Western culture is also part of the Islamist discourse in Arab culture. In November 2003 NewBoy Design Studio, based in Syria, introduced Fulla, a dark-eyed doll with "Muslim values"—in the following years Barbie dolls all but disappeared from the shelves of many toy stores in the Middle East. Fulla took their place. She roughly shares Barbie's size and proportions, but steps out of her shiny pink box wearing a black *'abāya* and matching head scarf: "It is nearly impossible to walk into a corner shop in Syria or Egypt or Jordan or Qatar without encountering Fulla breakfast cereal or Fulla chewing gum or not to see little girls pedaling down the street on their Fulla bicycles, all in trademark 'Fulla pink'" (Zoepf 2005). See the official site (in Arabic and English) at <http://fulla.com/> (last accessed 8 April 2016), where she is described as follows: "Fulla is sixteen years old. She's Arab, body and soul. She loves life and learning. She honors her parents and loves her family and friends. She's a good listener and cares about those around her [...] Hopeful and ambitious, Fulla doesn't let difficulties hold back her determination. She considers difficulties a part of life that builds character and makes us stronger. The greater the challenge, the greater the benefit [...] Fulla always tries to be of benefit to those around her and gives her best. She thinks giving enriches the soul and increases her ability to always excel. Fulla is the spirit of any girl who strives toward excellence, creativity, renewal, and peace. Fulla strives to make the world a better place for everyone".

poets who are wholly unknown to the canonical center of modern Arabic literature.[76] If, as seen above, we have incipient critical studies of Islamist literary production,[77] including the publication of bio-bibliographical sources,[78] such activities are generally carried out by scholars not belonging to the canonical center of Arabic literature.[79] In any event, Islamist Arabic fictional narratives have been translated into other languages of the Muslim world (for example, Turkish, Persian), which shows, according to one scholar, that there is an "increasing interest in establishing an international discourse of 'Islamic' literature."[80]

[76] See al-Amīnī 1964, especially pp. 37 (#85), 40 (#97), 49 (#139), 51–2 (#148), 89 (#314), 98 (#348 & 349), 106 (#384), 255 (#1013 and 1016), 266 (#1068), 297 (1206). Not all of the poets mentioned in the book write exclusively in *fuṣḥā*; some also write in *'āmmiyya* (e.g. p. 153 [#573]). In addition to Arabic, several poets also write in Persian and Turkish (e.g. p. 51 [#145]).

[77] Up to now, Islamist literature has not been a field of serious scholarly research in the West. To my knowledge, there is still no comprehensive study on this topic, though there are studies dedicated to specific works, such as Cooke 1994; Cooke 1998; and Cooke 2001, which deal with *Ayyām min Ḥayātī* (*Days of My Life*) by Zaynab al-Ghazālī (al-Jubaylī) (1917–2005) (al-Ghazālī 1980. On Zaynab al-Ghazālī's Islamic activism, see Hoffman 1985, pp. 233–54; and al-Ghazālī 1989; for her unique interpretation of the Qur'ān, see al-Ghazālī 1994); Malti-Douglas 1994, pp. 116–29 and Malti-Douglas 2000, pp. 389–410, which deal with *Qiṣṣat Ayyāmī: Mudhakkirāt al-Shaykh Kishk* (*The Story of My Days: Memoirs of Shaykh Kishk*) by Shaykh 'Abd al-Ḥamīd Kishk (1933–96) (Kishk 1986; on Shaykh Kishk, see also Kepel 1984, pp. 165–82; and Kepel 1985, pp. 172–90). In the Arab world, the research of Islamist literature is more developed, especially when it comes to poetry. For example, the first academic conference held at Birzeit University (17–19 May 1997) under the title *al-Adab al-Filasṭīnī Bayna al-Manfā wa-l-Iḥtilāl* ("Palestinian Literature between Exile and Occupation") included several lectures dealing with "Religious Discourse" (*Khiṭāb Dīnī*) in Palestinian poetry. Based on the project suggested in the present book, several MA students in the Department of Arabic Language and Literature at the University of Haifa studied various aspects of Islamist literature, among them Riḍā Ighbāriyya, whose study has already been published (Ighbāriyya 1997).

[78] One major source is the first volume of *Dalīl Maktabāt al-Adab al-Islāmī fī al-'Aṣr al-Ḥadīth* (*The Guide to the Library of Islamist Literature in the Modern Period*) (1993) compiled by 'Abd al-Bāsiṭ Badr and published by Dār al-Bashīr in Amman. The Guide contains several sections, including sections on children's literature (pp. 25–8), poetry collections (pp. 71–90), travel literature (pp. 91–2), narratives (pp. 93–105), memoirs (pp. 108–9), and plays (pp. 110–14).

[79] An example is Ḥasan Maḥmūd Abū 'Alyawī's PhD thesis *al-Ittijāhāt al-Waṭaniyya wa-l-Ijtimā'iyya fī al-Shi'r al-'Āmilī al-Mu'āṣir (1943–1975)* (*National and Social Trends in the Contemporary Poetry of Jabal 'Āmil* [in Lebanon] *[1943–1975]*); most of the poems discussed are by religious Shiite poets (*al-Bilād*, 26 March 1994, p. 42). Apart from publishers in Saudi Arabia known to be active in the production of Islamist books of all sorts, two publishers were quite active in the field of Islamist literature: the Jordanian Dār al-Bashīr (e.g. Jarrār 1984; Shihāb 1985; (especially) Badr 1993) and the Lebanese Mu'assasat al-Risāla (e.g. al-Jada' and Jarrār 1978–85; al-Kaylānī 1981; al-Kaylānī 1985; al-Kaylānī 1985a; al-Kaylānī 1986; al-Kaylānī 1986a; Khalīl 1987). See also al-Sārīsī 1996 and the details of scholarly activities in the field of Islamist literature in Jordan on pp. 15–20.

[80] Szyska 1995, p. 96. This discourse of *Islamist* literature since the 1980s is essentially differ-

Texts for Children

While medieval Muslim-Arab culture did not ignore cultural activities for children from either a religious or a literary standpoint,[81] Arabic children's literature did not emerge, however, until the twentieth century.[82] It was pioneered in Egypt by several writers, and the most prominent of them was Kāmil Kaylānī (1897–1959), who wrote, translated, and adapted numerous stories for children. The publisher Dār al-Maʿārif issued during the 1940s a series entitled *Makabat al-Aṭfāl* (*The Children's Library*), which included more than forty illustrated books for children, all of them written by Kaylānī himself.[83] He was also active in many other ways, one of which was setting up public libraries for children. The guidelines for future Arabic literature for

ent from that of *Islamic* literature as used by some Western scholars, especially prior to the 1980s. For example, speaking about "Islamic" literature, James Kritzeck in his *Anthology of Islamic Literature* refers to the literature of the vast community of Muslims throughout the world in various languages: "Islamic literature can be, and usually is, subdivided according to languages. Principal among them are Arabic, Persian, and Turkish; but Berber, Hausa, Swahili, Somali, Albanian, Kurdish, Uzbek, Tadjik, Pashto, Baluchi, Urdu, Panjabi, Bengali, Gajarati, Sindi, Telugu, Tamil, Malay, Javanese, Cham, and a good many others must be added [...] Quite obviously, therefore, a tremendous number of forms and styles are comprehended under so general a rubric as 'Islamic literature'" (Kritzeck 1964, p. 4). Needless to say, this kind of "Islamic literature" is more a generalization which refers to the external formal religious characteristics of the writers in the aforementioned languages. Seen thus, most Arabic literary production in modern times is "Islamic," while, from the 1980s "Islamist literature" has stood for literature that is written only by sincere Muslim writers and that does not contradict the divine law (*sharīʿa*).

81 Instruction for the rearing and education of children of the nobility and the upper classes is included in *waṣāyā* (injunctions) which fathers formulated for tutors (many of which can be found scattered throughout *adab* compilations) and in the "Mirrors for Princes" literature. Special emphasis was laid on the moral and physical education of princes and on enriching the curriculum of their elementary education, which consisted mainly of the Qur'ān and studies in language, history, and poetry. On the culture and education of children in Muslim-Arabic tradition, see Giladi 1992; Zalaṭ 1994, pp. 28–30; Giladi 1995, pp. 821–7; and Shuraydi 2014, pp. 199–216.

82 Several Arab writers argue that children's literature already existed in ancient Egyptian and Arabic-Islamic literature (e.g. Suwaylim 1987. Cf. Azeriah 1993, pp. 12–18). Others state that the first emergence of this literature was in the mid-nineteenth century (Zalaṭ 1994, p. 13). However, it was only in the 1930s that the term *adabiyyāt al-aṭfāl* (children's literature), referring to a separate genre, started to appear in the literary magazines; before that, literary books for children were classed among school books (Zalaṭ 1994, pp. 27–8). According to *al-Akhbār* (19 September 1982), the first book for children in Egypt was Muḥammad Ḥamdī's *al-Quṭayṭāt al-ʿIzāz*, which was published in 1912. And thus was the seventieth anniversary of children's literature celebrated in 1982 with the granting of special prizes for the "pioneers of children's books": Muḥammad Ḥamdī, Kāmil Kaylānī (1897–1959), Muḥammad Saʿīd al-ʿIryān (1905–64), Amīn Dawydār, Ḥusayn Bīkār (1913–2002), and Muṣṭafā Ḥusayn (1935–2014). On pioneering efforts in the field of children's literature in Arabic, see also Shablūl 1998, pp. 13–20; and Yaḥyā 2001, pp. 17–39.

83 See a commercial advertisement for the series appended to the end of al-ʿAqqād 1945.

children were that it must have didactic aims, observe correct albeit simple *fuṣḥā*,[84] and, for moral reasons, avoid vulgar stories.[85]

Among the poets and writers who have contributed to the development of children's literature in Arabic are Rifāʿa Rāfiʿ al-Ṭahṭāwī (1801–73), Muḥammad ʿUthmān Jalāl (1829–98), and Aḥmad Shawqī (1868–1932), who all achieved fame in other fields. There were also other, less well-known writers such as Maḥmūd al-Harāwī (1885–1939), who was given the nicknames *amīr shiʿr al-ṭufūla* (prince of children's poetry) and *rāʾid masraḥ al-ṭifl al-ʿArabī* (the pioneer of Arabic children's theater),[86] and Maḥmūd Abū al-Wafā (1902–79). One of the prominent activists of children's literature in Lebanon was Rashād Dārghawth (1907–84)[87] whose stories employed didactic methods for moral ends, as he did with *Fī al-ʿAshāyā* (*In the Late Evening*) (1963).[88] In *Maʾāthir al-Ṣaḥāba* (1994) (*The Glorious Deeds of the Companions* [of the Prophet]), he writes that "didactic committed literature (*al-adab al-tawjīhī al-multazim*) was and still is a part of our message."[89]

Although they have traditionally had their work published in special sections of various religious journals, Islamist children's authors also use electronic media to disseminate their literary creations.[90] Following the terrorist attacks carried out against the United States on 11 September 2001, radical Islamist discourse was confronted by moderate Islamist discourse, the latter being especially produced by the state media of Western-oriented Arab states. For example, in April 2006 a twenty-four-hour Arabic Islamic television channel was launched "to counter the misconception about Islam." The channel—*al Risālah* (The Message)—started to broadcast "open-minded viewpoints and the true message of Islam and its teachings." It broadcasts a variety of programs including educational shows, plays, music videos, and game shows purely in the Islamic context. This non-profit channel owes its creation to the personal financial contribution of Saudi Prince al-Walīd ibn Ṭalāl (b. 1955), Chairman of Kingdom Holding Company, who stated that

84 See his introduction to *al-Sindibād al-Baḥrī* (Tel Aviv: Orient, 1962 [1928]), pp. 5–6. Cf. Fāsha 1976, p. 159.

85 In his adaptations of *Alf Layla wa-Layla*, he omitted the sex episodes. On these episodes and their significance, see al-Khāzin and al-Yān 1970, p. 163; and Rosenthal 1979a, pp. 14–15. On the way of adaptation, see Yaḥyā 2001, pp. 141–8. On Kāmil Kaylānī, see Badawī 1999.

86 On al-Harāwī, see Yūsuf 1987; and Zalaṭ 1994, pp. 43–88.

87 According to Makarius 1964, p. 315, he was born in 1917.

88 Dārghawth 1963. On the book, which includes short stories, plays, and essays for children, see the comments of the author in al-Khāzin and al-Yān 1970, pp. 131–6.

89 Dārghawth 1994, p. 5.

90 See, for example, the video cassette *Arkān al-Islām*, which was produced and distributed by Safīr (Cairo) and includes stories, songs, short plays, and shadow theater. Cf. Werner 2001, pp. 212–13; and Anderson 2005, pp. 252–63.

Islam was "being hijacked and defamed by a group of deviants who operate in the name of religion in several parts of the world." According to him, "*al Risālah* targets the new knowledgeable young generation and open-minded Arab audience to counteract the negative image of Islam being portrayed in other societies of the world." He insists that Islam is a religion of tolerance and that people of other faiths lived harmoniously with Muslims during the time of the Prophet Muḥammad.[91]

At first, demands in the field of children's literature were met by translations and adaptations from stories written in foreign languages; original Arabic language stories came later.[92] That children's literature was receiving more and more attention is clear if we only look at the programs of major publishing houses in the Arab world, which put out numerous series for children between the 1970s and the 1990s. The Egyptian Dār al-Maʿārif had already published more than thirty different series for children by the mid-1970s, each including more than twenty books geared toward different age groups (for example, animal stories, adventure stories, fairy tales, adaptations of novels, and scientific stories). Two other Egyptian publishers of children's texts at the time were Maktabat Miṣr[93] and al-Markaz al-ʿArabī li-l-Nashr.[94] In Lebanon, Dār al-Kitāb, by the mid-1970s, had published three series for children according to age: the first included fifty-six books, the second included 108 books, and the third included forty-three books. Palestinian publishers have also been very active in this field: Dār al-Hudā from Kafr Qaraʿ, for example, published in the 1990s a series called *Qiṣaṣ al-Ḥayawānāt al-Ẓarīfa* (*Witty Animal Stories*) edited by the Palestinian writer Muṣṭafā Murrār (b. 1930). Each of the ten books in the series came with an audio cassette recorded by Īmān Qāsim Sulaymān. Similar series were published by companies in the West, such as the *Ladybird Series*, published in Arabic translation by the International Book Center in Troy, Michigan. This series includes preschool and elementary readers (for example, *Talkabout Baby, Bedtime, Animals, Clothes, Bedtime Stories, Children's Rhymes*), well-loved tales (for example, *Puss and Boots, The Princess and the Frog, William Tell, Peter Pan, Hansel and Gretel, Rapunzel*), adventure stories (for example, *Treasure Island, Robinson Crusoe, The Wind in the Willows, Gulliver's*

91 Habib Shaikh, "Islamic TV Channel Launched," *Khaleej Times Online*, 28 April 2006.

92 On the role of translation in enhancing Arabic children's literature, see Azeriah 2000, pp. 11–29.

93 See, for example, the series *al-Maktaba al-Ṣaghīra* (*The Small Library*) by Ilhām Saʿūdī, which includes twenty-five books written for children between the ages of seven and thirteen, and they come with special reading directions for both parents and children.

94 See, for example, the series *Iqra' wa-Lawwin* (*Read and Paint*), which includes twelve books.

Travels). *Ladybird* books also come with audio cassettes and CDs on which the works are read by native speakers. The same publisher produces the *Butterfly Series*, original stories written in Arabic with full-color illustrations that are also available in English translation, as well as a bilingual collection of story books written in English and Arabic for ages five and over. The US-Mid-East Performing Arts Council, a non-profit organization dedicated to promoting cultural relations between the United States and Middle Eastern countries through music and the arts, also introduced popular children's classics in bilingual editions (Arabic and English) accompanied by audio recordings. The first book published was Sergei Prokofiev's (1891–1953) popular children's classic *Peter and the Wolf*, which came with a preface written by Harlow Robinson, the latter's biographer and noted professor of Russian history and culture.

In the last few decades, more and more established Arab writers have been specializing in writing original texts for children. For example, the Egyptian writer Maḥmūd Qāsim (b. 1949), who received the State Prize for Children's Literature in 1989, only began his career in this field in the 1980s. Fu'ād Ḥijāzī (b. 1938), who received the same prize in 1993, only began writing for children in 1983 after he had been writing for adults for twenty years.[95] Their compatriot, Aḥmad Najīb (b. 1928), entered the field of children's literature after he had worked in education and then became a major activist in the field of children's literature (especially original didactic literature) in Egypt.[96] Since the early 1950s he has written about three hundred literary works for children, including songs and plays, and taken part in the production of many radio and television programs.[97] He has also been one of the pioneering researchers of Arabic children's literature and has taught in several Egyptian universities, such as the universities of ʻAyn Shams, Ṭanṭā, and Cairo, having held the position of Head of the Center for Children's Literature at the Cairo institution. He has also published thirteen studies in book form about the subject and proposed a detailed program for future studies.[98]

95 See Ḥusayn (Hamdī) 1993, pp. 24–9.

96 See, for example, the series *Mughāmarāt Ḥawla al-ʻĀlam* published by Idārat al-Kutub wa-l-Maktabāt in *Akhbār al-Yawm* (according to *October*, 22 May 1988, p. 36).

97 One of his original publications is a comprehensive poetry collection for children and youth (Najīb 1995). In the preface to the book (pp. 11–13), Samīr Sirḥān (1941–2006), head of al-Hay'a al-Miṣriyya al-ʻĀmma li-l-Kitāb at the time, praises Najīb for his pioneering work in the field of children's literature. The fact that the book was published with a preface written by the head of the most prestigious institution in Egyptian canonical cultural life bears witness to the role that children's literature began to play in cultural life in Egypt in the 1990s.

98 See Najīb 1982. A partial list of Najīb's literary works appears on pp. 195–7.

The growing awareness of the literary establishment of children's literature has meant that commercial firms and institutions have introduced programs to support it. Since the early 1980s Cairo has been hosting an annual international fair for children's books. For example, in the sixth fair (26 November–8 December 1989), sponsored by Egypt's then first lady, Mrs Suzanne Mubārak (b. 1941), more than 120 publishing houses from twenty-eight countries presented about three million books.[99] She also sponsored an annual competition for authors of children's literature and one for illustrators of children's literature.[100] Arab publishing houses also participated in international fairs for children's literature,[101] and many cultural organizations were set up to support it.[102] Greater attention is also being paid by the literary supplements and journals to such issues as people's and institutions' attitudes toward children's literature,[103] libraries for children,[104] the various kinds of books children like to read,[105] children's literacy levels (especially in rural areas),[106] graphics in children's literature,[107] and the prices of children's books.[108]

On 17 February 2007 the Arab League announced the establishment of an annual prize to be given to the best literary work written by a child in Arabic, be it in prose or in verse. The announcement was made during a conference held in Cairo entitled "The Language of the Arab Child in the Age of Globalization." The dominant theme at the conference was preserving the purity of the Arabic language amid the challenges it faced from some of the effects of globalization. The prize was meant to serve as a way

99 See *al-Hilāl*, January 1990, p. 117.

100 On the competition in 1994, see *al-Ahrām*, 15 July 1994, p. 9. It is significant to mention here a study made already in the 1950s by the artist Sa'd al-Khādim (1913–87) of the relations between art and social education based on children's drawings. See Berque 1969 [1960], p. 84 (English translation: Berque 1964, p. 74; Arabic translation: Berque 1982, p. 85).

101 See Shalabī 1990, pp. 146–50. The writer expresses her disappointment at the nature of Arab participation, which she called insufficient and negligible despite the many efforts made in the Arab world in this field. During the fair, Mrs Mubārak was granted a special award in appreciation for her efforts to promote Arab children's literature.

102 See, for example, al-Jam'iyya al-Kuwaytiyya li-Taqaddum al-Ṭufūla al-'Arabiyya (The Kuwaiti Association for the Development of Arab Childhood), which published a worldwide call to writers and illustrators of children's literature from all over the Arab world to participate in the project of the "Monthly Book for the Child" (*Domes* I.3 [Summer 1992], p. 81).

103 *Filasṭīn al-Thawra*, 2 July 1989, p. 37.

104 'Abd al-Hādī 1986, pp. 2–3.

105 Abū Zayd 1993, pp. 30–6; Darwīsh and Jawda 1994, pp. 54–7.

106 Al-Muṭī'ī 1993, pp. 12–17.

107 Shiḥāta 1993, pp. 18–23.

108 *Al-Aḥrār*, 27 January 1986, p. 9.

to promote children's literacy and strengthen children's command of the language.[109]

Still, an inventory of literary texts for children currently available mainly consists of adaptations of original and translated canonical literature for adults. In 1989 Dār al-Shurūq in Cairo and Beirut began adapting the works of Najīb Maḥfūẓ (1911–2006) for children.[110] Dār al-Fatā al-ʿArabī published a series of adaptations of Arabic poetry for children with illustrations (*Silsilat al-Shiʿr wa-l-Shuʿarā'*).[111] Works by other major canonical writers have also been adapted for children.[112] The rapid development of electronic media, especially television, and the rapid increase of Internet access worldwide have had a significant influence on the production and consumption of children's literature. Countering complaints that such developments have resulted in fewer people taking the time to read books, some writers argue that electronic media can be leveraged so as to be pedagogically beneficial and therefore have a positive influence on children.[113] The growing number of resources on the Internet (for example, stories, interactive websites, journals, libraries) are now helping form the so-called "electronic culture" of Arabic-speaking children.[114]

Despite the fact that the public started to pay more and more attention to Arabic children's literature following its commercial success,[115] scholarly, critical, and academic circles in the Arab world as well as in the West[116] have

[109] See <http://www.middle-east-online.com>, 18 February 2007 (last accessed 12 October 2016).

[110] See, for example, Najīb Maḥfūẓ, *ʿAjā'ib al-Aqdār: Muyassara* (illustrations by Ḥilmī al-Tūnī [b. 1934]) (Cairo and Beirut: Dār al-Shurūq, 1989). The nature of the project is illustrated in the introduction written by the editor, Muḥammad al-Muʿallim (p. 1).

[111] See, for example, *Saʿdī Yūsuf* (ed. Firyāl Jabūrī Ghazzūl; illustrations by Īhāb Shākir [b. 1933]) (Yūsuf 1989); and *Maḥmūd Sāmī al-Bārūdī* (ed. Muḥammad ʿAfīfī Maṭar [1935–2010]; illustrations by Nabīl Tāj [b. 1939]) (al-Bārūdī 1993).

[112] See, for example, *Dīwān Shawqī li-l-Aṭfāl* (Shawqī 1984). New modern editions of Shawqī's writings for children have been published since 1980 by al-Hay'a al-Miṣriyya al-ʿĀmma li-l-Kitāb (Cairo) and Dār Thaqāfat al-Aṭfāl (Baghdad). ʿAbd al-Tawwāb Yūsuf's presentation in the "Ḥāfiẓ and Shawqī" conference held in Cairo in October 1982 dealt with Shawqī's literary writings for children (ʿAbd Allāh 1982, p. 9). Yūsuf himself published a book on his experience writing for children (Yūsuf 1999).

[113] See, for example, al-Khāzin and al-Yān 1970, p. 135.

[114] See Shablūl 1999.

[115] Publication of children's literature has been developing constantly throughout the Arab world, especially since the 1970s. See, for example, the Egyptian *Nashrat al-Īdāʿ* (Legal Deposit Bulletin, National Bibliography Section, National Library), which from its first issue in January 1969 dedicated a special section to books for children (in addition to sections on general books and school books).

[116] To my knowledge, there is no scholarly project in English about Arabic literature for children aside from what was included in issue 17–18 of *Matatu: Journal for African Culture and Society*, entitled *Preserving the Landscape of Imagination: Children's Literature in Africa*

lagged behind in treating this literature as *literature*.[117] The prevailing opinion is that this literature is unworthy of any academic effort; only sporadically do we find dedicated scholars of canonical literature for adults turning to the study of children's literature.[118] The translation of Arabic literature for children into other languages is also very limited.[119] The Egyptian scholar Anas Dā'ūd (1934–93) published one book on children's poems[120] and was planning other books on the short story, the theater, and the researching of children's literature.[121] Yet most of the studies in this field so far have didactic,[122] social, and national aims.[123] In 1994 the Egyptian scholar Aḥmad Zalaṭ (b. 1952) still complained about the "lack of attention by the great writers, cultural, educational, and media circles to the child, especially its literature, and its culture in the wide sense, generally."[124] In a 400-page book

(Granqvist and Martini 1997). It should be noted that the above project is perceived by the editors not as a literary project but "as a contribution to the promotion of the rights of the child as they have been declared and discussed at so many fora and seminars in recent years" (Granqvist and Martini 1997, p. xii). Nevertheless, several contributions in the issue treat children's literature as *literature*.

117 For an exception, see Part VII of Fernea 1995 entitled "Children and Play, Children and the Arts" (pp. 421–68). Among the studies included in that part are "Children's Games and Songs in Egypt" by Mohammed Omran; "Children's Games and Songs from Tunisia" collected and translated by Sabra Webber; "Themes Reflected in Palestinian Children's Literature" by Taghreed Alqudsi-Ghabra; and "Iftah Ya Simsim (Open Sesame) and Children in Baghdad" by Misbah al-Khayr and Hashim al-Samira'i.

118 Cf. Azeriah 1993, p.1.

119 An exception is a project by Petra Dünges, a German translator who is interested in Arabic children's literature; she wrote several survey articles on the topic, translated Arabic children's books which were published in bilingual versions in Germany, and keeps a website on Arabic children's literature entitled "Kinder- und Jugendliteratur aus dem Arabischen, Übersetzungen" (<http://www.petra-duenges.de> [last accessed 20 May 2016]). She also collects Arabic children's books on behalf of the Gutenberg Museum Mainz, which is one of the oldest and most famous printing museums in the world (<http://www.gutenberg-museum.de> [last accessed 20 May 2016]).

120 Dā'ūd 1993.

121 Dā'ūd 1993, p. 3.

122 See, for example, Yūsuf 1983, pp. 99–143; Shiḥāta 1991; Abū Mughallā et al. 1993; al-Hawar 1994, pp. 50–4; Shiḥāta 1994; Abū Fanna and 'Azāyiza 1996; Brīghash 1996; Shiḥāta 1996; Shablūl 1998; and Ḥalāwa 2002. 'Abd al-Ra'ūf Abū al-Sa'd, Dean of the School of Education at the University of al-Manṣūra in Egypt, rejects all sorts of non-canonical texts for children (Abū al-Sa'd 1994, p. 7; see also pp. 26–8).

123 See, for example, *Annals of the Faculty of Arts* (Kuwait University) 14 (1993–4), special issue about the topic entitled "The Common Types of the Roles of Men and Women in the Literature of Children and School Books: Analytical and Evolutionary Study." See also Giladi 1985, pp. 157–86.

124 Zalaṭ 1994, p. 5. Only few exceptions may be mentioned, most of them being under the influence of Western concepts, such as al-Ḥadīdī 1969, pp. 49–53, which sees no essential difference between literature for adults and literature for children. In 1998 we find a study that charts, for the first time, a corpus of books for children and youth in Arabic, that is, Nitza Maoz's PhD thesis on the emergence of a system of Arabic children's literature in

published in 2002 dealing with newspapers and journals for children in the Arab world, covering fourteen Arab states, only a few pages were allocated to literary matters. The general orientation of the study is national–didactic: Referring to stories published in the journal *Samīr*, it is said that the journal published many translated stories which contained "concepts, habits, and customs which are far away from our concepts and our Arab and Islamic surroundings."[125] Referring to the field of translated songs which appeared in the journal, the scholar accuses the journal of helping the "cultural and ideological invasion" (*ghazw thaqāfī wa-fikrī*) of Arab and Islamic nations.[126]

Translated Texts

Unlike translated literary texts and their role in the rise of modern Arabic literature during the nineteenth century,[127] or even up to the 1930s,[128] contemporary translated texts for both adults and children are almost totally neglected in the scholarly research.[129] Moreover, when looking at transla-

the cultural sphere of Palestine between the years 1826 and 1918. The study shows that most of the books were used as textbooks, even though some had not been written specifically for that purpose. However, the study does not treat children's literature as *literature*. For example, the chapter that deals with belles-lettres (Maoz 1998, pp. 242–53) does not treat at all the literary aspects of the texts in question, even if most of them were originally written for didactic and educational purposes in order to meet the needs of new education systems.

125 Al-Ghabbāshī 2002, p. 306.

126 Al-Ghabbāshī 2002, p. 243. Another dimension of what is considered to be a "cultural and ideological invasion" is the emergence of a form of speech that mixes Arabic with English. Mixing Arabic with foreign languages has long been commonplace among Western-educated elites in Arab countries such as Lebanon and Algeria, but in recent years it has been widely used also among Western-educated elites in more traditional societies, drawing ire from language purists and exposing a widening social and economic gap in these societies. In Jordan, for example, this form of speech has been dubbed by some as "Arabizi"—a slang term for Arabic and "Inglizi," the Arabic word for English. It is also a means of expression for many young Jordanians who have been educated abroad and who do not share Jordan's conservative values. Linguists blame the growing use of English among young Jordanians on American pop culture inundating the Arab world. According to Haitham Sarḥan, a linguist and professor at Jordan University, "some young people look down on the Arabic language. They think it is old and that English represents life and desires" (Ibon Villelabeitia, "In Jordan, the Young and Hip Speak 'Arabizi,'" *Reuters*, 18 December 2005).

127 See, for example, Tājir 1945?; al-Shayyāl 1950; al-Shayyāl 1951; Abu-Lughod 1963, pp. 28–65; ʻAnānī 1976, pp. 8–25; Peled 1979, pp. 128–50; Somekh 1982, pp. 45–59; Cachia 1990, pp. 29–42; Khulūsī 1991, pp. 107–40; Ostle 1991, pp. 33–44; Somekh 1991, pp. 75–82; Sawāʻī 1999; Khoury 2004, pp. 48–95; and Bardenstein 2005.

128 See, for example, Badīr 1991.

129 For example, in Egypt from the 1950s to the 1980s the number of books translated from English exceeds 4,790, while the number of books translated from French exceeds 1,050 (Nuṣayr 1992, pp. 43–7). However, to the best of my knowledge, not a single study has

tions carried out in the nineteenth and twentieth centuries, scholars seem to be more interested in understanding what kind of influence the West may have had on Arab culture, and they thus concentrate on prose masterpieces from English, French, German, Russian, Italian, Spanish, and even Hebrew literature. Most of these translations were done within the Arab world, especially in Beirut and Cairo. For example, in the 1980s the Lebanese publisher Manshūrāt ʻUwaydāt put out a series of prose masterpieces under the title *Rawāʼiʻ al-Adab wa-l-Fikr* (*Masterpieces of Literature and Thought*). We have also witnessed initiatives by foreign publishers to put out Western classics in Arabic. Classics published by the International Book Center in Troy, Michigan, include Charlotte Brontë's (1816–55) *Jane Eyre*, Charles Dickens' (1812–70) *Oliver Twist*, Ernest Hemingway's (1899–1961) *A Farewell to Arms* and *The Sun Also Rises*, Harriet Beecher Stowe's (1811–96) *Uncle Tom's Cabin*, Victor Hugo's (1802–85) *Les Misérables*, and Pearl Buck's (1892–1973) *The Good Earth* (all of them having been translated by Munīr al-Baʻlabakkī [1918–99]). On November 2007 a non-profit initiative called *Kalima* (Word) was established in Abu Dhabi with the aim of funding "the translation, publication, and distribution of high-quality works of classic and contemporary writing from other languages into Arabic." It was funded by a grant from the Abu Dhabi Authority for Culture and Heritage and benefits from the backing of the Crown Prince of Abu Dhabi:

> Every year we will select 100 candidate titles of classic, contemporary and modern titles from around the world to be translated into Arabic. We hope this number will increase as our funding grows. In summary, *Kalima* will focus on the following activities:
>
> —selecting quality titles across all genres
> —funding quality publishing houses across the Arab World to translate, print and distribute the selected titles
> —supporting marketing and distribution initiatives for books by introducing new and effective distribution channels and upgrading existing ones
> —investing in new translators to encourage more and better quality translators in the future
> —becoming the first "marketers" of books in Arabic on a major scale.

been published yet about the nature of the literary works included among these translated books, the methods of their translation, and their division into genres. Moreover, it is not even known how many literary works there are among them. Mention should also be made of Abdul-Hai 1976, which includes a bibliography of Arabic translations of English and American poetry from 1830 to 1970, but without any attempt to study these translations. On the reception and translation of American literature in the Arab world, see Yousef 2000, pp. 73–86. On the need to control American translations in order to avoid the introduction of a "non-nationalist element in our modern nationalist culture," see Meijer 2002, p. 221.

According to ʿAlī ibn Tamīm, *Kalima*'s chief executive officer, *Kalima* is part of Abu Dhabi's vision to become a center of learning, cross-cultural understanding, and knowledge throughout the Middle East. In September 2008 *Kalima* launched a program inviting Americans to nominate works of American authors for translation. In an attempt to build "understanding between the United States and Arab speakers," Americans were invited to nominate novels, short stories, or poems that reflected American dreams, opportunities, and challenges, or which otherwise embodied the "American spirit." Eight years later, on *Kalima*'s website one could find a plethora of submissions spanning ten categories: general knowledge; philosophy and psychology; religion; social science; language; natural and exact sciences; arts, games, and sport; literature; history, geography, and biography; and children's literature.[130]

In addition, a call for chapters for the *Routledge Handbook of Arabic Translation*, which was issued in May 2015,[131] indicates that translation-related activities from and into Arabic have significantly increased in the last few years in both scope and scale and in turn have stimulated the need of research as well:

> The launch of a number of national translation projects, policies and awards in a number of Arab countries, together with the increasing translation from Arabic in a wide range of subject areas outside the Arab world—especially in the aftermath of the "Arab Spring"—have complicated and diversified the dynamics of the translation industry involving Arabic. Alongside an expanding Arabic translation market, Arabic translation pedagogy witnessed a remarkable progress, with the launch of many Arabic translation programmes at undergraduate and postgraduate levels, both inside and outside the Arab world. This gave rise to a new generation of Arabic translation scholars who embraced the double challenge of critically engaging with the recent innovations in the epistemology and methodology of Western translation studies and developing at the same time their own research tools and conceptual apparatuses that would effectively describe and theorise the unique and fast-evolving realities of Arabic translation.[132]

As for translated canonical literature for children, if we refer only to the 1990s mention should be made of the series *al-Maktaba al-ʿĀlamiyya li-l-Fityān wa-l-Fatāyāt* (*World Library for Young Men and Women*) published by Dār al-ʿIlm li-l-Malāyīn in Beirut. The series adopts the technique of *taʿrīb wa-talkhīṣ* (Arabization and Abridgment) and includes more than twenty

130 The details are according to *Kalima*'s website, <http://www.kalima.ae/> (last accessed 20 May 2016).

131 Editors: Sameh F. Hanna, Hanem El-Farahaty, and Abdel Wahab Khalifa.

132 The suggested publication date is December 2017.

books for elementary and intermediate pupils, including Charles Dickens' *Oliver Twist*, Daniel Defoe's (1660–1731) *Robinson Crusoe*, Alexandre Dumas' (1802–70) *The Three Musketeers*, Jules Verne's (1828–1905) *Around the World in Eighty Days*, Victor Hugo's *The Hunchback of Notre Dame*, and Miguel de Cervantes' (1547–1616) *Don Quixote*. Similar series of translated canonical adaptations were set up in the 1990s by Dār al-Biḥār in Beirut and Dār al-Hilāl in Cairo but with bilingual editions—the translated text (whether the original is in English or in any other language) is printed next to the Arabic translation. The International Book Center in Troy, Michigan, also published adaptations of famous classics as intermediate readers, including Charlotte Brontë's *Jane Eyre*; Charles Dickens' *Hard Times*; R. D. Blackmore's (1825–1900) *Lorna Doone*; Mary Shelley's (1797–1851) *Frankenstein*; and William Shakespeare's (1564–1616) *Merchant of Venice*, *As You Like It*, and *Twelfth Night*. There still exists, however, no study of the inventory of translated canonical texts undertaken from a *literary* point of view.[133]

NON-CANONICAL LITERATURE

Throughout its history Arab culture has regarded works written in dialect or in a mixture of *ʿāmmiyya* and *fuṣḥā* as subliterary.[134] The canonical center of the Arabic literary system, which controls the main cultural institutions, withholds recognition, prizes, and even publication from those writers who have made *ʿāmmiyya* their main literary linguistic medium.[135] In reaction to

133 For a case study of translational norms in children's literature translated into Arabic, see Azeriah 1993. For some observations on translated children's literature in Syria, see ʿAbbūd 1995, pp. 202–18.

134 On the metalinguistic Arabic discourse and the polarity of the linguistic practice, see Armbrust 1996, pp. 36–61.

135 Other factors adduced to militate against the use of *ʿāmmiyya* in literature are beyond the scope of this book; however, mention should be made briefly of two of them: first, texts written in dialect are generally fully intelligible only to those readers who are native speakers of that dialect; and second, dialects in the Arab world never developed successful writing systems of their own. See *Apollo*, January 1934, p. 247 (regarding songs in *ʿāmmiyya* included in the film *al-Warda al-Bayḍāʾ*). The Lebanese dramatist ʿIṣām Maḥfūẓ (1939–2006) suggested the "solution" of *fuṣḥā shaʿbiyya*, that is, the dramatic text in *ʿāmmiyya* is "translated" into *fuṣḥā*, but twelve "key terms" (*alfāẓ mafātīḥ*) are left in the Lebanese vernacular; see Maḥfūẓ 1988 [1970], p. 9; and Maḥfūẓ 1988 [1971], p. 14. See also Abdel-Malek 1972, p. 132; Somekh 1991, p. 26; and Somekh 1993a, pp. 177–8. On the issue of different writing systems for Arabic, especially for *ʿāmmiyya*, see Mūsā 1945, pp. 137–9; Madkour 1962?, pp. 108–11; and al-Jundī 1963, pp. 123–32, 244–6. The poet Saʿīd ʿAql (1911–2014), who published several collections of poetry in *fuṣḥā*, but who throughout his career has also written in *ʿāmmiyya*, devised a new script in Latin characters that would, in his view, adequately represent the distinctive features of the dialect. However, he failed to

this, some of those who fight for the canonization of *'āmmiyya* reject *fuṣḥā* as the sole language of literature. For example, defending the use of *'āmmiyya* in literature for children, Anīs Furayḥa (Frayha, Freiha) (1903–93) claims that canonical poetry in *fuṣḥā* has always remained confined to those belonging to certain sectors of society, such as kings, sultans, princes, aristocrats, and fighters.[136] Nevertheless, not every text written in *'āmmiyya* is considered to be non-canonical, and not every text written in *fuṣḥā* is in fact canonical. The canonicity or the non-canonicity of a text may also be a result of other aesthetic and/or non-aesthetic considerations and constraints. Here, too, scholarly research in the Arab world generally overlooks non-canonical texts, and most of the academic studies in this field are carried out by Western scholars. As for the Arab scholars who already do pay attention to these texts, they generally do so out of non-literary considerations (for example, searching for national roots, attempting to consolidate a particularistic territorial identity).[137] Only during the late 1980s and the beginning of the 1990s was

inspire a new generation of poets (Somekh 1991, pp. 69, 121. Cf. Shraybom-Shivtiel 2005, pp. 136–40, 156–7). In his weekly newspaper entitled *Lubnān*, founded in the mid-1970s and written entirely in the Lebanese *'āmmiyya*, 'Aql used to publish almost in each issue a short poem in the vernacular in Latin script. Here, for example, is a poem entitled "Baab en Naÿiim" ("The Gate of Bliss") (for lack of suitable fonts, the following letters I use here do not exactly reflect 'Aql's script: *ÿ*; *ș*; *ẓ*):

Xqiitellna, ya Rabb, ÿan baab en Naÿiim
Baddu l ÿazaab eș șeÿb zewwaadi:
L çakd sahl, byaÿmlu l ÿaadi,
Bass el ÿata baddu betulaat el ÿaẓiim

In standard Arabic script, it might be written as follows:

حكيت لنا، يا ربّ، عن باب النعيم
بـــدّو العذاب الصـــعب زوّادي
الأخد ســـهل، بيعمـــلو العـــادي،
بسّ العطـــا بدّو بطـــولة العظيم

You told us, O God, that the gate of happiness
Needs, as provisions, hard suffering
To take is easy, everyone is used to it,
But generosity needs the bravery of the great man (*Lubnān*, 24 December 1982, p. 4).

On efforts to promote *'āmmiyya* as a print language and to systematize it to be part of "colonial linguistic projects," see Sharkey 2004, pp. 131–49.

136 Furayḥa 1955, p. 152. Cf. Jubrān 1985, pp. 538–9.

137 See, for example, the articles included in the folkloristic Iraqi bimonthly *Majallat al-Turāth al-Sha'bī*, which has been published since 1969 by the Ministry of Culture and Information in Baghdad. A similar periodical is the quarterly *al-Ma'thūrāt al-Sha'biyya*, published by Markaz al-Turāth al-Sha'bī l-Duwal Majlis al-Ta'āwun al-Khalījī (al-Dawḥa). Since its first issue in January 1986, it has published articles on topics such as oral literature, traditional folk music and dance, material culture, arts and crafts, customs, traditions, beliefs, and conventions. See also the attention paid by Palestinian critics to various popular genres, which can be seen in the studies published by Mu'assasat Ibn Rushd in Jerusalem (e.g. al-

there some growing awareness of the literary aspects of these texts.[138] Due to a lack of space, and in order to avoid a lengthy discussion which will not contribute to the aim of the present study, I will analyze below the literary dynamics of non-canonical Arabic texts in synchronic cross-section without distinguishing between vernacular and popular literature.[139] And I will use the term "popular" to refer to both.

Texts for Adults

The inventory of non-canonical texts for adults includes popular prose and poetry, detective stories, spy thrillers, monster and science fiction stories, love stories, erotic, sex, and pornographic literature,[140] and comic

Khalīlī 1977; al-Khalīlī 1979; and ʻAllūsh 1981). However, ʻAlī al-Khalīlī (1943–2013), for example, did not employ the Palestinian dialect in his original literary writings, and even in his prose, not to mention his poetry, he used *fuṣḥā* in the dialogues as well. In addition, at the academic conference held at Birzeit University (17–19 May 1997) entitled *al-Adab al-Filasṭīnī Bayna al-Manfā wa-l-Iḥtilāl* (*Palestinian Literature between Exile and Occupation*), there were no scholarly presentations on popular Palestinian literature. See also the Syrian Muḥammad Jāsim al-Ḥumaydī's essay entitled *Limādhā Nataʻāmal bi-Ḥadhr maʻa al-Adab al-Shaʻbī* (*al-Thawra*, 29 August 1991, p. 6), which, while intending to deny the territorial national considerations behind the study of popular literature, paradoxically only asserts them. For example, the essay ends with the following words: "Many Arab countries acted ahead of us and published specific journals dealing with popular heritage, while nobody among us has thought of that yet."

138 See, for example, the special issue of *Oral Tradition* on "Arabic Oral Tradition" 4.1–2 (1989); and Caspi and Blessing 1993, pp. 355–80. See also Ṣafwat Kamāl's presentation at the conference held in Cairo on "The Reading of Literature" (according to *al-ʻĀlam*, 27 June 1992, p. 53).

139 On this distinction, see Khoury 2006, pp. 1–20.

140 In Arabic, the following terms are generally used: *adab al-jins, adab al-ithāra al-jinsiyya, al-adab al-makshūf, al-adab al-fāḥish,* and *al-adab al-ibāḥī*. On the issue of erotic non-canonical literature in Arabic, see the attitude of Arab intellectuals to *al-Rawḍ al-ʻĀṭir fī Nuzhat al-Khāṭir* (*The Perfumed Garden in the Trip of the Mind*) by Abū ʻAbd Allāh al-Nafzāwī from the fifteenth century (al-Nafzāwī 1983, pp. 3–71). For the complete text, see al-Nafzāwī 1990. For a survey of Arabic erotic literature and for details on translations of al-Nafzāwī's book into French (1886), German (1905), and English (1927), see the introduction by Jamāl Jumʻa in al-Nafzāwī 1990 (pp. 11–17); Meisami and Starkey 1998, I, pp. 572–3; and Lowry and Stewart 2009, pp. 309–21 (by L. A. Giffen). Cf. Jamāl Jumʻa's introduction to *Nuzhat al-Albāb fīmā lā Yūjad fī Kitāb* (*The Delight of the Hearts in What Is Not Found in Any Book*) by Shihāb al-Dīn Aḥmad al-Tīfāshī (1184–1253) (al-Tīfāshī 1992, pp. 15–42); Meisami and Starkey 1998, I, p. 772; Allen 1998, pp. 251–2; Antoon 2014; and Talib et al. 2014. When sexual desires are expressed in contemporary canonical literature, this is generally done in a highly refined fashion, and then mostly in the service of certain social or moral ideas (cf. Shukrī 1991; and Cobham 1975, pp. 78–88). See also the file "Kitāb al-Fann al-Shahwānī" published in *al-Kitāba al-Ukhrā* 21–2 (January 2000, pp. 177–274). Prostitution is a recurring theme in canonical works of male as well as female writers, where it serves to illustrate the oppression of women in Arab society, for example, Najīb Maḥfūẓ's *Zuqāq al-Midaqq* (Maḥfūẓ n.d. [1947]; English translation: Mahfouz

books[141] (although most Arab comics are destined for children).[142] Poetry differs from prose in the field of non-canonical literature for adults especially in regard to the function of the language: Poetry is generally considered to be non-canonical when written in *'āmmiyya* and canonical when written in *fuṣḥā*.[143] Prose is generally referred to as non-canonical when it deals with popular and so-called "inappropriate" themes, even when written in *fuṣḥā*. On the other hand, use of *'āmmiyya* in certain texts does not automatically mean that those texts are non-canonical, as we previously saw regarding the novel and social drama. In these cases, whereas social drama uses *'āmmiyya* because it consists of dialogues alone, the novel and the short story are written in *fuṣḥā* and have their dialogues in *'āmmiyya*; when written totally in *'āmmiyya*, however, they are typically accompanied by suitable "justifications."[144] However, the aforementioned equations (canonicity = writing in *fuṣḥā*; non-canonicity = writing in *'āmmiyya*) still dominates

1966; Mahfouz 1981) and Nawāl al-Sa'dāwī's *Imra'a 'inda Nuqṭat al-Ṣifr* (al-Sa'dāwī 1979; English translation: El Saadawi 1983). On the former, see Accad 1984, pp. 69–70 (Miriam Cooke argues that the portrayals of prostitutes as either main or subsidiary characters in Maḥfūẓ's works have in common not so much the commodification of the body for survival as an urge for independence [Cooke 1993a, p. 112]), and on the latter, see Malti-Douglas 1995, pp. 44–67. On the prostitute in Arabic literature in general, see Kishtainy 1982; Accad 1984, pp. 63–75; and Cooke 1993a, pp. 106–25. On male and female homosexuality in Arabic literature, see above, pp. 12–13. Needless to say, canonicity and non-canonicity in Arabic literary works dealing with sex and the erotic are not disconnected from religious considerations. Consequently, it is relevant to consider the standpoint of religious circles regarding the topic, as is illustrated for example by Muḥammad Ḥusayn Faḍl Allāh (1935–2010), the Lebanese Shiite religious scholar and a spiritual leader of Ḥizb Allāh: "The banning of some Arabic books dealing with sex does not mean that there is any negative attitude of Islam toward sex; only the people of the East live such negativeness [...] There is one point which does not have any relationship to the Islamic concept, that is the cheap writing about sex which does not grant you any artistic or creative value, and which, moreover, occasionally causes you to be sick" (Faḍl Allāh 1995, pp. 210–11. Cf. Ḥarb 1995, pp. 252–4. On Faḍl Allāh's general conceptions, see Esposito 1995, I, pp. 453–6). On the censorship of belles-lettres on moral grounds, see below, pp. 117–21, 128, 147, 275. On the tolerant attitude of medieval religious scholars to literary works dealing with sex, see al-Qishṭīnī 2001, pp. 7–10.

141 Comic books for adults in general have not taken off yet in the Arab world. On the general issue of comics, how they began as a popular kind of entertainment in England's press in the nineteenth century and how they reached their elevated status in the United States in the 1960s, see Gifford 1976; and Barker 1989. On Arabic comics for children, see below, pp. 84–5.

142 For a detailed inventory of "dialect literature," especially from Egypt and Lebanon (and relevant bibliographical references), see Versteegh et al. 2006, I, pp. 597–604.

143 Even the journal *Shi'r*, which during the late 1950s was the mouthpiece of modernism in Arabic poetry, published only in *fuṣḥā* even though its founder and editor Yūsuf al-Khāl (1917–87) supported poetic expression in the vernacular as part of the renaissance of Arabic literature (al-Khāl 1981 [introduction]).

144 Cf. al-Qa'īd 1994, p. 226. See above, pp. 36–8.

the Arabic literary system, despite successive attempts to have it abolished. Indeed, the frequent apologies made by Arab intellectuals and scholars wanting to justify the attention they give to non-canonical popular poetry show the persistent influence of this equation on literary culture.[145]

Non-canonical popular poetry refers mainly to *shi'r 'āmmī,* also known as *shi'r al-'āmmiyya* and *zajal,* a dialectal form of poetry which made its first appearance in written form in the twelfth century in medieval Spain[146] and which thereafter spread throughout the Arab world.[147] Traditional forms of this poetry,[148] such as *mawwāl,*[149] *'atābā, m'anna, shrūqī,* and *qarrādī,*[150] are commonly sung or recited in public gatherings, but the *zajal* is also rendered in more "elevated" styles and is published in magazines and individual collections. In Arabia and Iraq the terms *nabaṭī* and *shi'r 'āmmī* are preferred, respectively, while in Egypt, Lebanon, Syria, and Palestine *zajal* is the generic term for all kinds of colloquial poetry, oral and written. Although this type of poetry deals with nearly all subjects we find in canonical poetry, it is often

145 See, for example, 'Abbūd 1968, pp. 119–20; and al-Maqāliḥ 1978, pp. 6–13.

146 One of the earliest known *zajal* poets was Ibn Quzmān (1078–1160). For more on his work, see Deyoung and Germain 2011, pp. 175–86 (by James T. Monroe); and Monroe 2013, pp. 293–334. Many sources indicate that dialectal poetry had existed much earlier as an oral genre (Einbinder 1995, p. 254). An episode mentioned in al-Iṣfahānī's *Kitāb al-Aghānī* proves that such poetry existed as early as the Umayyad period: The leading singer and prolific composer Ma'bad ibn Wahb (d. 743) related that the Caliph al-Walīd ibn Yazīd (d. 744) enjoyed much more dialectal poetry than poetry in *fuṣḥā*; he even detested the singing of Ma'bad himself:

فلما طال عليه أمري قال الوليد: يا غلام، شيخنا شيخنا، فأتي بشيخ، فلما رآه هشّ إليه، فأخذ الشيخ العود فاندفع يغنّي:
سلّوْر في القدر ويلي عَلُوهْ جاء القطّ أكله ويلي عَلُوهْ
- السلّوْر: السمك الجريّ بلغة أهل الشأم - قال معبد: فجعل صاحب المنزل يصفّق ويضرب برجله طربا وسرورا
(...) قال معبد: وانسللت منهم فانصرفت ولم يعلم بي. فما رأيت قطّ غناء أضيع، ولا شيخا أجهل.

See al-Iṣfahānī 1927, I, pp. 55–6; and al-Iṣfahānī 1997, I, p. 74. In both editions, the following editorial remark is cited: "'*alūh* is probably a Syrian language (*lahja shamiyya*) for '*alyahi*." Cf. Fakhr al-Dīn 2007, pp. 73–5. See also the historical novel *Ma'bad Yanjaḥ fī Baghdād* (2005) by the Lebanese novelist Rashīd al-Ḍa'īf (Daïf) (b. 1945), in the center of which is the singer and composer Ma'bad (al-Ḍa'īf 2005, p. 66). It is interesting that *Kitāb Adab al-Ghurabā'* by Abū Faraj al-Iṣfahānī, which consists of medieval Arabic graffiti on the theme of nostalgia, consists of poetic graffiti only in *fuṣḥā*, although it is not improbable that graffiti had been written then in dialects as well (al-Iṣfahānī 1972; English translation: al-Iṣfahānī 2000).

147 See Stern 1974, pp. 166–203; Abbās 1985, pp. 252–79; and Reynolds 1997, pp. 233–6 (and the references on p. 236). On the contemporary *zajal,* see Meisami and Starkey 1998, II, pp. 819–20 (art *Zajal,* modern by D. Semah) as well as Khūrī 1999; Khūrī 1999a, pp. 97–128; Yaqub 2007; and Abū Zakī 2008. On Palestinian Arab music and the *maqām,* see Cohen and Katz 2006.

148 See Jargy 1970.

149 On the *mawwāl,* see Cachia 1977, pp. 77–103; and Fanjul 1977, pp. 104–22.

150 On these forms and others, see Khūrī 1999, pp. 105–75.

used in the service of politics, national and social struggles, and ideologies,[151] as well as for humorous purposes.[152] Already in 1910 the national Egyptian leader Muḥammad Farīd (1868–1919) mentioned in his introduction to a collection of *fuṣḥā* patriotic poems by his compatriot ʿAlī al-Ghāyātī (1885–1956) that the poets of the countryside (*shuʿarāʾ al-aryāf*) had written patriotic poems in *ʿāmmiyya* for the uneducated classes, and that these poems helped spread the spirit of patriotism among the masses.[153]

Interestingly, after 1948 Palestinian national themes appear in folk songs, especially those sung by Egyptian and Iraqi poets. Outstanding among the latter are the Egyptian Aḥmad Fu'ād Nigm (Najm) (1929–2013) and the Iraqi Muẓaffar al-Nawwāb (1934–2017). Nigm's song "Yā Falasṭīniyya" ("Oh Palestinians!") seems to be the first Egyptian folk song to raise the problem of the Palestinians.[154] Significant also is the use the Iraqi authorities made of *zajal* poetry for the glorification of Ṣaddām Ḥusayn (1937–2003). A specific association, Jamʿiyyat Shuʿrāʾ al-Shaʿb (The Association of People's Poets), was established in Iraq, with around eighteen thousand members, according to an anti-regime columnist, with the aim of producing "khaki poems" for nothing but "washing memory and praising persecution and wars." According to this columnist, these poems served as a kind of

> policeman in order to keep a political and social situation whose lines were drawn on all levels, including the historical level with all its immortal features and stances, offering it as a despised sacrifice of love and admiration for a despotic ruler.[155]

At the same time, the Iraqi authorities persecuted other poets who wrote in the vernacular, accusing them of composing poems against the president.[156]

151 Cf. Cachia 1975, pp. 86–98; Kishtainy 1985; Slyomovics 1986, pp. 178–85; Abdel-Malek 1988, pp. 162–78; Booth 1992, pp. 419–40; and Beinin 1994, pp. 191–215. See also Ṣāliḥ 1982, which includes sections like *Bayram wa-l-ʿArab* ("Bayram and the Arabs") (pp. 49–70) and *Mawāwīl Siyāsiyya* ("Political Colloquial Poems") (pp. 71–107). The political involvement of popular poets sometimes produced political pressure and censorship, especially in Syria and Palestine (e.g. ʿAbd al-Ḥakīm 1984, pp. 9–10). For a study of the ideology of the social life of the Bedouin Awlād ʿAlī in Egypt through their *ghinnāwa*s (short lyric poems), see Abu-Lughod 1986, that uses the term "ideology," broadly defined, to refer to "what many anthropologists might prefer to call culture," that is, "the stuff of definitions of the world, that which allows people to understand and act" (p. 276, n. 24). On the poetry of Awlād ʿAlī, see also Abu-Lughod 1990, pp. 24–45. On stories by and about women in the Awlād ʿAlī community, see Abu-Lughod 1993.

152 See, for example, Cachia 1983, pp. 60–6; and Furayḥa 1988, pp. 30–51.

153 Al-Ghāyātī 1947 [1910], p. 12.

154 Sulaiman 1984, p. ii. On Palestine in Egyptian colloquial poetry, see Radwan 2011, pp. 61–77.

155 Haddād 2002, p. 9.

156 See, for example, *al-Muʾtamar* (London) 312 (19–25 July 2002), p. 1.

Popular poetry in the vernacular, the prosodic conventions of which are still disputed among scholars,[157] has been regarded by the literary establishment, with only a few exceptions,[158] as an inferior type of poetry.[159] Moreover, songs written in the vernacular are not considered to be poetry at all, as Ghālī Shukrī (1935–98), one of the outstanding Arab cultural critics during the second half of the twentieth century, has observed:

> The masters of the official literature (*asātidhat al-adab al-rasmī*) chose to emphasize the artistic gap that exists, according to them, between the value of what is called *zajal*, that is, poetry written in the vernacular (*al-shi'r al-'āmmī*), and what is considered true poetry, that is, canonical poetry (*al-shi'r al-faṣīḥ*). These labels have been current for many generations, even amongst sectors of educated people and have shaped the social gap, as I see it, between the class sensitivity of those who defend poetry in *fuṣḥā* and the "mob" (*ghawghā'*) [who go for] poetry in the vernacular.[160]

Particularly since the 1950s we find efforts to have the *zajal* canonized and its literary value recognized, especially in Egypt,[161] which has been home to such

157 See Gorton 1975, pp. 1–29; Gorton 1978, pp. 32–40; Corriente 1982, pp. 76–82; Corriente 1986, pp. 34–49; Semah 1988, pp. 49–73 (= Semah 1995, pp. 115–40); Semah 1990, pp. 93–127 (= Semah 1995, pp. 141–82); Semah 1991a, pp. 187–200 (a review article on Bailey 1991; see also R. B. Serjeant's review in *Journal of Arabic Literature* 24.3 [1993], pp. 278–80); and Semah 1992, pp. 95–143 (= Semah 1995, pp. 183–238). See also R. Stoetzer's review of Semah 1995 in *Journal of Arabic Literature* 27.2 (1996), pp. 187–90, in which he discusses the theory of non-classical metrics with regard to Semah's view that strophic poetry has its antecedents in traditional poetry. See also Fakhr al-Dīn 2010, and Federico Corriente's review of the book in *Journal of Arabic Literature* 42.2–3 (2011), pp. 261–8.

158 For example, Louis Cheikho (1859–1927) published an article in *al-Mashriq* entitled "The Merits of the Colloquial Compared with the Classical Language," where he asserted that the dialects have their proper place as literary forms, pointing to the numerous pieces in the colloquial of nineteenth-century literature which he had published in *al-Mashriq* (Cheikho 1925, pp. 161–71. Cf. Campbell 1972, p. 100).

159 See, for example, Adnan Abbas' words on the attitude of scholars toward the Iraqi *band* which led to its gradual fall into oblivion in the twentieth century (Abbas 1994, p. 6. On the *band*, see also Ibrahim 2006, pp. 87–98). See also Pierre Cachia's comments in Naff 1993 (p. 21) about "the indifference not only of Western scholars but also of Arab colleagues who looked upon folk literature as a debased activity unworthy of serious attention, their disapproval sometimes mounting to active antagonism."

160 Shukrī 1978 [1968], pp. 56–7. See also Nigm's attitude to *zajal* before he became aware of its value: "I used to despise the lovers of Bayram's poetry and the melodies of Sayyid Darwīsh [1892–1925] and Zakariyyā Aḥmad [1890–1961]" (Nigm 1993, p. 205. Cf. 'Awaḍ 1963, p. 143; and 'Īd 1986, p. 232). Some newspapers and journals published *zajal* in different pages, an example being *al-Ra'y al-'Āmm* (Kuwait), 23 February 1990, which has a special page entitled *Min al-Adab wa-l-Shi'r al-Sha'bī* ("From Popular Literature and Poetry") (p. 15): The canonical poetry is published on another page (p. 4).

161 See Radwan 2004, especially pp. 221–6.

famous twentieth-century *zajal* poets as Bayram al-Tūnisī (1893–1961),[162] Ḥusayn Ṭanṭāwī (1914–86),[163] Ṣalāḥ Jāhīn (1930–86),[164] Aḥmad Fu'ād Nigm (Najm),[165] and ʻAbd al-Raḥmān al-Abnūdī (1938–2015).[166] In 1961 President Gamāl ʻAbd al-Nāṣir (1918–70), in what seemed to be a step toward improving the status of popular poetry,[167] granted Bayram al-Tūnisī the highest prize of the Supreme Council for Culture (*al-Majlis al-Aʻlā li-l-Thaqāfa*). Three years later Aḥmad Fu'ād Nigm was awarded the same prize.[168] However, external non-literary factors cannot impose canonical status on any literary system because whatever the social/cultural factors might be, their possible function in literary dynamics is one which is manifested/actualized through conversion (transformation). This conversion "is carried out with the means available to, and conditioned by, the literary system. Thus, while the need for change, its rate and tempo, may depend on the social/cultural norms (converted by the literary system), its manifestation/actualization is determined by the specific intra-literary conditions."[169]

Disregarded by the literary establishment, the *zajal* is also ignored by publishing houses, major literary journals, literary circles, and scholarly institu-

162 On Bayram al-Tūnisī, see al-ʻAzab 1981; Booth 1990; and Booth 1994, pp. 149–76. See also al-Tūnisī 2001, especially pp. 115–31; and Arroues 2011, pp. 31–51.

163 On Ṭanṭāwī, see ʻAbd al-Fattāḥ 1993a, pp. 35–62.

164 On Jāhīn, see Elmessiri 1976, pp. 65–7; Sayf 1986; ʻAbd al-Fattāḥ 1993a, pp. 123–47; Campbell 1996, pp. 410–12; Ziyāda 1996; and Radwan 2004, pp. 238–42.

165 On Nigm, see Makkī 1986, pp. 11–48 (published also as an introduction to Nigm 1986, pp. 5–38); Abdel-Malek 1990 (see also D. Semah's review article in *al-Karmil—Abḥāth fī al-Lugha wa-l-Adab* 12 [1991], pp. 153–61 and P. Kennedy's review in *Journal of Arabic Literature* 25.2 [1994], pp. 175–9); al-Mukhkh 1990; Farīda al-Naqqāsh's introduction to Nigm 1991 (pp. 2–20); and ʻAbd al-Fattāḥ 1993a, pp. 87–122. In the late 1970s Nigm and his wife, the singer ʻAzza Balbaʻ (b. 1956), together with the blind singer Shaykh Imām (1918–95) and the plastic artist Muḥammad ʻAlī were subjected to persecution and imprisoned by the Egyptian authorities; see the open letter Nigm issued "to the consciences of the noble writers, artists and intellectuals in Egypt and throughout the world [...] singing became a crime in the shadow of [Anwar] al-Sādāt's 'democracy' and that of his friend [Jimmy] Carter" (*al-Thaqāfa al-Jadīda* 4.13 [1979], pp. 180–1).

166 On al-Abnūdī, see *al-Ṭalīʻa*, August 1972, pp. 148–52; *al-Ikhā'*, April 1989, pp. 38–9; and Campbell 1996, pp. 173–5. See also al-Abnūdī's prose writings (al-Abnūdī 1998). Ibrāhīm al-Ḍamrānī considers al-Abnūdī to be the poet most committed to the national cause (*al-Ahrām*, 9 February 1994, p. 18).

167 On ʻAbd al-Nāṣir's attitude toward Umm Kulthūm before and after the revolution, see his words to her according to Nassib 1994, p. 206: "Je Lui [directeur de la radio] ai dit que le Nil et les Pyramides existaient aussi sous l'ancien régime, il n'a jamais été question de les interdire [...] Vous serez toujours plus grande. Vous étiez la voix de l'Égypte, la révolution fera de vous la voix des Arabes. Face au monde entier, vous verrez." The Arabic translation can be found in Turkiyya 1999, pp. 220–1.

168 See Abdel-Malek 1990, p. 18. On the rehabilitation of popular art in Egypt, see also Berque 1969 [1960], pp. 219–20 (English translation: Berque 1964, pp. 195–6; Arabic translation: Berque 1982, pp. 270–1).

169 Sebeok 1986, I, pp. 459–60.

tions. *Zajal* poets can never become members of the general association of poets and writers that exists in Egypt, and they have to make do with their own association (*Rābiṭat al-Zajjālīn*). In the mid-1980s the Egyptian scholar and critic ʿAbd al-Fattāḥ al-Bārūdī (1913–96), an indefatigable defender of popular poetry,[170] lashed out at the canonical literary establishment for the way it continues to ignore Muḥammad ʿAbd al-Munʿim Abū Buthayna (1905–79), who chaired the association for about fifty years and whose poetry was vastly popular.[171] In a short essay in *al-Akhbār*, he calls for Sanjar Street in Cairo, where Abū Buthayna's house still stands, to be renamed after the late poet: "Doesn't this poet deserve that Sanjar Street be named after him?! After all, who is Sanjar?!"[172] Likewise, the critic Ibrāhīm al-ʿArīs (b. 1946), literary editor of the Palestinian magazine *al-Yawm al-Sābiʿ* published in Paris during the 1970s and 1980s, complained about how Fu'ād Ḥaddād (1927–85), "Bayram al-Tunisī's successor,"[173] had been completely ignored. The Egyptian scholar Yusrī al-ʿAzab (b. 1947), himself a composer of *zajal* poems,[174] demanded from the Egyptian Ministry of Culture to start removing the "siege" (*muḥāṣara*) imposed on poetry in the vernacular.[175] Al-ʿAzab mentions the following five features of this "siege":

1. There are no *zajal* representatives on the poetry committee within the Supreme Council for Culture (*al-Majlis al-Aʿlā li-l-Thaqāfa*);

170 For example, he assumes the title *Ra'īs Jamʿiyyat Aṣdiqā' Mūsīqā al-Sayyid Darwīsh* (Head of the Association of the Lovers of al-Sayyid Darwīsh's Music) (Zakī 1992, pp. 36–7).

171 Abū Buthayna also wrote a study on the *zajal* and its development (Abū Buthayna 1973).

172 *Al-Akhbār*, 11 June 1986, p. 10. Al-Bārūdī quotes two verses of Abū Buthayna which illustrate the poet's awareness of the inferior status of his poetry:

يا ممثلين الفنّ انهار   والنقد كمل ع الباقي
ما عادشي للمسرح أنصار   أنصاره فين أنا مش لاقي

Oh actors, art is collapsing, critical writing has exterminated what has been left.
Theater does not have any supporters, where are they? I cannot find them.

On Abū Buthayna, see also ʿAbd al-Fattāḥ 1993a, pp. 7–34.

173 See *al-Ḥayāt*, November 1996, p. 19. Rajā' al-Naqqāsh (1934–2008) states that when he was the editor of *al-Hilāl* between 1969 and 1971, he published a poem by Ḥaddād which was the first to be published in the magazine in *ʿāmmiyya* since its first issue in 1892 (al-Naqqāsh 1992, p. 285). On Fu'ād Ḥaddād and his poetry, see ʿAbd al-Fattāḥ 1993b, pp. 63–86. See also the special file about the poet in *Adab wa-Naqd*, January–February 1986; and Radwan 2004, pp. 226–38.

174 See, for example, al-ʿAzab 1971. He also published *zajal* poems in the literary section of the newspapers in Egypt (e.g. *al-Akhbār*, 28 July 1993, p. 9).

175 *October*, 22 May 1988, p. 36. Cf. Rajā' al-Naqqāsh's observations following the death of Fu'ād Ḥaddād (al-Naqqāsh 1992, p. 291) as well as ʿIzzat al-Qamḥāwī's (b. 1961) note in the literary page of *al-Akhbār* (28 July 1993, p. 9) following the publication of two new *zajal* collections: one of them by Muḥammad al-Ghayṭī (al-Ghayṭī 1993) and the second by Ṭāhir al-Barnbālī (b. 1958) (al-Barnbālī 1993).

2. The *zajal* is excluded from literary magazines published by the Ministry of Culture, especially *Ibdāʿ* and *al-Qāhira;*
3. The status of this poetry is not recognized by the bibliographic journal *ʿĀlam al-Kitāb;*
4. The magazine *al-Shiʿr*, which specializes in poetry, never publishes *zajal* poems; and
5. The State Prizes Committee (*Lajnat Jawāʾiz al-Dawla al-Tashjīʿiyya*) does not recognize poetry in the vernacular as being worthy of nomination for its poetry prizes.

Al-ʿAzab also complains that the interests of electronic media organizations in poetry in the vernacular are confined to those poems which are set to music.[176] Recent years have witnessed some undeniable, though still small, changes in this situation. Since the mid-1970s calls within the literary system for the canonization of the *zajal* have been intensified. Al-Hayʾa al-Miṣriyya al-ʿĀmma li-l-Kitāb (The General Egyptian Book Organization), the central agent of the Egyptian literary canonical establishment, has started publishing *zajal* collections, and during the period from 1976 to 1986 it produced the *Complete Works* (*al-Aʿmāl al-Kāmila*) of Bayram al-Tūnisī (1893–1961).[177] Another project of al-Hayʾa al-Miṣriyya al-ʿĀmma li-l-Kitāb is a series of poetry collections in the vernacular under the title *Ishrāqāt Adabiyya* (*Literary Illuminations*). One of these collections, by the poet Aḥmad Ghāzī, includes twenty poems portraying the heroism of Egyptian soldiers in battles against the Israeli army and has an introduction by Yusrī al-ʿAzab.[178] Another collection is by Muḥammad al-Ghayṭī.[179] *ʿĀlam al-Kitāb*, which started appearing in 1984 and which is published by al-Hayʾa al-Miṣriyya al-ʿĀmma li-l-Kitāb, has reflected the change in attitude toward popular poetry. From its first issue,[180] this journal has included a section entitled *al-Fihrist al-ʿAṣriyya li-l-Waṭan al-ʿArabī* ("The Modern Index of the Arab World"), which has "category 800," a subsection dedicated to literature, entries on essays, poems, novels, and short stories, but not on vernacular poems. In the second issue,[181] category 800 included under modern poetry a collection by Aḥmad Fuʾād Nigm. In the third, fourth, and fifth issues, a few collections of

[176] The blind singer Shaykh Imām (1918–95) claimed that the main reason for the circulation of the *zajal* was a lack of attention from the electronic media (*al-Ḥurriyya*, 18 November 1984, pp. 41–2).

[177] Al-Tūnisī 1976–86 (10 volumes).

[178] According to *October*, 22 May 1988, p. 41.

[179] Al-Ghayṭī 1993. On the collection, see *al-Akhbār*, 28 July 1993, p. 9.

[180] *ʿĀlam al-Kitāb*, January–February–March 1984, pp. 24–5.

[181] *ʿĀlam al-Kitāb*, April–May–June 1984, pp. 36–7.

vernacular poetry were mentioned, and the sixth issue contained a new entry entitled *Ashkāl Ukhrā* ("Other Forms"),[182] where one can find listed the *maqāmāt* of Bayram al-Tūnisī and his *al-A'māl al-Kāmila* (*Complete Works*) as well as poetry collections by Aḥmad Fu'ād Nigm and Fu'ād Ḥaddād. Obviously, the editors still considered vernacular literature as not meriting inclusion on a par with literature in *fuṣḥā*, a policy that continued until the second issue of 1990,[183] with collections in *zajal* (especially those of Bayram al-Tūnisī) under *Ashkāl Ukhrā* always included (which also included items the editors did not know exactly how to classify). In the second issue of 1991[184] *Anwā' Adabiyya Ukhrā* ("Other Literary Genres") replaced *Ashkāl Ukhrā*, but included no vernacular literature at all even though it was clearly a rubric for miscellaneous items. Since then the policy has been to classify *zajal* poetry together with poetry in *fuṣḥā*.[185] The change may well have been precipitated by the many complaints from writers, critics, and readers (for example Yusrī al-'Azab's aforementioned demand), which had specifically criticized the policy of that bibliographic journal.

It should also be noted that the magazine *Adab wa-Naqd*, which began circulating at the start of 1984, has always shown an openness toward the poetry in the vernacular. It published vernacular poems, such as those by 'Abd al-Raḥmān al-Abnūdī[186] and Aḥmad Fu'ād Nigm,[187] as well as studies on vernacular poetry. During its first year of publication, one could find studies on the genre of the popular song (*ughniyya*),[188] on the commitment and aesthetic values in the songs of Shaykh Imām,[189] and on the role of words in popular songs,[190] a review of a book dealing with the popular Palestinian songs in Kuwait,[191] and an essay in memory of the Egyptian musician Riyāḍ al-Sinbāṭī (1906–81).[192] In addition, the magazine published files on popular

182 *'Ālam al-Kitāb*, April–May–June 1985, p. 37. The words *ākhar* and *ukhrā* have also been used to refer to non-canonical literary activities (see above, p. 21).

183 *'Ālam al-Kitāb*, April–May–June 1990, p. 224.

184 *'Ālam al-Kitāb*, April–May–June 1991, p. 176.

185 For example, *'Ālam al-Kitāb*, July 1995, includes the class "Arabic Poetry" which contains classical and modern poetry in both *'āmmiyya* and *fuṣḥā*. However, this class also includes the sub-class *al-Aḥājī wa-l-Nawādir wa-l-Fukāhāt* ("Riddles, Anecdotes, and Jokes"), which mainly contains items in *'āmmiyya*.

186 Vol. 4, May–June 1984, pp. 111–20; vol. 6, August 1984, pp. 104–15.

187 Vol. 7, September 1984, pp. 51–2.

188 Vol. 1, January 1984, pp. 26–38.

189 Vol. 1, January 1984, pp. 124-45. Shaykh Imām is the aforementioned Egyptian blind popular singer 'Īsā Imām (1918–95). On Shaykh Imām, see also Nigm 1993, pp. 242–8; *al-Ādāb*, September–October 1998; and al-Nābulsī 2001, p. 519.

190 Vol. 3, April 1984, pp. 25–48.

191 Vol. 6, August 1984, pp. 138–46.

192 Vol. 8, October–November 1984, pp. 158–60.

Egyptian cartoonists, such as Aḥmad Ibrāhīm Ḥijāzī (1936–2011),[193] Bahjat 'Uthmān (1931–2001),[194] and Jalāl al-Rifā'ī (1946–2012),[195] as well as on the Palestinian cartoonist Nājī al-'Alī (1938–87) with an introduction by the Palestinian poet Maḥmūd Darwīsh (1941–2008).[196] That this magazine was published by the ruling party in Egypt at the time, al-Tajammu' al-Waṭanī al-Taqddumī al-Waḥdawī, and that it defined itself on its cover as *Majallat Kull al-Muthaqqafin al-'Arab* ("The Magazine of All the Arab Intellectuals"), may indicate a political attempt, as in President Abd al-Nāṣir's endeavor in the 1960s (discussed above), to improve the status of popular poetry.[197]

The general negative attitude of the literary establishment toward the *zajal* had little effect on its great popularity.[198] Explanations for this phenomenon pointed to the *zajal*'s directness and simplicity as opposed to the complexities of poetry in *fuṣḥā*.[199] Al-Abnūdī explained the problem with writing in *fuṣḥā*:

> The classical language was very far from the minds of the *fellahin*, from their concerns and imaginations. When I started to write in the classically correct, formal style and language, I felt that a barrier had gone between me and my friends. I felt alienated, as if I were some kind of snob.[200]

In his introduction to Aḥmad Fu'ād Nigm's memoirs, Ṣalāḥ 'Īsā (b. 1939) describes what attracted, after the 1967 War, the attention of the masses to Nigm's poetry:

> This poetry blew in upon the rays of the sun, mingling with breaths of air, for our shocked and dazed hearts to smell, resembling a slaughtered bird flapping its wings out of sweetness of spirit. It restored to us the hope that the defeat was not the end of history, that a victory was possible, and that the enemy was not only beyond our borders, but also beneath our skins. The crowds would gather in that narrow room in that old house in one of the narrow alleys of the homeland, and we were shocked when we first saw him—a middle-aged poet, thin, coughing, together with a blind and helpless singer,[201] in a small room, which

193 Vol. 3, April 1984, pp. 165–72.
194 Vol. 4, May–June 1984, pp. 166–74.
195 Vol. 6, August 1984, pp. 177–91.
196 Vol. 2, February 1984, pp. 171–5.
197 Rushdī Ṣāliḥ (1920–80), one of the first scholars of Egyptian folklore, considered the 23 July 1952 Revolution as signaling the start of a new scientific period in the research of Arab popular arts (al-Jawharī 2003, pp. 307–8).
198 Cf. 'Abbūd 1968, p. 116.
199 Cf. Ḥāfiẓ 1971, pp. 136, 200.
200 *Al-Ahram Weekly*, 21 March 1991, p. 14 (according to Armbrust 1996, p. 37). Cf. al-Abnūdī 1998, pp. 9–10. In addition to his own vernacular writings, al-Abnūdī published five volumes of texts of *Sīrat Banī Hilāl* (1988–91).
201 The previously mentioned Shaykh Imām, Nigm's closest companion, who popularized

> had only two wooden sofas, a three-legged chair, a shelf and a broken mirror. The least we had expected was that this poor wretched poet would be the new voice of anger, and that this poor room, devoid of beauty and glory, would be an assembly for our new sorrows and a fountain of our deep dreams, though when one looked on the place and its inhabitants it lacked all the traditional qualifications.[202]

The popularity of the *zajal* owes much to the development of phonographs and records, and the advent of film, electronic media (that is, radio and television), and then the Internet.[203] Setting poems to music and having them played on the radio[204] and on television has proven to be a powerful and effective way to increase the popularity not only of the *zajal*, but also of poems in *fuṣḥā*,[205] precisely as adapting novels to the big screen has been proven to increase their popularity.[206] For *zajal* poems, this has been especially true when they were sung by such famous performers as Umm Kulthūm (1904–75),[207] Muḥammad ʿAbd al-Wahhāb (1910–90),[208] Farīd al-Aṭrash (1915–74),[209] his sister Amal al-Aṭrash, known as Asmahān (1912–44),[210]

his revolutionary *azjāl* by chanting them to the melodies of the *ʿūd* (Abdel-Malek 1990, pp. 18–19). On the break, in the beginning of the 1980s, between Nigm and Imām, see the interview with Shaykh Imām in *al-Ḥurriyya*, 18 November 1984, p. 42.

202 Nigm 1993, p. 19. Cf. Kishtainy 1985, pp. 158–9. On a similar attitude toward the poetry of Muẓaffar al-Nawwāb, see al-ʿAzzāwī 1997, pp. 95–6.

203 See, for example, the series *al-Silsila al-Fanniyya al-Muṣawwara* published by Dār al-Barāʿim li-l-Intāj al-Thaqāfī, which includes twelve books about the great singers of the Arab world, each book consisting of an introduction and the lyrics of the songs.

204 Nassib 1994, p. 251 (= Turkiyya 1999, p. 269) suggests that it was the circulation of the transistor radio which prompted the huge increase in the popularity of Umm Kulthūm.

205 See Abd al-Raḥmān 1960, pp. 5–6. On the nature of the relationship between music and poetry in the Arab world, it is instructive to quote O. Wright: "Despite the gradual emergence of important instrumental forms, music in the Islamic world has been (and still is) predominantly vocal, and vocal compositions have usually included, or consisted entirely of, settings of verse." See also H. Kilpatrick's comment: "As far as can be determined, there has always been a close connection between singing and poetry in Arabic culture [...] composers of songs for entertainment habitually set to music lines by recognized poets, not necessarily their own" (Meisami and Starkey 1998, II, pp. 554 and 724, respectively). On Arabic poems set to music, see Fransīs 2000; and Yawākīm 2013.

206 A good example is the recent series *Afrāḥ al-Qubba* (The Joys of al-Qubba), based on a novel by Najīb Maḥfūẓ, screened during the month of Ramadan in 2016 (<http://www.middle-east-online.com/?id=227132> [16 June 2016] [last accessed 12 October 2016]).

207 On Umm Kulthūm, see Fernea and Bezirgan 1977, pp. 135–65; Nassib 1994 (Arabic translation: Turkiyya 1999); Danielson 1997; Danielson 1998, pp. 109–22; Meisami and Starkey 1998, II, p. 795; al-ʿĀnī 1999, pp. 47–8; and al-Maḥlāwī 1999. See also *al-Ḥanjara al-Dhahabiyya: Ḥayāt wa-Aghānī Kawkab al-Sharq Umm Kulthūm—Majmūʿat Aghānīhā al-Kāmila* (Beirut: Manshūrāt Dār Maktabat al-Ḥayāt, 2000).

208 On Muḥammad ʿAbd al-Wahhāb, see Darwish 1998, p. 18; Meisami and Starkey 1998, I, p. 20; and Nassib 1994 (Arabic translation: Turkiyya 1999).

209 On Farīd al-Aṭrash, see Darwish 1998, p. 26.

210 On Asmahān, see Zuhur 1998a, pp. 81–107; and Zuhur 2000.

'Abd al-Ḥalīm Ḥāfiẓ (1936–77),[211] the Iraqi singer of Jewish origin Salīma Murād (1905–74)[212] and her husband Nāẓim al-Ghazālī (1921–63),[213] and the Lebanese singers Jeanette Feghali, known as Ṣabāḥ (1925–2014),[214] and the aforementioned Nuhād Ḥaddād, known as Fayrūz (b. 1935).[215] Umm Kulthūm's repertory of religious poems in the mid-1920s gave way to modern love songs that were composed especially for her. When, in the early 1940s, she asked the composer Zakariyyā Aḥmad (1890–1961) and the colloquial poet Bayram al-Tūnisī (1893–1961) to write poems in the vernacular for her, it was the commercial recordings she made that launched her life-long involvement with the mass media and that brought her the immense popularity she enjoyed until the end of her life. She could be heard on the radio the moment Egyptian National Radio began broadcasting in 1934; she first appeared in films in 1935; and she could be seen on television as early as 1960.[216] Umm Kulthūm was also one of the first Arab singers to be heard over the Internet.[217]

Now, the number of Arabic songs and singers on the Internet is immense. An interesting phenomenon, which emerged intensely following the development of Internet and satellite radio and television is the industry of video clips. For example, the popular Egyptian singer Sha'bān 'Abd al-Raḥīm (b. 1957), also known affectionately to his fans as Sha'bola, became a superstar following his political clips, especially those against Israel, such as "Ana ba-Krah Isrā'īl" ("I Hate Israel") released in 2001. He has also released a number of songs (written by Islām Khalīl) about the dangers of smoking cigarettes and marijuana (though he admitted to smoking both), unjust taxes, pollution of the Nile, the al-Aqṣa *Intifāḍa*, the US invasion of Iraq, the relationship between the United States and Israel, support for President Ḥusnī Mubārak's re-election campaign, and the *Jyllands-Posten* Muhammad cartoons.[218]

211 On 'Abd al-Ḥalīm Ḥāfiẓ, see Darwish 1998, p. 32; and *al-Jadīd* (Los Angeles) 24 (1998).

212 On Salīma Murād, see Shohet 1982, p. 127; Baṣrī 1983, pp. 87–8; Ingrams 1983, pp. 134–5; Sālim 1986, pp. 24–5; Baṣrī 1993, pp. 90–2; Obadyā 1999, pp. 125–9; and Zubaida 2002, pp. 219–22.

213 On Nāẓim al-Ghazālī, see Sālim 1986.

214 On Ṣabāḥ, see LaTeef 1997, pp. 72–7.

215 On Fayrūz, see Tomiche 1969, pp. 21–2; LaTeef 1997, pp. 23–7; and *al-Jadīd* (Los Angeles) 27 (1999).

216 On the development of Umm Kulthūm's career, see Danielson 1991, pp. 57–75; and Danielson 1997, pp. 42–125.

217 One of the first sites in the beginning of the 1990s was <http://edmund.hiof.no/almashriq/egypt/700.art/780.music/umKoulthoum/umkalthoum.html> (link no longer active).

218 On Sha'bān 'Abd al-Raḥīm, see Grippo 2006. Grippo distinguishes between two overlapping categories: *sha'bī* and *shabābī*. *Sha'bī*, literally "popular," but more accurately understood as "of the people," is the quintessential "music of the people," a sometimes populist

When, as happened several times, outstanding canonical poets also tried their hand at *zajal* poems, these poems were invariably relegated to the fringes of the literary system. Even the poets themselves referred to them as marginal and as certainly being inferior to their work in *fuṣḥā*. *Zajal* poems by Aḥmad Shawqī (1868–1932), for example, were not canonized and thus are not found in his "official" *Dīwān*.[219] The case of Aḥmad Rāmī (1892–1981) is even more instructive. Rāmī began his literary career as a poet in *fuṣḥā* and was soon embraced by the canonical literary circles of his day. In his early forties, however, he started composing poems in *'āmmiyya*,[220] which became hugely successful when Umm Kulthūm began including them in her repertoire. Rāmī had been introduced to her when the latter felt that she wanted to improve her skills in poetry, and he helped her deepen her command of literary Arabic and become familiar with Arabic poetry.[221] The poet and critic Ṣāliḥ Jawdat (1912–76) saw, however, this close collaboration between Rāmī and Umm Kulthūm as the main reason why the "value of his poetry" allegedly declined.[222] Be this as it may, it remains a fact that when he began publishing poems in *'āmmiyya* Rāmī soon had his canonical status "taken" away from him. In much the same way, when canonical universal poetic masterpieces are translated into *'āmmiyya* they are immediately relegated to the margins of the literary system.[223]

and sometimes popularized manifestation of urban folk music conventionally performed in lower-class life-cycle celebrations such as weddings and circumcisions. Its associations are with the lower rungs of the night club and cabaret business. *Shabābī* literally means "of the youth," and its most common gloss is "youth music." Both styles overlap class and cultural boundaries.

219 These poems were published in *al-Shawqiyyāt al-Majhūla* (Ṣabrī 1979; see also Boudot-Lamotte 1977, pp. 443–65). On the phenomenon of writers whose literary works are recognized only as far as they adhere to the canonical rules, see Ziyād Barakāt's observation (*al-Dustūr* [Jordan], 19 June 1992, p. 9). The phenomenon of not incorporating works considered to be of low status in the "official" main *Dīwān* is known from the non-canonical sector as well, where the differentiation is based on other considerations. For example, the Iraqi *zajal* poet Mullā 'Abbūd al-Karkhī (1861–1946) published a volume of obscene poems entitled *al-Adab al-Makshūf* (*Brazen Literature*). The volume, whose poems are not included in his main *Dīwān*, is undated and without indication of publisher or place (though the latter is probably London) (Zubaida 2002, p. 229, n. 28).

220 For songs in *'āmmiyya* written by Rāmī for the film *al-Warda al-Bayḍā'*, see *Apollo*, January 1934, p. 247, in which Rāmī was accused of "vain efforts to make the *'āmmiyya* a language of art."

221 See Nassib 1994 (= Turkiyya 1999).

222 See his introduction to Rāmī's *Dīwān* (Rāmī n.d., pp. 3–10). For Jawdat, "value" here is equivalent to "status in the literary system." On Rāmī's poetry, including his vernacular poems, see Gibb and Landau 1968, pp. 226–7; Wādī 1981, pp. 227–33; and Racy 2003, pp. 182–5.

223 For example, among the numerous Arabic translations of the *Rubā'iyyāt* of the Persian poet Omar Khayyām (1048–1131), there exists a *zajal* translation by the poet Muḥammad

Because of the leading cultural status of Egypt and the overwhelming popularity of Egyptian cinema, music, and theater since the 1920s, only a few *zajal* poets from other countries have gained the kind of fame which their Egyptian counterparts enjoyed. This does not mean that the *zajal* is less popular in other regions of the Arab world. On the contrary, Rashīd Nakhla (1873–1939) has been described as the prince of the Lebanese *zajal* (*amīr al-zajal al-Lubnānī*) and the "*primus inter pares*" (*za'īm awwal*) of vernacular poetry in Lebanon.[224] Famous, too, are Sa'īd 'Aql (1911–2014),[225] Michel Ṭrād (1912–98),[226] and the brothers Raḥbānī, 'Āṣī (1923–86) and Manṣūr (1925–2009).[227] Well-known *zajal* poets in Iraq are Mullā 'Abbūd al-Karkhī (1861–1946)[228] and Muẓaffar al-Nawwāb (1934–2017).[229] It is safe to say that the status of popular poetry and narrative in the Arabic literary system will be enhanced in the future: significant research has been done on this non-canonical form of literature in recent decades, the Internet as a medium can now reach more people than ever before,[230] and the *zajal* often flourishes with the rise of nationalist movements.[231] As we will see below in the case

Rakhā (1927–2003), a disciple of Bayram al-Tūnisī. However, because of the vernacular nature of the translation, it had to wait about thirty years before it was published, and even then it was published only thanks to the assistance of the governor of Suez, Muḥammad Badawī al-Khūlī (Rakhā's dedication in Khayyām 1974). On the translation of the *Rubā'iyyāt* into various languages, see Ṣarrāf 1960, pp. 310–22.

224 See al-Shaqīfī 1936, p. 541. See also *al-Adīb*, January 1943, pp. 42–3. For Nakhla's poetry, see Nakhla 1964; and 'Awwād 1983, pp. 85–94, 477. In a poem dedicated to Nakhla, the Lebanese poet Ilyās Abū Shabaka (1985, I, pp. 440–1) says:

وقالت لي الفصحى غبطت لسانه   فمن «لغوة» للشعر هُذّب عنصر
وإن ضاق هذا الشعر وهو محرّر   فما ضرّه إن الكريم محرّر

225 On 'Aql and his poetry in *'āmmiyya*, see 'Awwād 1983, pp. 241–57, 487–8; and Campbell 1996, pp. 955–7. On his symbolist poetry in *fuṣḥā*, see Jayyusi 1977, pp. 489–509. See also Norin and Tarabay 1967, pp. 119–22.

226 On Ṭrād and his poetry, see *Shi'r* (Beirut) 1 (1957), pp. 20–1; Norin and Tarabay 1967, pp. 144–5; Lyons 1968; 'Awwād 1983, pp. 258–66, 488; Asfour 1988, pp. 89–90; Campbell 1996, pp. 840–2; Fāḍil 1996, pp. 147–53; Meisami and Starkey 1998, II, p. 774; and Kallas 2003, pp. 447–63.

227 On them, see *al-Sha'b* (Jerusalem), 6 August 1986, p. 6; and *al-Jadīd* (Los Angeles) 26 (1999).

228 On al-Karkhī, see al-Karkhī 1956, I, pp. 1–32; al-Fattāl 1987; and Moreh 1993, pp. 351–73.

229 For al-Nawwāb's collected poetic works, see al-Nawwāb 1996. On the aesthetic value of his poetry, see al-Muḥsin 1993, p. 20; on his poetry in general, see al-Shāhir 1997; on his imprisonment in Iraq in the early 1960s, see al-'Azzāwī 1997, pp. 94–6; and on his reception in Palestinian culture, see al-Usṭā 1999.

230 See, for example, Rif'at Salām's words on *qaṣīdat al-'āmmiyya* (*al-Usbū' al-'Arabī*, 31 January 1994, p. 45): "The poets of *'āmmiyya* are the greatest poetic phenomenon during the 1990s, and in the following years their voices will be much more crystallized, deep, and unique."

231 The *zajal* poet Wilyam Ṣa'b (1912–99) attributed the rise and development of the *zajal* to the emergence of territorial nationalism in the Arab world (*al-Adīb*, January 1943, pp. 41–2).

of *Alf Layla wa-Layla* (*One Thousand and One Nights*), which was finally canonized after it had received widespread recognition in the West, the deep interest which Western scholarly circles have been taking in Arab oral poetry and narrative, not only from a linguistic and ethnographic point of view, but from an aesthetic one as well,[232] seems to similarly promise a bright future for the *zajal*.[233]

When it comes to popular prose, the situation is markedly different. Unlike popular poetry, most popular prose genres are still utterly neglected by scholarly research.[234] For example, research into the development of science fiction (*khayāl ʿilmī*) in Arabic literature is essentially limited to a few studies by Arab scholars who do not belong to the canonical center of the literary system.[235] These studies are mainly confined to the description of original Arabic works in this domain without investigating the background issue of how this genre developed through interference from Western culture. It is assumed that the development of original science fiction in Arabic began following the constant increase of public interest in various aspects of outer space. Technological achievements since the late 1950s have created a demand for literature about space, and this demand has been partly fulfilled by translations of relevant books, especially those in English.[236] In addition, public interest in strange phenomena, such as flying saucers, and the books published about them[237] have helped the development of the genre, initially

232 Sowayan 1992, p. xi. See also P. Marcel Kurpershoek's note about the Bedouin poet ʿAbd Allāh ibn Muḥammad ibn Ḥazayyim, generally known by the nickname al-Dindān (1917–98): "The more I came to know his work, the more I marvelled at the fact that a poor, illiterate bedouin like him should be able to match the artistry of the great classical and modern literate poets" (Kurpershoek 1994, p. ix).

233 See Reynolds 2007, pp. 33–76.

234 The non-canonical narrative genre that has gained the greatest attention from scholars is the folktale, though generally not for literary but for historical, social, and anthropological considerations. See, for example, Hejaiej 1996, which includes forty-seven tales told by three "Beldi" women and examines the role of tale-telling in their shared world and its significance in the life of the tellers. See also Pach 1968; El-Shamy 1980; Watson 1992; Early 1993; and Shaʿlān 1993. In different regions and over different historical periods, *Sīrat Banī Hilāl* has been performed not only as rhymed verse but also as "a complex tale cycle narrated entirely in prose" (Reynolds 1995, p. xiii).

235 Al-Shārūnī 1980, pp. 243–76; Qāsim 1993, especially pp. 199–255 (Chapter 8: "Science Fiction in Arabic Literature"). It seems that science fiction is not always clearly defined, and scholars sometimes confuse it with fantasy. See also Rāghib 1981, pp. 103–12; Bahī 1994; and Khaḍr 2001. On Arab science fiction for children, see the collection of articles *Adab al-Ṭifl al-ʿArabī* (Amman: Manshūrāt al-Ittiḥād al-ʿĀmm li-l-Udabāʾ al-ʿArab, 1995).

236 See, for example, Hirsch 1972 (a translation of Hirsch 1966).

237 See, for example, the series *Aghrab min al-Khayāl* (*Stranger than Fiction*) by Rājī ʿInāyat (b. 1929) published by Dār al-Shurūq (Cairo and Beirut). The series includes books such as *Sirr al-Aṭbāq al-Ṭāʾira* (1980); *Laʿnat al-Farāʿina Wahm am Ḥaqīqa* (1983); *Aḥlām al-Yawm Ḥaqāʾiq al-Ghad* (1984); and *al-Ashbāḥ al-Mushāghiba* (1995). Most of the books

through translations and adaptations of short stories in English that were published in journals[238] or in special anthologies.[239] The nature of these translations and the methods used to adapt them illustrate the nature of the problems that have accompanied the appearance of the genre in the Arabic literary system. Original Arabic works of science fiction have existed since the 1970s and have mainly taken the form of short stories,[240] though they have also taken the form of novels.[241] One of the most dedicated writers of Arabic science fiction was the Egyptian Nihād Sharīf (1932–2011).[242] His novel *al-Shay'* (*The Thing*)[243] is one of the prominent novels of Arabic science fiction illustrating the desire of some science fiction writers to have the genre canonized. This novel, which bears a pacifist message, is fundamentally based on Sharīf's short story "Imra'a fī Ṭabaq Ṭā'ir" ("A Woman in a Flying Saucer").[244] As we saw earlier, Islamist authors have taken to science fiction as a means to help them spread Islamic concepts because of the impact of this genre on the masses and because of its "utopian" aspect.[245]

Also enjoying wide circulation are detective stories and novels (*qiṣaṣ būlīsiyya* and *riwāyāt būlīsiyya*)[246] and love stories and novels (*rūmansiyyāt*). But here, too, scholarly interest is all but absent.[247] In Lebanon, Dār Rātib has

included in the series were published in more than one edition (e.g. *La'nat al-Farā'ina Wahm am Ḥaqīqa* was published in at least five printings).

238 See, for example, "al-Walīd al-Mur'ib" ("The Dreadful Newborn Baby") translated by Rājī 'Ināyat (*al-'Arabī*, August 1976, pp. 138–40).

239 See, for example, Silverberg 1986 (a translation of Silverberg 1983).

240 See, for example, Sharīf 1981.

241 Among the first novels in this field is Maḥmūd 1972.

242 On Nihād Sharīf's views on the reservations of the canonical center of Arabic literature about the genre, see the interview with him published in *al-Qāhira* (15 July 1988, pp. 40–3). Sharīf considers the roots of the genre as Arab, but "because of negligence and forgetfulness by the Arabs, they did not speak about that and enabled others to say that science fiction had been initiated by Westerners."

243 Sharīf 1989.

244 Sharīf 1981, pp. 121–33. On the emergence of science fiction in Arabic literature, especially on Sharīf's works, see Snir 2000, pp. 263–85; Snir 2002b, pp. 209–29. See also 'Asāqla 2011.

245 See, for example, *al-Bu'd al-Khāmis* (*The Fifth Dimension*) (Rā'if 1987) by Aḥmad Rā'if. The genre of science fiction for the propagation of Islamic ideas is also employed by non-Arabic Muslim writers (e.g. the Turkish novel *Uzay Çiftçileri* [*Space Farmers*] by Ali Nar [b. 1941]. See Szyska 1995, pp. 95–125).

246 According to Elkhadem 2001, pp. 25–8, two prominent Egyptian canonical writers contributed to the development of this genre, Najīb Maḥfūẓ in his *al-Liṣṣ wa-l-Kilāb* (1961) and Tawfīq al-Ḥakīm in his *Yawmiyyāt Nā'ib fī al-Aryāf* (1937).

247 Many outstanding Arab writers were, when young, ardent readers of detective novels. Najīb Maḥfūẓ, for example, even attempted to imitate Ḥāfiẓ Najīb's (1883–1948) detective stories, which were popular while he was young (Somekh 1973a, p. 37. Cf. Mahfouz 2001, pp. 3–21, 30; Dhinī 2002, p. 92; and Ayalon 2015, pp. 321–2). On the popularity of the detective novels in the Arab world, see also al-Faytūrī 1979, p. 11; Schami 1996, pp. 206–7; and the interview with 'Abd al-Wahhāb al-Bayyātī in *al-Ḥayāt*, 7 August 1999, p. 18).

published a series of original detective stories entitled *Silsilat al-Riwāyāt al-Būlīsiyya* (*The Detective Novel Series*) and another series of love novels entitled *Silsilat Rūmansiyyāt Nātālī* (*The Natali Romantic Story Series*). Another Lebanese publisher, Dār al-Nafā'is, has come out with a series of detective stories under the title *Silsilat al-'Uṣba al-Khafiyya* (*The Secret Gang Series*). Then, there are numerous non-canonical literary texts appearing in popular journals and magazines aimed at specific sections of the Arab public.[248] Given the fact that the canonical center of the Arabic literary system still refers to them as messengers of "invading cultures" (*thaqāfāt ghāziya*),[249] it is not surprising that these genres and texts have, for the most part, remained virgin territory for literary critics.[250]

The Egyptian Bahā' Ṭāhir (b. 1935) writes that "all readers, no matter what their intellectual and cultural level is, like from time to time to spend time reading detective novels or any other amusing work" (Ṭāhir 2006, p. 8). The Jewish writer of Iraqi origin Shimon Ballas (Sham'ūn Ballāṣ) (b. 1930) wrote in his youth a detective novel in Arabic entitled *al-Jarīma al-Ghāmiḍa* (The Mysterious Crime); however, he burned it before immigrating to Israel in 1951 (personal communication in Haifa, 4 April 2001; and S. Ballas, "Ṣuwar Mutaḥarrika," *Mashārif* [Haifa] 21 [Summer 2003], p. 22). Fedwa Malti-Douglas tried to find a similar genre in the classical Arabic heritage (Malti-Douglas 1988, pp. 108–27 [= Malti-Douglas 2001a, Chapter IX]; Malti-Douglas 1988a, pp. 59–91 [= Malti-Douglas 2001a, Chapter VII]). See also Cooperson 2008, pp. 20–39. On the detective novel, see also Rāghib 1981, pp. 95–102; Smolin 2007 (Smolin translated the first Arabic detective novel into English [Hamdouchi 2008]). See also Zachs and Bawārdī [forthcoming]. Alīf Farānsh from the Department of Arabic Language and Literature at Bar-Ilan University has submitted (2016) a PhD thesis on detective literature in Arabic.

248 A few examples are the Saudi weekly *Sayyidatī* as well *al-Fāris: Majallat al-Rajul al-'Aṣrī* and *Siḥr: Majallat al-Tajaddud wa-l-Fann wa-l-'Ā'ila*, both of them published by Dār al-Ṣayyād in Beirut. The popular nature of these magazines and their desire to generate profit sometimes become the *raison d'être* of the magazines. For example, Yārā Mash'ūr (Yara Mashour) (b. 1974), editor of *Laylak* (Nazareth), a feminist magazine first published in April 2000, says: "People ask me, isn't this rather shallow stuff? [...] But if you want deep, read a book!" (*The New York Times International*, 28 April 2000). In July 2016 Condé Nast International declared that it would launch a *Vogue Arabia* edition, with Saudi Princess Deena Aljuhani Abdulaziz (Dīnā al-Juhanī 'Abd al-'Azīz) (b. 1976) as its editor-in-chief, marking the publisher's long-awaited move into the Middle Eastern market. Condé Nast will first launch a website in Arabic and English to develop further insight into its audience spanning the Middle East and North Africa (MENA) region. The bilingual website will be followed by a print magazine in the spring of 2017 (<https://www.businessoffashion.com/articles/news-analysis/conde-nast-to-launch-vogue-arabia> [15 September 2016] [last accessed 12 October 2016]).

249 Abū al-Sa'd 1994, pp. 26–8. The term *ghazw thaqāfī* (cultural invasion) frequently appears in Islamist writings. One of the attempts to define this term is as follows: "Every idea or data or program or plan aiming, directly or indirectly, to destroy the ideological, intellectual, and cultural foundations of the Islamic nation" (Muḥammad 1994, p. 16). On cultural invasion, see also Kishk 1966; al-Ḥājj 1983; and al-'Aẓm 1992, pp. 153–62.

250 A step on the way to more research into such texts is the semiotic–historic examination of advertisements which were published in the Saudi weekly *Sayyidatī* from 1996 to 1998 (Zirinski 1999; Zirinski 2005). On the development of commercial advertising in Saudi

Texts for Children

The inventory of non-canonical original texts for children consists of adventure and police stories, thrillers, and comic books. Arab comic strips for children, for example, can be found in newspapers, but they can also be read in special comic books.[251] In their pioneering study on Arab mass culture, Allen Douglas and Fedwa Malti-Douglas go into great detail on the subject of children's comics. The most popular of these comics at the time the study was published was *Majīd*, which appeared in the United Arab Emirates and sold over 150,000 copies. Another comic, *Samīr*, published in Egypt, had a circulation of about 80,000 copies. But such well-known Western characters as Mickey Mouse and Donald Duck have also been popular in Arab comic strips. In these strips, however, they wear galabeas and celebrate Ramadan: Parts of Western culture are adapted to Arab culture.[252] Comics have been used for political and social criticism and to make ideological statements. Egypt's late president Gamāl ʻAbd al-Nāṣir (1918–70) appeared as a historical hero, the late Iraqi president ʻAbd al-Karīm Qāsim (1914–63) as a dictator, while the late Iraqi president Ṣaddām Ḥusayn (1937–2006) was frequently idealized and presented as a mythological hero.[253] One comic strip dealt with the theft of Egyptian archeological artifacts and their being smuggled to other countries and tells the story of the disappearance of the well-known statue of Ramses from its pedestal in front of a Cairo train station and how it was traced to and eventually recovered in Paris. Although this genre is non-canonical,

Arabia, see AlFardi 1989; Al-Yusuf 1989; and Al-Yusuf 1994. On journalism and the promotion of goods in Egypt (1890–1939), see Shechter 2004, pp. 179–90. See also the arguments of Muḥammad al-Musfir from Qatar in an interview with *al-Ra'y* (Amman), 8 December 1999, p. 45.

251 As previously mentioned, comic strips for adults have yet to become popular. The discussion of Arab comic strips for children is based on Douglas and Malti-Douglas 1994.

252 Cf. *Sayyidatī* 880 (17–23 January 1998), where Mickey Mouse is used in an advertisement for watches in Saudi Arabia (Zirinski 1999, pp. 44–5; Zirinski 2005, p. 41). In 2005 the Dubai-based Arabic MBC satellite channel began showing culturally modified, Arabic-dubbed versions of the iconic animated show *The Simpsons*. Given the title *Āl Shamshūn* in Arabic, bald, chubby underachiever ʻUmar Shamshūn (= Homer) works each day at the local nuclear power plant. Every evening, he comes home to a family that includes his blue-haired wife, Munā (= Marge), hyper-smart daughter, Bīsā (= Lisa), trouble-making son, Badr (= Bart), and the small girl Baṭṭa (= Maggie). The Arabic dialogue laid over existing shows is actually fairly faithful to the original script. Nothing seems to be censored, but episodes such as those featuring Homer's gay roommate or the visit to the Duff brewery are unlikely to be chosen for translation. Additionally, many of the more American inside jokes are simply glossed over (see a report by Ashraf Khalil and Jailan Zayan in *The Los Angeles Times*, 15 December 2006).

253 On shaping the images of contemporary Arab leaders in canonical literature, see Bengio 1998, pp. 77–9, 153–4, 196–7; and Snir 2000c, pp. 181–7.

> when Arab comics are destined for children (the majority of cases), their authors take them quite seriously as political and cultural products. The individuals who create Arab comics are among the best that their societies have produced in literature and the arts. Often they have already made a name for themselves as serious writers, painters or political cartoonists. They are motivated by the need for self expression [...] by political ambition, [...] but they are also concerned about the future of contemporary culture and particularly that of the children of their society.[254]

One of the interesting projects in the field of non-canonical literature for children in the late 1980s was the series *Silsilat al-Mashāhīr* (*The Series of the Well-known*), which was initiated by Dār Thaqāfat al-Aṭfāl in Baghdad. It contains a volume on the Egyptian poet Bayram al-Tūnisī (1893–1961) entitled *Bayram al-Tūnisī Shā'ir al-Ālām wa-l-Āmāl* (*Bayram al-Tūnisī: The Poet of Pains and Hopes*). In an obvious effort to have the literary work of this Egyptian poet canonized,[255] the writer 'Abd al-Ra'ūf al-Khanīsī (b. 1944) states in his introduction, "Wamḍa" ("Gleam of Light"):

> يعدّونه موليير مصر وأعدّه شكسبير العرب. عاش بين دمعة وابتسامة متذوّقا مرارة المنفى وعناء السفر والغربة، موقّعا في حزن عميق دفين:
>
> الأولة مَصر قالوا تونـــسي ونفوني جَزاة الخير وإحسـاني
> والثانية تونس وفيها الأهل جحدوني وحتى الغير ما واساني
> والثالثة باريس وفي باريس نكروني وأنا موليير في زمـاني
> الأوله أشتكيـــــها للّي أجرى النيل
> والثانية دمعي عليها غرّق الباستيل
> والثالثة الطشت فيها ممتثل وذليـل
>
> فهذا عمّك محمود بيرم التونسي. عمّك الذي سحرنا بشعره الفصيح وزجله العامّي وبأغانيه الوطنية والعاطفية والاجتماعية مستلهما عبقرية أمّته العربية التليدة وقوى الإبداع والإمتاع في حياة الناس اللّي تحت. لقد كان عمّك محمود بيرم التونسي سفينة أشواق وهوى، جابهت إعصار الظلمات وعواصف العسف والطغيان إلى شاطئ الأمان. فاقرأ تاريخ عمّك، وكن بحياته بصيرا وبتراثه أمينا.

> He is considered to be Egypt's Molière and I consider him the Shakespeare of the Arabs. He lived between teardrop and smile, tasting the bitterness of exile, and the hardship of travel and exile singing in deep hidden agony:
>
> First came Egypt, where they said [he is] Tunisian and expelled me in return for my good deeds and charity,

254 Douglas and Malti-Douglas 1994, pp. 5–6. On political cartoons in Arabic, especially during the Gulf War, see Awad 1992; Slyomovics 1992, pp. 93–9; Slyomovics 1993, pp. 21–4; Omri 1998, pp. 133–54; and Slyomovics 2001, pp. 72–98.

255 Attempts to have his poetry canonized were already underway during the 1930s, but at the time the *zajal* was not recognized for its literary value if it did not show a true effort to close the gap between *'āmmiyya* and *fuṣḥā*. See, for example, *Apollo*, January 1934, p. 247: "The literary writings of Bayram are a glorious attempt to promote *'āmmiyya*; moreover, the more he polishes his *zajal* the more he renders good services to the public and to *fuṣḥā*."

> Second came Tunis, its people rejected me, nor did others console me,
> Third came Paris, and in Paris they were ignorant of me, though I was the Molière of my time.
>
> I complain about the first to Him who made the Nile flow,
> The second, my tears upon which drowned the Bastille,
> And the third, the basin there obedient and despised.
>
> This is your uncle Maḥmūd Bayram al-Tūnisī. Your uncle who has charmed us with his eloquent poetry and popular *zajal* and with his national, emotional, and social songs seeking inspiration from his Arabic ancient nation's genius and the creative and pleasure forces in the life of the people that are beneath. Your uncle Maḥmūd Bayram al-Tūnisī was like a ship of longing and love, facing the whirlwinds of darkness and the storms of oppression and despotism, heading toward the safe coast line. Therefore, read the history of your uncle and be aware of his life and be faithful to his heritage.[256]

Al-Khanīsī here chooses a particular strategy to try to bring about the canonization of al-Ṭūnisī. First, the *fuṣḥā* he uses in this quote is highly elevated and not really appropriate for children. The only phrase in *ʿāmmiyya*, apart from the verses, is *al-nās illī taḥt*. Second, the verses he quotes, from al-Ṭūnisī's poem "Ḥayātī" ("My Life"),[257] use "high" *ʿāmmiyya*, that is, they may be read as *fuṣḥā*, with the exception of one word in the fourth verse (*li-llī*). Other vernacular elements appearing in the original were "improved" in order to bring them closer to the *fuṣḥā*: The vernacular words *tāniya* and *tālita* appear in their literary form *thāniya* and *thāliha*. Furthermore, the word *al-ulā* appears in the original الأوله, that is with *hā'* (ه) at the end instead of *alif maqṣūra* (ى); however, here *hā'* (ه) in the first verse was changed to *tā' marbūṭa* (ة) to be pronounced *al-ulatu*—a kind of pseudo-correction.[258] Third, al-Khanīsī emphasizes that al-Ṭūnisī was not only a poet in the vernacular but also in *fuṣḥā*, although the popularity he enjoyed can by no means be attributed to his canonical poetry. Poems in *fuṣḥā* by al-Ṭūnisī are frequently quoted throughout the book. In other words, it seems that Bayram al-Tūnisī was chosen to appear in this series for children not only because his poems in *ʿāmmiyya* are invaluable, but also because his poetry is important from a national and historical point of view. This idea is expressed in the following words:

> قبل أن يرحل عمّكم محمود، غنّاكم هذا الوطن الأمّ وبشّركم بالمستقبل، وأزال الفواصل والحواجز بين الأقطار والأمصار بفضل أدبه الرقيق، ولغته المميّزة الشفّافة، وشعبياته، وزجلياته، وفوازيره التي وحدها حافظت على كنوز شعبنا وذاكرته التاريخية والجمالية والروحية.

256 Al-Khanīsī 1989, p. 3. For another translation of the poetry verses, see Howarth and Shukrallah 1944, pp. 103–4.
257 Al-Tūnisī 1987, pp. 3–4.
258 Blau 1981, pp. 29–30.

> Before your uncle Maḥmūd passed away, he sang to you of this motherland and brought to you the good news of the future removing barriers and fences between states and countries thanks to his tender literature, peculiar delicate language, his folk pieces and popular melodies and his riddles which retained the treasures of our nation and its historical, aesthetic, and spiritual memory.[259]

Finally, among the forms of non-canonical literature for children that have generally been neglected, one should also include songs for children, games, popular tales, and nursery rhymes in *ʿāmmiyya*.[260] Many of these were recorded on cassettes,[261] and they may now be found on the Internet as well. What these texts have in common is that they are spoken or sung.

Translated Texts

Translated non-canonical literature is on the whole defined according to the content of the works in question and not according to the language in which they are written. The inventory of these texts includes detective novels, pornographic literature, science fiction, love stories, and adventure stories. According to the literary critic Saad Elkhadem (1932–2003), in Egypt the detective novel (in his words the "mystery novel") in translation from English and French experienced two golden ages: the first, from the dawn of the twentieth century to the First World War; and the second, from 1936, with the establishment of the series *Riwāyāt al-Jayb* (*Pocket Novels*), to the end of the Second World War. Readers of these translations generally belonged to the lower middle class, mostly students and junior civil servants. Tobacco and candy stores served at the time as bookstores and libraries, where it was possible to buy new editions of translated novels for ten *millimes*, to buy secondhand editions for five *millimes*, and to rent new editions for two *millimes*.[262] Najīb Maḥfūẓ, who was in his youth an ardent reader of translated literature ("for a while I was under the impression that this was because, somehow, they were important literary texts"), remembers that such was the popularity of translated crime novels that novels written

259 Al-Khanīsī 1989, p. 26.

260 I know of only a few studies in book form which examine that field: al-Khalīlī 1978 and Yūsuf 1992, the former mainly aiming to strengthen the Palestinian national consciousness (as indicated in the introduction of the poet and scholar Ḥannā Abū Ḥannā [b. 1928] to al-Ṣāliḥ 2004—an anthology of Palestinian lullabies [*Tahālīl* or *Aghānī Tanwīm al-Aṭfāl*]). See also al-Barghūthī 1979, pp. 36–44, 245–8; and Mursī 1983, pp. 221–5.

261 See, for example, the cassettes produced by the International Book Center in Troy, Michigan, which include *Arabic Nursery Rhymes and Songs* recorded by Elias Raḥbānī (b. 1938) and *Christmas Songs* recorded by Fayrūz.

262 Elkhadem 2001, pp. 23–4.

originally in Arabic in Egypt would often have the sentence "translated from French" emblazoned across their dust-jackets.[263]

Gamāl ʻAbd al-Nāṣir's *coup d'état* of 1952 put an end to the flourishing of the new genre because the so-called "Blessed Movement" demanded that all literary expressions be totally committed to the new ideals of the revolution, and because the regime placed new restrictions on imported goods, which included printing paper. According to Elkhadem, even after ʻAbd al-Nāṣir's death this kind of novel "has never experienced any genuine revival."[264] One cannot, however, ignore the popularity of the detective novels even during ʻAbd al-Nāṣir's time in power. For example, in the 1950s and 1960s the Egyptian publishers Dār al-Hilāl and al-Dār al-Qawmiyya li-l-Ṭibāʻa wa-l-Nashr put out twenty-four translations of detective stories by Agatha Christie (1891–1976).[265] The Lebanese publisher al-Maktaba al-Thaqāfiyya also published translations (all of them by ʻUmar ʻAbd al-ʻAzīz Amīn [1908–86]) of the same stories. Translated by Muḥammad ʻAbd al-Munʻim Jalāl, Christie's stories have also been put out by al-Markaz al-ʻArabī li-l-Nashr in Alexandria. The same goes for the International Book Center in Troy, Michigan, where they were translated by Munīr al-Baʻlabakkī (1918–99). In 1993 another Lebanese publisher, Ṣawt al-Nās (Beirut and Limassol), published a series, entitled *al-Silsila al-Būlīsiyya* (*The Detective Series*), of fifteen detective novels in full literary translation (by Bassām Ḥajjār [b. 1955], Sumayya ʻAbbūd, and others). Among them, apart from Agatha Christie, we can find translations of novels by Maurice Leblanc (1864–1941),[266] Georges Simenon (1903–89), Arthur Conan Doyle (1859–1930), and Raymond Chandler (1888–1959). The Lebanese publisher Manshūrāt Mu'assasat al-Zayn li-l-Ṭibāʻa wa-l-Nashr published the complete *Adventures of Tarzan* under the title *Mughāmarāt Ṭarāzān*. One may also mention Dār al-ʻAhd al-Jadīd li-l-Nashr, which published translations of more than thirty books by Maurice Leblanc on the adventures of Arsène Lupin. Its ambition was to publish a new book in this series every week. The Arabic of the translations was *fuṣḥā*.[267] Despite the abundance of non-canonical translated texts (as we

263 Mahfouz 2001, p. 30. On the popularity of the translated detective stories, see Manṣūr 1983, p. 59.

264 Elkhadem 2001, pp. 23–4.

265 For the details of the translations, see Badrān 1972, pp. 227–8. On the popularity of Christie's translations into Arabic at the American prison at Guantanamo Bay, see Caroline Drees, "Harry Potter Bewitches Guantánamo Bay Prisoners," *Reuters*, 9 August 2005.

266 Translation of novels by Maurice Leblanc into Arabic started in the first decade of the twentieth century (Pérès 1937, p. 301).

267 On the popularity of Arsène Lupin in Syria, see the words of Walīd Ikhlāṣī (b. 1935) in Campbell 1996, I, p. 225; and Schami 1996, pp. 206–7. Cf. al-Faytūrī 1979 (introduction), p. 11; and the memories of the Jewish Iraqi writer Samīr Naqqāsh (1938–2004) published

have just seen), I was unable to find even one significant study on any of their genres or subgenres.[268]

INTERNAL AND EXTERNAL INTERRELATIONSHIPS

The Arabic literary system, like any other cultural system,[269] is a network of functional interrelationships between various canonical and non-canonical original texts and translations.[270] Although non-canonical texts are not considered part of "true" literature, they are exploited as models or stock elements for canonical literature.[271] Literary elements, types, single works, and genres may wander not only from certain canonical genres to others[272] but also from non-canonical to canonical strata of the literary system and vice versa.[273] In this respect, translated texts constitute an initial channel for interference in both canonical and non-canonical subsystems—to what degree depends on the particular position that translated literature assumes in the literary system. Interference typically occurs first in the lower, peripheral subsystems of literature before it reaches the center. This interaction takes

in *al-Mu'tamar* (London) 325 (18–24 October 2002), p. 9. On Arsène Lupin in Arabic and colonial identities, see Selim 2010, pp. 191–210.

268 Another interesting phenomenon for our purposes is the advent of the first translations of Western masterpieces into the vernacular. The Lebanese poet Henri Zughayyib (b. 1948) translated Shakespeare's *Othello* and Gibran's *The Prophet* (Gibran 1924) into the Lebanese dialect (*Lubnān*, 24 December 1982, p. 4). On another translation of *Othello* into the Egyptian dialect, by Muṣṭafā Ṣafwān (b. 1921), see Hanna 2009, pp. 157–78; and Dūs and Davies 2013, pp. 169–74, 309–12. For a study that explores the history of *Othello* in the Arab world by examining its translations, adaptations, and interpretations, as well as its assimilation into the Arab literary system, see Ghazoul 1998, pp. 1–31.

269 Cf. the interrelationships between "high" and "low" within the system of religious symbols (Wasserstrom 1995, p. 213).

270 Unlike what is argued by Kritzeck 1964, p. 12, this interaction, or any aspect of it, is by no means a unique phenomenon of Arabic or "Islamic literature" alone.

271 See, for example, Mursī 1983, pp. 9–22; Badīr 1986; and Somekh 1991, pp. 59–60.

272 Cf. for example, the argument of the Lebanese writer Ilyās Khūrī (b. 1948): "The Arabic poetic heritage is an important part of the [Arabic] novel, to the point that sometimes we consider the novel nothing but a form which consists of a series of events constructed directly within a long poem, which means that the narrative form plays only a direct role, the role of communication, in order to let poetry be much more effective than the poetic form" (Khūrī 1974, p. 110).

273 See, for example, the employment of the models of wedding, children, and peasant songs by the Lebanese poet Ilyās Abū Shabaka (1903–47) such as in "'Urs fī al-Qarya" ("A Wedding in the Village"), "'Īd fī al-Qarya" ("A Festival in the Village"), and "al-Mi'ṣara" ("The Wine-Press") from the collection *al-Alḥān* (*Melodies*) (Abū Shabaka 1941). See also al-Ḥāwī 1980, III, pp. 113–15, 122–3, 128–9; and Abū Shabaka 1985, I, pp. 272–3, 281–3, 284–5. On the poetry of Abū Shabaka in this collection, see Razzūq 1970, pp. 205–18. See also the employment of the model of nursery rhymes by the Palestinian poet Jamāl Qa'wār (1930–2013) (Somekh 1991, pp. 125–6).

place through various channels and modes, such as religious frameworks,[274] feminist culture,[275] and translation activities. For example, the translation of European literary works into Arabic started with works that only occupied non-canonical or marginal sectors of the literary system.[276] This may well have been because the translation movement (*ḥarakat al-tarjama*) of the nineteenth century was directed in its first phases mainly at non-literary texts. But the impact that these translations were to have in the long run on the canonical models was immense. Furthermore, the study of the translational norms that have existed since the nineteenth century may shed some light on the overall development of literary norms.[277]

Canonization of non-canonical single works or an entire corpus may occur as a result of changes in the literary system or, alternatively, as a result of the loosening of extrasystemic constraints. Literary evolution, as Fredric Jameson suggests (following Victor Shklovsky), is not only a break with the dominant and existing canons, "it is the canonization of something new at the same time, or rather the lifting of literary dignity of forms until then thought to be popular or undignified, minor forms until then current only in the demi-monde of entertainment or of journalism."[278]

For example, until the nineteenth century, *Alf Layla wa-Layla* (*One Thousand and One Nights*), composed in a mixture of *fuṣḥā* and *ʿāmmiyya*, was considered to be lowbrow literature, hardly admissible into respectable households.[279] These stories were part of a folklore that was kept alive by

[274] See, for example, the role played in this regard by Christian liturgy as mentioned in Cohen and Cohen 1996, p. 21.

[275] Due to their traditionally more secluded social status, women used to adopt and take part in new cultural activities rejected by men. For example, the genre of the novel was considered in England in the eighteenth century to be literature for women. In the nineteenth century, the novel became the elevated genre that men were happy to adopt (Tuchman and Fortin 1989). On the high status of the novel in contemporary Arabic literature, see below, pp. 223–6.

[276] See Badr 1983, pp. 127–40.

[277] See, for example, the studies on Arabic translational norms with regard to the French didactic romance *Les aventures de Télémaque* (1699) by François de Salignac Fénelon (1651–1715) (Fénelon 1934 [1699]) and the English novel *Robinson Crusoe* (1719) by Daniel Defoe (1660–1731) (Defoe 1906 [1719]) (ʿAnānī 1976, pp. 8–25; Badr 1983, pp. 57–67; Somekh 1991, pp. 75–82; and Haist 2000, pp. 145–61) as well as the translations of the poetry of Percy Bysshe Shelley (1792–1822) (Abdul-Hai 1976, pp. 132–41; Raʾūf 1982 [see also a review of the book in *al-Karmil—Abḥāth fī al-Lugha wa-l-Adab* 8 (1987), pp. 197–202]; Abdul-Razak 1989; and Somekh 1991, pp. 109–17).

[278] Jameson 1972, p. 53.

[279] Aḥmad Ḥasan al-Zayyāt considers the popularity of this kind of "hallucinatory" literature to be a cause for the spreading use of drugs in Egypt (al-Zayyāt n.d., pp. 393–4. Cf. Elkhadem 1985, p. 55). For the negative attitudes of educated Arabs toward the popular *Sīra* romance literature, such as *Sīrat ʿAntara* (*The Story of ʿAntara*) and *Sīrat al-Iskandar wa-mā fīhā min al-ʿAjāyib wa-l-Gharāyib* (*The Story of Alexander with its Wondrous and

storytellers and were considered to have virtually no literary value. When Ibn al-Nadīm (d. 987) included *Alf Layla wa-Layla* in his comprehensive catalog of books entitled *al-Fihrist,* he described it as *kitāb ghathth bārid al-ḥadīth* ("a coarse book, without warmth in the telling").[280] That he decided to include it did not mean that it had canonical status in the literary system of his time, but that it enjoyed wide popularity and that it existed in a written version at the time. Franz Rosenthal attributes the survival of *Alf Layla wa-Layla* not only to its appealing contents but also to the fact that it was introduced into Arabic literature at an early stage, just when it was about to enter its golden age. Yet,

> Arabic stories of love and war incorporated in anthologies, the joke books and collections of facetious anecdotes, and the historical romances cover a vast ground and show the uniformly great demand for such entertaining literature all over the world of Islam. However, many more of the variations that were played upon the basic motifs probably never achieved literary permanence and are thus lost to us.[281]

In the nineteenth century, the religious, traditional intellectuals and the educated Arab elite still agreed that *Alf Layla wa-Layla* had a harmful influence

Marvelous Events), see Heath 1984, p. 29; and Doufikar-Aerts 2000, pp. 22–3. Ulfat al-Idlibī (1912–2007) considers the sexual episodes being incorporated into *Alf Layla wa-Layla* to be nothing but "cheap arousing" (*ithāra rakhīṣa*) (al-Idlibī 1992, p. 53. On the sexual themes in *Alf Layla wa-Layla,* see Irwin 1995, pp. 159–77).

280 Ibn al-Nadīm 1970, II, p. 714; Ibn al-Nadīm 1985, p. 605. Cf. Rosenthal 1979, p. 322; Kabbani 1986, p. 23; Hovannisian and Sabagh 1997, p. 8; and Kilito 2007, pp. 49–54. For a general account of *Alf Layla wa-Layla,* see Littmann 1960, pp. 358–64; Marzolph 2006; Marzolph 2007; and Reynolds 2007, pp. 77–86. On various aspects of the text, see the special issue of *Fuṣūl* 12.4 (Winter 1994) and al-Mūsawī 2000. On the evolution and formulation of the text in its various collections, see Walther 1987 (for a review of the book by J. Sadan, see *Journal of Arabic Literature* 25.1 [1994], pp. 81–5). On its relationship with other *ḥikāyāt,* see Sadan 1998, pp. 1–22 (see p. 7, n. 19 on the studies published during the last two centuries on the work). See also Sadan 1999, pp. 149–88; and Sadan 2001, pp. 169–84. For a motif index of *Alf Layla wa-Layla,* see El-Shamy 2005, pp. 235–68; El-Shamy 2006 (see also the review of the book by Robert Irwin in *Mamlūk Studies Review* 12.1 [2008], pp. 218–20). For a study of the text in comparative context, see Ghazoul 1996. For Western reception of the work, see Altoma 2000, pp. 221–62. For a comprehensive interdisciplinary collection on the work, see Marzolph 2006. For a bibliography of representative research publications on the *Arabian Nights* compiled by Ulrich Marzolph, see <http://wwwuser.gwdg.de/~umarzol/arabiannights.html> (last accessed 20 October 2016). For the Egyptian editions of the *Arabian Nights* (since 1835, when the first edition came out), see <https://albiblio.net/editions/> (last accessed 15 September 2016). A mention should be made as well of *Kitāb Mi'at Layla wa-Layla* (*The Book of A Hundred and One Nights*), which is likely much older than *Alf Layla wa-Layla,* drawing on Indian and Chinese antecedents (it was translated into English for the first time by Bruce Fudge and published by New York University Press, 2016).

281 Rosenthal 1979, p. 336.

on Arabic style, morals, customs, virtues, and even on the "mentality" of the Arab reader. This kind of literature was looked upon as "morbid, legendary, and popular," and the public was encouraged to read classical works of Arabic literature and science in order to revive the glorious past. Nawfal Ni'mat Allāh Nawfal (1812–87), for example, at the end of his book *Ṣannājat al-Ṭarab fī Taqaddumāt al-'Arab* (*The Castanet of Joy in the Progress of the Arabs*) laments about how classical Arabic sciences and arts have deteriorated, and how their place have been taken by Arabic romances:

> وتركت العرب كافّة تلك العلوم والفنون بعد أن كان دأبهم البحث عن استخراج درّها المصون وجوهرها المكنون ومن ثمّ تفرّق شملها ما بين فاقد وضائع وتقاصرت بخلوّها العقول أيضا عن السباق في حلبة الأعمال والصنائع بل قايض عليها الأكثرون من الشبّان بمطالعة كتب الخرافات كحكاية السندباد البحري والمحتالة دليلة أو قتل الأوقات عمدا بسماع حماس قصّة عنترة ومجون ألف ليلة وليلة.

> The Arabs abandoned all these sciences and arts after they had at first eagerly attempted to extract the virtuous pearls and hidden jewel they contain. Thereafter, the Arabs became scattered, in part deficient in part missing, and their empty brains no longer competed in the arena of actions and crafts; moreover, many young men instead read books of fables such as the story of Sindibād the Sailor or the [story of the] deceiver Dalīla, or deliberately passed the time by listening to the enthusiastic tale of 'Antara or the impudence of *Alf Layla wa-Layla*.[282]

Even Salīm al-Bustānī (1848–84), editor of *al-Jinān*, who in order to modernize Arabic literature dedicated a special section in the journal to folkloristic tales,[283] declaring that one of the aims of the journal was to liberate Arabic language from the chains of tradition,[284] considered the tales of 'Antara and *Alf Layla wa-Layla* as "works devoid of any literary principles, and their foundation is mere sensual delight of the body without serving the mind at all."[285]

Alf Layla wa-Layla was mainly associated with public performances and stories for amusement that were popular with the illiterate lower social classes.[286] It was only in the eighteenth and nineteenth centuries, when it was translated into European languages, especially English, French, and German,

282 Nawfal n.d., p. 464. Cf. Moreh 1979, pp. 369–70.

283 See, for example, *al-Jinān* VI (1875), pp. 540, 576, 612, 648. Cf. al-Bustānī (Salīm) 1990, p. 41.

284 *Al-Jinān* II (1871), p. 612. Cf. al-Bustānī 1990, p. 29. See below, p. 158.

285 *Al-Jinān* IV (1873), p. 32. Cf. al-Bustānī 1990, p. 38. On *al-Jinān* and its effort to develop a new Arabic narrative discourse, see Eissa 2000, pp. 41–9.

286 For example, Muhammad Ali Pasha's (1769–1849) first printed journal, *Jurnāl al-Khidīw*, was reported to have featured such stories "for attraction and amusement" (Ayalon 1995, p. 175).

that a slow process of canonization began.[287] Not only would it eventually become a canonical Arabic masterpiece, but it would come to be celebrated as a brilliant component of world literature.[288] What the West knew about Arabic literature before the modern period was, as Franz Rosenthal states, not what the Muslims themselves considered "its truly great and important products." And what were these products? Rosenthal continues:

> These, being the intimate property of Muslim culture, were simply not communicable. The more popular and lowly fringes of literary activity were. They were absorbed, and sometimes, it seems, were given greater weight than they originally were thought to possess, but again without altering the fundamental concerns of Western literature and its persistent efforts towards the literary expression of "reality."[289]

Through translation, *Alf Layla wa-Layla* received the status of literature in Europe, not in the least perhaps because Europeans saw it as a mirror of Eastern reality. European authors responded to the Oriental vogue with dozens of "Oriental tales," some of which came directly from *Alf Layla wa-Layla* and some of which were thinly veiled Orientalized versions of contemporary events.[290] Although these tales were highly popular throughout the eighteenth century, only *Vathek, An Arabian Tale* (published in 1786) by William Beckford (1760–1844) and the philosophical romance *The History of Rasselas, Prince of Abissinia* (first published in 1759 under the title *The Prince of Abissinia. A Tale*) by Samuel Johnson (1709–84) have been able to garner continual critical attention.[291] The Orient of the stories was adopted as a

287 Ṭāhā Ḥusayn in *al-Ayyām* describes how at the turn of the century his father was unpleasant when he and his brothers were reading *Alf Layla wa-Layla* or other popular stories (Ḥusayn n.d. [1929], pp. 202–3). Najīb Maḥfūẓ says that when he was young this work had a bad reputation and "we only read the abridged version—all the explicit scenes were censored" (Mahfouz 2001, p. 88). In his memoirs, the Iraqi-Jewish writer Samīr Naqqāsh (1938–2004) states that his father agreed that he would read it only after he had promised not to read "certain stories in the book" (*al-Mu'tamar* [London] 325 [18–24 October 2002], p. 9).

288 On the translations of that popular literary work, see Huart 1966, pp. 402–3; Ḥamāda 1992, II, pp. 201–4; Classe 2000, pp. 1390–92; and Fudge 2016, pp. 135–46. Even Antoine Galland (1646–1715), who first introduced this work to European readers at the beginning of the eighteenth century, did not consider it to be of high literary importance (MacDonald 1932, p. 398. On Galland and his translation, see Knipp 1974, pp. 44–54; Kabbani 1986, pp. 23–9; and Hopwood 1999, pp. 13–14. On Galland's *Arabian Nights* in the traditions of English literature, see Mack 2008, pp. 51–81). On the changing value of *Alf Layla wa-Layla Alf* for nineteenth-century Arabic, Persian, and English readerships, see Rastegar 2005, pp. 269–87.

289 Rosenthal 1979, p. 348.

290 On *Alf Layla wa-Layla* and Orientalism, see Yamanaka and Nishio 2006.

291 On these English works, see Stapleton 1985, pp. 737, 915. An exception is Martha Pike Conant's (1869–1930) book (Conant 1966 [1908]), which offers a comprehensive study of the subject.

framework for romanticism and as a metaphor for what the West saw as the moral beliefs of Muslim societies and peoples. Moreover, "often European writers projected their own repressed sexuality onto their image of the Orient."[292] In her *Europe's Myths of Orient: Devise and Rule*, Syrian cultural historian Rana Kabbani (b. 1958) writes that *Alf Layla wa-Layla* was

> greeted with great enthusiasm in an area that was fidgeting under the stern domination of rationalism, desiring imaginative space and relief from sobriety [...] The allure of *Les Mille et une nuits* led many Europeans to confuse the real East with the East of the stories.[293]

Richard Burton (1821–90), the translator of the first unexpurgated English version of *Alf Layla wa-Layla* (1885–88) projected, according to Kabbani, every imaginable kind of sexual perversion onto the Orient: "The Orient for Burton was chiefly an illicit space and its women convenient chattels who offered sexual gratification denied in the Victorian home for its unseemliness."[294] He "used the *Arabian Nights* to express himself, to articulate his sexual preoccupations. He made it serve as an occasion for documenting all manner of sexual deviation."[295] Burton's fascination with the *Arabian Nights*, Kabbani says, "was greatly enhanced by the fact that they upheld his own views on women, race and class."[296]

The reception of *Alf Layla wa-Layla* in Western culture led to a fundamental change in its status within the Arabic literary system.[297] After having been considered for centuries as harmful and damaging,[298] it became, especially

292 Sardar and Davies 1990, p. 51.

293 Kabbani 1986, pp. 28–9.

294 Kabbani 1986, p. 7.

295 Kabbani 1986, pp. 60–1. On the association of the Orient with sexual fantasies, see Said 1985 [1978], pp. 103–4, 190; and Hopwood 1999, pp. 180–2.

296 Kabbani 1986, p. 48. For a survey of Western sexual attitudes of the Arabs, see Hopwood 1999, pp. 147–61. On Burton's translation of the *Arabian Nights*, see Shamma 2005, pp. 51–67. On Burton's contribution to the shaping of the image of the Arabs in Victorian times and to what extent he was himself influenced by inherited ideas in his personal reactions to the Arabs, see Sulaiman 1991. For other views of Burton, see Nasir 1976, pp. 68–76; and Long 2014, pp. 31–75. On Burton's translation from the point of view of world literature, see Damrosch 2009, pp. 77–82.

297 ʿAbd al-Laṭīf al-Barghūthī describes the Arabs' appreciation of *Alf Layla wa-Layla* as a sort of "infection" (*ʿadwā*) under the influence of the attention the West paid to this work (al-Barghūthī 1988, p. 19).

298 In the introduction to his book *al-Ṭifl al-ʿArabī wa-l-Adab al-Shʿabī* (Yūsuf 1992, p. 5), the Egyptian writer ʿAbd al-Tawwāb Yūsuf (1928–2015) says that his father "forbade me to read *Alf Layla wa-Layla* in my childhood, but I read some of what Kāmil Kaylānī and others published based on it." See also the introduction written by Ṭāhā Ḥusayn to the study of Suhayr al-Qalamāwī (1911–97) about *Alf Layla wa-Layla* (al-Qalamāwī 1966, p. 8), in which he states that al-Qalamāwī "tried to improve the status of popular literature so that scholars would start to study it."

in the second half of the twentieth century, a major source of inspiration. Its significance for Arab culture has become a self-evident fact as reflected, for example, in the first sentence of a study on the work:

ألف ليلة وليلة نصّ مركزي في الثقافة العربية، أنتجت رمزيته رحلة طويلة في الذاكرة الجماعية، وجغرافية الإبداع، تحوّل معها إلى صور ذهنية، كثيفة، ملتبسة، وماتعة الأعطاف.

> *Alf Layla wa-Layla* is a central text in Arab culture, its symbolism has created a long journey in the collective memory and the geography of creativity, through which that work has taken the shape of mental, dense, ambiguous, and all-inclusive images.[299]

Although several Arab intellectuals wondered why the Arabic literary system should be allowed to be influenced by foreign literary systems,[300] the impact of *Alf Layla wa-Layla* today is evident in all genres of modern Arabic fiction, poetry, and theater for adults[301] and children,[302] not to mention other arts, such as music, sculpture, cinema, and television. The Iraqi scholar Muḥsin Jāsim al-Mūsawī (b. 1944) even argues that the "reclamation of Scheherazade" may stand for the whole postcolonial endeavor in Arabic

299 Mājdūlīn 2001, p. 5.

300 See, for example, Yāsīn Ṣāliḥānī al-Ma'aṭṭ's article published in *al-Thawra*, 6 December 1978 (according to al-Nafzāwī 1983, pp. 37–45), especially the following (p. 39):

لماذا لا نركّز اهتمامنا عادة إلا على الموضوعات والكتب التي حازت على إعجاب أوربا والغرب ولا نكون نحن الذين نلفت أنظار الغرب إلى ذلك التراث الرائع الذي يذخر به تاريخنا الأدبي؟ لماذا لا نقبل أن ننتظر حتى تهتمّ أوربا بكتاب من كتبنا أو أديب من أدبائنا حتى نصحو نحن إلى أهمّية ذلك الكتاب أو ذلك الأديب؟ لماذا لا نبدأ نحن بالمبادرة ونوجّه اهتمام أوربا إلى الجيّد من أدبنا بدل أن نترك لهم أسبقية الاختيار الذي كان دائما يبنى على ميل شخصي من مستشرق وقع مصادفة على كتاب - ما - أو سمع بأديب - ما - أعجبته فيه ناحية من النواحي وقد تكون أسباب الإعجاب شخصية بحتة أو مغرضة، لأسباب لا نقبل نحن بها إطلاقا؟

See also what Ḥusām al-Khaṭīb (b. 1932) wrote in *al-'Arabī* (Kuwait), November 1982 (according to al-Nafzāwī 1983, pp. 63–7), especially the following (p. 66): "Could an Arab scholar mention one book from the heritage which became famous because the Arabs themselves had discovered it?!"

301 See, for example, the novel, *Layālī Alf Layla* by Najīb Maḥfūẓ (Maḥfūẓ n.d. [1982]) (English translation: Mahfouz 1994. Cf. Allen 1998, p. 294. On the novel, see al-Musawi 2003, pp. 109–14, 375–87); the poem "Riḥla fī al-Layl" ("A Journey at Night"), by Ṣalāḥ 'Abd al-Ṣabūr (1931–81), from his first collection *al-Nās fī Bilādī* (*People in My Country*) (1957) ('Abd al-Ṣabūr 1972, pp. 7–13) (English translation: Abdel Sabour 1970, pp. 2–17); *Alf Yawm wa-Yawm* (*One Thousand and One Days*) by Ṭāhir Abū Fāshā (1908–89) (Abū Fāshā n.d.). Cf. Sa'd 1962; and Somekh 1991, pp. 4, 66–7. On the *Arabian Nights* and the contemporary Arabic novel, see Jarrar 2008, pp. 297–315.

302 On the adaptations of *Alf Layla wa-Layla* published by Kāmil Kaylānī since the 1920s, see above, p. 56n. In the 1950s Dār al-Ma'ārif in Egypt published a weekly illustrated magazine for children entitled *Sindibād* (according to advertisements published in the Lebanese journal *al-Adīb*, November 1956, p. 36). On the effect of *Alf Layla wa-Layla* on Arabic children's literature, see Yaḥyā 2001.

literature. However, "Scheherazade is reclaimed, but she is no longer the same. Nor is the tale."[303]

It is generally agreed that the canonization of *Alf Layla wa-Layla*, brought about by its interaction with foreign literary systems as well as by the great acclaim that the translations of this masterpiece received in those systems, embodied a radical change in how it was viewed in the Arabic literary system.[304] Moreover, the high status that this work attained in modern Arabic literature in the twentieth century following its translation into Western languages made some scholars forget that not long ago it was an absolutely marginal work vis-à-vis its relationship to the canonical center.[305]

But there are other similar classical literary works that have also received Western attention and yet have failed to gain canonical status in the modern Arabic literary system. *Al-Rawḍ al-ʿĀṭir fī Nuzhat al-Khāṭir* (*The Perfumed Garden in the Trip of the Mind*) by Muḥammad ibn Muḥammad al-Nafzāwī today belongs to the non-canonical pornographic literature which in Arabic is variously called *adab al-jins* (sex literature), *adab al-ithāra al-jinsiyya* (literature of sexual stimulation), *al-adab al-khalāʿī* (bawdy literature), *al-adab al-makshūf* (brazen literature), *al-adab al-fāḥish* (dirty literature), and *al-adab al-ibāḥī* (licentious literature). Wanting to reclaim for this book the canonical status it enjoyed in the past, some modern Arab intellectuals argue that, like other books dealing with sexual desire, *The Perfumed Garden* was written for the amusement of the elite and the high classes.[306] Indeed, as we have seen, the consumption of non-canonical literature was never confined exclusively to the lower social classes.[307]

303 Al-Musawi 2003, p. 389. On postcolonial theory and modern Arabic literature, see Hassan 2002, pp. 45–64.

304 Nevertheless, we can find residues of the negative attitude toward *Alf Layla wa-Layla* in the margins of contemporary Arabic literary system. Also, in 1985, an Egyptian court banned, on moral grounds, a new unexpurgated edition published by Dār al-Kitāb al-Miṣrī al-Lubnānī in Beirut (*al-Shaʿb* [Jerusalem], 11 November 1985, p. 4. Cf. al-Barghūthī 1988, p. 14; Slyomovics 1994, p. 392; and Miller 1996, p. 81). In one of the printings of the work published in eight volumes by Dār Miṣr li-l-Ṭibāʿa in Cairo and edited by Saʿīd Jawda al-Saḥḥār (1909–2005), we find in the introduction that the original version is preserved but in a certain condition (p. 4): "We made it suitable to be read by readers from any class or age and deserving to be bought by every family." Although more rarely, a negative attitude toward the work is sometimes expressed also by Western scholars. For example, about *The Arabian Nights* and the *Rubāʿiyyāt* of ʿOmar al-Khyyām, James Kritzeck says that "they are *rightly* regarded by the Arabs and Persians as quite inferior morsels of what their rich literatures contain" (Kritzeck 1964, p. 3, my emphasis).

305 See, for example, al-ʿĪsāwī 2001, p. 79.

306 See Ḥusām al-Khaṭīb's (b. 1932) essay in *al-Baʿth* (Damascus), 13 July 1978 (according to al-Nafzāwī 1983, pp. 19–20).

307 Cf. Sadan 1998, pp. 3–7, and see the episode in Maḥfūẓ 1988, pp. 33–4, in which a pornographic book—*Rujūʿ al-Shaykh ilā Ṣibāhu* (Ibn Kamāl Bāshā 1994)—is eagerly read.

As contemporary research into non-canonical sectors of Arabic literature is only in its infancy, the limited available research permits no detailed analysis of the intrasystemic, intersystemic, as well as extrasystemic interactions that may be at work. But even if we cannot always describe and explain these interactions, we can hypothesize, for example, that certain phenomena in the canonical sectors of Palestinian or Iraqi literature can be explained by pointing to certain developments in the non-canonical sectors of these literatures.[308] Already at the beginning of the twentieth century, the Jesuit scholar Louis Cheikho (Shaykhū) (1859–1927) asserted that certain vernacular poets of the nineteenth century were the inventors of new poetical forms which would later become an integral part of canonical poetry.[309] Conversely, it is beyond any doubt that the vernacular verses of young poets in Egypt has been highly influenced by modernist poetic approaches in canonical Arabic poetry.[310] Non-canonical texts in the Arabic literary system may influence canonical or non-canonical genres in foreign literary systems. *Alf Layla wa-Layla*, for example, which first emerged in classical Arabic literature as a result of interactions with foreign cultures, has in turn influenced, as an Arabic literary work, French prose writing and theater, German cinema and children's literature, and traditional Southeast Asian theater[311] (in addition to several canonical genres in the Arabic literary system).[312] It has also left traces in numerous novels by great writers, novels that still await adequate critical attention.[313]

308 See, for example, the words of Maḥmūd Darwīsh (1941–2008): "The first poetic influence upon my poetry was that of popular poets, the poets of celebrations and *zajal* poetic dialogues." Darwīsh states that in his poem "Qaṣīdat al-Arḍ" ("The Land Poem") (Darwīsh 1977, pp. 79–107; Darwīsh 1977a, pp. 513–41; Darwīsh 1988, pp. 618–31), he recalls the memory of a *zajal* singer whose poems were the first inspiration for his poetry (Bayḍūn 1995, pp. 78–9. Cf. Snir 2015, p. 44). See also the influence of Muẓaffar al-Nawwāb's *zajal* on canonical poetry in Iraq (al-Muḥsin 1993, p. 20). Muḥammad Maḥmūd al-Jawharī refers to the "interaction between the popular traditional heritage and the historical changes that occurred in the canonical culture" (al-Jawharī 1974, p. 133). On the interaction between folk literature and canonical poetry with regard to the folktale of Zarqā' al-Yamāma, as reflected in the poetry of Amal Dunqul (1940–83) and 'Izz al-Dīn al-Manāṣira (b. 1946), see Khoury 2008, pp. 311–28.

309 See Campbell 1972, p. 84.

310 See, for example, the poetic work of Majdī al-Jābirī (1961–99), which combines stream of consciousness, surreal images, prose poetry, and quotations from Sufi texts and modern thinkers (Burt 1997, pp. 152–6, 169–74).

311 Al-Khāzin and al-Yān 1970, p. 163; and Ghulam-Sarwar 1994, pp. 198, 254–5. On the impact of *Alf Layla wa-Layla* in the West, see al-Qalamāwī 1966, pp. 66–75; Kabbani 1986, pp. 23–36; al-Mūsawī 1986; al-Barghūthī 1988, p. 17; Haase 2004, pp. 261–74; and Marzolph 2007.

312 See, for example, al-Hasan 1984; and Metwali 1984, pp. 101–8.

313 As for example, traces of the *Thousand and One Nights* can be found in the works of Jorge Luis Borges (1899–1996). See Fishburn 2004, pp. 213–22.

The interplay of various canonical and non-canonical genres, models, and texts in the Arabic literary system might be illustrated on the level of the text as a synchronic reflection of the entire system. Some writers are so attuned to this interplay between the canonical and the non-canonical that their works almost become a sort of meta-literary declaration. For example, in 1965 the Egyptian poet and dramatist Najīb Surūr (1932–78) published a "novel in verse" (*riwāya shiʿriyya*) entitled *Yāsīn wa-Bahiyya* (*Yāsīn and Bahiyya*), which uses an admix of *ʿāmmiyya* and *fuṣḥa*.[314] Two quotations at the opening of the work reflect its meta-poetic aim; the first is in *ʿāmmiyya* and is written by the poet himself:

الشعر مش بس شعر
لو كان مقفّى وفصيح
الشعر لو هزّ قلبك
وقلبي شعر بصحيح

Poetry is not only when it
Rhymes and is in *fuṣḥā*
Poetry, if it moves your heart
And mine, is real poetry.

The second quotation, which the poet attributes to Ibn Rashīq,[315] is in *fuṣḥā*:

لعن الله صنعة الشعر ماذا   من صنوف الجهّال منه لقينا
يؤثرون الغريب منه على ما   كان سهلا للسامعين مبينا
ويرون المحال معنى صحيحا   وخسيس الكلام شيئا ثمينا[316]
يجهلون الصواب منه ولا يد   رون للجهل أنهم يجهلونا
فهم عند من سوانا يلامو   ن وفي الحقّ عندنا يعذرونا

God curse poetry! How many kinds of stupid [poets] have we met!
They prefer strange expressions to what would be easy and clear to the listener.
They consider the absurd a sound idea, and vile speech something precious.
They ignore what is right (in poetry). On account of their ignorance, they do not know that they are ignorant.
Not we, but others, blame them. We, in fact, find them excusable.[317]

314 See Surūr n.d. [1965]. Yāsīn and Bahiyya are the names of the protagonists. On this work, see also Frolova 1978, pp. 22–7; Somekh 1988, pp. 35–47; and Somekh 1991, p. 68.

315 These verses were not written by Ibn Rashīq but quoted by him in *al-ʿUmda* and attributed to al-Nāshī Abū al-ʿAbbās ʿAbd Allāh ibn Muḥammad (d. 905–6) (Ibn Rashīq 1963, II, p. 113). They also appear in Ibn Khaldūn's *Muqaddima* (Ibn Khaldūn 1979, III, p. 1308 [= Ibn Khaldûn 1967 [1958], III, p. 387]. See also Rosenthal's note about the poet in the English translation of the *Muqaddima*: Ibn Khaldûn 1967 [1958], III, p. 389, n. 1506).

316 In Surūr n.d. [1965]: مينا.

317 The translation is according to Ibn Khaldûn 1967 [1958], III, p. 387.

The wide acclaim that *Yāsīn wa-Bahiyya* received in Egyptian literary circles shows that the canonical center of the literary system is not all adverse to accepting that the interplay of various canonical and non-canonical sectors is an important part of canonization.[318] A similar kind of interplay is found in many canonical literary works that have been published since the 1960s, and there are critics who want to see it become even more pronounced.[319] Almost every contemporary canonical genre employs models and elements that are taken from non-canonical sectors in order to convey meaning. A full understanding of such works is only possible when one considers the interplay between those models and elements and the various canonical original and translated texts. This interplay is prominent, for example, in the genre of verse drama (*maṣraḥiyya shi'riyya*) from the 1960s. Since verse drama is a literary text both to be read and to be concretized on the theatrical stage, its interrelationships and interactions with other texts and genres traverse literary and non-literary systems and are not confined to limitations imposed by language. For example, the verse drama *Qaraqāsh* (1969) by the Palestinian poet and playwright Samīḥ al-Qāsim (1939–2014)[320] traverses Arabic, Hebrew, and Western canonical and non-canonical sectors, and it is an example of intrasystemic and intersystemic interrelationships that occur between various sectors of the Arabic literary system.[321]

318 *Yāsīn wa-Bahiyya* was staged in Cairo as a dramatic work in Masraḥ al-Jayb (on this presentation, see the notes and essays appended to Surūr n.d. [1965], pp. 114–43). Surūr wrote another two similar literary works: *Āh Yā Layl Yā Qamar* (Surūr 1980 [1968]) and *Qūlū li-'Ayn al-Shams* (Surūr n.d. [1972?]); however, he called each of them "tragedy in verse" (*ma'sāt shi'riyya*). According to Jalāl al-'Ashrī (1939–89), together with *Yāsīn wa-Bahiyya* they comprise an "epic trilogy" (*thulāthiyya malḥamiyya*) (Surūr 1980 [1968], p. 4). On this trilogy, see also Fārūq 'Abd al-Qādir's (1938–2010) essay in *al-Ṭalī'a,* March 1973, pp. 172–3. On Surūr's theory of drama, see Guth and Ramsay 2011, I, pp. 121–34 (by Monica Ruocco).

319 See, for example, Ṣafwat Kamāl's reference to children's literature during the conference held in Cairo about the issue of reading literature (*al-'Ālam,* 27 June 1992, p. 53).

320 The play was published in three printings: one by Dār al-Ittiḥād in Haifa (al-Qāsim 1970), a second by Dār al-'Awda in Beirut (al-Qāsim 1970a), and a third was incorporated into the fifth volume of al-Qāsim's complete works entitled *al-Masraḥ wa-l-Ḥikāya* (*Drama and Narrative*) (al-Qāsim 1991, pp. 9–69). On al-Qāsim, see Moreh and 'Abbāsī 1987, pp. 181–4. For a list of his works as well as a bibliographic list of studies, see Rajab 1995, pp. 178–98.

321 See Snir 1993g, pp. 129–47; Snir 1995e, pp. 63–103; and Snir 1996a, pp. 101–20.

Chapter 3

Outlines of Diachronic Intersystemic Development

In the introduction to *Poetry and the Making of Modern Egypt (1822–1922)* (1971), Mounah A. Khouri (1918–96) sets out some of the problems that the historian of literature ought to confront when dealing with Arabic poetry. For Khouri, poetry is the result of specific external correlates, and so one must therefore be able to provide a causal explanation for the social and intellectual meanings that it contains—that is to say, how the actual poetic expression of those meanings hangs together with biographical, social, psychological, and other environmental factors involved in its (that is, poetry) creation. In other words, the historian must assume the roles of other specialists and attempt to blend the insights yielded by different critical approaches, whether they be historical, psychological, functional, descriptive, or normative. At the same time, there are the effects that poetry itself produces.[1] And Khouri is aware of the difficulties that the literary historian faces when it comes to describing the various levels of interactions and relationships between the literary system and other systems, and when it comes to dealing with what the Formalists called the "communicative space (*literaturayj byt*) that mediates between author or text and reader."[2]

In the previous chapter, we investigated the literary dynamics of Arabic literature in synchronic cross-section, where both canonical and non-canonical literary texts are addressed in six subsystems explained as networks of relationships interacting on various levels. Here, I wish to examine the issue of the diachronic interactions that obtain between the Arabic literary system and various other literary and cultural systems as well as various extra-literary and extra-cultural systems. This will enable us to describe the diachronic intersystemic changes that have determined the historical course of Arabic literature since the nineteenth century. Not surprisingly, sociocul-

[1] Khouri 1971, p. 1.
[2] See Sebeok 1986, II, pp. 844–5.

tural changes have also been mentioned as factors by some Arab and Western scholars. For example, Ṭāhā Ḥusayn (1889–1973) focused on the liberty of the writer, the vast increase in the reading public, and the growing influence of electronic media.[3] But there has been no systematic study of these intersystemic interactions. One notable exception is the interaction between literature and gender,[4] which rapidly grew into an important research topic

[3] Ḥusayn 1945, pp. 25–7; and Ḥusayn n.d. [1958], pp. 30–2.

[4] Before the 1970s there was only a tiny amount of research on gender and feminist literature and on the representation of women in literature. However, during the last four decades this research has been significantly intensified. In Arabic, special attention should be given to pioneering studies published before the late 1990s such as Farrāj 1980; Ghurayyib 1980; Zaydān 1986; Fawzī 1987; Samarīn 1990; ʻAṭiyya 1992; al-Qāḍī 1992; Shaʻbān 1993, pp. 211–34; BenMasʻūd 1994; al-Zayyāt 1994; al-Fayṣal 1996; and Mansiyyah 1997. See also *Ibdāʻ*, January 1993, a special issue on "The Woman as a Writer"; and *Mawāqif* 73–4 (Autumn 1993–Winter 1994), a special issue on "The Problems of the Arab Woman." As for studies in other languages, especially in English, there are numerous publications that have come out since the late 1970s: Beck and Keddie 1978; Kilpatrick 1978, pp. 7–9; Mikhail 1979; Ingrams 1983, pp. 129–54; Accad and Ghurayyib 1985; Accad 1987, pp. 33–48; Cooke 1987; Cooke 1987a; Baron 1988; Tauzin 1989, pp. 178–87; Accad 1990, pp. 78–90; Badran and Cooke 1990; Keddie and Baron 1991; Malti-Douglas 1991 (see also Kilpatrick's review in *Bibliotheca Orientalis* LIII.3–4 [May–August 1996], pp. 566–9); Badawi 1992, pp. 443–62 (by Miriam Cooke); Abu-Lughod 1993; Accad 1993, pp. 224–53; al-Ali 1993; Badran 1993, pp. 129–48; Cooke 1993; Mehdid 1993; Stetkevych 1993, pp. 159–238; Arebi 1994; Baron 1994 (Arabic translation: Baron 1999); Cooke and Rustomji-Kerns 1994; Göçek and Balaghi 1994, pp. 139–73; al-Hassan 1994; Kadi 1994; Malti-Douglas 1994a, pp. 224–9; Roded 1994; Badran 1995; Brooks 1995; Nieuwkerk 1995; Zeidan 1995; Kandiyoti 1996; Snir 1996, pp. 65–72; Khan 1997; LaTeef 1997; Abu-Lughod 1998; Bennett 1998, pp. 283–91; Erickson 1998, pp. 37–65; Fernea 1998; Hartman 1998; Hatem 1998, pp. 369–90; Manisty 1998, pp. 272–82; Nashashibi 1998, pp. 165–82; Nelson 1998, pp. 95–120; Nieuwkerk 1998, pp. 21–35; Odeh 1998, pp. 263–71; Rejwan 1998, pp. 221–8; Lunt 1999, pp. 135–58; Meriwether and Tucker 1999; Moghissi 1999; Roded 1999; Handal 2000; Joseph 2000; Kahf 2000, pp. 147–71; Bahrani 2001; Cooke 2001; Deguilhem and Marín 2001; Joseph and Slyomovics 2001; Hartman 2002; Marín and Deguilhem 2002; Nieuwkerk 2002, pp. 231–51; Oleksy 2002, pp. 74–80; Zubaida 2002, pp. 212–30; Mikhail 2004; Bray 2006, pp. 47–87; Rausch 2006, pp. 291–304; Stephan 2006, pp. 159–80; Mehta 2007; Valassopoulos 2007; Suyoufie 2008, pp. 216–49; Taha 2008, pp. 193–222; Tijani 2008, pp. 250–69; Procházka 2009, pp. 235–55; Ritt-Benmimoun 2009, pp. 217–33; Zachs and Halevi 2009, pp. 615–33; El Hamamsy 2010, pp. 150–75; Regaïeg 2010, pp. 21–33; al-Ṭaḥāwī 2010, pp. 151–61; Abudi 2011; Gottesfeld 2011, pp. 75–101; Zachs 2011, pp. 332–57; Ball 2012; Khedr 2012, pp. 35–56; Abou-Bakr 2013, pp. 320–33; Alami 2013, pp. 443–53; Gottesfeld 2013, pp. 22–40; Salhi 2013; al-Samman 2015; Shitrit-Sasson 2015; and Zachs and Halevi 2015. For the history of modern Arabic writing by female authors, see Cooke 1986, pp. 212–16; Shaʻbān 1999; and Cooke 2001, pp. 1–28. Together with the development of research into feminist literature (cf. Afshar 1993, especially pp. 3–17), the number of translations of Arabic literature by women is increasing at a constant rate (e.g. Bagader et al. 1998). For a selection of titles on female-authored Arabic fiction available till the 1990s in English, see Altoma 1996, pp. 137–53; and Amireh 1996, p. 11. Garnet Publishing in London started a new series in 1995 entitled *Arab Women Writers*, in which the first translated novels published were *al-Waṭan fī al-ʻAynayn* by Ḥamīda Naʻnaʻ (b. 1946) (Naʻnaʻ 1979; translation: Naʻnaʻ 1995); *Ḥajar al-Ḍaḥk* by Hudā Barakāt (b. 1952) (Barakāt 1990;

in the 1970s, when the study of women in the Middle East was firmly established as a separate field[5] as a result of what the Syrian writer and scholar Kamāl Abū Dīb (Kamal Abu-Deeb) (b. 1942) calls "the collapse of totalizing discourses and the rise of marginalized/minority discourses."[6] Since women have been providing readers with fresh, nuanced portraits of the complex relationships and situations that exist within the domestic sphere and the public sphere, research into the intersection between literature and gender has made a significant contribution to our understanding of both society and politics. Additionally, the literary scene, as Roger Allen points out, has been changing as well, and women have been contributing in significant ways to experimental modes of literary creativity.[7]

I have not come across any systematic scholarly study dealing with the interaction between the literary system and the economic system, although its impact on literary production and consumption is obvious.[8] Some trends in sociological criticism refer to the basic social and economic influences that operate whenever works of art are produced. Marxist theory views a given work of art as a reflection of the class interests and the aspirations of its author, but it views it in terms of whether it will make a valuable or harmful contribution to the understanding of the true goals of society at large. The range of

translation: Barakat 1995); *ʻAyn al-Mir'ā* by Liyāna Badr (b. 1950) (Badr 1991; translation: Badr 1995); and *al-ʻAraba al-Dhahabiyya lā Taṣʻad ilā al-Samā'* by Salwā Bakr (b. 1949) (Bakr 1991; translation: Bakr 1995; on Salwā Bakr, see El Sadda 1996, pp. 127–44). Writing on the problems and defects found in these translations, Hilary Kilpatrick describes the series as "a tragic failure" and concludes her review article with the following words: "Ill-executed projects like this help to keep Arabic culture out of the international arena" (1996, p. 149). Garnet Publishing also put out a series of autobiographical essays in translation by thirteen Arab women writers entitled *In the House of Silence* (Faqir 1998), but the series seems to have been discontinued after two years of intense activity. On the problems and prospects of publishing Arabic feminist literature in the West, see Amireh 1996, pp. 10–11. On challenges facing Arab women writers, see al-Nsour 2012, pp. 625–7. On the legacy of Orientalism in Middle Eastern feminism, see Valassopoulos 2003, pp. 183–99.

5 Cf. Baron 1996, pp. 172–86. On the start of the interest in feminist studies in the Middle East, see Nikki Keddie's observations in Gallagher 1994, pp. 143–4. Leila Ahmed stresses the significance of women as writers in shaping cultural production and altering conventional mainstream discourses (Ahmed 1992, p. 214. Cf. al-Ali 1993, p. 119). On the discourse of "Islamic feminism," see Hatina 2011, p. 9.

6 Abu-Deeb 2000, p. 348.

7 Allen 2007, p. 257.

8 Even the history of printed Arabic books has been neglected in the scholarly research until recently; I know of only one study in book form dealing with this subject. Al-Ṭannāḥī 1996 concentrates on the history of the printed book in Egypt during the nineteenth century. For some important observations on book production and publishing in the Arab world, see Winkler 2001, pp. 159–73. But see now Ayalon 2016 on the Arabic print revolution, cultural production, and mass readership. Also, Elizabeth M. Holt plans to publish an historical materialist study of the simultaneous rise of the novel form and finance capital in Arabic in the late nineteenth century (Holt [forthcoming]).

issues that have economic relevance extends, however, beyond Marxist theoretical implications. Already in the late nineteenth century, when modern Arabic fiction was taking its first steps, Salīm al-Bustānī (1848–84), editor of *al-Jinān*, took into consideration while composing his novels the number of readers who would buy the journal issues in which the novels would be published. For example, he wrote that in order to attract female readers to his novels he would incorporate topics of concern to feminists into each of them.[9] Writing in the 1940s, Salāma Mūsā (1887–1958)[10] saw a close relationship between literary and economic systems, attributing what he called the "backwardness of Arabic literature" to the fact that economically as well as socially the Arab world lagged behind the West.[11] Likewise, for Hishām Sharābī (1927–2005), the hegemony of Western culture was due to the predominance of Western economic capitalism.[12] The literary critic Ghālī Shukrī (1935–98) argued that complaints about a crisis in Arabic literature or in Arabic literary criticism would remain unjustified as long as no systematic sociocultural field studies were carried out.[13] Also, since the 1930s, we occasionally find articles in such periodicals as the Egyptian *al-Risāla* and *al-Ṭalīʻa* or the Lebanese *al-Ādāb*[14] on the importance of the interaction between the literary system and the economic system, but this effort, together with brief references by the writers themselves,[15] comes nowhere near the sociocultural field studies that Shukrī had called for.[16]

This trickle of research into the relationship between literature and economics widens into a stream when we look at the work done on the connection between literature and politics in the Arab world. However, the most prominent scholarly outlook here considers literature to be a by-product of extra-literary events. The emphasis is on how political events are reflected

9 *Al-Jinān* IV (1873), p. 826. Cf. al-Bustānī 1990, p. 40.

10 That he was familiar with Marxist theory is clear from his article "al-Tafsīr al-Iqtiṣādī li-l-Lugha wa-l-Adab al-ʻArabiyyayni" ("The Economic Explanation of Arabic Language and Literature") (Mūsā 1945, pp. 129–31).

11 See his aforementioned article as well as his article entitled "al-Klasiyya Dāʼ al-Adab al-ʻArabī" ("Classicism is the Malady of Arabic Literature") (Mūsā 1945, p. 82).

12 Sharābī 1993, pp. 30–1 (based on the writings of the Egyptian-French Marxist economist Samīr Amīn [b. 1931]). Semiotic–historic research into advertisements published in the Saudi weekly *Sayyidatī* from 1996 to 1998 exposes how, through advertising, Western goods are made a part of Saudi culture (Zirinski 1999; Zirinski 2005).

13 Shukrī 1989, p. 90.

14 See, for example, Zakī 1934, p. 1374; al-Amīn 1936, pp. 381–3; al-Baʻlabakkī 1972, pp. 70–3; al-Fārisī 1972, pp. 77–80; Mūsā 1975, pp. 160–5; Qāsim 1993a, pp. 40–3; and Makhlūf 1998, p. 9.

15 For instance, in Maḥfūẓ's letters to his friend Adham Rajab from the 1940s he mentioned the influence of economic factors on the writing of literature (*October*, 11 December 1988, pp. 40, 46).

16 For the importance of such an endeavor, see Rainey 1999, pp. 33–69.

in literary works:[17] Only a few scholars look at how the literary system may influence the political system. The numerous works on the Arab–Israeli conflict make this abundantly clear,[18] as does the use of the term "political novel" (*riwāya siyāsiyya*), which generally stands for a literary product in which political events play a central role.[19] Needless to say, language and literature play a major role in nation-building; one only needs to look at how modern Hebrew literature has been harnessed to serve the goals of Zionism,[20] while Palestinian literature has been similarly harnessed to serve the goals of Palestinian nationalism.[21] In addition, a frequently occurring phenomenon in the Arab world is that of political figures engaging in literary activities.[22] At the end of the day, however, only rarely do studies deal with the role of literary texts in the political process.[23] Most often, when interactions between the political and the literary systems are expressed in works of art, we will find that political dimensions far outweigh literary considerations. This should perhaps be seen against the background of the nineteenth century, when the Arab world began witnessing the increasing marginalization of cultural aspects of society in favor of political ones.[24] Quite a few writers admit that cultural activities often serve to disguise political ideas,

17 See, for example, Aḥmad Muḥammad ʿAṭiyya's book *Ḥarb October fī al-Adab al-ʿArabī al-Ḥadīth* (*The October War in Modern Arabic Literature*) (ʿAṭiyya 1982).

18 See, for example, Ballas 1980.

19 See, for example, ʿAṭiyya 1981; and Wādī 1996.

20 See, for example, Ben-Yehuda 1995.

21 See Snir 2015, pp. 17–154. See also below, pp. 161, 168n, 172–3.

22 For example, Libya's late president Muʿammar al-Qadhdhāfī (1942–2011) published several short stories (al-Qadhdhāfī 1995), and Iraq's late president Ṣaddām Ḥusayn (1937–2006) published a novel (Bengio 2002, pp. 9–18). Also, Osama bin Laden (Usāma ibn Lādin) (1957–2011), al-Qāʿida's (Al-Qaeda) founder and leader, wrote poetry, about which Adūnīs said: "This is not poetry [...] All Arabs are poets, but 95 percent of them are rubbish" (*The New York Review of Books*, 16 April 2016. See also Haykal and Creswell 2015). Among the political leaders who excelled in literary writing against the background of their period, one can mention Maḥmūd Sāmī al-Bārūdī (1838–1904) and Imīl Ḥabībī (1921–96). The writer ʿAbd al-Wahhāb al-Amīn refers to the interaction between politics and literature from the point of view of writers who became politicians and put their writings in the service of their political ambitions, alluding to the "crimes of politics and the press carried out against literature" (*jināyat al-siyāsa wa-l-ṣiḥāfa ʿalā al-adab*) (al-Amīn 1936, p. 381).

23 The famous case is that of Tawfīq al-Ḥakīm's novel *ʿAwdat al-Rūḥ* (*The Return of Spirit*) (al-Ḥakīm 1933; English translation: al-Ḥakīm 1990) which chiefly deals with the author's youth and ends with the revolution of 1919, when the protagonist, Muḥsin, joins the demonstrations and rebellions (on the novel, see Allen 1982, p. 38; Brugman 1984, pp. 281–5; and Elkhadem 1985, pp. 44–5). President Gamāl ʿAbd al-Nāṣir (1918–70) liked the novel and even claimed it had helped him along the road to revolution (Elon 1980, p. 71; and al-Ḥakīm 1990, pp. 4, 22 n. 8 [introduction]).

24 Cf. this argument as presented by Muḥammad ʿĀbid al-Jābirī (Mohammed Abed al-Jabri) (1935–2010), a Moroccan critic and professor of philosophy and Islamic thought at Mohammed V University in Rabat (al-Jābirī 1993, p. 12).

and some argue alternatively that any cultural action or struggle is in and of itself political.[25] Very important in this regard is the strong involvement of literature with political life through the raising of people's awareness of the drawbacks and mistakes of their political leaders. At no time has this been clearer than during the start of the Arab Spring in 2011:

> The impact of that literature stems from the writers' attempts to expose the leaders and defame their unchallenged presence and influence on public and social life. Politicizing literature was and still is one of the mainstays of the movement that had always called for freedom of expression. It took the shape of unofficial civil movements that confronted the military and its unlimited authority. People needed some hope to revive any potential movement that would put some restrictions on the dictatorial behaviors. It is not strange at all that the conflict between the public and the dictatorships was crystallized through literature. Before it was expressed across the Arab Spring counties [sic], breaking the barrier of fear took shape in literary forms that continue to distress and deprive Arab dictators of the indefinite control over all aspects of life.[26]

Five years later, whether or not one considers the Arab Spring to have failed or succeeded, the genuine aspirations of the revolts across the Middle East continue to produce various literary experimental manifestations which will certainly change the face of Arabic literature despite the current frustrations and disappointment of many Arab men of letters.[27]

25 Cf. Adūnīs' statement (*Mawāqif* 34 [Winter 1979], p. 160): "By all means, we must emphasize that the cultural action cannot be separated from the political action, and that the cultural struggle is, in essence, a political action."

26 Kadalah 2014, pp. 439–48. See also Dabashi 2012; Seigneurie 2012, pp. 484–509; Elbousty 2013, pp. 159–63; Foley 2013, pp. 32–46; Erlich 2014; Larémont 2014; Abū Dīb 2015; Issa 2015; Booth 2015; Mamelouk 2015, pp. 100–22; al-Saleh 2015; Zartman 2015; Albakry and Maggor 2016; Baker 2016; and Gran 2016, pp. 1–15. See also Armbrust 2013, pp. 834–64; and Zoepf 2016. Armbrust's next study, *A Symbolic Revolution: Culture and Politics in Post-Mubarak Egypt*, is currently under contract with Princeton University Press (according to <http://www.orinst.ox.ac.uk/staff/iw/warmbrust.html> [last accessed 23 May 2016]). On the explosion of artistic production in the Arab world during the Arab Spring, see LeVine 2015, pp. 1277–313. On feminist writing following the Arab Spring, see <http://ofoq.arab-thought.org/?p=2443#.V9LTJyw9wLn.facebook> (last accessed 10 September 2016).

27 One only needs to read the essays that Adūnīs has published since the start of the Arab Spring in his regular column *Madārāt* (Orbits) in the London-based newspaper *al-Ḥayāt*. One of them reads: "The 'Arab Spring' has been lost / Yesterday I saw the Spring entering / Into the court of seasons / In order to change its name // I appreciated it and expected for it a shining and brimful future / But yesterday I heard it had died by poison / In water from a well he dug before his house" (*al-Ḥayāt*, 25 February 2016). Another one: "About our Spring, we can rightly say, seriously not jokingly, in light of what it has given us, we have not tasted from it but its smell" (*al-Ḥayāt*, 23 June 2016). See also his contributions, in the same column, on 24 April 2014; 15 May 2014; 29 May 2014; 1 October 2015; and 17 July 2016. Cf. Snir 2012, pp. 66–78).

The rapid development of the movie industry and electronic media,[28] the proliferation of home videos, and the spread of Internet communication[29] have done much to change the way culture is perceived. In the Arab world, it has also extensively influenced the ways in which Arabic literature is published as well as the very patterns of Arabic literature itself.[30] The adoption of the Internet with its various means of communication (that is, email, websites, message boards) changed both writers' and readers' attitudes toward literature:

> Readers are called to discover the identity behind the screen, making sense of pseudonyms, self-conscious narration, and hoaxes and gathering fragments of the author's real identity scattered through the [text] [...] [they] have to make their own way through the labyrinth of the open, multimedia text, by reading text together with pictures, selecting links and browsing different pages, playing music and videos [...] They can also have a say in the visual layout of the [text] and the stylistic features of the narrative.[31]

There were initial hopes that electronic media and the Internet would open up new horizons for canonical Arabic literature,[32] but it is now clear that their influence has mainly extended to non-canonical sectors of the Arabic literary system.[33] On the other hand, ever since the rise of radio and television, there has been much talk about the vanishing role of canonical poetry.[34] Such complaints are also frequent in the field of world literature, with some scholars predicting the death of literature following "the complex transformations of a social institution in a time of radical political, technological, and social changes."[35] Wolfgang Iser (1926–2007) wrote in 1989 that "the place

[28] For a survey of electronic media in the Middle East, see Boyd 1999.

[29] On the Arabic Internet, see Versteegh et al. 2006, II, pp. 380–7.

[30] Cf. Gibb and Landau 1968, pp. 192–3; and Bowen and Early 1993, pp. 251–3. On the lingual aspects of the emergence of mass media, see Somekh 1991, pp. 8, 9–14.

[31] Pepe 2015, p. 88.

[32] See, for example, "al-Radio wa-l-Shiʿr" ("Radio and Poetry") in *Apollo*, June 1934, pp. 899–900.

[33] See Reynolds 2015, p. 2: "[T]he technological revolution in broadcast and electronic communications in the form of hundreds of new satellite television channels and the advent of the Internet and social media has now put the spoken Arabic dialects in contact with one another in an unprecedented manner. Signs of rapid linguistic and cultural change are everywhere in the Arab World."

[34] See, for example, the statement of the Syrian poet Marwān al-Khāṭirī (*al-Bilād*, 20 May 1995, p. 51): "I have lost my trust in the role of poetry in the time of television."

[35] Kernan 1990, p. 10. For a critique of such arguments, see Walter E. Broman's review of Kernan 1990 (*Philosophy and Literature* 15 [1991], pp. 323–4). Cf. the complaint of the poet Rifʿat Salām (b. 1951) in *al-Usbūʿ al-ʿArabī*, 31 January 1994, pp. 44–5: "What can the poet do against the background of these institutions which decrease, every day, the need of the reader to read a poem? Nothing but adhering to the poem itself."

of literature in modern society is something that can no longer be taken for granted [...] the functional values of literature also change. Evidently literature has reached just such a turning point today."[36] It prompted Arab writers, poets, and critics to find ways to adapt to the new world that electronic media and the Internet were creating. According to the Egyptian critic Muḥammad Mandūr (1907–65), films, radio programs, and popular magazines were superficially helpful in providing speedy education for the masses, but the wide popularity which they enjoyed had a bad influence on literary taste in general. Mandūr foresaw dangers for the intellectual treasures of literature, and he called on responsible critics to watch out for these dangers.[37] Envisaging a comprehensive cultural project which he called "the memory of the nation" (*dhākirat al-umma*), Ghālī Shukrī saw "publication through electronic media as the most important medium of any possible culture."[38] The Iraqi poet Buland al-Ḥaydarī (1926–96) was one of the first canonical poets to recite their work on audio cassette.[39] He was convinced that canonical Arabic poetry was developing in a new direction under the creative influence of the medium of "video art," and he labeled the end result of this development as "video poetry." Shortly before his death he had started working on a "video poem" entitled "Picasso's *Guernica*."[40]

The information technology revolution in general and the ensuing development of the World Wide Web in particular have shown us that we are only at the very beginning of a period of significant change in the Arabic literary system—a change that will be felt at every level and in all sectors. At first, technical difficulties associated with using the Arabic script on the Internet held back the development of Arabic literary homepages and websites for some years, but even then many texts in Arabic managed to appear online, especially short popular poems such as those by Syrian poet and diplomat Nizār Qabbānī (1923–98).[41] Very soon, around the turn of the twenty-first century, the Internet became a virtual library for billions of Arabic literary texts housed on millions of websites. In addition, we have seen a sharp rise in the amount of research on Arabic literature being published online by both Western and Arab academic and cultural institutions.[42] Browsing on the

36 Iser 1989, p. 197.

37 Mandūr (1963 [1944]), pp. 11–12. Cf. Semah 1974, p. 187.

38 Shukrī 1993, p. 14.

39 *Words and Voice of the Poet Buland al-Haidari* (produced by Pan Middle East Graphics and Publishing [London] [n.d.]).

40 *Al-Waṭan al-ʿArabī*, 17 February 1995, p. 38.

41 One of the first Internet sites that presented Arabic texts at the start of the 1990s was Saud al-Hajeri's homepage (<http://www.liii.com/~hajeri/> [link no longer valid; last access date unavailable]

42 Among the first mailing lists in the field of Arabic Studies were *ARABIC-L*, the mailing

Internet, one could input Arabic script into a variety of search engines and get results rather easily. In April 2006 a European search engine, Seekport, unveiled plans to launch an Arabic version of its service. Seekport had teamed up with Saudi Arabia's MITSCo on the creation and design of a search engine to be called *Sawāfi* (Sandstorm). The collaboration was an attempt by the two companies to take advantage of the Arabic Internet market that analysts believed would have more than fifty million users in only a few years, but which at the time had been one of the least exploited markets in the world. Hermann Havermann, who had been managing the partnership under the name of Seekport Internet Technologies Arabia, said that this joint venture was doing pioneering work because it was the first Internet search engine to take up seriously the challenges of Arabic language and culture. He argued that it would present a strong challenge to international search giants such as Google, MSN, and Yahoo, which had only offered a basic Arabic search engine. *Sawāfi* was hoping to copy the success of the Chinese language search engine Baidu, which had made huge strides in a market with more than one hundred million Internet users. Havermann had this to say about the Arabic market: "There are only 100 million Web pages right now in Arabic, and that's nothing. It's only 0.2 percent of the total worldwide [...] There is not enough Arabic content available on the Internet. But there's no motivation to put more Arabic content on the Internet as long as you don't have a system to find the content."[43]

Before the rise of information technology, however, came the collision between the Arabic literary system and Western culture in the mid-nineteenth century, which did much to destroy the self-image of the Arab cultural world.[44] Although "nobody seems to know when the term *inḥiṭāṭ* was first used to denote 'decadence' as [expressing the] self-view of intellectuals of the Ottoman Empire,"[45] and although there have been Arab intellectuals and writers who refused to acknowledge its existence,[46] nowadays one

list for Arabic linguistics and Arabic language teaching sponsored by Brigham Young University, the Arabic Linguistics Society, and the American Association of Teachers of Arabic (mailserv@byu.edu); ADABIYAT, for the discussion of the literatures of the Middle East, especially Persian, Arabic, Turkish, and Urdu (adabiyat@listhost.uchicago.edu); and Arabic-Info, the communication network for Arabic Studies (arabic-info@indiana.edu).

43 *Reuters*, 26 April 2006. Unfortunately, that joint venture was unsuccessful.

44 Cf. P. Starkey's words: "Not only has the West's perception of the East been changed, but the East's perception both of the West and itself" (Starkey and Starkey 1998, p. 285). On the role of translations in the changes which the self-image of Arab culture has undergone, see Lefevere 1990, p. 27. See also above, pp. 27, 96, 102n, and below in the Conclusion.

45 Wild 1996, p. 386. On the use of term in the Western scholarly tradition, see Allen 2006, pp. 1–2. See also Hassan 2002, pp. 57–9; and Bauer 2007, p. 144.

46 Cf. the statement of Najīb al-Ḥaddād (1867–99) in his essay "Muqābala Bayna al-Shiʿr al-ʿArabī wa-l-Shiʿr al-Ifranjī" regarding the superiority of Arabic poetry over Western

can hardly find anyone who will deny that the crisis was real. The lecture that Buṭrus al-Bustānī (1819–83) delivered on 15 February 1859, *Khuṭba fī Ādāb al-'Arab* (*A Lecture on the Culture of the Arabs*), may be seen as the watershed moment that marked this radical change.[47] That it occurred within the politico-economic context of Europe's penetration of the East finds expression in many literary works written since that time. For example, in *'Alam al-Dīn* (*The Sign of Religion*) (1882) by 'Alī Mubārak (1824–93), the fictional Western narrative structure he adopted[48] is reinforced by the overriding theme that the West is far superior to the East and that the East is inferior to the West. For Mubārak, the self-deprecating attitude he portrays is made worse because the East is unaware of its inferior position.[49] Forty years later the *Mahjarī* poet and critic Mīkhā'īl Nu'ayma (1889–1988) expressed the same notion in his famous *cri de coeur* entitled "fa-l-Nutarjim" ("Let Us Translate") published in his book *al-Ghirbāl* (*The Sieve*) (1923).[50] It is not uncommon even today to find statements to the effect that the status of Arab culture has undergone little change or that its image in the eyes of its own people has remained low, unlike that of Western culture.[51] But it is no longer difficult to find literary Arab vanguards who have been defining their place in relation to the West and provoking their audiences to confront its influence "in order to criticize the Westernization of their home culture."[52]

Besides being a target for other literatures and cultures, Arabic and Islamic literature and culture were also important sources of influence for certain cultures.[53] However, we must not talk about this influence in the sense of

poetry (1954, p. 138; cf. Somekh 1991, p. 50. On al-Ḥaddād's main contribution to modern Arabic literary criticism through the aforementioned essay, see Fanous 1980, pp. 146–54; and van Gelder 1996, pp. 144–52).

47 Al-Bustānī 1859; al-Bustānī (Buṭrus) 1990, pp. 101–17. On this speech and its importance, see Sheehi 2004, pp. 19–45. See also Abu-Lughod 1963, pp. 135–6; Sharabi 1970; Ayalon 1995, p. 178, and below, pp. 233–4. For a translation of the speech, by Stephen Sheehi, see El-Ariss [Forthcoming].

48 The work belongs to the genre of travel literature (*adab al-riḥla*). In the introduction to the book, Mubārak describes it as *ḥikāya laṭīfa* (a fine story) (Mubārak 1882, p. 7). On Mubārak, see Muḥammad 'Imāra's introduction to Mubārak's *Complete Works* ('Imāra 1979, pp. 17–300). On the book, see Haist 2000, pp. 173–4; and Ouyang 2007, pp. 331–58. See also below, p. 235.

49 Cf. al-Qāḍī 1981, pp. 27–9.

50 Nu'ayma 1964 [1923], p. 126. On this *cri de coeur*, see below, p. 231.

51 See, for example, a *cri de coeur* similar to that of Nu'ayma's in 'Abd al-Wahhāb 1995, pp. 10–12.

52 Szyska 1997, p. 144. Yusrī al-'Azab (b. 1947) sees a fundamental difference between past and present, emphasizing the cardinal contributions of medieval Arab culture to Western civilization (al-Rāwī 1982, pp. 249–50). Ghālī Shukrī emphasizes the huge gap between material and intellectual development in the Arab world (Shukrī 1978 [1968], pp. 18–19).

53 See, for example, Hitti 1962, pp. 48–63; Southern 1962; Hunke 1965 (Arabic translation: Hunke 1979); Conant 1966 [1908]; Watt 1972; Hilāl 1977, pp. 55–68; Metlitzki

the polemical statement by the Syrian poet and critic Adūnīs (ʿAlī Aḥmad Saʿīd) (b. 1930) that "there is nothing in the West that the West did not take from the East,"[54] or Gustave E. von Grunebaum's (1909–72) hyperbolic statement that "there is hardly an area of human experience where Islam has not enriched Western tradition."[55] Samuel Miklos Stern (1920–69) argued that "not even the most fanatical advocate of the case for Arabic influence on the West would seek to set out a long catalogue" of literary loans after the twelfth century.[56] Among the exceptions to this, however, is Sufism, which proved to be a living tradition that shielded Islam against its assailants and at the same time stimulated cross-cultural interaction:

> This interaction cast doubt on the validity of the view that cultural transfer in modern times was unidirectional, from Europe to the Arab-Muslim world. A striking example of this phenomenon was to be found in the cultural dialogue that emerged at the end of the Ottoman era between Muslims and Christians in Cairo, Rome, and Paris. The players in this dialogue highlighted the spirituality of Islam, and advocated rapprochement between East and West at a time of

1977; Rosenthal 1979, pp. 345–9; Semaan 1980; Bushrūʾi 1982, pp. 153–9; Menocal 1985, pp. 61–78; Kabbani 1986, pp. 23–36; al-Mūsawī 1986; Menocal 1987; Caracciolo 1988; Saad el Din and Cromer 1991; Ḥamāda 1992; Agius and Hitchcock 1993; Engels and Schreiner 1993; Sharfuddin 1994; Lewis 1995, p. 13 (and the references on pp. 83–4, n. 1); Bosworth 1996, pp. 155–64; Starkey and Starkey 1998, pp. 179–230 (contributions by M. Taymanova, M. Orr, P. Whyte, J. W. Weryho, and J. D. Ragan); and Reeves 2000. Canonical Arabic literature has been a source of direct and indirect loans mainly for literature in Muslim societies since the Middle Ages, while popular Arabic literature has been a source of loans mainly for Western societies, especially since the nineteenth century. See, for example, the widespread circulation of the canonical model of the *qaṣīda* in classical and modern cultures, such as those that wrote in Persian, Turkish, Urdu, Indonesian, Swahili, and Hausa. On various classical and modern *qaṣīda* traditions in Islamic Asia and Africa, see the articles, original poems, and translations appearing in Sperl and Shackle 1996 and Sperl and Shackle 1996a which came about as a result of the London *Qaṣīda* Conference which took place at SOAS (London) in July 1993. On the traveling of the *Qaṣīda* structure in Asia and Africa, see al-Musawi 2015b, pp. 34–45. For popular Arabic literature as source literature for modern Western literary traditions, see the case of *Alf Layla wa-Layla* dealt with above (p. 97). Mention should also be made of the substantial influence that Arabo-Spanish popular strophic poetry had on emerging Romance lyrics and the troubadours (Nykl 1946; and Gorton 1974, pp. 11–16). For a symbolic Islamo-European encounter in prosody between *muwashshaḥāt, azjāl*, and Catalan troubadours, see Sanaullah 2010, pp. 357–400. On Arabic poetry and the songs of the troubadours, see Jafri 2004a, pp. 374–87; and Nieten 2006, pp. 253–61. For a comprehensive study of the relationship and interaction between Islam and the West, see al-ʿAẓma 1996.

54 See Adūnīs 1980, pp. 330–1; and *Mawāqif* 36 (Winter 1980), pp. 150–1. For a critical response to Adūnīs' argument, see al-ʿAẓm 1992, pp. 109–19. Cf. the argument of the Palestinian poet and critic Jabrā Ibrāhīm Jabrā (1919–94) that the European Renaissance was nothing but the result of the translation of Arab investigation and creativity into Latin (Jabrā 1992, p. 191).

55 Von Grunebaum 1953, p. 342.

56 Stern 1974, p. 204.

growing friction. They sought to position their agenda at the forefront of the discourse of their respective communities.[57]

As for literary interaction, although the reading of Arabic literature in the original outside the Arab world is still mainly confined to a limited number of academic circles, there has been an upsurge of translations of Arabic literature into various foreign languages.[58] The impact, albeit minor, of these translations[59] cannot be overlooked. In addition, the number of Arab

57 Hatina 2007a, p. 404.

58 On translations of Arabic literature into English, see Howarth and Shukrallah 1944; Alwan 1972, pp. 195–200; Alwan 1973, pp. 373–81; Anderson 1980, pp. 180–207; Allen and Hillmann 1989, pp. 104–16; Le Gassick 1992, pp. 47–60; Altoma 1993, pp. 160–79; Altoma 1993a; Allen 1994, pp. 165–8; Johnson-Davies 1994, pp. 272–82; Altoma 1996, pp. 137–53; Altoma 1997, pp. 131–72; Classe 2000, pp. 62–71; France 2000, pp. 139–58; Altoma 2005; Altoma 2009, pp. 307–19; Altoma 2010; and Reynolds 2015, pp. 108–10 (by Shawkat M. Toorawa). On translations of Arabic literature into French, see Jackman 1992, pp. 43–57; Nuṣayr 1992, pp. 43–7; Altoma 1993a; and Tomiche 1993, pp. 152–6. On translations of Arabic literature into Spanish, see Comendador et al. 2000, pp. 115–25; Comendador and Fernández-Parrilla 2006, pp. 69–77; Amo 2010, pp. 239–57; and Fernández-Parrilla 2013, pp. 88–101. On translations of Arabic literature into Italian, see Ruocco 2000, pp. 63–73; Avino 2001, pp. 53–66, 115; Camera d'Afflitto 2001, pp. 11–16, 109–10; Corrao 2001, pp. 17–21, 110–11; Giorgio 2001, pp. 23–8, 111–12; and Ruocco 2001, pp. 29–37, 112. On translations of Arabic literature into Romanian, see Feodorov 2001, pp. 35–45; and Dobrişan 2004, pp. 29–32. On translations of Arabic literature into Swedish, see Stagh 1999, pp. 41–6; and Stagh 2000, pp. 107–14. On translations of Arabic literature into Russian, see Frolova 2004, pp. 143–9. On translations of Arabic literature into German, see 'Abbūd 1995, pp. 31–53; Trudewind 2000, pp. 49–51, as well as the review sections of *Fikr wa-Fann*, which has been published since the early 1960s by Inter Nations in Bonn, Germany. On the reception of Arabic literature in Germany in the shadow of *The Arabian Nights*, see Fähndrich 2000a, pp. 95–106. On the situation of contemporary Arabic literature in German-speaking countries in general, see Fähndrich 2000, pp. 167–80. On translations of Arabic literature into European languages in general, see Gibb and Landau 1968, pp. 317–19; and Cachia 1990, pp. 222–8. On translations of Arabic literature into Hebrew, see Gibb and Landau 1970, pp. 195–7; Somekh 1973, pp. 141–52; Amit-Kochavi 1996, pp. 27–44; Amit-Kochavi 1999; Amit-Kochavi 2000, pp. 53–80; Amit-Kochavi 2003, pp. 39–68; Amit-Kochavi 2004, pp. 190–210; and Amit-Kochavi 2006a, pp. 100–9.

59 See, for example, Allen 1993, pp. 87–117. Maḥfūẓ is the most popular Arab writer in the West, especially after he won the Nobel Prize (on his reception in American publications, see Altoma 1993, pp. 160–79. See also El-Enany 2014, pp. 89–94). Maḥfūẓ himself considered the Nobel Prize as the world's recognition of Arab culture (Larry Luxner, "A Nobel for the Arab Nation," *Aramco World* 40.2 [March–April 1989], pp. 15–16 [according to Lawall 1993, p. 25, n. 21]). Almost all of Maḥfūẓ's novels and short story collections have been translated into English (for a list of these translations, see Cachia 1990, p. 226; Gordon 1990, pp. 141–2; Altoma 1993, pp. 169–70, 174–5; and Altoma 1996, pp. 137–53. On issues related to the translation of his work, see Etman 1993, pp. 355–8). The impact of his literary works might be inferred also from the fact that scholarly study of his work is carried out even by academics who do not read Arabic and use translations (e.g. Gordon 1990). However, it seems that his popularity in the West might be explained by the sociopolitical value of his work (see Lūwīs 'Awaḍ's [1915–90] opinion in *al-Muṣawwar*, 11 August 1989, p. 35. See also below, p. 262). A different example is the popularity of *Alf Layla wa-Layla*

authors writing in foreign languages is increasing.[60] Interference between the Arabic literary system and other literary systems is occurring throughout the world at an ever-increasing pace.

Two major examples of reciprocal interference between Arabic and Western literatures in the twentieth century and the start of the twenty-first century are Arabic and English,[61] and Arabic and French.[62] Especially noteworthy is the participation of Arab writers in the French literary system, which already in the 1930s was seen as an inspiring way for enriching the Arabic poetic tradition.[63] This phenomenon, which was also criticized,[64]

in the West, which is mainly due to literary considerations (al-Qalamāwī 1966, p. 65. See also below, p. 263). In the nineteenth century, E. W. Lane (1801–76) considered *Alf Layla wa-Layla*'s value to lie in the "fullness and fidelity with which they describe the character, manners and customs of the Arabs" (Lane 1859 [1839–41], III, p. 686. Cf. Kabbani 1986, pp. 37, 44). Lane, who translated *Alf Layla wa-Layla* into English (first published in parts from 1838 onward), "was primarily a scholar, not a *littérateur*" (Starkey and Starkey 1998, p. 246).

60 On this general phenomenon, see Adūnīs 1993, pp. 95–6.

61 For example, Jubrān Khalīl Jubrān's works written originally in English: *The Madman* (Gibran 1918); *The Forerunner* (Gibran 1920); *The Prophet* (Gibran 1924); *Sand and Foam* (Gibran 1926); *Jesus, the Son of Man* (Gibran 1928); *The Earth Gods* (Gibran 1931); *The Wanderer: His Parables and His Sayings* (Gibran 1932); *The Garden of the Prophet* (Gibran 1933); *Lazarus and His Beloved* (Gibran 1973; Gibran 1982); and *The Blind* (Gibran 1982). Except for the last two, all of these works were translated into Arabic by Anṭūnyūs Bashīr (1898–1966) and were published in one volume under the title *al-Majmūʿa al-Kāmila li-Muʾallafāt Jubrān Khalīl Jubrān al-Muʿarraba ʿan al-Inklīziyya* (*The Complete Collection of Jubrān Khalīl Jubrān's Writings Translated into Arabic from English*) (Jubrān 1981). For Jubrān's Arabic works, see Jubrān 1985. For a list of the English translations of most of these works, see Bushrūʾi 1987, pp. 91–2. For a general bibliography on Jubrān, see Bushrūʾi 1987, pp. 93–4; and Altoma 2000, pp. 255–7. On Lebanese literature in English in general (in fact on Jubrān, as well as on Amīn al-Rīḥānī [1876–1940] and Mīkhāʾīl Nuʿayma [1889–1988]), see Bushrūʾi 2000. Among the other writers in English, mention can be made of Jabrā Ibrāhīm Jabrā (1920–94), who also translated literary works from English into Arabic (Luʾluʾa 1989, pp. 26–31). On Palestinian writers in English, see Jayyusi 1992, pp. 333–66. On the "experimental encounter" with English, see "The Smell of Writing" by ʿAbd al-Qādir al-Janābī (b. 1944) (El Janabi 1996, pp. 55–6). For the development of Arab-American culture, see, for example, the journal *Mizna*, "A Forum for Arab American Expression," which started to appear in 1999 (<http://www.mizna.org/> [last accessed 21 May 2016]); Kadi 1994; Hatem 1998, pp. 369–90; Akash and Mattawa 2000; Barakat 2000, pp. 304–20; Al Maleh 2009; Hassan 2011; Hout 2012; Gana 2013; and Reynolds 2015, pp. 109–10 (by Shawkat M. Toorawa).

62 See Déjeux 1973; Bouraoui 1980, pp. 129–44; Joyaux 1980, pp. 117–27; Accad 1990, pp. 78–90; Achour 1991; Benarab 1995; and Giovannucci 2008. See also the series *Écritures Arabes*, edited by Marc Gontard (Paris: Éditions L'Harmattan), in which more than one hundred literary works (poetry, short stories, novels, and plays) of Arab writers in French were published. On the relationship between Arabic and French writing and the bilingual phenomenon, see Bamia 1992, pp. 61–88; and Amanṣūr n.d., pp. 79–98. On the influence of French literature on the Arabic novel, see El Beheiry 1980.

63 See ʿAql 1935, pp. 381–93.

64 On the negative attitude of cultural circles in the Arab world toward writers and intel-

has begun attracting the attention of Arab critics.[65] Among the winners of France's most prestigious literary award, the *Prix Goncourt*, we find three Arab writers: the Moroccan writer Tahar Ben Jelloun (al-Ṭāhir ibn Jallūn) (b. 1944), who won in 1987 for his *La nuit sacrée*,[66] the Lebanese writer Amin Maalouf (Amīn Maʿlūf) (b. 1949), who won in 1993 for his *Le rocher de Tanois*, and the Moroccan novelist Leïla Shimani (Layla al-Sulaymani) (b. 1981), who recently won for *Chanson Douce* (2016).[67] Another novel by Maalouf, *Samarkand*,[68] was given the *Prix de Maison de la Presse*. Other distinguished Arab authors who wrote in French include Georges Schéhadé (1905–89), Andrée Chedid (1920–2011), Driss Chraïbi (1926–2007), Kātib Yāsīn (Kateb Yacine) (1929–89), Assia Djebar (1936–2015), Muḥammad Barrāda (Mohammed Berrada) (b. 1938), and ʿAbd al-Kabīr al-Khaṭībī (Abdelkebir Khatibi) (1938–2009). The participation of these writers in French literature by no means came about as a result of their abandoning of their original cultural identities. In fact, most of them were appreciated at home as well as abroad. For example, Maalouf, who was formerly the director of the weekly international edition of the leading Beirut daily *al-Nahār* and editor-in-chief of *Jeune Afrique*, dedicated his novel "to the memory of the man with the broken wings"—an allusion to *al-Ajniḥa al-Mutakassira* by Jubrān Khalīl Jubrān (Gibran) (1883–1931),[69] who was himself successful at writing in a foreign language and "the only Arab or Arabic-speaking author who succeeded in authoring a book that has had this extensive presence in the four corners of the earth."[70] Inevitably, however, along with the role (which was sometimes even subversive)[71] that these writers have taken

lectuals writing in French, see the interview with Algerian writer and scholar Mālik Shibl (b. 1953) published in *al-Ḥayāt*, 11 March 1996, p. 11.

65 See, for example, Qāsim 1996.

66 Ben Jelloun 1987. For more on Ben Jelloun, see M'henni 1993; and Elbaz 1996.

67 Maalouf 1993 (English translation: Maalouf 1995).

68 Maalouf 1989 (English translation: Maalouf 1994).

69 Jubrān n.d. [1912] (English translation: Gibran 1957).

70 Shahīd 2000, p. 321. The book is *The Prophet* (Gibran 1924), which has been translated into more than forty languages. On Jubrān Khalīl Jubrān's significance and role in Arabic and world literature and his creative reception around the world, see Michalak-Pikulska 1999, pp. 93–100.

71 See, for example, the way Robert Elbaz interprets the Arabic words in Ben Jelloun's novels: "Ces signes arabes, c'est le surplus textuel, le supplément qui vient combler l'absence du signifiant premier. Et comme ils sont disséminés à travers tout le Texte, ils brisent la surface textuelle, démantèlent la séquence narrative, et fonctionnent comme des réservoirs virtuels dans lesquels on pourrait emmagasiner tout ce qu'incorpore l'espace discursif maghrébin. Ils s'infiltrent, se posent comme objets sur la surface du Texte, et l'empêchent d'accéder à une transcendance, étant donné que le rapport terme à terme entre le monde et le Texte est affecté. Ces signes ne s'intègrent pas dans la séquence, ils la sapent. Ils la fragmentent" (Elbaz 1996, p. 16).

up in foreign literary systems came the slow decline of the high status they had once occupied in their original literary systems.[72]

In the French literary system, the participation of Arab writers is indeed quite high, but even in literary systems which see lower rates of participation when it comes to Arab writers one can still find reciprocal interference. Compared to English and French literatures (and we can add Russian literature to this list as well), German literature did not, until recently, manage to attract much attention in Arab society, and this is probably due, as the Russian Orientalist I. J. Krachkovskii indicates, to the limited direct colonial influence of Germany in the Middle East.[73] Yet, we do find the writer ʻAlī Aḥmad Bākathīr's (1910–69) subversive recasting of the Goethean tragedy of *Faust*, the aim of which was "to provoke an audience while confronting it with patterns from its own culture in the disguise of foreign settings and characters in order to criticize the Westernization of the own culture."[74] We also see striking similarities between the novels of Jurjī Zaydān (1861–1914) and the historical novels of the German Egyptologist George Ebers (1837–98).[75] And finally, Aḥmad Shawqī (1868–1932), in his *Riwāyat Dal wa-Taymān aw Ākhir al-Farāʻina* (*Dal and Taymān or the Last Pharaohs*) (1899) freely adapted Ebers' *Eine Ägyptische Königstochter* (1864), which he had read in Arabic translation.[76] Conversely, Arab participation in German culture has not traditionally been high, but one can still find important examples of literary interaction.[77] Two of the most prominent Arab writers in German are

72 This was clearly illustrated by the irony with which the literary critic of one of the Arab journals described Maalouf's visit to his homeland, Lebanon (Shūmān 1994, p. 41). Maalouf's novels have been translated into Arabic and published by Manshūrāt Milaff al-ʻĀlām al-ʻArabī in Beirut.

73 Primarily through its support of Istanbul as of the end of the nineteenth century. Cf. Krachkovskii 1989, p. 23. Omitted from Edward Said's *Orientalism* (Said 1985 [1978]), the influence of German scholarship in and about the Middle East remains also relatively unexplored. During the past few years, there have been some movements in that direction: *Comparative Studies of South Asia, Africa, and the Middle East* published in 2002 a call for papers on this topic. Volume 24.2 (2004) of the journal published a section on German Orientalism with only five contributions, none of them relating to literary issues. In September 2003 the Institute of Germanic Studies and the School of Oriental and African Studies, University of London, published a call for papers on the topic of "Oriental Motifs in 19th- and 20th-Century German Literature and Thought." The aim was to examine "the strengths and weaknesses of the German contribution to what was chiefly a literary and intellectual Orientalism and one comparatively unencumbered by imperialistic ambition."

74 Szyska 1997, p. 144.

75 See Elkhadem 1985, p. 18 (and n. II.4 on p. 58).

76 See Elkhadem 1985, p. 21 (and n. II.12 on p. 59).

77 On immigrant Muslim writers in Germany, see Stoll 1998, pp. 266–83; and the special file in *Fikr wa-Fann* (Bonn), issue 80 (2004) on immigrant authors writing in German. An interesting case is the inspiration which the German director Wolfgang Becker's (b. 1954) film *Good Bye, Lenin!* (2003) apparently drew from *Saʻdūn al-Majnūn* (al-Ramlī 1992) by

the Syrian-Christian Rafik Schami (pseudonym of Suhayl Fāḍil; b. 1946),[78] who never published in Arabic, and the Bedouin Palestinian writer Salīm Alafenisch (b. 1948).[79] In addition, there are many German translations of Arabic works,[80] many of which have been put out by the Cologne-based publisher Al-Kamel Verlag (*Manshūrāt al-Jamal*), which is headed by the Iraqi poet Khālid al-Ma'ālī (b. 1956). Among its main activities are the publication of classical and modern literary works and poetry collections, including those of German poets,[81] and the publication, since the mid-1990s, of the magazine *'Uyūn*. Al-Ma'ālī himself translated many Arabic poems into German, some of which he translated in collaboration with his German colleagues.[82] Until recently, only a few German literary authors have been translated into Arabic[83] with the exception of J. W. von Goethe (1749–1832), whose works were not only translated into Arabic, but reprinted in multiple

the Egyptian dramatist Līnīn (Lenin) al-Ramlī (b. 1945). The way this inspiration reached Becker has been still unexplored.

78 See, for example, Schami 1987 (English translation: Schami 1993). On the book, see Schami 1989 (Hebrew translation: Schami 1996); Schami 1995; Amin 2000, pp. 211–33; and Schami 2004 (English translation: Schami 2009). The first Arabic translation has been published in Israel (Shāmī 1997), where few articles have been published on his literary work: *Ha'aretz* (weekly supplement) (Tel Aviv), 7 February 1997, pp. 30–2 (Hebrew); *Yediot Aḥronoth* (literary supplement), 7 March 1997, p. 28 (Hebrew); Schami 1996, pp. 237–42 (Hebrew); and Shāmī 1997, pp. 219–30. The publisher Manshūrāt al-Jamal in Cologne planned to publish an Arabic translation of Schami's *Der geheime Bericht über den Dichter Goethe* (1999) (*al-Ḥayāt*, 27 October 2004). On Schami, see Khalil 1994, pp. 217–24; Khalil 1995, pp. 521–7; and *Banipal* 14 (Summer 2002), pp. 66–70.

79 On him, see Khalil 1995, pp. 521–7; Berman 1998, pp. 271–83; and *Yediot Aḥronoth*, literary supplement, 29 December 2000, p. 26.

80 See, for example, Māhir 1970; and Māhir 1974.

81 On Arab-German literature in general, see Khalil 1995, pp. 521–7. In 2001 a new bilingual Arabic–German magazine appeared with the title *Dīwān: Majalla li-l-Shi'r al-'Arabī wa-l-Almānī/Diwan: Zeitschrift für arabische und deutsche Poesie*, its aim being to strengthen the Arab-German cultural dialogue (first issue came out in May 2001). The magazine has two sections: The Arabic section includes works by German writers in Arabic translation, and the German section includes works by Arab writers in German translation. The editor is the Iraqi poet Amal al-Jubbūrī (Jubouri) (b. 1968). Adūnīs, who is a member of the editorial board, says in his opening remarks to the first issue that the aim of the magazine was to traverse the dualism between East and West and get rid of the "mentality of domination" (*'aqliyyat al-haymana*) (on the magazine, see also *Fikr wa-Fann* 74 [2001], pp. 68–9). See also Midad (Midād)—Deutsch–Arabisches Literaturforum (<http://www.goethe.de/ins/eg/prj/mal/> [last accessed 14 October 2016]).

82 See, for example, Boulus 1997, with Stefan Weidner, and the file on Arabic literature published in *Die Horen: Zeitschrift für Literatur Kunst und Kritik* 189 (1998), pp. 61–134, with Mona Naggar and Heribert Becker. On the translation of Badr Shākir al-Sayyāb's poetry into German, see *Barīd al-Janūb*, 27 October 1997, p. 17. On the cultural achievements of Arab authors in Germany, see Weidner 2012, pp. 68–74.

83 See, for example, Benn 1997.

editions.[84] Due to the immigration of many intellectuals from the Arab world to the West, we can find Arab writers who publish in other languages as well. In general, these writers stopped writing in Arabic and started to concentrate on composing in the language of their adopted country. For example, the Iraqi poet ʿAī al-Bazzāz (Ali Albazzaz) (b. 1958), who published several poetry collections in Dutch, was the only Arab poet included in an anthology of one hundred and twenty poets from the Netherlands and Belgium writing in Dutch.[85] Of interest too is the emergence of Palestinian writers in Hebrew, especially the bilingual writers Naʿīm ʿArāyidī (1950–2015) and Anton Shammās (b. 1950).[86]

Do to lack of space, only four diachronic interactions that obtain between the Arabic literary system and social and cultural extra-literary systems will be discussed in the following pages, and only two of them will be examined in some detail.

LITERATURE / RELIGION

The nature of Arabic literature from the seventh century until our own times has largely been determined by the interaction between the Arabic literary system and Islam, the religious system to which the overwhelming majority of Arabs subscribe. For Ṭāhā Ḥusayn, Islam—and more specifically the Qur'ān—were prominent in consolidating the principles that ensured modern Arabic literature could only be a direct extension of classical Arabic literature.[87] With the rise of Islam, the Arabic literary system—like Arab civilization in general[88]—was given a well-defined ideological and cultural framework within which it could develop. With time, the Arabic literary system (and Islamic civilization as a whole) admitted such contributions from outside as would help it keep its identity under changing conditions

[84] See, for example, Goethe 1964; Goethe 1966; Goethe 1967; Goethe 1968; Goethe 1978; Goethe 1980; Goethe 1980a; Goethe 1999; and Goethe 1999a. For translations of Goethe's works, see also Badrān 1972, p. 108. For a comparative study on "the fortunes of Faust in Arabic literature," see al-Mousa 1998, pp. 103–17.

[85] See Anna Enquist, *Gedichten voor het hart: troostende woorden uit de Nederlandse en Vlaamse poëzie* (Amsterdam: Maarten Muntinga, 2006).

[86] On the Hebrew writing of Palestinian authors, see also Snir 1991a, pp. 245–53; Manṣūr 1992, pp. 63–6; Snir 1995, pp. 163–83; Snir 1995a, pp. 29–73; Snir 1997, pp. 141–53; and Snir 2001a, pp. 197–224. See also below, pp. 226–7n. On translations of Hebrew literature into Arabic, see Zipin 1980; Kayyal 2000; Kayyal 2006; and Kayyal 2016.

[87] Ḥusayn 1945, p. 11; Ḥusayn n.d. [1958], p. 12.

[88] Some Arab intellectuals label Arab civilization prior to Islam as deficient. Cf. the conception of the Egyptian Islamist intellectual Muḥammad Jalāl Kishk (1919–93): "The Arabs did not have a complete and perfect civilization but after the rise of Islam!" (Kishk 1966, pp. 18–19).

and at the same time broaden "its base beyond the limitations inherent in the koranic text." This meant that

> while Islam for many a century continued liberal in accepting information, techniques, objects, and customs from all quarters, it was careful to eliminate or neutralize any element endangering its religious foundation, and it endeavored consistently to obscure the foreign character of important borrowings and to reject what could not be thus adjusted to its style of thinking and feeling.[89]

As many cases attest,[90] most Arabic literary works published during the twentieth century—and certainly those published within the Arab world—continued to adhere to this Islamic framework; it is only in the margins that we find dissenting voices. Censorship or the banning of books for religious reasons or for the harm they may do to public morality has been a frequent occurrence in the Arab world[91] and has even included classical works such as various Sufi books[92] and the *Maqāmāt* by Badī' al-Zamān al-Hamadhānī (969–1008).[93] Publishers in the Arab world have generally censored classical works which are considered to be a threat to public morals. For example, the aforementioned *al-Rawḍ al-'Āṭir fī Nuzhat al-Khāṭir* (*The Perfumed Garden in the Trip of the Mind*) by Muḥammad ibn Muḥammad al-Nafzāwī in its unabridged version has never been published in the Arab world—the only printed versions in existence are shorter, popular editions. Maktabat Usāma in Damascus published a partial edition of the book, which includes several articles about the book and its reception.[94] An unabridged edition was put out by the London-based publisher Riyāḍ al-Rayyis.[95] The same publisher also released what it called *al-Nuṣūṣ al-Muḥarrama* (*The Forbidden Texts*),

89 Von Grunebaum 1953, p. 321.
90 See Ballas 1992.
91 For example, fifty-five books were banned in Egypt during the first five months of 1989 (*al-Ahālī*, 7 June 1989, p. 11).
92 See, for example, Schimmel 1982, p. 39; and Shukrī 1994a, p. 68, n. 19.
93 In the introduction to his edition of al-Hamadhānī's *Maqāmāt*, the Egyptian religious scholar and liberal reformer Muḥammad 'Abduh (1849–1905) writes that for moral considerations he omitted *al-Maqāma al-Shāmiyya* entirely and made some changes and omissions in other works (al-Hamadhānī 1983 [introduction], p. 7). For example, in *al-Maqāma al-Bishriyya*, he changed words which refer to sexual intercourse, such as *khalā bihā* (p. 247) and *waṭi'a* (pp. 255–6), to *tazawwaja* and *qārana* (married). For the original of *al-Maqāma al-Shāmiyya* and *al-Maqāma al-Bishriyya*, see al-Hamadhānī, AH 1298, pp. 43–5, 92–5. It is interesting that other editions of al-Hamadhānī's *Maqāmāt* followed 'Abduh's edition without alluding to the changes and omissions (e.g. al-Hamadhānī 1993). On al-Hamadhānī, see Deyoung and Germain 2011, pp. 38–51 (by Jaakko Hämeen-Anttila). On al-Hamadhānī as a model of the scholar as a humanist of his time, see al-Musawi 2015b, pp. 53–6.
94 Al-Nafzāwī 1983.
95 Al-Nafzāwī 1990.

that is, the book containing *mujūn* (ribald poetry) from the *Dīwān* of Abū Nuwās (c. 755–c. 813), which was generally omitted from the editions published in the Arab world.[96]

One of the most famous examples of morality-based censorship was the case of the Lebanese writer Laylā Baʿlabakkī (b. 1936) and her collection of short stories entitled *Safīnat Ḥanān ilā al-Qamar* (*A Space Ship of Tenderness to the Moon*), which was first published in 1963.[97] The public prosecutor of the Lebanese Court of Appeals, Saʿīd al-Barjawī, summoned the writer in accordance with Section 532 of the Lebanese criminal law, and he accused her of harming public morality and demanded that the court hand down a sentence of one to six months in prison and that she pay a fine of ten to 100 liras. At the same time, members of the Beirut vice squad confiscated the remaining copies of the book from bookstores. On 23 August 1964, however, after discussing the case, the court's unanimous verdict was to stop proceedings against Baʿlabakkī, to waive the payment of any fine, to overturn the original decision to confiscate the copies of the book, and to return the confiscated books to their rightful owners.[98] Copies of the Hebrew translation of Baʿlabakkī's novel *Anā Aḥyā* (*I Am Alive*) (1958), published in 1961, were confiscated from bookstores in Israel for harming public morality and for the alleged anti-Jewish sentiment expressed in the novel.[99] A few other well-known cases are as follows: Iḥsān ʿAbd al-Quddūs (1919–90) was accused of provoking "sexual disturbances" (*shaghab jinsī*) with his novel *al-Banāt wa-l-Ṣayf* (*The Girls and the Summer*)[100]—even President ʿAbd al-Nāṣir expressed

96 Abū Nuwās 1994. The book was first published in a separate edition in 1316H under the title *al-Fukāha wa-l-Ītinās fī Mujūn Abī Nuwās* (*Jesting and Sociability in the Ribald Poetry of Abū Nuwās*) without mentioning the place of publication (probably Cairo), but indicating that "expenses were covered" by Manṣūr ʿAbd al-Mutʿāl and Ḥusayn Afandī Sharaf. When the German Orient-Institut Beirut published the second volume of *Dīwān Abī Nuwās* (Abū Nuwās 1972), the Imprimerie Catholique, run by the Jesuits of Beirut, who did the printing, refused their name to be mentioned in the volume for fear that Muslim intellectuals might attack the Catholic Church in Lebanon for "poisoning the minds of Muslims." I thank Stefan Wild for this observation. On *mujūn* in Arabic literature, see the various contributions in Talib et al. 2014.

97 Baʿlabakkī 1964 [1963]. For an English translation of the title story, see Johnson-Davies 1981 [1967], pp. 128–34; Fernea and Bezirgan 1977, pp. 274–9; and Khalaf 2006, pp. 25–32.

98 For an account of the trial and the court decision, see Fernea and Bezirgan 1977, pp. 280–90; and Allen 1987, pp. 72–3.

99 Cf. Amit-Kochavi 1999, pp. 269–72. On the uproar that the novel created in Beirut due to Baʿlabakkī's outspokenness and her critical approach to most aspects of Lebanese society, see Salem 2003, p. 59.

100 ʿAbd al-Quddūs 1959. A popular film based on the book was produced in 1960 by Aflām al-ʿĀlam al-ʿArabī. The film was based on three of the book's five stories. ʿAbd al-Ḥalīm Ḥāfiẓ (1929–77) and Suʿād Ḥusnī (1943–2002), two of the greatest stars of Egyptian cinema, took part in the third story (based on the book's fifth story) (on the film, see Qāsim 2002, p. 332).

reservations concerning this work because of its explicit sexual passages;[101] *Ḥikāyat Zahra* (*The Story of Zahra*) (1980) by the Lebanese writer Ḥanān al-Shaykh (b. 1945), which nine publishers in Beirut turned down before the author decided to publish it herself, was dismissed as pornography and banned in some Arab countries;[102] *Ḥadīqat al-Ḥawāss* (*The Garden of the Senses*) (1993), written by al-Shaykh's younger contemporary ʿAbduh Wāzin (b. 1957), was also banned throughout the Arab world;[103] and, finally, the Arabic translation of Dan Brown's *The Da Vinci Code* (2003) was banned in Lebanon because the book (and those like it) "harmed Christian beliefs."[104]

The most notorious case of scholarly censorship may well have been that of Ṭāhā Ḥusayn's controversial study of pre-Islamic poetry, *Fī al-Shiʿr al-Jāhilī* (*On Jāhilī Poetry*) (1926). In it, Ḥusayn claimed that most pre-Islamic poetry was forged. He also doubted the historical validity of some sections in the Qur'ān, stating, for example, that the reference to Ibrāhīm in itself did not prove that he had been in Mecca.[105] The book raised a storm of protest and unleashed a wave of publications criticizing it.[106] Al-Azhar, Egypt's supreme Muslim authority, brought legal charges against the author, and the chief prosecutor, Muḥammad Nūr, issued his decision on 30 March 1927.[107] Consequently, in that same year Ṭāhā Ḥusayn published a toned-down

101 Fawzī 1988a, pp. 169–72. On ʿAbd al-Quddūs' status in the Arabic literary system, see above, p. 41.

102 The novel was translated into English by Peter Ford as *The Story of Zahra* (London: Readers International, 1986). On the banning of the novel, see *The Guardian*, 7 July 2001.

103 Wāzin 1993. On the novel and the sensuality of the text, see Meyer 2001, pp. 213–22; and Salem 2003, pp. 227–29.

104 The *Daily Star*, 16 September 2004. The Arabic translation, entitled *Shifrat da Vinci*, was done by Sima Muḥammad ʿAbd Rabbihi and published by al-Dār al-ʿArabiyya li-l-ʿUlūm in Beirut in 2004.

105 See Ḥusayn 1926, p. 26. On the intellectual and philosophical sources from which Ḥusayn derived his skepticism, see Mahmoudi 1998, pp. 56–7, 120–4, 171–3, 198–202. On the liberal discourse of historicization and rationalization of the Qur'ān as part of the depoliticization of Islam, see Hatina 2011, p. 10.

106 Some of them appeared immediately after the publication of Ḥusayn's book, for example Muḥammad Farīd Wajdī's (1878–1954) *Naqd Kitāb al-Shiʿr al-Jāhilī* (*A Criticism of the Book* [*Fī*] *al-Shiʿr al-Jāhilī*) (Cairo: Maṭbaʿat Dā'irat Maʿārif al-Qarn al-ʿIshrīn, 1926); and Muḥammad al-Kahḍr Ḥusayn's (1876–1958) *Naqḍ Kitāb al-Shiʿr al-Jāhilī* (*The Refutation of the Book* [*Fī*] *al-Shiʿr al-Jāhilī*) (Cairo: al-Maṭbaʿa al-Salafiyya, AH 1345). For the main arguments against the book, see *Taḥta Rāyat al-Qur'ān* (*Under the Flag of the Qur'ān*) by Muṣṭafā Ṣādiq al-Rāfiʿī (1880–1937) (al-Rāfiʿī 2000). For an historical and critical survey of the case, see Salāma 1998.

107 The text of the prosecution's decision against Ṭāhā Ḥusayn was published in a thirty-two-page booklet under the title *Qarār al-Niyāba fī Kitāb al-Shiʿr al-Jāhilī* (Cairo: Maṭbaʿat al-Shabāb, n.d.). A photocopy of the book was published in *Fuṣūl* 9.1–2 (October 1990), pp. 193–225. See also the text in Khayrī Shalabī, *Muḥākamat Ṭāhā Ḥusayn* (Alexandria: Dār wa-Maṭābiʿ al-Mustaqbal, 1994 [1974]), pp. 55–99.

version of the book entitled *Fī al-Adab al-Jāhilī* (*On Jāhilī Literature*), but he remained an advocate for liberal ideas.[108] As late as 1980, Ṭāhā Ḥusayn was still described in certain Arab-Muslim circles as "aiming to destroy Islam."[109] On the other hand, modernist liberal and secularist circles in the Arab world thought the book sparked a revival of Arab-Muslim civilization and thought.[110]

Other well-known cases of censorship in Egypt before and after the Ṭāhā Ḥusayn case centered on intellectuals who "resorted to rationalism in their examination of the Muslim canon."[111] The fact that some of these cases are

108 Ḥusayn 1927. On this issue, see Cachia 1956, pp. 145–9; Abdel-Malek 1965, pp. 136–9; Brugman 1984, p. 363; Hourani 1986 [1962], p. 327; Erlich 1989, pp. 78–9; Adūnīs 1993, pp. 57–9; Rejwan 1998, pp. 43–53; Ibrāhīm 1999, pp. 13–51; and Ayalon 2009, pp. 98–121.

109 Shukrī 1992, pp. 297–8. Cf. al-Jundī 1977a; al-Muḥtasib 1978; and al-Jundī 1979. See also Abū Ḥamda 2003, which deals in detail with each argument in *Fī al-Shiʿr al-Jāhilī*, referring to Ṭāhā Ḥusayn as launching attacks against Muslims and seeing his writing style as being "in harmony with the wickedness of the Orientalists and the hidden hatred of the Jews" (p. 14).

110 See the introduction to a new edition of the book published by Dār al-Maʿārif li-l-Ṭibāʿa wa-l-Nashr in Sūsa, Tunis, 1997, pp. 5–7. In February 1996, the magazine *al-Qāhira* republished the original *Fī al-Shiʿr al-Jāhilī* in its entirety. The Jordanian scholar Shākir al-Nābulsī (b. 1940) dedicated his book *al-Lībarāliyūyn al-Judud—Jadal Fikrī* (2005) "to the memory of Ṭāhā Ḥusayn."

111 Al-Azmeh 1996, p. 44. A famous case is that of ʿAlī ʿAbd al-Rāziq (1888–1966), who in 1925 published a book entitled *al-Islām wa-Uṣūl al-Ḥukm* (*Islam and the Principles of Governance*) (ʿAbd al-Rāziq 1925). The book elicited a violent reaction in religious circles and was denounced by a council of leading scholars of al-Azhar, pronouncing the author unfit to hold any public office. For a new edition of the text of the book as well as the judgment of the council and related documents, see ʿAbd al-Rāziq 1988 (for the text of the judgment, see also *al-Manār* 26.5 [September 1925] pp. 363–83). On the case, see Abdel-Malek 1965, pp. 81–6; Hourani 1986 [1962], pp. 183–92; Meisami and Starkey 1998, I, p. 18; Rejwan 1998, pp. 43–53; and Polka 2000, pp. 215–20. Cf. the case in the early 1950s, in which al-Azhar demanded the banning of a book by Khālid Muḥammad Khālid (1920–96) (Khālid 1959, pp. 9–14. Cf. ʿAwaḍ 1974, p. 51). On other cases involving Tawfīq al-Ḥakīm (1898–1987) for his series of *munājayāt* (conversations [with Allāh]) published in 1983 in *al-Ahrām*, whose title *Aḥādīth maʿa Allāh* was changed—through pressure exerted by Muḥammad Mutawallī Shaʿrāwī (1911–98)—into *Aḥādīth maʿa Nafsī* and Lewīs ʿAwaḍ (1915–90) for his *Muqaddima fī Fiqh al-Lugha al-ʿArabiyya* (*An Introduction to Arabic Philology*) (1980), which was eventually banned (see Shukrī 1994a, pp. 68–9). On the general problem of the freedom of speech in Egypt under ʿAbd al-Nāṣir and al-Sādāt, in addition to thirteen case studies on the censorship of prose works, see Stagh 1993 (for a review of the book, see Gonzalez-Quijano 2000, pp. 87–93). For an attempt to map out some of the most significant cultural battles in Egypt, focusing specifically on the Mubārak era, see Mehrez 2008. The Egyptian cultural critic Ṣalāḥ Faḍl (b. 1938) argues that banning a book in the Arab world has become now a guarantee for its greater circulation (<http://www.elaph.com>, 2 April 2005 [last accessed 15 October 2016]). On censorship of theatrical productions in Egypt between 1923 and 1988, see Ismāʿīl 1997. See also Amin 2008, pp. 181–4. On state censorship of books and literature in the Arab world in general, see Makiya 1993, p. 281; Meisami and Starkey 1998, I, pp. 171–2; and Hafez 2001, p. 10. The journal *al-Ādāb* published a series of dossiers about the intricacies of censorship and cultural production in the Arab world. The first of them, in vol. 50.7–8 (July–August

quite recent only serves to illustrate how influential religious circles have remained to the present day. In June 1995 Naṣr Ḥāmid Abū Zayd (1943–2010), an Egyptian professor of Arabic literature at Cairo University, was declared an apostate by a religious court, which meant that his marriage to his wife, Professor Ibtihāl Kamāl Yūnus (b. 1958), was declared illegal. The court accepted a claim, brought by Muslim fundamentalists, that Abū Zayd's writings[112] proved that he was an apostate from Islam and therefore forbidden from marrying a Muslim woman.[113] Arguments against him were reminiscent of those voiced against Ṭāhā Ḥusayn;[114] however, unlike the latter, Abū Zayd enjoyed strong support among Arab liberal intellectuals; his situation was compared to that of the philosopher Ibn Rushd (better known as Averroës in the West) (1126–98) and the astronomer Galileo Galilei (1564–1642).[115] 'Azīz al-'Aẓma (Aziz al-Azmeh) (b. 1947) from Central European University reacted by writing that "the reality of modern Arab history leads in the direction of secularism, which has been responsible for the progress of our societies, cultures and lives in general."[116]

2002), presents the case of censorship in Syria (on this dossier, see *al-Ḥayāt,* 20 July 2002, p. 16); the second, in vol. 50.11–12 (November–December 2002), in Egypt; the third, in vol. 51.9–10 (October–November 2003), in Morocco; and the fourth, in vol. 52.7–8 (July–August 2004), on general issues of censorship in the Arab world, such as censorship confronting publishing houses, self-censorship, and party censorship. On censorship of the press in the Arab world in general, see Ayalon 1995, pp. 79–80, 115–17 (Egypt); 84–7, 121–2 (Syria); 90–1 (Lebanon); 98–100 (Palestine). See also Rugh 1979 (index). For the history of censorship in Islamic societies, see Mostyn 2001. For censorship of Arabic literature in the Middle East, see the chapter written by an anonymous author in Peleg 1993, pp. 94–109 (the editor added the following note: "It is, no doubt, an apt reflection of the contents of this chapter that the author prefers to remain anonymous." On the theoretical dimensions of censorship in Muslim societies, see Arkoun 2002, especially pp. 9–36. On freedom of expression and censorship in medieval Arabic literature, see Szombathy 2007, pp. 1–24; Hirschler 2012, pp. 88–9; and al-Musawi 2015b, p. 172.

112 Especially Abū Zayd 1990; Abū Zayd 1992; and Abū Zayd 1995. Cf. Kassab 2010, pp. 183–94.

113 Olivier Roy considers the case as part of the process where Islamization went beyond state control (Roy 2004, pp. 92–9).

114 See, for example, Fāyid 1995, pp. 2–7.

115 Kermani 1994, p. 42; and Wild 1996, p. 390.

116 Al-'Aẓma 1995, pp. 3–7. Cf. the speech delivered by Taslima Nasreen (b. 1962) before the 63rd International Congress of the Poets', Essayists', and Novelists' Club (PEN) in Mexico on 8 November 1996, in which she said that "secularism is a must for democracy. Religious law and democracy are totally contradictory [...] If we want to enjoy democracy, we have to separate religion and state" (according to *al-Akhbār* Muslim World News list—"IAP" <iapinfo@iap.org> [10 November 1996]). Nasreen, a practicing gynecologist and writer, fled Bangladesh for Sweden in August 1994 after receiving death threats for allegedly insulting Islam in her novel *Lajja* (*Shame*) (1993). On the Nasreen affair, see Ghosh 2000, pp. 39–83. On the religious and the secular in contemporary Arab life, see al-Azmeh 1996, pp. 41–58. On Arab liberal discourse and the role of Abū Zayd, see Hatina 2011, pp. 3–20.

In August 1996 two Egyptian civil rights groups warned that the decision by Egypt's highest court upholding the order of Abū Zayd to divorce his wife constituted a license for Muslim extremists to murder the couple; in the words of the Egyptian Organization for Human Rights (EOHR), the court's decision was a "death sentence," making Abū Zayd and his wife targets "for armed violent groups trying to carry out Islamic sentences." The Center for Human Rights Legal Aid (CHRLA) warned that the ruling could be perceived by radicals as "a green light to practice lethal intellectual terrorism." Both groups cited the case of the liberal intellectual Faraj Fawda (Farag Foda) (1946–92), who had been assassinated by Muslim extremists just days after al-Azhar had described him as being "full of animosity against whatever is Islamic."[117] On 23 September 1996 an unprecedented coalition of international human rights organizations condemned the court-ordered divorce[118] because it was "a flagrant violation of one of the most cherished of human rights—the right of a legally married couple to remain married so long as both parties so desire—as well as the basic right of free expression, including academic freedom." The coalition called on President Ḥusnī Mubārak to speak up publicly for the rights of Abū Zayd and Yūnis and to support the application by their lawyers to the Court of Cessation to overturn the ruling. "By upholding the right of a civil court to declare an Egyptian citizen an apostate," the coalition asserted, "the ruling has a severely chilling effect on freedom of expression."[119] Only in December 1996 did an appeals court indefinitely suspend the ruling that Abū Zayd must divorce his wife.[120]

In addition to works that criticized Islam or the Qur'ān, feminist writings were also thought to pose a danger to traditional society and therefore incurred the wrath of the Islamist campaign in Egypt,[121] especially when the values they espoused were frequently seen to be synonymous with those of the West.[122] Threats against Nawāl al-Sa'dāwī (b. 1931) meant that her name was included on the death lists of radical Islamist groups. Her novel *Suqūṭ al-*

[117] According to adabiyat@listhost.uchicago.edu (15 August 1996). On Fawda, see *Arab Studies Journal* 1 (Spring 1993), pp. 16–19.

[118] The coalition included twenty-two human rights, Arab-American, women's rights, academic, and other organizations.

[119] According to adabiyat@listhost.uchicago.edu (22 September 1996). On the affair, see also Kermani 1994, pp. 25–49; Ḥarb 1995, pp. 234–9; Chalala 1996, p. 8; Maḥmūd 1996, pp. 107–9; Ajami 1998, pp. 212–21; Sfeir 1998, pp. 402–14; Ayalon 1999, pp. 3–6 and the bibliographical references on p. 43, n. 2. Abū Zayd himself published a book which includes various documents relating to the affair (Abū Zayd 1995a) as well as a collection of articles and essays by writers and intellectuals supporting his case (Abū Zayd 1995b). See also Abu Zaid with Nelson 2004, in which Abū Zayd tells the story of his life and works.

[120] *The Washington Post*, 20 December 1996, p. A49.

[121] Cf. Miller 1996, p. 70.

[122] Fernea 1998, p. 414.

Imām (*The Fall of the Imam*) (1987) was seen as a condemnation of ideological religious circles for taking part in the oppression of Arab women.[123] The setting of *Jannāt wa-Iblīs* (*Jannāt and Iblīs*) (1992), seen as a sequel to *Suqūṭ al-Imām*,[124] is an insane asylum where God and Satan are confined together as patients, and this is all it took for Muslim radicals to be quick in branding the book as blasphemy.[125] In an open letter sent in May 2001 over the Internet following the start of their state-sponsored divorce proceedings, al-Sa'dāwī and her husband Sharīf Ḥitāta (Sherif Hetata) (b. 1923) asked intellectuals and writers all over the world to launch a campaign in support of them.[126] Al-Sa'dāwī gave an interview in March 2001 to the Egyptian weekly *al-Maydān*, where she was quoted as saying that the rituals in the Muslim *Ḥajj* pilgrimage had pre-Islamic origins; she also called for sexual equality in Muslim inheritance laws. The Egyptian Mufti issued a statement regarding her opinions, saying that they transgressed the laws of Islam. A few days later, the Islamist lawyer Nabīh al-Waḥsh filed a case against her, arguing that she must divorce her husband on the basis of the concept of *Ḥisba*.[127] On 30 July 2001 a Cairo court threw out the petition, ruling that no individual

123 Al-Sa'dāwī 1987. For an English translation, see El Sa'adawi 1995. On the novel, see Malti-Douglas 1995, pp. 91–117 (for a review of Malti-Douglas' book, see *Yearbook of Comparative and General Literature* 43 [1995], pp. 175–7). Some Arab intellectuals argue that the fact that Arabic is considered a holy language is the cause (even if indirect) for the oppression of the female (al-Jazzār 2002, p. 142).

124 Al-Sa'dāwī 1992. For the English translation entitled *The Innocence of the Devil*, see El Sa'adawi 1994. On the novel, see Malti-Douglas 1995, pp. 118–41; and Malti-Douglas' introduction to El Sa'adawi 1994, pp. xi–xiv. In other novels, al-Sa'dawī mentions how Islam is being abused to oppress women, such as in *Mawt al-Rajul al-Waḥīd 'alā al-Arḍ* (1978 [1974]), which was published in English as *God Dies by the Nile* (1985). For a view of the novel from a socialist feminist perspective, see Balaa 2013, pp. 187–211.

125 Cf. Malti-Douglas 1995, pp. 6, 95. On al-Sa'dāwī's attitude toward the Islamist discourse, see her essay about al-Ṣādiq al-Nayhūm's book *al-Islām fī al-Asr* (al-Nayhūm 1991) published in al-Nayhūm 1994, pp. 297–301 (published originally in *al-Nāqid* 49 [July 1992]. On al-Nayhūm, see also below, p. 129). Nawāl al-Sa'dāwī has been mentioned as one of the principal sources from whom the English writer Rosalind Miles (b. 1943) in *The Women's History of the World* (Miles 1988) and Salman Rushdie in *The Satanic Verses* (Rushdie 1988) garnered the diatribes against Islam (Sardar and Davies 1990, p. 168). Miles sees monotheistic religions as conspiracies against women, as "the result of divine inspiration transmitted from a male power to males empowered for this purpose, thereby enshrining maleness itself as power" (Miles 1988, p. 59; cf. Sardar and Davies 1990, pp. 165–76). On the Rushdie affair, see below, pp. 138–47.

126 Already in 1983, Sharīf Ḥitāta described the insecurity and fear in Egypt (see Khalafallah and Walmsley 1983, pp. 23–4).

127 According to email messages from Sherifa Zuhur on 5, 11, and 17 May 2001. Zuhur and Sondra Hale launched a campaign in support of al-Sa'dāwī against the attempt to force her separation from her husband on grounds of her apostasy. On the case, see also the *Daily Telegraph*, 25 April 2001; *al-Ādāb*, May–June 2001; and the news release issued on 27 July 2001 by the Amnesty International Secretariat (according to ainews@amnesty.org).

could petition a court to forcibly divorce another person. Al-Saʿdāwī, who did not attend the court session, said afterward that she would campaign for *Ḥisba* to be removed from the law books entirely.[128]

Similar cases occurred in Egypt quite frequently. For example, in May 2000 the Islamist-oriented opposition Labor Party and its newspaper *al-Shaʿb* led a public campaign against the novel *Walīma li-Aʿshāb al-Baḥr (Nashīd al-Mawt)* (*A Banquet for Seaweed* [*The Hymn of Death*]) by the Syrian Ḥaydar Ḥaydar (b. 1938), which they said defamed Islam. They subsequently demanded the resignation of the Culture Minister because his ministry reprinted the novel.[129] Claiming that the novel denigrated the Prophet Muḥammad and the Qur'ān, Islamist students organized demonstrations in which dozens of them were wounded in clashes with the Egyptian police. Ḥaydar himself said that the campaign against the novel, first published in 1983, was based on passages taken out of context.[130] Following the clashes the Egyptian authorities effectively froze (on a temporary basis) the activities of the Islamist-oriented opposition Labor Party and shut down its newspaper *al-Shaʿb*.[131] The writer and foreign editor of *al-Ahrām*, Muḥammad Salamāwī (b. 1945), explained that the demonstrations should be seen as an attempt by the Muslim extremists to gain political power.[132]

In a press release published on 9 May 2000, the Egyptian Organization for Human Rights expressed its alarm over the campaign against Ḥaydar and the Egyptian writer Idwār (Edward) al-Kharrāṭ (1926–2015), warning that judging creative works on anything other than artistic grounds was tantamount to imposing a religious and/or political filter on human thought. The organization said that past experience had proven that the intensity of

128 *Reuters*, 30 July 2001. *Ḥisba* is the divinely sanctioned duty of the ruler to intervene and coercively "enjoin good and forbid wrong" in order to keep everything in order and in accordance with Islamic law.

129 Ḥaydar 2000. The first edition of the novel, which was written between 1974 and 1983 in Algeria, Lebanon, and Cyprus, was published in Beirut at the author's expense (Ḥaydar 1983) after publishers had refused to put it out. A second edition was published by Dār Amwāj in Beirut (Ḥaydar 1988). On the novel, see *Adab wa-Naqd* 21 (April–May 1986), pp. 25–54. For excerpts from the novel translated into English, see *Edebiyât* 13.1 (2003), pp. 37–48. A translation of the entire novel by Allen Hibbard and Osama Esber is expected to be published (see <http://arablit.org/2013/10/02/a-banquet-for-seaweed-finally-coming-to-english-read-an-excerpt/ > [last accessed 21 May 2016]).

130 According to the *Associated Press* (13 May 2000).

131 *Reuters*, 20 May 2000.

132 *BBC World Service*, 9 May 2000. On the controversy surrounding Ḥaydar's novel and the political protest that the novel ignited, see also *The New York Times*, 9 May 2000, p. A5; and *AlJadid* (Los Angeles) 31 (2000). In *al-Ādāb*, July–August 2000, the Syrian critic ʿAbd al-Razzāq ʿĪd (b. 1950) argues against a "secular" interpretation of the novel that, while "protecting" the writer from possible death, "kills" the literary value of the work. On the case, see also Abbās 2001.

the persecutorial discourse could lead to violence. It cited previous cases in which a number of writers and artists who were exposed to similar campaigns ended up as victims of physical violence. These cases included the assassination of Faraj Fawda (Farag Foda) (1946–92) and the attempts during the 1990s to assassinate novelist Najīb Maḥfūẓ (1911–2006) and journalist Makram Muḥammad Aḥmad (b. 1935). Noting that the perpetrators of these crimes had never even read the works of their victims but were incited instead by the very discourse of violence, the organization called upon intellectuals to work against the phenomenon of cultural violence and urged the Egyptian authorities to duly protect freedom of expression and belief as well as literary and artistic creativity.[133] In 2003 the Academy of Islamic Research, the highest institute of al-Azhar, issued a *fatwā* confiscating the poetry collection *Waṣāyā fī 'Ishq al-Nisā'* (*Commandments in the Love of Women*) by the Egyptian poet Aḥmad al-Shahāwī (b. 1960) for "the glorification of sexual pleasure" and for using phrases from the Qur'ān and the *Ḥadīth* in inappropriate contexts.[134] In 2016 the writer Aḥmad Nājī (b. 1985) was sentenced to two years in prison for defaming Egypt's public morals in his novel *Istikhdām al-Ḥayāt* (*The Use of Life*), which contains numerous sex and drug references.[135] I was personally exposed as well to a campaign of defamation when my book *Rak'atān fī al-'Ishq: Dirāsa fī Shi'r 'Abd al-Wahhāb al-Bayyātī* (*Two Rak'as in Love: A Study of 'Abd al-Wahhāb al-Bayyātī's Poetry*) (2002) was published.[136] On 17 November 2015 the Palestinian poet Ashraf Fayyāḍ (b. 1980) was sentenced to death by a Saudi Arabian court for apostasy. On 2 February 2016 the sentence was modified to eight years in prison and 800 lashes.[137] Also, Dārīn Tātūr (Dareen Tatour) (b. 1982), a Palestinian citizen of Israel, was accused that her poetic posts on social media "are incitement to violence and terrorism, and support for a terrorist organization." She faces up to eight years in prison, if convicted on all charges. Her case is still pending.[138] The poet Muḥammad al-'Ajamī (b. 1975) from Qatar was jailed for life in 2012 for a poem he wrote about authoritarian rule in the region, in which he expressed his support for the uprising in Tunis. According to al-'Ajamī,

133 According to EOHR's website (<http://en.eohr.org/> [last accessed 14 October 2016]).

134 See *al-Riyāḍ*, 4 November 2003; and <http://www.albawaba.com> (4 November 2003) (last accessed 14 October 2016).

135 BBC, 20 April 2016. For the text of the novel, see <http://ketab4pdf.blogspot.co.il/2016/02/pdf-Download-novel-use-life-book-Ayman-Ahmed-Naji-Zargani.html> (last accessed 16 September 2016). The novel was publihsed in Italian translation: *Vita: istruzioni per l'uso* (2016).

136 See <https://archive.is/3mS8D> (3 September 2008) (last accessed 14 October 2016).

137 *The Guardian*, 2 February 2016.

138 See <http://www.haaretz.com/israel-news/.premium-1.720418>(21 May 2016) (last accessed 14 October 2016).

"we are all Tunisia in the face of the repressive elite." He also denounced "all Arab governments" as "indiscriminate thieves." The sentence was reduced to fifteen years on appeal in 2013. In March 2016 he was freed after receiving a pardon from the emir.[139]

Similar cases even occurred in Arab countries known for their openness. This included Lebanon, which has long been regarded as "the most liberal state in the Arab world."[140] For example, in December 1969 the scholar Ṣādiq Jalāl al-ʿAẓm (1934–2016) was jailed for several days following the publication of his book *Naqd al-Fikr al-Dīnī* (*A Critique of Religious Thought*) (1969).[141] Although it is a multi-religious society, Lebanon has laws prohibiting the slander of religion, and al-ʿAẓm and the Lebanese thinker Bashīr al-Dāʿūq (1931–2007), owner of the Lebanese publisher Dār al-Ṭalīʿa, were accused of offending Christianity and Islam. In July 1970, however, both of them were found not guilty.

In September 1996 the Lebanese composer, *ʿūd* (oud) player, and singer Mārsīl Khalīfa (Marcel Khalife) (b. 1940) was charged with blasphemy and with "defaming" Islam for setting to music a poem that included a verse from the Qur'ān about the biblical figure of Joseph; his song "Anā Yūsuf Yā Abī" ("Oh, My Father, I am Yūsuf") was released in 1995 on the album *Rakwat ʿArab* (*Arabic Coffeepot*). According to the chief prosecutor of Beirut, Khalīfa—a Maronite Christian who has won a cult following in the Arab world and the Arab diaspora through his nationalistic songs and who has been nicknamed in the West "the Bob Dylan of the Middle East"[142]—was alleged to have "insulted Islam." The music of the song is Khalīfa's, while the lyrics are based on a poem by the Palestinian poet Maḥmūd Darwīsh (1941–2008) from his collection *Ward Aqall* (*Fewer Roses*), which was inspired by the Lebanon War (1982) and its aftermath:

أنا يوسف يا أبي. يا أبي، إخوتي لا يحبّونني، لا يريدونني بينهم يا أبي. يعتدّون عليّ ويرمونني بالحصى والكلام. يريدونني أن أموت لكي يمدحوني. وهم أوصدوا باب بيتك دوني. وهم طردوني من الحقل. هم سمّموا عنبي يا أبي. وهم حطّموا لعبي يا أبي. حين مرّ النسيم ولاعب شعري غاروا وثاروا عليّ وثاروا عليك، فماذا صنعتُ لهم يا أبي؟ الفراشات حطّت على كتفيّ، ومالت عليّ السنابل، والطير حلّق فوق يديّ. فماذا فعلت أنا يا أبي، ولماذا أنا؟ أنت سمّيتني يوسفا، وهمو

139 See <http://www.bbc.com/news/world-middle-east-35830372> (last accessed 16 March 2016).

140 Hafez 2001, p. 27.

141 For the book, see al-ʿAẓm 1988 [1969]. Some documents of the trial of the writer and the publisher appear in an appendix (pp. 146–60). See also al-Azm 2014; al-Azm 2014a; and al-Azm 2014b. Cf. Kassab 2010, pp. 74–81.

142 WNYC, New York Public Radio, 24 October 2005.

أوقعوني في الجبّ، واتّهموا الذئب؛ والذئــب أرحم من إخوتي، أبت!
هل جنيت على أحد عندما قلت إني رأيت أحد عشر كوكبا، والشمـــــس
والقمر، رأيتهم لي ساجدينْ.

Oh, my father, I am Joseph. Oh father, my brothers neither love me nor want me in their midst, Oh
Father, they assault me and cast stones and words at me. They want me dead so
They can eulogize me. They closed the door of your house and left me outside. They expelled me from the field. Oh, my father, they
Poisoned my grapes. They destroyed my toys. When the passing gentle breeze caressed my
Hair they were jealous, they flamed up with rage against me and you. What did I do to them, Oh my father?
The butterflies landed on my shoulder, the ears of grain bent down to me and the bird hovered over
My hands. What have I done, Oh my father? And why me? You named me Joseph and they
Threw me into the well and accused the wolf and the wolf is more merciful than my brothers, Oh, my father!
Did I wrong anyone when I said that I saw eleven stars, and the sun
And the moon; I saw them bowing down before me.[143]

The last lines use the fourth verse from *Sūrat Yūsuf*, in which Joseph addresses his father, Jacob (both Joseph and Jacob were revered in Islam as prophets):

إِذْ قَالَ يُوسُفُ لأَبِيهِ يَا أَبَتِ إِنِّي رَأَيْتُ أَحَدَ عَشَرَ كَوْكَبًا، وَالشَّمْسَ وَالْقَمَرَ رَأَيْتُهُمْ لِي سَاجِدِينَ.

When Joseph said to his father, “Father, I saw eleven stars, and the sun and the moon; I saw them bowing down before me.”[144]

As in other poems included in *Ward Aqall*, Darwīsh describes the suffering of Palestinian Arabs at the hands of other Arabs.[145] Without any intent to violate the sacredness of the Qur'ān, the poet employs the story of Joseph and his brothers in the same way that he uses the story of Cain and Abel in the poem “Yu'āniqu Qātilahu” (“Embracing His Killer”),[146] from the same collection, to illustrate how the Palestinian Abel strives desperately to elicit the mercy of a brother who is about to slay him.[147]

143 Darwīsh 1987a, p. 77. For another translation, by Manal Swairjo, see *AlJadid* 28 (Summer 1999), p. 16.
144 *Yūsuf* 4. The translation is according to Arberry 1979 [1964], p. 226.
145 On *Ward Aqall*, see Snir 2004–5, pp. 17–85; Snir 2008, pp. 123–66; and Snir 2015, pp. 89–111.
146 On this story as an archetypal conflict in classical and modern Arabic literature, see Günther 1999, pp. 309–36.
147 Darwīsh 1987a, p. 33. One cannot ignore the possibility of other interpretations. The Iraqi

The chief prosecutor of Beirut charged Khalīfa with blasphemy, even though the singer had obtained permission from Lebanon's General Security Censorship Bureau to release the song. If Khalīfa had been convicted he would have faced six months to three years in prison. The Lebanese thinker and lawyer ʻAbd Allāh Zakhyā (b. 1930), a close friend of Khalīfa, considered the charge a dangerous precedent undermining the freedom of expression in Lebanon: "The move takes us back to the Dark Ages. I fear this could be a precedent for silencing all voices, not only political, but also cultural." In a reference to the Egyptian court's decision regarding Abū Zayd, Zakhyā said that the charge against Khalīfa "is as ugly as what is happening in Egypt."[148]

Khalīfa's was an interesting test case, because while some Muslim scholars maintain that all singing of the Qur'ān is forbidden, others have had no qualms about making lyrical recordings of the Qur'ān, and tapes of clerics singing verses from Islam's holy book can be bought in many places.[149] Also, Qur'ānic verses, whether in the original Arabic or translated into Persian, have been routinely used in Iranian revolutionary songs since 1979. Perhaps that was the reason why the Higher Shiite Council in Lebanon, while issuing a statement that Islamic law does not allow verses from the Qur'ān to be included in popular songs, disagreed with the drive to place Khalīfa on trial.[150] On charges against Khalīfa, Stephen P. Sheehi, an American intellectual and scholar of Lebanese descent, had this to say:

poet and scholar Sinan Antoon (b. 1967), for example, believed that the poem was reflecting the suffering caused by fellow Arabs, since the different Palestinian rival factions were being manipulated and used as tools by Arab regimes. As for the Cain and Abel myth, Antoon saw it as reflecting the rivalry between Arabs and Jews. Antoon based his interpretation upon the presentation of the poem as a song by Marcel Khalīfa, who for a long time was a member of the Lebanese Communist Party, and the fact that most of his songs focus on the Palestinian and Lebanese resistance in southern Lebanon and on the *Intifāḍa* in the Occupied Territories. Antoon also mentioned that Khalīfa's songs had been banned in a number of Arab countries and that the first time he was allowed to perform in Jordan was during the 1991 Jarash festival. "Every reading is a misreading," according to Antoon, "however, and without delving into theories of interpretation, I doubt that Marcel Khalife would have chosen this poem if it highlighted Palestinian–Palestinian violence. That would defeat the purpose of his work, as manifested in numerous interviews and on many occasions" (quoted from Sinan Antoon's message in *adabiyat* <adabiyat@listhost.uchicago.edu, 24 September 1996). For another poem, by the Palestinian poet Mūsā Ḥawāmida (b. 1959), which employs the story of Joseph, see Faḍl 2002, pp. 165–7.

148 Based on a *United Press International* wire report from Beirut, 19 September 1996 (according to adabiyat@listhost.uchicago.edu [19 September 1996]).

149 According to early Islamic tradition, listening to the recital of the Qur'ān accompanied by music is considered by certain scholars to be a sin of disobedience to God (Kister 1999, p. 61). On the issue of setting verses of the Qur'ān to music, see Baybars 1970, pp. 118–27.

150 Chalala 1999, p. 7.

> This is a politically motivated witch hunt by Prime Minister Ḥarīrī [1944–2005]. For some time, he has had an active campaign to intimidate, if not silence, his critics. In addition to threatening directly or indirectly innumerable right- and left-wing opponents, left-wing artists like Ziyād Raḥbānī [b. 1956] have been physically threatened by al-Ḥarīrī's squadrisimi.[151]

Likewise, Muslim and Christian poets, writers, and journalists said they were disgusted by charges against Khalīfa, calling them bizarre and reminiscent of campaigns waged against intellectuals in certain other Islamic countries. The poet Paul Shā'ūl (b. 1942) said that this edict was comparable to those edicts issued in Egypt, Sudan, India, and Pakistan "and before them the Inquisition courts of the dark Middle Ages." Another poet, Shawqī Bazīgh (b. 1951), said the charges against the writer al-Ṣādiq al-Nayhūm (1937–94) and the confiscation in 1991 of those of his books that were considered to be an offense against Islam[152] "falsify Beirut's spirit and role" as a cultural center.[153] Another poet wrote: "It is as if we face a new version of the saga of Youssef Chahine [Yūsuf Shāhīn; 1926–2008] and his film *The Emigrant* [*al-Muhājir*, 1994]."[154] Darwīsh himself criticized the legal proceedings in an interview on 10 October 1999 with the Lebanese daily *al-Diyār*, stating that fundamentalism is in the process of stifling culture and creation in the Arab world: "We should all be ashamed. If Khalīfa is found guilty, it will be an insult to culture."[155]

On 2 October 1999 the newly appointed investigating judge, 'Abd

151 According to adabiyat@listhost.uchicago.edu (20 September 1996).

152 On al-Ṣādiq al-Nayhūm's outlook and the reactions to it, see al-Nayhūm 1991; and al-Nayhūm 1994.

153 Cf. *AlJadid* (Los Angeles) 28 (Summer 1999), pp. 8–9.

154 Based on a *Reuters* report from Beirut dated 21 September 1996 (according to adabiyat@listhost.uchicago.edu [22 September 1996]). Following this case, the journal *AlJadid* (Los Angeles) dedicated an entire issue to the freedom of artists, intellectuals, and media outlets in Lebanon (2.11 [September 1996]). Among the articles published in this issue were "Arab Artists, Intellectuals, Condemn Charges against Khalife as Attack on Liberty, Civil Freedom," by Elie Chalala; "We Turn the Page from City to City" by Marcel Khalīfa himself; "Marcel Khalife and the Modern Inquisition" by Paul Sha'ūl; and "Lebanese Media Restrictions Stir Broad Opposition" by Michelle A. Marzahn. On the case, see also *AlJadid* (Los Angeles) 28 (Summer 1999). On the general issue of the freedom of expression in Lebanon, see Samāḥ Idrīs' (b. 1961) editorial in *al-Ādāb* 11–12 (1999). On how Shāhīn's controversial film narrowly escaped being banned for allegedly depicting Joseph, see Wild 1996, pp. 379–90 and the references in nn. 21 and 22; and Ayalon 1999, p. 33. On the film, see Qāsim 2002, pp. 911–12. At the 50th Cannes Film Festival (May 1997), a special lifetime achievement award was presented to Shāhīn (on Shāhīn in general, see Cluny 1978, pp. 161–72; al-Ṣāwī 1990; Culhane 1995, pp. 49–56, 71–5; Darwish 1998, p. 43; and Russell 1998, pp. 47–50). On the attempt to ban Umm Kulthūm's singing of Aḥmad Rāmī's translation of *Rubā'iyyāt al-Khayyām* (Khayyām 1977), see Turkiyya 1999, pp. 208–11.

155 According to Human Rights Watch <hrwatchnyc@igc.org> (1 November 1999). Cf. Chalala 1999, p. 7.

al-Raḥmān Shihāb, recommended that prosecutors bring criminal charges against Khalīfa for "insulting religious values," and the next day senior Sunnī Muslim clerics in Lebanon ruled that singing verses from the Qur'ān was absolutely unacceptable. Under article 473 of Lebanon's penal code, blasphemy in public is punishable by one month to one year in prison. Article 474 of the penal code authorizes imprisonment for six months to three years for publicly insulting a religion. The highest Sunnī Muslim religious authority in Lebanon, Grand Mufti Muḥammad Rāshid Qabbānī (b. 1942), maintained that "there is a limit to freedom of expression. One limit is that it should not infringe on people's religious beliefs." In reply Hanny Megally (b. 1953), executive director of the Middle East and North Africa division of Human Rights Watch, said that this case was a direct legal challenge to the right to freedom of expression in Lebanon and that the court had the opportunity to establish an important legal precedent by issuing a verdict in Khalīfa's favor.[156] In another move, the American-Arab Anti-Discrimination Committee (ADC) encouraged intellectuals throughout the world to sign a petition on behalf of the singer, saying that the charges against him were a

> flagrant violation of intellectual freedoms which should be guaranteed to artists in all countries [...] In fact, the song is dedicated to the people of Lebanon and Palestine, referring symbolically to their suffering, using the narrative of the Prophet Joseph's famous story. We are shocked to see Lebanon—the country that has long prided itself as a haven for artists and intellectuals—embark on prosecuting one of its best artists even as the country celebrates its capital, Beirut, as the cultural capital of the Arab world.[157]

In the middle of December 1999 Khalīfa was acquitted by the court.[158] This was not the first time that charges of blasphemy had been leveled against singers in the Arab world. Two major instances were of poems that the Egyptian musician and singer Muḥammad 'Abd al-Wahhāb (1901–91) set to music and sang: "al-Ṭalāsim" ("The Talismans"), written by the *Mahjarī* poet Īliyyā Abū Māḍī (1889–1957),[159] and "Min Ghayr Leh" ("Without Asking Why"), written by 'Abd al-Wahhāb himself.[160]

[156] According to Human Rights Watch <hrwatchnyc@igc.org> (1 November 1999).

[157] According to msanews@msanews.mynet.net (*MSANEWS*) (19 October 1999).

[158] According to *Ha'aretz* (Tel Aviv), 19 December 1999, p. A3.

[159] For the original poem, known for its repeated phrase *lastu adrī* ("I do not know"), see Abū Māḍī n.d., pp. 191–214. On an ironic poetic allusion to Abū Māḍī's poem, see Adūnīs' poem "Bayna 'Aynayki wa-Baynī" ("Between Your Eyes and Mine")—the persona in the latter goes even further than Abū Māḍī's naïve and innocent wanderings, adopting divine knowledge, which "justifies" the image of Adūnīs as a heretic and saboteur among Islamist circles.

[160] On the poem and the attempt to ban it, see Nieuwkerk 1995, p. 65. The Jewish writer of Iraqi origin Mnashshī Za'rūr (1897–1972) mentioned in an interview (*al-Sharq*, May–June

Arabic literature that developed after the rise of Islam is still sometimes described by several scholars as Islamic literature.[161] It is a generalized ideological approach to literature that sees the Arabic literary system as a cultural product of Islam, overlooking the interactions between the literary texts and the discursive contexts within which they were produced and effacing the diverse literary and social movements which developed over time. For these scholars, Islam, as a system of symbols, is the most significant explanatory mechanism for Arab cultural, intellectual, and literary history. However, although the Arabic literary system had, since the seventh century, generally existed within the confines of Islam and been controlled by the cultural heritage that had become nearly as sacred as religious law, it has never been an entirely religious phenomenon.[162] In the 1950s a strong tendency appeared which had as its aim the separation of Arabic literature from its Islamic base in order to let it follow its natural course as an emerging modern secularized literature.[163] There is no better illustration of this development than the deep rift that one can see between the Egyptian poet and prose writer Muḥammad Tawfīq al-Bakrī (1870–1932) and the Syrian poet Adūnīs (b. 1930).[164]

Al-Bakrī was a typical representative of "neoclassical" Arabic rhetorical prose style and the author of *Ṣahārīj al-Lu'lu'* (*The Reservoirs of Pearls*),[165] which he said was an attempt to achieve the eloquence of al-Ḥarīrī (1054–1122) and the language of Ru'ba ibn al-'Ajjāj (685–762). This by no means religious work contains three travel accounts (two from France and one from Constantinople in the Ottoman Empire), an ode to solitude, the

1977, p. 63) that Abū Māḍī's poem is similar to an Iraqi popular song, the concluding words of which are as follows:

أنـــا مـنـين   وأنـــت منـين
تايه دلوني   الطريق منين

Where am I from? Where are you from?
I am lost, please guide me to take the right road.

161 See, for example, Ullah 1963, pp. 172–211; Kritzeck 1970; and Allana 1973.

162 Cf. Shukrī 1978 [1968], p. 19.

163 This trend, supported mainly by Arab writers and intellectuals living in the West, was represented by avant-garde journals like *Mawāqif* (Paris and Beirut) and much more radically by *Farādīs* (Cologne and Paris). The latter's editor, 'Abd al-Qādir al-Janābī (b. 1944), considers Arab-Muslim classical heritage as merely a linguistic one (personal communication, 17 August 2005). For an illustration of the main conceptions of this trend, see al-Bīṭār 1969, pp. 34–50; and Sharabi 1988. See also the articles and literary texts published during the last two decades by al-Janābī on the liberal Arab website <http://www.elaph.com> (last accessed 15 October 2016).

164 The history of Arabic literature provided many examples of Christian contributions being significant in changing literary norms, but these changes only came about after the participation of Muslim writers in reformist efforts (Moreh 1976, pp. 57–8).

165 See al-Bakrī 1907. On using such terms as "neoclassical" for describing trends in modern Arab poetry, see below, p. 193n.

description of a ball in Vienna, a glorification of Saladin, and, finally, the announcement of the birth of the author's son. In the travel accounts, al-Bakrī tried his hand at imitating French poetic prose when he described the Bois de Boulogne and the Battle of Austerlitz, but the result was artificial and stiff, and full of allusions to Arabic proverbs and historical events. Since he was fond of employing *gharīb* (arcane words), frequent similes, and classical poetic diction (sometimes even for romantic themes), the author's style is hardly "modern." Al-Bakrī's poetry and prose writings were considered to be canonical by the literary establishment of his time.[166] According to ʿAbbās Maḥmūd al-ʿAqqād (1889–1964), al-Bakrī's love poem "Dhāt al-Qawāfī" ("Endowed with Rhymes") was the first to use *shiʿr mursal* (blank verse).[167] Al-Bakrī, however, was not only a distinguished poet from the canonical center of the Arabic literary system, but he was also a religious notable who belonged to the Bakriyya Sufi brotherhood (*ṭarīqa*). He was eventually appointed Sheikh of this brotherhood and promoted to the leadership of all Sufi brotherhoods (*Mashyakhat al-Mashāʾikh* [Sheikdom of Sheiks]) and of the organization which registered the descendants of the Prophet (*Niqābat al-Ashrāf* [Society of Sherifs]).[168]

Since the 1930s no poet has succeeded in being a central figure in the Arabic literary system and a traditional religious notable at the same time; literary modernism has not been able to live in harmony with traditional religious concepts. The literary vision of Adūnīs, perhaps the most significant representative of the canonical center in contemporary Arabic poetry, differs radically not only from that of al-Bakrī but also from that of the whole of canonical Arabic literature in the first half of the twentieth century. The "Arabic-Islamic concept," as Adūnīs himself refers to the old framework in his comments about Aḥmad Shawqī's poetry,[169] has been supplanted by a new concept which holds that the Islamic literary heritage is a purely literary and cultural heritage.[170] Adūnīs sees two major trends in the 1950s in the

[166] He was, for example, among the six poets whom Khalīl Muṭrān (1872–1949) wrote about in detail in his essay "The Contemporary Poets" published in 1912 in an anthology edited by Muṣṭafā Luṭfī al-Manfalūṭī (1876–1924). The other poets were Ismāʿīl Ṣabrī (1854–1923), Aḥmad Shawqī (1868–1932), Ḥāfiẓ Ibrāhīm (1872–1932), Maḥmūd Sāmī al-Bārūdī (1838–1904), and Ibrāhīm al-Yāzijī (1847–1906) (al-Manfalūṭī 1954 [1912], pp. 65–76).

[167] On al-Bakrī and his literary activities, see Brockelmann 1937–49, *Suppl.*, III, pp. 81–2; al-Dasūqī 1959, II, pp. 401–36; Kaḥḥāla 1960, IX, p. 141; Moreh 1976, pp. 130–3; Fahmī 1982; Brugman 1984, pp. 80–2; al-Ziriklī 1984, VI, pp. 65–6; and Meisami and Starkey 1998, I, p. 131.

[168] Among al-Bakrī's works is also *Bayt al-Ṣiddīq*, in which he outlined his autobiography as well as his religious and literary career (al-Bakrī 1905, pp. 11–26).

[169] See Adūnīs 1982, pp. 18–22.

[170] Adūnīs' conceptions are presented here only from a literary point of view. As to his world-views, they have gone through several stages since the late 1940s. Ṣādiq Jalāl al-ʿAẓm

field of Arabic poetic modernism, one stressing the national Arab identity and the other inspired by Marxist communism. There is, however, according to him, a third trend which reads Arabic heritage in a different way, namely, that it not only consists of *Jāhiliyya* (pre-Islamic) poetry but of literary works from cultures with which Arabs have interacted over the centuries, including the Sumarian, Babylonian, and Canaanite cultures:

> هكذا اتّخذت العروبيّة في هذه النظرة بعدا آخر: لم تعد عروبيّة العرق أو الجنس، وإنما أصبحت عروبيّة اللغة والثقافة بحيث تنصهر في هذه العروبيّة اللغوية الثقافية تلك الموروثات القديمة كلّها. كانت هذه النـظرة ترى، بتعبير آخر، إلى الموروث الشعري-الثقافي العربي، لا من حيث أنه كلّيّة منفصلة قائمة بذاتها، بل من حيث أنه استمرار حيّ لتراث حضاري يرقى إلى خمسة آلاف سنة. وعلى هذا، فإن اللغة العربية لا تأخذ فرادتها وخصوصيّتها من استيعابها الهائل للتراث الجاهلي-الإسلامي وحسب، وإنما تأخذها كذلك من غناها، وسعتها، وقابليّتها المستمرّة للتجدّد والاتّساع أي من عبقريّة احتضانها ذلك العالم القديم الذي سبقها، ومن أنها امتداده التاريخي، وتكامله الخلاّق.

In that conception, Arabism took on another dimension: It was not an Arabism of race and nation but an Arabism of language and culture so that all ancient heritages are melted in this linguistic and cultural Arabism. In other words, this conception considered the Arabic cultural poetic heritage not as a separate independent bloc but as the living continuity of a civilized heritage going back some five thousand years. Hence, the Arabic language does not only take its individuality and particularity from the fact of its containing the whole of the pre-Islamic and Islamic heritage, but also from the fact of its richness and continuing capacity to revive and widen, that is, from its genius to absorb that ancient world that preceded it, and from being its historical extension and creative completion.[171]

refers to Adūnīs' intellectual stage in the 1990s as *dāʿiya min duʿāt al-istishrāq al-islāmānī al-maʿkūs* ("one of the propagandists of reversed Islamist Orientalism") (al-ʿAẓm 1992, p. 67). That stage is illustrated by his arguments following Iran's Islamic revolution in 1979 (e.g. *Mawāqif* 34 [Winter 1979], p. 158), which contradicted his outlook ten years earlier (e.g. *Mawāqif* 6 [October–December 1969], p. 3). According to al-ʿAẓm, Adūnīs' intellectual stage at the time can be summarized by the following (al-ʿAẓm 1992, p. 71): "Adūnīs takes the side of the East precisely as the majority of the Orientalists have taken the side of the West; he considers Western thought as being based on material factors while arguing that Eastern thought is based on spiritual factors, and who could dare now to prefer the material over the spiritual?!" Al-ʿAẓm also ridiculed Adūnīs' frequent ideological transformations, and he mentions that the latter's current rejection of nationalism, secularism, socialism, Marxism, communism, and capitalism should be viewed against the background of his previous nationalism, secularism, Nasserist socialism, and radical leftism (al-ʿAẓm 1992, p. 70). On Adūnīs' intellectual development and his "reverse Orientalism" as viewed against the background of Edward W. Said's *Orientalism* (Said 1985 [1978]), see also al-ʿAzm 1981, pp. 5–26 (= al-ʿAzm 1984, pp. 349–76); and al-ʿAẓm 1992, pp. 49–85. On Adūnīs' conceptions, see also Snir 2006, pp. 117–30; and Snir 2012, pp. 11–108.

171 Adūnīs 1993, pp. 101–2. Cf. the views expressed by Ṭāhā Ḥusayn in his *Mustaqbal al-Thaqāfa fī Miṣr* (*The Future of Culture in Egypt*) (Ḥusayn 2001 [1938]; English translation: Hussein 1954). The literary critic Jihād Fāḍil distorts this conception when he speaks of Adūnīs' attempt to "fragment the Arab-Islamic heritage and divide it into [different]

In order to illustrate this new concept of modernism, let us take a look at "neo-classical" poetry's attitude toward the Qur'ānic text, on the one hand, and the attitude of the new poetry advocated by Adūnīs, on the other. Shawqī's poem "al-Jāmi'a al-Miṣriyya" ("The Egyptian University"),[172] recited during the inauguration of the university's institutions in 1931, includes a clear allusion to the Qur'ān:

إسكندرية، عاد كنزك سالما　　حتى كأن لم يلتهمه ضـــرام
لمّته من لهب الحريق أنامل　　برد على ما لامست، وسلام

Alexandria, your treasure has returned safe, as if the fire never swallowed it up.
It was gathered from the flames by fingertips, coolness be with what they have touched, and safety.

These verses indicate that the city, which in antiquity had been one of the great cultural centers, is regaining its glory in modern Egypt. Mentioning the fire that is said to have destroyed Alexandria's Royal Library, Shawqī alludes to a Qur'ānic verse:

قُلْنَا: يَا نَارُ كُونِي بَرِدًا وَسَلامًا عَلى إبْراهِيمَ.

We said: "O fire, be coolness and safety for Abraham!"[173]

This allusion is considered entirely within the linear mode of the intertextuality,[174] that is, it draws on the Qur'ānic image in a way that is in full agreement with the religious discourse. Such a linear intertextual allusion to the same Qur'ānic verse is found also in the poetry of non-Muslim Arab poets, an example of which can be found in two trope-laden verses composed by the Christian Nāṣīf al-Yāzijī (1800–71):[175]

في فتح عكّـا بردُ نارِ معاطبٍ　　دارِ الخليل وللديار به البُكـــا
رأسَ الثمانِ وأربعين بِطيـــّهِ　　مئتان مَعْ ألف فبارَك ربُّكـــا

The weeping over the remains of the encampment [of the beloved] during the occupation of Acre, the dwelling place of the lover, cools the flames of the destructions.
May God bless the beginning of forty eight together with two hundreds with one thousand.[176]

We can find such intertextual linear allusion to the same Qur'ānic verse also in the writing of the Egyptian-Jewish writer Murād Faraj (1866–1956).

'heritages'" (*shardhamat al-turāth al-'Arabī al-Islāmī wa-tafkīkuhu ilā turāthāt*) (Fāḍil 1996, p. 334).

172 Shawqī n.d., IV, pp. 10–13.

173 *Al-Anbiyā'* 69. The translation is according to Arberry 1979 [1964], p. 328.

174 Cf. Somekh 1991, p. 53. See also this linear use in prose: Turkiyya 1999, pp. 36, 245.

175 Al-Yāzijī 1904, p. 21.

176 On these verses, see below, p. 156.

Elaborating on a verse by the Jewish Andalusian poet Ibrāhīm ibn Sahl al-Ishbīlī al-Isrā'īlī (1208–59), which alludes to this Qur'ānic verse, Faraj says:

فاتّقاد وجنتيه تورّدا كنار إبراهيم بردا وسلاما.

His cheeks burned and became flushed like the fire of Abraham, be coolness and safety.[177]

That same discourse is totally rejected by Adūnīs in his poem "al-Mawt" ("Death"), subtitled "Thalāth Marthiyāt ilā Abī" ("Three Elegies for My Father"), from the collection *Qaṣā'id Ūlā* (*First Poems*) (1957). In the second elegy, he writes:

يا لهب النار الذي ضمّه
لا تك بردا، لا ترفرف سلامْ
في صدره النار التي كُوّرت
أرضا عبدناها وصيغت أنام.
لم يفنَ بالنار ولكنّه
عاد بها للمنشأ الأولِ
للزمن المقبلِ
كالشمس في خطورها الأولِ
تأفل عن أجفاننا بغتةً
وهي وراء الأفق لم تأفل.

Oh, the flames of the fire that embraced him
Do not be coolness, do not flutter safety
In his heart is the fire that was rolled up
Into a land we worshipped and that was shaped as men.
He did not die in the fire but
Took it back to the first source
To the coming time
As the sun in its first rising
Goes down suddenly from our eyelids
But over the horizon it did not go down.[178]

177 Faraj 1929, p. 35. See also the Iraqi-Jewish poet Shmuel Moreh (b. 1933) in "Ḍaḥkat al-Qadar" ("The Laugh of Destiny") (*al-Sharq*, March 1972, p. 8; Moreh 1998a, pp. 111–12). We may find it also in prose by Arabized Jews: In his autobiography *'Azza, Ḥafidat Nefertiti* (*'Azza, the Granddaughter of Nefertiti*), the Egyptian-Jewish writer Maurice (Mūrīs) Shammās (Abū Farīd) (1930–2013) used it with evident allusion to the Qur'ānic verse (Shammās 2003, p. 150. On the familiarity of Shammās with the Qur'ān, see Shammās 2003, pp. 5, 93). The Iraqi-Jewish writer Samīr Naqqāsh (1938–2004) in his novel *Nzūla wa-Khayṭ al-Shayṭān* (*Tenants and Cobwebs*) (1986) used the same allusion in a sexual context (Naqqāsh 1986, p. 21. Cf. Naqqāsh 1971, p. 104):

أنت الساعة يا صبرية في حضن افرايم، مشتعل الجمش والخمش والحضن والتقبيل، وبلا آخر ينهال على بدنك، يمطرك بردا وسلاما. يطفئ جمرة مستعرة في أعطافك.

178 Adūnīs 1988, I, pp. 39–40. This version of the elegy omits four lines of the original version

The ironic mode of the intertextuality[179] here is evident: While God commands fire to "be coolness and safety for Abraham," the speaker demands the very opposite. Not only does the Qur'ānic allusion function in a radically different way from what we find in the writing of Shawqī, Faraj, al-Yāzijī, and many others, but Adūnīs' text might also be seen as making a sarcastic comment on the original sacred verse.[180] In any case, according to Adūnīs the Qur'ān itself and the classical studies which deal with the Qur'ānic text justify the ironic poetic intertextuality. It is based on the new emerging aesthetic and critical principles that prompted the transformation from the "poetics of *Jāhilī* orality" (*shi'riyyat al-shafawiyya al-Jāhiliyya*) to the "poetics of writing" (*shi'riyyat al-kitāba*). Among these principles, Adūnīs mentions writing without imitation of any pre-existing model, the rejection of clarity, and the preeminence of ambiguity and obscurity as well as leaving behind the routine, the common, and the traditional.[181]

In the aforementioned poem of Adūnīs, the speaker assumes the role of God, that is, of the almighty power that can guarantee eternal life for his dead father. This experience of being parallel to or one with God has appeared in quite a few of Adūnīs' poems since the 1950s. For example, in "Asrār" ("Secrets"), the speaker says:

يضمّنا الموت إلى صدره
مغامرا زاهدا
يحملنا سرّا على سرّه
يجعل من كثرتنا واحدا.

(Adūnīs 1971, I, p. 117). On Adūnīs' attitude toward the Qur'ānic text, see Adūnīs 2000 [1985], pp. 33–55 (English translation: Adonis 1990, pp. 35–53); and Adūnīs 1993a, pp. 19–37. On the issue of the changing versions of his poems and his concept of "final version" (*ṣīgha nihā'iyya*), see the aesthetic and poetic justifications in Adūnīs 1988, I, pp. 5–7; and Snir 2012, pp. 57–64. Nevertheless, it goes without saying that several of Adūnīs' poems, especially from the early 1950s, were revised in subsequent editions because they reflected the Syrian ideology which he later abandoned. Adūnīs' first collection, *Qālat al-Arḍ* (*The Earth Says*) (Adūnīs 1954), for example, was changed in its subsequent editions to the point that it became "not a revised poetry but a new poetry" (Dāghir 1996, p. 16). Dār al-Jadīd in Beirut described the new edition of *Qālat al-Arḍ* in 1996—which is a faithful copy of the 1954 edition—as a "pirate edition" (*ṭab'a muqarṣana*), since it appeared without Adūnīs' approval. See also Bawārdī 1998, pp. 180–211.

179 On this mode in Arabic poetry, see Somekh 1991, p. 61.

180 Cf. the following lines by al-Bayyātī from "Qamar Shīrāz" from the eponymous collection (1979) (al-Bayyātī 1979, p. 517; al-Bayyātī 1984, p. 105):

أخفي فاجعة تحت قناع الكلمات. أقول لجرحي:
«لا تبرأ» ولحزني «لا تبرد» وأقول «اغتسلوا بدمي» للعشاق

181 Adūnīs 2000 [1985], pp. 52–5 (English translation: Adonis 1990, pp. 50–3).

Death embraces us on His breast[182]
Risking [His life], renouncing [worldly pleasures]
Bearing us as a secret on His secret
Making from our plurality One.[183]

"Poetry is against religion," says Adūnīs, "you will not find even one poet in Arab history who was religious."[184] Against this background, it is little wonder that radical religious circles considered Adūnīs to be a *mulḥid* (heretic) or *mukharrib* (saboteur).[185] However, interestingly, in contrast to the lives of other Muslim writers who deal with the Prophet in their work,[186] Adūnīs' life has never been under threat. Timothy Brennan states that there has traditionally been less tolerance toward attempts at humanizing Muhammad and historicizing the Qur'ān than at attempts to critique God himself.[187] The outstanding example is the Urdu poem "Shikwah" ("Complaint") by Muḥammad Iqbāl (1875–1938), in which he accuses God of infidelity. He catalogs all that Muslims have done for God over the centuries, yet God has neglected them and allowed the Muslim world to be destroyed. In one of the more startling lines of the poem, Iqbāl exclaims:

At times You have pleased us, at other times
(it is not to be said), You are a whore.[188]

Iqbāl was angrily denounced as a blasphemer, but his life was never in any danger.[189]

Adūnīs' new poetic vision has gradually made it to the center of the Arabic literary system. There is no better proof of this development than the sharp reactions to this vision from both ends of the literary system: On the one

182 An allusion to the death–rebirth cycle, probably also alluding to the *Iliad* (Homer 1983, p. 129).

183 Adūnīs 1988, I, p. 37. For the last line, see also Adūnīs' collection *Mufrad bi-Ṣīghat Jam'* (*Singular in the Form of Plural*) (1975).

184 *The New York Review of Books*, 16 April 2016. Cf. Kassab 2010, pp. 128–35.

185 See, for example, the Egyptian journal *al-I'tiṣām*, April 1989, p. 6, in which the poet is described as *al-muslim al-murtadd wa-l-mutanaṣṣir* ("the Christianized apostate Muslim"). When the Yemenite poet and scholar 'Abd al-'Azīz al-Maqāliḥ (b. 1939) was declared *mulḥid* by a Saudi journal, following the publication of one of his poems (*al-Majalla al-'Arabiyya*, May 1985, as quoted in Adūnīs 1993a, pp. 191–2), Adūnīs wrote some comments on the issue of poetry and blasphemy that might be considered a defense on his part against the accusations leveled at al-Maqāliḥ (Adūnīs 1993a, pp. 183–90). For Adūnīs' views regarding the traditional Islamic framework of Arabic culture, see his introduction to Shawqī 1982, pp. 5–19; Adūnīs 1992, pp. 66–70; and Adūnīs 1993, pp. 154–9.

186 See the cases of Salman Rushdie and Najīb Maḥfūẓ (below, pp. 138–47).

187 Brennan 1989, p. 146.

188 Brennan 1989, p. 143.

189 In another place, Iqbal says: "You can deny God, but you cannot deny the Prophet!" (Schimmel 1982, p. 209).

hand, the conservative and religious circles consider it as heresy and a great danger to Islam,[190] and, on the other hand, postmodernist circles refer to Adūnīs' revolutionary vision as being traditional.[191] Still, it never gained much popularity among the Arab masses, and Adūnīs himself and those postmodernist circles opposing his vision are mainly active in the West.

That it will take time for Adūnīs' modernist conceptions to be accepted is clear from the cases involving Najīb Maḥfūẓ and Salman Rushdie (b. 1947). Maḥfūẓ's long allegorical novel *Awlād Ḥāratinā* (*Children of Our Alley*) (1959)[192] was published in book form in Egypt only in 2006[193] due to the outcry of the Islamist circles who claimed that it treated the sacred beliefs of Islam without the appropriate reverence.[194] The international furor engendered by Rushdie's *The Satanic Verses* (1988)[195] and the subsequent death

190 See, for example, al-Jundī n.d.

191 See, for example, al-Janābī 1994, published as the first work in a series entitled *Faḍḥ al-Sā'id* (*The Disgrace of the Prevailing Situation*) (later it proved to be the only work published within the series, a fact which may be interpreted as having been planned from the start in order to magnify the critical attitude of the author to Adūnīs). Cf. also the journal *Farādīs*, edited by ʻAbd al-Qādir al-Janābī (b. 1944) and published in Cologne and afterwards in Paris (first issue: July 1990), and the journal *al-Laḥẓa al-Shiʻriyya*, edited by Fawzī Karīm (b. 1945) and published in London (first issue: Summer 1992).

192 Serialized in *al-Ahrām* from 21 September to 25 December 1959 and first published as a book by Dār al-Ādāb in Beirut (Maḥfūẓ 1967). On the differences between these two versions of the novel, see Stewart 2001, pp. 37–42. The novel was translated into English by Philip J. Stewart under the title *Children of Gebelawi* (Mahfouz 1981a). Following the awarding of the Nobel Prize to Maḥfūẓ, Stewart was invited to have his translation included among the official translations being produced by the AUC Press and Doubleday. However, having seen that other translators of the novel had been subject to attack, he refused, and Peter Theroux translated the book again with the title *Children of the Alley* (Mahfouz 2001a. Cf. Johnson-Davies 2006, pp. 42–3. For the translator's tale, see Theroux 2001–2, pp. 666–71).

193 Maḥfūẓ 2006.

194 Cf. Maḥfūẓ 1968, pp. 85–6. On the novel and its various interpretations, see Snir 1994a, pp. 51–75; and Allen 2011a, pp. 33–58 (with accompanying bibliographical information in both articles). On the banning of the novel and on the religious objections to and attacks on it, see Stagh 1993, pp. 157–70. The argument that the novel was written "purely to curry favour with the Nasser regime in Egypt" (Ruthven 1990, p. 123) is very odd, as it was accepted since the early 1970s that Maḥfūẓ's novel was intended mainly as a manifesto against ʻAbd al-Nāṣir's regime (Snir 1994a, p. 61. Cf. Ghālī Shukrī's interpretation in ʻUmar 2000, pp. 90–1. On literary representations of ʻAbd al-Nāṣir's regime, see also Snir 2007b, pp. 181–208; Litvin 2012). See also al-Naqqāsh 2006, pp. 155–67. Samia Mehrez used the novel and its representation of the status of the scribe of the alley as an extended metaphor—the alley as the nation—to look at the politics of the cultural battles in Egypt since the second half of the 1990s (Mehrez 2008). On Maḥfūẓ as an oppositional writer, see also Sazzad 2013, pp. 194–212.

195 Rushdie 1988. On the novel against the background of the Rushdie affair, see Brennan 1989, especially pp. 143–66; and Erickson 1998, pp. 129–60. On the Rushdie affair in general, see Appignanesi and Maitland 1990; Ruthven 1990; Sardar and Davies 1990; "Eine Chronik des Falls Salman Rushdie," *Zeitschrift für Kulturaustausch* 4 (1992(, pp. 539–88;

sentence issued against Rushdie by the *fatwā* of Ayatollah Ruhollah Moosavi Khomeini (1902–89), spiritual leader of Iran after the revolution of 1979,[196] incited the radical religious circles again in the late 1980s against Maḥfūẓ and his novel.[197] Of the typical books written in the Islamic world[198] to defend

Esposito 1992, pp. 190–3; Hawley 1998, pp. 1–31; Majid 1998, pp. 84–92; Reeves 2000, pp. 271–300; and Ibn Warraq 2003, pp. 3–33. For the treatment of the affair with regard to Orientalism and postcolonial discourse, see Majid 2000, pp. 22–49. The title of the novel is based on verses which were allegedly transmitted by the Prophet Muḥammad as part of the Qur'ānic revelation. In these verses, Satan inspired Muḥammad to praise the idols al-Lāt, al-Uzza, and Manāt, calling them *al-gharānīq al-'ulā* (the lofty cranes). The Prophet later realized that he had been tricked by Satan and withdrew the verses (*Sūrat al-Ḥajj* 52 says: "Allāh abrogates that which Satan proposes"), transmitting others in their place (*Sūrat al-Najm* 19–23). Rushdie deals with this story in the second chapter of the novel entitled "Mahound," which concludes thus: "Mahound has reached his oasis: Gibreel is not so lucky. Often, now, he finds himself alone on the summit of Mount Cone, washed by the cold, falling stars, and then they fall upon him from the night sky, the three winged creatures, Lat Uzza Manat, flapping around his head, clawing at his eyes, biting, whipping him with their hair, their wings. He puts up his hands to protect himself, but their revenge is tireless, continuing whenever he rests, whenever he drops his guard. He struggles against them, but they are faster, nimbler, winged. He has no devil to repudiate. Dreaming, he cannot wish them away" (Rushdie 1988, p. 126). On the story of this *naskh* (abrogation), entitled in Muslim tradition *riwāyat al-gharānīq* ("the story of the cranes"), see al-Ṭabarī 1961, pp. 338–40; and al-Azmeh 1996, p. 115 (as well as n. 54 on p. 125). For an analysis of the early traditions on this incident, see Ahmed 1999; and Jones 2001, pp. 125–33. For an analysis of this story in relation to Rushdie's novel, see al-'Aẓm 1992, pp. 276–83. See also Netton 1992, p. 226.

196 "I inform the proud Muslim People of the world that the author of *The Satanic Verses*, which is against Islam, the Prophet and the Qur'an, and all involved in its publication who are aware of its content are sentenced to death. I request brave Muslims to quickly kill them wherever they find them so that no one ever again would dare to insult the sanctions of Muslims. Anyone killed in trying to execute Rushdie would, God willing, be a *shaheed* (martyr). In addition, anyone who has access to the author of the book but does not have the strength to execute him should introduce him to the people so that he receives punishment for his action" (Sardar and Davies 1990, pp. 193–4; and Ruthven 1990, p. 112). This *fatwā* was particularly prompted by the aforementioned allusion to *riwāyat al-gharānīq* as well as the description in the chapter "Return to Jahilia" of the popular brothel entitled *Hijab* in the city of Jahilia, where each of the whores assumed the identity of one of Mahound's wives: "The fifteen-year-old whore 'Ayesha' was the most popular with the paying public [...] The oldest, fattest whore, who had taken the name of 'Sawdah' [...] The whore 'Hafsah' grew as hot-tempered as her namesake [...] 'Umm Salamah the Makhzumite' and, snootiest of all, 'Ramlah' [...] And there was a 'Zainab bint Jahsh', and a 'Juwairyah' [...] and a 'Rehana the Jew', a 'Safia' and 'Maimunah', and, most erotic of all whores, who knew tricks she refused to teach to competitive 'Ayesha': the glamorous Egyptian, 'Mary the Copt'. Strangest of all was the whore who had taken the name of 'Zainab bint Khuzaimah'" (Rushdie 1988, pp. 381–2).

197 See, for example, *al-I'tiṣām*, April 1989, pp. 5–7.

198 Similar books were written in various languages in addition to Arabic. For example, in 1996 Iran's Ministry of Islamic Guidance published a book by Ahmad Zomorodian entitled *Who is the Satan?*, which, according to its introduction, was written in order to expose the "anti-Islamic propaganda" in Rushdie's novel and to stop the spread of "spiteful nonsense"

Islam against Rushdie and Maḥfūẓ, one book opens with the following Qur'ānic verse:

يُرِيدُونَ لِيُطْفِئُوا نُورَ اللهِ بِأَفْوَاهِهِمْ وَاللهُ مُتِمُّ نُورِهِ وَلَوْ كَرِهَ الْكَافِرُونَ

They desire to extinguish with their mouths the light of God; but God will perfect his light, though the unbelievers be averse.[199]

Inspired by things the late Syrian president Ḥāfiẓ al-Asad (1930–2000) had said,[200] and convinced that Zionists were behind the publication of Rushdie's book,[201] the writer Ṣā'ib Sa'ūd addresses Maḥfūẓ with the following words:[202]

أما كفاك الرمز والغمز بابن الحارة[203] (...) فالإسلام ليس حقلا للتجارب لمشروعاتكم الأدبية (...) وليست مقدّساته رمزا لرغائبكم الوضيعة وأهوائكم القذرة، فالإسلام روح إنسانية سامية وجمرات ذكية قدسية لا تحويها أجسادكم وأرواحكم القذرة شانكما شأن ذلك الفاسد بن الملعون في روايته ليلة القدر. وما يدريه ما ليلة القدر؟[204]

Was it not enough for you to allude to and slander the son of the alley[205] [...] Islam is not a field of experiments for your literary projects [...] its sanctities are not symbols for your vulgar desires and filthy tendencies. Islam is elevated human spirit and fragrant holy firebrands which your filthy bodies and spirits fail to compass, just as with that wicked son of the damned in his novel *Laylat al-Qadr*. He does not even know what *Laylat al-Qadr* means![206]

Another book, by Nabīl al-Sammān, ends its diatribe against Rushdie and his Arab supporters with the following call to Arab writers:

إن الكتّاب العرب مدعوّون دعوة جادّة للكتابة عن العرب والمسلمين باللغات العالمية الحيّة، بأسلوب يفهمه الغربيون، وتطوير هذه الدراسات الإسلامية والعربية في أوطانهم ومن مصادرهم التراثية، بدلا من الاعتماد على ما وضعه المستشرقون عن الإسلام والعرب، ودسّوا فيه ما شاءت لهم أهواؤهم وميولهم العدائية لكل ما هو عربي ومسلم، بدءا من الحروب الصليبية وحتّى العصر الحاضر.

Arab writers are earnestly called upon to write about Arabs and Muslims in living international languages in a style that Westerners will understand, and to develop these Islamic and Arabic studies in their homelands and based on their own heritage, instead of on the Orientalists' writings about Islam and Arabs, which they infused with their hostile desires and tendencies against everything

designed to undermine the pillars of religion (according to adabiyat@listhost.uchicago.edu [7 September 1996]).

199 *Al-Ṣaff* 8. The translation is according to Arberry 1979 [1964], p. 581.
200 See, for example, Sa'ūd 1991, pp. 9, 37–8.
201 Sa'ūd 1991, pp. 40–2, 67–77.
202 Sa'ūd 1991, pp. 77–8.
203 Writer's note: إشارة إلى روايته أبناء حارتنا
204 Writer's note: إشارة إلى الكاتب الطاهر بن جلون
205 Writer's note: "an allusion to his novel *Abnā' Ḥāratinā*" [sic].
206 Writer's note: "an allusion to the writer al-Ṭāhir ibn Jallūn."

that is Arabic and Muslim, beginning with the Crusades and until the modern period.[207]

Wanting to show that Western and Christian writers also have other images of Islam, in 1989 the Egyptian writer Sayyid Ḥāfiẓ Abū al-Futūḥ (b. 1952) published *Qālū ʿan al-Islām: Rasāʾil ilā Salmān Rushdī min Kibār Mufakkirī wa-Falāsifat al-ʿĀlam al-Masīḥī* (*They Said of Islam: Letters to Salman Rushdie from the Greatest Intellectuals and Philosophers of the Christian World*). The book opens with the following Qur'ānic verse:

وَأَمَّا الزَّبَدُ فَيَذْهَبُ جُفَاءً.

As for the scum, it vanishes as jetsam.[208]

The book's first section presents the views on Islam of such writers as Johann Wolfgang von Goethe (1749–1832), Alphonse de Lamartine (1790–1869), Karl Marx (1818–83), George Bernard Shaw (1856–1950), and Leo Nikolayevich Tolstoy (1828–1910).[209] The second section presents the views on Islam of Christian-Arab writers such as Shiblī Shumayyil (1860–1917), Rashīd Salīm al-Khūrī (1887–1984), Mīkhāʾīl Nuʿayma (1889–1988), and Jurjī Zaydān (1861–1914).[210]

Another book, by Rifʿat Sayyid Aḥmad (b. 1957), Head of the Jaffa Research Center in Cairo, opens with the following Qur'ānic verse:

وَلَنْ تَرْضَى عَنْكَ الْيَهُودُ وَلاَ النَّصَارَى حَتَّى تَتَّبِعَ مِلَّتَهُمْ.

Never will the Jews be satisfied with thee, neither the Christians, not till thou followest their religion.[211]

In an appendix, the author lists the names of the "most famous Western Orientalists," the majority of whom he believed "offended Islam," "did not understand Islamic civilization," and "distorted its various symbols." The more than 380 scholars are divided into seven sections according to their nationality—French, German, Italian, Spanish, British, American, and Soviet.[212] As for the attitude of Muslim writers and intellectuals toward

207 Al-Sammān 1989, p. 117.

208 *Al-Raʿd* 17. The translation is according to Arberry 1979 [1964], p. 241.

209 Abū al-Futūḥ 1989, pp. 23–139.

210 Abū al-Futūḥ 1989, pp. 141–61.

211 *Al-Baqara* 120. The translation is according to Arberry 1979 [1964], p. 15.

212 Aḥmad 1989, pp. 187–93. For other books and articles attacking Rushdie, see Ayyūb 1989; al-Fāsī 1989; Daydāt 1990; al-Mahājarānī 1993; and Yūsuf (ʿAbd al-Qādir) 1999, pp. 9–25. For one of the few books in Arabic which acknowledge the author's right to create his or her own autonomous fictional world, see Darwīsh and ʿAbd al-Rāziq 1989. The Egyptian critic Ghālī Shukrī argues that most of the Muslim intellectuals who have attacked Rushdie never actually read the novel (*al-Waṭan al-ʿArabī*, 17 March 1989, pp. 22–7. Cf. al-ʿAẓm 1992, p. 230).

Rushdie's novel, the author argues that "the reaction of the Muslim collective mind (which is comprised of the nation's writers, intellectuals and scholars) varied between complete rejection of the novel—this being the dominant reaction—and a qualified rejection."[213] However, he mentions three Muslim writers who supported Rushdie's novel "without any reservation"—Najīb Maḥfūẓ, Waḍḍāḥ Sharāra (b. 1942) from the Lebanese University, and Ḥamīd al-Azrī.[214] Alluding to Maḥfūẓ's 1988 Nobel Prize for Literature, he describes the prize as "controlled by Jews who are hostile to Islam." Still, unlike most Islamist writers commenting on the Rushdie affair, the author does present every aspect of Maḥfūẓ's attitude toward Rushdie's novel—although supportive of Rushdie's right to free expression, Maḥfūẓ does not agree with its content.[215]

While he personally rejected the notion of any similarity between *Awlād Ḥāratinā* and *The Satanic Verses*,[216] it seems that it was Maḥfūẓ's decision to condemn Rushdie's death sentence which prompted radical Islamists to react. The blind mufti of the radical Egyptian group *al-Jihād*, 'Umar 'Abd al-Raḥmān (Sheikh Omar Abdel-Rahman) (1938–2017), delivered a *fatwā* against Maḥfūẓ himself in April 1989.[217] He argued that had such a *fatwā* been published when Maḥfūẓ's *Awlād Ḥāratinā* first came out, Rushdie would never have dared to publish his blasphemies.[218] 'Abd al-Raḥmān's

213 Aḥmad 1989, p. 150.

214 Aḥmad 1989, pp. 174–5. Ḥamīd al-Azrī, according to the author, became an apostate from Islam following the death sentence issued against Rushdie. For a full presentation of Sharāra's outlook, see Sharāra 1995, pp. 59–80.

215 Aḥmad 1989, pp. 174–5. The *fatwā* against Rushdie was renewed. See <http://www.dailymail.co.uk/news/article-2560683/Iranian-mullah-revives-death-fatwa-against-Salman-Rushdie-Satanic-Verses-25-years-issued.html> (16 February 2014) (last accessed 15 October 2016).

216 *Al-Ahrām*, 2 March 1989, p. 7. Cf. Maḥfūẓ's interview in *Der Spiegel*, no. 9, 1989 (according to Appignanesi and Maitland 1990, pp. 140–2); Mehrez 1993, p. 67; and Mehrez 1994, pp. 23–4. On the reaction of Islamist writers to Maḥfūẓ's argument, see al-Sammān 1989, p. 23. Philip J. Stewart, who wrote the first thesis on the novel (Stewart 1963) and published an English translation of it (Mahfouz 1981a), posited that Maḥfūẓ had been influenced by the play *Back to Methuselah* by George Bernard Shaw (1856–1950), a writer he held in great esteem (Shaw 1954). Based on personal communication with Maḥfūẓ in 1962, Stewart states that Maḥfūẓ considered this play to be his favorite piece by Shaw and that there are important similarities between the two works: each is a history of mankind in five parts; each includes the theme of immense longevity; and, most importantly, both works protest against the tyranny of a false God and contain a plea for the revival of true religion (Stewart 1991, pp. 213–20).

217 *Al-Ahālī*, 12 April 1989, p. 13.

218 Ruthven 1990, p. 116; Miller 1996, p. 53. In an interview in the *New Yorker*, on 30 January 1995, 'Abd al-Raḥmān denied that he had issued such a *fatwā*, asserting that his comments had been misunderstood (Miller 1996, p. 481, n. 41).

fatwā aroused many protests in the Arab world,[219] as did Khomeini's *fatwā* against Rushdie.[220] Moreover, stating that no Muslim could be executed without a fair trial, the Grand Mufti of Egypt, Muḥammad Sayyid Ṭanṭāwī (1928–2010), categorically rejected the *fatwā* against Maḥfūẓ.[221] The *fatwā* of ʻUmar ʻAbd al-Raḥmān is believed to have incited the assassination attempt on Maḥfūẓ in Cairo on 14 October 1994.[222] It should be noted that, prior to its publication in Egypt in 2006, *Awlād Ḥāratinā* had not been published in Egypt in book form and had not appeared on the lists of Maḥfūẓ's works habitually appended to his books.[223]

219 See, for example, *al-Ahālī*, 7 June 1989, p. 11; *al-Akhbār*, 17 May 1989, p. 9; *al-Hadaf*, 9 April 1989, pp. 40–3; *al-Shirāʻ*, 15 May 1989, p. 52; and *al-Wafd*, 30 May 1989, p. 9.

220 Cf. *For Rushdie: Essays by Arab and Muslim Writers in Defense of Free Speech*, trans. Kenneth Whitehead and Kevin Anderson (New York: George Braziller, 1994). Among the writers are the Syrian Adūnīs (b. 1930), the Palestinians Maḥmūd Darwīsh (1941–2008), Imīl Ḥabībī (1921–96), Anton Shammās (b. 1950), and Liyāna Badr (b. 1952); the Saudi ʻAbd al-Raḥmān Munīf (1933–2004); the Egyptian Ṣunʻ Allāh Ibrāhīm (b. 1937); the Lebanese Ḥanān al-Shaykh (b. 1945) and Amin Maalouf (Amīn Maʻlūf) (b. 1949); and the Moroccans Mohamed Berrada (Muḥammad Barrāda) (b. 1938) and Tahar Ben Jelloun (al-Ṭāhir ibn Jallūn) (b. 1944).

221 *Al-Ahālī*, 3 May 1989, p. 3; Ruthven 1990, pp. 115–16.

222 See *al-Kifāḥ al-ʻArabī*, 24 October 1994, pp. 51–2. On the assassination attempt, see al-Naqqāsh 1998, pp. 345–60. ʻUmar ʻAbd al-Raḥmān, whose name has been associated with calls for violence and terrorism in the name of religion, left Egypt in 1990 and was able to take up residence in the United States thanks to what American officials admitted were administrative errors. In 1994 he was tried in Egypt in absentia, convicted, and sentenced to seven years in prison. However, by then he was about to stand trial in New York for his role in a plot to blow up the United Nations and other New York buildings (Miller 1996, p. 53). He is currently serving a life sentence at the Butner Federal Medical Center, which is part of the Butner Federal Correctional Complex in Butner, North Carolina. On ʻUmar ʻAbd al-Raḥmān, see Esposito 1995, I, pp. 10–11.

223 On the connection between the Rushdie and Maḥfūẓ affairs, see Shukrī 1992, pp. 307–46; Netton 1996; and Shepard 2014, pp. 55–73. On the controversy surrounding Maḥfūẓ' book, see Kishk 1989. After meeting Maḥfūẓ in early 1994, Judith Miller observed that the silence of intellectuals was not officially enforced but rather voluntary—although intellectuals had been terrified into passivity. Even before Maḥfūẓ was attacked, he had softened his own defense of Salman Rushdie to avoid antagonizing militants. According to Maḥfūẓ, Rushdie's work, which he said he had not read, was "very disturbing." Rushdie had "insulted Islam," and insults had "consequences." Miller said she "was saddened by Mahfouz's retreat on such a critical principle of free expression," saying that "his revised position was not all that different from that of the Muslim brotherhood or, for that matter, from that of Sheikh Abdel Rahman in jail in New York" (Miller 1996, p. 71). On the other hand, we find Maḥfūẓ saying on 3 June 1999 that "it is absolutely inadmissible that a book or a painting be banned because it is supposedly base. If we were to start condemning works on moral grounds, we would be unable to stop. We can, at most, give our opinion: it is not our right to prevent others from doing the same" (Mahfouz 2001, p. 71). On this issue, see also al-Naqqāsh 1998, pp. 139–46, 243–4, 326–7. Also, Jamāl al-Ghīṭānī (1945–2015) criticized the wave of religious fanaticism: "You can't apply morals to an artistic work, what about Abu Nawass [sic] whose work has been read for more than a thousand years and became part of our heritage. All of a sudden the Ministry of Culture judged the

A good illustration of the way in which the Islamist literary discourse takes on the secular canonical center of the Arabic literary system, as seen against the background of the Rushdie and Maḥfūẓ affairs, is given by the literary critic Ṣādiq Jalāl al-ʿAẓm (1934–2016) in his book *Dhihniyyat al-Taḥrīm* (*The Proscribing Mentality*) (1992):

> في الواقع إذا دفعنا منطق الإسلامانيين إلى حدوده القصوى يكون من الأفضل لو لم يعرف العالم العربي ظواهر مثل طه حسين أو توفيق الحكيم أو نجيب محفوظ أو أدونيس أو خليل حاوي، لأن كلّ واحد منهم يمثّل شكلا من أشكال التعبير الفكري والفنّي المستورد من الغرب هي على التوالي: النقد، والمسرحية، والرواية والشعر الحديث.

> Actually, if we follow Islamist thinking to its logical conclusion, it would have been better had the Arab world never known of phenomena such as Ṭāhā Ḥusayn or Tawfīq al-Ḥakīm or Najīb Maḥfūẓ or Adūnīs or Khalīl Ḥāwī, since each of them represents a mode of intellectual and artistic expression which is imported from the West: criticism, theater, the novel, and modern poetry.[224]

Al-ʿAẓm's main argument is that all attacks against Rushdie have been based on the assumption that literature, and art in general, must kowtow to Islamic concepts; that is, the literary discourse is hardly independent and must remain within the limits of the religious discourse. Al-ʿAẓm quotes from an article entitled "Nihilistic, Negative, Satanic" authored by Syed Ali Ashraf (1925–98), Director-General of the Islamic Academy in Cambridge, regarding Rushdie's novel; Ashraf poses such questions as,

> How could the two characters Gibreel (Gabriel) and Saladin fall from the sky and still be alive? How could they get transformed and how could they become normal again? How could they have the normal human body and how could they at the same time move about and influence people across space and time?[225]

man as obscene and confiscated some of his work. I can't expect worse" (*al-Ahram Weekly*, 10–16 March 2005).

224 Al-ʿAẓm 1992, p. 82. Cf. Sharabi 1988, pp. 110–11. In a note, al-ʿAẓm quotes what the Lebanese writer Ilyās Khūrī (b. 1948) wrote in *al-Safīr* (26 November 1990): Khūrī accused the Islamist groups of attempting to return to the pre-modern genres such as the *qaṣīda* and to al-Khalīl's prosody. For a critical response to al-ʿAẓm's views, see Barqāwī 1995, pp. 81–114. For subsequent arguments by al-ʿAẓm, see his *Mā Baʿda Dhihniyyat al-Taḥrīm: Qirāʾat al-Āyāt al-Shayṭāniyya, Radd wa-Taʿqīb* (*Beyond the Proscribing Mentality: Reading the Satanic Verses, Reply and Commentary*) (al-ʿAẓm 1997. The original title of the book was shorter, *Qirāʾat al-Āyāt al-Shyṭāniyya*, but the publisher changed it to the present title, alluding to its relationship to the first book [Abū Fakhr 1998, p. 46], and indeed the book does include articles written in reply to al-ʿAẓm's *Dhihniyyat al-Taḥrīm* as well as his own comments. For al-ʿAẓm's views on the topic, see Abū Fakhr 1998, pp. 67–78).

225 Al-ʿAẓm 1992, pp. 237–8. Ashraf's article was originally published in *Impact International* (London), 28 October–10 November 1988, and republished in Appignanesi and Maitland 1990, pp. 18–21.

The clash between religious and secular discourses by no means entails absolute consensus within each camp. For example, religious notables sometimes oppose the prevailing views among Islamist circles. A collection of articles entitled *al-ʿUnf al-Uṣūlī: Muwājahāt al-Sayf wa-l-Qalam* (*Fundamentalist Violence: The Clash of the Sword and the Pen*) (1995) mainly consists of pieces about the Rushdie affair by secular intellectuals denouncing the Islamist position.[226] The Lebanese Shiite spiritual leader of Ḥizb Allāh Muḥammad Ḥusayn Faḍl Allāh (1935–2010), is the sole contributor to a section of the book entitled "Islamiyyūn Ḍidd al-Taʿaṣṣub" ("Islamic Personalities against Fanaticism"). In his "Hawā al-Sharq wa-Huwiyyat al-Islam" ("Love of the East and the Identity of Islam"), Faḍl Allāh does not adopt the usual religious stance vis-à-vis Rushdie[227] and states at the end of the article that no topic is closed to discussion, that historically Islam has been culturally diverse, and that "this diversity has made Islam a civilization and the Muslim a rich human being."[228]

The collection opens with an article by ʿAzīz al-ʿAẓma (Aziz al-Azmeh) entitled "Riwāya Kāfira" ("Novel of Unbelief") that attacks the Islamist position in the Rushdie affair.[229] Al-ʿAẓma ironically points out that the Islamist radicals base their attitude toward the novel, "as they are wont to do," upon the "notion" that "ignorance is a sign of piety."[230] He concludes the article with the following lines:

> ما ادّعاء الإسلاميين بأنهم يتكلّمون باسم «الشعب» وأنهم يمثّلون الأكثرية إلا علامة وهمية على طموح سياسي جامح، وما الدعوى بأن سلمان رشدي وغيره ممن لا يرى رأيهم ليس إلا خارجا على تاريخه وأصالته وتراثه وداعية للغرب ضدّ الإسلام، إلا إشارة إلى التعارض الذي يعيشونه ليس مع الغرب- فالأنظمة السياسية الإسلامية على وئام معه - بل مع الحداثة والرقيّ في بلدانهم عينها. ويجب التأكيد على أن وهم التمثيل الكلّي للتراث ومحاولة مصادرة كل قول فيه شأن يدلّ على هوس بمصادرة المستقبل وإرساء الاستبداد الجامع باسم ماض لا تاريخ فيه، وهذا برنامج يفتخر به كل طموح إلى فاشستية بائسة متخلّفة.

The claim of the Islamists that they are speaking in the name of "the people" and that they are representing the majority is nothing but an imaginary expression

226 The book published by Riyāḍ al-Rayyis in London is a selection of articles appearing in the journal *al-Nāqid* (London) ever since the outbreak of the Rushdie affair.

227 See Faḍl Allāh 1995, pp. 197–213. On Faḍl Allāh's outlook in that domain, see also Aḥmad 1989, p. 166. On Faḍl Allāh's general conceptions, see Esposito 1995, I, pp. 453–6; and Baroudi 2016, pp. 94–114.

228 Faḍl Allāh 1995, p. 213.

229 Al-ʿAẓma 1995a, pp. 13–21. For a critical approach to al-ʿAẓma's article, see al-Jazāʾirī 1995, pp. 23–38. Al-Jazāʾirī rejects the analogy made by al-ʿAẓma between *The Satanic Verses* and *Awlād Ḥāratinā* (p. 35): "*Awlād Ḥāratinā* is a human-historical diagnosis in a new narrative discourse, while *The Satanic Verses* is an assassination attempt, a willful attempt to exterminate an ancient human heritage."

230 Al-ʿAẓma 1995a, p. 17.

> for an indomitable political desire. The claim that Salman Rushdie and others that do not agree with the Islamists are rising against their own history, nobility, and heritage and are propagandists for the West against Islam is nothing but proof of the conflict the Islamists are living in, not with the West—since the political Islamist regimes are in harmony with it—but with modernity and progress in their own countries. We should emphasize that their illusion of totally representing the heritage, and their attempt to confiscate every important saying, point to a craze to confiscate the future in order to lay down foundations for a comprehensive dictatorship in the name of a past devoid of any history. This is a program that anyone desiring any poor backward [form of] fascism could be proud of.[231]

Al-ʿAẓma explains elsewhere that "in many third-world countries, *The Satanic Verses* is characterized as the work of a self-hater eager to ingratiate himself with the coloniser simply because the novel challenges the most conservative instincts of those groups claiming Muslim 'nativism.'"[232]

The clash between the Islamist discourse and the modernist discourse demonstrates the fact that Arab culture is still somehow fettered by religious restrictions. In this, as we have already seen, there is no difference between the various genres. Thus, Homi K. Bhabha's reading of Rushdie's blasphemy, following Yunus Samad's analysis,[233] seems to be on shaky ground, at least from the standpoint of Arabic literature. According to Bhabha,

> it is the medium Rushdie uses to reinterpret the Koran that constitutes the crime [...] By casting his revisionary narrative in the form of the novel—largely unknown to traditional Islamic literature—Rushdie violates the poetic license granted to critics of the Islamic establishment [...] Rushdie's sin lies in opening up a space of discursive contestation that places the authority of the Koran within a perspective of historical and cultural relativism. It is not that the "content" of the Koran is directly disputed; rather, by revealing other enunciatory positions and possibilities within the framework of the Koranic reading, Rushdie performs the subversion of its authenticity through the act of cultural translation—he relocates the Koran's "intentionality" by repeating and reinscribing it in the locale of the novel of postwar cultural migrations and diasporas.[234]

Looking for any differentiation among the various genres, one can start by assessing the popularity of a particular genre: The more popular the literary work, the greater the demand to see it shackled by traditional religious

[231] Al-ʿAẓma 1995a, p. 21. Cf. al-ʿAẓm 1992, pp. 74–5. Cf. the argument of Riyāḍ Najīb al-Rayyis (b. 1937) (al-Rayyis 1996, pp. 27–8): "The Rushdie affair is an internal Iranian affair related to the struggle of power in which Islam was used as a weapon against the West."

[232] Al-Azmeh 1989, pp. 16–17. Cf. Brennan 1989, p. 145.

[233] Samad 1991, pp. 507–19.

[234] Bhabha 1994, p. 226.

fetters. Thus, Darwīsh's aforementioned poem "Oh, My Father, I am Yūsuf" did not excite a public storm before Khalīfa sang it. The same could be said about Maḥfūẓ's novel *Children of Our Alley*, whose "danger" increased only with the Rushdie affair following the publication of *The Satanic Verses*. And at this point, it should also be mentioned that Arab writers and intellectuals frequently complain that censorship is one of those cliché things that Westerners get worked up about. During the Frankfurt Book Fair in 2004, the Omani author Sa'īda Khāṭir al-Fārisī (b. 1956) accused earnest European authors and the Western public of being strangely obsessed with the issues of censorship, sexual taboos, and the "repression" of women in Arab society.[235]

To sum up, the greater part of the Arabic literary system is still essentially governed by a religious framework, and most contemporary literary activities carefully avoid any violation of basic Islamic precepts. At the same time, unlike medieval Arabic literature, contemporary Arabic writing is no longer the product of an international cultural community, but is once more becoming—as it was in the pre-Islamic period—a literature of the Arabs alone. In the Abbasid period, many of the central literary figures were of non-Arab descent, quite a few of them Persians. From about the tenth century onward, Muslim Persian authors began to replace Arabic with Persian as the dominant literary language, a process that was continued elsewhere outside Arabic-speaking countries. Nevertheless, in the eighteenth century we can still find an eminent poet such as the Indian Ghulām 'Alī Āzād Bilkrāmī (Bilgrāmī) (1704–86) writing poetry in Arabic while authoring books in Persian and Urdu (because of his versatile grasp of Arabic he was nicknamed "Ḥassān al-Hind" after the poet of the Prophet, Ḥassān ibn Thābit [d. 674]).[236] Even in the nineteenth century and at the beginning of the twentieth century, Arab poets of non-Arab descent could still find their way to the center of the literary canon. For example, Aḥmad Shawqī, *Amīr al-Shu'arā'* ("The Prince of Poets"), was of Kurdish and Arab descent on his paternal side, and of Turkish and Greek descent on his maternal side.[237] Today, the three major peoples of the Middle East—the Arabs, the Turks, and the Iranians—have become intellectually isolated from one another. In Iran, Arabic is still taught as a classical and scriptural

235 *Expatica*, 7 October 2004. The translator Stefan Weidner said during the fair that "German book-lovers evidently had little interest in 'authentic' Arabic literature. They preferred 'worn-out oriental clichés'" (*Expatica*, 8 October 2004).

236 On Bilkrāmī, see Lowry and Stewart 2009, pp. 91–7 (by Shawkat M. Toorawa). Cf. al-Musawi 2015b, pp. 17, 44.

237 Brugman 1984, pp. 35-36. On this issue, see Zaydān 1973, p. 125:

إن الأرض بتراثها قد جعلت من ابن الرومي ومهيار وأبي نواس وبشّار وشوقي أعرابا هم في لسانهم أقوى عراقة من مستعرق عربي قد استعجم لسانه.

language in schools, and in Turkey it has been reintroduced into religious seminaries. However, Cairo, Tehran, and Istanbul are nevertheless culturally very remote from one other.[238] Only rarely do scholars pay attention to the limitations of nationalistic frameworks that characterized Middle Eastern Studies. One such scholar is C. Ceyhun Arslan, who organized a seminar at the annual conference of the ACLA (American Comparative Literature Association), held at Harvard University on 17–20 March 2016, entitled "Comparative Middle Eastern Literatures: Forging a Discipline." The purpose of this seminar was to analyze interactions among diverse Middle Eastern literary traditions and understand the region's literary and cultural networks:

> Previous comparative works emphasized the Western influence on Turkish, Persian, or Arabic literatures, but rarely analyzed the interactions among these three traditions. Furthermore, the field has given scant attention to many literary traditions including but not limited to Armenian, Greek, and Kurdish. To rewrite a new literary history that includes these traditions and comparative methodologies will yield a more accurate understanding of the region's cultural networks. By chartering literary networks in the Middle East, this seminar also questions the fundamental assumptions that govern today's prominent fields that emphasize cultural networks—world literature and digital humanities. Although these fields achieved laudable success in undermining Eurocentric biases, they often risk making theoretical claims with little attention to specific cultural contexts. To analyze Middle Eastern literatures within the framework of larger debates in humanities will thus contribute to the most pressing questions in comparative literature.[239]

Also worth mentioning are the minor, but sometimes important, Christian and Jewish contributions to Arabic literature.[240] There is no doubt that the contribution of Christian-Arab writers and intellectuals to this literature in its formative stage in the nineteenth century and the beginning of the twentieth century was highly significant.[241] Also, the influx into Egypt of Syrian-

[238] See Lewis 1968, p. 73. Cf. the rationale behind the study of Islamic popular literature and the literary relationship between Arabs, Turks, and Persians, as alluded to in al-Miṣrī 2001, especially pp. 5–9, 229–40; al-Miṣrī 2001a, especially pp. 5–7; and al-Miṣrī 2003, especially pp. 7–28. It should be noted that even comparative studies between Arabic, Persian, and Turkish literatures are rare. On some recurrent motifs in late-twentieth-century Arabic and Turkish novels, see Guth 2003, pp. 121–37; and Guth 2007, pp. 25–49. On Turkish and Ottoman motifs in Arabic literature from the *Nahḍa* to the end of the Caliphate, see Daniels 2005, pp. 99–128.

[239] According to "Arabic Lit Scholars" list, 4 August 2015.

[240] On the contribution of Christian poets to Arabic poetry after the rise of Islam, see Cheikho 1967.

[241] I. J. Krachkovskii, however, asserts that the literary work of the Christian Nāṣīf al-Yāzijī (1800–71) was the first to violate the principle of *al-ʿArabiyya lā tatanaṣṣaru* ("Arabic

Christian intellectuals and writers in the nineteenth century, when they pioneered free journalism and various cultural activities, was a contributory factor to the lead taken by that country in the Arab *Nahḍa* (Renaissance).[242] Syrian-Christian writers were also at the core of intensive Arabic literary activities in the *Mahjar* (the Arab diaspora), especially in North and South America.[243] Still, Arab Christianity has never been isolated from Arabic-Islamic social and cultural systems, and Christian writers in Arabic have never entered the canonical center of the literary system without adopting the Arabic-Islamic literary heritage.[244] Unlike the formative stage of modern Arabic literature in the nineteenth century, the number of Christian writers since the twentieth century has constantly decreased; they were also the first to adopt other languages as new media for literary creation.[245]

language cannot become Christian"), which means that "Arabic literature cannot grant recognition to Christian writers" (Krachkovskii 1989, p. 24. Cf. Ajami 1998, pp. 42–3; and Allen 2010, p. 380).

242 On the *Nahḍa*, see Patel 2013; Rastegar 2013, pp. 227–31; and Reynolds 2015, pp. 54–74 (by Yoav Di-Capua). On a possible "theory" of the *Nahḍa*, see Sheehi 2012, pp. 269–98. On a critical pedagogy of the *Nahḍa* in American comparative literary studies, see Tageldin 2012, pp. 227–68. For the dilemma of the *Nahḍa* as unfinished mission, rewriting it as "the other appellation for Arab modernity," and interrogating it through a postcolonial critique, see Muhsin al-Musawi's two-part article in *The Cambridge Journal of Postcolonial Literary Inquiry* entitled "The Republic of Letters: Arab Modernity?" (al-Musawi 2014, pp. 265–80; and al-Musawi 2015, pp. 115–30) and the four responses to al-Musawi's article within the "Forum on Literary World Systems" in the same journal (El-Ariss 2015, pp. 260–6; Ganguly 2015, pp. 272–81; Helgesson 2015, pp. 253–60; and Orsini 2015, pp. 266–72. See also al-Musawi 2015a, pp. 281–6; and al-Musawi 2015b).

243 For some misconceptions about the *Nahḍa* and the role of the Christians, see Tibawi 1974, pp. 304–14. For the *Mahjar* as being synonymous with the *Nahḍa*, and the example of Amīn Rīḥānī (1876–1940), see Dakhli 2013, pp. 164–87. For a study which addresses the *Nahḍa* "as a sociopolitical movement encapsulating and questioning issues of gender, language, community, and literature," see Khaldi 2012 (the quotation is from p. 1). On the question of whether women had a *Nahḍa* as well, see Zachs and Halevi 2015, especially pp. 149–52.

244 See the Christian writers mentioned in Kilpatrick 2004, pp. 33–51. Kilpatrick shows, for example, how Carl Brockelmann omits in his *Geschichte der Arabischen Litterature* (*GAL*) (<http://referenceworks.brillonline.com/browse/brockelmann> [last accessed 15 October 2016]) all texts by Jews and Christians intended only for their co-religionists—"Arabic literature is essentially Islamic" (p. 34). Cf. Ilyās Khūrī's statement in his introduction to a collection of articles dealing with the Arab Christians (Khūrī 1981, p. 9): "Arab Christianity is an integral part of the Arab and Islamic social and cultural reality; it cannot separate itself of that reality; otherwise, it will lose its identity and distinctiveness." Khūrī even refers to himself as Christian-Muslim (*Masāhārif* [Haifa] 17 [2002], pp. 253–4).

245 The writing of Arabic literature by Christians, however, has never been confined to secular intellectuals who accept the Muslim framework of Arabic culture. Even during the twentieth century, we could find Christian religious notables who were engaged in the writing of traditional Arabic poetry. One outstanding example is the Pope of the Coptic Church in Egypt, Pope Shenouda III of Alexandria (1923–2012), who composed poems in the form of *qaṣīda* and recited them in public gatherings (*al-Ahrām*, 8 February 1994, p. 14).

The phenomenon of Arabic literary writing by Jews has been rare in the cultural history of Jews under the rule of Islam, at least according to the sources at our disposal. We know of the existence of Jewish poets writing in Arabic in pre-Islamic Arabia, but after the rise of Islam in the seventh century AD it was only during the era of Muslim rule in Spain that Jewish poets became well versed in literary Arabic, even winning a degree of fame.[246] One of the interesting phenomena that can help shed light on the interaction between language, literature, ethnicity, and religion is the short episode of Jewish-Arabic literary writing in the twentieth century, especially Arabic belles-lettres penned by Iraqi-Jewish writers since the early 1920s:[247] When it flowered in Iraq in the 1920s and 1930s, some authors showed obvious signs of Islamization.[248]

Contemporary Arabic literature by writers of other religions, such as those of the Druze[249] and Bahai,[250] is also very limited and remains remote from the canonical center of the literary system. Again, as we saw above, the religious constraints on the literary system by no means imply that Arabic literature is traditional or inclined toward religious themes. A poet or writer may exploit religious themes and at the same time attempt to break through the Islamic framework of Arabic literature, as we find, for example, in the neo-Sufi trend in Arabic poetry.[251]

LITERATURE / TERRITORY

As a linguistic culture, a given literature is generally rooted in a particular territory and related to the community in that territory. While the world's Arab population may still be seen as one community with a shared linguistic culture, it is today spread out over different territories, and much of Arabic literature is being produced and consumed in places that are remote from its original source. Since the rise of Arabic literature as a high form of artistic expression, the canonical center of the literary system has moved diachronically from one place to another: Ḥijāz, Damascus, Baghdad, Cairo, Andalus in the Middle Ages, and Cairo, Beirut, Baghdad, and New York in the modern era. Whereas in the first half of the twentieth century Egypt's

[246] On the linguistic situation in al-Andalus, see Wasserstein 1991, pp. 1–15.

[247] On the writing of Arabic literature by Jews and for relevant studies, see my publications in the References. On ethnicity and the Arabic language in general, see Versteegh et al. 2006, II, pp. 58–65.

[248] See Snir 1994b, pp. 161–93.

[249] See, for example, the Druze writers acting in Israel mentioned in Moreh and ʿAbbāsī 1987.

[250] See, for example, Bushrū'i 1979; and Moreh and ʿAbbāsī 1987, pp. 9–10 (about Mu'ayyad Ibrāhīm [1910–87]).

[251] On the neo-Sufi trend and for relevant studies, see my publications in the References.

literary leadership was still beyond any doubt,[252] contemporary Arabic literature is no longer produced in Arab countries alone, but throughout the entire world, and important centers of literary activity, such as Paris and London, have sprung up in the West.[253] A salient phenomenon in the diachronic development of the literary system has been the constant struggle that communities throughout the Arab world have undertaken to get at its center. If, in the past, such efforts were territorial and nationalist in nature,[254] in recent years one finds communities that modernity had pushed into the margins of the literary system joining forces to gain some literary prominence (and in some cases even literary leadership).[255]

One outstanding example of this is the volume *The Literature of Modern Arabia* (1988) sponsored by King Saud University of Riyadh and edited by the Palestinian poet and scholar Salma Khadra Jayyusi (Salmā al-Khadrā' al-Jayyūsī) (b. 1926), one of the leading figures in Western scholarly research into modern Arabic literature.[256] Here, for the first time, we have representative selections in English translation from the works of ninety-four creative authors in the Arabian Peninsula, most of them totally unknown to the canonical center of the literary system. In her preface, the editor neatly illustrates the marginal status of Arabic literary production in Arabia:

252 See, for example, the special project of the Egyptian magazine *al-Risāla* in 1936 mentioned below, p. 168n. Most of the reports about the "literary life" (*al-ḥayāt al-adabiyya*) in various regions of the Arab world recognized the central position of Egypt in Arabic culture and the marginal position of other countries. Most scholarly surveys in English on modern Arabic literature until the 1980s were still Nile-valley-centered; unlike these studies, Tomiche 1993 covers a wider area, that is, from the Gulf to the Atlantic (cf. Hartmut Fähndrich's review of the book in *Journal of Arabic Literature* 27.2 [1996], pp. 182–3). During the last few decades, as shown in the present study, scholarly activities have covered other regions.

253 For example, among the literary Arabic journals which were published in London alone: *al-Ightirāb al-Adabī* (first issue: 1985. On the nature of that journal, see Lu'lu'a 2002, pp. 143–99); *al-Nāqid* (first issue: 1988); *al-Laḥẓa al-Shi'riyya* (first issue: 1992); and *al-Kātiba* (first issue: 1993). In addition, London-based Arabic newspapers and periodicals such as *al-Ḥayāt*, *al-Sharq al-Awsaṭ*, *al-Majalla*, and *al-Quds al-'Arabī* come out with large literary supplements. Cf. also Gibb and Landau 1968, p. 270. In the twentieth century, London became an important center for the publishing of Arabic magazines, books, and newspapers (El Sharkawi 1992).

254 See below, p. 000.

255 Cf. the field of Islamic beliefs and practices as expressed by the contributions in Manger 1999. In his introduction, Manger indicates that "the variety of cases, and the variety of beliefs and practices presented, certainly point beyond any simple Orientalist notion of an unchanging world of Islam. Similarly they point beyond a notion of any 'culture core' of Islam, defined by its place of origin, Arabia, and by Arabic language and culture only. Within Islamic studies such assumptions have led researchers studying Islam in Africa and in Asia to believe they were 'on the margins,' that the religious beliefs they saw represented 'peripheral Islam' and that the religious practices they encountered were 'syncretist.' Such assumptions are shaken by studies from within the Middle East itself" (Manger 1999, p. 3).

256 See Jayyusi 1988.

> No single work on the literature of the whole area exists. Even individual genres such as poetry, for example, are not covered comprehensively. Books of criticism, literary history and even anthologies are usually devoted to the poetry of this country, or to the short story or drama of that, or of a specific group of countries (such as the Gulf states, for example). The most flagrant omissions occur in books that treat modern Arabic literature in general. These general studies make little or no mention of the varied and flourishing literature which the Peninsula has produced in modern times. It was clear from the outset that, for some reason, the literature of Arabia, once the fountainhead of literary creativity in classical times, has veered away in modern times from the mainstream of Arabic literature, and for the most part critics and literary historians of Arabic literature in general have left it untreated.[257]

In her *Trends and Movements in Modern Arabic Poetry* published more than a decade earlier (1977), Jayyusi dealt in great detail with the development of Arabic poetry in Egypt, Syria and Lebanon, Iraq, Palestine, Tunisia, Transjordan, and North America, but made no mention of what she now describes as the "varied and flourishing" poetry of the Arabian Peninsula. Needless to say, besides the scholarly interest of its editor, the publication of *The Literature of Modern Arabia* was also inspired by the efforts of the literary establishment in Arabia, especially Saudi Arabia, to enhance the status of the local literary system in the general Arabic literary system.[258] In a review of Jayyusi's *Anthology of Modern Palestinian Literature* (1992), Kamāl Abū Dīb (Kamal Abu-Deeb) (b. 1942) writes:

> In the present climate of entanglement of literary, political, ideological, ethnic, gender and other such issues, translation often assumes a significance unrelated to the literary worth of the writing. The works of certain categories of writers appear to be guaranteed immediate, uncritical and unquestioning interest in the West. These include writers who are women, Palestinian, Kurds, Berbers, or citizens of an oil-rich country that matters economically to the West or that can fund translations of the outputs of its literary figures. Soon, to be a Muslim fundamentalist will qualify a writer to even greater accolade. There are Arab poets and writers of genuine importance who have been writing for decades and who have made significant contributions to Arabic literature, but who have not been "blessed" with being translated and anthologized in English, or any other language for that matter. On the other hand, there are minor figures who have been writing for a few years and have failed to attract attention

[257] Jayyusi 1988, p. 18. In her studies since the late 1980s, Jayyusi started to give the literature of Arabia much more prominence; see also Jayyusi 2003; and Jayyusi 2005.

[258] See, for example, the reference in the Acknowledgments to "the esteemed President of King Saud University, Dr Mansour al-Turki and the university's Academic Council for making it possible for us, through a generous grant and much moral support, to prepare this volume" (Jayyusi 1988, p. 15).

in the Arab world itself, but whose work now appears in English translation. Salma Jayyusi's work has helped substantially to achieve this unbalanced state of affairs.[259]

For other areas, however, the situation is less fortuitous. The Arabic literature of India, for example, is almost unknown. A 1929 dissertation by Zubayd Aḥmad, about the contribution of Indo-Pakistan to Arabic literature, dealt only with works published until 1857.[260] 'Abd al-Ḥayy al-Ḥusnī (1869–1923) prepared a survey of Islamic culture in India,[261] paying little attention to Arabic belles-lettres.[262] Finally in 1998 Aḥmad Idrīs published a book on the Arabic literature of the Indian Peninsula until the end of the twentieth century.[263] The Arabic literature of Sicily as well found itself at the center of some scholarly attention.[264] The Arabic literature of Africa has been almost totally neglected by the canonical establishment of the literary system in both the Arab world and the West. Interest here has come from historians rather than literary scholars as illustrated by the research project initiated by J. O. Hunwick and R. S. O'Fahey. The aim of their planned six-volume series is to provide a bio-bibliographical overview of the Arabic literature of Saharan and sub-Saharan Africa. What prompted the editors was their awareness that the

> Muslim regions of Africa, although rich in writings in Arabic and in various local languages in most of the branches of the Islamic sciences and literary genres, are poor in those research tools that are the essential foundation for such an overview: catalogues of manuscript collections, biographical dictionaries of local scholars or monographs on specific literary traditions or schools. The study of Muslim Africa's political and social history has advanced considerably further

259 *The Middle East Journal* 51.2 (Spring 1997), p. 298.

260 The dissertation, submitted to the University of London, was first published in book form only in 1946 (Ahmad 1968 [1946]).

261 The survey was published only in 1958 in Damascus (al-Ḥusnī 1958). Needless to say, the delayed publication of Ahmad 1968 [1946] and al-Ḥusnī 1958 only testifies to the lack of interest in Arabic literature written in India. On India's contribution to Arabic literature, see also Yusuf 1967, pp. 54–66; Akbarabadi 1968, pp. 24–8; and Nadwi 2002, pp. 161–6. For a survey and classification of the uses of Arabic in India, compared with the uses of Persian, see Qutbuddin 2007, pp. 315–38.

262 See al-Ḥusnī 1958, pp. 42–54. However, the writer has little appreciation for the literary Arabic works of Indian writers "as prominence in literature is only the right of the eloquent Arab scholars [...] the people of India are devoid of any such science" (p. 43).

263 In the opening of his introduction, he writes: "I wish that one thousand or half a thousand scholars would spread out in the libraries of the Indian subcontinent (India, Pakistan, and Bangladesh) and shake off the dust from the thousands of Arabic books [...] because what has been written by the children of those countries exceeds the imagination of any Arab person" (Idrīs 1998, p. 3).

264 See al-Jamal 1996.

> than that of its intellectual and literary traditions. Although much research has been done, the results are scattered, often inaccessible and very uneven.[265]

Four volumes have appeared so far. The first volume deals with the literature of Eastern Sudanic and Saharan Africa to c. 1900, that is, the eastern part of the medieval Arab geographers' *Bilād al-Sūdān*, an area more or less congruent with the eastern regions of the Sahara, which include the Fezzan, the Muslim sultanates to the east of Lake Chad, and the Muslim regions of the present-day Republic of the Sudan.[266] The second volume deals with Arabic writings in Central Sudanic Africa—that is, the area lying between the present-day Republic of the Sudan and Mali, including Nigeria,[267] which has produced a voluminous and varied Arabic-Islamic literature—and the lesser-known Arabic literary traditions of Chad, Cameroon, and Niger.[268] The third volume covers the Islamic writings of Northeastern Africa.[269] The fourth volume is about the writings of Western Sudanic Africa.[270] The last two planned volumes will cover the writings of Eastern Sudanic Africa from c. 1900 onward and the writings of the Western Sahara.[271] Up to the present time, the study of Arabic literature written outside the Arab world has been in its infancy and still has a long way to go before it will receive the attention it deserves.[272]

The poet ʿAbd al-Qādir al-Janābī (b. 1944) argues that the notion of a cultural and literary center has disappeared from the Arab world. Instead, there are many local centers, but none of them could claim that it is a center whose influence could be compared to the influence that Cairo, Baghdad, or Beirut once held in the past.[273] However, it seems that the changing definition of

265 O'Fahey 1994, p. ix.

266 O'Fahey 1994.

267 On modern Arabic literature in Nigeria, see Raji 1986; Abdul-Rahmon 1995, pp. 315–25; Folorunsho 1996, pp. 287–93; Hunwick 1997, pp. 210–23; Abdul-Samad 2004, pp. 368–90 (which deals with Senegal as well); and Abdul-Samad 2009, pp. 335–61. On the influence of the Maghreb on the Arabic literary tradition of northern Nigeria, see Usman 2009, pp. 207–26. On Arabic in Nigeria as an indigenous language and a national heritage, see Amuni 2005, pp. 108–22. On Arabic-Islamic scholarship in Yorubaland, the cultural region of the Yoruba people which spans parts of modern-day Nigeria, Benin, and Togo, see Abubakre 1980; Sanni 1995, pp. 427–50; and Abubakre 1997, pp. 183–209.

268 Hunwick 1995.

269 O'Fahey 2003.

270 Hunwick 2003.

271 According to O'Fahey 1994, p. x.

272 A promising sign was the first issue of *Mundus Arabicus* (July 1981) entitled *al-Kuttāb al-ʿArab fī Amrīkā* (Cambridge: Dār Mahjar li-l-Nashr wa-l-Tawzīʿ). For a review of this issue, see *al-Ādāb*, September–October 1981.

273 See <http://www.elaph.com>, 24 July 2005 (last accessed 15 October 2016). It was published as an introduction to a series of articles by Arab writers and intellectuals on the notion of space in Arabic literature.

a literary and cultural center has much to do with the decreasing status of literature as such, as well as with the marginalization of printed literary texts in the cultural system—instead one can easily discern the emerging influence of the satellite mass media and Internet communication outlets, whose notion of culture is much broader. Additionally, the fact that al-Janābī's lamentation was published in the cultural section of an Internet newspaper is evidence of the emergence of a new center which does not have any fixed abode.[274]

LITERATURE / LANGUAGE

Given that literature is a lingual art, it is impossible to separate the diachronic development of Arabic literature from the way in which the Arabic language itself developed through the ages. That is, the interaction between them is fundamental to our understanding of both. Two factors are important here: first, the high reverence accorded to Arabic as the language of the Qur'ān[275] and the canonical medieval texts, and second, the state of diglossia between *'āmmiyya* and *fuṣḥā*, which has been a fact of the interaction between literature and language since the Middle Ages.[276] This interaction has been treated in various studies by Arab and Western scholars, especially from a stylistic point of view[277] and from the point of view of translation.[278] Here, I will focus on the general issue of the status of language in the literary system.[279]

274 Cf. Sharbal Bu'aynī, "al-Markaz al-Jadīd li-l-Thaqāfa al-'Arabiyya huwa al-Intirnit" ("The New Center of Arab Culture is the Internet"), <http://www.elaph.com>, 21 July 2005 (last accessed 15 October 2016). However, the territorial literary abode, practically and metaphorically, has not been neglected, as can be seen by recent publications such as Mehrez 2010; Mehrez 2011; and Snir 2013.

275 See Chejne 1969, pp. 8–13. The Prophet Muḥammad was quoted as saying: "Love the Arabs for three things: Because I am an Arab, and the Qur'ān is in Arabic, and the tongue of the people in Paradise is Arabic" (al-Nahrawānī 1987, III, p. 348). Muṣṭafā Ṣādiq al-Rāfi'ī (1880–1937) argued that a true renaissance of the Arab East could only be based on Islam and the Arabic language (al-Rāfi'ī 1960, III, p. 200). H. R. Culhane used the above saying (her translation "I love the Arabs" is based on the reading *uḥibbu*, while the correct form is *aḥibbū*) in the conclusion of her book to illustrate the importance of religion and language for the Arab identity of Egyptian cinema (Culhane 1995, pp. 195–9). The aforementioned Muḥammad 'Ābid al-Jābirī does not think Arabic became a sacred language because of religious considerations (al-Jābirī 1994, p. 276): "Religion did not have a cardinal role in the love of the Arabs for their language; cultural and linguistic belonging caused the Arabs to love their language."

276 On the nature of the diglossia with regard to the literary system, see Somekh 1991, pp. 5–10.

277 See, for example, 'Āmir 1967; Cachia 1967, pp. 12–22; Beyerl 1971; al-Sāmarrā'ī 1980; Cachia 1989, pp. 65–76; Cachia 1990, pp. 43–75; and Somekh 1991.

278 See, for example, Somekh 1991, pp. 75–82, 109–17.

279 The following remarks benefited from Berque 1969 (1960), pp. 213–35 (English translation: Berque 1964, pp. 190–210; Arabic translation: Berque 1982, pp. 261–93).

Thanks to the gradual interaction over time between the literary and lingual systems, language in modern Arabic literature after the post-classical period is no longer an end in itself, as was often the case with traditional poetry (for example, *qaṣīda*) and prose (for example, *maqāma*).[280] One result of this process interaction is the bridging of the gap between *ʿāmmiyya* as the language of reality and *fuṣḥā* as the language of canonical literature.[281] In the literary system of the mid-nineteenth century, texts in which language was an end in itself could still occupy the center of the literary canon. A good example is the trope-laden poetry of the aforementioned Nāṣīf al-Yāzijī (1800–71). During the nineteenth century, verses like the following were considered canonical:[282]

في فتح عكّـا بردُ نارِ معاطبٍ　　　دارِ الخليل وللديار به البُكـا
رأسَ الثمانِ وأربعين بِطيـــّهِ　　　مئتان مَعْ ألف فبارَك ربُّكـا

It is hard to detect any reasonable content in both verses, and they make some sense only if we read them in the correct order:

البُكا للديار في فتح عكّا، دارِ الخليل، بردُ نارِ معاطب
فبارَك ربُّكا رأسَ الثمانِ وأربعين بِطيّهِ مئتان مَعْ ألف

> The weeping over the remains of the encampment [of the beloved] during the occupation of Acre, the dwelling place of the lover, cools the flames of the destructions.
> May God bless the beginning of forty-eight together with two hundreds with one thousand.

These verses, written in praise of Ibrāhīm Pasha (1789–1848) in AH 1248/AD 1832 to commemorate the occupation of Acre, use *ḥisāb al-jummal*, that is, a method of recording dates of past or future events by using letters of the alphabet according to their numerical value.[283] Thus, the date 1248 appears in these two verses twenty-eight(!) times: For example, 1248 is the sum of the numerical value of all the letters of each hemistich, of all the letters *without* and of all the letters *with* diacritical points in each verse, and of each

[280] Cf. Haykal 1965, pp. 35–42.
[281] Cf. Shraybom-Shivtiel 1995, pp. 207–15.
[282] Al-Yāzijī 1904, p. 21.
[283] It is known as *ramz* or *taʾrīkh*. On *ḥisāb al-jummal*, see De Vaux 1934, p. 672; Colin 1971, p. 468; Bauer 2003, pp. 501–31; and al-Yousfi 2006, pp. 68–9. In Arabic literature, the genre of *tawārīkh* was very popular in the eighteenth and nineteenth centuries, and al-Yāzijī's son Ibrāhīm al-Yāzijī (1847–1906) devoted most of his *Dīwān* to it (al-Yāzijī 1983, pp. 144–99). On *ḥisāb al-jummal* and other rhetorical forms and embellishments which were dominant in the poetics of the premodern period, as reflected in *ʿAjāʾib al-Āthār fī al-Tarājim wa-l-Akhbār* (*The Marvelous Compositions of Biographies and Chronicles*) by the Egyptian historian ʿAbd al-Raḥmān al-Jabartī (1754–1825), see also Moreh 2000, pp. xvi–xviii.

hemistich's letters *without* diacritical points together *with* each hemistich's letters *with* diacritical points. It is mentioned in full in the second verse as well. Al-Yāzijī was able to reach this result by making each hemistich consist of an equal numerical value of the letters *with* or *without* diacritical points, that is, 624. Thus, as we have eight units with the same numerical value and as each pair consists of 1248, we can present the following arithmetical progression or series (that is, a sequence in which each term is obtained by reducing a constant number from the preceding term): 7+6+5+4+3+2+1 = 28. The two aforementioned verses, however, were only the beginning of another complicated "poetic project" by al-Yāzijī:[284]

ولمّا بلغ إبراهيم باشا البيتان أرسل يطلب منه قصيدة على نسق قصيدة السيّد شاكر النحلاوي
التي مدح بها الشيخ عبد الغني النابلسي بدمشق فنظم هذه القصيدة وقد جعل كل شطر منها تاريخا
وصدّرها ببيتين قد ضمّن كل شطر منهما تأريخين ووزّع حروف البيت الأول على أوائل أبيات
الغزل من القصيدة وحروف البيت الثاني على أوائل أبيات المديح منها أمّا البيتان فهما قوله:
أنت الخليل وفي الأطلال برد لظى أطلال عكا ورفض الرعب والحذرِ
١٢٤٨ ١٢٤٨ ١٢٤٨ ١٢٤٨
كن بالغا أوج سعد ما به ضرر أو غالبا لم يزل في أوّل الظفر
١٢٤٨ ١٢٤٨ ١٢٤٨ ١٢٤٨
أما القصيدة فهي قوله (...)

In the introduction to his *Majma' al-Baḥrayn* (*Confluence of the Two Seas*), al-Yāzijī speaks of his futile attempts to match the highest achievement of al-Hamadhānī (969–1008) and al-Ḥarīrī (1054–1122),[285] and he clearly believed that literary contributions of this kind guaranteed their author a place within the canon. However, al-Yāzijī's *maqāmāt* are more like linguistic acrobatics and culminate in fourteen verses that can be read from right to left and vice versa.[286] Consider, for example, the following verse:

قمر يفرط عمدا مشرق رش ماء دمع طرف يرمق

As with the following thirteen verses, the sole "poetic" achievement—in the modern sense—of this verse stems from the poet's skill in finding words

284 Al-Yāzijī 1904, pp. 22–7.

285 See, for example, al-Yāzijī 1958, p. 9:

إني قد تطفّلت على مقام أهل الأدب من أيّمة العرب بتلفيق أحاديث تقتصر من شبه مقاماتهم على اللقب.

286 Al-Yāzijī 1958, pp. 121–2. On the similarity of al-Yāzijī's literary exercises to those of al-Ḥarīrī's, see, for example, *al-Maqāma al-Marāghiyya* (al-Ḥarīrī 1985, pp. 48–56), *al-Maqāma al-Maghribiyya* (al-Ḥarīrī 1985, pp. 129–36), *al-Maqāma al-Qahqariyya* (al-Ḥarīrī 1985, pp. 137–43), and *al-Maqāma al-Raqṭā'* (al-Ḥarīrī 1985, pp. 205–12). Cf. Hämeen-Anttila 2002, pp. 351–7. On the literary exercises and artificial compositions of al-Ḥarīrī, see al-Ḥarîri 1969 [1867], pp. 524–5. Cf. the *maqāmat* of Ibn Ṣayqal al-Jazarī (d. 1301), which were even considered to be superior to those of al-Ḥarīrī (Stewart 2006, pp. 152–3). On the revival of the *maqāmat* of al-Ḥarīrī in the eighteenth century, see Gran 1979, pp. 57–63.

that letter by letter, or combined together, can be read both backwards and forwards. The modern reader is likely to come away from a reading of such verses "with the feeling that the author was better equipped to be a crossword or sudoku champion than an author of imaginative literature."[287] These kinds of palindromes are more like the verbal ornamentation so characteristic of the period immediately preceding the *Nahḍa* and make it dubious whether al-Yāzijī can at all be considered as belonging to the "neoclassical" trend in Arabic poetry.[288] If, curiously, this kind of poetry "seemed to satisfy generation after generation of men who were neither fools nor uncultured,"[289] this probably means that in the mid-nineteenth century the canonical center of the literary system viewed it as a touchstone of literary taste. Because of that, it is not surprising to see other poets of the second half of the nineteenth century following in al-Yāzijī's footsteps. For example, the Lebanese poet Shākir Shuqayr (1850–96)[290] wrote two verses to commemorate Khedive Ismāʿīl's being awarded a medal by the Emperor of Austria in AH 1287/AD 1870 using *ḥisāb al-jummal*. But unlike al-Yāzijī, Shuqayr used the Hijri calendar only six times and the Christian calendar eight times. He also wrote other verses imitating al-Yāzijī's poetic and linguistic acrobatics.[291]

With the gradual change in attitude toward language in poetry since the late nineteenth century, such literary phenomena no longer had a place at the center of the literary system, especially from the 1950s onward. Already in 1871 Salīm al-Bustānī (1848–84), editor of *al-Jinān*, wrote in one of his opening articles in the journal that one of his aims was to liberate the Arabic language from these chains after "ignorance resulted in the view that the real eloquence stemmed from the sound of the rhyme."[292] Later, Fu'ād Afrām al-Bustānī (1906–94) in his preface to a selection of poems by al-Yāzijī not only expressed his strong reservations about such "poems," but refused to consider them as poetry at all.[293]

287 Allen 2010, p. 380. For another view about al-Yāzijī, see Bauer 2006, pp. 49–118.

288 See, for example, Somekh 1991, pp. 48, 109.

289 Cachia 1988, p. 219. Cachia qualifies his argument by concluding that this poetry did not satisfy "an entire society, but a restricted elite, steeped in uniform learning" (p. 225).

290 On him, see Ṭarrāzī 1913, II, pp. 188–92; and Meisami and Starkey 1998, II, pp. 715–16.

291 Ṭarrāzī 1913, II, pp. 190-191.

292 *Al-Jinān* II (1871), p. 612. Cf. Al-Bustānī 1990, p. 29.

293 Al-Bustānī 1950, pp. 26–8:

إذا به ينحطّ إلى أسمج التلميحات الصرفية والنحوية والبديعية والعروضية أيضا (...) لا لوم عليه لأنه قلّد «أيّمة الأدب» وهو قد طُبع على ذلك (...) أمّا ما زاد فيه على غيره من أنواع التقليد كنظم تلك الألغاز والأحاجي وسبك القصائد العواطل وعواطل العواطل والخيفاء والرقطاء والمعجمة والملمعة وأمثلة العكس والطرد وترتيب التواريخ من مفردة ومزدوجة فلا مجال للبحث فيها وليست من الشعر في شيء.

In the third volume of the autobiography of Ṭāhā Ḥusayn (1889–1973), *al-Ayyām* (*Thy Days*) (1973), which refers to his life from 1910 to 1922, we can find an anecdote which testified to the above change in Arabic poetic sensibilities. The author—"the young man" (*al-fatā*)—is called to an interview with Shukrī Bāshā, the Sulṭān's *Chef de Bureau* (*Ra'īs al-Dīwān al-Sulṭānī*), who had an interest in Arabic literature, that is, the "Arabic literature which was favored by people of the last [nineteenth] century." Shukrī Bāshā talked about various rhetorical embellishments—*jinās*, *ṭibāq*, *ḥusn al-fukāha*, and *barā'at al-tawriya*—illustrating them with verses of "belated" (*muta'akhkhir*) poetry. However, the young man only remembered one:

أخذ الكِرى منّي وأحرمني الكرى   بيني وبينك يا ظلوم الموقف

He took the money from me, and cut me off from sleep, between me and you, O thou defrauder, is *al-mawqif*.[294]

On hearing the verse, the young man burst out laughing. The *Chef de Bureau* then said in a somewhat sorrowful tone: "This verse we used to find quite enchanting, and here you are, the leading youth of today, laughing at it and making a joke about it and its like."[295] The irony with which the young man reacted to this verse is the essence of the new modernist poetic sensibilities. This change owed much to the development of the press,[296] the growing influence of dialects, and the advent of various sociocultural changes, prominent among which was the sharp increase in the number of readers. In *al-Dīwān fī al-Adab wa-l-Naqd* (1921), 'Abbās Maḥmūd al-'Aqqād (1889–1964) and Ibrāhīm 'Abd al-Qādir al-Māzinī (1890–1949) neatly summed up the poetic ideal of the nineteenth century as follows:

فقد كان العهد الماضي عهد ركاكة في الأسلوب وتعثّر في الصياغة تنبو به الأذن، وكان آية الآيات على نبوغ الكاتب أو الشاعر أن يوفّق إلى جملة مستوية النسق أو بيت سائغ الجرس فيسير مسير الأمثال وتستعذبه الأفواه لسهولة مجراه على اللسان.

The previous period was a period of weakness in style and broken composition which grated on the ear, and the surest sign of a writer's or poet's talent was his success in producing a well-ordered sentence or an enjoyable verse which could be used as a proverb, was pleasant for the mouth, and could be used easily in speech.[297]

Another phenomenon related to the interaction between literature and language that deserves mention here is the increasing number of Arab authors

294 *Al-mawqif* means both the place where the donkeys gather in order to carry people where they want to go, as well as the place where souls gather in advance of the judgment.
295 Ḥusayn n.d. [1973], pp. 151–2. The translation is based on Husain 1976, pp. 148–9.
296 Cf. Ayalon 1995, especially pp. 173–82.
297 Al-'Aqqād and al-Māzinī n.d. [1921], I, p. 12.

writing in foreign languages, many of whom struggled with issues of identity.[298] And most of those Arab writers who wrestled with these issues were non-Muslims.[299]

LITERATURE / STATE NATIONALISM

There is general agreement among contemporary social historians that, as a direct corollary of modernity, nationalism appeared on the historical scene only fairly recently. Accepted, too, is the notion that it has its basis in invention, construction, and what noted historian Eric Hobsbawm has termed "social engineering":

> "Invented traditions" [...] are highly relevant to that comparatively recent historical innovation, the "nation," with its associated phenomena: nationalism, the nation-state, national symbols, histories and the rest. All these rest on exercises in social engineering which are often deliberate and always innovative, if only because historical novelty implies innovation.[300]

Elsewhere, but again stressing the "element of artefact," Hobsbawm approvingly quotes social anthropologist Ernest Gellner:

> Nations as a natural, God-given way of classifying men, as an inherent [...] political destiny, are a myth; nationalism, which sometimes takes pre-existing cultures and turns them into nations, sometimes invents them, and often obliterates pre-existing cultures: that is a reality.[301]

The history of the modern Middle East provides ample evidence of how effective this reality can be.[302] The nation-states that arose there after the

298 See, for example, the work of the Moroccan writer ʻAbd al-Kabīr al-Khaṭībī (Abdelkebir Khatibi) (1938–2009), especially his novel *al-Dhākira al-Mawshūma* (*The Tattooed Memory*) (translated from the French by Buṭrus al-Ḥallāq) (al-Khaṭībī 1984, especially pp. 7–10, 137–41. For the original novel, see Khatibi 1971). His poetry was also translated into Arabic, an example being *al-Munāḍil al-Ṭabaqī ʻalā al-Ṭarīqa al-Tāwiyya* (*The Fighter of Class in the Taoist Manner*) (translated by Kāẓim Jihād) (al-Khaṭībī 1986. For the original collection, see Khatibi 1976. Cf. also the two studies about al-Khaṭībī's work, by Christine Buci-Glucksmann and Muḥammad al-Zāhīrī, included in this collection [pp. 55–111]). On al-Khaṭībī, see also the special issue of *Revue CELFAN* (7.1–2, November 1988–February 1989) published by Le Centre d'Études sur la Littérature Francophone de l'Afrique du Nord (at Tulane University, New Orleans).

299 For example, among Christian and Druze writers in Hebrew (Snir 1991a, pp. 245–53; Snir 1992b, pp. 6–9; Snir 1995, pp. 163–83; and Snir 1997, pp. 141–53. See also below, p. 226n).

300 Eric Hobsbawm's "Introduction: Inventing Traditions," in Hobsbawm and Ranger 1992 [1983], p. 13.

301 Hobsbawm 1992, p. 10; emphasis in original quote from Gellner 1983, pp. 48–9.

302 It is interesting here to quote Bernard Lewis: "The introduction of the secular heresy of nationalism, of collective self-worship, is the best founded and least mentioned of the many grievances of the Middle East against the West" (Lewis 1968, p. 70).

First World War clearly serve as evidence of how politics, language, and literature all contributed to the fostering of nationalistic sentiment. Writing more than sixty years ago on developments in the West, Boyd C. Shafer already remarked that "nationalism embraces not only the political but all phases of life—men have come to work and produce and live not only for themselves but for the nation; even their truths and their Gods have become national."[303] On the subject of the national character of literature, he added:

> By the twentieth century the student seldom studied drama, poetry, or novel as such but the English, the French, or American drama, poetry, or novel. The extreme was again to be reached in the totalitarian states of the second quarter of the twentieth century when few literary works or studies of any kind could be published unless they patriotically supported the policies of the national government. By 1955, even in a democratic country like the United States, popularly elected governmental officials were examining all forms of artistic production to root out any ideas that were "un-American."[304]

This holds a fortiori for the nation-states in the Middle East, where during the last decades of the twentieth century critics and scholars have spoken of the separate Arabic literatures of Egypt, Syria, Iraq, and Lebanon. But by now it is obvious that one should also study the role that literature—or even the creation of literature—has played and still plays in the social engineering that has gone into the making of the nation-state. To return to Hobsbawm:

> Israeli and Palestinian nationalism or nations must be novel, whatever the historic continuities of Jews or Middle Eastern Muslims, since the very concept of territorial states of the currently standard type in their region was barely thought of a century ago, and hardly became a serious prospect before the end of World War I. Standard national languages, to be learned in schools and written, let alone spoken, by more than a smallish élite, are largely constructs of varying, but often brief, age.[305]

303 Shafer 1955, pp. vii–viii. On developments in Western-based cultural scholarship on nationalism, see Lazarus 1997, pp. 28–48.

304 Shafer 1955, pp. 190–1. On national character in general, see also Barakat 1993, pp. 182–90. Actual studies of national character are open to severe criticism on methodological grounds. The large majority of them provide insights into and interpretations of phenomena without undertaking the systematically controlled and detailed comparative studies that would be required for any scientific proof of the assertions made (Mitchell 1979, pp. 130–1). On the issue of national literatures, see the discussion published in the 1980s in the *Yearbook of Comparative and General Literature* following the publication in English translation of Ernst Elster's article "World Literature and Comparative Literature" (Elster 1986, pp. 7–13), first published in German at the beginning of the twentieth century (Elster 1901, pp. 33–47). See especially Clüver 1986, pp. 14–24; Clüver 1988, pp. 134–9; Clüver 1988a, pp. 143–4; Konstantinovic 1988, pp. 141–2; and Steinmetz 1988, pp. 131–3. See also above, pp. 27n, 93, regarding the concept of "world literature."

305 Eric Hobsbawm's "Introduction: Inventing Traditions" in Hobsbawm and Ranger 1992

Thus, along with the search for the gradual legitimization of the Arab nation-state came the invention, for each of them, of a particularist "national" past which was then disseminated through cultural campaigns in various fields and the inevitable shifts in educational and cultural policies in the service of indoctrination.[306] As state control of cultural organs and electronic media always comes into play here, caution is required when one encounters nationalistic themes in modern literature with regard to the conclusions one may draw from them. A case in point is Iraq, where writers and artists were "encouraged to derive their inspiration from the civilization and cultures that flourished in Mesopotamia-Iraq from remote antiquity to the modern age."[307] But then to argue that poets such as Badr Shākir al-Sayyāb (1926–64) and ʿAbd al-Wahhāb al-Bayyātī (1926–99) relied heavily on Mesopotamian themes because of their own strong sense of territorial *waṭaniyya* (patriotism)[308] would be to miss the point. Mesopotamian mythology[309] has by no means been used by Iraqi poets alone, but by poets from various Arab nation-states. Arab poets themselves seem to dismiss the

[1983], pp. 13–14. He continues: "As a French historian of Flemish language observed, quite correctly, the Flemish taught in Belgium today is not the language which the mothers and grandmothers of Flanders spoke to their children: in short, it is only metaphorically but not literally a 'mother tongue'" (p. 14). In Hobsbawm 1992 (p. 54), he writes: "National languages are therefore always semi-artificial constructs and occasionally, like modern Hebrew, virtually invented. They are the *opposite* of what nationalist mythology supposes them to be, namely the primordial foundations of national culture and the matrices of the national mind" (my emphasis).

306 For the regional school or theory (*madhhab* or *naẓariyyat al-iqlīmiyya*) in Egypt since the 1930s, whose main proponents were Aḥmad Ḍayf (1880–1945) and Amīn al-Khūlī (1895–1966), see al-Ḥuṣrī 1985, pp. 11–20. This tendency even took on an excessive aspiration, such as the desire of the Lebanese poet Saʿīd ʿAql (1911–2014) for the "Lebanonization of the world" (*Labnanat al-ʿālam*) (ʿAql 1947 [1944], p. 22). On the Phoenician tendency in literature, see ʿAwwād 1983, especially the introduction (pp. 7–11); Bawārdī 1998, pp. 48–179; and Bawārdī 2000–1, pp. 7–79.

307 Baram 1990, p. 425. See also Baram 1994, pp. 279–319. In his last, comprehensive book-length study, published twenty years later, Baram mentions the Mesopotamian themes (Baram 2014, pp. 7–8) but attributes to them much less importance and avoids referring to relevant works of poetry. On the politics of national celebrations and the "market of symbols" in modern Iraq, see Podeh 2011, pp. 108–67.

308 Baram 1983, pp. 282–7. The problematic relationship between the lingual and literary expressions based on the educational and cultural environment and on the psychological structure of each writer may be clarified by a similar relationship existing in the expression of the mystical experience in various religions: Although it is assumed that the experience is essentially the same, each mystic draws upon the specific symbols he is familiar with from his own culture. History shows us, again and again, according to the Anglo-Catholic writer Evelyn Underhill (1875–1941), "the great mystics as faithful sons of the great religions" (Underhill 1961, pp. 95–6).

309 In Arabic, it has been called *al-Mīthūlūjyā al-Tamūziyya* or *al-Rāfidayniyya* (e.g. Jabrā 1992, pp. 220–1).

"territorial" tendency in Arabic literature. According to al-Bayyātī himself, for example,

من مظاهر الانهيار الثقافي التي نراها الآن ظهور النعرة الإقليمية بحيث أننا أصبحنا نرى أن كل قطر عربي بدأ يؤصّل أسلوبا وتأريخا وهميين للحركة الأدبية في داخل هذا القطر أو ذاك.

> one of the visible signs of current cultural deterioration is the appearance of territorial chauvinism to the point that we can see each Arab nation-state beginning to establish foundations of imaginary style and history for the literary movement in the framework of this or that state.[310]

The same distinction between political territorialism, which he sees as positive, and cultural territorialism, which is a threat to "Arabic cultural sensitivity," was made by the aforementioned critic Ibrāhīm al-ʿArīs (b. 1946).[311] In other words, we find that in the contemporary Arab world the idea of "national culture" has fluctuated between two poles: general national Arab culture (*thaqāfa qawmiyya*) and the culture of the territorial nation-state (*thaqāfa waṭaniyya*).[312] Sāṭiʿ al-Ḥuṣrī (1880–1968), for example, is usually seen as one of the great defenders of the unity of Arabic literature, especially in light of the articles and essays he published in the 1950s.[313] And even as intensive territory-based cultural activities were always made under the cover of strengthening Arab unity, they nevertheless started to pose a threat to the "unity of Arab culture" in the eyes of those at the canonical center of the Arabic literary system.

One of the signs of this development came in February 1970, when the Egyptian magazine *al-Majalla*, which defined itself as "Sijill al-Thaqāfa al-Rafīʿa" ("The Register of High Culture"), published an editorial by its associate editor Shukrī ʿAyyād (1921–99) under the title "Ḥawla Waḥdat al-Thaqāfa al-ʿArabiyya" ("On the Unity of Arab Culture"). ʿAyyād complained about the absence of literary magazines, which could take on the role played by journals such as *al-Risāla* and *al-Hilāl* during the first half of the twentieth century. Although most of them were published in Cairo, they reflected the "general Arab culture." However, in the 1970s each Arab state started to foster its own territorial culture in an attempt to reach a kind of cultural "self-sufficiency" (*iktifāʾ dhātī*). Against this background, ʿAyyād

310 *Al-Majalla* (London), 27 March–2 April 1982, p. 64.

311 *Al-Yawm al-Sābiʿ*, 4 September 1989, p. 31. On the opposition to the territorial tendency in Arabic literature and its dangers, see ʿAmmār 1979, pp. 18–23. On other aspects of the territorial tendency, especially with regard to modernism in poetry, see Dāghir 1995, p. 17.

312 On the terms *waṭan* and *qawm*, see Lewis 1968, pp. 75–8, 88. On *waṭaniyya* and *qawmiyya*, see Bengio 1998, pp. 87–97. On the general national cultural identity in contemporary Arabic literature, see Ismāʿīl 1999. On *waṭan* in classical Arabic poetry, see Noorani 2016, pp. 16–42; in modern Arabic literature, see Günther and Milich 2016.

313 See, for example, al-Ḥuṣrī 1985, pp. 11–20, 143–58. Cf. Ṣāghiyya 1999, pp. 55–71.

presented *al-Majalla* as a general national Arab magazine (*majalla adabiyya qawmiyya*).[314] In the years that followed, general cultural literary activities started to gain favor in the Arab world: From 6 May to 11 May 1972, the Arab League Educational, Cultural and Scientific Organization (ALECSO) held a conference in Cairo, which came out strongly against territorial national cultural activities in the Arab world. In the proceedings, entitled *al-Waḥda wa-l-Tanawwu' fī al-Thaqāfa al-'Arabiyya al-Mu'āṣira* (*Unity and Diversity in Contemporary Arab Culture*), published in *al-Ādāb*,[315] the *maḥalliyya* (localism) and *iqlīmiyya* (territorialism) versus *qawmiyya* (nationalism) and *waḥda* (unity) dichotomy in Arab culture stands out in sharp relief, as can be seen in the text's introduction:

> لا شكّ أن حقيقة التنوّع والوحدة في الثقافة العربية ليست وليدة العصر الحاضر. فلقد عرفت الثقافة العربية في عصورها السابقة ألوانا من التنوّع، ترتدّ في المقام الأول إلى عاملين: أوّلهما أن الثقافة العربية امتدّت فشملت رقعة واسعة جدّا من الأرض، تنوّعت فيها أنماط المعيشة وتفاوتت فيها درجات التحضّر. وثانيهما، أن الثقافة العربية كانت منفتحة على الثقافات السابقة عليها والمعاصرة لها، فاستقبلت تيّارات فكرية متعدّدة جاءت إليها من المشرق والمغرب، فضلا عن حصيلة ضخمة من التراث السابق كانت تعيش في البيئات العربية نفسها وتتفاعل مع ثقافتها الجديدة. ومع هذا، فقد ظلّ للثقافة العربية في مختلف مجالات الإنتاج، طابع مميّز، جعل لها شخصية مستقلّة حين تقارن بثقافات الأمم الأخرى في العصور القديمة والوسيطة، والدارسون المحدثون مهما اختلفت أحكامهم على الحضارة العربية، يعترفون بهذا التنوّع من التميّز والاستقلال ويجد فيه ورثة الثقافة العربية مصدرا من مصادر الخصب ووفرة العطاء (...) تمكين الجماهير في كل قطر عربي أن تظلّ قادرة على فهم الإنتاج الثقافي لأبناء سائر الأقطار العربية الأخرى والاستفادة منه، لتذكير الأجهزة الثقافية الكبرى في الأقطار العربية بمهمّتها في هذا المجال ليكون هذا التنوّع مصدرا وعاملا في إثراء الثقافة العربية واكتمال وحدتها.

There is no doubt that the essence of diversity and unity in Arab culture is not a product of the contemporary period. Arab culture has known in its previous periods various kinds of diversity, which can fundamentally be explained by two causes: first, Arab culture spread to and included very wide territories, where the ways of life were of various kinds and the levels of civilization were different. And second, Arab culture has been open to preceding and contemporary cultures and has been influenced by many intellectual trends from East and West, in addition to the interaction of this new culture with the wide range of ancient heritage embedded in the same Arab environment. Nevertheless, Arab culture has retained its special nature in various domains of creativity and it is this which gives it its own identity, if we compare it with other cultures in ancient and medieval times. Whatever the opinions of the new scholars regarding Arab civilization are, they admit that in this diversity of distinction and independence the inheritors of the Arab legacy find one of the sources of their fertility and abundance of giving [...] It enables the masses from each Arab state to under-

314 'Ayyād 1970, pp. 2–3.
315 *Al-Ādāb*, June 1972, pp. 81–114.

> stand and benefit from the cultural creation of peoples from other Arab states, in order to emphasize before the large cultural apparatuses in Arab states their role in this domain so that this diversity continues to be a source of and a cause for enriching Arab culture and completing its unity.[316]

Quite a few intellectuals in the Arab world refer to conferences such as the ALECSO conference as paying lip-service to the unity of Arab culture. In the same month that *al-Ādāb* published the proceedings of the ALECSO conference, the Egyptian writer Bahā' Ṭāhir (b. 1935) wrote in another magazine that such conferences with great titles were not useful because they failed to yield practical results.[317] Nevertheless, the efforts to strengthen Arab cultural unity would continue for the next decades. In the 1990s Aziz al-Azmeh ('Azīz al-'Aẓma) discerns an Arab culture that transcends boundaries:

> Arab nationality has thus in the course of many decades become an accomplished and cultural fact, not only because a high-cultural, "modular" cohesion has been accomplished, but also because the mass-cultural field has been to a large extent homogenized, and in the same breath, commodified. One would cite here, for example, the circulation of a largely but by no means exclusively Egyptian output of television serials, films, songs, and school teachers: a mixed blessing, as it should really more aptly be described as low, rather than popular, culture. Much like the crassness of the gutter press in Britain and the United States, it has the effect of obliterating entire regions of lived culture and substituting for them a cultural surface which might be read as a text no less canonical for being, or rather for becoming, popular. This by no means implies the disappearance of local particularisms, and such ethnographic distinction, indeed distinctiveness, is the normal condition of all societies, although England, Holland, and parts of the Nordic countries bespeak a homogenization of a thoroughness that is truly original, not matched by conditions in, say, France or Germany.[318]

Yet, here too we find that the attempt to bring particularist cultural activities under one general Arab umbrella stems from the realization that the long-cherished dream of pan-Arabism, of a united Arab state, or even of a coherent Arab political bloc had to be abandoned.[319] It is small wonder that

316 *Al-Ādāb*, June 1972, p. 81. For a similar collection of articles, more than twenty years later, see *Waḥdat al-Thaqāfa al-'Arabiyya: Abḥāth Nadwat 'Ammān (10–12 Kānūn al-Awwal 1993)* ('Ammān: Manshūrāt al-Ittiḥād al-'Āmm li-l-Udabā' wa-l-Kuttāb al-'Arab, 1995).

317 See *al-Ṭalī'a*, June 1972, p. 202.

318 Al-Azmeh 1995b, pp. 11–12. See also al-Azmeh's observations in al-Khūlī 1998 (pp. 355–6). Cf. Ṣāghiyya 1999, pp. 78–103.

319 In the early 1990s Bernard Lewis wrote that pan-Arabism no longer counts as a political force: "It survives among diminishing groups of intellectuals, mainly outside the Arab lands; it is still cherished by a variety of special interests, often for reasons unrelated to the concerns or well-being of the Arabs themselves. But it is not a factor in international or inter-Arab or even domestic politics. Is this change irreversible? Nothing is impossible, and

the Jordanian scholar Shākir al-Nābulsī (b. 1940), "the most systematic of the Arab liberals,"[320] preferred to conclude an analysis of the last stage of the development of the national Arab discourse with the following lines by the aforementioned Iraqi poet 'Abd al-Wahhāb al-Bayyātī:

طحنتنا في مقاهي الشرقِ
حرب الكلماتْ
والسيوف الخشبيّةْ
والأكاذيب
وفرسان الهواء (...)
شغلتنا الترهات
فقتلنا بعضنا بعضا
وها نحن فتات.

The war of words in the cafés of the East
Has crushed us
So have the wooden swords
And the lies
And the airy knights [...]
The lies have kept us busy
We have killed each other
And here we are only crumbs.[321]

A similar phenomenon occurred in the field of culture and literature,[322] especially when literature was not conceived of as an isolated activity in society regulated by laws exclusively and inherently different from those governing all other human activities, but as an integral, often central, and very powerful force in society.[323] During the 1980s and 1990s one could seldom find in the

it may be that the US or Israeli governments will succeed where all the Arab governments have failed, in reviving the cause of pan-Arabism and recreating an Arab political bloc. What is much more likely, however, is that the position of the Arab world will more closely resemble that of Latin America—a group of countries linked by a common language and culture, a common religion, a common history, a common sense, even, of destiny, but not united in a common polity" (Lewis 1992, p. 101. Cf. Landau 1995, p. 247; and Ṣāghiyya 1999, especially pp. 9–19). For what may be seen as a new breed of Arab nationalist thought in the writings on Arabism and a revived assessment of Arab nationalism in the 1980s, see Jawani 1996. For the broad issue of the interactions between language, culture, and nationalism in the Arab world and for relevant bibliographical references, see Suleiman 2003; Suleiman and Muhawi 2006; and Versteegh et al. 2006, I, pp. 527–36.

320 On al-Nābulsī's "Liberal Manifesto," see Hatina 2011, pp. 12–16. The words in quotation marks are from p. 12.

321 Al-Nābulsī 2001, p. 92. The lines are from the poem "Bukā'iyya ilā Shams Ḥazīrān" ("An Elegy for the Sun of June") published in *'Uyūn al-Kilāb al-Mayyita* (*The Dead Dogs' Eyes*) (1969) (al-Bayyātī 1979, II, pp. 284–5). Due to an inaccuracy in the lines quoted by al-Nābulsī, they are quoted here as they appear originally in the poem.

322 Cf. Ṣāghiyya 1999, pp. 73–86.

323 Cf. Even-Zohar 1990, p. 2.

Arab world a reference to "Arabic literature" as such, but instead to "Egyptian literature," "Palestinian literature," "Syrian literature," and even "Kuwaitian literature," "Bahraini literature," and "Omani literature."[324] Thus, it is small wonder that already in the beginning of the 1980s a Saudi cultural magazine dedicated a section to Saudi literature (*rukn al-adab al-Saʿūdī*)[325] and an Egyptian scholar in his book on the Arabic short story dealt separately with the literary production of nineteen national Arab states.[326] Scholars in the West have followed suit. For example, in the *Encyclopedia of World Literature in the 20th Century,* the entry "Arabic Literature" includes references to the entries on Algerian, Egyptian, Iraqi, Lebanese, Moroccan, Nigerian, Palestinian, Somali, Sudanese, Syrian, and Tunisian literatures.[327]

324 I have collected hundreds of studies published during the few last decades in periodicals, magazines, and books about particularist territorial national literatures in the Arab world. For lack of space, mention here is being made only of some early studies of territorial national literary entities from the late 1980s and the 1990s, such as *al-Adab al-Imārātī* (the literature of the United Arab Emirates) (Muḥammad 1993, p. 22. On the building of a new nation in the United Arab Emirates, see Alqassime 1996); *al-adab al-Mūrītānī* (Mauretanian literature) (al-Naḥawī 1979); *al-Adab al-Qaṭarī* (Qatarian literature) (*al-Akhbār*, 20 December 1989, p. 11); and *al-Adab al-ʿUmmānī* (Omani literature) (al-Shārūnī 1990; see also the special issue on the short story published in *al-ʿAlam al-Thaqāfī* [Rabat], 29 October 1994. In his introduction, the editor, Najīb Khadārī [b. 1933], speaks about the "effective and propagated presence" [*ḥuḍūr fāʿil wa-mutawālid*] of modernism in ʿUmānī literary creation [p. 1]). The territorial tendency in Arabic literature has also brought about the publication of special bibliographical lists and books of local national literatures, such as those on Algerian literature (Bois 1992, pp. 103–11) and Tunisian literature (e.g. Fontaine 1992, pp. 183–93; Fontaine 1997; and Fontaine 2010, pp. 117–44). Jean Fontaine wrote extensively about modern Tunisian literature. For a list of his books on the topic, see Fontaine 1997, p. 4. For earlier bibliographical lists of Tunisian literature published by Fontaine, see *Journal of Arabic Literature* 13 (1982), pp. 151–3; 17 (1986), pp. 151–4; 19 (1988), pp. 84–7; and 20 (1989), pp. 213–15. The same journal published similar lists about Moroccan literature (by L. K. De Voogd in 13 [1982], pp. 149–50) and Syrian literature (by B. Seekamp in 22 [1991], pp. 176–81).

325 See *al-Majalla al-ʿArabiyya*, April 1981, pp. 20–2, 28–31. For a comprehensive survey of "modern Saudi literature," whose history, so it is argued, starts at the beginning of the twentieth century "together with the establishment of the Saudi state," see Mujalī 2005; the quotation is from p. 18.

326 Wādī 2001.

327 Klein 1982, I, p. 104. Cf. also Gibb and Landau 1968, p. 193 ("Die Aufteilung erfolgt deshalb geographisch, weil es ungeachtet der thematischen Gleichförmigkeiten und der Ähnlichkeit, die sich auf die Art des Dargebotenen bezieht, dennoch offenkundige Unterschiede nach dem Entwicklungsstand der Literatur gibt und lokal bedingte Nuancen zumindest in einem Teil der arabischen Länder"). See also Gibb and Landau 1968, p. 288 and the method of presentation in Tomiche 1993, chapters two, three, and four. International scholarly journals started to publish during the last few decades studies dealing with particularist Arab literatures: see Michalak-Pikulska 1994, pp. 23–8; Baldissera 1995, pp. 89–100; Michalak-Pikulska 1998, pp. 184–201; Michalak-Pikulska 2001, pp. 59–65; Ramsay 2006, pp. 211–16; Michalak-Pikulska 2008, pp. 28–33; Michalak-Pikulska 2009, pp. 39–48; Raven 2010, pp. 201–17; Fadhila 2011, pp. 301–21; Liebhaber 2011, pp. 249–65; Suvorov 2012,

This tendency might be considered a setback if we read what Salma Khadra Jayyusi wrote in the late 1970s:

> The forties, however, were the last decade in which poetry in the Arab world was first recognized by its country of origin. The modern poetic movement which flourished in the fifties was to be a unifying movement which was to unite the energy of poets all over the Arab world. In the fifties Arab poets were usually recognized not as Egyptians, Syrians, Iraqis, Lebanese, etc., but as followers of the new movement or as conventional poets.[328]

While modern Arabic poetry, and literature in general, may artistically be referred to as a unifying movement, there has been in each Arab nation-state a strong tendency to emphasize, more than ever,[329] the particularist characteristics of its own relevant territorial national literature, including its folk heritage.[330] In the 1960s the French scholar Charles Pellat (1914–92)

pp. 24–30; Alami 2013, pp. 443–53; Idrissi 2013, pp. 60–75; Almaiman 2014; McManus 2014, pp. 322–33; and Ruocco 2014. Similar studies in languages other than Arabic have been published as chapters in books, though only a sample of them appear in the References.

328 Jayyusi 1977, p. 242.

329 It is instructive to compare the territorial cultural tendencies in the Arab world since the 1980s with the findings that came out of a special project initiated by the Egyptian magazine *al-Risāla* in 1936: Writers from all over the Arab world were asked to report on the state of the "literary life" (*al-ḥayāt al-adabiyya*) in their respective areas; their responses were then published in successive issues. These areas comprised Baghdad (al-Amīn 1936, pp. 381–3); Damascus (al-Ṭanṭāwī 1936, pp. 214–16); Lebanon (al-Shaqīfī 1936, pp. 540–1); Palestine (Ṭūqān 1936, pp. 2047–8); East Jordan (al-Qassūs 1936, pp. 865–7); Tunis (al-Ḥalīwī 1936, pp. 1062–4); Ḥijāz (Shabkashī 1936, pp. 586–7); and Morocco (Ibn Jallūn 1936, pp. 743–4; K. 1936, pp. 984–6). Significantly, all reports, directly or indirectly, were in favor of a united Arab culture. For some of the writers, the project of the magazine itself illustrated a response to the "narrow territorial idea" (*al-fikra al-iqlīmiyya al-ḍayyiqa*), that is, they saw *al-Risāla* not only as an Egyptian magazine but primarily as an Arab one (al-Ṭanṭāwī 1936, p. 214). Most of the reports mentioned the central status of Egypt in Arabic culture and the marginality of other regions. The report on Lebanon briefly mentions the Lebanese poetry in *'āmmiyya*, though without indicating any territorial cultural tendency (al-Shaqīfī 1936, p. 541).

330 The interest in folklore has generally much to do with nation-building, as exemplified by the Palestinian case (see, for example, the anthology of Palestinian folktales, that is, Muhawi and Kanaana 1989, especially p. 12 [Arabic version: Muhawwī and Kanā'ina 2001, especially pp. 5–6]. In March 2007 the Hamas-run Ministry of Education ordered this anthology to be pulled from school libraries and destroyed because the folktales contained sexually explicit language. Kanaana said he believes that "The Little Bird," a tale in a chapter entitled "Sexual Awakening and Courtship," was one of the reasons the book was banned because it mentions genitals. In their notes, the authors explain that the bird in the story is a symbol of femininity, adding that the use of sexual subjects in Palestinian folklore is a principal source of humor [*Associated Press*, 6 March 2007]. After several days, the Education Minister reversed the ban after protesters had taken to the streets and marched to the Ministry of Education in Ramallah with banners that read: "No to Ignorance. Yes to Enlightenment" [*Associated Press*, 10 March 2007]). On this topic, see also Ṣāghiyya 1999, pp. 87–103. Al-'Antīl 1987, on the other hand, concentrates on the general issue of folklore. On Arab folklore in general, see Reynolds 2007.

could still write that "some modern Arabic authors are trying hesitantly to revive the ancient themes in order to make of them truly literary works, but it is quite certain that, on the whole, folklore hardly inspires contemporary writers, who are more interested in imitating the West, neglecting this traditional material."[331] The great amount of attention paid in recent decades to the folkloric heritage of each Arab state is by no means due only to cultural and literary motives; it has been spurred on by a territorial national cultural tendency.[332] Even the thematic allusions in modern Arabic fiction to famous ancient narratives are not generally justified by purely literary considerations; rather, they are frequently motivated by territorial national causes.[333]

The close relationship between Arabic literature and Arab politics, territorialism, and nationalism is generally quite clear, and nowhere is this relationship more evident than in the case of Oman: "The history of modern Omani literature," according to the Egyptian writer and critic Yūsuf al-Shārūnī (b. 1924), "is the history of the Omani renaissance which began in 1970 when the Sultan Qābūs ibn Sa'īd (b. 1940) came to power."[334] The Syrian critic Khaldūn al-Sham'a (b. 1941) has lambasted this particularist cultural phenomenon as a "baseless territorial narcissism which is devoid of prerequisite minimal credibility" (*narjasiyya quṭriyya majjāniyya taftaqiru ilā al-ḥadd al-adnā min al-miṣdāqiyya al-maṭlūba*), adding that with the entry of other states into the Arab League, we might soon expect to hear about a Djiboutian or Mauretanian novel.[335] This particularist cultural trend, namely, the tendency of the literary system to be tightly connected to the political system, is gaining so much strength that the term "Arabic literature" is sometimes considered to be essentially identical with the term "European literature." That is, the Arabic language is expected to play the same role as Latin once did in Europe when the latter's fall "exemplified a larger process in which the sacred communities integrated by old sacred

331 Pellat 1960, p. 371.

332 See, for example, al-Barghūthī 1986, pp. 8–9 on the role of popular songs in the consolidation of territorial national identity. See also Armbrust 1992, pp. 525–42.

333 See, for example, the allusion to the popular story of 'Antara in *al-Arḍ* (*The Land*) (1953) by the Egyptian 'Abd al-Raḥmān al-Sharqawī (1920–87): Shaykh Yūsuf's national enthusiasm grows when he is reading the story of this black slave hero who defeated the oppressors (al-Sharqawī 1968 [1953], pp. 200–2. For a partial English translation of these pages by D. Stewart, see al-Sharqawi 1990 [1962], pp. 147–8). Aida Adib Bamia used a passage from these pages as a motto for the chapter "The Power of Folk Poetry" in her book on Algerian folk poetry (Bamia 2001, p. 11).

334 Al-Shārūnī 1990, p. 9. See also al-Shārūnī 1990a.

335 Al-Sham'a 1989, p. 78. When al-Sham'a wrote these words, he did not notice that his "prophecy" had already come true, as indicated above.

languages were gradually fragmented, pluralized, and territorialized."[336] For the Lebanese writer Yūsuf Ḥabashī al-Ashqar (1929–92), there is no such thing as the "Arabic novel." There are only "Egyptian novels," "Syrian novels," and "Lebanese novels" (among others) written in Arabic.[337] Likewise, in a discussion with the Syrian writer ʿAlī ʿUqla ʿArsān (b. 1940), an advocate of one shared Arab culture, the literary critic Jihād Fāḍil argued that traditional Arab culture was nothing but a daydream.[338] In fact, Fāḍil is one of the most outspoken literary critics inveighing against what he describes as *al-nazʿa al-shuʿūbiyya*[339] in modern Arabic literature, especially as expressed in the works of Adūnīs and Nizār Qabbānī.[340]

The development of independent national literatures sharpened the conflict in the Arabic literary system between distinctiveness and unity, that is, between Arab identity and local territory-specific identities.[341] It is too early to state whether or not Arabic literature is going to lose its unity and be replaced by distinct local literatures. However, one cannot be as certain as Sāṭiʿ al-Ḥuṣrī (1880–1968), who in the late 1950s exclaimed that "there is not and there will never be Egyptian literature, Iraqi literature, or Syrian and Tunisian. But there are and there will be Egyptian, Iraqi, Syrian, and Tunisian writers."[342] A prominent factor in any future development will certainly be whether religion and the language of the Qur'ān will be able to maintain their role as unifying cultural forces.[343] Given that the process of standardizing classical Arabic was mainly motivated by the desire to keep

336 Anderson 1991, p. 19. On this issue in the Arab world, see Kazziha 1981, pp. 154–64; and al-Ḥuṣrī 1985, pp. 33–50.

337 Al-Shamʿa 1989, p. 78.

338 *Al-Ḥawādith*, 17 September 1993, p. 45: "We speak about general national Arab thought in a time when Arab nationalism is deteriorating in one way or another, if we want it or not."

339 An allusion to the movement within the early Islamic commonwealth of nations which refused to recognize the privileged position of the Arabs.

340 See, for example, Fāḍil 1989, especially pp. 16–19, 69–75, and 135–49.

341 On this issue, see, for example, the case of Syria (Snir 1992c, pp. 61–4; Snir 1996b, pp. 165–82; Cooke 2007). The same conflict also exists in other fine arts such as cinema. See, for example, al-Naḥḥās 1986; and Armbrust 1994–5, pp. 6–20.

342 Al-Ḥuṣrī 1985, p. 19. Against the background of this statement, it is interesting to note that in 1937 Ṭāhā Ḥusayn, then Rector of the Egyptian University, suggested that a special chair for Islamic Egyptian literature should be founded. Commenting on this suggestion, historian Muḥammad ʿAbd Allāh ʿAnān (1898–1986) wrote in *al-Risāla* that Ṭāhā Ḥusayn's call was not due only to national motives but also due to "scientific, cultural, and historical motives, which make Islamic Egyptian literature an independent literary component among general Arabic literary heritage" (ʿAnān 1937, p. 249).

343 Cf. al-Ḥusaynī 1966, p. 17; and ʿImāra 1991, pp. 170–94. The French Orientalist Clément Huart (1854–1926) emphasized the close relationship between language and religion in the Arab world (Huart 1966, pp. 443–6). In the 1920s G. Young could still write that "it is not impossible that in the distant future, Egypt will substitute French for Arabic" (Young 1927, p. 284). Some North African writers in French, such as the Algerian writer Kātib Yāsīn

the Qur'ān intelligible to Muslims,[344] it is being argued that it is the use of *fuṣḥā* in literature which keeps the holy book intelligible for Arabs everywhere, while the use of *'āmmiyya* in literature could have the exact opposite effect.[345] For the time being, as the Islamist theorist Muḥammad 'Imāra (b. 1931) states, "the Muslims are one nation that came out from one book and its lands, peoples, tribes and nationalities are nothing but verses and chapters in this book."[346] Should Islam lose its dominant cultural role, the development of independent literatures may well accelerate. At the same time, while the use of local dialects in literature is now considered as a kind of "conspiracy against the unity of the Arab homeland,"[347] they may well come to replace *fuṣḥā* as the major medium of literary production.[348] At present, those at the canonical center of Arabic literature reject any change in this

(Kateb Yacine) (1929–89), rejected writing in Arabic, which he saw as fossilized much like Latin (*al-Bilād*, 8 January 1994, pp. 50–1).

344 Ibn Khaldûn 1967 [1958], II, p. 444; Ibn Khaldūn 1979, III, p. 1031.

345 Cf. Farrūkh 1961, pp. 151–220.

346 'Imāra 1991, p. 194. Cf. the view of the Saudi writer 'Abd Allāh Mannā' (b. 1939) on the cultural fragmentation in the Arab world (*al-Shurūq*, 1–8 September 1993, p. 40). For more on the relationship between Islam and nationalism, see Polka 2000, pp. 127–33.

347 Al-Qa'īd 1994, p. 226 (the comment of the publisher). Cf. Qāsim 1980, pp. 391–7. At different times, several European scholars, such as John Selden Willmore (1856–1931), Socrates Spiro (1868–19??), and William Willcocks (1852–1932), all resided in the Arab world, called for the replacement of *fuṣḥā* by *'āmmiyya* as the main language of writing, and were consequently considered as sharing in and even directing such a conspiracy against united Arab culture. On the issue known as *ma'ārik al-'āmmiyya wa-l-fuṣḥā* ("the battles between *'āmmiyya* and *fuṣḥā*") or *al-da'wa ilā al-'āmmiyya* ("the propaganda for *'āmmiyya*"), see al-Jundī 1963, especially pp. 54–68, 99–105, and 227–36; Maṭlūb 1968, pp. 130–40; Sa'īd 1980; al-Ḥuṣrī 1985, pp. 29–32; and Sharkey 2004, pp. 131–49. The call for the replacement of *fuṣḥā* by *'āmmiyya* was reinvented several years ago in Israel, but without referring at all to the aforementioned European scholars' call and its subsequent failure. However, this new "preaching" seems to have been motivated more by a narrow political and national agenda than by solid scholarship: "Nationalism that is based on a standard language that artificially unites a large variety of dialects, many of which cannot be easily understood by other speakers, [carries] the seeds of destruction. The symptoms may vary, taking the form of racism, religious fanaticism, dictatorship, fascism, world war, or murderous terrorist attacks upon civilians, but the underlining disease is the same" (Myhill 2006, p. 280).

348 Contrary to literature, in the sciences *fuṣḥā* is gradually losing its position, and foreign languages, especially English, French, German, and Russian, and even *'āmmiyya*, are taking its place. Interesting evidence for this development may be found in an article published by Ramaḍān 'Abd al-Tawwāb (1930–2001), formerly Dean of the Faculty of Humanities at the Egyptian 'Ayn Shams University entitled "Arabic is the Language of Science." In it the author calls for the "Arabization of sciences" (*ta'rīb al-'ulūm*), but mentions only one successful attempt, in his view, to employ *fuṣḥā* in the teaching of sciences, that is, in the faculties of medicine in Syria (*Minbar al-Islām* 54.2 [July 1995], pp. 72–6. Cf. Ṭalfāḥ 1976, p. 4; and Abū Bashar 1991, pp. 25–52. See also the special issue of *al-Ādāb*, February 1975, on the question of Arabization). This matter has preoccupied the minds of Arab intellectuals since the beginning of the *Nahḍa* in the nineteenth century (e.g. Mubārak 1936, pp. 15–26). On the status of Western languages in the Arab world, see Lemu 1993, pp. 34–6.

direction. In his book *al-Adab al-Ḥadīth fī Lubnān—Naẓra Mughāyira* (*Modern Literature in Lebanon—A Different Outlook*) (1996), Jihād Fāḍil reveals his negative attitude toward any sort of "canonization of the vernacular" (*taqnīn al-'āmmiyya*), and he caricatures attempts that were made in this direction in Lebanon.[349] His main objection is not to the writing of literature in the vernacular, but to the desire to canonize this literature and have it replace the literature written in *fuṣḥā*. Referring to the poetic works of Michel Ṭrād (1912–98), he says:

> على أن ما يسيء إلى تجربة ميشال طراد الشعرية الشعبية، ليس كتابة القصيدة العامّية، بل التنظير لهذه العامّية، ووعي الشاعر بأنه يؤسّس شعرا بلغة جديدة هي اللغة اللبنانية، أو «اللغا اللبنانيي» حسب تعبيره وتعبير مواطنه الزحلاوي الشاعر سعيد عقل (...) فهو شاعر لا أيديولوجي وليته اكتفى بالزجل دون ولوج باب التنظير لأن الشاعر الذي ينظم أجمل الكلمات من الغبن أن يقع في أسوأ النتظيرات.

> What harms Michel Ṭrād's poetic vernacular experience is not the writing of *qaṣīda* in *'āmmiyya* but rather presenting theoretical foundations for it, and the poet's awareness that he is introducing a poetry in a new language, that is Lebanese language, or *al-Lughā al-Libnāniye* as it is called [in the Lebanese dialect] by him and by his compatriot from Zaḥla Sa'īd 'Aql [...] He is a poet, not a man of ideology and I wish he had confined himself to writing *zajal* and refrained from insinuating himself in the space of theory because for a poet who composes the most beautiful words it is wrong to fall prey to the worst theories.[350]

There are others who see no danger in literature in *'āmmiyya*, although it is hard in general to ignore the nationalistic motives behind their arguments. For example, the Tunisian writer 'Izz al-Dīn al-Madanī (b. 1938) wrote in 1973 that the time had come "to reconsider the past and to eliminate the holiness that surrounds it, including the holiness of the Arabic language, which is in urgent need of deconstruction (*tafkīk*) and reconstruction (*i'ādat al-tarkīb*), and in need of being infused with its various dialects."[351] Fifteen years later the Palestinian scholar 'Abd al-Laṭīf al-Barghūthī (1928–2002) rejected the fear of a decline in the status of the Qur'ān or *fuṣḥā* as a result of the improvement in the status of popular literature:

> إن ذلك التخوّف على اللغة الفصحى، وبالتالي على القرآن الكريم، وعلى تراث اللغة العربية الفصحى بأسره، أمر عفا عليه الدهر، ولم يعد ذا بال، لأن القرآن ولغة القرآن، أقوى وأرسخ من أن يزعزعهما، أو يهدمهما، أي اهتمام بلهجة عربية عامّيّة، هما في واقع الحال المعين الذي تستمدّ منه حياتها. والذي يجب أن يخشى عليه من التغيّر، والانتقاص، والاندثار، والزوال، في ظلّ الظروف الراهنة المعادية، هو ليس القرآن، ولا لغة القرآن، وإنما هي اللهجة العربية الفلسطينية الدارجة، التي لا وطن لها، ولا سند، سوى من يحملونها من أبنائها، وهم قوم تكالبت عليهم الأيّام، فجعلتهم عرضة

349 Fāḍil 1996, pp. 71–81.
350 Fāḍil 1996, pp. 148, 153.
351 See al-Madanī 1973, p. 67.

للضياع والهلاك، وذلك بدوره يجعل لهجتهم عرضة لأن تضيع بضياعهم، وتهلك بهلاكهم، إذا لم نسارع إلى رصدها، ودرسها، وتدوينها، قبل أن تفوت الفرصة السانحة، وتضيع الغاية المرموقة.

> That fear for the *fuṣḥā*, and consequently for the Holy Qur'ān and the whole heritage of *fuṣḥā*, is obsolete and is no longer relevant. The Qur'ān and the language of the Qur'ān are too strong and too powerful to be devastated and destroyed by any attention paid to any Arabic dialect; moreover, they actually are the spring from which the dialect draws its life. What has to be guarded against change, deterioration, perdition, and extinction, in these current hostile circumstances, is not the Qur'ān or the language of the Qur'ān, but the Arabic Palestinian dialect. This dialect has no homeland and no support, with the exception of its children who speak it, against whom times have rushed and have made a target for perdition and extinction. This puts their dialect in danger of perdition, together with their extinction, if we do not hurry to preserve, study and record it before the passing of the present opportunity and the loss of the desired aim.[352]

The nationalistic motives (in this case Palestinian nation-building) that inspire 'Abd al-Laṭīf al-Barghūthī's arguments are undeniable. Discussing Arabs' attitudes toward their respective dialects, Charles Ferguson observed that Arabs tend to feel that their own dialect is the best spoken Arabic and that it is the closest to classical Arabic.[353] This phenomenon reflects both a regional pride in the national dialect and, for the time being, an adherence to the *fuṣḥā*. Thus, the Arabic literary system is still considered to be a united system, although, much as in the past,[354] certain local territorial literatures have shown their distinctiveness.[355] However, the development of the Internet and its associated communications technologies during the last few decades, the advent of globalization, and the recent teetering of the nation-state in parts of the Arab world—in addition to the rise of cosmopolitanism (the fact that we can no longer take it for granted that society is equated with

352 Al-Barghūthī 1988, pp. 20–1.

353 Ferguson 1968 [1959], pp. 379–80. Cf. Nader 1968, p. 279. Summarizing sociolinguistic interviews with Cairenes, Niloofar Haeri, however, observed that while Egyptians generally seemed to believe that their language is the most widely understood, they did not think that their own dialect was the closest to classical Arabic. In fact, they often cited Jordanians, or natives of the Gulf countries, as the ones whose dialects were closer to classical Arabic (Haeri 1996, p. 219).

354 See, for example, the regional literature in Egypt and Yemen (Ashtiany et al. 1990, pp. 412–68).

355 See, for example, the North African Arabic literary system (al-Salāwī 1986; al-Sa'dī 1989; Ostle 1991, pp. 193–212; *al-Ādāb*, February 1995 [special issue on Moroccan literature]; and Campbell 2013). Another prominent example is the relationship between Palestinian literature and the contemporary process of Palestinian nation-building (Snir 1990, pp. 244–68; Snir 1991b, pp. 202–5; Snir 1995a, pp. 29–73; Snir 2015, pp. 17–154). On the other hand, Arabic literature in certain territories is sometimes considered part of literary systems (e.g. African literature) whose distinctiveness is based on geographical factors. For the case of African literature, see Irele 2009.

the nation-state), and the belief in the necessity to avoid treating identities as fixed and absolute entities[356]—all have recently brought about the feeling that national cultures, in many instances, have been replaced by a single globalized culture. When I write these words, I recall Ignác Goldziher's (1850–1921) report on the books brought from the East for the Hungarian Academy of Sciences (1874),[357] where it was clear that Goldziher understood national sentiment in the Arabic texts as reflecting pan-Arabism and not as reflecting a territorial identity. Since then, many nation-states were established in the Arab world and each has had significant influence on the Arabic literature within its borders; but the last decade has witnessed the modern structure of the nation-state chafe under constant pressure from the forces of globalization.[358] Consequently, the diachronic intersystemic interaction between literature and state nationalism calls for renewed investigation.

356 See below, the Conclusion.
357 Mestyan 2015, pp. 443–80.
358 Zajda 2009, p. 8.

Chapter 4

Literary Dynamics in Generic and Diachronic Cross-section

The study of the literary dynamics of Arabic literature in generic and diachronic cross-section aims at an investigation that is restricted to the historical development of each genre and the diachronic relationships between genres. Each genre, as well as each subgenre, should be examined in its own right and on its own terms, but the historical interrelationships and interactions that obtain between the components of the literary system are just as important. Any scholarly examination into this topic should take into account the developing innovations in and discussions of genre theory and seek to answer the question, "What is a genre?"[1] It must also look into the transtextual and transgeneric writing and the intergeneric relationships in modern Arabic literature.[2] Finally, it has to find an answer to the important question of periodization: How does one define a "literary period"? Just as any world history needs to divide up the temporal continuum and offer ways in which to trace the evolution of mankind, so too an examination of literature must of necessity schematize the history of its development.[3] As has been shrewdly pointed out, "the division of history into periods is not a fact, but a necessary hypothesis or tool of thought, valid in so far as it is illuminating, and dependent for its validity on interpretation."[4] Also, as Frank Kermode argued in the late 1980s, "although periods are often detected long after they are over, it is not unusual for people to think they are actually in one; such is the case with the 'Postmodernism' of the present moment."[5] The methodological problems that arise from a definition of periods or

1 For an account of the state of the research in this field, see Taha 2000, pp. 101–19. See also Szyska and Pannewick 2003, especially the introduction (pp. 1–9).

2 See Jābir 2006; and Allen 2007, pp. 256–7.

3 Cf. Momigliano 1987, pp. 31–57.

4 Carr 1965, p. 60.

5 Kermode 1988, p. 122.

movements in cultural history, such as those explained by E. H. Gombrich,[6] need to be clarified and explicated. Therefore, we will have to look at how plausible some explanatory models of literary change are for our purpose—both literary and extra-literary.[7] And we should not forget that our choices will inevitably be "controlled by the desires of the mind and even by the desire for power."[8]

As always, how we define the relationship between modern and classical Arabic literature remains fundamental to our understanding of the contemporary literary system and the way in which it developed historically.[9] In other words, the question is whether modern Arabic literature is an extension of classical Arabic literature or whether it is a new creation whose relationship with its medieval predecessor is tenuous.

PERIODIZATION

Periodization, which is a way of "ordering the past" and "so making it accessible to valuation,"[10] aims at describing the different systems of poetic norms that characterize literary works written at different points in time, and it seeks possible explanations for why and how these systems changed. Studying periodization can do justice to literary change, as it emphasizes such relative–contrastive phenomena as novelty, borrowing, revival, imitation, parody, inversion, and transformation within a historical framework. It also helps us more accurately interpret works written in previous ages, since it locates them in their historical contexts, contexts which it places within the history of literary forms. We may take the automatization/de-automatization opposition, considered to be the *differentia specifica* of art, as the major law for systemic shift when it comes to literary change. As Fredric Jameson put it, it has three signal advantages: it serves as distinguishing the purely literary system from other verbal modes; it allows for the establishment of a hierarchy within the literary work itself; and it brings forth a new concept of literary history as "not that of some profound continuity of tradition characteristic of idealistic history, but one of history as a series of abrupt discontinuities, of ruptures with the past, where each new

[6] Gombrich 1969, pp. 35–8.

[7] This chapter benefited from Glowinski 1969, pp. 14–25; and Margolin 1969, pp. 5–13. See also Wellek 1941, pp. 73–93; Lovejoy 1948, pp. 1–13; Teesing 1948; Wellek 1966; Crane 1967, II, pp. 3–175; Crane 1971; Cohen 1974; Miftah and Boushsane 1997; and Miftāḥ 1999.

[8] Kermode 1988, p. 125.

[9] For the meaning of "classical" in the context of Arabic literature, see Bauer 2007, pp. 138–41; and van Gelder 2013, pp. xiv–xv.

[10] Kermode 1988, p. 118.

literary present is seen as a break with the dominant artistic canons of the generation immediately preceding."[11]

With time, genres, modes of writing, and literary devices wear out as a result of repetitive usage and undergo automatization, that is, they start functioning as "automatic stock" and thus stop fulfilling their original poetic function.[12] De-automatization (defamiliarization) is then necessary in order to revitalize the literary system—on the level of the text, it is the only way to overcome stereotypy and loss of contact with the real world. The defining features (elements and structures) on any level of an individual work can be divided up as follows:[13] individuality—showing features unique to this particular work; innovation—showing features common to this work and other works written at the same time-section but having no precedent in the literary history of the relevant genre; renovation—showing features common to this work and works written in a previous time-section, except for the immediately preceding one;[14] and continuity—showing features common to this work and works written in the immediately preceding time-section.

A literary period may be defined by innovation or renovation, that is, when we can point to several features that many works of literature written during a given time-section have in common and when these features have either no precedent at all or only have a precedent or precedents but not in the immediately preceding time-section. In other words, each period should be seen as a unique phenomenon characterized by the conjoint occurrence of the same group of features in a large number of works written during a

11 Jameson 1972, pp. 52–3.

12 Sebeok 1986, I, pp. 66–7. Cf. Shklovsky 1965, pp. 3–24. Alluding to the reason why it is a blind imitation to use new Western literary forms which are not suitable to Arabic literature, Najīb Maḥfūẓ points to the difference between Arabic literature and Western literatures: "The literary form in Europe would move to a new stage only after it has become absolutely fed up with the old [stage] and has consumed it. [At the same time] we have not begun yet [with that old stage]" (al-Nuʿaymī 2001, p. 16).

13 According to Margolin 1969, pp. 5–13.

14 The Arabic word *nahḍa* ("rising," "awakening," "revival," "renaissance"), which commonly refers to the renaissance of Arabic literature and culture from about the mid-nineteenth century, is the closest term to the idea of renovation; the term implies "a historical sequence of past greatness, recent decadence, and a current effort to revive greatness" (Esposito 1995, III, p. 217). A good example of renovation has been provided by Jaroslav Stetkevych in his last book on the hunt in Arabic poetry: Modernist Arab free-verse poets such as ʿAbd al-Wahhāb al-Bayyātī (1926–99), Aḥmad ʿAbd al-Muʿṭī Ḥijāzī (b. 1935), and Muḥammad ʿAfīfī Maṭar (1935–2010) published modernist hunt poems, even if these poems were considered to be part of the "idea-sphere of formal contemporary Arabic poetry" or were written in "a poetic manner that is strongly idiosyncratic and, as such, studiedly allusive, masked, and metamorphic" (Stetkevych 2016, pp. 225–79. The quotations are from p. 225 and p. 243, respectively). On rereading Arabic literary tradition in light of contemporary literature, see also El-Ariss 2016, pp. 62–90.

given time-section. This group of features or system of norms is preferably drawn from all the levels of the literary work and dominates the literary scene for a certain time. But while a particular combination of features is unique to each period, separately these features may, and do, occur in some other period or periods as well. The levels of the work from which the defining features are drawn undergo changes in the course of literary history, but the starting point and the extent of change vary considerably from one level to another. In addition, periods are defined according to a system of canonical norms, as these are incorporated into many works written within a certain time-section. There are no uniform time-sections with just one incontestable system of norms, but in any time-section there exists only one system of canonical norms.

Given the theoretical background outlined above, one is struck by the absence of clear concepts of literary periodization in virtually every study of modern Arabic literature currently available.[15] *Modern Arabic Literature* (1992) by Muhammad Mustafa Badawi (1925–2012) begins as follows:

> Compared with earlier *periods* of Arabic literature the Modern *period*, often referred to in Arabic as *al-Nahḍah* (= renaissance), requires an approach that is at once simpler and more complicated. While Classical Arabic literature can safely be regarded as fundamentally a continuum, Modern literature constitutes in certain important respects an entirely new departure, even though its break with the Classical has sometimes been exaggerated, for despite its borrowing

[15] One of the few exceptions is Roger Allen's *The Arabic Literary Heritage: The Development of Its Genres and Criticism* (1998). Being more aware than any other scholar in the field of Arabic literature of the problems that the traditional modes of periodization raise, even deliberately avoiding the use of the word "history" in the title of his books, Allen writes the following in "An Essay on Precedents and Principles": "The present work seeks to strike a balance, one that will privilege the literary dimension over the historical. It will make use of categories that are those of literature studies, although there will be frequent reference to political and societal contexts. The chronological dimension will always be implicit. The difference that I hope to establish can perhaps be illustrated by considering the organising principles that have been applied in many other works on this topic in Arabic and other languages, and in particular the method of periodisation that *mutatis mutandis* has been applied in most cases" (Allen 1998, p. 4 [Cf. the abridged version, Allen 2000, p. 2]. For a review of the book, see *Journal of Arabic Literature* 30.2 [1999], pp. 193–5 [by Muhsin al-Musawi]. See also Allen 2006, pp. 1–21; and van Gelder 2013, p. xv). An example of the new direction recommended by Allen, which "will privilege the literary dimension over the historical" and "will make use of categories that are those of literature studies," but where the "chronological dimension will always be implicit," is Huda J. Fakhreddine's *Metapoesis in the Arabic Tradition: From Modernists to Muḥdathūn* (Fakhreddine 2015). Through the lens often used to study modernist poetry, Fakhreddine examines the self-reflexive attitude in the poetry of the first century of Abbasid poets, detaching it from chronology and consequently refreshing our sense of what is "modernist" or "poetically new." On the issue of periodization, see also Miftāḥ and BūḤasan 1996; Miftah and Bouhsane 1997; Hirschler 2006, pp. ix–x; Bauer 2007, pp. 137–48; and Hirschler and Savant 2014, pp. 6–19.

> of European forms such as drama and the novel, Modern literature never really completely severed its link with its past.[16]

The way the term "period" is introduced in the first sentence leaves it unclear as to whether Badawi is referring to historical or literary periods.[17] The confusion this creates is prominently illustrated by the chronological table of historical events at the opening of the book, which starts in 1787 ("Death of Muhammad ibn Abd al-Wahhab, founder of the Wahhabi Movement in Arabia") and runs until 1991 ("[March] expulsion of Iraqi soldiers from Kuwait by Allied forces of the United Nations"),[18] as well as the map of the Arab world with population figures of the various states,[19] although modern Arabic literature was never confined to the Arab world alone.[20] Moreover, to find long descriptions of historical events in an introduction to a literary history of modern Arabic literature is strikingly odd, as if the book is to be understood as another short survey of Middle Eastern history. Take, for example, the following paragraph:

> France invaded Algeria in 1830, Britain occupied Aden in 1839, France occupied Tunisia in 1881, Britain Egypt in 1882, Italy seized Libya in 1911–12, and in 1920 France acquired mandates over Syria and Lebanon, while the mandates for Palestine, Transjordan and Iraq went to Britain. Even Morocco, which had retained its independence for a long time, fell prey to the ambitions of France and Spain which in 1904 concluded a secret agreement that divided Morocco into two spheres of influence between them, and in 1912 Morocco was declared

16 Badawi 1992, p. 1 (my emphasis of the first two words). Cf. Somekh 1991, p. 3: "Arabic literature is thought, by at least some of its practitioners and students, to consist of two separate literary systems, not merely two different periods." Referring to Badawi's paragraph cited above, and comparing it with a paragraph included in an article by the same writer written in Arabic (Badawī 1984, p. 98), Walter Armbrust indicates that when writing for an English-speaking audience, "the association of classical heritage and religion is comparatively muted" (Armbrust 1996, pp. 45–6).

17 Cf. Bakalla 1980, pp. 113–16: "Arabic literature is generally divided into six periods [...] the pre-Islamic period [...] the Early Islamic age [...] the Umayyad literature [...] the Abbasid period [...] the Mamlūk literature extends from 1258 [...] until 1800, the year which marks the beginning of Modern Arabic literature." Cf. also Khouri 1976, p. 17 (Arabic translation: Khūrī 1990, p. 38): "Arabic literary history is generally divided into six periods: the Jahiliyyah, or pre-Islamic (500–622); the early Islamic and Umayyad (622–750); the Abbasid (750–1258); the Hispano-Arabic in Muslim Spain (750–1492); the post-Abbasid (1258–1800); and the modern renaissance (1800 to the present)." It should be noted that when Louis Cheikho divided his book on Arabic literature of the nineteenth and twentieth centuries (Cheikho 1924; Cheikho 1926; Cheikho 1926a), he acknowledged doing it only for the convenience of the reader (Cheikho 1924, p. 18. Cf. Campbell 1972, p. 76). On this topic, see also al-Zayyāt 1996, p. 8; and Arazi 1997, p. 449.

18 Badawi 1992, pp. viii–xi.

19 Badawi 1992, pp. xii–xiii.

20 See, for example, above, p. 150.

> a French protectorate. Britain imposed her authority upon the Arab rulers of the small Persian Gulf states by means of treaties which go as far back as the 1820s.[21]

In this respect, it seems that Badawi's critical approach to the history of modern Arabic poetry had not changed since the mid-1970s. When Edward W. Said reviewed his *A Critical Introduction to Modern Arabic Poetry* (1975), he found a similar conception of historical poetics:

> Dr Badawi is a scholar whose optic—to use a usefully up-to-date term—is not critical (or is critical only in a very limited sense), but archival; for him modern Arabic poetry is a record of births and deaths, themes, images, a list of adjectives, general terms like "spontaneity," "sincerity" and "natural," all of which are contained in envelopes [...] Too often he sounds more like a harassed cataloguer than a literary critic.[22]

When Badawi comes to the issue of periodization, it is therefore not surprising to find him choose the following method:

> The history of modern Arabic literature could be divided into three main periods: the first from 1834 to 1914, which may be termed the Age of Translations and Adaptations as well as Neoclassicism; the second is the inter-war period, which may be described as the Age of Romanticism and Nationalism; the third is from the end of World War II to the present: it embraces a wide variety of schools, approaches and styles, but may conveniently be called the Age of Conflicting Ideologies.[23]

Alluding to Badawi's model of literary history, in which

> all typical period divisions mobilized by Western literatures for structuring their own master narratives of literary development following the Middle Ages are redeployed to serve as a scaffolding for developing a discursive episteme centered on a collection of texts whose differences from Western literary texts risk being lost in a litany of similarities,[24]

Terri DeYoung writes:

> The greatest danger of this otherwise quite useful period scheme: the notion that Arab romanticism as well as Arab neoclassicism, were simply repetitions of their Western counterparts—and thus, in a very significant sense, a waste of time, that had to be "gotten through" so that one could arrive at the teleologically determined endpoint of modernism, which alone had value because

21 Badawi 1992, p. 5.

22 Said 1976, p. 1559. In his response to the review, Badawi scarcely touched upon that critical observation, let alone most of the other observations made by Said (Badawi 1977).

23 Badawi 1992, p. 16.

24 DeYoung 1998, p. 152.

> it represented the arrival of Arabic literature at a point where it was fully integrated with "modernity" and could unproblematically assume a leading role on the stage of world literary activity. Such a set of syllogisms may be empowering for Arab modernist writers and those who identify with them, but the opposite obtains for the study of earlier writers and their works, which are rendered simply superfluous and without functional importance.[25]

Basic terms in Western historical poetics, which have become an essential part of the lexicon of anyone writing a literary history (for example, automatization, de-automatization, individuality, innovation, renovation, and continuity) are absent from Badawi's discussion. To define periodization in a literary study according to political dates (1834, 1914, 1939), while ignoring the many studies that deal with the issue of defining the literary period,[26] is a problematic course of action, especially as some definitions are too common. For example, René Wellek and Austin Warren argue that "a period is thus a time section dominated by a system of literary norms, standards and conventions,"[27] and Hubert Paul Hans Teesing maintains that "Perioden sind Zeiträume, die in sich relativ einheitlich sind und sich in charakteristischer Weise von anderen unterscheiden [...] Periode ist eine einmalige Verbindung gewisser Merkmale, die ein individuelles Gepräge zeigt."[28] In 1989 the Egyptian literary critic Ghālī Shukrī warned that "in literature there exist no generations in the chronological simplified sense, but only through connection in time with the new experiences and outlooks that divide between one period and another."[29] When viewed in this light, the way Badawi treats the historical poetics of Arabic literature rests upon a simplistic approach to the history of events, wholly inappropriate when it comes to explaining the development of literary systems.[30]

25 DeYoung 1998, p. 159. For the full critical approach of DeYoung to Badawi's model of literary history, see DeYoung 1998, pp. 151–85.

26 On the confusion between political history and literary history, see Abū al-Khashab 1984, pp. 37–8.

27 Wellek and Warren 1963, p. 265.

28 Teesing 1948, pp. 8, 38–9.

29 Shukrī 1989, p. 232. Cf. Maẓlūm 1996, pp. 136–43; and al-ʿAzzāwī 1997, pp. 348–9, n. 5, especially with regard to *jīl al-sittīnāt* ("the sixties generation") in Iraq. On the emergence of "the sixties generation" in Egypt and the anxiety over categorization, see Guth 2011, pp. 104–9; and Ramadan 2012, pp. 409–30.

30 For a review of Badawi 1992 and Badawi 1993 (*A Short History of Modern Arabic Literature*), for which the author employs the same method as Ignác Goldziher (1850–1921) in his famous classical study (*A Short History of Classical Arabic Literature*) (Goldziher 1966), see Snir 1994, pp. 61–85.

CLASSICAL VIS-À-VIS MODERN LITERATURE

As I have already pointed out, the way we view the relationship between modern and classical Arabic literature is essential to our understanding of the nature of the contemporary literary system. The question is whether modern literature is an extension of classical literature or whether it is a new creation that has hardly any relationship at all with its medieval predecessor. It is no coincidence that Arab, especially Muslim, scholars tend to adopt the former view, whereas Western scholars tend to adopt the latter. For example, in his article "al-Adab al-ʿArabī Bayna Amsihi wa-Ghadihi" ("Arabic Literature between its Past and Future"),[31] which in October 1945 led the first issue of his journal *al-Kātib al-Miṣrī*, Ṭāhā Ḥusayn asserts the continuity of Arabic literature. Unlike Greek and Latin literatures, which have no direct contemporary extension, modern Arabic literature, according to Ḥusayn, is a direct linear extension of classical literature:

> The historical existence of Arabic literature has never been cut off, and it seems that it will never be cut off. The connection between this literature and contemporary generations in the lands of the Arab East, from the Persian Gulf to the Atlantic Ocean, and in various Arab lands here and there, is still strong and fertile, like the connection between Arabic literature and the Arab nation during the period of al-Mutanabbī and Abū al-ʿAlāʾ [...] Arabic literature is very traditional and at the same time very modern. *Its ancient past has been directly mingled with its modern present without any break or bend* [...] Our Arabic literature is a living being and resembles, more than anything else, a huge tree the roots of which have been consolidated and extended into the depths of the earth, while its branches have risen and spread out in space. The water of life is still ample and running in its steady roots and its high branches [...] Our Arabic literature is definitely a traditional one, possessing an old Arab-Bedouin character that it never relinquished, nor will it ever do so [...] The way in which we see things might change as ages, regions, and circumstances change. But our way of portraying things, even if it takes different shapes, will always go back to a set of traditional principles which cannot possibly be avoided, because such avoidance means killing this literature and breaking the connection between it and the new time as well as deterring it from the road of the continuous life of the living literatures into the road of cut-off life which the Greek and Latin literatures took.[32]

This direct extension of classical into modern literature has been guaranteed, according to Ḥusayn, by the continuous equilibrium that Arabic literature maintained until modern times between aspects of continuity and change:

[31] Ḥusayn 1945, pp. 4–27. The article was also incorporated into Ḥusayn n.d. [1958], pp. 5–32.
[32] Ḥusayn 1945, pp. 10–11; Ḥusayn n.d. [1958], pp. 11–13 (my emphasis).

> The revival of ancient Arabic literature[33] was, and still is, turning modern Arab minds toward the past, highlighting elements of stability and steadfastness. On the other hand, the contact with modern European literature has been pushing Arabic literature into a different direction, stressing elements of mobility and change. It is surprising that the Arab mind has maintained its equilibrium in spite of this fierce conflict. Indeed, it has benefited from it immensely.[34]

By preserving some traditional principles to ensure its distinctive identity and, at the same time, incorporating a variety of innovations both in form and content, Arabic literature, according to Ḥusayn, has proven its vitality down through the ages.[35]

The contrary view we find neatly summarized by Hamilton Gibb, one of the first Western scholars to systematically study modern Arabic literature,[36] in an article published in 1928:

> It may be asked [...] by what right Arabic literature is called a young literature. To all appearances, it is entitled to claim a history of thirteen centuries, a longer period of continuous literary activity than any living European language can boast. But beneath the apparent linguistic continuity, Arabic literature is undergoing an evolution comparable, in some respects, to the substitution of Patristic for Classical Greek literature and idiom. Neo-Arabic literature is only to a limited extent the heir of the old "classical" Arabic literature, and *even shows a tendency to repudiate its inheritance entirely*. Its leaders are, for the most part, men who have drunk from other springs and look at the world with different eyes. Yet the past still plays a part in their intellectual background, and there is a section among them upon whom that past retains a hold scarcely shaken by newer influences. For many decades, the partisans of the "old" and the "new" have engaged in a struggle for the soul of the Arabic world, a struggle in which the victory of one side over the other is even yet not assured. The protagonists are (to classify them roughly for practical purposes) the European-educated classes of Egyptians and Syrians on the one hand, and those in Egypt and the less advanced Arabic lands whose education has followed traditional lines, on the other. Whatever the ultimate result may be, however, there can be no question that the conflict has torn the Arabic world from its ancient moorings, and that *the contemporary literature of Egypt and Syria breathes, in its more recent developments, a spirit foreign to the old traditions.*[37]

33 That is, through the editing and disseminating of classical texts since the mid-nineteenth century.

34 Ḥusayn 1945, p. 17; Ḥusayn n.d. [1958], p. 20.

35 Cf. Semah 1974, p. 122.

36 See "Studies in Contemporary Arabic Literature," in Gibb 1962, pp. 245–319, which is based on a series of articles Gibb first published in *Bulletin of the School of Oriental Studies* (*BSOAS*) (IV.4 [1928], pp. 745–60; V.2 [1929], pp. 311–22; V.3 [1929], pp. 445–66; VII.1 [1933], pp. 1–22).

37 Gibb 1962, pp. 246–7 (my emphasis).

Regarding the modern Arabic literary system as a new creation[38] means accepting the view that Arabic literature prior to the nineteenth century had somehow collapsed and been abandoned by its own community, as though the Arabs during the eighteenth and nineteenth centuries had in one way or another exchanged all or parts of their culture for another. Of course, slippage or collapse may occur, and a given community may let go of its literature when changes in its sociocultural conditions fail to leave their mark on that literature, but long before this happens one should be able to detect certain signals, such as the literature being pushed to the periphery of the cultural system. In any event, it is an unsupported and unjustifiable assumption to refer to classical, medieval, and premodern Arabic literature as a case of collapse and abandonment, side by side with Latin, Byzantine Greek, and Church Slavonic literatures.[39] It is also an unsupported assumption to refer to Arabic literature as consisting of "two separate literary systems" or "two different periods."[40] Any student of Arabic literature familiar with literary production prior to the nineteenth century, especially with the various branches of non-canonical literary production before the encounter between Arabic literature and Western culture, would hesitate to speak of "two separate literary systems." I. M. Filshtinsky, after describing in length the popular romances and tales of the late Middle Ages,[41] concluded his book *Arabic Literature* (1966) with the following passage:

> The Arab literary tradition was never totally broken. This was a favourable factor during the period of the Arab literary renaissance in the 19th century. The starting point of the Arab political and cultural advance is usually placed in the early years of the 19th century, and is associated with the struggle of the Egyptians against the invading armies of Napoleon Bonaparte. From that moment, in the Arab countries, the long struggle for independence was launched; it was in these conditions that the new literature came into existence, closely linked with contemporaneity, yet resting upon, and adhering to, the age-old literary tradition.[42]

38 ʻAfīf al-Bahnasī refers to this general conception as *siyāsat al-batr*, i.e. "the policy of amputation" (al-Bahnasī 1997, p. 62).

39 I. Even-Zohar in Sebeok 1986, I, p. 461. Cf. Sasson Somekh, "A Literature in Search of Language," Inaugural Lecture, The Irene Halmos Chair of Arabic Literature, Tel Aviv University, 23 October 1983, p. 4: "[Modern Arabic literature] emerged after a period of hundreds of years of virtual isolation, during which Arabic literature suffered from stagnation and triviality."

40 See Somekh 1991, p. 3.

41 Filshtinsky 1966, pp. 205–24.

42 Filshtinsky 1966, p. 224. On this topic, specifically on the attitude to Mamluk period, "one of the apogees of Arabic literature," see Bauer 2005, pp. 105–32: "Mamluk literature is fascinating because it transcends boundaries: the boundaries between everyday and literary communication; between popular and high literature; between poetry and prose; between

As the present study seeks to underline, modern Arabic literature is connected with the ancient Arabic literary heritage in all aspects of its development. Every signal innovation is based *on* or is introduced *against* that literary background. Moreover, no Arab poet, writer, or playwright has ever succeeded in gaining fame or becoming canonical without a deep knowledge of the Arabic literary heritage.[43] This makes it impossible to refer to modern Arabic poetry as lending itself "to Western modes of composition" and to claim that "it is hardly recognizable as a direct offspring of classical Arabic poetry in the output of the most representative Arab poets today."[44] For example, Adūnīs, probably the most sophisticated of all contemporary canonical Arab poets, because of his poetic innovations, has been accused of betraying Arabism and Islam.[45] However, all his writings are deeply rooted in the ancient Arabic poetics and the classical Sufi heritage.[46] Even the most avant-garde Arab poets, championing poetic iconoclasm and the abrogation of poetic values long held sacred, are deeply rooted in their traditions—if only in the way they oppose or challenge them.[47] Modern Arabic literature

the private and the public; between theory and praxis. Colonial delusions have thus far prevented a proper appreciation of this culture" (p. 130). See also Bauer 2007, pp. 137–67.

43 In a proposal for a seminar at the annual conference of the ACLA (American Comparative Literature Association), which was held at Harvard University on 17–20 March 2016, entitled "The Classical in the Modern: Specters of Arabic Literature," Muhsin al-Musawi and Yasmine Khayyat write that "contemporary debates in Arabic literary production often posit artificial borders between Classical and modern literary production such that Arabic literature allegedly stagnated for hundreds of years, until modern Arabic literature emerged with European intervention in the region. As that account of Arabic literature's history would have it, Classical Arabic's rich repertoire of poetry and prose was either put aside or rejuvenated by the ostensibly purely modern themes and forms preoccupying authors and poets since Napoleon arrived in Egypt in 1798." The proposal pushes against this sharp divide, probing the intersections of modern Arabic literature with tropes and motifs of the Classical period, asking how Classical Arabic poetry, storytelling, myth and prose affected Arabic literary production in the last two centuries (according to "Arabic Lit Scholars" list, 25 July 2015).

44 Somekh 1991, p. 4. On the issue of foreign influence on modern Arabic poetry, see the various contributions in Ṣāliḥ 1995. In his introduction to the book, Fakhrī Ṣāliḥ (b. 1957) criticizes both Arab and Western critics for the methods they have used to examine that influence (pp. 11–12).

45 See, for example, al-Malā'ika 1983 [1962], pp. 213–27. Cf. a review of Moreh 1988 in *al-Karmil—Abḥāth fī al-Lugha wa-l-Adab* 10 (1989), pp. 161–71.

46 Nevertheless, the Egyptian poet Muḥammad Ādām (b. 1954), who considers his poetry a continuation of the Sufi heritage, contends that Adūnīs writes Arabic with "European pronunciation" (*lukna ūrūbiyya*) (*al-Ḥawādith*, 6 April 1990, p. 53).

47 Cf. Kronholm 1993, pp. 20–2; Burt 1995, pp. 91–9; and Allen 1998, pp. 203–17. See also what 'Abd al-Wahhāb al-Bayyātī (1926–99) said before his death (*al-Ḥayāt*, 7 August 1999):

حداثة شعر الروّاد جاءت من أو خرجت من معطف الشعر العربي، يعني هي مولود أصيل، ولد ولادة عسيرة ولكنه كان ابن أبيه، كما يقال.

has been influenced by Western literary models and concepts, but this influence has not changed the awareness in the Arab world that the present literary creation is a direct extension of ancient production.[48] Quite a few Arab authors, critics, and scholars regard even those genres considered to be a direct result of Western influence (such as the novel, the short story, and theater) as stemming from or inspired by the classical and medieval Arab literary tradition or as at least benefiting from early Arab and Islamic literary forms.[49] Najīb Maḥfūẓ even argued that his initial understanding of the novel was formed by the stories of the Qur'ān which attracted him as a fine form of the art of storytelling. These stories follow the most modern principles of novel-writing:

> They do not begin, like nineteenth-century novels, by setting the stage for the drama, then build up toward a climax, before reaching a resolution in the last pages. They are more like twentieth-century literary experiments, in which events do not follow a monotonous sequence but move according to dramatic requirements, which dictate where the different parts of the story are located. In modern European novel writing, this represented a revolution, as can be seen in the works of Joyce or Proust. In the Qur'ān, the story of Mary, for example, is distributed among various *suras*. Each of these contains part of the story. For this reason, the Qur'ānic stories, with their noble content and style, were the first to provide me with a concept of the novel that I felt I could use in my writing.[50]

Naturally, Maḥfūẓ cannot but completely disagree with such decisive statements as Charles Vial's (b. 1928) on the birth and evolution of Arabic fictional literature:

> The modern *ḳiṣṣa* owes nothing to Arab tradition. It is linked neither with the folklore of the *Thousand and One Nights* nor with tales of chivalry nor with narratives of *adab*. The tradition of classical *maḳāma*, although taken up by two

48 It was illustrated during the conference held in Philadelphia University in Amman, 5–7 December 1999, under the title "Modernism and Post-Modernism" (on the contributions to the conference, see the reports in *al-Ra'y*, 6 December 1999, p. 41; 7 December 1999, p. 50; and 8 December 1999, p. 45).

49 See Maḥmūd 1979; al-Ghīṭānī 1986, p. 9; al-Ghīṭānī 1986a, p. 9; al-Ghīṭānī 1986b, p. 9; al-Ghīṭānī 1986c, p. 9; al-Ḥakīm 1986, p. 9; Zaydān 1992, pp. 48–9; Badrān 2001; and Wādī 2001, pp. 21–60. See also Khaldūn al-Sham'a's essay in *al-Thawra* (Damascus), 24 June 1978 (according to al-Nafzāwī 1983, pp. 9–11). Cf. Snir 1993, pp. 149–70. See also Elkhadem 1985, p. 55 about the *maqāma* that "has often been regarded as a forerunner of, if not a model for, the European picaresque novel." Cf. also Wilpert 1964, p. 406; and al-Bustānī 1990, p. 125.

50 Mahfouz 2001, p. 66. In another place, however, Maḥfūẓ states that "there had not been any [Arabic] fictional heritage which I could use as a basis" (al-Ghīṭānī 2006, p. 149). Maḥfūẓ was probably referring to an actual modern heritage of fiction writing.

> men of imagination and dual culture (Fāris al-Shidyāḳ for *al-Sāḳ ʿalā ʾl-Sāḳ*, 1855; and Muḥammad al-Muwayliḥī [for *Ḥadīth ʿĪsā b. Hishām*], 1907), has left no legacy. It is from Europe that the Arabs have borrowed this literary genre totally unfamiliar to them, sc. the novel.[51]

And one does not have to look far to find Arab intellectuals for whom the encounter between Islamic culture and European culture in Andalus, Sicily, or in other parts of Europe during the Crusades was a major factor in the renaissance of Western culture.[52] One should mention as well Miguel de Cervantes' (1547–1616) *Don Quixote* and the metafictional reflection on the identity of the author;[53] and some even went so far as to argue that William Shakespeare was of Arab origin and that his original name was al-Shaykh Zubayr.[54] That such an argument seems, even to the majority of Arab scholars, to have no basis in reality does not change their feeling that Islamic culture has not received sufficient credit for the development of modern civilization. A corollary of this is the view that it was the impact of Western culture in the nineteenth century that directly caused Arab culture to slide into a state of inferiority.[55] Adūnīs goes one step further by stating that "creative ability" (*al-ibdāʿ*) is an essential characteristic of the East:

> التقنية «تقدّم» في إعادة إنتاج النموذج. الإبداع ليس تقدّما تقنيا أو نموذجيا، إنه انبثاق - اكتشاف للأصل لا نهاية له. إبداعيا، أعني على مستوى الحضارة بمعناها الأكثر عمقا وإنسانية، ليس في «الغرب» شيء لم يأخذه من الشرق. الدين، الفلسفة، الشعر (الفنّ، بعامّة) «شرقية» كلّها. ويمكنكم أن تستأنسوا بأسماء المبدعين في هذه الحقول، بدءا من دانتي حتى اليوم. فخصوصية «الغرب» هي التقنية، لا الإبداع. لذلك يمكن القول إن الغرب، حضاريا، هو ابن للشرق. لكنه، تقنيا، «لقيط»: انحراف، استغلال، هيمنة، استعمار، إمبريالية، إنه، في دلالة أخرى، تمرّد على الأب. وهو، الآن،

51 Vial 1986, p. 187.

52 See, for example, al-Ṭawīl 1990, pp. 142–69. See also the following argument by Jabrā Ibrāhīm Jabrā (1920–94) (Jabrā 1989, pp. 16–17. Cf. Krachkovskii 1989, p. 20):

> في القرون الوسطى، بعد اكتساح العرب للأندلس، وانتشارهم على سواحل البحر الأبيض المتوسّط وبثّ فنونهم الأدبية والحضارية في أرجاء أوربا التي أخذت عندها تستيقظ من ظلمات التردّي والجهل، أعطى العرب كتّاب الفرنسية والإيطالية لا المادّة فقط لملاحمهم البطولية، بل الكثير من أسلوبها الشعري بالذات. وظهرت «الروماسات» (كذا!) المطوّلة في الآداب الأوربية شعرا، وقد يكون بعضها في آلاف من الأبيات. وكان الفنّ الروائي عندهم فنّا شعريا، لحمته الفروسية والحبّ - وكلاهما مستقى عن النموذج العربي أصلا - وسداه الصيغ الإيقاعية والقوافي التي تلقّنها شعراء الإفرنج عن العرب، فأضافوها إلى الصيغ اللاتينية القديمة لديهم، أو حوّروا بموجبها الصيغ الميسّرة في لغاتهم.

53 See Kilito 2001, pp. 91–7. See also Rodenbeck 1997, pp. 55–72.

54 See al-Nāshif 1989, pp. 36–41. For more on that argument, search الشيخ زبير on the Internet.

55 See, for example, the extreme position of Muḥammad Farīd Abū Ḥadīd (1893–1967) (Abū Ḥadīd 1935, p. 207):

> فالحقّ أن شعب مصر في القرن الثامن عشر كان آخذا في سبيل نهضة حقيقية في كل جوانبه نهضة وطنية صرف لا تشوبها رطانة أجنبية ولا لوثة أعجمية ولا سيطرة غربية. نهضة لو سارت في سبيلها وبلغت قصارها لكانت مصر اليوم في مستوى اليابان وإيطاليا أو فيما هو فوق ذلك. غير أن القرن الثامن عشر، واحسرتاه، انتهى بنكبة شاملة وداهية فادحة بإغارة الفرنسيين على مصر، واكتساحهم كل آثار تلك النهضة الشابّة فقضى عليها ولمّا يتمّ نموّها، وحفرت بين ماضي مصر وحاضرها هوّة عميقة تقطع تيّار الرقيّ الوطني، وتقف في سبيل وصل الطارف بالتالد.

لم يعد يكتفي بمجرّد التمرّد، وإنما يريد أن يقتل الأب (...) لهذا كانت الإبداعات الكبرى في الغرب،
سواء أكانت دينية أو فنّية أو فلسفية، تجاوزا للتقنية، أي «شرقية» الينابيع. إنها نوع من شَرْقَنَة الغرب.

Technical ability is "progress" in the reproducing of a known pattern. Creative ability is not technical progress or progress from the point of view of reproduction according to some pattern. It is emanation—a never-ending discovery of the essence. From the point of view of creative ability, I mean on the level of culture in its deepest and most human sense, there is nothing in the "West" that was not taken from the "East." Religion, philosophy, poetry (art, in general), all of them are originally Eastern. You can include the names of the creators in those fields, since Dante until now. The obvious feature of the "West" is its technical rather than creative ability. Therefore, we could say, from the cultural point of view, that the West is the son of the East, but actually it is a "foundling": deviation, exploitation, domination, Colonialism, Imperialism; in other words, revolt against the father. Moreover, it is now no longer content with revolt, but is willing to kill the father [...] That is why the great creations of the West—religious, artistic or philosophical—traversed technicality, that is, they had "Eastern" roots. They were a sort of Easternization of the West.[56]

It is, however, generally accepted that canonical and non-canonical Arabic literary models helped guide the emergence of the new modern Arabic genres, but the marginal status of certain non-canonical models changed only after their interaction with their Western equivalents.[57] The case of *Robinson Crusoe* (1719) by Daniel Defoe (1660–1731)[58] is highly instructive in this respect, as its translation into Arabic in the nineteenth century was one of the factors that helped shape the norms of the emerging Arabic novel.[59]

56 *Mawāqif* 36 (Winter 1980), pp. 150–1; Adūnīs 1980, pp. 330–1. For a critical response to Adūnīs' argument, see al-'Aẓm 1992, pp. 109–19. Adūnīs' aforementioned argument that "the West is the son of the East" by no means reflects his great disappointment at the failure of the Arabs to regain their ancient glory. In dozens of essays he has published under the title *Madārāt* (*Orbits*) during the last decade in the London-based newspaper *al-Ḥayāt*, he expressed his sadness over the deterioration of the Arabs: "From what is called the 'Period of Renaissance' (*'Aṣr al-Nahḍa*) until today, the Arabs have deteriorated on all levels, relatively and comparatively to the progress of others, in education and culture, in economic and social growth and in human rights and democratic freedom" (*al-Ḥayāt*, 6 January 2009). He also wrote: "We, the Arabs, have a strong presence throughout the world on the level of form, and, at the same time, we are absent of the world on the level of meaning" (7 January 2016. Cf. his essays on 24 April 2014; 11 December 2014; 1 October 2015; and 7 January 2016).

57 Cf. the argument of 'Abd al-Raḥmān Yāghī (b. 1924) regarding the development of Arab theater (Yāghī 1980, p. 86).

58 Defoe 1906 [1719].

59 On the norms of translation for this novel, see 'Anānī 1976, pp. 8–25; Badr 1983, pp. 57–67; and Somekh 1991, pp. 75–82. See above, p. 90n. It is interesting to note that even in the 1990s Arab scholars still used Buṭrus al-Bustānī's translation of the novel for their studies on *Robinson Crusoe* (e.g. al-Khaṭīb 1995, pp. 123–38).

However, it seems that *Robinson Crusoe* was not just a purely English cultural product but also the outcome of the interaction between English and Arab culture in general and between *Robinson Crusoe* and the philosophical tale *Ḥayy ibn Yaqẓān* by Abū Bakr Ibn Ṭufayl (1100–85) in particular.[60] A comparative study by Ḥasan Maḥmūd ʿAbbās arrives at the conclusion that Defoe was highly influenced by Ibn Ṭufayl's tale.[61] It is also possible that *Ḥayy ibn Yaqẓān*, together with other classical Arabic autobiographical works[62] (though it cannot be considered an autobiography according

60 Ibn Ṭufayl 1940. For an English translation of this tale, see Goodman 1972, pp. 95–166. On an earlier translation by the Elder Edward Pococke (1604–91), see Nahas 1985, pp. 88–90.

61 See ʿAbbās 1983, especially the conclusions on pp. 249–52, which end with the following:

ولم يغرب عن بالنا أن الأدب والفكر العربيين كانا طيلة عهودهما عرضة للتأثير والتأثّر، وذلك هو شأن الأدب الإنكليزي وآداب الأمم الأخرى جميعا. فلا يعلي من شأن هذا الأدب أن يؤثّر ولا ينتقص من شأن ذلك الأدب أن يتأثّر، فالتأثير والتأثّر قائمان ما دامت الصلات الثقافية قائمة بين الشعوب.

62 Such as *al-Munqidh min al-Ḍalāl* by Abū Ḥāmid al-Ghazālī (1059–1111) (al-Ghazālī 1956. English translation in Watt 1963) and *Kitāb al-Iʿtibār* by Usāma ibn Munqidh (1095–1188) (Ibn Munqidh 1930. English translation: Ibn-Munqidh 1987). On autobiography in classical Arabic literature, see al-Ghamdi 1989; Kilpatrick 1991, pp. 1–20; Kilito 1999, pp. 69–80; and Cooperson 2000. See also Reynolds 2001, which is a survey of premodern Arabic autobiography. The book examines a corpus of more than 100 Arabic autobiographies from the ninth to the nineteenth centuries and includes thirteen translated selections as well as an annotated bibliography of approximately 140 pre-twentieth-century primary sources. On autobiography in Arab culture in general, see ʿAbd al-Dāʾim 1975; Shuiskii 1982, pp. 111–23; Malti-Douglas 1988b; Sharaf 1992; Philipp 1993, pp. 573–604; al-Qāḍī 1993, pp. 207–32; al-Hassan 1994; al-Bāridī 1997, pp. 68–80; Rooke 1997; Enderwitz 1998, pp. 1–19; Ostle et al. 1998 (for a review of the book, see *IBLA* 184 [1999], pp. 221–3); Enderwitz 1999, pp. 29–50; Machut-Mendecka 1999, pp. 510–22; Mowafy 1999; Wild 1999, pp. 349–61; Enderwitz 2000, pp. 189–99; Kattānī 2000–1, pp. 315–63; Fay 2001; Malti-Douglas 2001; Enderwitz 2002, pp. 49–72; Shākir 2002; Golley 2003; al-Bāridī 2005; Reynolds 2005, pp. 261–84; Musʿid 2006; Lowry and Stewart 2009; al-Qāḍī 2009, pp. 241–51; Allen 2010; DeYoung and Germain 2011; Guth and Ramsay 2011, II, pp. 139–65 (by Christian Junge); Sheetrit 2012, pp. 102–31; and Anishchenkova 2014. For essays in Arabic on the genre of autobiography from both critical as well as literary points of view, see the study of Iḥsān ʿAbbās (1920–2003) on the genre (Abbās n.d. [1956]) and his own autobiography (Abbās 1996). See also Robert B. Campbell's two-volume *Aʿlām al-Adab al-ʿArabī al-Muʿāṣir: Siyar wa-Siyar Dhātiyya* (*Contemporary Arab Writers: Biographies and Autobiographies*) (Campbell 1996). The autobiography in Arabic literature was also the topic of a conference held on 10 March 1997 at the University of Haifa with papers such as "Can Self-Exposure Be Considered Autobiography?" (by A. Arazi); "Autobiographical Elements in *Adab* Books" (by I. Geries); "Autobiographies in Modern Literature" (by S. Wild); and "Autobiographies of Contemporary Arab Poets" (by R. Snir). For lack of space, we cannot discuss here the relevance of the genre in Arabic literature, both modern and classical, to the various presuppositions behind the prevalent definitions of the autobiographic genre, especially the "typological" and the "dynamic" as well as to the problematic relationship between fact and fiction (e.g. Elbaz 1988, especially pp. 1–16). The adoption of the Internet has favored the proliferation of new forms of autobiographical writing and literary creativity all over the world. Blogs in particular are used by Internet users worldwide to record and share their writing (Pepe 2015, pp. 73–91).

to Philippe Lejeune),[63] played an important role in the development of the apprenticeship novel (*Bildungsroman*) in modern Arabic literature.[64]

According to the view that claims a break between medieval and modern Arabic literature, it is not hard to recognize the Orientalist attitude that has characterized so much of Western scholarship on Arab and Islamic culture in the twentieth century.[65] But unlike the undifferentiated patronizing attitude toward Arabic literature that was predominant until the nineteenth century,[66] a new attitude emerged among the Orientalists with the rise of modern Arabic literature—one that saw modern Arabs culturally as an *umma bā'ida* (extinct nation), that is, a nation which has an ancient culture but no modern one.[67] This was presumably due to a classicist bias that viewed the

[63] "A retrospective prose narrative produced by a real person concerning his own existence, focusing on his individual life, in particular on the development of his personality" (Lejeune 1982, p. 193). Cf. Genette 1992, p. 79. See also Lejeune 1975 (two chapters of that book [pp. 13–46, 311–41] were translated into Arabic in Lejeune 1994); and Lejeune 1989. On the dilemma of literary theory with regard to Arabic literature, see R. Ostle's introduction to Ostle et al. 1998 (pp. 18–24). See also the roundtable "Theory and Arabic Literature in the United States" in *International Journal of Middle East Studies* 43.4 (2011) with an introduction (Selim 2011, p. 721) and contributions of five literary scholars (Aboul-Ela 2011, pp. 725–7; Colla 2011, pp. 722–4; Omri 2011, pp. 731–3; Selim 2011a, pp. 734–6; and Tageldin 2011, pp. 728–30).

[64] Cf. al- Ḥakīm 1990, p. 6 (introduction). The Egyptian science-fiction writer Nihād Sharīf (1932–2011) considered *Ḥayy ibn Yaqẓān* to be among the Arab roots of science fiction in the West (*al-Qāhira*, 15 July 1988, p. 41).

[65] We can mention here also the phenomenon of Westerners confirmedly writing about Muslim and Arab culture while hardly knowing Arabic (e.g. Hever 1987, pp. 47–76; Hever 1989, pp. 30–2; Gordon 1990; Hever 1991, pp. 129–47; Shenberg 1998, pp. 21–9; Brenner 1999, pp. 85–108; and Brenner 2003). And see below what Edward W. Said wrote in his review of *God Has Ninety-Nine Names: Reporting from a Militant Middle East* by Judith Miller (Miller 1996).

[66] See, for example, the speech T. B. Macaulay (1800–59) made before the General Committee on Public Instruction shortly after he reached India in 1834. In the speech entitled "Minute on Indian Education," he said: "I am quite ready to take the Oriental learning at the valuation of the Orientalists themselves. I have never found one among them who could deny that a single shelf of a good European library was worth the whole native literature of India and Arabia [...] I certainly never met with any Orientalist who ventured to maintain that the Arabic and Sanskrit poetry could be compared to that of the great European nations" (Macaulay 1972, p. 241. Cf. Anderson 1991, pp. 90–1).

[67] On the marginality assigned to modern Arabic literature in general in Oriental or Middle Eastern Studies, see Altoma 1996, p. 137. Stating that "Islamic literature has for the most part remained so unappreciated in the West," J. Kritzeck does not refer only to belles-lettres and neither does he distinguish between Western scholarly attitudes toward classical or modern literature or between various branches of Islamic literature (Kritzeck 1964, p. 5. Cf. Krachkovskii 1989, pp. 15–16). On the other hand, it seems somewhat exaggerated to argue that the negative attitude toward modern Arab culture is shared by Arab scholars as well. It is true that "when a modern Arab thinks of his cultural heritage, he is inclined to skip over the last one thousand years or so, reaching back to the glorious centuries of Islamic civilizations" (Ayyad and Witherspoon 1999, p. 1), but that is not because "the golden age of

artistic work of the late Middle Ages and early modern period as essentially decadent without any aesthetic merit and thus not deserving of scholarly attention. As I have already pointed out, until the 1960s modern Arabic literature, among all the other modern literatures of the East, received singularly little attention in the West. When M. M. Badawi came to teach at Oxford in 1964, modern Arabic literature as a subject "was barely known" there:

> I found myself continually engaged in attempts to persuade some of my colleagues that Arabic literature had not really ceased, as was commonly believed, with Ibn Khaldun (who died in 1406), but that a sizable body of writing of considerable literary merit had been and was being produced by the Arab of today, and that Taha Husayn's autobiography *al-Ayyam* was not a solitary phenomenon. All too often modern Arabic literature was dismissed by scholars who did not take the trouble to read it.[68]

Roger Allen (b. 1942), who was among the very first pioneers specializing in what was then (the early 1960s) a radically new and somewhat disparaged field—that of "modern Arabic literature studies"—was in fact the first Oxford graduate student to obtain a doctorate in that subject (1968). Allen, a professor emeritus of Arabic and comparative literature at the University of Pennsylvania, indicates that modern Arabic texts were taught at Oxford before that decade, but were considered a "special subject"—something "that you might dabble in if you so desired, but only after you had studied the texts of the major canon (or, at least, the Oxonian version thereof)."[69] As late as 1971 John A. Haywood still complains in his *Modern Arabic Literature 1800–1970* that "modern Arabic literature has been largely neglected until the last few years."[70] And in 1974 Ilse Lichtenstadter wrote in her *Introduction to Classical Arabic Literature* that the Arabs "have rested on their ancient laurels and so far have failed to create new masterpieces."[71]

A probable explanation, already given by Gibb, is that the small body of Europeans who read Arabic with any ease were "occupied with researches into the rich historic past of Islam and the Islamic peoples that the present holds no interest, or possibly no attraction, for them."[72] Another possible

Islam [...] does not seem to link up with the present" (Ayyad and Witherspoon 1999, p. 2). The golden age serves as a kind of lost paradise from the point of view of the relationship between Arab civilization and other civilizations; it is by no means due to a low regard for the present culture (Snir 2000b, pp. 263–93. See also Martínez Lillo 2011, pp. 57–86). On the concept of "golden age," see Bauer 2007, p. 144.

68 Badawi 2000, pp. 129–30. See also Allen and Ostle 2015, pp. 1–2, 47–8.

69 Allen 2007, p. 248.

70 Haywood 1971, p. 1.

71 Lichtenstadter 1974, p. 119. Cf. P. Cachia's comments in Naff 1993, p. 17; Aboul-Ela 2001, pp. 42–4; and Aboul-Ela 2011, pp. 725–7.

72 Gibb 1962, p. 245.

explanation is the general negative attitude in the West toward Arabic literature as a *literary* phenomenon. Gibb himself alluded to this attitude, the strongest variant of which may well be George Young's dictum that "nearly all national movements—for example, those of Turkey, Greece, Ireland, and other modern nations—begin with a renascence of the national language, legends, and literature. This, in time, leads to a political rebellion against the alien authority or *ancien régime*. But *Modern Egypt has no language, no literature, no legends of its own*."[73]

Despite increased interest in the field, particularly since Najīb Maḥfūẓ was awarded the Nobel Prize in 1988, this attitude toward Arabic literature has basically remained the same.[74] The new interest is mainly due to non-aesthetic (for example, political, sociological) reasons, some viewing Arabic literature as a means to familiarize oneself with the Arab world and its many societies.[75] From the literary–aesthetic point of view, however, literary texts written since the Arab world had its first intensive cultural contacts with the West cannot be studied separately from medieval Arabic literary texts. Some phenomena and features in modern literature first appeared in medieval literature and have either remained essential components of Arabic literature throughout its history (that is, continuity) or have disappeared only to be revived in modern times (that is, renovation) under the impact of the West. A good example is the rationale that the Bahraini poet Ibrāhīm al-ʿUrayyiḍ (1908–2002) gives in the introduction to his *Min al-Shiʿr al-Ḥadīth 1900–1950* (*From Modern Poetry 1900–1950*) for the way he put together his anthology of modern Arabic poetry:

> كانت أمامي في عهد صباي- لمختار الشعر مجموعتان قديمتان، إحداهما عربية وهي حماسة أبي تمام، والثانية إنكليزية وهي «الذخيرة الذهبية» لمؤلّفها بالغريف، وكنت معجبا بالاثنين لمخضهما زبدة الشعر في كلّ من اللغتين. ولكني كنت أشدّ إعجابا بهما لاشتراكهما معا في ظاهرة نادرة هي سلكهما القطع المختارة كلّها على نظام القلادة في سلك منظّم بحيث كانت تتساوق القطعة التالية مع التي تسبقها في الغرض والموضوع (...) فخطر لي أن أنتخب من الشعر الحديث مختارا أجري فيه على نهج أبي تمام وبالغريف وأصنع صنعهما في الاختيار والترتيب.

> In my youth I had before me two ancient collections of selected poetry, one of them in Arabic, that is, Abū Tammām's *Ḥamāsa*, and the second *The Golden Treasury* by Palgrave. I admired both of them since they contain the best poetry in both languages. However, I admired them more due to a common rare phenomenon, that is, the chaining of all the selected poems—as in a necklace—in an organized string. Each poem is in harmony with the preceding one as regards the purpose and theme [...] Therefore, it came to me to select from modern

[73] Young 1927, p. x (my emphasis).
[74] See the various contributions in Beard and Haydar 1993.
[75] Cf. below, p. 262.

poetry an anthology after the pattern of Abū Tammām and Palgrave, and to do as they did from the point of view of selection and arrangement.[76]

The *Ḥamāsa* by Abū Tammām Ḥabīb ibn Aws (d. 845) is the most widely known anthology of classical Arabic poetry.[77] Similarly, *The Golden Treasury* by Turner Francis Palgrave (1824–97) compiled in 1861 is perhaps the most famous anthology of poems and lyrics in the English language,[78] and during the first half of the twentieth century it was one of the factors behind the gradual change in the poetic models of Arabic poetry.[79] But, as al-ʿUrayyiḍ indicates, features of Western culture have most appealed to modern Arab poets when they could see them as being synonymous with features of continuity or renovation as they pertained to various aspects of the Arab heritage.

THE DEVELOPMENT OF THE GENRES

The study of the literary dynamics in the generic and diachronic development of Arabic literature requires that we first look at each genre and subgenre separately and then demarcate interrelationships and interactions that bind them, that is, between genres and between genres and subgenres, and so on. It will not be effective, for example, to offer a general study of the diachronic development of poetry without looking systematically and separately at poetry aimed at adults and poetry aimed at children (subgenres) in the three different frameworks (that is, *fuṣḥā*, *ʿāmmiyya*, and translation). Only after we have done this can we study the interrelationships and interactions that obtain among them. And the same holds true for the sub-subgenres in each subgenre. When it comes to poetry in *fuṣḥā* for adults, for instance, we need to study separately the so-called "neoclassical" poetry, "romantic poetry," "free verse" (*al-shiʿr al-ḥurr*), and "the prose poem" (*qaṣīdat al-nathr*), among other forms.[80] If we then delineate the relationships between

76 Al-ʿUrayyiḍ 1958, p. 5.

77 See Abū Tammām n.d.

78 See Palgrave 1906 [1861]. The book changed with The World's Classics edition of 1907, which carried additional poems, and the 1928 edition, which included more work by contemporary poets. Further contemporary poems were included in The World's Classics edition of 1941. Finally, a complete fifth book was added to the existing four by John Press (Oxford Standard Authors, 1964), bringing the anthology up to date. The same text is used in The World's Classics edition of 1964 (on the various editions, see Palgrave 1906 [1861], pp. vii–xix; and Stapleton 1985. p. 667).

79 Palgrave's anthology was a major inspiration for Arab writers, especially during the first half of the twentieth century; see Semah 1974, p. 193; Badawi 1975, pp. 88–90; Moreh 1976, p. 56; Badīr 1982, pp. 50, 152; Somekh 1991, p. 109; and Badawi 1992, p. 90. On the importance of the poems included in *The Golden Treasury* to Arabic poetry in general and to Nāzik al-Malāʾika's poetry in particular, see Abdul-Razak 1989.

80 I am using these terms here only for the sake of clarifying my views. On the problems with

these sub-subgenres we will arrive at a better understanding not only of each of these sub-subgenres but of the development of poetry in general as well. Here, the best we can do is set the stage, as much research still needs to be done before we can embark on the kind of detailed analysis such a study requires. Thus, what follows are only a few general remarks in regard to the three general canonical genres (poetry, fiction, and theater) without ignoring the fact that those are Western categories and "the disregard of indigenous categories can never do justice to any other culture than the Western."[81]

Poetry

No feature is probably more characteristic of the general development of Arabic poetry in *fuṣḥā* since the early nineteenth century, or perhaps even since the emergence of that poetry in its unified meter-and-rhyme scheme in the pre-Islamic period, than the breaking of the traditional norms of the *qaṣīda* in the twentieth century.[82] Frank Kermode was right when he argued that "although periods are often detected long after they are over, it is not unusual for people to think they are actually in one,"[83] but most if not all contemporary scholars of Arabic poetry are unified in that the last century was decisive in the development of Arabic poetry. In a proposal for a seminar at the annual conference of the ACLA held at Harvard University on 17–20 March 2016 entitled "The Arabic *Qasida*: An Aesthetics for the 21st Century," Suzanne Stetkevych writes that

> for classical Arabic poetry, as for Arab culture in general, the 20th century was a tumultuous period. For 1,500 years the *qasida* had reigned as the preeminent Arabic poetic form and as the matrix from which other poetic forms (*ghazal*, hunt poem, wine poem, etc.) emerged [...] the *qasida* reached its apogee in the rhetorical triumphalism of the Abbasids. After the 10th c., the *qasida* dissipated into other and lesser forms, settling into the ornate stylization of Post-Classical Prophetic praise poems. Its final flourish came in the late 19th-early 20th c. Arab Renaissance, when the Neo-Classical poets claimed the Classical

using such terms, see DeYoung 1998, pp. 151–85. ʻAbd al-Fattāḥ al-Bārūdī says that there is no justification at all to use these Western terms for Arabic poetry, which should be understood based on terms stemming from the nature of Arabic literature, its peculiarities, and its functions (*al-Akhbār*, 27 April 1986, p. 8).

81 See Bauer 2007, pp. 148–51. The quotation is from p. 149. Cf. Harris and Reichl 1997, pp. 249–75 (by Wolfhart Heinrichs) and pp. 277–94 (by Dwight Reynolds).

82 For an analysis of this development, see a review article of Moreh 1986 and al-Ghadhdhāmī 1987 in *al-Karmil—Abḥāth fī al-Lugha wa-l-Adab* 9 (1988), pp. 167–89. On the norms of the *qaṣīda* in various Islamic traditions, see Sperl and Shackle 1996; and Sperl and Shackle 1996a.

83 Kermode 1988, p. 122.

> *qasida* as both source and model for Arab-Islamic civilization [...] The remainder of the Modern period discredited the *qasida* tradition [...] For their part, the Orientalists, who were not without influence on Arab critics, reduced the classical *qasida* tradition to a corpus of realistic depictions and rhetorical tropes, or else of philological specimens beyond the scope of literary aesthetics.[84]

It is in general accepted that canonical poetry in *fuṣḥā* throughout the nineteenth century and at the beginning of the twentieth was largely of an epigonic nature, being in general little more than undisguised imitation of previous poems (exceptions existed, but they occupied the margins of the literary system). For example, the Egyptian poet Muḥammad ʿAbd al-Muṭṭalib (1871–1931) insisted on close adherence to the classical manner of writing and opposed all forms of innovation to the point that his poetic models were not the Abbasid, but the pre-Islamic and Umayyad poets. His traditional linguistic education had such a firm hold on him that even when he tried his hand at describing modern realities, he did not bother to consider newer and more appropriate styles but preferred instead to follow the traditional one. In one of his poems, "al-ʿAlawiyya al-Ūlā,"[85] in homage of the Caliph ʿAlī ibn Abī Ṭālib (d. 660), ʿAbd al-Muṭṭalib substituted the modern airplane for the camel of ancient poetry, describing its flight as "rising to set tents upon the clouds." Using the convention of addressing imaginary companions, he asks two of his friends to carry him into the skies, saying "perhaps I can meet the Imām on the clouds:"

أصغر الأرض وما فيها مقاما   فاعتلى يضرب في السحب الخياما
حسد الطير على الجوّ فسر   عان ما حلّق في الجوّ وحاما
يزجر الريح فتجري تحته   أينما ولّى بها تلوي الزماما
سابحا فوق ابنة النار على   مسرح النجم جنوبا وشآما
فإذا شاء أسفّت في الثرى   وإذا شاء بها شقّ الغماما
أخوَذيات إذا ما هزّمت   تملأ الأفق رغاء واهتزاما
سفن في الجوّ إلا أنها   في السرى تطويه كالطيف لماما
ليت شعري أين يبغي بعدما   غلب النسر عليها والحماما
يا خليليّ احملاني فوقها   علّني ألقى على السحب الإماما
أو أحيى ذلك البرق الذي   شقّ من نجد إلى مصر الظلاما

No translation can possibly do justice to this poem, whose peculiarities cannot be understood without being aware of, and being absorbed into, the period in which it was written and the readership which it targeted. ʿAbd al-Muṭṭalib's poetic imagination hovered around ancient Arabia, as if he himself were one of the ancient classical poets, and it earned him the

[84] According to the "Arabic Lit Scholars" list, 21 July 2015. See also the various significant contributions included in Stetkevych 2009 as well as the book's introduction (pp. xiii–xxix).

[85] ʿAbd al-Muṭṭalib n.d., pp. 268–70. On the poem, see Moreh 1988, pp. 41, 44.

nickname of the "Bedouin poet."[86] Nevertheless, this kind of poetry never reached the level of visionary power so characteristic of some of the ancient poets,[87] and before long we find some of the contemporary poets creating new techniques and discovering new themes, though always within this same narrow framework.[88] In this regard, such Egyptian poets as Maḥmūd Sāmī al-Bārūdī (1839–1904), Aḥmad Shawqī (1868–1932), Ḥāfiẓ Ibrāhīm (1871–1932), Aḥmad Muḥarram (1871–1945), ʻAlī al-Jārim (1881–1949), and Ismāʻīl Ṣabrī (1885–1923) stand out, but so too do such Iraqi poets as Jamīl Ṣidqī al-Zahāwī (1863–1936), Maʻrūf al-Ruṣāfī (1875–1945), and Muḥammad Mahdī al-Jawāhirī (1900–97). Their foremost concern, according to most critics, was to free Arabic poetry from the impurities that vitiated it in the intervening centuries and to recapture the grand poetic style of the golden age.[89] One way of attaining this goal was the frequent practice of *muʻāraḍa*, that is, a kind of contrafactum: composing poems for which rhyme, meter, and sometimes even the topic were borrowed from a specific classical poem.[90] The central poetic conception of the so-called "neoclassi-

86 On ʻAbd al-Muṭṭalib, see Kaḥḥāla 1960, X, p. 253; Qabbish 1971, pp. 96–8; Brugman 1984, pp. 51–2; al-Ziriklī 1984, VI, p. 247; and Abū al-Khashab 1984, pp. 329–38. Cf. Meisami and Starkey 1998, I, p. 15.

87 Cf. Adūnīs 1996 [1964–8], I, pp. 14–15:

> ما نسمّيه عصر النهضة، بعد انحطاط دام ألف سنة، لم يكن إلا تقليدا للنماذج التراثية. ولم يتناول هذا التقليد الروح الداخلية في هذه النماذج (...) لكنه تناول الشكل، وفوق ذلك لم يفهم من الشكل إلا جانبه اللغوي. لهذا كانت النهضة، إذا جاز لنا أن نسمّيها كذلك، إحياء لأساليب اللغة القديمة (...) هذا الإحياء لم يفهم روح اللغة العربية: نظر إليها من زاوية النحو والصرف، لا من زاوية الشعر والإبداع. لذلك لم يفهم الشعر العربي ولا الروح العربية.

Cf. Jayyusi 1996, p. 28 (concerning the poetry of ʻAbd al-Muḥsin al-Kāẓimī [1866–1935] of Iraq). However, most of Jayyusi's article aims at asserting the important role of well-known "neoclassical" poets, especially Aḥmad Shawqī, as "propagators"—"those who develop an already established trend to its fullest potential enriching it and imbuing it with flair and sophistication" (p. 31).

88 The innovations in the literary works of the "neoclassical" poets ("the classical as innovation," according to Larkin 2008, pp. 117–21) generally fell behind their innovative critical theories and literary views. For example, the modernist views expressed by al- Maḥmūd Sāmī al-Bārūdī (1838–1904) in the preface to his *Dīwān* (al-Bārūdī 1954, pp. 1-9) hardly find their reflection in his poetry, which, even if different from the well-known poetry of his time, remains rather conventional. Cf. Badawi 1975, pp. 17–20, where he minimizes the importance of this gap. On al-Bārūdī in the context of contemporary poetry, see Solaiman 1999, pp. 185–96.

89 Cf. al-ʻAqqād and al-Māzinī n.d. [1921], I, p. 12 about the poetic ideal of the nineteenth century:

> فقد كان العهد الماضي عهد ركاكة في الأسلوب وتعثّر في الصياغة تنبو به الأذن، وكان آية الآيات على نبوغ الكاتب أو الشاعر أن يوفّق إلى جملة مستوية النسق أو بيت سائغ الجرس فيسير مسير الأمثال وتستعذبه الأفواه لسهولة مجراه على اللسان.

90 On the "neoclassical trend," see Moreh 1973, pp. 155–79; Badawi 1975, pp. 14–67; Moreh 1976, pp. 1–2; Boudot-Lamotte 1977; Jayyusi 1977, pp. 46–54; Brugman 1984, pp. 26–56; Somekh 1992, pp. 36–81, 491–4; Kadhim 2004; and Starkey 2006, pp. 42–59. On the specific

cal" poets was basically the same: The *qaṣīda* is the sacred form of poetry, and the relationship between the poet and his readers is like that between an orator and his audience. This kind of poetry is thus often called *shi'r minbarī* (platform poetry), *shi'r khiṭābī* (oratorical poetry), or *shi'r al-munāsabāt* (poetry of occasions). Moreover, as can be seen in nearly every poem of the great "neoclassical" poets, the audience "imposes" a particular method of writing on the poet. This comes most clearly to the fore in poems intended to be recited at public gatherings, such as the poem that Shawqī wrote for a celebration held by Nādī Madrasat al-Mu'allimīn al-'Ulyā (The High Teachers College's Club) in Cairo, whose opening verse is:

قم للمعلّم وفّه التبجيلا   كاد المعلّم أن يكون رسولا

Stand up for the teacher and honor him, the teacher is almost like a prophet.[91]

Or the poem with which he showcased the inauguration of Bank Miṣr (The Bank of Egypt) that begins with the following verse:

قف بالممالك وانظر دولة المال   واذكر رجالا أدالوها بإجمال

Halt by the kingdoms and observe the realm of money, and remember the people who made it happen.[92]

In both poems, the particular occasion for which the poem was written determined not only the rhetorical framework but also the content—honoring the teachers in the first poem and the people of finance in the other. Even

issue of *mu'āraḍa*, see Nawfal 1983; and 'Abd al-Waḥid 2003. Cf. Meisami and Starkey 1998, II, p. 534. On *mu'āraḍa* in modern Arabic poetry and some examples from the work of Badr Shākir al-Sayyāb, see DeYoung 1994, pp. 217–45; and Larkin 2008, pp. 117–21.

91 Shawqī n.d., I, pp. 180–4. Emphasizing the nature of these verses as "poetry of occasions," the Palestinian poet Ibrāhīm Ṭūqān (1905–41) wrote an ironic *mu'āraḍa*, opening with:

شوقي يقول وما درى بمصيبتي   قم للمعلّم وفّه التبجيلا
اقعد، فديتك، هل يكون مبجلا   من كان للنشء الصغار خليلا
ويكاد يفلقني الأمير بقوله: كاد المعلم ان يكون رسولا
لو جرّب التعليم شوقي ساعة   لقضى الحياة شقاوة وخمولا
حسب المعلم غمّة وكآبة   مرآى الدفاتر بكرة وأصيلا

(Ṭūqān 1975, pp. 126–7; Qabbish 1981, p. 354). Also, in the second part of Najīb Maḥfūẓ's trilogy, *Qaṣr al-Shawq*, Shawqī's poem is treated ironically: "Books document strange and supernatural matters. For example, you read at times in them 'the teacher is almost like a prophet,' but have you ever encountered a teacher of whom that was true? Come with me to al-Naḥḥāsīn School or recall any of your teachers you please. Show me one of them deserving the title 'human being,' let alone that of 'prophet'" (Maḥfūẓ n.d. [1957], p. 60. Translation is based on Mahfouz 2002, p. 57). On the role of teachers in Shawqī's poems, see Abubakar 2000, pp. 47–75.

92 Shawqī n.d., I, pp. 184–7. The bank, which was established on 13 April 1920 and which was instrumental in promoting Egyptian economic development, was identified with the national revival (Davis 1983, pp. 3–4).

when they already attempted to break the traditional norms, "neoclassical" poets did so in a conventional way. An example of this is Ḥāfiẓ Ibrāhīm's ars-poetic poem entitled "al-Shi'r" ("Poetry"):[93]

ضعت بين النهى وبين الخيال   يا حكيم النفوس يا ابن المعالي
ضعت في الشرق بين قوم هجود   لم يفيقوا وأمّة مكسال
قد أذالوك بين أنس وكأس   وغرام بظبية أو غزال
ونسيب ومدحة وهجاء   ورثاء وفتنة وضلال
وحماس أراه في غير شيء   وصغار يجرّ ذيل اختيال
عشت ما بينهم مذالا مضاعا   وكذا كنت في العصور الخوالي
حملوك العناء من حبّ (ليلى)   و(سليمى) ووقفة الأطلال
وبكاء على عزيز تولّى   ورسوم راحت بهنّ الليالي
وإذا ما سموْا بقدرك يوما   أسكنوك الرحال فوق الجمال
آن يا شعر أن نفكّ قيودا   قيدتنا بها دعاة المُحال
فارفعوا هذه الكمائم عنا   ودعونا نشمّ ريح الشمال

Ḥāfiẓ Ibrāhīm laments the stranglehold of conventions on Arabic poetry and calls for its liberation, but he does so in a poem which itself is a typical example of the traditional form of poetry.

Breaking with the *qaṣīda* form was to come only with those poets who were called by some scholars, following the development of Western poetic traditions, "pre-romantic" or "romantic" poets and who heralded the onset of a change in canonical poetics.[94] The term "pre-romantic" was ascribed to poets such as Khalīl Muṭrān (1872–1949) and the members of the *Dīwān* group—'Abd al-Raḥmān Shukrī (1886–1958), 'Abbās Maḥmūd al-'Aqqād (1889–1964), and Ibrāhīm 'Abd al-Qādir al-Māzinī (1890–1949).[95] The term "romantic" referred, for the most part, to those poets belonging to the two literary groups of the Egyptian *Apollo* and the New York-based *al-Rābiṭa al-Qalamiyya* (The Pen League). In the Eastern branch of the "romantic" school we find Muslim poets such as the Egyptians Aḥmad Zakī Abū Shādī (1892–1955), Ibrāhīm Nājī (1898–1953), and 'Alī Maḥmūd Ṭāhā (1902–49); the Tunisian Abū al-Qāsim al-Shābbī (1909–34); and the Sudanese al-Tījānī Yūsuf Bashīr (1912–37).[96] In the Western branch we find Christian poets

93 Ibrāhīm n.d., I, pp. 237–8. For a similar example in the classical period, see Ṣanāwī 1994, pp. 20–1.

94 The first serious critical attempt to break the hegemony of the "neoclassical" trend and to introduce a new poetics appeared in al-'Aqqād and al-Māzinī's *al-Dīwān fī al-Adab wa-l-Naqd* (1921), which contained "some of the best practical criticism produced in Arabic in the first half of the century" (Badawi 1975, p. 89). Actually, the book concentrates more on breaking the poetic idols of the past than presenting the poetics of the future, as is indicated by the authors in the preface (al-'Aqqād and al-Māzinī n.d. [1921], I, p. 4).

95 On these poets, see al-Zubaidi 1970, pp. 36–48; Ostle 1971, pp. 116–26; Badawi 1975, pp. 68–114; and Mawāsī 1995.

96 On "romantic" poets in the East, see Badawi 1975, pp. 115–78; and Ostle 1991a, pp. 202–12.

such as Jubrān Khalīl Jubrān (1883–1931), Mīkhā'īl Nu'ayma (1889–1988), Nasīb 'Arīḍa (1887–1946), Īliyā Abū Māḍī (1889–1957), and Rashīd Ayyūb (1872–1941).[97] Of course, the terms "pre-romantic" and "romantic" might be misleading, since only some of the characteristics of their poetry are reminiscent of their assumed Western counterparts, but it is probably correct to say that all of the aforementioned poets allowed themselves to be inspired more by inner personal experiences than by outside stimuli, and after a while most of them left behind the accepted classical forms and opted instead for strophic forms in a great number of their poems, introducing new types of metaphorical and poetic language.[98] Scholarship has referred in general to "romantic" poetry as having emerged especially in the interwar period, with the so-called "neoclassical" poetry gradually being pushed to the margins (but never outside) of the literary canon. But the temporal limits are misleading, and poems which might be described as "neoclassical" or "romantic" continue to be written to the present day.

It is when we come to the late 1940s and the rise of *al-shi'r al-ḥurr* (free verse) that we encounter significant deviations from classical metrics, which succeeded in gaining canonical status. For traditional critics, "free verse" signaled that the framework of the ancient, sacred form of Arabic poetry had finally been broken.[99] Based on the earlier experiments of Arab poets who were influenced by English poetry, the essential concept of "free verse" poetry entails reliance on the free repetition of the basic unit of conventional prosody—the use of an irregular number of a single foot (*taf'īla*) instead of a fixed number of feet. The poet varies the number of feet in a single line according to need. The new form, which is closely associated with the names of the Iraqi poets Nāzik al-Malā'ika (1923–2007) and Badr Shākir al-Sayyāb (1926–64), found acceptance virtually throughout the Arab world. Which of the two poets was the first to introduce "free verse" has been the subject of much controversy, and claims of priority have been made for both of them. This issue was complicated by the fact that both poets published their first

[97] On "romantic" poets in the West, see Krachkovskii 1927, pp. 193–213; Badawi 1975, pp. 179–203; and Duraković 2000, pp. 265–96. On *al-Rābiṭa al-Qalamiyya*, see Nijland 1993, pp. 329–41; and Popp 2001, pp. 30–52. For an annotated bibliography of literary criticism and biography in Western languages on *Mahjari* literature, see McNulty 1981, pp. 65–88.

[98] On "romantic" Arabic poetry in general, see Abdul-Hai 1972, pp. 72–89; Moreh 1976, pp. 54–195; Jayyusi 1977, pp. 54–176, 361–474; Brugman 1984, pp. 56–62, 94–204; al-Hussein 1989; al-Sādāt 1992; Abu-Haidar 1996, pp. 3–17; and Starkey 2006, pp. 60–78. See also a review of Ra'ūf 1982 in *al-Karmil—Abḥāth fī al-Lugha wa-l-Adab* 8 (1987), pp. 198–202. On the *Apollo* school's early experiments in "free verse," see Zubaidi 1974, pp. 17–43.

[99] On the issue of terminology regarding the "free verse," see al-Tami 1988, pp. 70–105; and al-Tami 1993, pp. 185–98.

poems in the new experimental form—al-Malā'ika's "al-Kūlīrā" ("Cholera")[100] and al-Sayyāb's "Hal Kāna Ḥubban?" ("Was It Love?")[101]—in the same month (December 1947).[102] The controversy surrounding the first poet to write a free-verse poem, however, is actually rather unimportant and marginal, for the year 1947 only marked the end of a long process in which we see the *qaṣīda* gradually being pushed from the center of the literary system to the margins. What is more significant is that the rise of "free verse" in the late 1940s should be viewed as another outcome of the inescapable process of automatization that the traditional *qaṣīda* had undergone throughout the last few centuries.[103] As its conventional literary devices had worn out through endless repetition, the necessity of destroying "the automatism of perception"[104] became far more urgent to revitalize the poetic discourse and to overcome stereotyping. Nāzik al-Malā'ika's preface to the fourth edition of her book *Qaḍāyā al-Shi'r al-Mu'āṣir* (*Issues in Contemporary Poetry*) (1962) illustrates this process quite clearly:

> لو لم أبدأ حركة الشعر الحرّ لبدأها بدر شاكر السياب يرحمه الله، ولو لم نبدأها أنا وبدر لبدأها شاعر عربي آخر غيري وغيره، فإن الشعر الحرّ قد أصبح في تلك السنين ثمرة ناضجة حلوة على دوحة الشعر العربي بحيث حان قطافها، ولا بدّ من أن يحصدها حاصد ما في أيّة بقعة من بقاع الوطن العربي، لأنه قد حان لروض الشعر أن تنبثق فيه سنابل جديدة باهرة تغيّر النمط الشائع، وتبتدئ عصرا أدبيا جديدا كلّه حيوية وخصب وانطلاق.

> If I had not started the "free verse" movement, the late Badr Shākir al-Sayyāb would have started it and if neither of us, me and Badr, had started it, it would have been another Arab poet. "Free verse" in those years [the late 1940s] had become a ripe sweet fruit on the tall tree of Arabic poetry ready to be plucked, and it was inevitable that someone somewhere in the Arab homeland would pluck it. That is because time had come in the gardens of poetry so that gleaming new spikes should burst forth and change the common course in order to announce a new literary period full of vitality, fertility, and freedom.[105]

Many writers balked at the modernization of the structure of Arabic poetry. The previously mentioned 'Abbās Maḥmūd al-'Aqqād is a notable example.[106]

[100] Al-Malā'ika 1979, II, pp. 138–42.

[101] Al-Sayyāb 1971, I, pp. 101–3.

[102] On this issue, see Moreh 1976, pp. 198–200; Jayyusi 1977, pp. 558–9; DeYoung 1998, pp. 191–2; and Ḥijāzī 1999, pp. 93–4.

[103] Poets in the eighth and ninth centuries already made sarcastic remarks about normative poetical forms and wrote outspoken parodies mocking the traditional approach to poetry and the classical canon itself (Bakkār 1981, pp. 93–100; and Filshtinsky 1984, pp. 65–70).

[104] Eichenbaum 1965, p. 114.

[105] Al-Malā'ika 1983 [1962], p. 17. Cf. al-Nuwayhī 1971 [1964], pp. 249–309; and Niyāzī 1999, pp. 64–5. See also al-Bayyātī's attitude toward the question of priority in this field (al-Sayyid 1999, p. 14).

[106] During the 1950s and the beginning of the 1960s, al-'Aqqād served as the head of the

But the success of "free verse" was assured the moment the literary establishment realized that the canons of prosody could no longer be treated as a sacred revelation. As Ṭāhā Ḥusayn put it:

> I cannot reject poetry merely because it takes liberties with the established norms, or because it deviates from the poetic meters laid down by al-Khalīl. I do, however, reject it when it fails to fulfill two conditions, namely, that it shows sincerity, strength, beauty, and novelty of imagery, and that it be written in an Arabic that is unmarred by corruption or banality.[107]

Ṭāhā Ḥusayn was especially critical of the changes in the form of Arabic poetry when they included the use of dialects and when literary texts threatened to become "a kind of popular literature which rightly or wrongly we despise."[108] The new kind of poetry presented by the advocates of "free verse" was still based on the traditional meters, as the work of its first practitioners shows.[109] Yet, the innovations were not confined to metrics, and senior literary critics at the center of the literary system were soon describing the other innovative characteristics of this poetry.

For example, the Egyptian literary critic ʻIzz al-Dīn Ismāʻīl (1929–2007), one of the main defenders of "free verse," maintains that a distinction should be made between verse that reflects the superficial side of modern life and the kind of poetry that succeeds in representing the spirit of the age. He argues that the aesthetic concept that inspires the new poetry stems from the heart of the literary work itself—it attempts to explore the essence of life, reflects the culture of the age on a universal scale, and expresses a poetic

poetry committee within the Supreme Council for Culture (*al-Majlis al-Aʻlā li-l-Thaqāfa*) in Egypt, and he used to send all the "free verse" poems in the competitions held by the council to the prose committee. After al-ʻAqqād had banned the participation of Ṣalāḥ ʻAbd al-Ṣabūr (1931–81) and Aḥmad ʻAbd al-Muʻṭī Ḥijāzī (b. 1935) in the poetry festival held in Damascus in September 1961, Ḥijāzī reacted by writing a scathingly critical retort in traditional meter (*basīṭ*) in which he described al-ʻAqqād as "he who speaks on everything but almost does not master anything" and addressed him directly: "You live in our period only as a guest but vilify us; we sing and delight" (*al-Ḥayāt*, January 2006, <http://www.arood.com/vb/archive/index.php/t-466.html> [last accessed 16 October 2016]). See also Ṣalāḥ ʻAbd al-Ṣabūr's article "Radd ʻalā al-Ustādh al-ʻAqqād: Mawzūn ... w-Allāhi al-ʻAẓīm," first published in *Akhbār al-Yawm* on 17 June 1961 and then incorporated into ʻAbd al-Ṣabūr 1971, pp. 73–8. Cf. Moussa-Mahmoud 1996, p. 63. It is ironic that Ḥijāzī himself, when serving in the 1990s as the head of the same poetry committee, was accused by the poets of the "prose poem" as vilifying them even more than al-ʻAqqād had vilified him (<http://www.al-akhbar.com/node/138206> [4 August 2007] [last accessed 16 October 2016]).

107 *Al-Ādāb*, February 1957, p. 8. Cf. *al-Adīb*, May 1960, p. 56; and Semah 1974, pp. 122–3.

108 Ḥusayn n.d. [1958], p. 15.

109 See, for example, al-Malāʼika 1983 [1962], pp. 67–137.

experience that is not confined to personal emotions but seeks new forms and techniques as determined by changing experiences.[110]

Another staunch defender of "free verse" is the Egyptian literary critic Muḥammad al-Nuwayhī (1917–80). He argues against the use of the term "free verse" because it implies that this poetry, like English "free verse" or French *vers libre*, is free from meter, which it is not. The new form, according to al-Nuwayhī, is the only way to revive Arabic poetry and make it the appropriate vehicle to bring about the intellectual and artistic well-being of the Arab world. His book *Qaḍiyyat al-Shi'r al-Jadīd* (*The Case of the New Poetry*)[111] was written in support of the new poetry. Based on T. S. Eliot's article "The Music of Poetry" (1942),[112] al-Nuwayhī claims that poetry ought to reflect daily life and speech, though he is aware that among minor poets this could encourage exaggerated realism and ambiguity. For al-Nuwayhī, the new poetic form is to prepare the way for a new type of rhythm and meter based on stress. He discusses the possibility of having accentual rather than quantitative measures in the future, claiming that modern poets have already started resorting to accentual measures in *al-khabab* and other meters, especially in *al-rajaz*. Because it allows the poet's language to come closer to common daily speech and the spirit of the people, the suggested prosody, which he calls *al-niẓām al-nabrī* (the tonal system), will revive Arabic poetry and save it from stagnation, inject new blood into the Arabic language, and prevent it from being dominated by the colloquial language.[113] That two such senior scholars and critics, 'Izz al-Dīn Ismā'īl and Muḥammad al-Nuwayhī, devoted their major writings to defending the "free verse" option is perhaps the clearest proof that this kind of poetry had reached the center of the literary system.

Recent developments in Arabic poetry, however, have already seen the gradual pushing of "free verse" to the margins of the literary system.[114] Its place has been taken over by prose poetry, especially *qaṣīdat al-nathr* (the prose poem), with its varied types and forms.[115] During the late 1950s Adūnīs

110 Ismā'īl 1978. Cf. Moreh 1976, pp. 260–1; Jayyusi 1977, pp. 597–8; and Meisami and Starkey 1998, I, p. 399.

111 Al-Nuwayhī 1971 [1964].

112 Eliot 1969, pp. 26–38 (Arabic translation: Khūrī 1966, pp. 24–31); al-Nuwayhī 1971 [1964], pp. 19–25.

113 On al-Nuwayhī and his critical views, see Green 1984, pp. ix–xxiv; Semah 1974, pp. 148, 195–201; Moreh 1976, pp. 263–6; and Jayyusi 1977, pp. 638–9. Cf. Meisami and Starkey 1998, II, p. 590.

114 See the symposium in *Barīd al-Janūb* (Paris), 21 June 1999, pp. 14–15 held under the title "al-Qaṣīda al-'Arabiyya Hal Tashhadu Mawtahā am Istikmāl Wilādatihā?" ("Arabic Qaṣīda: Does it Witness its Death or the Completion of its Birth?").

115 See Moreh 1988, pp. 1–31; and Adūnīs 1993, pp. 168–75. See also the review article of Moreh 1988 in *al-Karmil—Abḥāth fī al-Lugha wa-l-Adab* 10 (1989), pp. 161–71. On this process, see also the articles in al-Khaṭīb 1996; and al-Khaṭīb 1996a.

and his colleagues claimed that the change in the form of Arabic poetry, following the adoption of "free verse" technique, had only been external and had not affected "the essence of the Arabic *qaṣīda,*" which they argue remained unchanged.[116] At any rate, prose poetry is still in the process of development and change, be it at the hand of the pioneers of the genre or due to the effort of younger generations. Significant contributions to the process of canonization of the new genre were made in the journals *Shi'r* and *Mawāqif* by Adūnīs and the poets who followed him,[117] as well as by young poets of the 1970s, 1980s, and 1990s,[118] and by poets such as the *Farādīs* group in Paris, which was headed by the exiled Iraqi poet 'Abd al-Qādir al-Janābī (b. 1944),[119] and by various other groups of exiled poets.[120]

116 Adūnīs 1959, p. 83: "We can follow the direction of the development of the Arabic *Qaṣīda*, and we can see some change in its form, but this change has been only marginal and never touched the essence of the *Qaṣīda* which has remained without change." It seems that it was these words as well as the modernist attempts of Adūnīs since the late 1950s that prompted the sharp accusations leveled against him and his followers—for example, al-Malā'ika's essay "Qaṣīdat al-Nathr" ("The Prose Poem") first published in *al-Ādāb*, April 1962, pp. 5–7 (a critical review of this essay appeared in *al-Ādāb*, May 1962, pp. 60–2), later incorporated in al-Malā'ika 1983 [1962], pp. 213–27. Al-Malā'ika describes the modernist poetic attempts as *kidhba* (lie) and *khiyānat al-lugha al-'Arabiyya wa-l-'Arab anfusihim* (a betrayal of the Arabic language and the Arabs themselves) (al-Malā'ika 1983 [1962], p. 222). Cf. al-Naqqāsh 1992, p. 45, about Adūnīs as *kārih li-l-'Arab wa-rāfiḍ li-l-turāth al-Islāmī* (hating the Arabs and rejecting the Muslim heritage).

117 See Adūnīs' essays in *Shi'r* and *Mawāqif* as well as the introduction to the second edition of his complete works, in which he speaks about *nathr ākhar* (a different kind of prose) (Adūnīs 1988, pp. 5–7).

118 See, for example, the works published in the Egyptian magazine *al-Kitāba al-Ukhrā* (*Another Writing*), such as volumes 5–6 (September 1993); and 7 (June 1994). The same group also published a series of poetry collections entitled *Kitābāt Ukhrā* (*Other Writings*), such as *'Alā Bu'd Khuṭwa* (*At a Distance of a Step*) by 'Alī Manṣūr (b. 1956) (on the collection, see 'Alā' al-Dīb's article in *Ṣabāḥ al-Khayr*, 2 July 1992, p. 66). See also the various issues of the Egyptian magazines *Aṣwāt* and *Iḍā'a*. On these poetic activities, see *al-Usbū' al-'Arabī*, 31 January 1994, pp. 44–5; and Mehrez 1994a, pp. 177–96. Clarissa Burt deals with the "Nineties' Poets," who started to appear in print primarily in 1990, and is a group of "young poets and poetic aspirants, now for the most part in their mid- to late twenties and early thirties [...] [they are] the harbingers of radical change in literary values and cultural underpinnings in Egyptian society" (Burt 1997, pp. 141–78).

119 See, for example, *Farādīs* 6–7 (1993), especially pp. 57–141. On al-Janābī's conception of the development of Arabic poetry since the 1950s, see El Janabi 1999, especially pp. 7–24. On his surrealist writings, see Irwin 2000, pp. 14–15. See also al-Janābī's articles and literary texts on <http://www.elaph.com> (last accessed 15 October 2016).

120 See, for example, *al-Laḥẓa al-Shi'riyya* (London), especially the article by Fawzī Karīm (b. 1945) in the first issue, "Thiyāb al-Imbarāṭūr: Maqāla fī al-Siyāq al-Shi'rī al-Sā'id" ("The Emperor's Clothes: An Essay on the Prevailing Poetic Context") (Karīm 1992, pp. 68–80). See also al-'Azzāwī 1997, which describes the experience of "sixties generation" (*jīl al-sittīnāt*) and the activities of the Kirkūk's group (*Jamā'at Kirkūk*) (1955–64) in Iraq (especially pp. 279–340).

We may call this development of Arabic poetry a renovation, as it employs features common to works written in some other time-section in the distant past, namely in the pre-*qaṣīda* period, when even the canonization of what would become the "sacred form" of Arabic poetry was still far off. As we lack sources for pre-Islamic poetry, it is impossible at present to argue that the latest development in contemporary Arabic poetry constitutes a return to that "primitive" form of poetry which the standardization of the *qaṣīda* then had made less "advanced" or less "civilized."[121] However, hypothesizing the existence of such poetic "primitivism" might not be so unreasonable. The earliest known verses date from a period in which the form, meter, rhyme, and theme of Arabic poetry were already fully developed. In other words, as Reynold A. Nicholson indicates, "their elaborate form and technical perfection forbid the hypothesis that in them we have 'the first sprightly runnings' of Arabian song" and, like the *Iliad* and *Odyssey*, "they are works of highly finished art, which could not possibly have been produced until the poetical art had been practised for a long time."[122]

What may have been the nature of the poetry that was widespread before the emergence of the "advanced" type of *qaṣīda* is still a subject of dispute among scholars.[123] We might have only one extraordinary rare glimpse into that period when "primitive" poetry was at the center of the literary system, and that is a short Arabic inscription that was discovered in 1979 engraved on a rock above the gorge of 'En 'Abdat in the Negev desert.[124] This sort of "primitive" poetry was pushed to the margins of the literary system with the standardization of the *qaṣīda*, which would remain the dominant canonical model until the twentieth century. As is well known, even such a popular poetic mode as the *muwashshaḥ* (an Arabic poetic genre in strophic form

[121] On the general phenomenon of "primitivism" in poetry, see Preminger 1974, pp. 663–4.

[122] Nicholson 1969 [1907], p. xxii. Cf. Gibb 1963 (1926), p. 14. Some of the ancient poems allude to earlier poets and poems: for example, 'Antara 1905, p. 77; Imru' al-Qays 1964, p. 114; and al-Suyūṭī. n.d., II, pp. 476–7. Cf. Ḍayf n.d., p. 183.

[123] On this dispute, see for example Sowayan 1985 (who argues that *nabaṭī* poetry is a direct descendant of ancient pre-Islamic Arabic poetry); Monroe 1972, pp. 1–53; and Zwettler 1978 (concerning the improvisatory, oral-formulaic character of pre-Islamic poetry). On outbursts of Arabic poetry during the fourth century AD, in the lower Euphrates in and around Ḥīra, see Shahīd 1984, pp. 21–2, 438–9 (and n. 94 on p. 439), 559–60, 569. Al-Furayjāt (1994, pp. 20–1) suggests that the history of Arabic poetry can be attributed to the "songs the Arabs used to sing to their Assyrian masters in the seventh century BC"(!). See also Reynolds 2007, pp. 29–33; and Webb 2016, pp. 60–109.

[124] The inscription was first presented in Negev 1986, pp. 56–60. For a literary analysis of the inscription, see Snir 1993a, pp. 110–25. See also Bellamy 1990, pp. 73–9; Hämeen-Anttila 1991, pp. 33–6; Noja 1993, pp. 183–8; Ambros 1994, pp. 90–2; Beeston 1994, pp. 234–43; Kropp 1994, pp. 165–74; Testen 1996, pp. 281–92; and Larsen 2009, pp. 5–21. On early inscriptions in Arabic, see Versteegh 2014, pp. 33–41.

developed during the eleventh and twelfth centuries) in Muslim Spain could not manage to acquire canonical status and push the *qaṣīda* to the margins.[125] Since the second half of the twentieth century "the prose poem" (*qaṣīdat al-nathr*) may be seen as a renovation of the "primitive" pre-*qaṣīda* type of poetry which is "returning" to the center of the literary system while the *qaṣīda* is being pushed to the margins.[126] Yet, the dominance of certain norms in a given period by no means implies the absence of other non-canonical norms in the same period. In the contemporary Arabic literary system, we find side-by-side Arabic poetry written according to various norms: *qaṣīda*, strophic verse, "free verse," prose poetry, and others. In the 1990s the struggle for control of the center was between "free verse" and "the prose poem," whereas all the other poetic models, especially the traditional *qaṣīda*, had been pushed to the margins.[127] At the start of the new

125 That Ibn Bassām al-Andalusī (d. 1147) showed a dismissive attitude toward the genre of the *muwashshaḥ* makes it clear that in the mid-twelfth century knowledge of early *muwashshaḥāt* had already disappeared (Ibn Bassām 1979, I, p. 469. Cf. Jones 1988, pp. 11–13; and Abu-Haidar 1991, pp. 115–16) and testifies to the non-canonical status of this genre. Moreover, the thirteenth-century historian ʿAbd al-Wāḥid al-Marrākushī claimed that it was not customary to include *muwashshaḥāt* in well-regarded literary or historical works: "*al-ʿāda lam tajri bi-īrād al-muwashshaḥāt fī al-kutub al-mujallada al-mukhallada*" (al-Marrākushī 1963, p. 146 [including the editor's note]. In fact, al-Marrākushī's book, which contains many poems in the form of *qaṣīda*, does not include even one poem in the *muwashshaḥ* form; cf. Abbās [Iḥsān] 1985, pp. 217–18; and Abu-Haidar 1991, p. 121, n. 3). The non-canonical status of the *muwashshaḥ* should be placed within the framework of the canonical status of Arabic literature in the East, which for the Andalusians was their example of excellence. Ibn Ḥazm (994–1064) illustrated that attitude through the following verse:

أنا الشمس في جوّ العلوم منيرة ولكن عيبي أن مطلعي الغرب

("I am the sun shining in the spheres of sciences / but my shortcoming is that I rise in the West") (ʿAbbās 1969, p. 321. Cf. Nykl 1946, p. 102; and Abu-Haidar 1991, p. 116. See also ʿAbbās 1969, pp. 127–8). On the non-canonical status of the *muwashshaḥāt*, we can also learn from the popular models (whether Eastern, according to M. Hartmann, or Spanish, according to García Gómez) that inspired the Andalusian poets who composed them (Monroe 1974, pp. 30–3; Kennedy 1991, pp. 68–9; and Zāhir 1999–2000). Monroe considers the *muwashshaḥ* as the daughter of the non-canonical genre of the *zajal* (Monroe 1993, p. 413). On the close relationship between these two genres, see Einbinder 1995, pp. 252–70. On the intimate association of the *muwashshaḥāt* with folk music, see Shiloah 1995, p. 77. On these genres as a simple development from the Arabic literary tradition of the East without any significant outside influence, see Abu-Haidar 1992, pp. 63–81; and Abu-Haidar 1993, pp. 439–58 (both studies were incorporated in Abu-Haidar 2001, pp. 126–38, 147–67, and spread out through other sections of the book). On the *muwashshaḥāt* in general, see Stern 1974.

126 It is ironic that some "prose poems" make use of the *maqāma* style (e.g. those published by Ilyās ʿAwaḍ [1922–84] in *Shiʿr* [Beirut] 31–2 [1964], pp. 42–53).

127 The status of the various models is illustrated by the status of their advocates in the literary system: For example, Ghālī Shukrī (1935–98), a well-known contemporary Arab literary critic, states that the marginality of the *qaṣīda* is now beyond any doubt (*al-Majalla*

millennium it seems that "the prose poem" is consolidating its position at the center of Arabic poetry.

The attempt to describe the changes in the norms of prosody of Arabic poetry is only one example of the sort of systematic research waiting to be carried out as part of the study of the literary dynamics of Arabic poetry in generic and diachronic cross-section. That is, further studies should similarly refer to other aspects of the development of poetry, such as changes in the norms of simile, metaphor, language, enjambment, meter, and theme.[128]

Fiction

Unlike poetry, which parted ways only gradually with traditional "sacred" norms, the development of fiction has faced no major obstacles. Within less than one century, traditional canonical prose genres, such as *maqāma* and *risāla*, almost totally disappeared from the literary system,[129] and the short story and the novel became the leading prose genres. Together with other classical genres,[130] both *maqāma* and *risāla* played a role in the development of the new prose genres, but the exact nature of that role is still a matter of

[London] 467 [1989], p. 54). Lūwīs 'Awaḍ (1915–90), another major figure of the canonical center, in reply to a question about the possible comeback of the *qaṣīda*, presented the same argument as his colleague, but even more sharply (*al-Muṣawwar*, 11 August 1989, p. 36): "The [traditional] *qaṣīda* will never return again [...] it is like a lifeless corpse." Unlike Shukrī and 'Awaḍ, the Lebanese poet George Shakkūr (b. 1935) published a collection of poems in *qaṣīda* form and declared that the "neoclassical" *qaṣīda* still dominated the literary arena (*al-Usbū' al-'Arabī*, 6 July 1992, p. 48).

128 This does not exclude other tendencies in scholarly research, such as the one represented by Kamal Abu-Deeb's statement that fragmentation is "the dominant force shaping Arabic poetry today" (Abu-Deeb 1997, p. 114).

129 Among the few writers of *maqāmāt* in the twentieth century, mention should be made of the Egyptian *zajal* poet Bayram al-Tūnisī (1893–1961) (al-Tūnisī 1976 [vols. 8 and 9 of his *Complete Works*]. On his *maqāmāt*, see Armbrust 1996, pp. 55–8) and his compatriot Fu'ād Qā'ūd (1936–2006) ('Abd al-Fattāḥ 1993a, pp. 165–96). On the *maqāma* in general, see al-Hamaḏāni 1957, pp. 1–53 (by R. Blachère and P. Masnou); al-Ḥarîri 1969 [1867], I, pp. 1–102; Yāghī 1969; Beeston 1971, pp. 1–12; al-Ḥarīrī 1971 [1850], pp. 2–22; Abu-Haidar 1974, pp. 1–10; Nemah 1974, pp. 83–92; 'Awaḍ 1979; Mattock 1984, pp. 1–18; 'Abbās (Ḥasan) 1985; 'Abbās 1986; Ḍayf 1987; Murtāḍ 1988; Ashtiany et al. 1990, pp. 125–35 (by A. F. L. Beeston); Muṣṭafā 1991; Pellat 1991, pp. 107–15; Richards 1991, pp. 89–99; Hämeen-Anttila 2002; al-Musawi 2006, pp. 114–17; and Stewart 2006, pp. 143–58. On the *risāla* in general, see Arazi and Ben-Shammay 1995, pp. 532–9; and al-Musawi 2006, pp. 109–22. From the second half of the eleventh century, many sources confuse *risāla* with *maqāma*: "Certain *risāla*s, on account of their lofty literary qualities, were considered to be *maḳāma*s" (Arazi and Ben-Shammay 1995, p. 538. Cf. Bauer 2007, p. 157). On English translations of the *maqāmāt*, see Classe 2000, pp. 912–13.

130 Such as *ayyām al-'Arab*, *qiṣaṣ al-anbiyā'*, *al-faraj ba'da al-shidda* as well as various parts of the *adab* literature.

dispute.[131] What is clear is that the new genres developed quickly thanks to the popularity of non-canonical narrative literature, with *Alf Layla wa-Layla*, *Siyar al-Anbiyā'* and the various epics of 'Antara, Baybars, and Banū Hilāl all paving the way for modern narrative prose.[132] The spread of novels translated into Arabic and original Arabic works of popular fiction during the second half of the nineteenth century and the first quarter of the twentieth century[133] was a necessary stage in the development of the novel as a canonical genre.[134]

Much has already been written about the development of Arabic narrative discourse,[135] and the short story[136] and the novel in particular,[137] and there

131 See, for example, the introduction by R. Blachère and P. Masnou to al-Hamadānī 1957, pp. 49–53; Ḥasan 1974; and Moreh 1979, pp. 367–94. See also the radical argument of the Lebanese writer Ilyās Khūrī (b. 1948): "The novel had not been part of our literary heritage [...] We do not see after the rise of Islam or before it any narrative development [...] Any attempt to argue that this genre had ancient roots, such as done by al-Ṭayyib Ṣāliḥ (1929–2009) (*Majallat al-Ma'rifa* [Damascus], August 1973), causes a collective convincing of the self that harms scholarly research [...] The novel arrived to our literary culture through the interaction with European ideas and thought and by the invading European armies" (Khūrī 1974, pp. 11–12).

132 On the relationship of the non-canonical ancient narrative literature with the new narrative genres, see Krachkovskii 1989, pp. 15–22. Cf. Snir 1993, p. 154. The examination of narrative techniques in the *Arabian Nights* by S. Naddaff and D. Pinault (Naddaff 1991; Pinault 1992) points to a close generic affinity between non-canonical narratives and modern narrative genres. See also D. F. Reynolds' account of Banū Hilāl's epic in Lowry and Stewart 2009, pp. 77–91.

133 See Selim 2006, pp. 35–58.

134 The fact that the ascendance of the genre of the novel in English literature was attributed to the Orient by some Arab scholars has been generally referred to as an understandable "patriotic" Arab tendency, but such a "hypothesis" had already been presented as well by English critics early in the 1830s, mentioning *Alf Layla wa-Layla* as its best exemplar (Rastegar 2007, p. 3).

135 See, for example, Moosa 1983; and Hafez 1993.

136 On the development of the short story, see (in Western languages) Abdel-Meguid 1955; Beyerl 1971; Sakkut 1971; Vial 1986, pp. 187–93; and Badawi 1992, pp. 270–328 (by Sabry Hafez). On the art of the short story of particular writers, mention should be made of studies on Yūsuf Idrīs' work (e.g. Kurpershoek 1981; Somekh 1984; and Mikhail 1992). See also the collections of translated stories of Idrīs, which reflect the interests of current scholarship: Allen 1978; Idris 1978; Idris 1984; and Idris 1992. For a bibliographical list of Egyptian short stories from 1910 to 1961, see al-Nassāj 1972. For a general bibliographical list of collections of short stories arranged alphabetically according to the authors' names, see Badawi 1992, pp. 514–30; for critical studies in Arabic, see Badawi 1992, pp. 530–2; and for critical studies in English and French, see Badawi 1992, pp. 532–4 (all three lists were prepared by Sabry Hafez).

137 On the development of the novel, see (in Western languages) Gabrieli 1967, pp. 283–91; Sakkut 1971; Moussa-Mahmoud 1973; Kilpatrick 1974; Allen 1982; Jad 1983; Elkhadem 1985; Vial 1986, pp. 187–93; Badawi 1992, pp. 180–269 (by Roger Allen and Hilary Kilpatrick); Stagh 1992, pp. 63–72; Elad 1994; Meyer 2001; Taha 2002; al-Musawi 2003; Selim 2004a; Caiani 2007; Elad 2007; Siddiq 2007; and Campbell 2013. For a retrospective

are a number of studies on the changing norms in dialogue and narration.[138] Due to a lack of space, only a few observations are possible here on the rapid canonization of both the short story and the novel. First, as in poetry, the development of narrative discourse has involved a constant process of innovation, renovation, automatization, and de-automatization. For example, the emergence of the *muḍāri‘* (*yaf‘alu*) in fiction, corresponding to the style of the historical present,[139] might be considered an innovation, an outcome of interference from Western fiction, where the use of the historical present is widespread. On the other hand,[140] it may equally be seen as an updated version of the classical style used by the medieval poet and philosopher Abū al-‘Alā’ al-Ma‘arrī (973–1057) in his *Risālat al-Ghufrān* (*The Epistle of Forgiveness*). Take the following excerpt for example:

> ويحُمُّ فإذا هو بأسد يفترس من صيران الجنّة وحسيلها فلا تكفيه هنيدة ولا هند فيقول في نفسه (...) فيلهم الله الأسد أن يتكلّم، وقد عرف ما في نفسه، فيقول: (...) فيذهب، عرّفه الله الغبطة في كلّ سبيل، فإذا هو ببيت في أقصى الجنّة، كأنه حفش أمة راعية، وفيه رجل ليس عليه نور سكّان الجنّة، وعنده شجرة قميئة ثمرها ليس بزاك. فيقول (...)

> And he proceeds till suddenly he sees a lion devouring a herd of celestial cattle with their calves, not being satisfied with a hundred nor yet with two. And he says to himself [...] And God inspires the lion to speak, after He has known what he has had in his thought. And he says [...] And, may God make him happy wherever he goes, he proceeds further until he comes upon a house on the farthest confines of Paradise, as small as a shepherd's hut. In it there is a man who has not the light of the denizens of Paradise upon him, and besides it there is a stunted tree bearing unripe fruit. And he says [...][141]

look at the parameters of literary history as applied to the Arabic novel, see Allen 2007, pp. 247–60. On the art of the novel of particular writers, mention should be made of studies about Najīb Maḥfūẓ (e.g. Somekh 1973a, Peled 1983; Le Gassick 1991; Beard and Haydar 1993; and Milson 1998). The aforementioned books include references to many Arabic-language contributions to the field. For a bibliographical list of Egyptian novels from 1867 to 1969, see Ḥāfiẓ 1970, pp. 43–79. The development of the novel in the Arab world has brought about an attempt to further develop it in the field of children's literature (e.g. Abū Hayf 1992, pp. 89–120). On Arabic novels in translation, see Moussa-Mahmoud 1976, pp. 151–3.

138 See, for example, Somekh 1991, pp. 24–35.

139 That is, the present tense used in narrating a past event as if it were happening at the time of narration. See Somekh 1991, pp. 33–4. Alan Jones refers to the *māḍī* (*fa‘al*) in several verses of al-Shanfarā's *Lāmiyat al-‘Arab* (verses 32–5) as denoting the "storytelling 'historic present'" which has to be translated by the present in English (Jones 1992, p. 162).

140 Sasson Somekh argues "that this usage is virtually non-existent in classical Arabic" ("A Literature in Search of Language," Inaugural Lecture, The Irene Halmos Chair of Arabic Literature, Tel Aviv University, 23 October 1983, p. 8).

141 Al-Ma‘arrī 1975, pp. 135–6. Translation is based on al-Ma‘arrī 1943, pp. 121–2, which uses the past tense even though the original uses the *muḍāri‘* (for a new translation, see al-Ma‘arri 2016). Somekh considers this use of *yaf‘alu* as an historical present, "since the ref-

The similarity of al-Maʿarrī's style to that of Najīb Maḥfūẓ in *Ḥikāyāt Ḥāratinā* (*Tales of Our Alley*) (1975) is striking (although the use of the historical present in Maḥfūẓ's work is not systematic):

> ويختفي ذات يوم غنّام أبو رابية فلا تراه عين. يتردّد السؤال عنه في البيت والمقهى، بين المعارف والأقارب والحسّاد. لا يظفر أحد بجواب حاسم، ثمّة غموض يكتنف الموضوع ويثير الحيرة والريب. ليس الرجل مريضا ولا على سفر ولا صلة له بالسياسة مدّها وجزرها، ولا خصوم له على الإطلاق، فلم يبق إلا أن تحوم الظنون حول أمور غاية في الحساسية وأن تختلف فيها الآراء تبعا للنوايا والعواطف الشخصية، فنسمع حينا أنه هرب، ونسمع حينا آخر أنه قتل. ويظهر غنّام أبو رابية ذات يوم كما اختفى فجأة. ويتزاحم المهنّئون في داره (...) ومع الأيام تناقل الناس حكاية جديدة عن غياب غنّام أبو رابية (...) يقال أن غنّام أبو رابية استغلّ مركزه كمشرف مالي على الأموال السرّية فاختلس منها عشرة آلاف من الجنيهات (...) أدرك منذ بادئ الأمر أنه في الموقع الأقوى وتلقّى كافة التهديدات بسخرية وقال لهم: ألوف وألوف (...)

> One day Ghannām Abū Rābiya completely disappears. People ask after him at home, in the cafe, among his friends, relatives and envious acquaintances. Nobody gets a straight answer. His absence is shrouded in mystery, which of course leads to suspicion. He's not sick or away on business; he has no enemies, no connection with the ups and downs of politics. Suspicion hovers over the only things left, matters of extreme sensitivity, and each person works out a theory that matches his own character and inclination. Some say he's simply run away, others that he's been murdered. And then one day Ghannām Abū Rābiya appears every bit as suddenly as he disappeared. People crowd his house to welcome him back [...] Some time later, a new story about Ghannām's disappearance begins to make the rounds [...] It is said—God knows best—that Ghannām Abū Rābiya took advantage of his position as supervisor of the secret budget to embezzle ten thousand pounds [...] Dealing from a position of strength, he met their threats with mockery: "Thousands and thousands" [...][142]

The use of the historical present in Arabic fiction, though found already in the 1940s,[143] has never been so frequent as to risk becoming "automatic stock" and remains very efficient from the point of view of its assumed literary

erence in that work is not to past events but to a hypothetical action. In other words, *tafʿal* in al-Maʿarrī's *Risāla* is translatable as 'if you do' or 'it is likely that you do'" (Somekh 1991, p. 33). However, one can argue that the actions in this quotation from *Risālat al-Ghufrān*, which is typical of the entire text, are not always "hypothetical."

142 Maḥfūẓ n.d. [1975], pp. 137–9 (translation according to Mahfouz 1991a, pp. 90–1, with minor modifications).

143 One of the first successful attempts to use this style was by the Iraqi-Jewish writer Shālom Darwīsh (1913–97) in his short story "Qāfila min al-Rīf" ("A Caravan from the Countryside") (Darwīsh 1948, pp. 1–29. On the story and relevant bibliographical references, see Snir 1997a, pp. 128–36; and Snir 2005a, pp. 174–81). It seems that Darwīsh was influenced by the style of Ṭāhā Ḥusayn in *al-Ayyām* (Ḥusayn n.d. [1929]), in which the narrator not only relates the events of the past from the point of view of the present but also describes the events of the past in the present tense. On the relationship of the narration in *al-Ayyām* to the genre of autobiography, see al-Qāḍī 1993, pp. 207–32.

function in fiction. This also means that it would be premature to speak of canonization.[144] Where we do find automatization is in headlines in newspapers and the electronic media. For example, when a headline in a newspaper now uses the past tense, the reader faces a de-automatization process, that is, the journalistic discourse is revitalized, stereotypicity is overcome, and the automatism of perception is destroyed.

Another example of renovation in fiction is the revitalization of medieval stylistic features, such as the technique of the *maqāma* ironically alluded to by Imīl Ḥabībī (1921–96),[145] or the technique of the historical chronicles as used by Jamāl al-Ghīṭānī (1945–2015).[146] The features of renovation in Ḥabībī's and al-Ghīṭānī's works are in some sense innovative as well and come as a result of interference from Western models.[147] In both cases, these features are intermingled with highly sophisticated political criticism. In the

144 See, for example, Somekh 1991, p. 34.

145 See, for example, Ḥabībī 1974 (English translation: Habiby 1985; French translations: Habibi 1980; Habibi 1987). See Allen 1987, pp. 104–7. Yāsīn Fā'ūr considers the sources of Ḥabībī's irony, for example, to be rooted in the texts of writers such as al-Jāḥiẓ (776–886), al-Ma'arrī (973–1057), and al-Hamadhānī (969–1008) (Fā'ūr 1993, p. 42).

146 See, for example, *al-Zaynī Barakāt* (al-Ghīṭānī 1974 [1971]. French translation: Ghitany 1985. English translation: al-Ghitani 1988. On the novel, see Mehrez 1994, pp. 96–118); and *Khiṭaṭ al-Ghīṭānī* (al-Ghīṭānī 1981 [1980]. On the novel, see Mehrez 1994, pp. 58–77). On al-Ghīṭānī's literary works, see also Mehrez 1985, which is a study of al-Ghīṭānī's narrative structure and narrative modes, as well as Allen 1987, pp. 100–4; and al-Kakalī 1992.

147 Such as the pastiche, burlesque, or parody, or even specific Western novels like *Candide* by François-Marie Arouet Voltaire (1694–1778) (Voltaire 1959 [1759]) and *Tristram Shandy* by Laurence Sterne (1713–68) (Sterne 1964 [1760–7]). Apart from the indirect allusion to *Candide*—the Arabic translation of which by 'Ādil 'Umar Zu'aytir (1897–1957) (Cairo: Dār al-Ma'ārif, 1958) inspired Ḥabībī's novel *al-Waqā'i' al-Gharība fi Ikhtifā' Sa'īd Abī al-Naḥs al-Mutashā'il* (translated as *The Secret Life of Saeed: The Pessoptimist*) (1974) (Wild 1996, p. 388, n. 17)—Ḥabībī admits the influence of Voltaire's *Candide* in the chapter *al-Shabah al-Farīd Bayna Candide and Sa'īd* ("The Unique Similarity between Candide and Sa'īd") (Ḥabībī 1985, pp. 117–21. On the relationship between these two literary works, see Fā'ūr 1993, pp. 180–7. On the relationship between Ḥabībī's *al-Mutashā'il* and Jaroslav Hašek's (1883–1923) *The Good Soldier Švejk*, see Fā'ūr 1993, pp. 188–91). Needless to say, Ḥabībī's tendency toward the style of *maqāma* is not without allusions to the various attempts at imitating this style that have appeared since the nineteenth century, such as that of Aḥmad Fāris al-Shidyāq (1804–87) in *al-Sāq 'alā al-Sāq fī mā Huwa al-Fāryāq* (al-Shidyāq 1855; al-Shidyāq 2014). The debt that al-Shidyāq owed to Western novels, such as *Tristram Shandy*, is not in any doubt (e.g. Alwan 1970, pp. 179–93; and Jubrān 1991, pp. 23–4). On the other hand, the *maqāma*, whose tales, even by Western critics, generally "come into the category of picaresque" (Cuddon 1986, p. 381), "has often been regarded as a forerunner of, if not a model for, the European picaresque novel" (Elkhadem 1985, p. 55. See also Wilpert 1964, p. 406). Referring to that assumption, Jaakko Hämeen-Anttila is very skeptical about any possible influence, as long as no credible source can be shown: "The incredible popularity of maqāma among Arabic-speaking literati in Dār al-Islām did not provide the stimulus for it to cross the boundaries to Dār al-Ḥarb, Christian Europe" (Hämeen-Anttila 1994–5, pp. 108–10).

latter, al-Ghīṭānī establishes a conscious link between the creative writer and the historian, especially against the background of Arab genres of historiography which persisted well into the nineteenth century. He uses narrated discourse in which no "I" is to be held responsible as a political strategy vis-à-vis an increasingly repressive political system. What is narrated is not by necessity what was said. In this way, al-Ghīṭānī challenges any claim to objectivity and invites the reader to reread the representations not only of Egypt's past but of its present as well.[148]

Another observation regarding the canonization of the novel has to do with the changing status of the novel in the literary system.[149] Written according to the Western concepts of the genre and published in the first quarter of the twentieth century, Arabic novels were considered marginal and inferior in the literary system, even derided by respected writers. When the Egyptian author Muḥammad Ḥusayn Haykal (1888–1956) published *Zaynab* (1913), he did so under the pseudonym *Miṣrī Fallāḥ* ("Egyptian of Peasant Origin") out of fear that his career as a lawyer may be in jeopardy if he were to use his real name.[150] Efforts to canonize the novel had begun already in the middle of the nineteenth century: Khalīl al-Khūrī (1836–1907), who owned the Beirut newspaper *Ḥadīqat al-Akhbār* (1858–1911), believed that an adoption of a new Western literary genre into the traditional Arabic literary tradition would provide Arab culture with tools for reviving the Arabic language and create new styles of expression. *Ḥadīqat al-Akhbār* was the first Arabic newspaper to publish translations from Western narrative fiction, especially from French romance stories. Khalīl al-Khūrī also published narrative fiction of his own such as *Wayy, Idhan Lastu bi-Ifranjī* (*Alas, I'm Not a Foreigner*) (1859–61).[151] This literary activity played a substantial role in changing the aesthetic literary taste of the period and paved

148 According to Mehrez 1994, pp. 58–77, 96–118. Cf. Allen 2007, pp. 255–6.

149 Cf. also al-Bataineh 1998.

150 Haykal 1968 [1913], p. 7. (English translation: Haikal 1989. On the pioneer role of *Zaynab* in the history of the Arabic novel, see Barrāda 1996, pp. 32–3). On Haykal and his novel, see Badr 1983, pp. 322–37; Brugman 1984, pp. 234–43; Elkhadem 1985, pp. 26–8; Allen 1987, pp. 31–5; Badawi 1992, pp. 190–2, 223–6; and Allen 1998, pp. 303–4. A film based on the novel was directed by Muḥammad Karīm (1896–1972) and presented in Cairo in 1930 (Qāsim 2002, p. 16; and Shafik 1998, p. 133). *Zaynab* has been generally regarded as the first Arabic artistic novel, albeit, as Roger Allen indicates, "the ascription of 'firstness' to such a work and the total confusion in placing its antecedents into some sort of narrative categories or developmental sequence provide an excellent illustration of the consequences of the unbalanced picture presented by the failure of the scholarly community to come to terms with the nature of generic change as it was affected by attitudes to modernity and pre-modernity during the 19th century" (Allen 2007, pp. 253–4). For more on "how *Zaynab* became the first Arabic novel," see Colla 2009, pp. 214–25.

151 Published in *Ḥadīqat al-Akhbār* from issue 93 (November 1859) to issue 151 (March 1861).

the way for the birth of authentic Arabic narrative fiction and then for its canonization.[152]

On the other hand, the use of the novel for non-literary (especially historical and national) aims was very popular and accepted as canonical during the nineteenth century. Salīm al-Bustānī (1848–84) published serially in the early 1870s in *al-Jinān* three didactic historical novels that he wrote under the title of *fukāhāt* ("humorous texts") for the purpose of entertainment and in order to transmit ideas of Syrian patriotism to the younger generation.[153] *Al-Jinān* was one of the first Arabic periodicals to publish such literary works in the original and in translation. The aforementioned Jesuit scholar Louis Cheikho (Shaykhū)[154] published serial novels in his *al-Mashriq*, starting with the first issue of the journal, in which he put out the first instalment of the serial novel *Kharīdat Lubnān* (*Lebanon's Virgin*) written by the Belgian Jesuit scholar Henri Lammens (1862–1937).[155] Immediately after publishing the last instalment of this novel, another serial novel by Lammens started to appear: *Riwāyat al-Shaqīqatayn* (*The Story of the Two Daughters*).[156] It is interesting that *Kharīdat Lubnān* had in its last instalment a metafictional message regarding the relationship between poetry and the new emerging genre of the novel: The events of the novel could have been written in verse, but only by accident were they narrated by a prose writer.[157] It means, at least according to Lammens, that not only should the art of the novel not be considered less expressive than the art of poetry,[158] but that both arts were even capable of serving similar functions.

Jurjī Zaydān (1861–1914), for his part, wrote historical novels in which he subordinates the narrative to the historical structure to such an extent that the end result is more history than novel. In the introduction to his *al-Ḥajjāj ibn Yūsuf al-Thaqafī* (1902), Zaydān declares that he wants to write history in the form of a story or a novel.[159] The tradition of the historical novel was

152 See Bawārdī 2008, pp. 170–95.

153 See al-Bustānī 1990, pp. 35–41.

154 See above, p. 97.

155 First instalment: 1 January 1898, pp. 39–42; last instalment: 1 April 1898, pp. 326–32. In a lecture addressed by Louis Cheikho in Kulliyyat al-Qiddīs Yūsuf and entitled "Dars al-'Arabiyya" ("Learning Arabic"), he mentioned that many of the monks among the faculty of the college were foreigners who had left their countries and cut their relations with their relatives of their own free will in order to come to Lebanon and adopt its language and culture (*Al-Mashriq*, 1 August 1898, p. 702).

156 First instalment: 15 April 1898, pp. 376–9; last instalment: 15 August 1898, pp. 757–63.

157 *Al-Mashriq*, 1 April 1898, p. 332.

158 Contrary to what Abbās Maḥmūd al-'Aqqād argued, as mentioned below, p. 217.

159 Zaydān 1902, introduction (without page numbers):

وقد رأينا بالاختبار أن نشر التاريخ على أسلوب الرواية أفضل وسيلة لترغيب الناس في مطالعته والاستزادة منه وخصوصا لأننا نتوخّى جهدنا في أن يكون التاريخ حاكما على الرواية لا هي عليه كما فعل كتبة الإفرنج وفيهم من جعل غرضه الأول تأليف الرواية وإنما جاء بالحقائق التاريخية لإلباس الرواية ثوب الحقيقة فجرّه ذلك إلى التساهل

taken up by other writers after Zaydān, the most prominent of whom being Muḥammad Farīd Abū Ḥadīd (1893–1967), one of the most prolific Arab writers of historical novels,[160] and 'Alī al-Jārim (1881–1949).[161] Unlike them, Najīb Maḥfūẓ in his historical novels used the historical material only as raw matter for the fictional worlds that he constructed.[162]

The low status of the novel, and fiction in general, until the first quarter of the twentieth century was illustrated in a metafictional way in Najīb Maḥfūẓ's *Qaṣr al-Shawq* (*Palace of Desire*) (1957). Set in the 1920s, the novel contains the following dialogue between Kamāl,[163] Ḥusayn, and 'Āyida:

> 'Āyida asked pleasantly:
> —Do you want to be an author?
> Swept by a tidal wave of happiness rarely experienced by human beings, Kamāl answered:
> —Perhaps!
> —Poet or prose writer?
> Then, leaning forward so she could observe him, she added:
> —Let me see if I can tell by my *firāsa* (thought-reading).

في سرد الحوادث التاريخية بما يضلّ القراء. وأما نحن فالعمدة في رواياتنا على التاريخ وإنما نأتي بحوادث الرواية تشويقا للمطالعين فنبقي الحوادث التاريخية على حالها وندمج في خلالها قصّة غرامية تشوّق المطالع إلى استتمام قراءتها فيصحّ الاعتماد على ما يجيء في هذه الروايات من حوادث التاريخ مثل الاعتماد على أيّ كتاب من كتب التاريخ من حيث الزمان والمكان.

On Zaydān and his historical novels, see Philipp 1979 (for a review of the book by M. M. Badawi, see *Journal of Arabic Literature* 14 [1983], pp. 98–100); Brugman 1984, pp. 218–224; Elkhadem 1985, pp. 18–20; and Krachkovskii 1989, pp. 23–43. On Zaydān's Beirut beginnings as an aspiring Syrian Protestant College medical student and his becoming one of the most prolific editors, authors, and novelists of the *Nahḍa*, see Holt 2016, pp. 273–9. The Zaidan Foundation has so far commissioned the translation into English of five of Zaydān's historical novels, and more are being planned (<http://zaidanfoundation.org/ZF_Website_HistoricalNovels.html> [last accessed 20 October 2016]). While it has been clearly shown that Zaydān's novels were influenced by the novels of Walter Scott (1771–1832) (Allen 1982, p. 27), it remains to be confirmed "that the striking similarities between Zaydān's works and the historical novels of the German Egyptologist George Ebers (1837–98), which were known, admired, and imitated in Egypt, are not based on coincidence only" (Elkhadem 1985, p. 18 and n. II.4 on p. 58). Literary experts divide the historical novel into two categories: traditional historical novels and postmodernist historical novels. Based on that classification, Maman Lesmana examined historical novels by Zaydān and al-Ghīṭānī (Lesmana 2014, pp. 83–92). For a general bibliography on Zaydān and his works, see Philipp 2014, pp. 419–31 (see also the review of the book by Stephen Sheehi in *Journal of Arabic Literature* 47.1–2 [2016], pp. 214–217). On the poetics and politics of historical fiction in Egypt, see Kilpatrick 1998, p. 115; and Mahmood 2013, pp. 265–84.

160 On Abū Ḥadīd's historical novels, see Brugman 1984, pp. 310–13.

161 On al-Jārim's historical novels, see Brugman 1984, pp. 313–14.

162 On the relationship between history and fiction in Arabic literature, see Mehrez 1994 as well as the review of the book in *Journal of Arabic Literature* 27.3 (1996), pp. 281–5.

163 In an interview, Maḥfūẓ admitted that Kamāl reflects his own experiences (al-Ghīṭānī 2006, p. 171).

I've exhausted all the resources of poetry in a secret conversation with your dream-vision. Poetry is your sacred tongue. I won't try to make a living from it. My tears have drained their wells during dark nights. How happy I am to have you look at me, and how wretched I am! I am living under your gaze, like the earth, which is living by the eye of the sun.
—A poet! Yes, you're a poet!
—Really? How do you know? [...]
—If you don't like the idea of being a poet, then don't be one [...]
—Have you read any French stories?
—Some by Michel Zévaco, in translation. You know I can't read French.
She said enthusiastically:
—You won't be an author until you master French. Read Balzac, George Sand, Madame de Staël and Loti. After that write a novel.
Kamāl said disapprovingly:
—A novel?! That's a rather marginal genre. I aspire to do serious work.
Ḥusayn said earnestly:
—In Europe the novel is considered a serious art. Some writers there concentrate on it to the exclusion of all other types of writing. That is the way they've achieved the status of immortals. I'm not throwing praise around blindly. The French professor confirmed that to me.
Kamāl shook his large head skeptically, and Ḥusayn resumed speaking:
—Be careful not to make 'Āyida angry. She's a reader who delights in French novels. In fact, she's one of their heroines.
Kamāl leaned over a little to observe her reaction to Ḥusayn's comment, seizing this opportunity to fill his eyes with the gorgeous sight. Then he asked:
—How did that happen?
—She gets all caught up in novels, and her head is crammed with an imaginary life. Once I saw her strutting in front of a mirror. When I asked her what she was doing, she said: "Aphrodite used to walk like this along the beach at Alexandria."
Frowning and smiling at the same time, 'Āyida said:
—Don't believe him. He's more immersed in the world of the imagination than I am. But he's not satisfied until he accuses me of things that aren't true.
Aphrodite? What's Aphrodite compared with my beloved? By the truth of your perfection, I'm sad to have you imagine yourself in any form but your own!
He commented sincerely:
—You're not to blame. The heroes of al-Manfalūṭī and Rider Haggard have made a big impression on my imagination.
Ḥusayn laughed delightedly and cried out:
—How fitting it would be for all of us to be united in a single book. Why should we stay here on the ground, since we're so drawn to the world of the imagination? It's up to you. Bring this dream to reality. I'm not a writer and don't want to be, but you would be able to bring us together, if you so desired, in one book.[164]

[164] Maḥfūẓ n.d. [1957], pp. 188–90. The translation is based on Mahfouz 1991, pp. 183–84. The

In his report on the books brought from the Orient for the Hungarian Academy of Sciences (1874), Ignác Goldziher mentioned the

> tasteless Arabic translation of French works, which are, by the way, absolutely unnecessary in Egypt [...] French literature is so much the exact opposite of everything that the Arab reader needs and would read with interest that serving such exotics to a people who can boast of the most beautiful literature discloses the total misunderstanding of their spirit.[165]

Reflecting, however, as it does the negative attitude at the center of the Arabic literary system in the early twentieth century toward the novel and the latter's popularity among readers,[166] the aforementioned dialogue in Maḥfūẓ's novel may serve as a way in which to trace how fiction started to move from the margins of the Arabic literary system into its center:[167]

1. Contemporary status in the Arabic literary system: Kamāl's disapproving statement about the novel as insignificant and "a rather marginal genre" illustrates the status that the novel occupied during the nineteenth century and the first quarter of the twentieth century. This view of the novel is reminiscent of the status of the novel in England during the late seventeenth century and at the start of the eighteenth century as illustrated, for example, in *Northanger Abbey* (1817) by Jane Austen

term *qiṣṣa* (story) was translated as "novel," unlike in the published English translation. In this dialogue, Maḥfūẓ reflects the literary terminology employed in the beginning of the twentieth century when *qiṣṣa* was not only a story but also a novel (Haykal 1968 [1913], pp. 7–12 [introduction]). On the term *qiṣṣa,* see also Pellat 1986, pp. 185–7; and Vial 1986, pp. 187–93. It seems that in this dialogue Maḥfūẓ was inspired by a similar dialogue from Thomas Mann's (1875–1955) *Buddenbrooks* (1902), considered to be one of the works which influenced him while writing the trilogy (on his general inspiration, see Hafez 2006; and Somekh 2008, pp. 100–1). In that dialogue, from the seventh chapter of part three of the novel, Morten refers to *Die Serapionsbrüder* (1819–21; translated as *The Serapion Brethren,* 1886–92) by the German author E. T. A. Hoffmann (1776–1822), which Tony is reading, by saying: "Yes, that's very pretty. But, it is more for ladies. Men want something different, you know" (Mann 1970, pp. 105–6).

165 Mestyan 2015, p. 455.

166 See, for example, the public demand for reading novels as reflected in the Egyptian newspaper *al-Muqaṭṭam* in the 1890s (Abū 'Arja 2001, pp. 84–5).

167 Referring to Maḥfūẓ's *Aṣda' al-Sīra al-Dhātiyya* (*Echoes of an Autobiography*) (1995; first serialized in *al-Ahrām* between 11 February and 8 April 1994) (Maḥfūẓ 1995; English translation: Mahfouz 1997), Roger Allen considers the Maḥfūẓ's trilogy as "representative of a particular phase in the career of a writer who has continually been anxious to develop his fictional techniques." What the author preferred to do in *Aṣda' al-Sīra al-Dhātiyya* is, according to Allen, to continue his exploration of those structures and modes of narration that have characterized his contributions to fiction since then and "perhaps one might say that the source of these 'echoes' is the autobiographical element in those very fictional narratives" (Allen 1998a, pp. 214–16). On Maḥfūẓ's experimentation with the form of the novel and the influence of the Western forms on him, see al-Ghīṭānī 2006, pp. 174–6.

(1775–1817). In a dialogue with Catherine, John Thrope says: "I never read novels; I have something else to do [...] Novels are all so full of non-sense and stuff."[168]

2. Contemporary status in a foreign but influential literary system: Ḥusayn presents the status of the Western novel by saying that "in Europe the novel is considered a serious art" and that "some writers there concentrate on it to the exclusion of all other types of writing. That is the way they've achieved the status of immortals."
3. The beginning of interference: Only when people in a given culture realize that the status of a component of the literary system needs to change does such change actually occur. And change does not come without intrasystemic and intersystemic interaction.[169]
4. The intrasystemic interaction: the relationship and interaction between the various components of the literary system, such as that between poetry and the novel—Ḥusayn challenges Kamāl to write novels: "Bring this dream to reality. I'm not a writer and don't want to be, but you would be able to bring us together, if you so desired, in one book."
5. The intersystemic interaction: It is illustrated by the exposure of the people in the culture to foreign models through translation—ʿĀyida became a "reader who delights in French novels." Moreover, "she's one of their heroines."

Through that metafictional dialogue, Maḥfūẓ presents the condition of the literary system during the early twentieth century, when poetry was as yet firmly at the center of the system but was then gradually being pushed to the margins by the short story and the novel. The dialogue has a metafictional significance, since it appears in a novel considered to be the major novel of contemporary Arabic literature written by an author who had begun his literary career by writing traditional poetry and then more "modernist" poetry.[170] Alluding to the poems he wrote in the mid-1920s, some of whose verses were without meter, Maḥfūẓ even considered himself as "the pioneer of the modern school of poetry."[171] As it is, not only has the novel become the leading genre in the Arab literary system, it was this specific novel that

168 Austen 1965 [1917], p. 39. Cf. Hunter 1990, pp. 4, 225–6.

169 A good illustration for this stage is what the Egyptian author Muḥammad Ḥusayn Haykal (1888–1956) wrote in 1965 on "the art of fiction" and "the reason for the weakness of fiction" (Haykal 1965, pp. 67–77, 78–95).

170 See Somekh 1973a, p. 37. On Maḥfūẓ's love for poetry, see El-Enany 1993, p. 14. The statement that Maḥfūẓ "did not write poetry or incorporate verse into his many novels and short stories" (Reynolds 2015, p. 97 [by Shawkat M. Toorawa]) is inaccurate. See al-Naqqāsh 2006, pp. 133–47.

171 Duwāra 1965, pp. 276–7. Cf. Moreh 1976, p. 205.

more than anything else qualified Maḥfūẓ for the Nobel Prize in Literature in 1988.[172] In the second part of the trilogy, Kamāl dreams of writing a book: "It would not be poetry [...] the book would be prose. It would be a large, bound volume about the size and shape of the Holy Qur'ān."[173] Finally, in the third part of the trilogy entitled *al-Sukkariyya*, Sawsan predicted the change in the literary system:

> أمّا القصّة فذات حيل لا حصر لها، إنها فنّ ماكر، وقد غدت شكلا أدبيا شائعا سوف ينتزع الإمامة في عالم الأدب في وقت قصير، ألا ترى أنه ما من كبير من شيوخ الأدب إلا وهو يثبت وجوده في مجال نشاطها ولو بمؤلّف واحد؟
>
> Fiction contains unlimited artifices. It's a cunning art, which has become such a prevalent form it will soon wrest leadership from all the others. Don't you see that there is not a single prominent literary figure who hasn't tried to make a name for himself in this genre, if only by publishing one literary text?[174]

In 1945 Maḥfūẓ reacted to what 'Abbās Maḥmūd al-'Aqqād (1889–1964) had said, that fiction could never reach the level of poetry and that he personally would never read fiction whenever he could read poetry,[175] by saying that

> أجل إن القصّة لا تزال أعظم انتشارا من الشعر ولكن أكان هذا لسيّئة فيها أم لحسنة؟ إن الخاصة التي تقرأ الشعر الرفيع وتتذوّقه تقرأ القصّة الرفيعة وتشغف بها، وإذا كان العقّاد لا يقرأ القصّة إلاّ مضطرا فطه والمازني والحكيم وأيزنهاور يقرؤونها بغير اضطرار.
>
> Indeed, fiction is still more circulated than poetry, but is it because of a disadvantage in it or advantage? Those educated who read high poetry and enjoy it thoroughly read fiction as well and are extremely fond of it. And if al-'Aqqād reads fiction only when he is obliged to, Ṭāhā [Ḥusayn] and [Ibrāhīm 'Abd al-Qādir] al-Māzinī and [Tawfīq] al-Ḥakīm and [Dwight D.] Eisenhower read it without any compulsion.[176]

172 Maḥfūẓ himself admits that the appearance of the trilogy in French must have helped to ensure his nomination and led the Arts Committee of the Nobel Academy to select him as the recipient of the 1988 prize (Allen 1993a, p. 28; Jayyusi 1993, p. 18; Allen 2007, p. 254). Besides, Maḥfūẓ sees the translation of Arabic literature into other languages as the only way for it to transform into an international literature (Maḥfūẓ 1996, pp. 171–2). On Maḥfūẓ and the Nobel Prize, see also Fawzī 1988, pp. 29–44.

173 Maḥfūẓ n.d. [1957], p. 61. The translation is based on Mahfouz 2002, p. 58. The novel *Awlād Ḥāratinā* (*Children of Our Alley*), which was published in 1959, has 114 chapters like the number of the *suras* of the Qur'ān!

174 Maḥfūẓ n.d. [1957a], p. 209. The translation is partly according to Mahfouz 1992, p. 191. Cf. 'Āmir 1970, p. 26; and 'Aṭiyya 1977, pp. 174–5.

175 Al-'Aqqād argues that fiction is "not among the best of what minds can create" (*lastu aḥsibuhā min khayrat thimār al-'uqūl*), justifying his position by citing two criteria. First, he measures the "tool" (*adāt*) compared to the "outcome" (*maḥṣūl*)—whenever the "tool" is smaller and the "outcome" is bigger, the value of the relevant art is higher and vice versa—and second, he states that poetry is read by the higher social classes (al-'Aqqād 1945, pp. 27–9).

176 *Al-Risāla*, 3 September 1945, pp. 952–3 (as for the aforementioned criteria al-'Aqqād

As with poetry, further studies should refer to other aspects of the development of prose, in particular changes in the norms of both the short story and the novel.

Theater

It is not only Western Orientalists, but Arab scholars as well who have claimed that "the Arab theatre is a creation *ex nihilo*,"[177] namely, that before the nineteenth century theater was virtually unknown in the Arab world. Others have suggested that it is simply not feasible that the rich Arab culture could not have known drama, and they have pointed to the dramatic dimensions in classical canonical Arabic poetry[178] and the many references in Arab culture to semi-theatrical and semi-dramatic phenomena to make their case. Among these phenomena are the "shadow theater" (*khayāl al-ẓill*),[179] the storytellers (*ḥakawātī*; *shā'ir*),[180] and the peep show, that is, the "Box of

presents for the higher value of poetry, Maḥfūẓ states that in good art the dissonance between "tool" and "outcome" disappears, and that details in fiction are by no means a kind of unnecessary stuffing. As for readers, says Maḥfūẓ, the fact that some art is spread among certain classes does not mean anything as long as the reasons for that are not investigated). Cf. al-Naqqāsh 2006, pp. 194–205. Interestingly, in one of Maḥfūẓ's letters from the 1940s to Adham Rajab, he mentions Tawfiq al-Ḥakīm as describing the art of narrative prose as *fann al-niswān* (the art of women): "Tawfiq al-Ḥakīm wrote an article in *Akhbār al-Adab* in which he attacked narrative prose and what is described as literature of life; he says that it is the art of women and that true literature is thinking; from that time all my friends call me saying: 'oh, woman!'" (published in *October*, 11 December 1988, p. 41). Already in the late nineteenth century, when the modern Arabic novel was taking its first steps, Salīm al-Bustānī (1848–84), editor of *al-Jinān*, mentioned that many female readers had been attracted to his novels (*al-Jinān* IV [1873], p. 826. Cf. al-Bustānī 1990, p. 40).

177 Berque 1969 (1960), p. 221 (English translation: Berque 1964, p. 197; Arabic translation: Berque 1982, p. 273). Cf. Aḥmad al-Ḥajjājī's statement: "In 1870, the Egyptian theater was born, one year after the opening of the Suez Canal" (quoted in Murshid 1980, p. 5).

178 See, for example, the dramatic monologues of Abū al-'Alā' al-Ma'arrī (Cachia 1970, pp. 129–36).

179 On *khayāl al-ẓill*, see Ḥamāda 1963; Wiet 1966, p. 269; Badawi 1982, pp. 83–107; al-Khozai 1984, pp. 19–30; Moreh 1987, pp. 46–61; and Ḥusayn (Kamāl al-Dīn) 1993, pp. 111–19. See also Kahle 1992 and the reviews of the book in *British Journal of Middle Eastern Studies* 20.2 (1993), pp. 268–70 (by Marilyn Booth); *Bulletin Critique des Annales Islamologiques* 11 (1994), pp. 15–17 (by Abdallah Cheikh-Moussa); *Bulletin of the School of Oriental and African Studies* 56 (1993), pp. 364–5 (by Robert G. Irwin); *Journal of the American Oriental Society* 114 (1994), pp. 462–6 (by Everett K. Rowson); and *Die Welt des Islams* 34.1 (1994), pp. 126–9 (by Shmuel Moreh). *Khayāl al-ẓill* is even considered to be an earlier stage of the cinema. Cf. Abdel Wahab 1966, pp. 32–6; and al-'Alāylī 1978, p. 142.

180 On the *ḥakawātī*, the *shā'ir*, and storytellers in the Islamic world, see Lane 1954 [1908], pp. 397–431; And 1963–4, pp. 28–31; 'Arsān 1983, pp. 353–9; Slyomovics 1987; al-Ṭālib 1987, pp. 106–13; Khūrshīd 1991, pp. 166–7; Slyomovics 1994, pp. 390–419; Berkey 2001; and Hanna 2003, pp. 66–8. See also the first section of chapter eight in Ibn al-Nadīm's *al-Fihrist* entitled "Fī Akhbār al-Musāmirīn wa-l-Mukharrifīn wa-Asmā' al-Kutub fī al-Asmār

Wonders" or the "Magic Box" (*ṣundūq al-dunyā* or *ṣundūq al-'ajab*).[181] Then there are the religious festivals, such as the traditional birthday (*mawlid*) of the Prophet or the birthdays of saints (*mawālid*), the night-time shows during the fast of Ramadan, and the theatrical elements that can be found in other places in the Islamic world[182] in popular peasant cultures, such as the *dabka* dances.[183] These scholars insist that premodern Arab culture could not have witnessed shadow theater without (secular) live parallels. It has also been argued that long before the end of the tenth century the oral genres of *ḥikāya* and *khayāl*, in the sense of live theater, preceded both the *khayāl al-ẓill*, which reached Arab society from the Far East sometime during the tenth and eleventh centuries, and the *maqāma*, which adopted the dialogues of the existing oral farce tradition.[184] As this live theatrical tradition persisted in Arab society and culture until the nineteenth century, it formed

wa-l-Khurāfāt" ("With Accounts of Those who Converse in the Evening and the Tellers of Fables with the Names of the Books which [they Composed] about Evening Stories and Fables") (Ibn al-Nadīm 1970, II, pp. 712–24; Ibn al-Nadīm 1985, pp. 605–13). On the role of the religious storytellers (*quṣṣāṣ*) in the first decades of the Islamic era, see Tottoli 2002, pp. 86–96 and the references on p. 92, n. 2. For a comparative study of modern and classical storytelling in Arabic literature, see Mustafa 1997.

181 The itinerant storyteller carries the box on his back, puts it down on a trestle at street corners, invites children to part with a small coin to peer through a row of holes at a succession of crude pictures on a roll which he unwinds as he speaks of the deeds of some folk hero (Cachia 1990, p. 135, n. 4; on *ṣundūq al-dunyā,* see also Ḥusayn [Kamāl al-Dīn] 1993, pp. 125–6). Modern Palestinian playwrights used *ṣundūq al-dunyā* to allude to the traditional Palestinian theatrical heritage (e.g. Mu'īn Bsīsū's [1927–84] *Thawrat al-Zanj* [Bsīsū 1988, pp. 119–20, 163–5, 183–5] and Imīl Ḥabībī's *Luqa' ibn Luqa'* [Ḥabībī 1980, pp. 9–14]. The folkloristic dimensions in the play are also emphasized in a reportage on the staging of the play in 1981 in Damascus by Firqat al-Mukhtabar al-Masraḥī al-Sūrī [*Filasṭīn al-Thawra,* 22 May 1981; according to *al-Jadīd,* June–July 1981, pp. 13–16]. See also Snir 2005c). See also the role of the *ḥakawātī* in *Mughāmarat Ra's al-Mamlūk Jābir* by Sa'd Allāh Wannūs (1941–97) (Wannūs 1989. Cf. al-Ṭālib 1987, pp. 322–31). According to Margaret MacDonald (1999, p. 325), until the 1950s this phenomenon of peep show could ordinarily be seen in Egypt, but after the spread of television and videos it began to gradually disappear.

182 Cf. And 1963–4, pp. 53–61.

183 These dances, in which a group of dancers link arms and stamp out the rhythm and sing, still figure prominently in various Palestinian cultural activities. On the popular dances, especially the *dabka,* see al-Barghūthī 1979, pp. 72–82. On the songs accompanying the *dabka,* that is, *Dal'ūnā,* see al-Barghūthī 1979, pp. 137–58; and Khūrī 1999, pp. 159–60.

184 See Moreh 1992; and Moreh and Sadgrove 1996, pp. 13–16. On the theatrical and semi-theatrical dimensions of the medieval Arab cultural heritage and the relationship between them and modern Arab theater, see also Tomiche 1969, pp. 15–16, 40–55; Murshid 1980, pp. 4–69; 'Arsān 1983; al-Khozai 1984, pp. 1–18; al-Ṭālib 1987; Mortensen 1992, pp. 104–13; Ḥusayn (Kamāl al-Dīn) 1993; Janabi 1993, pp. 55–61; Snir 1993, pp. 149–70; Knio 1994; Sadgrove 1996, pp. 11–26; al-Sheddi 1997; and Zeidan 1997, pp. 173–91. For other references, see Moreh 1992, p. ix, n. 1. For more on entertainment in the early Islamic tradition, see Kister 1999, pp. 53–78.

a fertile ground for Western theatrical influences. A survey of the developments of the Arabic theater in the nineteenth century reveals important links between traditional Arabic live theater and modern theater. One such link can be found in the first known printed Arabic play, Abraham Daninos' (1797–1872) *Nazāhat al-Mushtāq wa-Guṣṣat al-ʿUshshāq fī Madīnat Ṭiryāq fī al-ʿIrāq* (*The Pleasure Trip of the Enamored and the Agony of Lovers in the City of Ṭiryāq in Iraq*).[185] This Algerian play, published in 1847, was written under Western influence but has many similarities with *Ḥikāyat Abī al-Qāsim al-Baghdādī* (*The Tale [Play] of Abū al-Qāsim al-Baghdādī*) composed about 1010 by Abū al-Muṭahhar al-Azdī (d. 1011) which is one of the few extant textual versions of a medieval Arabic dramatic variation on the *maqāma*.[186]

By the mid-nineteenth century, we find clear evidence of pioneering Arab ventures into modern drama in Egypt, though the very first attempt came from Syria.[187] In February 1848, after visiting Europe, the Syrian-Christian merchant Mārūn al-Naqqāsh (1817–55), being particularly impressed by Italian opera, wrote and produced at his own house in Beirut a play entitled *Riwāyat al-Bakhīl* (*The Play of the Miser*), which drew heavily on Molière's *L'Avare*, though it was not a direct translation and involved a great deal of singing.[188] The play was written in a mixture of *fuṣḥā* and *ʿāmmiyya* for the speech of educated and illiterate characters, respectively.[189] After Mārūn al-Naqqāsh's death, his nephew Salīm al-Naqqāsh (1850–84) immigrated to Alexandria, where he took part in the rapid development of the Egyptian theatrical movement. Since the second half of the nineteenth century, there has been an influx of Syrian-Christian men of letters into Egypt, who, by pioneering free journalism[190] and various other cultural activities, have contributed significantly to Egypt's leading role in the modern Arab cultural renaissance. Stimulated as well by Napoleon Bonaparte's expedition at the turn of the century and by the drive for modernization embarked upon by the dynasty of Muḥammad ʿAlī (1769–1849), Egypt soon became the

185 See Moreh and Sadgrove 1996, pp. 1–42 (Arabic text).

186 See Moreh and Sadgrove 1996, pp. 13–14; Moreh 1998, pp. 37–45; and Moreh 2000a, pp. 409–16. On other links between the traditional Arabic live theater and the modern one, see Landau 1986, pp. 120–5; Moreh 1992, pp. 152–63; and Woidich and Landau 1993. On performativity and mobility in Middle Eastern traditions, see Pannewick 2009, pp. 215–49.

187 In his essay "al-Shaʾāmiyyūn wa-Fann al-Masraḥ al-Muʿāṣir" ("The Syrians and the Art of Contemporary Theater"), the Egyptian critic Muḥammad Mandūr (1907–65) emphasizes the role that Syrian people played in the development of Arab theater (Mandūr 1984, pp. 3–17. See also Moosa 1972, pp. 106–17).

188 See Landau 1958, pp. 57–8. For the speech which al-Naqqāsh gave before the staging of *Riwāyat al-Bakhīl*, see al-Khaṭīb 1994, pp. 415–20.

189 Landau 1958, pp. 57–8.

190 On their role in this field, see Ayalon 1995, pp. 39–58, 144–5.

center of the Arab theatrical movement and produced the first notables in modern Arab theater, such as the Egyptian-Jew Ya'qūb Ṣanū' (Jacob Sanua) (1839–1912) and the Syrian Abū Khalīl Aḥmad al-Qabbānī (1836–1902). After emigrating from Syria to Egypt, al-Qabbānī was the first Muslim to rise to prominence in this field, and, unlike Ṣanū', he used the technique of rhyming in *fuṣḥā*.[191]

With the exception of the stage directions, dialogue—which in other genres is only one textual component among others—makes up the entire text in theater. Thus, language has become far more of a problem for the newborn Arab theater than for any other genre. Since the beginning of modern drama, Arab playwrights have grappled with this problem, especially the wavering between *fuṣḥā* and *'āmmiyya*. A play is written to be staged and performed by actors who are supposed to speak the natural language of dramatic characters, that is, *'āmmiyya*. At the same time, the canonical language of the literary system is *fuṣḥā*. Insofar as dramatists write their plays with a stage performance in mind, it is the presence of an active, professional theater that will stimulate them to write plays[192] and that will also determine the choice of register. The presence of an active theater in Egypt, for example, or in the Palestinian Occupied Territories since the 1970s, has often led to playwrights opting for *'āmmiyya*. The choice of register is also influenced by the type of play being performed: In historical and translated plays, *fuṣḥā* has usually been chosen, but with farce and social comedy *'āmmiyya* usually prevails.[193]

Arab theater has come a long way since the nineteenth century, and in the second half of the twentieth century it was not only a major cultural medium but also an outlet for various political ideologies and a tool in the nation-building process.[194] Mention should also be made of the "Islamic theater" that started to develop in the 1980s.[195] What has greatly encouraged the spread of dramatic art is the development of electronic media, especially television, as shown, for example, by the popularity of satirical plays and musicals by

[191] On the development of Arabic drama and theater, see Najm 1956; Badawi 1988; Badawi 1988a; al-Khaṭīb 1994; and al-Khaṭīb 1994a.

[192] Cf. Jabrā 1961, p. 224.

[193] Cf. Somekh 1991, pp. 37–9. On the issue of language in the Arab theater, see also Tomiche 1969, pp. 117–32; and al-Khaṭīb 1994a, pp. 779–933. Some theatrical troupes in the Arab world also perform in other languages, especially in English and French, although to very limited audiences (e.g. in Lebanon; see Tomiche 1969, pp. 149–50). On the factors determining the choice of language in Tawfīq al-Ḥakīm's plays, see Somekh 1991, pp. 41–5.

[194] See, for example, the case of Palestinian nation-building and the rise of Palestinian political theater (Snir 1993g, pp. 129–47; Snir 1995a, pp. 29–73; Snir 1995e, pp. 63–103; Snir 1996a, pp. 101–20; Snir 1998b, pp. 57–71; Snir 2005b, pp. 5–29; Snir 2005c).

[195] See above, pp. 49–51.

Durayd Laḥḥām (b. 1934) and Muḥammad al-Māghūṭ (1934–2006). Videocassette performances of their plays, especially those in which Laḥḥām plays the role of Ghawwār, were exceedingly popular and were sold and rented throughout the entire Arab world during this period. Ghawwār's popularity was similar to that of the traditional storyteller (*ḥakawātī*) and the shadow puppeteer of earlier times.[196] The development of new media and Internet technologies in the Arab Middle East, however, has opened up new horizons and provided new possibilities for Arab theater. As with poetry and prose, further studies and investigations into Arab theater should refer to all aspects of its development, especially in view of the changes in theatrical norms since the beginning of the nineteenth century.

GENERIC INTERRELATIONSHIPS

Classical poetry, which recorded the very appearance of the Arab nation, was its principal channel of literary creativity and was considered to be the true annals and public register of the Arab people (*al-shiʿr dīwān al-ʿArab*).[197] There is a famous passage by Ibn Rashīq al-Qayrawānī (1000–63) which reflects the high status that poetry enjoyed not only in the ancient Arabic literary system but also in Arab society as a whole:

> كانت القبيلة من العرب إذا نبغ فيها شاعر أتت القبائل فهنّأتها بذلك وصنعت الأطعمة واجتمع النساء يلعبن بالمزاهر كما يصنعن في الأعراس وتتباشر الرجال والولدان لأنه حماية لأعراضهم وذبّ عن أحسابهم وتخليد لمآثرهم وإشادة لذكرهم وكانوا لا يهنّئون إلا بغلام يولد أو شاعر ينبغ فيهم أو فرس تنتج.

> When a poet appeared in a tribe of the Arabs, the adjacent tribes would gather together and wish that tribe the joy of their good luck. Feasts would be got ready, the women of the tribe would join together in bands, playing upon lutes, as they were wont to do at bridals, and the men and boys would congratulate one another; for a poet was a defence for the honour of them all, a weapon to ward off insult from their good name, and a means of perpetuating their glorious deeds and of establishing their fame forever. And they used not to wish one

[196] See Kishtainy 1985, pp. 159–64; and Bowen and Early 1993, pp. 264–70. On the carnivalesque satires directed and staged by Laḥḥām (*Ḍayʿat Ṭīshrīn* [1974]; *Ghurba* [1976]; *Kāsak Yā Waṭan* [1979–82] [all three plays written jointly by Laḥḥām and al-Māghūṭ]; *Shaqāʾiq al-Nuʿmān* (written by al-Māghūṭ) (1983); and *Ṣāniʿ al-Maṭar* (written by Laḥḥām) [1990–3]), see Ḥamdān 1996; Ḥamdān 1998; Ḥamdān 1999, pp. 63–96; and Hamdan 2005. On Laḥḥām, see also al-Jammāl 2002.

[197] This saying is found in many different forms in various works which deal with ancient Arabic poetry (e.g. Ibn Qutayba 1928, II, p. 185; and al-Suyūṭī n.d., II, p. 470). Cf. Lyall 1930, p. xv. For an examination of this saying with regard to the change in the perception of poetry and its function while Arab-Islamic society was emerging, see Ouyang 1997, pp. 56–60.

another joy but for three things: the birth of a boy, the coming to light of a poet, and the foaling of a noble mare.[198]

Medieval literature provides a variety of narrative prose texts: historical, semi-historical, fictional, official, popular prose, and drama. Since the nineteenth century, other genres have come to prominence, such as the short story, the novel, and modern drama. Nevertheless, poetry maintained its primacy in the literary system and remained the leading literary genre throughout the first half of the twentieth century. For example, in a poem written by Jamīl Ṣidqī al-Zahāwī on 22 March 1932, poetry figures not only as the public register of the Arab people, but also as the epitome of all literature. Furthermore, he argues that thanks to poetry the renaissance of the Arabs in the East had materialized: "If prose is made of silver, poetry is made of gold."[199]

It was only during the second half of the twentieth century that poetry was pushed to the margins of the literary canon,[200] with prose, especially the novel, taking its place as the leading genre.[201] In the early 1970s the Egyptian magazine *al-Ṭalīʿa* dedicated an edition to the genre of the novel with the title *al-Riwāya Mirʾāt al-Shaʿb* ("The Novel is the Mirror of the People"),[202] structurally imitating the above saying *al-shiʿr dīwān al-ʿArab*. More than twenty years later, upon his nomination in August 1993 as the head of the prose committee at the Egyptian Supreme Council for Culture, the Egyptian ʿAlī al-Rāʿī (1920–99), a leading Arab scholar of Arabic theater, gave an excellent illustration of this new development by making the following declaration: "This is the time of the novel [...] The novel is the new annals of the Arabs (*al-riwāya dīwān al-ʿarab al-jadīd*) [...] Through the novel, one can express freely and in a strong and lasting manner the nation's sorrows and interests."[203] Elsewhere, al-Rāʿī attributes to the novel an historical role in

198 Ibn Rashīq 1963, p. 65; al-Suyūṭī n.d., II, p. 473. The translation is according to Lyall 1930, p. xvii, with minor modifications. See also Nicholson 1969 [1907], p. 71.

199 Al-Zahāwī 1972, pp. 557–60.

200 Muḥammad ibn Ismāʿīl refers to the marginalization of Arabic poetry in relation to politics as a metaphor for the rupture between poetry and culture in the contemporary Arab world (*Fikr wa-Fann* 72 [2000], pp. 44–8).

201 The Lebanese poet Muḥammad ʿAlī Farḥāt (b. 1945) sees this development as corresponding to the disappearance of the "spirit of the countryside" (*al-rūḥ al-rīfiyya*) and the dominance of the town in the Arab world (*al-Wasaṭ*, 2 March 1992, p. 51). On town and country in modern Arabic poetry, see Moreh 1984, pp. 161–85.

202 *Al-Ṭalīʿa*, August 1971, pp. 10–57.

203 *Al-Akhbār*, 11 August 1993, p. 11. Cf. the special volume of *Fuṣūl* 12.1 (Spring 1993) entitled *Zaman al-Riwāya* (*The Time of the Novel*) and the declaration of the Egyptian novelist Ṣunʿ Allāh Ibrāhīm (b. 1937): "*al-riwāya tulad al-ān wa-l-mustaqbal lahā wasyʾtī yawm takūnu ʿamūd al-ʿarab*" ("The novel is being born now, the future belongs to it, and the day will come when it will be the pillar of the Arabs") (*al-Majalla*, 25–31 July 1989, p. 56);

what may even be considered an intertextual ironic allusion to the passage of Ibn Rashīq al-Qayrawānī cited earlier:

> المجد للرواية العربية! لقد جعلها أفضل المبدعين فيها لسان حال الأمّة، وديوانا جديدا للعرب، ومستودعا لآمال وآلام أمّتنا العظيمة المقطّعة الأوصال. لا تزال شعوب هذة الأمّة ترنو إلى التوحّد من جديد، لا تزال تناضل الحدود الزائفة ومؤامرات الأجنبي وقصر نظر الحكام المحليين.

> Glory to the Arabic novel! The best of its writers have made it a mouthpiece of the nation, the new annals of the Arabs, and a reservoir of the hopes and pains of our great but fragmented nation. The peoples of this nation are looking forward to reunification, they are struggling against artificial boundaries, foreign conspiracies, and the shortsightedness of local rulers.[204]

A book published in 2001 by the Egyptian Ṭāhā Wādī (1937–2008) bears the title *al-Qiṣṣa Dīwān al-ʿArab* (*Fiction is the New Annals of the Arabs*). Wādī explains that narrative genres have become the new annals of the Arabs because "they truly reflect their general and personal reality, both social and subjective."[205] Following Maḥfūẓ's death, Tahar Ben Jelloun wrote:

> Balzac said that because the novel is the private history of nations, a real novelist must be able to plumb the depths of society. Mahfouz fitted this description perfectly. You can't understand Egypt without Mahfouz—without his characters, with whom every reader, Arab or not, can identify.[206]

In the introduction to his poetical works, the Lebanese novelist Rashīd al-Ḍaʿīf (Daïf) (b. 1945) explains that what is considered by his critics to be his poetical works is nothing but the "free expression" of feelings that he has experienced. He stopped writing such texts because he began to be categorized as a poet, and he found that upsetting when he had to face his parents and brothers, who were working hard to make a living and raise children. He was equally upset when publishers were displeased and feeling pity when facing poets wishing to publish their work. But most of all, he now writes novels because of the time in which he is living, for "the novel, not poetry, is the passion of the present time (*hawā hādhā al-zamān*)."[207]

as well as Iḥsān ʿAbbās' (1920–2003) saying that "'*aṣrunā huwa ʿaṣr al-riwāya dūna adnā rayb*" ("Our time is undoubtedly the time of the novel") (Abbās 1996, p. 230). See also Jabrā 1989, pp. 11–26; al-ʿĪd 2005, p. 183; and Barrāda 2011, pp. 109–11. Ilyās Khūrī (b. 1948) thinks that any attempt to compare literary genres in order to determine which is superior or deserves preference is useless (*al-Ḥayāt*, 4 May 2016). On the "novelization" of Islamic literatures and the intersections of Western, Arabic, Persian, Urdu, and Turkish traditions, see Omri 2007, pp. 317–28.

204 Al-Rāʿī 1991, p. 19.

205 Wādī 2001, p. 9.

206 Ben Jelloun 2006.

207 Al-Ḍaʿīf 2007, pp. 9–10.

In April 2007 the International Prize for Arabic Fiction was officially launched in Abu Dhabi in association with the Booker Prize Foundation and with the support of the Emirates Foundation. In March 2008 the Egyptian Bahā' Ṭāhir (b. 1935) was named the inaugural winner of the prize for his *Wāḥat al-Ghurūb* (*Sunset Oasis*) (2007), which explores one man's existential crisis. The events of the novel take place in Sīwa, a location rarely used in Egyptian literature. What drew Ṭāhir to Sīwa, according to his preface to the novel, was Maḥmūd 'Azmī, the *ma'mūr* (police chief) of Sīwa who blew up the temple of Umm Ubayda in 1897. Trying to understand why he did what he did, the novel is a series of first-person accounts by characters such as Maḥmūd 'Abd al-Ẓāhir; his Irish wife Catherine; Sheikh Ṣābir, one of Sīwa's tribal sheikhs; Sheikh Yaḥyā, the enlightened leader; and Alexander the Great, whose temple in Sīwa is one of the main locations in the book. "When I write a novel," Ṭāhir says, "I am not writing a story. A novel is a complex world. In my book, *Fi Madīḥ al-Riwāya* (*In Praise of the Novel*), I say that a novel represents a vision of the world; it is the novelist's vision of the individual, society and the metaphysical questions a human being asks."[208]

Unlike Rashīd al-Ḍa'īf and Bahā' Ṭāhir, Adūnīs and Maḥmūd Darwīsh, two of the most prominent authors of contemporary Arabic poetry, reject the idea that the novel is the new *dīwān* of the Arabs. The fact that poetry is now marginal in Arab culture does not bother Adūnīs, who in the current condition of Arab society sees that the readership for the revolutionary Arab poet consists not of consumers (*mustahlikūn*) but of producers (*muntijūn*).[209] Commenting on the value of Arabic poetry, Adūnīs says that "our success has been substantially and paradoxically due to our marginality."[210] Maḥmūd Darwīsh sees the current prominence of the novel as a temporary phenomenon. Furthermore, the future belongs to poetry because poetry belongs to the novel.[211] No one, however, including Adūnīs and Maḥmūd Darwīsh,[212] has any doubt that poetry is now in retreat among the Arab reading public and that the novel occupies the center of the literary system. Yet, one should remember that literature as a whole lost the power it previously had to electronic media and to the Internet. Bahā' Ṭāhir writes, for example, that the

208 Manal el-Jesri, "Bahaa Taher," *Egypt Today* 28.6 (June 2007). For a for a sharp criticism against the prize's committee and the selection process of the winners, and "the killing of all that is good, artistic, and experimental and, instead, sanctifying all that is bad and weak," see the Egyptian cultural critic Maḥmūd al-Ghīṭānī's article in <http://mynewar.blogspot.co.il/2016/08/blog-post.html> (16 August 2016) (last accessed 20 October 2016).

209 Adūnīs 1972, pp. 95–6. Cf. Snir 2002, p. 146; and Snir 2004–5, pp. 17–85.

210 Adūnīs 1993, p. 180.

211 Interview in Wāzin 2006, pp. 90–1. Cf. Sa'dī Yūsuf's (b. 1934) arguments in an article he posted on Facebook on 3 September 2016.

212 See, for example, Darwīsh 2007, pp. 131–3.

influence of any novel is now limited to only a few readers.[213] The change in the status of poetry and prose is not exclusive to Arabic literature,[214] but is a worldwide phenomenon and has much to do with the hermetic nature of the new poetry. This gradual change has been illustrated both by the aforementioned testimonies of Maḥfūẓ in his own fictional writing as well as by the tendency of poets to write novels or other prose genres, especially autobiography.[215]

213 Ṭāhir 2006, p. 12.

214 Asked on such statements as "this is the time of the novel," Adūnīs says: "The Arabic novel, compared to poetry, is still in its beginnings because the achievement of Arabic poetry is a great universal achievement far beyond the borders of Arabic language" (Būmsahūlī 1998, p. 132. Cf. Adūnīs 1996 [1964–8], I, p. 12).

215 Cf. Wādī 2001, p. 8. For this tendency in Palestinian literature, especially in the 1980s, see al-Qāsim 1977 (on the novel, see Sulaymān 1995, pp. 104–33); al-Qāsim 1980; Ṭūqān 1985 (English translation: Tuqan 1990. On the book, see Odeh 1998, pp. 263–71); Darwīsh 1987 (English translation: Darwish 1995. On the book, see Gonzalez-Quijano 1998, pp. 183–91; and Hallaq 1998, pp. 192–206. It is interesting that Maḥmūd Darwīsh does not consider it a novel; moreover, he says he never thought of writing a novel, since the novel "needs efforts and patience which I don't have"; see interview in Wāzin 2006, pp. 89–90); Jabrā 1987 (on the novel, see Neuwirth 1998, pp. 115–27); and Ṭūqān 1994. In addition, Samīḥ al-Qāsim had declared that he would write another novel (*Zu Haderekch*, 19 July 1989), and even revealed its title and content (Brumm 1995, pp. 85–6), but he did not publish it. On the Palestinian novel in general, see Taha 2002. Mention should be also made of the novels of two bilingual Israeli-Palestinian poets, Na'īm 'Arāyidī and Anton Shammās: Shammās 1986 (English translation: Shammās 1988) and 'Arāyidī 1992. On the bilingual writing of the Israeli-Palestinian writers and their status in Israeli culture, see my publications in the References. Of special interest is the case of Sayyid Qashshū'a (Sayed Kashua) (b. 1975), who never wrote in Arabic and has acquired a significant status in Israeli culture and the press since the late 1990s. See his novels *Aravim Rokdim* (*Dancing Arabs*) (Ben-Shemen: Modan, 2002; a monodrama based on the novel was performed in September 2005 by Norman 'Īsā [b. 1967] in a joint production of the Haifa Municipal Theater and the Arab-Hebrew Theater in Jaffa), *Va-Yehi Boker* (*Let It Be Morning*) (Jerusalem: Keter, 2004; English translation: Sayed Kashua, *Let It Be Morning* [trans. Miriam Shlesinger] [New York: Black Cat, 2006]), and *Guf Sheni Yaḥid* (*Second Person Singular*) (Jerusalem: Keter, 2010; English translation: Sayed Kashua, *Second Person Singular* [trans. Mitch Ginsburg] [New York: Grove Press, 2013]). Cf. the interview with Qashshū'a in *Yediot Ahronoth* (*7 Days*), 11 January 2002, pp. 20–6 as well as the reviews by H. Hofman in *Yediot Ahronoth* (supplement), 1 February 2002, pp. 26–7; A. Karp in *Kolbo* (Haifa), 15 February 2002, p. 90; and Y. Meltyzer in *Maariv* (literary supplement), 13 February 2004. In 2007 a prime-time situation comedy that he wrote, *'Avoda 'Arabit* (*Arab Labor*), was presented on Israel's commercial Channel 2 television. The series, which dealt with Israeli prejudices through the eyes of a Muslim Arab family, was popular with the Jewish audience but was considered by the Arabic local press as an act of treachery (*International Herald Tribune*, 7 January 2008; *Ha'aretz*, 12 February 2008). On Sayyid Qashshū'a's novels and how he articulates his identity, see Elkad-Lehman 2008, pp. 119–54. In 2015 Qashshū'a published a new book, which is a collection of his personal weekly columns in Hebrew for *Ha'aretz* newspaper: *Ben Ha'aretz* (English title: *Native* [Literally: *Son of Ha'aretz* (= the Land)]) (Jerusalem: Keter, 2015). Most Israeli-Palestinian intellectuals have adopted a cynical approach toward the phenomenon of Palestinians writing in Hebrew, admitting

When we come to the study of the relationships between the various literary genres and subgenres, an indispensable feature will be the transtextual, transgeneric, and intergeneric connections—as well as the intratextual and intertextual relationships[216]—between texts of various genres, be they modern or ancient.[217] These interrelationships should be examined diachronically between various sectors of the literary system, including children's literature and theater. For example, the Palestinian writer and dramatist Īmīl Ḥabībī (1921–96), in an interview about the new Palestinian theatrical movement,[218] mentions that when he was a student, before 1948, he had acted in a play based on *The Hunchback of Notre Dame* (*Notre-Dame de Paris)* (1831) by Victor Hugo (1802–85).[219] The dramatic adaptation of the novel to school theater followed a film made at the beginning of the century based on the novel. However, the novel has also been translated into Arabic under the title *Aḥdab Notre Dame*,[220] and there are various adaptations for children. It is these diachronic interrelationships between various sectors of the literary system that must be taken into account when one sets out to gauge the meaning of the short story Ḥabībī wrote after the 1967 War, "Wa-Akhīran Nawwara al-Lawz" ("Finally the Almond Blossomed"),[221] in which he returns to the character of Pierre Gringoire from Hugo's novel.

that nothing can be done against the backdrop of the rejection of Arab cultural values in Israeli society. A response to such an approach can be found in two novels by another Israeli-Palestinian writer in Hebrew, Ayman Siksak (Sikseck) (b. 1984), *El Yafo* (*To Jaffa*) (2010) and *Tishrin* (English title: *Blood Ties*) (2016). The first has a motto from "I Write in Hebrew" by the Israeli-Palestinian poet Salmān Maṣālḥa (b. 1953): "I write in Hebrew / Which is not my mother tongue, / In order to lose myself in the world. / He who doesn't get lost, will never / find the whole." As I argued in my studies on this issue, the relationship between those writers and the Hebrew literary system is not balanced; few have expressed such a "one-way" relationship more eloquently than Anton Shammās: "One-wayness is one of the rules of the Game. Amichai / Comes out of the Hebrew poetry and hangs a sign / 'Will be back soon.' I don't, I don't. I / Send postcards in the morning, to my very dear friends / In order to notify them that I send them / Postcards in the morning" (Shammās 1979, p. 13).

216 Based on the terms introduced in Fitch 1982, pp. 89–108.

217 See, for example, Somekh 1989, pp. 105–17.

218 Daoud 1995, p. 108.

219 See Hugo 1956 (English translation: Hugo 1937).

220 Two translations are available: Hugo 1959 and Hugo 1989.

221 Ḥabībī 1985, pp. 13–22. The English translation by Anthony Calderbank can be found in Elmessiri 1996, pp. 175–85.

Conclusion

In "Canon and Period," from his *History and Value* (1988), Frank Kermode writes that notions of value in literature more often than not involve, as a rule rather obscurely, our views of the relationship of a work to its historical context. Judgments of value, from abolitionism ("the anarchic or nihilistic attitude which would abolish the work along with the past as a whole") to the latest elaborations of Marxism ("the work may in its later existence have value that was not evident in its original form, the passage of time having made available its true relation to a necessarily false ideology enshrined in it"), cannot possibly avoid assumptions about the operations of history. It is necessary, therefore, according to Kermode, to say something rather general and elementary about the ways in which history is manipulated in the interests of literary valuation:

> There seem to be two main ways in which we try to make history manageable for literary purposes: by making canons that are in some sense transhistorical; and by inventing historical periods. They enable us to package historical data that would otherwise be hopelessly hard to deal with; and they do so by making them *modern*.[1]

Kermode also ponders the idea that periodization is colonial politics, which makes "period" as wicked an idea as "canon." Both are used "to serve our interests, which may be colonialist or political." But, both also help us give meaning to the past and secure access to "*something in the past that can be made new, made valuable for the present*."[2]

Unlike that of Kermode, our conception is descriptive and excludes evaluative judgments: We argue that Arabic literature can be more adequately analyzed as an historical phenomenon when conceived of as a system that

1 Kermode 1988, pp. 108–9.
2 Kermode 1988, p. 123 (my emphasis).

replaces the search for data about material aspects of literary phenomena with the uncovering of the functions these aspects have. This literary system is inclusive and consists of all *literary* texts (even potential ones) for adults and children, including those that are translations, regardless of any hierarchies of value. In other words, it consists of all texts that in a given culture or community have been imbued with cultural value, which allows for higher levels of complexity and significance in the way they are constructed. That is, any Arabic text perceived of in a certain span of time as *literary* by any Arab community is referred to as part of the literary system, which is a network of relations between *all* forms of literary texts. Our distinction between "serious" literature and "light" literature differentiates between presentational compositions designed to convey different kinds of values for different communities. When we speak of *value*, we by no means speak of its literary worth (which is always relative as *literature* for different communities, sometimes for the same community in various periods), but of the status of the text in a given period of time, at a particular point within the system, which is its synchronic *value*. Diachronic *value* is assigned to it by its paradigmatic position in the succession of synchronic systems, which acquire retrospective significance.

Both processes suggested by Kermode, making canons and inventing periods, have been studied here as integral components of a unified comprehensive framework, a functional dynamic historical model whose main purpose is to give meaning to the production of Arabic literature and make it valuable for the present—be it right now at the moment I am writing these lines or reading them, or in any another "present" in the future. As previously indicated, the aim is to "package" the enormous data available and make the investigation of the literary texts manageable for scholarly purposes. We have been descriptive in our analysis and have avoided as much as we can any evaluative judgments, trying to reflect the values and judgments of the communities toward their literary texts in different stages and periods.

Three categories of investigation have been used in this book: The first is the investigation of the literary dynamics in synchronic cross-section—potential inventories of canonized and non-canonized literary texts in three sections or subsystems: texts for adults, texts for children, and translated texts for adults and children. The internal and external interrelations and interactions between the various subsystems need to be studied if we wish to arrive at a comprehensive understanding of the modern Arabic literary system. The second category consists of the study of the historical outlines of the modern Arabic literary system's diachronic intersystemic development. I have emphasized the need to refer to the changes and interactions with other extra-literary systems that have determined the historical course of

Arabic literature since the nineteenth century. Due to a lack of space and due to the absence of relevant studies, I discussed in some detail only a few such interactions and mentioned some others sporadically. The third category is intended to concentrate on the historical diachronic development that each genre underwent and on the relationships between the various genres. Since literary genres do not emerge in a vacuum, the issue of generic development cannot be confined to certain time spans; emphasis must be laid on the relationship between modern literature, on the one hand, and classical and post-classical literature, on the other.

The model suggested here substitutes the discourse about the relationships between cultures and literatures in impressionistic subjective terms with a more "objective," evidence-based framework and refers to the interaction between cultural and literary systems mutually interfering in each other's activities. This framework offers scholars the possibility to analyze and examine the production of Arabic texts by concentrating on two vectors, the synchronic and the diachronic, which will enable them to have a systematic look at the literary system and, at the same time, provide potential insights into its various texts, agents, sectors, and processes. From the synchronic point of view, any "present" necessitates newer research into "fresh" phenomena and their interrelations with older ones, while leaving the door open for a diachronic, historical, and systematic study of the development of these literary phenomena and their corresponding cultural interactions from any temporal point in the past.

The model, however, is flexible and open-ended, always turning attention to the need to trace the diachronic interactions between the literary system and other, literary and non-literary systems. For example, one of the most important and most disputed phenomena in the debates concerning the historical development of Arabic literature is its interaction with Western culture (in fact, this is one of the most hotly debated issues concerning the Arab world in general). Examining this multilayered and complicated interaction as a diachronic historical interrelation between two different systems, each with its own complexities and intricacies, makes us hesitate to deal with this topic in a simple manner by drawing conclusions about the development of Arabic literature based only on terms such as "change," "adjustment," "transformation," "impact," "influence," "inspiration," "adoption," and "borrowing." Conversely, the approach which sees this interrelation in a more complex, intrasystemic manner requires extreme caution when it comes to generalizations and one-sided impressionistic conclusions, and turns our attention instead toward the various circumstances of each system in any time span and to the particular factors and unique contexts of their interaction. For now, it is sufficient to refer to one example that can show us how exploring what seems to be only one component of the interaction might provide us with valuable understanding of the development of Arabic literature by clarifying the ways in which the agents of the Arabic literary system—writers, critics, scholars, editors, publishers—related to Western culture.

In 1923 the Lebanese-Christian *Mahjari* poet Mīkhā'īl Nu'ayma (1889–1988) called on Arab authors to concentrate on translating Western literary masterpieces as a necessary step toward bringing Arabic literature into the ambit of world literature and the universal human spirit. Alluding to the urgent need for Arab culture to benefit from its contacts with the West, Nu'ayma wrote the following in his "Fa-l-Nutarjim" ("Let Us Translate"), which was published in his book *al-Ghirbāl* (*The Sieve*):

> نحن في دور من رقيّنا الأدبي والاجتماعي قد تنبّهت فيه حاجات روحية كثيرة لم نكن نشعر بها من قبل احتكاكنا الحديث بالغرب. وليس عندنا من الأقلام والأدمغة ما يفي بسدّ هذه الحاجات. فلنترجم! ولنجلّ مقام المترجم لأنه واسطة تعارف بيننا وبين العائلة البشرية العظمى.

> We are at a stage of our literary and social evolution in which many spiritual needs have awakened which we did not feel before our new contact with the West. As we have no pens and brains that can fulfill those needs, let us then translate! Let us honor the status of translator because he is an agent of acquaintance between us and the larger human family.[3]

Nu'ayma's call did not emerge in the Arab world or on the international scene *ex nihilo*. We can see similar calls in other societies, especially during the nineteenth century when writers and scholars felt that their local culture should benefit from Western culture. For example, in *A House of Gentlefolk* by Ivan Sergeyevich Turgenev (1818–83),[4] we find the following at the beginning of Chapter XXXIII:

> Panshin was the only guest. He was stimulated by the beauty of the evening, and conscious of a flood of artistic sensations, but he did not care to sing before Lavretsky, so he fell to reading poetry; he read aloud well, but too self-consciously and with unnecessary refinements, a few poems of Lermontov (Pushkin had not then come into fashion again). Then suddenly, as though ashamed of his enthusiasm, [he] began, a propos of the well-known poem, "A

[3] Nu'ayma 1964 [1923], p. 126. Cf. Badawi 1975, p. 182; and Ostle 1991, p. 42. See also the introduction to Nu'ayma's play *al-Ābā' wa-l-Banūn* (*Fathers and Sons*) (Nu'ayma 1989 [1917], pp. 11–19). The title of the play evokes a novel with the same title (1862) by I. S. Turgenev. The introduction was also published in al-Khaṭīb 1994a, pp. 443–9. Twelve years after the publication of Nu'ayma's article, his compatriot Sa'īd 'Aql (1911–2014), in the course of a review of several works of Lebanese poets in French, issued a similar *cri de coeur* ('Aql 1935, especially pp. 381–4). There have been many similar calls, and even sixty years later we find such a call in 'Abd al-Wahhāb 1995, pp. 10–12.

[4] Turgenev 1951 [1917].

> Reverie," to attack and fall foul of the younger generation. While doing so he did not lose the opportunity of expounding how he would change everything after his own fashion, if the power were in his hands. "Russia," he said, "has fallen behind Europe; we must catch her up. It is maintained that we are young—that's nonsense. Moreover we have no inventiveness: Homakov himself admits that we have not even invented mouse-traps. Consequently, whether we will or no, we must borrow from others. We are sick, Lermontov says—I agree with him. But we are sick from having only half become Europeans, we must take a hair of the dog that bit us ("le cadastre," thought Lavretsky). "The best head, *les meilleures tâtes*," he continued, "among us have long been convinced of it. All peoples are essentially alike; only introduce among them good institutions, and the thing is done. Of course there may be adaptation to the existing national life; that is our affair—the affair of the official (he almost said 'governing') class. But in case of need don't be uneasy. The institutions will transform the life itself."

When Nuʿayma published his own call, translations had already been the primary channel of interaction between Arabic literature and Western culture for several decades. Already in 1890 we find the Egyptian philologist Aḥmad Zakī (1867–1934), known as the "Dean of Arabism" (*Shaykh al-ʿUrūba*), saying that "we are at a time in which composing (*taṣnīf*) is decreasing and translation (*taʿrīb*) is increasing; how often an Arabic book is described as being composed while it is nothing but a translation or a summary of a European book."[5] In retrospect, then, "Fa-l-Nutarjim" seems less an attempt to boost the process of cultural borrowing from the West—at the time in full progress and in no need for such a call—and more a kind of a persistent lament over the state of Arab culture. Although "nobody seems to know when the term *inḥiṭāṭ* was first used to denote 'decadence' as self-view of intellectuals of the Ottoman Empire,"[6] we can hardly find anyone who has denied the collapse of the Arabs' cultural self-image and the significant decline in their self-esteem in modern times. The movement that sought to translate Western classics into Arabic, which began in the nineteenth century, reflected the state of Arab culture and the frustration of its agents.[7] Emphasizing the intellectual backwardness of the Arab world, forty-five years after Nuʿayma published his essay, the Egyptian critic Ghālī Shukrī (1935–98) still finds no comfort in the state of Arab culture. Furthermore, unlike Nuʿayma, he seems to have no hope for the near future:

> No cultural unity connects the Arab poet with his counterpart in Western or Eastern Europe. We are living under the influence of an undeveloped civiliza-

[5] *Al-Muqtaṭaf* 15 (October 1890), p. 269.
[6] Wild 1996, p. 386.
[7] Cf. Lefevere 1990, p. 27.

> tion compared to Western civilization [...] The modern Arab poet stands on the mouth of a volcano boiling for about a hundred years with strange and complex interactions. No less than four centuries, the temporal distance between the European renaissance and that of the Arabs, separate the Arabic poet from the caravan of human civilization at the peak of its artistic expression in Europe.[8]

Considering Nu'ayma's and Shukrī's comments about the decline of the Arabs' cultural self-esteem and the change in the self-image of the very culture they are part of, it is no accident that both writers are not Muslim. They are part of a long list of Christian intellectuals and men of letters for whom the high reverence accorded to Arabic not only as the language of the Qur'ān but also as the language of their own literary heritage did not prevent them, as it prevented Muslim intellectuals, from voicing dissatisfaction at the state and status of their own culture. The aforementioned lecture *Khuṭba fī Ādāb al-'Arab* (*A Lecture on the Culture of the Arabs*), delivered on 15 February 1859 by the Christian scholar Buṭrus al-Bustānī (1819–83), seems to be one of the first sharp statements reflecting that essential change in the Arabs' self-esteem. Concentrating on the culture of the Arabs in his time, at the beginning of the third chapter of his screed al-Bustānī complains in metaphorical language that the contemporary Arabs in his time are satisfied with the low state of their literature and are at the same time falsely considering themselves as having obtained the highest levels of science:

> إن العرب في أيّامنا هذه قنعون جدّا في أمر الآداب. فإنهم يكتفون بأقلّها، ويحسبون أنفسهم أنهم قد وصلوا إلى أعلى طبقات العلم، مع أنهم لم يقرعوا بابه. ومن تعلّم منهم كتاب الزبور، والقرآن، يقال إنه قد ختم علمه، وإذا تعلّم شيئا من أصول الصرف والنحو يقال فيه أنه قد صار علاّمة زمانه وإذا نطق بالشعر فلا يبقى عندهم لقب يصفونه به. وما ذلك إلا لأن ظهور نور قليل في العاقل كاف لأن يغشى على عيني الجاهل، لأنهم إلى الآن لم يقفوا على شاطئ أوقيانوس العلوم ويروا عظمته واتّساعه. ومع أننا نعتقد بأن عرب هذه الأيّام هم من نسل العرب القدماء، لا نرى فيهم ما رأيناه في أولائك المجاهدين من الثبات والجهاد في ميدان العلوم، ولا نقدر أن نسلّم بأن النسل قد فسد، وذلك لأن جودة عقول العرب، وحسن استعدادها في هذه الأيام لتحصيل العلوم، ببرهان النقيض. ولكن ذلك ناتج من أحوال كثيرة وأسباب متنوّعة نودّ لو سمحت لنا الأوقات لبيانها لكي نخفّف عمن هم من لحمنا ودمنا اللوم الواقع عليهم من الأجانب الذين لا نشكّ بأنهم كانوا وصلوا إلى حالة أردأ من حالتنا لو ألقاهم الدهر في ظروف كظروفنا. ولكن مهما كانت الأسباب فلا سبيل إلى إنكار كساد بضاعة العلم عند العرب، وعدم رواج سوقها بين جماهيرهم، وعلى الخصوص أكابرهم.

> The Arabs in our time are very satisfied with the matter of culture. They are satisfied with the minimum of it, considering themselves having arrived at the highest levels of science, although they have never even knocked on its door. It is said that any one of them who studies the *Book of Psalms* and the Qur'ān has finished his study, and if he studies something from the principles of *'ilm al-ṣarf* [morphology] and *'ilm al-naḥw* [grammar], it is said of him that he has

[8] Shukrī 1978 [1968], pp. 18–19.

> become the scholar of his time, and if he composes poetry, they find a difficulty in finding a suitable phrase to describe his greatness. We cannot explain this but for the fact that a small light for the intelligent man is sufficient to cause blindness in the eyes of the ignorant; that because they have not stood on the shore of the ocean of sciences they cannot know its greatness and wideness. Although we think that the Arabs of our time are the offspring of the ancient Arabs, we do not see in them the firmness and struggle in the field of sciences that we have seen in those ancient fighters. We cannot agree that the progeny has become spoiled, because the quality of the brains of the Arabs and their good ability to acquire sciences bear witness to the opposite. However, this is due to many circumstances and various reasons we wish we had enough time to explain in order to ease the blame laid upon those who are of our flesh and blood by the foreigners who would have been in worse shape than us if fate had decreed to them circumstances such as ours. However, whatever the reasons, we cannot deny the dullness of the Arab science market and the absence of its popularity among their masses, especially their senior members.[9]

Viewing al-Bustānī's complaint about the attitude toward the Other that prevailed among the Arabs several centuries before his time illuminates the abysmal collapse of the Arabs' cultural self-image. For example, in his *Kitāb al-I'tibār* (*The Book of Esteem*), Usāma ibn Munqidh (1095–1188) refers to the Franks as follows:

> سبحان الخالق البارئ إذا خبر الإنسان أمور الإفرنج سبّح الله تعالى وقدّسه ورأى بهائم فيهم فضيلة الشجاعة والقتال لا غير، كما في البهائم فضيلة القوّة والحمل. وسأذكر شيئا من أمورهم وعجائب عقولهم. كان في عسكر الملك فلك بن فلك فارس محتشم إفرنجي قد وصل من بلادهم يحجّ ويعود. فأنس بي وصار ملازمي يدعوني «أخي» وبيننا المودّة والمعاشرة. فلمّا عزم على التوجّه في البحر إلى بلاده قال لي: «يا أخي، أنا سائر إلى بلادي. وأريدك تنفّذ معي ابنك، وكان ابني معي وهو ابن أربع عشرة سنة، إلى بلادي يبصر الفرسان ويتعلّم العقل والفروسيّة. وإذا رجع كان مثل رجل عاقل». فطرق سمعي كلام ما يسمع من رأس عاقل. فإن ابني لو أُسر ما بلغ به الأسر أكثر من رواحه إلى بلاد الإفرنج. فقلت «وحياتك، هذا الذي كان في نفسي. لكن منعني من ذلك أن جدّته تحبّه وما تركته يخرج معي حتّى استحلفتني أني أردّه إليها». قال «وأمّك تعيش؟» قلت «نعم». قال «لا تخالفها».

> Mysterious are the works of the Creator, the author of all things! When one comes to recount cases regarding the Franks, he cannot but glorify Allah (exalted is he!) and sanctify him, for he sees them as animals possessing the virtues of courage and fighting, but nothing else; just as animals have only the virtues of strength and carrying loads. I shall now give some instances of their doings and their curious mentality. In the army of King Fulk, son of Fulk, was a Frankish reverend knight who had just arrived from their land in order to make the holy pilgrimage and then return home. He was of my intimate fellowship and kept such constant company with me that he began to call me "my brother." Between us were mutual bonds of amity and friendship. When he resolved to

[9] Al-Bustānī 1859, p. 31; al-Bustānī (Buṭrus)1990, pp. 113–14. Cf. Allen 2006, pp. 13–17.

> return by sea to his homeland, he said to me: "My brother, I am leaving for my country and I want thee to send with me thy son (my son, who was then fourteen years old, was at that time in my company) to our country, where he can see the knights and learn wisdom and chivalry. When he returns, he will be like a wise man." Thus there fell upon my ears words which would never come out of the head of a sensible man; for even if my son were to be taken captive, his captivity could not bring him worse misfortune than carrying him into the lands of the Franks. However, I said to the man: "By thy life, this has exactly been my idea. But the only thing that prevented me from carrying it out was the fact that his grandmother, my mother, is so fond of him and did not this time let him come out with me until she exacted an oath from me to the effect that I would return him to her." Thereupon he asked, "Is thy mother still alive?" "Yes." I replied. "Well," said he, "disobey her not."[10]

In the next century the geographer Zakariyyā ibn Muḥammad al-Qazwīnī (1203–83) mentions a city on the Atlantic called Shlashwīq (Schleswig, a town located in northeastern Schleswig-Holstein, Germany) which was visited by someone who said: "I have never heard singing more terrible than that of the people of Shlashwīq. It is a sound that emerges from their mouths like the barking of dogs or much worse than that."[11]

Against this background, it is highly instructive to find that none other than "The Prince of Poets," Aḥmad Shawqī (1868–1932), described in the introduction to the first edition of his *Dīwān* the expeditions sent out in the nineteenth century to Europe to benefit from the achievements of Western civilization as "learning wisdom."[12] Bernard Lewis writes that it is difficult for a Westerner to appreciate the magnitude of such a change, in a society accustomed to despise the infidel barbarians beyond the frontiers of civilization, because "even traveling abroad was suspect; the idea of studying under infidel teachers was inconceivable."[13] No sooner had the first expeditions returned, then the change was noticed on the level of literature as well. For example, *'Alam al-Dīn* (*The Sign of Religion*) (1882) by 'Alī Mubārak (1824–93), described as *ḥikāya laṭīfa* (fine story) and as belonging to the literature of travel (*adab al-riḥla*),[14] was written in a narrative structure which had not entirely followed the usual Arabic literary norms of the time. From a

10 Ibn Munqidh 1930, p. 132; translation according to Ibn-Munqidh 1987, p. 161. Cf. Hitti 1962, pp. 184–7; and Ayyad and Witherspoon 1999, pp. 3–18. On Ibn Munqidh, see DeYoung and Germain 2011, pp. 364–71 (by Terri DeYoung). The term "Franks" (*al-Ifranj*) was used by earlier Arabic authors to refer to all Western Europeans (Hermes 2012, pp. 48–55, 65–6).

11 Al-Qazwīnī 1960, p. 602. Cf. Abdullah 1997, pp. 78–9. On the European "Other" in medieval Arabic literature and culture, see Hermes 2012.

12 Mandūr 1970, p. 43.

13 Lewis 2003, p. 43.

14 Mubārak 1882, p. 7.

thematic point of view, the West in that work proves to be far superior to the East, insofar as the author produces an almost degrading image of an East which is yet unaware of its inferior position.[15]

Significantly enough, even 100 years later that awareness was still deeply rooted in the minds of Arab intellectuals. Pointing out the build-up of literary criticism in the 1980s, the Egyptian poet and critic Yusrī al-ʻAzab (b. 1947) finds no way forward but to benefit from the West. Emphasizing the contributions that medieval Arab culture made to universal civilization compared with its present, gloomy state, he indicates that "since we became petty states, splinters, we have been moving in circles in the ideological and cultural orbit of others. There is no other way but to benefit from their estates, even in the field of literature and criticism."[16] Even in 2006 the Libyan writer Ibrāhīm al-Kawnī (al-Koni) (b. 1948) argues that the real crisis facing Arab culture is that Arabs have not yet admitted their weakness:

> أزمتنا قبل أن تكون سياسية أو ثقافية أم غيرها هي أزمة أخلاقية (...) من المستحيل أن يستشفي إنسان من مرض ما دام هذا الإنسان يرفض أن يعترف بمرضه. أزمتنا لهذا السبب أخلاقية لأننا أمّة لا تريد أن تعترف بعلّتها المميتة ما دامت تصرّ أنها خير أمّة أخرجت للناس وتتجاهل الوصيّة الإلهية (...) التي كانت سرّ قيام، بل واستمرار الحضارة الأوروبية، والمنقولة على لسان سقراط «إعرف نفسك!» (...) المحنة الأخلاقية (هي) المتمثّلة في اليقين المسبق بتميّز موهوم (أو فلنقل غابر) (...) هذا في حين تسلّح المخاطب (أو الآخر) بيقين بسيط كان سرّ سلطانه دائما ألا وهو «إعرف نفسك!»

> Our crisis, before it is a political or cultural or other, is a moral crisis [...] man cannot find a cure for his malady as long as he does not admit it. Our crisis thus is moral because we are a nation which does not want to admit its fatal malady as long as it insists it has been the best nation emerged to human beings and ignores the divine command [...] that was the secret of the emergence, moreover, of the continuation of European civilization, that was transmitted by Socrates: "know yourself!" [...] the moral ordeal is that which is expressed in the premature certitude of imagined advantage (or, in fact, let us say bygone [advantage]) [...] while in the meantime the addressee (or the Other) has armed himself with a simple certitude, which was always the secret of his power, namely, "know yourself!"[17]

More than thirty-five years earlier, the Egyptian poet Ṣalāḥ ʻAbd al-Ṣabūr (1931–81) had alluded to the same position by considering Socrates' aforementioned saying as the turning point in the history of humanity—it was the first time that a human being turned his attention to himself:

> لأن الإنسان هو الموجود الوحيد الذي يستطيع أن يعي ذاته، فهو إذن وعي الكون فالكون قوّة عمياء، أو جسم عملاقي فائر. الإنسان هو عقله ووعيه وعظمة ذلك العقل أنه يستطيع أن يعقل ذاته، وجلال

[15] Cf. Hopwood 1999, pp. 248–9.

[16] Al-Rāwī 1982, pp. 249–50.

[17] Quoted on <http://www.elaph.com>, 1 August 2006 (last accessed on 15 October 2016).

الإنسان أنه يقدر أن يواجه نفسه، أن يجعل من نفسه ذاتا وموضوعا في نفس الآونة، ناظرا ومنظورا إليه ومرآة، أن ينقسم ويلتئم في لحظة واحدة.

> Because the human being is the sole creature who is able to become aware of himself, he is thus the consciousness of the universe. The universe is a blind force, or a giant boiling body whose mind and consciousness is the human being. The greatness of this mind is that it is able to realize itself and the greatness of the human being is that he is able to confront himself and make himself the subject and the object at the same time, the observer and the observed as well as a mirror, to be split up and combined in the same moment.[18]

Examining the repeated lamentations by Arab intellectuals and writers about the status of Arab culture and literature throughout the last two centuries, the nuances and wording of each of them enable the student of Arabic literature to understand the complicated attitude toward the West in light of the decline of the Arabs' cultural self-image and the huge gap between the august status enjoyed by Arab culture in the Middle Ages and its feeble modern counterpart. And here, and against the background of the aforementioned lamentations, it is necessary to mention that there are different views and opinions regarding the relationship and connections between premodern Arab culture, before the encounter with the West, and modern Arab culture, the role of modernist Arab intellectuals in that encounter inclusive. In the Introduction, I mentioned Muhsin Jassim al-Musawi's more recent significant contributions, especially his original and trail-blazing book *The Medieval Islamic Republic of Letters: Arabic Knowledge Construction* (2015), which I read while I was preparing the manuscript of the present book for publication. I have examined al-Musawi's challenging, sometimes provoking hypotheses as well as his profound interpretations of the texts he uses. I plan to refer at length to this book in an independent study, but as both al-Musawi's book and my present book offer general frameworks for the investigation of Arabic texts in their various contexts, the relationship with the West included, albeit in different periods and based on varying methodologies and theoretical conceptions, I will proffer here a few relevant comments:

First: terminology. Al-Musawi borrows the term "republic of letters" (*république des lettres*) from Dena Goodman's *The Republic of Letters: A Cultural History of the French Enlightenment* (1994) and Pascale Casanova's *The World Republic of Letters* (2004). Coined by Pierre Bayle (1647–1706) to indicate a network of intellectuals who created and sustained cultural

[18] 'Abd al-Ṣabūr 1969, p. 6. Cf. Snir 2006, p. 93.

exchange, this term is used by al-Musawi to refer to "a conceptual framework, an edifice, to account for a literary world-system in which Arabic functions as the dominating language," but "its appropriation in this book entails no equation between Latin and Arabic in relation to national languages."[19] For such a study which is considered to be, as Suzanne P. Stetkevych writes in her endorsement of the book, "the starting point for a new generation of scholarship" on premodern Arabic literature, the intelligible use of terms and the justifications for the use of each of them is crucial. That is why it is important to clarify in detail what makes the term "republic of letters" suitable to be used as an "umbrella term" (p. 305) in a study on *Arabic* literature. And if the term's appropriation "entails no equation between Latin and Arabic in relation to national languages," the question is this: What justifies the borrowing of this very term from a specifically "literary world-system" where the relationship between the major language (= Latin) and national languages is fundamental? Casanova's conceptions, which are indebted to world-systems theory as developed by Fernand Braudel and his concept of an "economy-world" as well as to Pierre Bourdieu's concepts of symbolic capital and the cultural field, make a case for international theory space which has developed its own standards, canons and values operating separately from national literary systems. According to Goodman, the "French Republic of Letters rose with the modern political state out of the religious wars of the sixteenth century, out of the articulation of public and private spheres, citizen and state, agent and critic." Furthermore, the basics of this Republic were established in the "Parisian salons, from which networks of social and intellectual exchange were being developed to connect the capital with the four corners of France and the cosmopolitan republic." Its aim was "to serve humanity"; its project was to define the nature of Enlightenment.[20] However, apart from brief references to both studies mainly in his *Preliminary Discourse*, nowhere does al-Musawi provide any coherent explanation for the shared conceptions between either Goodman or Casanova's republic and his. At the same time, justifying his focus on rhetoric, perhaps in an attempt to imitate the authors of the postclassical or premodern period,[21] al-Musawi refers to the Arabic translation of the term "republic":

> The recourse in rhetoric to indirection, or *laḥn al-qawl* (i.e., implicitness), and to *taʿrīḍ* (dissimulation, connotation, concealment) signifies the other side of

[19] Al-Musawi 2015b, p. 9. Hereafter, only references from this book will be cited within the text.

[20] Goodman 1994, p. 2 and p. 52, respectively.

[21] Hereafter, the terms "post-classical" and "premodern" are in general used interchangeably. On what makes that period both post-classical and premodern, see Allen 2006, pp. 8–17.

> written and verbal transactions in this *jumhūr* (majority) of littérateurs, which is the basis for Arab and Muslim modernists' application of the term *jumhūriyyah* (i.e., republic). In this verbal domain, the root and conjugation of the verb *jamhara* also connote dissimulation. Hence, both verb and noun are loaded in Arabic in a binary structure, negation, or *taḍadd* (based on opposites or contrasts—*aḍdād*), implying both revelation and concealment (pp. 2–3).[22]

Al-Musawi implies here that the etymology of the Arabic term for "republic" is relevant to his concept of the "republic of letters" and that, since "both verb and noun are loaded in Arabic in a binary structure, negation, or *taḍadd*," negation is relevant to his concept. Al-Musawi, however, does not further elaborate on his claim. The original meaning of the verb *jamhara*, from which the term *jumhūriyya* (republic) is derived, is "[to collect] together a thing or earth, or dust." The same verb also denotes dissimulation: Thus, *jamhara 'alayhi* (or *lahu* or *ilayhi*) *al-khabara* means "he acquainted him with a part of the news, or story, and concealed what he desired or meant"; or "he acquainted him with a part of the news, or story, incorrectly, or not in the proper manner, and omitted what he desired, or meant." Moreover, in one source only is there a view that the verb *jamhara* is of the category *aḍdād*, which is to say it is a "*ḍidd*" (plural: *aḍdād*), the Arabic term for a word with two basic meanings with one meaning being the opposite of the other: thus, *jamhar lak al-khabara jamharatan* means "he acquainted you with a minor part of the news and concealed its main part."[23] However, this is not an obvious case of the category of *aḍdād*, since *jamhar* in its main meaning, from which the word *jumhūriyya* is derived, as well as in its marginal meaning, does not connote a meaning and its opposite such as, for example, the word *jawn* which means both "black" and "white," or *jalal* which means both "great" and "small," or *ḍidd* itself which ironically has the contrary meanings "opposite" and "equal."[24] On the other hand, it is not clear what the benefit is to al-Musawi's argument for the "republic of letters" if "both verb and noun are loaded in Arabic in a binary structure, negation, or *taḍadd*."[25] In any event,

22 Lane 1968 [1865], I.2, pp. 461–2 (*jamhar*).
23 Abū al-Ṭayyib al-Lughawī 1963, p. 182.
24 Lane 1968 [1874], I.5, p. 1775 (*ḍidd*).
25 In an interview with the Arabic press before the publication of his book, al-Musawi referred to its title as *Jumhūriyyat al-Adab fī al-'Aṣr al-Islāmī al-Wasīṭ* (*al-Sharq al-Awsaṭ*, 22 January 2013), but after its publication he preferred to translate it as *Jamharat al-Ādāb fī al-'Aṣr al-Islāmī al-Wasīṭ* (*al-Khalīj*, 30 June 2015). He justifies the use of *Jamharat al-Ādāb* for "republic of letters" arguing wrongly(!), as I have shown above, that the word alludes to contrary meanings: *jam' wa-tafrīq* (joining and separating) (*al-Bayān*, 30 June 2015):

> لأن جمهر تعني الجمع والتفريق، وهي أصل للجمهورية كمفردة توازي ما درج عليه الفرنسيون، فدلالتها ديمقراطية لاسيما أنها تشتمل على الضدين، وتتيح عبر الجمع والتفريق، الاحتجاج واختلاف الرأي والجدل والمناقشة. وبالتالي، إحياء الفضاء العام اللازم لتنامي الظواهر المختلفة مؤسساتياً ومعرفياً.

al-Musawi writes about a period in history when the term *jumhūriyya* did not exist and the terms concerning literary and cultural activities were different from those that have been used since the late nineteenth century. Thus, there is a need to clarify terms used throughout the study such as "cultural production" and "cultural activity" vis-à-vis "literary production," "literary life," and "literary value." The aforementioned term "literary world-system" is also used without clear definition, sometimes by indirect allusion to Casanova's arguments or to an interpretation of one of her book's reviews (p. 89).[26] In the present study, I have explained what I mean by terms such as "literature," "culture," and "system" (among others), but my definitions seem to differ from those of al-Musawi—even as his definitions are, as I have just said, rather unclear.

Second: temporal spaces and borders. Al-Musawi's book refers to the "postclassical era (approximately the twelfth through the eighteenth centuries)" (p. 1), but one wonders about the uniformity of this long time span and the difference between it and other periods such as the eleventh and the nineteenth centuries. The essential characteristics of *literary* production in Arabic did not dramatically change between the tenth and twelfth centuries. Furthermore, in Chapter Two al-Musawi deals with the tenth-century encyclopedic work *Ikhwān al-Ṣafā'* (*The Brethren of Purity*), referring to it as the "prototype for an Islamic republic of letters" (p. 15) and thus only complicates the issue of the temporal spaces and borders of his "republic." In any event, before the late nineteenth century, modern literary conceptions had not as yet penetrated Arabic literature, and more explanation is needed for the particular characteristics of the "twelfth through the eighteenth centuries" and how they can be distinguished from those of other periods, previous and subsequent. Here, theoretical studies dealing with periodization may help as well as contributions by other scholars of Arabic literature who have dealt with this issue. For example, in the introduction to *Arabic Literature in the Post-Classical Period* (2006), Roger Allen explains in detail why the volume he edited together with D. S. Richards treats "the vast period between approximately 1150 and 1850 as a separate entity."[27] Also, I

In a review of the book, Shīrīn Abū al-Najā translated it as *al-Jumhūriyya al-Islāmiyya li-l-Ādāb* (Abū al-Najā 2016). Casanova's book was translated into Arabic as *al-Jumhūriyya al-'Ālāmiyya li-l-Ādāb* (trans. Amal al-Ṣabbān) (Cairo: al-Majlis al-A'lā li-l-Thaqāfa, 2002).

26 Where al-Musawi bases his argument on a partial and inaccurate quotation of Cleary 2006, p. 202.

27 Allen and Richards 2006, p. 20. For a review article of the book, see Bauer 2007, pp. 137–67. And see as well the response of Salma Khadra Jayyusi, whose article in the book was described by Bauer (p. 159) as falling "far short of scholarly standards" (Jayyusi 2008, pp. 193–207).

have dealt previously with the topic of periodization from a *literary* point of view, and the parameters I have used to distinguish between periods may be relevant to al-Musawi's study as well.[28]

Third: territorial, physical, and metaphorical spaces. Casanova's book, on which al-Musawi relies, is concerned with what one might call the geopolitics of literature. Terry Eagleton writes the following in his review of the book:

> Literary works, so it claims, are never fully intelligible in themselves; instead, you have to see them as belonging to a global literary space, which has a basis in the world's political landscape, but which also cuts across its regions and borders to form a distinctive republic of its own. Like geopolitical space, this literary republic has its frontiers, provinces, exiles, legislators, migrations, subordinate territories and an unequal distribution of resources. It is a form of intellectual commerce in which literary value is banked and circulated, or transferred from one national currency to another in the act of translation [...] Like the political sphere, too, the republic of letters is wracked by struggle, rivalry and inequality between the literary haves and the have-nots. There are "peripheral" or "impoverished" literary spheres [...] Such underdeveloped pockets are poor in literary capital, lacking publishers, libraries, journals and professional writers. Dominating their cultural resources is Old Europe, with its literary capital located firmly in Paris.[29]

Al-Musawi refers to Cairo of the post-classical era as the literary capital of the medieval Islamic republic of letters—a "cosmopolitan" city by virtue of its place and because of its being a

> nexus that witnesses a dialogue among schools of thought, scholastic controversies, scientific achievements, poetic innovations and shifts in expression, the massive use of prose for statecraft, and soaring heights of Sufi poetry that simultaneously derive and refract worldliness from common tropes.[30]

Moreover, "the influx of scholars, poets, travelers, and entrepreneurs continued markedly into the nineteenth century and played a significant role in giving the city its cosmopolitan features" (pp. 6–7). Scholars from all over the Islamic world "settled in Cairo or at least stopped there for a while.

28 See below, pp. 176–81.

29 *New Statesman*, 11 April 2005.

30 In a review of al-Musawi's book, Mohammad Salama argues that "one of the book's persuasive arguments is that we give Egypt, especially Cairo, its long overdue literary recognition that Casanova assigns exclusively to Paris" (*SCTIW Review*, 19 November 2015, p. 2). However, it seems that al-Musawi does not see Paris and Cairo competing on the same track; he argues instead that Cairo "stood to the postclassical Islamic world as Paris stood to Europe" (al-Musawi 2015b, p. 7).

Others were satisfied with an imaginary stopover, which was sustained and given shape through Sufi networks and an innovative reliance on the antecedent tradition of poetry and writing" (pp. 45–6). Additionally, Cairo escaped destruction and as "a safe enclave, it functioned in a way similar to its multiplying compendiums and lexicons" (p. 51).

But, can we consider Cairo as "cosmopolitan space," as al-Musawi argues (p. 71), against the backdrop of his own argument that following the fall of Baghdad the "Arab center could not hold for long" (p. 25)? Al-Musawi himself admits that the emergence of "an alternative center in Cairo was accepted, but not as wholeheartedly as had been the case with Baghdad" (p. 132). In Casanova's view, because of its long accumulation of literary prestige and its relative freedom from political concerns, Paris serves as the Greenwich meridian of literature, which "makes it possible to estimate the relative distance from the center of the world of letters of all those who belong to it."[31] Cairo by no means can be considered as the Greenwich meridian of Arabic literature during the post-classical or premodern period. For Casanova's republic, the central hypothesis is that "there exists a 'literature-world,' a literary universe relatively independent of the everyday world and its political divisions, whose boundaries and operational laws are not reducible to those of ordinary political space."[32] That being said, the "literature-world" is not, as Joe Cleary explains in his review of Casanova's book, "some free-floating cosmopolitan cultural zone that transcends or is independent of political space either." It does have "its own capitals, its own core and peripheral cultural regions, and its own laws of canonization and capital accumulation."[33] In addition, we can measure the power, prestige, and volume of linguistic and literary capital of a language not in terms of "the number of writers and readers it has, but in terms of the number of cosmopolitan intermediaries—publishers, editors, critics, and especially translators—who assure the circulation of texts into language or out of it." Also, "the great, often polyglot, cosmopolitan figures of the world of letters act in effect as foreign exchange brokers, responsible for exporting from one territory to another texts whose literary value they determine by virtue of this very activity."[34]

Theoretical research on the topic of cosmopolitanism has seen significant developments during recent decades, including its use in relation to the Middle East; this will be shown below when I will deal with Alexandria as a cosmopolitan city at the turn of the twentieth century and when I will

[31] Casanova 2004, p. 88.
[32] Casanova 2004, p. xii.
[33] Cleary 2006, p. 199.
[34] Casanova 2004, p. 21.

refer to the "cosmopolitan turn" following the intensified period of globalization. It is assumed that there is a need for certain urbane, social, and cultural dimensions for a city to be considered as cosmopolitan or for a global society to have cosmopolitan features. Such was the case, for example, with Baghdad after its establishment in 762, when the city enjoyed a pluralistic and multi-confessional atmosphere with multicultural ethnic and religious gatherings of Muslims, Christians, Jews, Zoroastrians, pagans, Arabs, Persians, and various other Asian populations. This cosmopolitan atmosphere was inspired by the leadership of the Caliph al-Mansur (754–75), who from Baghdad propagated an open and multicultural policy toward religious minorities.[35] The political, religious, and cultural supremacy of Baghdad as the center of the flowering of Mansur's Islamic empire encouraged the multicultural environment not only in the city itself, but throughout other cities, close and remote alike. A contemporary text describing typical gatherings that would take place in the southern city of Basra in the year AH 156 (AD 772–3) may serve to illustrate the city's pluralistic environment (the fact that those gatherings were held in Basra, the site of the production of the aforementioned encyclopedic work *Ikhwān al-Ṣafā'* [*The Brethren of Purity*], depicted by al-Musawi as a "prototype for an Islamic republic of letters," is not a coincidence):

> Khalaf ibn al-Muthannā related: Ten persons used to meet in Basra regularly. There was no equivalent to this gathering for the diversity of the religions and sects of its members: al-Khalīl ibn Aḥmad—a *sunnī* (Sunni), and al-Sayyid ibn Muḥammad al-Ḥimyarī—*rāfiḍī* (Shiite), and Ṣāliḥ ibn 'Abd al-Qaddūs—*thanawī* (dualist), and Sufyān ibn Mujāshi'—*ṣufrī* (Khārijī), and Bashshār ibn Burd—morally depraved and impudent, and Ḥammād 'Ajrad—*zindīq* (heretic), and the exilarch's son—a Jew, and Ibn Naẓīr—*mutakallim al-naṣārā* (a Christian theologian), and 'Amrū the nephew of al-Mu'ayyad—*majūsī* (Zoroastrian), and Rawḥ ibn Sinān al-Ḥarrānī—*ṣābi'ī* (Gnostic). At these gatherings they used to recite poems, and Bashshār used to say: your verses, Oh man, are better than *sūra* this or that [of the Qur'ān], and from that kind of joking and similar things they declared Bashhār to be a disbeliever.[36]

35 Micheau 2008, pp. 221–45.

36 Al-Dhahabī 1988, p. 383. For another version of this episode, see Ibn Taghrībirdī 1930, II, p. 29 (= edition 1992, II, pp. 36–7); on that liberal cultural atmosphere, see also Yāqūt 1991, III, pp. 242–4. For another translation and some remarks, see Tobi 2004, pp. 33, 62. On the atmosphere of freethinking in Basra and on the participants in such gatherings, see also Ibn Warraq 2003, pp. 254–6, who uses the historical materials for his own purposes. Ibn Warraq (b. 1946) is the pen name of a secularist author of Pakistani origin and founder of the Institute for the Secularization of Islamic Society; he believes that the great Islamic civilizations of the past were established in spite of the Qur'ān, not because of it, and that only a secularized Islam can deliver Muslim states from "fundamentalist madness." On the

Nowhere in the historical chronicles about Cairo, and nowhere in its literary heritage, can we find a similar text. Notwithstanding that the glorious and multicultural cosmopolitan image of Baghdad concealed a day-to-day reality of a city which suffered from all kinds of difficulties and troubles, just like any other medieval city, its cosmopolitan nature has remained in the Arab cultural imagination for many centuries. European travelers visiting Baghdad during the sixteenth and seventeenth centuries reported that, although several of its quarters were neglected, the city was a center of commerce with a cosmopolitan and international atmosphere, where three main languages (Arabic, Persian, and Turkish) were spoken. Even during the 1920s and 1930s, as well as during the 1960s, Baghdad was known for its remarkable religious tolerance, multicultural cosmopolitan atmosphere, and ability to bear witness to the peaceful coexistencce of all of its inhabitants.[37] Also, unlike Casanova, from whose book he borrows the term "republic of letters," al-Musawi argues that the pervasive Islamic consciousness that takes the Arabic language as its pivotal point seems more important here than a metropolitan-peripheral demarcation:

> Under precarious and ever-shifting politics, centers at any given time may be replaced by other centers, and scholars are compelled to develop their own counterstrategies in a vast Islamic domain where theological studies hold sway. Thus, the issue of centers and peripheries is secondary in relation to cultural activity (p. 2).

Apart from the premise that the very use of the term "republic of letters" demands the adoption of the center-periphery binary, it seems unlikely that the issue of centers and peripheries could be "secondary in relation to cultural activity" in any "republic of letters." Studies of the hierarchy of cultural activities indicate that the very idea of any literary or cultural system is based on the hypothesis that all cultural activities should be taken into account—those of the center as well as those of the periphery—and that the activities within a periphery, any periphery, essentially differ from those at the center.[38] According to Casanova's study, which provided the theoretical foundations for al-Musawi's book, Paris established itself as the city with the most literary prestige on the face of the earth: "The exceptional concentration of *literary* sources that occurred in Paris over the course of several centuries

open debate in the classical Muslim world, which included the Jews, see also Fischel 1938, pp. 181–7; Baron 1957, V, pp. 83–5; MacDonald 1960 [1903], p. 194; al-Ḥumaydī 1989, I, pp. 175–6; and Wasserstrom 1995, p. 113 and the references in n. 71.

37 Duclos 2012, pp. 391–401. See also Snir 2013, pp. 5–8.

38 As proposed in my present book on pp. 19–34.

gradually led to its recognition as the center of the *literary* world."[39] Quoting this very sentence, al-Musawi writes that "such description is no less applicable to Cairo; it stood to the postclassical Islamic world as Paris stood to Europe" (p. 7), but no scholar of Arab-Islamic civilization can testify to that. Moreover, al-Musawi does not refer to only *literary* texts and activities, stating that his "interdisciplinary critique conforms to a contemporaneous definition of the term *adab*, one through which aesthetics, the sciences, and crafts of professions transform the cultural landscape at the same time as they undergo ruptures and shifts" (p. 14). In Chapter Six, al-Musawi quotes the definition offered by George Makdisi (1920–2002) for the very same term:

> *Adab* is a field of knowledge by virtue of which mutual understanding is achieved; it is acquired through word-signs and writing. The word and writing are its subject-matter as part of their role in the communication of ideas. The benefit of *adab* is that it discloses intentions in the mind of one person and communicates them to another, whether present or absent. *Adab* is the ornament of both tongue and fingertips. By virtue of *adab* man is distinguished from the animals. I have begun with the concept of *adab* because it is the first element of perfection; he who is devoid of it will not achieve perfection through another human mode of perfection (pp. 180–1).[40]

Al-Musawi adds the following:

> The term *adab* refers to both a field and a practice, meaning that there is a littérateur, *adīb*, who is distinctly different from the "scientist" or *ʿālim*, especially when both terms can be inclusive of all learned people [...] Throughout the course of Islamic history and before the advent of a European modernity, the term *adab* as literature was inclusive of poetry and prose but not restricted to them. Its semantic field included refinement and good manners, in the tradition of the notion of belles-lettres, while at the same time partaking of an all-inclusive network of knowledge with no specific boundaries. It was only with the arrival of European modernity through colonization or incorporation that *adab* became institutionalized as a term referring specifically to literary writing, a process mediated through colleges fashioned after French and British models, all the way to the Higher Teachers' Colleges in Egypt and later Baghdad. Those colleges also happened to include among their graduates the most influential literary figures associated with literary modernity (pp. 181–2).[41]

39 Casanova 2004, p. 54 (my emphasis).

40 Makdisi 1990, p. 93. It is quoted from *Kitāb Irshād al-Qāṣid ilā Asnā al-Maqāṣid* by Muḥammad ibn Ibrāhīm Ibn al-Akfānī (d. 1348) (Ibn al-Akfānī 1998, p. 18).

41 For other references and indications for the term *adab*, see also al-Musawi 2015b, pp. 369–70, n.7. See also Makdisi 1981, pp. 79, 214, 306–7, 309; and the numerous mentions in Makdisi 1990 (see index).

Unlike Casanova, and because there is no equation between belles-lettres and *adab* in its premodern sense, al-Musawi argues that the premodern Islamic republic is not merely *literary*.[42] In respect to *adab* in its *modern* sense—the *literary* dimensions of cultural production—one can perhaps agree that Cairo in the modern period, at least during the first half of the twentieth century,[43] stood in relation to the Arab world as Paris did to Europe. However, there is no consensus between scholars regarding Cairo as the *literary* center throughout the time span of the post-classical Islamic era, particularly against the backdrop of the fragmentization of the Arab literary center after the fall of Baghdad.

Fourth: the corpus. As indicated above, the "extensive corpus" of texts which al-Musawi examined "through various lenses" (p. 8), and the potential texts which he considered as belonging to the "republic," do not include only *literary* texts, as we have just seen from al-Musawi's definition of the term *adab*. When the texts al-Musawi deals with are *literary*—whatever definition of the term is adopted—they are in fact largely limited to what I describe in the present book as non-canonical. Indeed, because of the diglossia of the Arabic language, there is no doubt that the literary production in *ʿāmmīyya* should be an important part of the Arabic corpus in any "Islamic republic of letters." Such non-canonical production has unfortunately been largely ignored by most "canonical" scholarship, and al-Musawi rightly does not ignore it. From this point of view, al-Musawi's study is very important, especially in its concentration on such texts within their relevant contexts and against the backdrop of the traditional scholarship. Arabic underwent, according to al-Musawi, "some of its most serious transformations, in the form of non-classical modes and practices" as well as the "upsurge of the so-called *ʿāmmī* (colloquial) poetry" (p. 7). And also: "There was an equally large production of works of *lesser merit* over these centuries, which were intended to nourish a broad populace in quest of knowledge" (p. 11, my emphasis). Al-Musawi emphasizes that these activities "are no less foundational for cultural capitals than the belletristic cultural tradition" (p. 50) and that along with bringing canonical works into communal use—poetry and rhetoric "are no longer

[42] There is a view that the "Arabic concept of *adab* carries much the same sense as eighteenth-century French literature: "learning and good breeding" (D'haen et al. 2013, p. 321).

[43] See Snir 2005a, p. 75, n. 192. See also the aforementioned findings that come out of the special project initiated by the Egyptian magazine *al-Risāla* in 1936: Writers from all over the Arab world were asked to report on the state of the "literary life" (*al-ḥayāt al-adabiyya*) in their region. This report was published in successive issues; most of the reports mentioned the central status of Egypt in Arabic culture and the marginality of other regions (above, pp. 151n, 168n).

the monopoly of the elite" (pp. 166–7). The cultural creativity of the "street" (quotation marks in the original) and popular responses are mentioned as "part of this vibrant encounter and unfolding" within the "republic of letters" as "opposed to scholars and other elites" (for example, pp. 9, 43, 62), that is, popular performances in public urban spaces such as markets, mosques, hospices, and colleges, as well as Sufi *dhikr*, mourning rituals, festivities, and epics (along with an increasing awareness in compendiums of such activities) (pp. 17–18, 48–50, 79, 120, 270–2, 298–303). All these activities allude to the "democratization of space as a central characteristic of the republic of letters" (p. 43) and the "increasing power of the Arab-Islamic street" (pp. 119–20).[44] Also, the "street," understood as the language of common people, "made its way into the writing and compilations of highly recognized scholars and poets" (p. 245). The "street" is "the stage on which the body and its physiological expressions in terms of eating and drinking practices are given free rein, which takes them far beyond normative conservative restraints" (p. 286). According to al-Musawi, the republic of letters transcends the boundaries of learned scholars and reaches into the very fringes of society:

> Nonclassical poetic subgenres, especially the ones with street registers, cover the lands of Islam from Andalusia and North Africa to Musul in the North of Iraq and bring into circulation words, images, and rhythms that also raise serious questions regarding the efforts of current scholarship to assign specific geographical and territorial locations and identities to popular literature (p. 134).

The republic of letters "was forced to expand its parameters so as to host the street, and it did so in the relative absence of the court, whose role as a literary and cultural center had diminished since the decline of the caliphate" (p. 263). Unfortunately, none of the book's chapters concentrate on the genres of *zajal* or *muwashshaḥ*. Also, various popular cultural activities such as the semi-theatrical entertainment in this period should have been mentioned.[45] One of the literary works included in the non-canonical corpus al-Musawi examined is the *Thousand and One Nights*, on which he had already published extensively,[46] but he uses these stories only for thematic purposes

[44] On "street poetry," see al-Musawi 2015b, pp. 263–70.

[45] See, for example, Moreh 1992; and Snir 1993, pp. 149–70. Al-Musawi mentions incidentally and cursorily the assemblies and memorial processions and practices to commemorate the tragedy at the Battle of Karbalā' in AD 680, which "possessed sufficient resilience to resist elite censorship or repression," and scholars tend to regard them as being separate from literate culture. Brief mentions are also made of several popular epics (pp. 48–50) and of *khayāl al-ẓill* (puppet shadow theater) (p. 26).

[46] See, for example, al-Musawi 1981; al-Mūsawī 1986; al-Mūsawī 2000; al-Musawi 2009b; and al-Mūsawī 2016. On the growth of modern Arabic fiction against the background of the increasing interest in *Thousand and One Nights*, see also al-Musawi 2003.

such as for "a testimony to the power of knowledge" (p. 12). When referring to their "successful entry into Europe" (pp. 12, 311), it should have been noted that their entry into Europe would later be the cause for the gradual change of its status in the Arabic literary system.[47]

The emergence of popular genres and the achievements of the "street" poets and writers in the post-classical era justify the rejection of the Orientalist discourse regarding the decadence and decline of Arab culture during this period.[48] That very Orientalist discourse reflects the paradigm that sees political changes as pivotal in their effects on cultural life. For example, the destruction of Baghdad in 1258 by Hulagu has been unjustifiably engraved on the Arabs' memory as the fundamental reason for the destruction of their great medieval civilization and the cause of its cultural stagnation until the renaissance (*Nahḍa*) in the nineteenth century.[49] Prompted by European Orientalists, Arabs placed emphasis on the descriptions of the killing of many of the scholars and men of letters by the Mongol army, the destruction of cultural institutions, the burning of libraries, and the throwing of books into the Tigris and the using of these books as a bridge to cross the river. While I was writing the introduction for *Baghdad—The City in Verse* (2013), I encountered many such texts in historical books, literary histories, as well as in poetry and prose. Furthermore, modern Arab officials have used the devastation caused by Hulagu for their own aims as did, for example, the late Egyptian president Gamal 'Abd al-Nasir (1918–70). Also, a high-level Syrian government official was quoted as saying, "in deadly earnest," that "if the Mongols had not burnt the libraries of Baghdad in the thirteenth century, we Arabs would have had so much science, that we would long since have invented the atomic bomb. The plundering of Baghdad put us back centuries."[50]

The emphasis laid by al-Musawi on non-canonical literature is a very fresh approach to the scholarship of Arabic literature, and the present study provides the rationale and reasoning for the inclusion of non-canonical production from the point of view of aesthetic legitimization and from the point of view of the attitude of the actual people who are constituent of Arabic cul-

[47] See references to this work above, pp. 90–7.

[48] He mentions briefly and without any detailed elaboration popular epics such as *Sayf ibn Dhī Yazan*, *al-Amīra Dhāt al-Himma*, *al-Sīra al-Hilāliyya*, and *al-Ẓāhir Baybars* (p. 50), the colloquial *mawwāl* (p. 96), and the *zajal* (p. 126).

[49] On this, see Allen 2006, p.13: "[W]ithin a literary-historical context the year 1258 cannot serve as a useful divide [...] the most significant processes of change in that context belong to an earlier period."

[50] On Hulagu's destruction of Baghdad and what has been engraved on the Arabs' memory (with references), see Snir 2013, pp. 26–31.

ture.[51] Nevertheless, the "layered structure," according to al-Musawi, which held together the "seemingly disparate modes of writing, rewriting, compilation, revision, commentary, and disputation in nearly every field of knowledge" (p. 8), seems to be incomplete and unbalanced, as there is almost no mention of what was considered in the premodern period to be *canonical* poetry and prose. This absence in such an important study that aspires to explore "the large-scale and *diverse* cultural production in Arabic in the post-classical era" (my emphasis) is unjustifiable, certainly when it is expected to inspire the new generation of scholars of premodern Arabic literature. A brief look at the contents of *Arabic Literature in the Post-Classical Period* (2006) reveals the wealth of "elite poetry" and "elite prose" that existed side by side with "popular poetry" and "popular prose."[52] Thomas Bauer's contributions in this regard are very much important as well.[53]

Fifth: the "revolutionary vernacularizing thrust." Al-Musawi argues that the concentration of scholars, authors, and copyists in Cairo and other Islamic centers valorized Arabic but also prompted what he calls, based on Casanova's conceptions, the "revolutionary vernacularizing thrust that was noticeable throughout the Islamic world." Al-Musawi refers to that "thrust" as making

> heavy use of lexical transmission, appropriation, and transference of Arabic grammar, rhetoric, and poetics. National languages also brought into Arabic their own distinctive traits [...] Arabic itself underwent some of its most serious transformations, in the form of nonclassical modes and practices that were theorized by several prominent scholars, and in the upsurge of the so-called *ʿāmmī* (colloquial) poetry. Hence, in spite of linguistic divergence, a common Islamic literary, theological, and symbolic field emerged that warrants the present discussion of an Islamic republic of letters. The massive production that has unsettled Arab modernists attests to this cultural space (p. 7).

I will refer below to al-Musawi's argument that "the massive production [has] unsettled Arab modernists" and only concentrate here on al-Musawi's different approach to the "vernacularizing thrust." Casanova, based on the work of Benedict Anderson,[54] speaks of the "revolutionary vernacularizing thrust of capitalism" as the first stage in the genesis of world literary space that "saw the exclusive use of Latin among educated men give way first to a demand for intellectual recognition of vulgar tongues, then to the creation of modern

51 See above, pp. 14–19.
52 Allen and Richards 2006, pp. v–vi. See also Allen 2006, pp. 17–21.
53 See, for example, Bauer 2005, pp. 105–32; Bauer 2007, pp. 137–67.
54 Anderson 1991, p. 39.

literatures claiming to compete with the grandeur of ancient literatures."[55] The second major stage in the enlargement of the literary world, according to Casanova, corresponds to the "philological–lexicographic revolution" that saw the appearance in Europe of new nationalist movements associated with the invention or reinvention of national languages and the creation of popular literatures. The final stage was the process of decolonization "marking the entry into international competition of contestants who until then had been prevented from taking part."[56] Nothing of these three stages exists in al-Musawi's analysis of the genesis of world *Islamic* literary space. Here it is instructive to refer to Abdelfattah Kilito's important observation regarding the subdivision of the literary output in the post-classical period because it is relevant in the present context:

> To us it seems more appropriate to regard Arabic poetics on its own terms and so to avoid treating the subject as some kind of deviation from a model realized in other times and under other skies. The governing principle should be derived from characteristics that are intrinsic to it, not those of works from some other poetics.[57]

Sixth: the role of Sufism. Al-Musawi frequently mentions the challenge posed to dominant ways of thought through the agency of Sufism because it "involved a liberated sensibility in a loving God's universe" and because it was "a challenge to official schools of thought since it disturbs and unsettles their paradigms of self-righteousness and dogma" (pp. 78–9). Also, "Sufi terminology strips language of its denotative role and sets it free. Words and nature leave their signifiers behind and assume new life in the soaring of the liberated Sufi experience, which may be seen as a partial anticipation of *postmodern musings on madness and poetry*" (pp. 142–3, my emphasis). Sufi orders as well

[55] Casanova 2004, pp. 47–8.

[56] Casanova 2004, p. 48.

[57] Kilito 1983, p. 136. Translation according to Allen 2006, p. 20. For Arabic translation, see Kilito 1993, p. 114. Cf. Phillips 2008, p. 297 regarding the attempt to apply Gérard Genette's model of hypertextuality to Najīb Maḥfūẓ's *Malḥamat al-Ḥarāfish* (1977). For the need for "homegrown modernity" and the issue of extroversion and introversion, see Helgesson 2015, pp. 253–60. See also Ricci 2011; unlike al-Musawi who posits his analysis as a counter-narrative to the European impact on Arabic literary modernity, Ricci deals with the inter-Asian travels of Arabic and brings into focus an Arabic cosmopolis in South and Southeast Asia (cf. Ganguly 2015, pp. 278–9). See also Thomas Bauer's suggestion concerning the need to "listen patiently to Mamluk authors and carefully analyze their texts, to elucidate their own aesthetic standards, and judge their texts by this rather than apply a yardstick of heroism that does not match the participational aesthetics of the Mamluk middle class" (Bauer 2013, pp. 21–2. Cf. Bauer 2007, p. 144).

> turned Sufism into a poetic enterprise and practice in a God-loving universe [...] its significance for the republic of letters extends even beyond its deconstruction of the prosaic and the mundane; for its striking freedom and newness in vision and illumination also necessarily downplay structures of authority and power (p. 309).

Because I extensively wrote on the intersection between Arabic literature and Sufism from the latter's rise until the second half of the twentieth century, suffice it to say here that one must distinguish between the role of early Sufism in reviving Arab society and culture, the various literary genres included, and the negative phenomena attributed to Sufi orders, especially in the premodern period.[58] I will elaborate more on this topic in the study I plan to write in response to al-Musawi's book.

Seventh: culture, scholarship, and accountability. Al-Musawi's book has been nominated for the 2016 Sheikh Zayed Book Award for "Arabic Culture in Other Languages" because

> it presents a compelling argument against the commonly held opinion that Arabic literature, since the glorious peak of the Abbasids, has somehow failed to be modern, and instead became locked in conventions that were stultifying and rarefied, created only for a small circle of initiates who were themselves censored and censuring.[59]

In his endorsement of the book, Roger Allen writes that al-Musawi's study refutes "the orientalist-inspired notion of a 'period of decadence' in the Arabo-Islamic cultural heritage [...] With al-Musawi's work, the medieval Arabo-Islamic 'slough of despond'—to cite Bunyan's well-known English phrase—can, one hopes, be forever laid to rest." And al-Musawi is absolutely right in his rejection of the aforementioned paradigm that sees political changes as pivotal in their effects on cultural life; in fact, he argues, there was not any cultural decline but only "political disintegration." However, scholarship aside, one cannot ignore al-Musawi's sharply critical attitude throughout many sections of his book toward those he calls "Arab and Muslim modernists" or "architects of [Arab] modernity," who, according to al-Musawi, failed to dissociate the "political disintegration" from "the ongoing cultural dissemination and exchange across the Islamic world" (p. 11; see also p. 144). He accuses them of misreading their past (p. 5), of

58 See my publications in the References, especially Snir 1986; Snir 2002; and Snir 2006. On the Sufi experience and on "musings on madness and poetry," which are not necessarily postmodern, see Snir 1993b, pp. 74–88.

59 According to <http://www.middle-east-online.com/english/?id=75978> (17 July 2016) (last accessed 27 October 2016).

falling back "on a series of negations and denials of [its] merit" (pp. 308–9), and of internalizing the "European Enlightenment disparagement of the Middle Ages [...] in their zealous duplication of a seductive Europe" (p. 15). The failure to connect effectively with the rich culture of the past and to establish emotive and cultural links with the Muslim populace, according to al-Musawi, can "easily induce *architects of regression* to involve regions and peoples in schisms and disorder" (p. 11, my emphasis). Al-Musawi also holds the "modernists" accountable for the failed education system in the newly emerging *Islamic* nation-states because of the "depreciation of pre-modern Arabic cultural production" which "amounts to a substantial disengagement from a tradition that was much needed for the promotion of education and culture in the newly emerging *Islamic* nation-states" (p. 45, my emphasis). In short, the experienced reader has the feeling that in his book al-Musawi functions not only as a scholar and literary critic but as an active participant in Arab cultural life and, moreover, as an integral part of the Arab-Islamic community in its struggle against foreign powers and their internal collaborators.[60]

Unlike most Western scholars of Arabic literature, al-Musawi could be seen as somewhat justified in his effacement of the borders between research and participation in a culture. Al-Musawi is now an integral part of the Western community of scholars and critics of Arabic literature that warmly adopted him and, moreover, made him one of its doyens, perhaps the first one. Born in al-Nāṣiriyya in Iraq in 1944, and having obtained his PhD from Dalhousie University in Nova Scotia, Canada, in 1978, al-Musawi now holds the prestigious Chair for Arabic Literature at Columbia University. Since 1999 he has been a member of the editorial board of the *Journal of Arabic Literature* (*JAL*), the only professional journal dedicated to the study of Arabic literature, and in recent years he has been serving as its general editor. Before moving to the West, physically, metaphorically, and spiritually, al-Musawi had been for more than two decades an integral part of literary, cultural, academic Arab life and its *jumhūr* of *littérateurs*, sensing its vibrant rhythm and vivacious beating heart, feeling its pains, and looking for ways to push it forward. As an active writer, he published five Arabic novels, and

[60] More than forty years earlier, al-Musawi published a book on Iraqi oil, the struggle with the oil companies, and "the great robbery of the Iraqi people's treasures" (al-Mūsawī 1973. The quotation is from p. 7). Reading now both books, one can sense the parallel lines, according to al-Musawi, between the material and spiritual robbery of Arab-Islamic treasures and the role of the "modernists" in such a robbery on the intellectual level (Cf. al-Mūsawī 1973a, pp. 5–10; al-Mūsawī 1993; al-Mūsawī 2001; and al-Mūsawī 2005, pp. 63–9). Al-Musawi plans to publish a monograph on *Arab Modernists' Struggle with the Past* (according to al-Musawi 2015a, p. 282).

as a scholar he published numerous scholarly books and articles in Arabic. He taught at major Arab universities such as Baghdad University, Amman National University, San'a University, Tunis University, and the American University of Sharjah. Also, he played a dominant role in government cultural institutions in Baghdad, serving as the director of the publishing house Dār al-Shu'ūn al-Thaqāfiyya al-'Āmma, the president of the board of directors of another publishing house al-Adīb al-'Arabī, and the editor-in-chief of the journal *Istishrāq*.[61] He also served as the editor-in-chief of *Āfāq 'Ārabiyya* in Tunis.

But who are those "modernists" whom al-Musawi holds accountable for the failed education system in the newly emerging Islamic nation-states? And with whom does al-Musawi debate, sometimes less as an unbiased literary critic and historian and more as an active proponent with a very clear agenda for the present and particularly for the future? In his *Preliminary Discourse*, al-Musawi mentions the prominent writers and intellectuals Aḥmad Ḥasan al-Zayyāt (1885–1968), Salāma Mūsā (1887–1958), and Ṭāhā Ḥusayn (1889–1973), who "have long internalized a European Enlightenment discourse and looked with suspicion and distrust in the past and its massive accumulation in cultural capital" (p. 5). At the end of Chapter One, al-Musawi refers to the "hasty conclusions of the kind often encountered in the writings of many Arab and Afro-Asian modernists" (p. 58), but he did not mention any other names apart from the three names mentioned above, all of them Egyptian.[62] In what follows, I will respectfully disagree with al-Musawi's position not as a proponent of any agenda, of course, but as a student of Arabic literature who has read most, if not all, of his writings and of those of the three "modernists" he named.

I previously referred to the unjustifiable attitude of some Orientalists to premodern Arabic literature at large as a "period of decadence," but nowhere could I find in the writings of al-Zayyāt, Mūsā, or Ḥusayn any sweeping

61 Al-Musawi's brother 'Azīz al-Sayyid Jāsim (1941–91) was executed in prison upon the orders of Ṣaddām Ḥusayn (for his profile, see al-Musawi 2006b, pp. 144–6. On his views, see the same book, which is dedicated to his memory). Al-Musawi himself, who served in his various positions in Iraq under Ṣaddām Ḥusayn, was accused, for no fault of his own, of collaborating with the regime, even after the murder of his brother (see the reactions of readers to a report on al-Musawi, especially comments 2 and 7, at <http://www.alarabiya.net/articles/2011/07/14/157569.html> [14 July 2011] [last accessed 27 October 2016]).

62 On p. 111, al-Musawi mentions the Egyptian Jurī Zaydān (1861–1914) as well. In an interview before the publication of his book, al-Musawi argues that the project of the Arab *Nahḍa* failed because of "the rupture between the rural areas (*rīf*) and the city, namely, the intellectual started to deem himself above his roots and despise them, like what Ṭāhā Ḥusayn has done in *al-Ayyām* (*The Days*)" (<https://www.alaraby.co.uk/portal> [21 October 2014] [last accessed 27 October 2016]). For an earlier version of al-Musawi's accusations against the "modernists," see al-Musawi 2013, pp. 51–2.

statements, as al-Musawi attributes to them, that the *whole* "literary output of the medieval Arab and Islamic nation-states is *ineffectual*" (p. 5, my emphasis).[63] Sensing that literary sensitivity should be altered in order to enable an overhaul of Arabic literature, they indeed rejected some literary values of the post-classical period but did this following previous writers who had in various ways already expressed their criticism of the state of the culture in their own era. One of these writers was Yūsuf al-Shirbīnī (1591?–1688), whose *Kitab Hazz al-Quhūf bi-Sharḥ Qaṣīd Abī Shādūf* (*Brains Confounded by the Ode of Abū Shādūf Expounded*)[64] is a humorous account of the lifestyles and habits of speech of peasants during the period of Ottoman rule in Egypt in a mixture of genres, styles, and diction. Writing that this work "plays havoc with a solid canon that staunchly adhered to verisimilitude and truth, while at the same time enrolling in its ranks jurists of disputable and unreliable knowledge" (p. 83), al-Musawi himself refers to its "dashing satire on elitism, pedantry in scholarship, and the compendious and commentarial surplus, and its biting irony directed toward certain religious circles and sham Sufism" (p. 96).

Referring to the "modernists" as the "reluctant heirs" of the medieval body of knowledge, al-Musawi argues that their "disillusion with [that] cultural production was primarily informed by a European discourse but was also driven by a misreading of the compendious and commentarial effort of the period." He explains that they

> could not discern the significant redirection of cultural capital to escape imitation, while simultaneously assimilating ancient and classical knowledge. In fact, by appropriating and classifying these sources rather than duplicating them, postclassical scholars and littérateurs embarked on what Pascale Casanova terms a "diversion of assets" (p. 5).

63 In a detailed note, al-Musawi quotes publications by the "modernists" which are intended to prove that they "looked at with suspicion and distrust in the [medieval Arab, and Islamic] past and its massive accumulation in cultural capital" (al-Musawi 2015b, p. 324, n. 10. Sahar Ishtiaque Ullah [2016, pp. 203–25] duplicates al-Musawi's arguments, accusing the "modernists" of "misreading of a massive corpus of evidence and at worst a deliberate neglect of an incredibly vast undertaking of postclassical literary production"). Checking closely those references, it is difficult to find how the relevant writings could support these sweeping arguments; suffice it here to mention Mūsā 1947, pp. 75–80; Mūsā 1962, pp. 137–41; al-Jābirī 1982, pp. 34–8; as well as what is cited in Allen 2006, pp. 14–15. One can find citations of Arab intellectuals who found themselves confronting the dilemmas of the cultural transformation that followed the interaction of the Arab world with the West (see, for example, Amīn 1965, p. 7. Cf. Allen 2006, p. 2). However, even these citations should not be taken literally, but as another indication of the aforementioned decline of the Arabs' cultural self-image and the huge gap between the august status enjoyed by Arab culture in the Middle Ages and its feeble modern counterpart.

64 See al-Shirbīnī 2005; and al-Shirbīnī 2007. On al-Shirbīnī's work, see al-Musawi 2015b, pp. 147–74. See also Peled 1986, pp. 57–75; Abū Fāshā 1987; and Omri 2000, pp. 169–96.

First, al-Musawi's argument that a "seductive Europe" was the root of all evil and the driving force behind the "modernists" in their role as "architects of regression" by internalizing the "European Enlightenment disparagement of the Middle Ages" does not, to say the least, do Arab culture any justice. Kilito's aforementioned call "to regard Arabic poetics on its own terms" and "to avoid treating the subject as some kind of deviation from a model realized in other times and under other skies" should guide us here as well. Tarek El-Ariss refers directly to al-Musawi's thesis, including the latter's argument about the *Nahḍa* as "the other appellation for Arab modernity,"[65] suggesting that the *Nahḍa* texts be freed from the *Nahḍa* as a "'modernity' project" and from "the dominant narrative of rise and decline, and from their intertextual and ideological dependency on European modernity as a model to be borrowed or resisted." El-Ariss argues that the *Nahḍa*'s "civilizational practices could not be reduced to notions of civilization associated with Orientalism as [a] system of othering and cultural superiority," referring to it as "this potential, this vague thing that everyone is practicing without knowing what it looks like or whether it will be achieved or not or to what end." It is a speech act: Let there be *Nahḍa*! Therefore, there is a need to decolonize the *Nahḍa* and "allow it to make its own meaning, however contradictory and inconsistent with historical narratives and ideological critique."[66]

Second, The term "diversion of [literary] assets"[67] is used by Casanova, following Joachim du Bellay (1522–60), to refer to the redirection of "the gains of Latinist humanism—a vast collection of knowledge derived from translation and commentaries on ancient texts" to the profit of French, a language that was less "rich." As a result, by the time of Louis XIV France reigned as the "dominant literary power in Europe."[68] Nothing similar to that happened in the medieval Islamic republic of letters if only for the simple reason that, to use Casanova's words, the gains of Arab classical humanism, though helping other Muslim nations consolidate their cultures, were by no means used to

65 Al-Musawi 2014, p. 265.

66 El-Ariss 2015, pp. 260–6; the quotations are from pp. 261, 264, 265, 266. In his response to El-Ariss' intervention, al-Musawi (2015a) does not respond directly to El-Ariss' major arguments regarding the *Nahḍa*, but mainly reiterates his accusations against the "modernists," who were those "prominent intellectuals [who] thought of themselves as leaders of thought like the European Enlightenment figures, locating themselves in that European moment of a century earlier, cutting themselves doubly from their immediate history and the challenge to the age of reason brought about by the rising imperial culture of nineteenth-century Europe" (p. 281).

67 Casanova 2004, p. 54. Casanova uses as well the terms "diversion of literary wealth" (p. 46), "diversion of [literary/symbolic] capital" (pp. 53, 99, 157, 235, 284) and "diversion of resources" (p. 233).

68 Casanova 2004, pp. 53–4.

the benefit of another single specific language in a way that would result in establishing a new dominant literary power replacing the dominance of Arabic. Furthermore, even if we adopt al-Musawi's use of Casanova's conception, as far as I know no "modernist," certainly not al-Zayyāt, Mūsā, or Ḥusayn, has ever decried those works that successfully assimilated ancient and classical knowledge while redirecting cultural capital to escape imitation. They have rightly decried texts that, in al-Musawi's words, failed in the act of "redirection of cultural capital to escape imitation." If there is any blame to be leveled against the "modernists," it is their elitist attitude toward the popular cultural production consumed by the masses, which in turn caused them to decry and even to ignore such texts and activities.[69] According to the conceptions adopted in my present study, and in that I completely agree with al-Musawi, texts and activities of this nature should be considered as an integral part of any cultural system.

In a passionate apologetic section entitled "The Fight for Culture: Compendiums and Commentaries" (pp. 97–103), al-Musawi denounces the "modernists" for their tendency to negate rhetoric as superfluity and denigrate the tradition of commentaries and compendia in the premodern Arab-Islamic period (pp. 98–99, 118). Emphasizing the importance of the tradition of *shurūḥ* (commentaries), *dhuyūl* (supplements), and *ḥawāshin* (marginal notes)—"a paper empire, of words on words, and *kalām 'alā kalām* (metadiscourse)"[70]—which flourished during the post-classical period, al-Musawi takes refuge in Michel Foucault's (1926–84) *The Order of Things: An Archaeology of the Human Sciences* (French: *Les mots et les choses: Une archéologie des sciences humaines*) (1966).[71] After Foucault, al-Musawi quotes Michel de Montaigne (1533–92): "There is more work in interpreting interpretations than in interpreting things; and more books about books than on any other subject; we do nothing but write glosses about each other." Foucault comments on de Montaigne's words: "These words are not a statement of the bankruptcy of culture buried beneath its own monuments; they are a definition of the inevitable relation that language maintained with itself in the sixteenth century." Al-Musawi argues that Foucault's analysis is an attempt to define commentary and gloss as the infinite proliferation of the interpretation that justifies what Foucault describes as the "sovereignty of an original text." It is the text "that offers its ultimate revelation as the promised reward of the commentary." Thus, it is the "interstice occurring between the primal Text and the infinity of Interpretation" that accounts

69 Ṭāhā Ḥusayn opposed the dialects in literature; see above, pp. 28–32.
70 Cf. Yaḥyāwī 2015.
71 Al-Musawi relies on Foucault 1966, pp. 38–46 ("The Writing of Things").

for the proliferation in interpretation, commentary, and gloss, which take writing to be a substantial part of the "fabric of the world."[72] Al-Musawi relies as well on Jorge Luis Borges' (1899–1986) idea of "a minutely drawn map that negates the original" and Christine Brooke-Rose's (1923–2012) argument that "disclaiming rhetoric is itself a figure of rhetoric" (p. 118). He suggests that the "strikingly widespread recourse to compendiums, the rise of the polymath, and the vogue of *shurūḥ*, of explications of an original text, all suggest a process in which designated classification and centers of institutionalized knowledge were being undermined" (p. 132). In short, arguing that the "lengthy pre-modern era remains relatively understudied, especially in terms of what Brinkley Messick associates with a 'calligraphic state,'" (p. 98), al-Musawi makes use of texts by Foucault, Borges, and Brooke-Rose in defense of the tradition of commentaries and compendia of the premodern Arab-Islamic period.

These texts, however, by no means support al-Musawi's arguments, but, for lack of space, I will make here only a few short comments: First, it seems that Messick's "calligraphic state" is irrelevant to al-Musawi' arguments. Messick traces "connections between the literary processes behind the constitution of authority *in* texts and the social and political processes involved in articulating the authority of texts." The specific types of text involved in Messick's research activity, intended to contribute to the specific history of Yemen, are basic manuals of *sharīʿa* jurisprudence and their commentaries.[73] Second, there is a substantial difference between sixteenth-century European commentaries according to Montaigne and the *shurūḥ* tradition.[74] Moreover, the "modernists" voiced their criticism in real time when they were endeavoring to change the face of Arab culture and save it from what they considered to be the negative phenomena of the premodern tradition; al-Musawi's criticism of them is possible thanks to their efforts. Third, Yūsuf al-Shirbīnī's aforementioned *Kitab Hazz al-Quhūf bi-Sharḥ Qaṣīd Abī Shādūf* would not have parodied "an ongoing and firmly established *shurūḥ* tradition" (p. 158) unless that tradition had seemed at the time to be superfluous in essence. That is why, even according to al-Musawi, al-Shirbīnī "dislodges the entire practice of these commentaries, not only by creating a distance between a hilarious ode and the commentator, but also by giving himself the freedom to poke fun at many practices that are normally buttressed by serious material or apocryphal detail" (p. 153).

72 Al-Musawi 2015b, pp. 98–9. The quotations are from Foucault 1966, p. 45. For an earlier version of these arguments, see al-Musawi 2013, pp. 51–2.

73 Messick 1993, pp. 1–12.

74 For the discussion of the trends of "compilation and elaboration" in the post-classical period against the backdrop of what had preceded them, see Allen 2006, pp. 8–13.

All in all, al-Musawi speaks assertively against the "modernists" and about their "wholesale" and "sweeping" "resistance," "rejection," and "denigration" of their past and its "cultural values" and "intimidating cultural capital" (pp. 9, 11, 14, 24, 97–8). In one section, he takes refuge in Casanova's book and one of the in-depth reviews of it:

> What is lost on modernists is a simple premise expressed by Casanova in her *The World Republic of Letters*: "It is necessary to be old to have any chance of being modern or of decreeing what is modern." In a review of her book, Joe Cleary puts this point as follows: "Only countries that can claim a venerable and distinguished historical stock of literary capital get to decree what is and is not 'fashionable' in literary terms" (pp. 11–12).[75]

The context of Casanova's aforementioned "premise" is her argument that "the ability to decree without fear of challenge what is or is not 'fashionable,' in the domain of haute couture and elsewhere, permitted Paris to control one of the main routes of access to modernity [...] Paris managed to sustain its position—at least until the 1960s—as the center of the system of literary time." Only then Casanova adds the following:

> The temporal law of the world of letters may be stated thus: *It is necessary to be old to have any chance of being modern or of decreeing what is modern*. In other words, having a long national past is the condition of being able to claim a literary existence that is fully recognized in the present.[76]

In his review of her book, Joe Cleary refers to Casanova's argument, but unfortunately al-Musawi in the quotation above does not quote Cleary's full text:

> In other words, only countries that can claim a venerable and distinguished historical stock of literary capital get to decree what is and is not "fashionable" in literary terms. But, since what constitutes up-to-dateness or the literary present is constantly changing—"the only way in the literary world to be truly modern is to contest the present as outmoded—to appeal to a more present present, as yet unknown, which thus become the newest certified present."[77]

In his attack against the "modernists," al-Musawi argues that they did not understand what Casanova describes as the "temporal law of the world of letters," namely, the condition of being able to claim a literary existence that is fully recognized in the present as having a long national past. But Cleary

[75] See also al-Musawi 2015b, pp. 111–14: "A number of things that are lost on most modernists [...] The enhanced devotion to rhetoric that has engendered so much negative criticism against the so-called age of superfluity" (p. 114. See also pp. 135, 142–3, 159–62).

[76] Casanova 2004, pp. 89–90 (emphasis in the original).

[77] Cleary 2006, pp. 199–200. The quotation is from Casanova 2004, p. 91.

adds that this is because "what constitutes up-to-dateness or the literary present is constantly changing," and here he quotes, with some inaccuracies, Casanova's saying, in a section entitled "What Is Modernity?," that "the only way in the literary *space* to be truly modern is to contest the present as outmoded—to appeal to a *still* more present present, as yet unknown, which thus becomes the newest certified present."[78] In other words, contrary to what al-Musawi attributes to the "modernists," they did exactly what Casanova recommends—they tried to contest the outmoded present by appealing to another present in order to make it "the newest certified present." Also, when Casanova speaks about the "fashionable" in literary terms, she is only referring to belles-lettres.[79]

In any event, al-Musawi's book is thought-provoking and an eye-opener for scholars, but at the same time it acts as an incentive to ponder his motivation beyond mere scholarship. He refers to the "Islamic constellation of knowledge as a movement with its own identifiable features and regenerative processes that *could have nourished the present and led it safely out of wars, disasters, and colonial incursions*" (p. 306, my emphasis). And he alludes to "complexity, diversity, and magnitude of medieval cultural production, which has daunted modernists and their counterparts in the West and caused them to fall back on a series of negations and denials of merit" (pp. 308–9). He accuses the "modernists" of depreciating certain "Islamic practices" and of considering them to be "regressive and hence not conductive to progress and modernity" (p. 310). Another unjustified charge he levels against the "modernists" is that they adopted a basic equation between secularism, on the one hand, and humanism and modernism, on the other (pp. 310–11). And here, al-Musawi expresses his opposition to the argument presented by Hamid Dabashi that Arab humanism "remained canonical in its commitment to the imperially imposed language of the Arab conquerors and their tribal racism."[80] Al-Musawi has reservations about defining Arab humanism as necessarily being tied to conquest and gain:

> The republic as the dialogic space for poetics and politics claims its freedom from power as the condition for its humanist conversations. Hence, the use of Arabic and the spread of a culturally oriented Islamic identification in no way negate the racial manipulation of genealogical divides to ensure privilege in times of conquest (p. 56).

78 Casanova 2004, p. 91. The words in italics are those which Cleary does not quote Casanova accurately.

79 See the anecdote told by Ṭāhā Ḥusayn about his interview with Shukrī Bāshā, the Sulṭān's *chef de bureau* (*Ra'īs al-Dīwān al-Sulṭānī*) (above, p. 159).

80 Dabashi 2012a, pp. 79–80 (quoted in al-Musawi 2015b, p. 54. See also pp. 40, 46–7, 54–7).

In alluding to Jean Le Rond d'Alembert's (1717–83) *Preliminary Discourse* that accompanied the first volume of Diderot's *Encyclopedia of Arts and Sciences* (1751), al-Musawi's *Preliminary Discourse* is instructive; it shows that al-Musawi is not satisfied with academic investigations alone. In this regard, the final lines of the *Conclusion* (*Al-Khātima*)[81] are illuminating:

> Hence, the long-established Western equation between secularism and humanism needs to be challenged whenever it is applied outside the specific domain of a European Renaissance. *Only through better engagement with this past, with rigorous interrogation of its successes and failures, can modernists build up a sustainable view of the present and thus be at peace with themselves.* Diversity and dissent constitute a marked feature of Islamic culture, one that valorizes and invigorates a republic of letters with its many conspicuous or discrete worlds in what amounts to no less than seismic *Islamica* (p. 311, my emphasis with the exception of the last word).

I disagree with al-Musawi when he accuses the "modernists" of "a substantial disengagement from a tradition that was much needed for the promotion of education and culture" and of failing to engage with their past and build up "a sustainable view of the present." A brief look at the articles Ṭāhā Ḥusayn published in the Egyptian press over almost sixty years gives a completely different picture.[82] However, I leave it for another time to give a detailed response to al-Musawi's arguments and wish to quote on this occasion only some recent lines by Adūnīs, perhaps the greatest of all contemporary Arab "modernists" (not because I agree with all what Adūnīs writes, but in order to illustrate the attitude of contemporary Arab "modernists" toward the premodern period):

> منذ سقوط بغداد وقيام السلطنة العثمانيّة،
> تحوّل الدين إلى مجرّد أداة عنفيّة لخدمة السلطة.
> لا نجد، على سبيل المثل، في تاريخ السلطنة العثمانيّة كلّها، على مدى أكثر من
> أربعة قرون، مفكّراً عربيّاً واحداً، أو فنّاناً واحداً، أو موسيقيّاً واحداً، أو شاعراً واحداً، أو عالماً واحداً.

[81] In his *Khuṭbat al-Kitāb* (*Preliminary Discourse*) (pp. 1–20) and *Al-Khātima* (*Conclusion*) (al-Musawi 2015b, pp. 305–11), al-Musawi imitates, mainly through the wording of the titles he selects, the style of the post-classical Arabic writers as well that of Jean le Rond d'Alembert, who was until 1759 co-editor with Denis Diderot (1713–84) of the *Encyclopédie* (*Encyclopedia of Arts and Sciences*) (1751–72), one of the large collaborative ventures of the republic of letters (see al-Musawi 2015b, p. 323, n. 2, as well as pp. 103, 144).

[82] See *Turāth Ṭāhā Ḥusayn—al-Maqālāt al-Ṣuḥufiyya min 1908–1967* (Cairo: Maṭba'at Dār al-Kutub wa-l-Wathā'iq al-Qawmiyya, 2002). From the numerous articles that refute al-Musawi's accusations, I will mention only two: an article published in *Majallatī* (1 June 1936) entitled "Tanẓīm al-Nahḍa" ("Organizing the Renaissance") (pp. 419–23); and another article published in *Musāmarāt al-Jayb* (18 January 1948) entitled "Mushkilat al-Lughāt al-Ajnabiyya" ("The Issue of Foreign Languages") (pp. 610–11).

هكذا كان لا بدّ من مجيء أتاتورك للأتراك،
ومن أن تبدأ حركة النهوض العربيّ.

Since the fall of Baghdad and the establishment of the Ottoman Sultanate,
Religion has become only a harsh tool in the service of authority.
We do not find, for example, throughout the history of the Ottoman Sultanate, during more than
Four centuries, even one Arab intellectual, or one artist, or one musician, or one poet, or one scientist.
That is why it was necessary that Atatürk would come to the Turks,
And that Arabic renaissance would start.[83]

Notwithstanding al-Musawi's campaign against the "modernists," examining the attitude of Western intellectuals toward Arab culture reveals that Arab culture has been and still is considered extremely marginal in Western eyes. The Arabs themselves are sometimes seen as "one dimensional—a flowing traditional robe, a catchy tune or a subtitled movie about fundamentalism."[84] As I have mentioned before, in spite of a small increase in interest in Arabic literature, particularly since Najīb Maḥfūẓ was awarded the Nobel Prize in 1988, Western attitudes toward the subject remain, in general, somewhat simplistic and patronizing.[85] Arabic literature is consistently denied representation in most multinational anthologies of world literature. Consulting at random some of the numerous American anthologies of world poetry and fiction, Salih J. Altoma rarely finds a representative work from Arabic, though other non-Western literatures are included in them.[86] There are extra-literary considerations which seem "to subvert the 'literary merit' principle when Arabic literature is involved." This negative approach extends at times "to the Arab people and their culture as a whole [...] even where least expected."[87] Emphasizing that American writing on Arabic literature invokes the tenacity of a long-standing prejudice, a fair amount of ignorance, and dominant Eurocentric orientations, Altoma mentions the tendency to judge Arabic literature on the basis of the Western literary canon and the attitude toward Arabic as a "linguistic Iron Curtain."[88] The boom in the

83 Adūnīs, "Madārāt—Lafẓ Yuwaḥḥid wa-'Amal Yubaddid," *al-Ḥayāt*, 29 May 2015.
84 Aboul-Ela 2001, p. 42.
85 See, for example, the contributions in Beard and Haydar 1993.
86 Even in anthologies of modern literatures of the non-Western world, the representation of Arabic authors is negligible and accidental (see, for example, Clerk and Siegel 1995).
87 Altoma 1993, p. 162.
88 Altoma 1993, pp. 165–6. In his polemic "Embargoed Literature," Edward Said spoke about an "iron curtain of indifference and prejudice" that "ruled out any attention to texts that did not reiterate the usual clichés about 'Islam,' violence, sensuality, and so forth" (Said 1990; Said 1994a, p. 374). Referring to Said's polemic, Hosam Aboul-Ela's "Challenging the Embargo: Arabic Literature in the US Market" ends with the following: "For just

study of Arabic in the West, especially in the United States following the attacks of 11 September 2001, has been mostly attributed to military and security needs and not to cultural considerations.[89] Moreover, this boom has not fundamentally changed the attitude toward Arabic as an aesthetically marginal language. In fact, it has sometimes even worsened it, particularly when the massacre of thousands of innocent people is frequently described, in the popular media and elsewhere, as having been motivated by a "barbaric culture."

Najīb Maḥfūẓ himself considered his winning of the Nobel Prize as the world's recognition of Arab culture as a whole,[90] but one can see only slowly increasing visibility for no other author than Maḥfūẓ himself in American publications:[91] beginning with a marginal presence (1950–70), moving toward expanded representation, which was still, however, largely restricted to a scholarly audience (1970–87), all the way to where it is today.[92] In a study published in 1996, Altoma finds that since 1988 contemporary Arabic fiction "has experienced a steadily growing interest among Western publishers and readers."[93] Yet, as I have mentioned earlier, this new interest is mainly due to non-aesthetic reasons.[94] The Egyptian author and literary critic Lūwīs 'Awaḍ (1915–90) argues that even Maḥfūẓ's popularity in the West is mainly due to the sociopolitical value of his works.[95]

One can see some difference between the European and American reception of Arabic literature. While historically enjoying a more visible presence in Europe, even if it is minor,[96] Arabic literature in the United States has been

as Hollywood came to learn that viewers would buy tickets to movies starring African-Americans, and publishers learned to sell magical realism in literature and film, a truer, subtler front can force publishers and curious readers to look at Arabic fiction with new eyes" (Aboul-Ela 2001, p. 44).

89 See, for example, Benjamin Sutherland, *YaleGlobal Online*, 19 January 2005: "Primary motivation for American students of the language is to land a job with a government security agency" (cf. *Herald Tribune*, 15 February 2005).

90 See Lawall 1993, pp. 25, 177, n. 21.

91 For bibliographical documentation relevant to the American reception of Maḥfūẓ, see Altoma 1993, pp. 160–79.

92 Altoma 1993, pp. 165–6.

93 Altoma 1996, p. 137.

94 See above, p. 192.

95 See *al-Muṣawwar*, 11 August 1989, p. 35. For an attempt to refute this claim, see al-Naqqāsh 2006, pp. 62–8. For a list of Maḥfūẓ's translations into English, see Altoma 1993, pp. 169–79 (the bibliography—a. translations; b. book reviews; and c. selected studies, interviews, and other items—is divided into two parts: pre-1988 publications and post-1988 publications). See also Classe 2000, pp. 890–2; and France 2000, pp. 157–8.

96 An example of that visibility is *The Little Black Book: Books. Over a Century of the Greatest Books, Writers, Characters, Passages and Events that Rocked the Literary World* (Daniel 2007), a reference work consisting of one thousand articles by various hands, covering literature from more than sixty countries from the late nineteenth century to the present day.

met "with neglect, indifference, and seemingly *deliberate exclusion* [...] confirming the view that there is perhaps an *inherent hostility* to Arabo-Islamic culture in general."[97] In a special issue of *Michigan Quarterly Review* on the Middle East that he edited in 1992, the Palestinian writer Anton Shammās (b. 1950) explains that "modern Arabic literature is under-represented in the US. Except for quite a few leading authors (Mahfouz, Munif), the uninitiated American reader—unlike the British—is virtually oblivious of the literary scene in the Middle East."[98] One exception, and here there is no difference between the European and American reception of Arabic literature, is the case of *Alf Layla wa-Layla* (*One Thousand and One Nights*), whose popularity probably stems from literary and aesthetic considerations, although one cannot rule out that the "exotic" nature of the stories—as demonstrated by the attitude of the aforementioned Richard Burton (1821–90), the translator of the first unexpurgated English version of the work—played a role in their reception among readers and critics. The circumstances of *Alf Layla wa-Layla*'s translation into various foreign languages and its process of absorption into the Western canon, as presented above, were however quite unique and cannot be applied to Arabic literature in general. For now, the impact of Arabic literature in the West is minimal—the reading of original Arabic literature is still confined mainly to limited circles of intellectuals of Arab origin and scholars.[99] The impact of the growing number of translations—the primary channel of interference and reception—of Arabic literature into foreign languages is limited,[100] and it seems that so far the impact of Arabic literature on Western culture has mainly come from a number of Arab authors moving to write originally in foreign languages.[101] Referred

The articles focus variously on key books, writers, passages, characters, and events, as well as mainstream literature, popular genres, and children's writing. Arabic literature is represented in the book by seven authors: Muḥammad Ḥusayn Haykal (1888–1956) (p. 101), Tawfīq al-Ḥakīm (1898–1987) (p. 238), al-Ṭayyib Ṣāliḥ (1929–2009) (p. 418), Imīl Ḥabībī (1921–96) (p. 555), Idwār al-Kharrāṭ (1926–2015) (p. 596), Alīfa Rifʿat (1930–96) (p. 620), and Yūsuf Idrīs (1927–91) (p. 679), in addition to Ahdaf Soueif (b. 1950), an Egyptian author writing in English (p. 731).

97 Altoma 1993, p. 162 (my emphasis).

98 Shammās 1992, p. 456.

99 In 2001 al-Ṭayyib Ṣāliḥ (1929–2009) expressed his view that there is a much wider potential readership for Arabic literature than publishers are prepared to admit; see Shaheen 2001 pp. 82–5.

100 For example, Allen 1993, pp. 87–117. For a study that shows that literature in translation has a tremendous impact on students' learning in an increasingly interdependent world and that Arabic young adult literature in English plays an important role in classroom instruction in Arabic- and non-Arabic-speaking countries, see Anati 2012, pp. 168–93. See also above, pp. 111–16.

101 On this general phenomenon, see Adūnīs 1993, pp. 95–6.

to as a significant phenomenon since the 1930s,[102] Arab authors in English[103] and French[104] have played a major literary role writing in those languages. Especially noteworthy, during the last quarter of the twentieth century, is the participation of Arab writers in the French literary system, which, unlike in the past,[105] has attracted the attention of Arab critics as well.[106]

The underestimation of Arab and Muslim culture is illustrated as well by the fact that journalists and scholars in the West sometimes write about it with little, if any, knowledge of Arabic.[107] In his review of *God Has Ninety-Nine Names: Reporting from a Militant Middle East* by the *New York Times* reporter Judith Miller (b. 1948), Edward W. Said (1935–2003) encapsulates this phenomenon quite neatly by saying that

> writing about any other part of the world, Miller would be considered woefully unqualified. She tells us that she has been involved with the Middle East for twenty-five years, yet she has little knowledge of either Arabic or Persian. It would be impossible to be taken seriously as a reporter or expert on Russia, France, Germany or Latin America, perhaps even China or Japan, without knowing the requisite languages, but for "Islam," linguistic knowledge is unnecessary since what one is dealing with is considered to be a psychological deformation, not a "real" culture or religion.[108]

102 See, for example, al-Shaqīfī 1936, p. 541.

103 See, for example, Jubrān Khalīl Jubrān's works written originally in English (above, p. 112n).

104 See above, pp. 112–14.

105 For example, only in the 1990s did the Lebanese thinker Ghassān Tuwaynī (1926–2012) found in Beirut the *Turāth* (*Heritage*) series published by Dār al-Nahār in an effort to "revive the literary Lebanese heritage written in French" (*al-Ḥayāt*, 1 November 1996, p. 20). Among the texts published in that series are the *Complete Works* of the Lebanese poets Shukrī Ghānim (1861–1929), Fu'ād Ghibriyāl Naffā' (1925–83), and Nādiyā Tuwaynī (1935–83). The publication of one of the books in the series, the *Complete Works* of Fu'ād Abī Zayd (1914–58), was accompanied by articles published in the Lebanese and international Arabic press regretting that the talented poet had been forgotten (*Mulḥaq al-Nahār*, 9 November 1996, pp. 4–5; *al-Ḥayāt*, 1 November 1996, p. 20).

106 Although the usual phenomenon is that of a writer or poet in Arabic moving on to write in a Western language, there are also contrary examples, albeit very few. One such example is the poet Ibrāhīm al-'Urayyiḍ (1908–2002). Born in India, the son of a Bahraini father and an Iraqi mother, he grew up in an environment scarcely exposed to Arabic language and culture. Consequently, his first poetic attempts were in Urdu and in English, in which he subsequently published a collection entitled *Sonnets* (1932). After returning to Bahrain, at the age of twenty, he started to read avidly in classical and modern Arabic literature and to distinguish himself by his writing in both. His first Arabic collection was published in 1931, but his poetry drew the attention of Arab critics only after *al-'Arā'is* (*The Brides*) (1946) and *Arḍ al-Shuhadā': Malḥama Shi'riyya 'an Ma'sāt Filasṭīn* (*The Earth of Martyrs: An Epic about the Tragedy of Palestine*) (1951) were published (Meisami and Starkey 1998, I, p. 795).

107 In the Israeli-Hebrew case, see studies by Hannan Hever, Haim Gordon, Galia Shenberg, and Rachel Feldhay Brenner.

108 See *al-Jadīd* (Los Angeles) II.10 (August 1996), p. 6. On American journalists' lack of lin-

All in all, in the present book, I have proposed a theoretical framework and suggested an historical model for the research of modern Arabic literature with the full awareness that they must continuously undergo modifications in order to provide better tools for the study of modern Arabic literature. These modifications will be necessary against the backdrop of the speedy development of Internet technologies, which have fostered "politically and aesthetically subversive transformations in Arabic literature"[109] and the emergence of new generations of writers. The Internet, as one of the factors and manifestations of globalization, has been embraced so far by 49.2 percent of the world's population (in the Middle East, 57.4 percent of the population).[110] As with any other technological inventions, the Internet makes our lives easier—human beings, even those of us who speak out against technology and science in favor of spirituality and a natural life, tend to adopt and adapt to new inventions immediately after they become available. And here there is another related significant development which, during the last two decades, started to have a fundamental impact on culture and which, together with the Internet, will certainly have a deep impact on literature in general. I am referring to the fragmentation of the notion of identity and belonging. Discussions about the concept of identity during the last two decades were conducted within a variety of disciplinary areas, all of which were in one way or another critical of the notion of an integral, originary, and unified identity. Here is Stuart Hall:

> The critique of the self-sustaining subject at the centre of post-Cartesian western metaphysics has been comprehensively advanced in philosophy. The question of subjectivity and its unconscious processes of formation has been developed within the discourse of a psychoanalytically influenced feminism and cultural criticism. The endlessly performative self has been advanced in celebratory variants of postmodernism. Within the antiessentialist critique of ethnic, racial and national conceptions of cultural identity and the "politics of location" some adventurous theoretical conceptions have been sketched in their most grounded forms.[111]

In 2009 Zygmunt Bauman wrote that the "discursive explosion" around the concept of identity "has triggered an avalanche." It is too soon "to wish

guistic competence as a reason for their distortive reporting, see also Altoma 1993, p. 165. On the general conceptions of Edward Said, see his *Orientalism* (Said 1985 [1978]) and the numerous publications (by him and by others) that followed it. For critical notes on *Orientalism*, see Irwin 2006, pp. 277–309 ("Obviously I find it impossible to believe that [Said's] book was written in good faith" [p. 309]).

109 Pepe 2015, p. 75.

110 See the Internet usage statistics on <http://www.internetworldstats.com/stats.htm> (last accessed 4 September 2016).

111 Hall 1996, p. 1.

identity 'goodbye,'"[112] but in fact questions such as those raised by Stephen Frosh and Lisa Baraitser in "Goodbye to Identity?" are no longer rare.[113] They suggest that a more definitive idea is that identities are mere fictions: This idea seems to be less helpful now than when our priorities were to resist coercive normative identity formations.[114] In our fluid world "identities are for wearing and showing, not for storing and keeping." It is because we are endlessly forced to twist and mold our identities and are not allowed to cling to one identity, even if we want to, "that electronic instruments to do just that come in handy and tend to be embraced by millions."[115] Communication through the Internet, more than through any other medium, encourages us to refrain from adhering to a single identity and instead to toy with adopting other identities, even to create fake identities. The deconstruction of the concept of identity and the development of the world of blogging and other new modes of artistic and literary creation have highly influenced all literary systems on various levels, including the interaction between print and digital texts. It is evident that online literary texts have unique features and that the techniques for studying texts in print cannot be applied to them without a significant amount of due diligence. In 1997 Alberto Melucci described human beings as migrant animals in the labyrinths of the metropolis: "In reality or in the imagination, we participate in an infinity of worlds." And each of these worlds, the world of literature included, has a culture, a language, and a set of roles and rules to which we must adapt whenever we migrate from one to another:

> Thus we are subjected to mounting pressures to change, to transfer, to translate what we were just a moment ago into new codes and new forms of relation. We transform ourselves into sensitive terminals, transmitting and receiving a quantity of information which far exceeds that of any previous culture. Our means of communication, our work environment, our interpersonal relationships, even our leisure, generate information addressed to individuals who must receive, analyse and store in the memory, and almost always respond with further information.[116]

Since these words were published, all the phenomena and processes which Melucci mentioned have been intensified in such a way that any journey into "the labyrinths of the metropolis," where "migrant animals" wander, has become so complicated with so many refuges (with, at the same time, a

[112] Bauman 2009, p. 1.
[113] See Du Gay 2007, p. 1.
[114] Frosh and Baraitser 2009, pp. 158–69.
[115] Bauman 2004, pp. 89–90.
[116] Melucci 1997, p. 61.

multitude of dead ends) that traditional notions of identity seem to have lost their conceptual strength. One can argue that the Arab world must wait for these developments to become as fully widespread and effective as they are in the West, but any examination of the impact of Internet technologies on Arab societies will prove the opposite: Globalization seems to be the major war cry in contemporary Arab societies as well!

Also, no-one can ignore what could now be called the "new cosmopolitan" turn of the start of the twenty-first century. Only three years before the turn of the century, Ilios Yannakakis declared "the death of cosmopolitanism." His identically named essay was published in a book dealing with Alexandria as "cosmopolitan community" during the late nineteenth century and the early twentieth century. He wrote that "interpretations and definitions of cosmopolitanism run up against each other and are self-defeating" and that "cosmopolitanism filled only an instant of history." Cosmopolitan people were "those who had the world for their culture and mankind as their nation." Referring specifically to Alexandrian cosmopolitanism, Yannakakis mentions its urbane nature and European cultural roots. The "cosmopolitan spirit" in Alexandria blossomed when economic growth "made it possible for the wealthy merchants to begin a certain social activity within their respective communities." The steady increase of community schools widened the social base of new elites fascinated by modernity; the "increased familiarity with others among a relatively young population encouraged an interest in the outside world and emancipated the mentality." French had acquired a dominant position in the eastern Mediterranean and at this time was thought to be the lingua franca of the region. From the end of the 1880s thousands of immigrants had flowed into Alexandria, filling up the city, and "it was external cultural inputs, especially European, that propped up the community identity." However, soon "cosmopolitanism became diluted by the adopted national culture," since "cosmopolitanism and a strong national sentiment are incompatible." Yannakakis concluded his essay by saying that "cosmopolitanism was the product of a limited period and singular history—that of the crumbling Ottoman Empire. It lived to the age of a sturdy human being, before disappearing forever."[117]

117 Yannakakis 1997, pp. 190–4. Cf. Levi 2012, pp. 33–7. For another view, see Hanley 2013, pp. 92–104 ("The conventional image of cosmopolitan Alexandria fails to describe its historical reality because it requires the conjuring of a faceless, voiceless non-cosmopolitan mainstream of poor Muslim Arab Egyptians who, by definition, cannot be cosmopolitan. They exist, submerged as a sort of human ballast, in order to elevate the cosmopolitan pinnacle. They are the context that creates cosmopolitan Alexandria, from which they are excluded by definition" [the quotation is from p. 100]). On Alexandrian cosmopolitanism, see also Starr 2008; Halim 2014.

When Yannakakis' lament for cosmopolitanism was published, some aspects of the Alexandrian cosmopolitanism were emerging in their entirety and even with much more intensity. The Internet generation has been considerably much more global than "those who had the world for their culture and mankind as their nation." Instead of French as a lingua franca, we have English (or "Globish"[118]) in our global village, and migration has never been as intense as it has been in the last few decades. In addition, the national cultures that caused the dilution of cosmopolitanism have, in many instances, been replaced by globalized culture. Speaking of cosmopolitanism in the Middle East and the Arab world, one should be extremely cautious because of the fluidity of the concept and the frequent tendency by some to use it as anti-nationalist and anti-traditionalist teleology and to grieve for the Ottoman prenationalist paradise lost. Although a contested concept, cosmopolitanism has come to indicate detachment from "parochialisms emanating from extreme allegiances to nation, race, and ethnos."[119] Will Hanley shows how cosmopolitanism in Middle Eastern studies is characterized by the fantasizing that clings to scholarly and popular accounts of the Middle East. Focusing on elites and the invocation of a tag rather than the pursuit of an idea, the general tone of these accounts is that of grieving nostalgia. Evidence of social diversity in the modern Middle East can be found in literature, memoir, and film, rather than in historiography, since historians have not provided the means to measure cosmopolitanism or to evaluate the claims and respond to the needs of non-specialists interested in diversity. The Middle East's past, Hanley says, is a victim of its moribund present. Prenationalist Middle Eastern modernity did not exist so as to condemn late-twentieth-century nation-states. At this point, the cosmopolitan-decline-teleology schema must be overturned, since truly cosmopolitan phenomena are of grave importance to the globalized Middle East and can only be recognized as such when the concept is rid of its romanticism.[120] Taking Hanley's arguments on the necessity to avoid using prenationalist Middle Eastern modernity as a means of condemning late-twentieth-century nation-states into consideration, what now makes it possible to talk about some kind of cosmopolitan tendency is the belief that it is necessary to avoid treat-

[118] McCrum 2010.

[119] Anderson 1998, p. 267. Cf. Starr 2008, pp. 10–11.

[120] Hanley 2008, pp. 1346–67. In his article, Hanley provides a critical discussion of most of the scholarly contributions on cosmopolitanism in Middle East Studies and, in particular, of Sami Zubaida's (b. 1937) contributions to the field (e.g. Zubaida 1999, pp. 15–33). These he sees as displaying elitism and grieving nostalgia: "Although the plebian majority is necessary to the existence of the cosmopolitan elite, its preponderance is an occasion for grief and nostalgia for a lost age" (p. 1350).

ing identities as fixed and absolute. Subjectivities are always unfinished and unfinishable, and their characteristics shift widely between multiple perspectives—no single analytical framework can fully account for the inner lives of people and their intersubjective relations. We are not using the notion of cosmopolitanism here as a refuge from the nation-state paradigm, as a label or tag devoid of meaningful content, or for the sake of nostalgia; it serves here as another dimension of the fragmentation of the notion of a fixed identity and as a tool to escape the confines of the binary analytical methods frequently found in the humanities and social sciences.

Speaking of "binary analytical methods" in an article published in 2006,[121] Ulrich Beck and Natan Sznaider argue that, from the beginning of the twenty-first century, we have been witnessing a global transformation of modernity which calls for a rethinking and a reconceptualization of the humanities and the social sciences by asking for a "cosmopolitan turn." As previously indicated, there is no uniform interpretation of cosmopolitanism, and the boundaries separating it from competitive terms such as globalization, transnationalism, universalism, and glocalization are not distinct; internally, the term is traversed by all kinds of fault lines.[122] Yet, all other concepts presuppose basic dualisms, such as domestic/foreign, national/international, local/global, and us/them, all of which in reality have become ambiguous. In fact, all of these dualisms have dissolved and merged together in new forms that require new conceptual analysis. The underlying idea is that the light of the great cultural problems has moved on from a nation-state definition of society and politics—"the modern construct of the nation state is under constant pressure from the forces of globalisation"[123]—to a cosmopolitan outlook. This means that in doing research or theorizing we can no longer take it for granted that society is equated with national society; the unit of analysis should no longer be the national society or the nation-state, or the combination of both. The principle of cosmopolitanism can be found in specific forms on every level and can be practiced in every field of social and political action: in international organizations, in bi-national families, in neighborhoods, in global cities, in transnationalized military organizations, in the management of multinational corporations, in production networks,

[121] Beck and Sznaider 2006, pp. 1–23.

[122] When the British historian Tony Judt (1948–2010) used the term "globalization," referring to "the last great era of internationalization" in the "imperial decades preceding World War I," he probably meant, as I intend in the present study, the era of cosmopolitanism. In any event, Judt argued that "the story of globalization combines an evaluative mantra ('growth is good'), with the presumption of inevitability: globalization is with us to stay, a natural process rather than a human choice." In his view, however, "we should by now have learned that politics remains national" (Judt 2010, pp. 190–7).

[123] Zajda 2009, p. 8.

in human rights organizations, among ecology activists, and in the paradoxical global opposition to globalization.[124]

The recent changes and developments in the attitude toward the notion of identity are a natural outcome of the intense globalization, wide migration, growing social and political uncertainty and insecurity, development of communication technologies, and turnabout in cosmopolitanism in the above sense: all this in addition to the heritage of postmodernism, post-structuralism, psychoanalysis, and post-feminism. These changes and developments, however, could not have happened without what has been described as the market triumphalism in our era that witnessed "the expansion of markets and market-oriented reasoning into spheres of life traditionally governed by non-market norms."[125] We are all "*in* and *on* the market," according to Zygmunt Bauman, "simultaneously customers and commodities. No wonder that the use/consumption of human relations and so, by proxy, also our identities [...] catches up, and fast, with the pattern of car use/consumption, imitating the cycle that starts from purchase and ends with waste disposal."[126] Bill McKibben describes how we surrendered a fixed identity—a community, an extended family, deep and comforting roots—for, "quite literally, the chance to 'make something of ourselves.' Now we create our own identities." And this "making something of yourself" is, more than anything else, an economic task. We are interested in longer lives, fuller tables, warmer houses, and the community is no longer necessary to provide these things. We change our religions, spouses, residences, and professions with ease; "our affluence isolates us ever more. We are not just individuals; we are hyper-individualists such as the world has never known."[127] Also, these changes and developments in the notion of identity could not have happened without what may be termed the "classlessness of the bourgeoisie": "If we had once again to conceive of the fortunes of humanity in terms of class," Giorgio Agamben says,

> then today we would have to say that there are no longer social classes, but just a single planetary petty bourgeoisie, in which all the old social classes are dis-

124 On moral cosmopolitanism, see Appiah 2006. According to Appiah, cosmopolitanism is a dynamic concept based on the idea that we have responsibilities to others that are beyond those based on kinship or citizenship, and that although other people have different customs and beliefs from ours, these customs and values still have meaning and value.

125 Sandel 2009, p. 265. Sandel's hero is Robert F. Kennedy (1925–68), who tried to confront what he called "the poverty of satisfaction": "But even if we act to erase material poverty, there is another great task. It is to confront the poverty of satisfaction—a lack of purpose and dignity—that inflicts us all. Too much and too long, we seem to have surrendered community excellence and community values in the mere accumulation of material things" (18 March 1968).

126 Bauman 2004, p. 91.

127 McKibben 2007, p. 96.

> solved: The petty bourgeoisie has inherited the world and is the form in which humanity has survived nihilism.[128]

Furthermore, if the petty bourgeoisie is willing to stop looking for "a proper identity in the already improper and senseless form of individuality," and if one accepts his or her "proper being-thus" not as belonging to an identity but as a "singularity without identity," then and only then might there be a chance that the bourgeoisie will enter into community without presuppositions and without subjects:

> The fact is that the senselessness of their existence runs up against a final absurdity, against which all advertising runs aground: death itself. In death the petty bourgeois confront the ultimate expropriation, the ultimate frustration of individuality: life in all its nakedness, the pure incommunicable, where their shame can finally rest in peace [...] This means that the planetary petty bourgeoisie is probably the form in which humanity is moving toward its own destruction. But this also means that the petty bourgeoisie represents an opportunity unheard of in the history of humanity that it must at all costs not let slip away. Because if instead of continuing to search for a proper identity in the already improper and senseless form of individuality, humans were to succeed in belonging to this impropriety as such, in making of the proper being-thus not an identity and an individual property but a singularity without identity, a common and absolutely exposed singularity—if humans could [...] be only the thus, their singular exteriority and their face, then they would for the first time enter into a community without presuppositions and without subjects, into a communication without the incommunicable. Selecting in the new planetary humanity those characteristics that allow for its survival, removing the thin diaphragm that separates bad mediatized advertising from the perfect exteriority that communicates only itself—this is the political task of our generation.[129]

"Global capitalism," René ten Bos explains, "is indifferent to whether products are being sold to Moslems, Christians, Buddhists, Hindus, or atheists. It is also indifferent to national or political identities. It only takes an interest in anonymous and acquisitive citizens."[130]

To sum up: The wide migration, the speedy development of Internet technologies, globalization, the deconstruction and the fragmentization of the concept of identity, the "cosmopolitan turn," and the "classlessness of the bourgeoisie," all have freed human beings from many limitations and chains, real or imagined. They have exerted as well their impact, in various ways,

128 Agamben 2003 [1993], p. 63.
129 Agamben 2003 [1993], p. 65.
130 See ten Bos 2005, p. 22.

on Arab culture, even if that impact is still not parallel to that on Western culture and even if scholarship has not been able so far to properly assess the results of the current processes that Arabic literature has been undergoing. The idea that we are free of any community permits us, at least in our imagination, to engage with all people everywhere: "This is why so much international literature is about freedom and favors rebellions against institutions."[131] It is certainly relevant to Arab culture as well, but the collapse of the Arabs' cultural self-image vis-à-vis Western culture necessitates cautious assessment of the development of Arabic literature during the last few decades and in the foreseeable future. Having begun to consume the spiritual and materialistic aspects of Western civilization, the Arabs became aware that most branches of their own culture were lacking the sufficient repertoire for the newly needed functions of the modern world. That awareness fueled the translation movement from Western literatures into Arabic, boosting the development of all genres and creating new ones. The translation movement created "a dynamic space of negotiation" that tended to unseat any literary monopoly.[132] Unlike the major role of Western culture in its relationship with Arabic literature as target literature, the reverse impact is still minor. Despite the growing number of translations of Arabic literature into foreign languages and a tendency of some Arab authors to move to write in foreign languages, the Arabic literary impact on foreign literatures is still limited to only several works and authors, and the reading of original Arabic literature outside the Arab world is still confined to a limited number of academic and literary circles. These unstable and asymmetrical connections have cast their shadow on the activities in the Arabic literary system since the nineteenth century.

The interplay between Arabic literature and Western culture is part of the diachronic interactions between the Arabic literary system and other systems, literary (also within the conception of world literature[133]) and non-literary, suggested by the present study. The proposed model allows for greater economy of analysis in that it replaces large numbers of catego-

131 Tim Parks, "Are You the Tim Parks Who?" *New York Review of Books*, 30 August 2012, <http://www.nybooks.com/blogs/nyrblog/2012/aug/30/are-you-tim-parks-who/> (last accessed 27 October 2016).

132 I use here the wording of Muhsin al-Musawi (2015b, p. 47) regarding the translation as unseating the medieval linguistic monopoly.

133 See Muhsin al-Musawi's two-part article in *The Cambridge Journal of Postcolonial Literary Inquiry*, "The Republic of Letters: Arab Modernity?" (al-Musawi 2014, pp. 265–80; and al-Musawi 2015, pp. 115–30) and the four responses to al-Musawi's article within the "Forum on Literary World Systems" in the same journal (El-Ariss 2015, pp. 260–6; Ganguly 2015, pp. 272–281; Helgesson 2015, pp. 253–60; and Orsini 2015, pp. 266–72. See also al-Musawi's response in al-Musawi 2015a, pp. 281–6).

ries of a classificatory nature with a small number of parameters, which can be viewed as governing rules. This can be considered to be a step toward accomplishing what has always been believed to be the goal of any scientific endeavor, namely, the detection of those relatively few rules that govern the great diversity and complexity of phenomena, both observable and non-observable. Arabic literature has been postulated here to constitute a system or polysystem—a heterogeneous, multi-stratified, and functionally structured system-of-systems—kept in motion by a permanent struggle between canonical and non-canonical texts and models. The cultural Arabic consciousness in general identifies *fuṣḥā* with canonicity and *ʿāmmiyya* with non-canonicity, and canonization still depends on this equation. However, the development of Internet technologies has opened up new possibilities for writing in the colloquial.

The evaluation of the systems of successive periods springs from the oscillating movement between the periphery of the system and its center. The relations between center and periphery in the literary system are a series of oppositions that actually make it possible to hypothesize more than one center, although in most historical cases centers are stratified in such a way that only one succeeds in dominating the whole. Each text forms a system and at the same time is an element of a larger whole, that is, also a system, which is itself, in turn, a part of the greater system of the Arabic literary environment. It is placed, at each given period of time, at a particular point in the system, which is its synchronic value. Diachronic value is assigned to it by its paradigmatic position in the succession of synchronic systems, which acquire retrospective significance. Consequently, the diachronic correlativity of a text is to be considered alongside the synchronic orientation of the text toward other texts. The purpose is to define the general taste of a given period, the horizon of the collective native readers of the era to which an author relates. In the process, the study of second- and third-ranking authors proves to be far more productive than the parade of literary "generals."

The theoretical framework proposed in the present study is wide enough to include *all* that is related to Arabic literature whether it concerns the literary texts themselves as *literature* or as texts relevant to extra-literary contexts. The fact that all my publications related to the study of Arabic literature appear in the References and that they are used in one way or another in the footnotes to exemplify or illustrate various phenomena testifies to the inclusiveness of this framework. I have successfully examined that inclusiveness with the entire corpus of publications of several other scholars active in the field. The proposed model, however, is not in any way a closed, narrow, static, and finished framework, but an open, flexible, adaptable, and dynamic one. The tools for the study of modern Arabic literature, like those for the study of any other literature, which include the intersection between the investigation of text and theory,[134] will never be complete and will always involve a constant rewriting of literary history as part of the study of Arab culture.

My hope is that the historical model which I have set out in the present study, which is based on the theoretical framework I have suggested, will enable a systematic study of modern Arabic literature as a whole, enhance our understanding of the elements that together make up that literature, and throw light on various phenomena, especially in the areas of literary production, that have traditionally been neglected. At the same time, I am well aware of the fact that we lack sufficient information on most sectors of the literary system and that the current paucity of relevant studies means that some of the theses introduced here are preliminary in nature. My true objective, then, may perhaps only be achieved if this study succeeds in stimulating others to take up the fascinating challenge of mapping out all those areas of modern Arabic literature that are yet to be explored.

Last point: The rapid development and spread of Internet technologies have done much to change the way culture is perceived and have changed dramatically the way literature in general—Arabic literature included—is created and consumed. A year ago, when I started writing the last draft of the present book, I attempted to interact with various Arab poets, writers, critics, and scholars using social media (that is, through "friendship requests" on Facebook).[135] Only a few authors born in the 1930s and 1940s are currently active on the Internet, but (fortunately) the opposite is true for authors born in the following generations. Many responded positively, especially Iraqi, Syrian,

134 See, for example, the roundtable "Theory and Arabic Literature in the United States" in *International Journal of Middle East Studies* 43.4 (2011) with an introduction (Selim 2011, p. 721) and contributions from five literary scholars (Aboul-Ela 2011, pp. 725–7; Colla 2011, pp. 722–4; Omri 2011, pp. 731–3; Selim 2011a, pp. 734–6; and Tageldin 2011, pp. 728–30).

135 It was not at all easy for an Israeli-Jewish scholar of Arabic literature to communicate with Arab writers, to get friendship approvals, or to be active on the Internet, especially against the background of ongoing BDS (Boycott, Divest, Sanction) activities (<https://bdsmovement.net/> [last accessed 27 October 2016]). In any event, in order to prove my scholarly "innocence" I put the cover of my book *Baghdad—The City in Verse* (Cambridge, MA: Harvard University Press, 2013) as my profile picture. Surprisingly, or not, Western scholars of Arab origin are the most hesitant in their connections with Israeli-Jewish scholars, something I knew quite well from my experience during the last few decades. Only a recent example: On 12 May 2016 I saw a Call for Papers on "Transcultural Identity Constructions in a Changing Arab World" issued by Eid Mohamed and Ayman El-Desouky (<https://networks.h-net.org/node/73374/announcements/124242/call-papers-chapter-abstracts-and-funded-workshop-doha> [last accessed 27 October 2016]). Since I had recently published a book on Arab-Jewish Identity (Snir 2015), I sent an email to one of the editors proposing a topic that could be of interest for the conference. Unfortunately, I did not receive a response.

Palestinian, and Egyptian men of letters. I now have around 270 friends, and I can hardly read even a small part of their writing every day despite my desperate "quest for knowledge." After a year of activity on Facebook, I can definitely say that the face of Arabic literature has been changing and that the present book is probably the last scholarly contribution of one of its loving students who is totally *aware* of the change caused by Internet technologies but who has not availed himself of their usefulness. That is why one of the most important conclusions of the present book, which summarizes research on modern Arabic literature before the advent of the Internet, is that scholars and students of Arabic literature should be encouraged to carry out research on the literature that is now available online and in social media.[136]

All in all, the impact of the Internet on Arabic literary writing has been gradually intensifying, and there are signs that Arabic literature is changing in many respects. First of all, it is the quantity of the literary texts, including translations—particularly of poetry—that is increasing, and I have no doubt that quantity will make quality in the long run. Where the Internet is available (without strict governmental interventions), there is no censorship, no publishing limitations, no need for literary editors, and no need for financial resources to publish whatever you want. The temporal distance between writing and publishing has now become shorter, if it really exists at all. Poets use the Internet not only to publish new works but also to show works that they wrote and never published and/or republish what they consider to be their best works. Complaints against "the publishing situation," like the aforementioned complaint that was voiced in the 1990s by a representative of the Egyptian *Aṣwāt* group, that "our work remains in the drawers,"[137] are now senseless.

Internet technologies are also behind what seem to be essential poetic changes in literary writing, such as the preference for short texts and the blurring of the boundaries between prose and poetry. These gradual changes deserve to be researched, and such research has yet to be conducted. One can easily see in the field of poetry, for example, the sheer superiority of the prose poem over the "free verse" and certainly over the traditional *qaṣīda*. Also, because the prose poem has become the leading contemporary poetic genre, poets tend to publish prose poems they had already published many years ago in order to prove their pioneering role in the field. And, also,

136 Only few of them so far have done that, but I know of some who plan to do that. Tarek El-Ariss, for example, intends to publish a book that will examine the way that online modes of confrontation, circulation, and exhibitionism shape contemporary writing practices and critiques of power in the Arab world and beyond (see <http://liberalarts.utexas.edu/mes/faculty/profile.php?id=te3347> [4 September 2016] [last accessed 27 October 2016]).

137 Mehrez 1994a, p. 182.

thanks to the Internet, there are as well daily literary discussions on various topics such as the feminist writing that followed the Arab Spring or whether we are still at "the time of the novel" or returning to "the time of poetry." For example, the Palestinian author Saḥar Khalīfa (b. 1942) wrote in a Facebook post that the novel is "the new public register of the Arab people" (8 August 2016), and the Syrian poet Ḥamza Rastanāwī (b. 1974) immediately gave the following response:

> لم تعد الفنون الكتابية بكل أشكالها ديوانا للعرب! كم نسبة القراءة؟ الصورة والفضائيات ومواقع التواصل الاجتماعي هي ديوان العرب! ربما تكون الرواية ديوانا للنخبة العربية المثقفة القارئة وهي شريحة ضيقة، نعم هذا صحيح، ولكن ليس العرب بإطلاق!

> Writing arts are no longer the public register of the Arabs! What is the percentage of [literary] reading now? The picture and satellite and social media are the true public register of the Arabs! Perhaps the novel is the public register of the reading intellectual elite, yes, indeed, that is correct, but this elite is a small group, [the novel is not the public register] of all the Arabs.

More importantly, poetic creativity has never been so rich and spontaneous like it has in recent years online; in some sense, it is reminiscent of the poetic activities of the pre-Islamic period, the Jāhiliyya, when poets used to recite verses on every occasion they deemed suitable according to the famous saying *li-kull maqām maqāl* ("every session has a different discussion"). Arab writers and poets are aware of the dramatic change in Arabic literary writing. The Iraqi poet Ṣalāḥ Fā'iq (b. 1945), who has been living since 1993 in the Philippines, has testified to this change:

> بفضل الفيسبوك، لي الآن أصدقاء وقراء
> أتقدم بجزيل الشكر إلى نفسي
> لأني أنجزت هذا!

> Thanks to Facebook, I have now friends and readers.
> Many thanks to myself,
> Because I have made it! (Facebook, 12 August 2016).

Without the Internet, Fā'iq would have been totally excluded from the Arabic literary scene, but now I can read his poetic texts on a (more or less) daily basis. His compatriot Hātif al-Janābī (b. 1952) has stated that the

> Internet brought about a great leap, facilitating our writing and its checking and revising; it enables us to be familiar over the net with the experiences of others; it makes easy our connection with intellectuals and writers so we can see them on the palm of our hand. The advantages of the Internet are innumerable despite its disadvantages."[138]

[138] See <https://www.alaraby.co.uk> (16 August 2016) (last accessed 27 October 2016).

On the occasion of publishing a new anthology of Arabic poetry, the Iraqi poet Nāṣīf al-Nāṣirī (b. 1960) wrote the following:[139]

> في سنوات الثمانينيّات من القرن الماضي، كان أكثر الذين يُهيمنون على الإعلام طبعاً أصدقاء وأساتذة أجلاّء، رئاسة تحرير المجلاّت الأدبية، الصحف، دوائر الإبداع، الخ، يتّهمون الشُعراء الشباب آنذاك بقلّة الثقافة وقلّة الوعي، وعدم الموهبة، والسعي إلى تدمير التراث. طبعاً من غير المعقول أن يسعى الشاعر الشاب الذي يحاول ويُجرّب أن يسعى إلى هدم تراث عمره أكثر من 1700 سنة. الآن وأنا أغْطسُ في أعماق هذا التراث الكبير منذ أكثر مِن 36 سَنَة، أشعرُ أنَّ آبائي الشعراء الكُثار آلهة عُظماء، تجارب كبيرة ومختلفة، وأجملُ ما في الشعر العربي، هي الديمومة. ماكو شاعر أحْسَن مِن شاعر. لكلّ شاعر تجاربه وأساليبه وموضوعاته وأحلامه.

> In the 1980s, most those who controlled the media were, of course, friends and great scholars, such as editors of literary magazines, of departments of literary creation; they accused the young poets at the time of lack of culture and lack of awareness and talent and in attempt to destroy the heritage. Of course, it is unreasonable for a young poet who is trying and experimenting to be able to destroy a heritage of 1,700 years. Now, when I have been diving for the last 36 years into the depths of this great heritage, I feel that my many ancestors, the great poets, they were great gods and they have great and various experiences. Each poet has his own experiences, styles, themes, and dreams (Facebook, 10 September 2016).

In short, Arabic literature is now in another place, but its scholarship needs time to adapt to the dramatic change it has undergone. And I write this without ignoring the negative phenomena of the Internet which Arab writers are aware of. For example, the Moroccan writer Fātima al-Zahrā' al-Rayūwī (Fatima al-Zohra al-Rghioui) (b. 1974) says:

> تلك النصوص الفايسبوكية شبه اليومية، فأنا لا أسميها كتابة حقا. لا أعرف كيف أسميها. إنها كتابة قلقة أيضا، وملحة، ولكنها لا تشبع رغبتي في الكتابة، وإنما تزيد الظمأ.

> Those Facebook texts, I cannot refer to them as real [literary] writing. I do not know how to call them. This is a restless writing, pressing, but it cannot satisfy my desire for writing, only intensify the thirst.[140]

But it seems that a recent post by the Iraqi poet 'Alī Nwayyir (b. 1950) on Facebook, whose title is "I Salute You, I Am the Facebook Poet," is representative of most Arab writers who have started to be active on the Internet. Among what Nwayyir wrote is the following:

> قالوا: شاعرٌ فيسبوكيّ.
> وقالوا: شاعرةٌ فيسبوكيّة.

139 I only made minor modifications to the punctuation.

140 See <http://elmawja.com/blog/> (2 September 2016) (last accessed 27 October 2016).

وأقول: ليس ثمّة أجمل من فضائهما الأزرق هذا، من قبلُ وربما من بعد. هذا الكائن الخرافيّ بأجنحته السحرية ومداه اللامنتهي هو أكثر واقعيّةً ممّا نعتقد ويعتقدون، حيث يضعنا في قلب العالم الحيّ، ويُدخِل العالم كلّه بلا استئذان الى القلب والروح والوجدان.

They say: A Facebook poet.
And they say: A Facebook poetess.
And I say: There is nothing more beautiful than their blue space, there was not before and will perhaps be not even after. This mythological creature with his magic wings and its infinite space is much more realistic than we and they think; it puts us in the heart of the living world and inserts, without any permission, the whole world into [our] heart and spirit and emotional life (Facebook, 1 September 2016).

References[1]

Aarseth, Espen J. 1997. *Cybertext: Perspectives on Ergodic Literature*. Baltimore: The Johns Hopkins University Press.

Abbas, Adnan. 1994. *The Band as a New Form of Poetry in Iraq, 17th Century*. Poznan: Adam Mickiewicz University Press.

ʻAbbās, Ḥasan. 1985. *Nash'at al-Maqāma fī al-Adab al-ʻArabī*. Cairo: Dār al-Maʻārif.

——. 1986. *Fann al-Maqāma fī al-Qarn al-Sādis*. Cairo: Dār al-Maʻārif.

ʻAbbās, Ḥasan Maḥmūd. 1983. *Ḥayy ibn Yaqẓān wa-Robinson Crusoe: Dirāsa Muqārina*. Beirut: al-Mu'assasa al-ʻArabiyya li-l-Dirāsāt wa-l-Nashr.

ʻAbbās, Iḥsān. n.d. [1956]. *Fann al-Sīra*. Beirut: Dār al-Thaqāfa.

——. 1969. *Ta'rīkh al-Adab al-Andalusī: ʻAṣr Siyādat Qurṭuba*. Beirut: Dār al-Thaqāfa.

——. 1977. *Malāmiḥ Yūnāniyya fī al-Adab al-ʻArabī*. Beirut: al-Mu'assasa al-Jāmiʻiyya li-l-Dirāsāt wa-l-Nashr.

——. 1985. *Ta'rīkh al-Adab al-Andalusī: ʻAṣr al-Ṭawā'if wa-l-Murābiṭīn*. Beirut: Dār al-Thaqāfa.

——. 1996. *Ghurbat al-Rāʻī*. Beirut: Dār al-Shurūq.

ʻAbbās, Muḥammad. 2001. *al-Waʻy Yanzifu min Thuqūb al-Dhākira*. Cairo: Maktabat Madbūlī.

ʻAbbūd, ʻAbduh. 1995. *Hijrat al-Nuṣūṣ: Dirāsāt fī al-Tarjama al-Adabiyya wa-l-Tabādul al-Thaqāfī*. Damascus: Manshūrāt Ittiḥād al-Kuttāb al-ʻArab.

ʻAbbūd, Mārūn. 1968. *al-Shiʻr al-ʻĀmmī*. Beirut: Dār al-Thaqāfa.

ʻAbd al-ʻAzīz, Aḥmad. 1983. "Athar Federico Gracia Lorca fī al-Adab al-ʻArabī al-Muʻāṣir." *Fuṣūl* 3.4, pp. 271–99.

ʻAbd al-Dā'im, Yaḥyā Ibrāhīm. 1975. *al-Tarjama al-Dhātiyya fī al-Adab al-ʻArabī al-Ḥadīth*. Beirut: Dār Iḥyā' al-Turāth al-ʻArabī.

ʻAbd al-Fattāḥ, Sayyid Ṣiddīq. 1993. *Tarājim wa-Āthār Udabā' al-Adab al-Sākhir*. Cairo: al-Dār al-Miṣriyya al-Lubnāniyya.

——. 1993a. *Ḥayāt wa-Aʻmāl Shuʻarā' al-Adab al-Sākhir*. Cairo: al-Dār al-Miṣriyya al-Lubnāniyya.

ʻAbd al-Hādī, Muḥammad Fatḥī. 1986. "Maktabāt al-Aṭfāl." *ʻĀlam al-Kitāb*, pp. 2–3.

ʻAbd al-Ḥakīm, Shawqī. 1984. *al-Shiʻr al-Shaʻbī al-Fulklūrī ʻinda al-ʻArab*. Beirut: Dār al-Ḥadātha.

[1] The definite article *al* is not taken into consideration in the alphabetical order. It appears in this form throughout the entire book before solar and lunar letters. Titles of Arabic books and articles are transliterated into English. Titles of Hebrew books and articles are translated into English and identified as such at the end of the translated title.

'Abd al-Ḥayy, Muḥammad. 1977. *al-Usṭūra al-Ighrīqiyya fī al-Shi'r al-'Arabī al-Mu'āṣir.* Cairo: Dār al-Nahḍa al-'Arabiyya.

Abdallah, Anouar. 1994. *For Rushdie: Essays by Arab and Muslim Writers in Defense of Free Speech* (trans. Kenneth Whitehead and Kelvin Anderson). New York: George Braziller.

'Abd Allāh, Muṣṭafā. 1982. "Mithl La Fontaine Kataba Shawqī li-l-Aṭfāl." *al-Ahrām*, 28 October, p. 9.

'Abd al-Muṭṭalib, Muḥammad. n.d. *Dīwān* (ed. Ibrāhīm al-Abyārī and 'Abd al-Ḥafīẓ Shalabī). Cairo: Maṭba'at al-I'timād.

'Abd al-Quddūs, Iḥsān. 1959. *al-Banāt wa-l-Ṣayf.* Cairo: Dār Rūz al-Yūsuf.

——. 1973. *al-Banāt wa-l-Ṣayf.* Beirut: Dār al-Qalam and al-Maktaba al-Ḥadītha.

'Abd al-Raḥmān, Muṣṭafā. 1960. *Ughniyyat al-Kifāḥ.* Cairo: al-Dār al-Qawmiyya li-l-Ṭibā'a wa-l-Nashr.

'Abd al-Rāziq, 'Alī. 1925. *al-Islām wa-Uṣūl al-Ḥukm.* Cairo: Maṭba'at Miṣr.

——. 1988. *al-Islām wa-Uṣūl al-Ḥukm.* Beirut: al-Mu'assasa al-'Arabiyya li-l-Dirāsāt wa-l-Nashr.

'Abd al-Ṣabūr, Ṣalāḥ. n.d. *Madīnat al-'Ishq wa-l-Ḥikma.* Beirut: Dār Iqra'.

——. 1969. *Ḥayātī fī al-Shi'r.* Beirut: Dār al-'Awda.

——. 1971. *Riḥla 'alā al-Waraq.* Cairo: Maktabat al-Anglo al-Miṣriyya.

——. 1972. *Dīwān.* Beirut: Dār al-'Awda.

'Abd al-Salām, Fātiḥ. 1999. *Ḥalīb al-Thīrān.* Beirut: al-Mu'assasa al-'Arabiyya li-l-Dirāsāt wa-l-Nashr.

'Abd al-Wahhāb, Zuhayr. 1995. "Ḥājatunā ilā al-Tarjama." *al-Qāfila* (al-Ẓahrān), July–August, pp. 10–12.

'Abd al-Wāḥid, 'Umar Muḥammad. 2003. *Dawā'ir al-Tanāṣṣ: Mu'āraḍāt al-Bārūdī li-l-Mutanabbī—Dirāsa fī al-Tafā'ul al-Naṣṣī.* al-Minyā: Dār al-Hudā li-l-Nashr wa-l-Tawzī'.

Abdel-Malek, Anouar (ed.). 1965. *Anthologie de la littérature arabe contemporaine: La essais.* Paris: Éditions du Seuil.

Abdel-Malek, Kamal. 1988. "The *Khawāga* Then and Now: Images of the West in Modern Egyptian *Zajal*." *Journal of Arabic Literature* 19.2, pp. 162–78.

——. 1990. *A Study of the Vernacular Poetry of Aḥmad Fu'ād Nigm.* Leiden: Brill.

——. 1995. *Muhammad in the Modern Egyptian Popular Ballad.* Leiden: Brill.

——. 2005. *The Rhetoric of Violence: Arab-Jewish Encounters in Contemporary Palestinian Literature and Film.* New York: Palgrave Macmillan.

——. and Wael Hallaq (eds). 2000. *Tradition, Modernity, and Postmodernity in Arabic Literature: Essays in Honor of Professor Issa J. Boullata.* Leiden: Brill.

Abdel-Malek, Zaki N. 1972. "The Influence of Diglossia on the Novels of Yuusif al-Sibaa'i." *Journal of Arabic Literature* 3, pp. 132–41.

Abdel-Meguid, Abdel Aziz. 1955. *The Modern Arabic Short Story.* Cairo: Dār al-Ma'ārif.

Abdel-Messih, Marie-Thérèse. 2009. "Hyper Texts: Avant-Gardism in Contemporary Egyptian Narratives." *Neohelicon* 36.2, pp. 515–23.

Abdel Sabour, Salah. 1970. *A Journey at Night* (trans. Samar Attar). Cairo: al-Hay'a al-Miṣriyya al-'Āmma li-l-Ta'līf wa-l-Nashr.

Abdel Wahab, Hassan. 1966. "Shadow-Shows and the Cinema." In Georges Sadoul (ed.), *The Cinema in the Arab Countries*, pp. 32–6. Beirut: Interarab Centre of Cinema and Television.

Abdul-Hai, Muhammad. 1972. "Shelley and the Arabs: An Essay in Comparative Literature." *Journal of Arabic Literature* 3, pp. 72–89.

——. 1976. "Bibliography of Arabic Translations of English and American Poetry (1830–1970)." *Journal of Arabic Literature* 7, pp. 120–50.

Abdullah, Thabit. 1997. "Arab Views of Northern Europeans in Medieval History and Geography." In David R. Blanks (ed.), *Images of the Other: Europe and the Muslim World: Before 1700*, pp. 73–80. Cairo: The American University in Cairo Press.

Abdul-Rahmon, M. Oloyede. 1995. "An Approach to the Stylistic Appraisal of Arabic Poetry of Nigerian 'Ulamā'." *Islamic Studies* 34.3, pp. 315–25.

Abdul-Razak, H. M. 1989. *Keats, Shelley and Byron in Nazik al-Mala'ikah's Poetry*. PhD thesis, University of Glasgow.

Abdul-Samad, Abdullah. 2004. "Arabic Poetry in West Africa: An Assessment of the Panegyric and Elegy Genres in Arabic Poetry of the 19th and 20th Centuries in Senegal and Nigeria." *Journal of Arabic Literature* 35.3, pp. 368–90.

——. 2009. "Intertextuality and West African Arabic Poetry: Reading Nigerian Arabic Poetry of the 19th and 20th Centuries." *Journal of Arabic Literature* 40.3, pp. 335–61.

Abi-Rached, Naoum (ed.). 2004. *Les problématiques de la traduction arabe, hier et aujourd'hui*. Strasbourg: Université Marc Bloch.

al-Abnūdī, 'Abd al-Raḥmān. 1986 [1964]. *al-Arḍ wa-l-'Iyāl*. Cairo: Madbūlī.

——. 1986 [1970]. *al-Fuṣūl*. Cairo: Madbūlī.

——. 1998. *Ākhir al-Layl*. Cairo: Mu'assasat Rūz al-Yūsuf.

Abou-Bakr, Omaima. 2013. "Rings of Memory: 'Writing Muslim Women' and the Question of Authorial Voice." *Muslim World* 103.3, pp. 320–33.

Abou-Bakr, Randa. 2011. "Egyptian Colloquial Poetry: A Neglected 'Genre'?" In Stephan Guth and Gail Ramsay (eds), *From New Values to New Aesthetics: Turning Points in Modern Arabic Literature (Proceedings of the 8th EURAMAL Conference, 11–14 June, 2008, Uppsala / Sweden). 2. Postmodernism and Thereafter*, pp. 13–32. Wiesbaden: Harrassowitz Verlag.

Aboul-Ela, Hosam. 2001. "Challenging the Embargo: Arabic Literature in the US Market." *Middle East Report* 219, pp. 42–4.

——. 2011. "Our Theory Split." *International Journal of Middle East Studies* 43.4, pp. 725–7.

Abrahamov, Binyamin (ed.). 2000. *Studies in Arabic and Islamic Culture* (Vol. 1). Ramat Gan: Bar-Ilan University Press.

Abū 'Arja, Taysīr. 2001. *al-Funūn al-Ṣuḥufiyya fī Jarīdat al-Muqaṭṭam al-Miṣriyya 1889–1952*. Amman: Dār Majdalāwī li-l-Nashr.

Abubakar, Isa A. 2000. "Knowledge, Learning, and the Role of a Teacher as Contained in Aḥmad Shauqī's Poems." *Islamic Culture* 74.2, pp. 47–75.

Abubakre, Razaq 'Deremi. 1980. *The Contribution of the Yorubas to Arabic Literature*. PhD thesis, University of London.

——. and Stefan Reichmuth. 1997. "Arabic Writing between Global and Local Culture: Scholars and Poets in Yorubaland (Southwestern Nigeria)." *Research in African Literatures* 28.3, pp. 183–209.

Abū Bashar, Kamāl. 1991. "al-Lugha wa-l-Thaqāfa." *Majallat Majma' al-Lugha al-'Arabiyya* (Cairo), May, pp. 25-52.

Abū Buthayna, Muḥammad 'Abd al-Mun'im. 1973. *al-Zajal al-'Arabī: Māḍīhi wa-Ḥāḍiruhu wa-Mustaqbaluhu*. Cairo: Dār al-Hilāl.

Abu-Deeb (Abū Dīb), Kamal. 1997. "Conflicts, Oppositions, Negations: Modern Arabic Poetry and the Fragmentation of the Self/Text." In Issa J. Boullata and Terri DeYoung (eds), *Tradition and Modernity in Arabic Literature*, pp. 101–33. Fayetteville, AR: University of Arkansas Press.

——. 2000. "The Collapse of Totalizing Discourse and the Rise of Marginalized/Minority Discourses." In Kamal Abdel-Malek and Wael Hallaq (eds), *Tradition, Modernity, and Postmodernity in Arabic Literature: Essays in Honor of Professor Issa J. Boullata*, pp. 335–66. Leiden: Brill.

——. 2015. *Simfūniyyat Sūriyya*. Amman: Dār Faḍa'āt.

Abudi, Dalya. 2011. *Mothers and Daughters in Arab Women's Literature: The Family Frontier*. Boston: Brill.

Abū Fakhr, Ṣaqr. 1998. *Ṣādiq Jalāl al-'Aẓm: Ḥiwār bi-lā Ḍifāf*. Beirut: al-Mu'assasa al-'Arabiyya li-l-Dirāsāt wa-l-Nashr.

Abū Fanna, Mūḥammad and Khālid 'Azāyiza. 1996. *Āfāq Jadīda: Dirāsāt wa-Abḥāth fī Adab al-Aṭfāl wa-l-Manāhij wa-l-Asālīb*. Nazareth: Wizārat al-Ma'ārif wa-l-Thaqāfa.

Abū Fāshā, Ṭāhir. n.d. *Alf Yawm wa-Yawm*. Cairo: Madbūlī.

——. 1987. *Hazz al-Quhūf bi-Sharḥ Qaṣīdat Abī Shādūf*. Cairo: al-Hay'a al-Miṣriyya al-'Āmma li-l-Kitāb.

Abū al-Futūḥ, Sayyid Ḥāfiẓ. 1989. *Qālū 'an al-Islām: Rasā'il ilā Salmān Rushdī min Kibār Mufakkirī wa-Falāsifat al-'Ālam al-Masīḥī*. Cairo: Madbūlī.

Abū Ḥadīd, Muḥammad Farīd. 1935. "Majālis al-Adab fī al-Qarn al-Thāmin 'Ashar." *al-Risāla*, 11 February, pp. 205–7.

Abu-Haidar, Jareer. 1974. "*Maqāmāt* Literature and the Picaresque Novel." *Journal of Arabic Literature* 5, pp. 1–10.

——. 1991. "The *Muwaššaḥāt* in the Light of the Literary Life that Produced Them." In Alan Jones and Richard Hitchcock (eds), *Studies on the Muwaššaḥ and the Kharja*, pp. 115–22. Reading: Ithaca Press.

——. 1992. "The *Muwashshaḥāt*: Are They a Mystery?" *Al-Qanṭara* 13, pp. 63–81.

——. 1993. "The Arabic Origins of the *Muwashshaḥāt*." *Bulletin of the School of Oriental and African Studies* 56.3, pp. 439–58.

——. 1996. "Romanticism and Modern Arabic Literature." In J. R. Smart (ed.), *Tradition and Modernity in Arabic Language and Literature*, pp. 3–17. Richmond: Curzon.

——. 2001. *Hispano-Arabic Literature and the Early Provençal Lyrics*. Richmond: Curzon.

Abū Ḥamda, Muḥammad 'Alī. 2003. *Fī al-'Ubūr al-Ḥaḍārī li-Kitāb fī al-Shi'r al-Jāhilī li-l-Duktūr Ṭāhā Ḥusayn*. Amman: Dār 'Ammār li-l-Nashr wa-l-Tawzī'.

Abū Hayf, 'Abd Allāh. 1992. "Naḥwa Riwāya 'Arabiyya li-l-Aṭfāl wa-l-Fityān." *al-Ma'rifa* Vol. 30, issue 340, pp. 89–120.

AbuKhalil, Asad. 1993. "A Note on the Study of Homosexuality in the Arab/Islamic Civilization." *Arab Studies Journal* 1.2, pp. 32–4.

Abū al-Khashab, Ibrāhīm 'Alī. 1984. *Ta'rīkh al-Adab al-'Arabī fī al-'Aṣr al-Ḥāḍir*. Cairo: al-Hay'a al-'Āmma li-l-Kitāb.

Abu-Lughod, Ibrahim. 1963. *Arab Rediscovery of Europe: A Study in Cultural Encounters*. Princeton: Princeton University Press.

Abu-Lughod, Lila. 1986. *Veiled Sentiments: Honor and Poetry in a Bedouin Society*. Berkeley: University of California Press.

——. 1990. "Shifting Politics in Bedouin Love Poetry." In Catherine Lutz and Lila Abu-Lughod (eds), *Language and the Politics of Emotion*, pp. 24–45. Cambridge: Cambridge University Press.

——. 1993. *Writing Women's Worlds: Bedouin Stories*. Berkeley: University of California Press.

——. 1998. *Remaking Women: Feminism and Modernity in the Middle East*. Princeton: Princeton University Press.

Abū Māḍī, Īliyyā. n.d. *Dīwān*. Beirut: Dār al-'Awda.

Abū Mughallā, Samīḥ et al. 1993. *Dirāsāt fī Adab al-Aṭfāl*. Amman: Dār al-Fikr.

Abū al-Najā, Shīrīn. 2016. "'al-Jumhūriyya al-Islāmiyya' li-l-Ādāb kamā Yarāhā Muḥsin Jāsim al-Mūsawī." *al-Ḥayāt*, 28 February.

Abū Niḍāl, Nazīh. 1981. *Adab al-Sujūn*. Beirut: Dār al-Ḥadātha.

Abū Nuwās. 1972. *Diwān Abī Nuwās al-Ḥasan ibn 'Alī al-Ḥakamī* (ed. Ewald Wagner). Wiesbaden: Franz Steiner.

——. 1994. *al-Nuṣūṣ al-Muḥarrama* (ed. Jamāl Jum'a). London and Limassol: Riyāḍ al-Rayyis.

Abu-Rabi', Ibrahim M. 2004. *Contemporary Arab Thought: Studies in Post-1967 Arab Intellectual History*. London: Pluto Press.

Abū al-Riḍā, Sa'd. 1993. *al-Naṣṣ al-Adabī li-l-Aṭfāl Ahdāfuhu wa-Maṣādiruhu wa-Simātuhu: Ru'ya Islāmiyya*. Amman: Dār al-Bashīr.

Abū al-Sa'd, 'Abd al-Ra'ūf. 1994. *al-Ṭifl wa-'Ālamuhu al-Adabī*. Cairo: Dār al-Ma'ārif.

Abū Saʻūd, Fakhrī. 1934. "al-Athar al-Yūnānī fī al-Adab al-ʻArabī." *al-Risāla*, 11 June, pp. 968–9.

Abū Shabaka, Ilyās. 1941. *al-Alḥān*. Beirut: Dār al-Makshūf.

——. 1985. *al-Majmūʻa al-Kāmila fī al-Shiʻr* (ed. Walīd Nadīm ʻAbbūd). Jūnya: Dār Ruwwād al-Nahḍa & Dār al-Aūdīsiyya.

Abū Shamāla, Fāyiz. 2002. *al-Sijn fī al-Shiʻr al-Filasṭīnī 1967–2001*. Ramallah: al-Mu'assasa al-Filasṭīniyya li-l-Irshād al-Qawmī.

Abū Ṣūfa, Muḥammad. 1993. "Ḥadīth fī al-Masraḥ al-ʻArabī wa-l-Islāmī." *al-Ra'y* (Jordan), 24 December, p. 11.

Abū Tammām. n.d. *al-Ḥamāsa*. Cairo: Muḥammad ʻAlī Ṣabīḥ.

Abū al-Ṭayyib al-Lughawī, ʻAbd al-Wāḥid. 1963. *Kitāb al-Aḍdād fī Kalām al-ʻArab* (ed. ʻIzzat Ḥasan). Damascus: al-Majmaʻ al-ʻIlmī al-ʻArabī.

Abu-ʻUksa, Wael. 2016. *Freedom in the Arab World: Concepts and Ideologies in Arabic Thought in the Nineteenth Century*. Cambridge: Cambridge University Press.

Abu Zaid, Nasr with Esther R. Nelson. 2004. *Voice of an Exile: Reflections on Islam*. Westport, CT: Praeger Publishers.

Abū Zakī, Ṭāriq Bahīj. 2008. *Shuʻarā' al-Zajal fī Qaḍā' al-Shūf*. n.p. [Lebanon]: n.pub.

Abū Zayd, Madīḥa. 1993. "Mādhā Yaqra'ūn al-Ān." *ʻĀlam al-Kitāb*, October, pp. 30–6.

Abū Zayd, Naṣr Ḥāmid. 1990. *Mafhūm al-Naṣṣ: Dirāsa fī ʻUlūm al-Qur'ān*. Beirut and Casablanca: al-Markaz al-Thaqāfī al-ʻArabī.

——. 1992. *al-Khiṭāb al-Dīnī: Ru'ya Naqdiyya*. Beirut: Dār al-Muntakhab al-ʻArabī li-l-Dirāsāt wa-l-Nashr wa-l-Tawzīʻ.

——. 1995. *Naqd al-Khiṭāb al-Dīnī*. Cairo: Madbūlī.

——. 1995a. *al-Tafkīr fī Zaman al-Takfīr: Ḍidd al-Jahl wa-l-Zīf wa-l-Khurāfa*. Cairo: Sīnā li-l-Nashr.

——. 1995b. *al-Qawl al-Mufīd fī Qaḍiyyat Abū* [sic] *Zayd*. Cairo: Madbūlī.

Accad, Evelyne. 1984. "The Prostitute in Arab and North African Fiction." In Pierre Horn and Mary Beth Pringle (eds), *The Image of the Prostitute in Modern Literature*, pp. 63–75. New York: Frederick Ungar.

——. 1987. "Freedom and the Social Context: Arab Women's Special Contribution to Literature." *Feminist Issues* 7.2, pp. 33–48.

——. 1990. *Sexuality and War: Literary Masks of the Middle East*. New York: New York University Press.

——. 1993. "Rebellion, Maturity, and the Social Context: Arab Women's Special Contribution to Literature." In Judith Tucker (ed.), *Arab Women: Old Boundaries, New Frontiers*, pp. 224–53. Bloomington: Indiana University Press.

——. and Rose Ghurayyib (eds). 1985. *Contemporary Arab Women Writers and Poets*. Beirut: Institute for Women's Studies in the Arab World.

Achour, Christiane. 1991. *Dictionnaire des oeuvres algériennes en langue française: essais, romans, nouvelles, conts, récits autobiographiques*. Paris: L'Harmattan.

Adab al-Ṭifl al-ʻArabī. 1995. Amman: Manshūrāt al-Ittiḥād al-ʻĀmm li-l-Udabā' al-ʻArab.

Adonis (Adūnīs). 1954. *Qālat al-Arḍ*. Damascus: al-Maṭbaʻa al-Hāshimiyya.

——. 1959. "Muḥāwala fī Taʻrīf al-Shiʻr al-Ḥadīth." *Shiʻr*, June, pp. 79–90.

——. 1971. *al-Āthār al-Kāmila*. Beirut: Dār al-ʻAwda.

——. 1972. *Zaman al-Shiʻr*. Beirut: Dār al-ʻAwda.

——. n.d. [1975]. *Mufrad bi-Ṣīghat Jamʻ*. Beirut: Dār al-ʻAwda.

——. 1980. *Fātiḥa li-Nihāyāt al-Qarn: Bayānāt min Ajl Thaqāfa ʻArabiyya Jadīda*. Beirut: Dār al-ʻAwda.

——. 1982. "Aḥmad Shawqī: Shāʻir al-Bayān al-Awwal." *Fuṣūl* 3.1, pp. 18–22.

——. 1988. *al-Aʻmāl al-Shiʻriyya al-Kāmila*. Beirut: Dār al-ʻAwda.

——. 1990. *An Introduction to Arab Poetics* (trans. Catherine Cobham). London: Saqi Books.

——. 1992. "al-Sharʻ wa-l-Shiʻr." *Fuṣūl* 11.3, pp. 66–70.

——. 1993. *Hā Anta, Ayyuhā al-Waqt*. Beirut: Dār al-Ādāb.

——. 1993a. *al-Naṣṣ al-Qur'ānī wa-Āfāq al-Kitāba*. Beirut: Dār al-Ādāb.

——. 1996 [1964–8]. *Dīwān al-Shi'r al-'Arabī*. Beirut: Dār al-Madā li-l-Thaqāfa wa-l-Nashr.

——. 2000 [1985]. *al-Shi'riyya al-'Arabiyya*. Beirut: Dār al-Ādāb.

Afshar, Haleh (ed.). 1993. *Women in the Middle East: Perceptions, Realities and Struggles for Liberation*. London: Macmillan Press.

Agamben, Giorgio. 2003 [1993]. *The Coming Community* (trans. Michael Hardt). Minneapolis: University of Minnesota Press.

Aghacy, Samira. 2009. *Masculine Identity in the Fiction of the Arab East since 1967*. Syracuse: Syracuse University Press.

Agius, Dionysius and Richard Hitchcock (eds). 1993. *The Arab Influence in Medieval Europe*. Reading: Ithaca Press.

Aḥmad, Rif'at Sayyid. 1989. *Āyāt Shayṭāniyya: Jadaliyyat al-Ṣirā' Bayna al-Islām wa-l-Gharb*. Cairo: al-Dār al-Sharqiyya.

Ahmad, S. Maqbul (ed.). 1968. *India and the Arab World: Proceedings of the Seminar on India and the Arab World*. New Delhi: Indian Council for Cultural Relations.

Ahmad, Zubaid M. G. 1968 [1946]. *The Contribution of Indo-Pakistan to Arabic Literature*. Lahore: Sh. Muhammad Ashraf.

Ahmed, Leila. 1992. *Women and Gender in Islam: Historical Roots of a Modern Debate*. New Haven: Yale University Press.

Ahmed, Mohammed Shahab. 1999. *The Satanic Verses Incident in the Memory of the Early Muslim Community: An Analysis of the Early Riwāyahs and Their Isnāds*. PhD thesis, Princeton University.

A Hundred and One Nights. 2016. (ed. and trans. Bruce Fudge). New York: New York University Press.

Ajami, Fouad. 1998. *The Dream Palace of the Arabs: A Generation's Odyssey*. New York: Pantheon Books.

Akash, Munir and Khaled Mattawa (eds). 2000. *Post Gibran: Anthology of New Arab American Writing*. West Bethesda, MD: Kitab.

Akbarabadi, Sa'id Ahmed. 1968. "The Contribution of India to Arabic Language and Literature Since Independence." In S. Maqbul Ahmad (ed.), *India and the Arab World: Proceedings of the Seminar on India and the Arab World*, pp. 24–8. New Delhi: Indian Council for Cultural Relations.

Akers, Deborah S. and Abubaker A. Bagader (eds. and trans.). 2008. *Oranges in the Sun: Short Stories from the Arabian Gulf*. London and Boulder, CO: Lynne Rienner Publishers.

Alagha, Joseph. 2011. "Pious Entertainment: Hizbullah's Islamic Cultural Sphere." In Karin van Nieuwkerk (ed.), *Muslim Rap, Halal Soaps and Revolutionary Theater: Artistic Developments in the Muslim World*, pp. 149–75. Austin: University of Texas Press.

Alami, Maryame. 2013. "Gender Representation in First Wave Moroccan Life Writing: Focus on Abdelmajid Benjelloun's Autobiographical Novel 'In Childhood.'" *Journal of North African Studies* 18.3, pp. 443–53.

Al-Alaya'a [sic], Zaid. 2006. "The Media and Writers—Their Role in the Decline of Standard Arabic." *Yemen Observer*, 10 April.

al-'Alāylī, 'Abd Allāh. 1978. *Ayna al-Khaṭā'?* Beirut: Dār al-'Ilm li-l-Malāyīn.

Alcalay, Ammiel. 1993. *After Jews and Arabs: Remaking Levantine Culture*. Minneapolis: University of Minnesota Press.

Alexander, Tamar et al. (eds). 1994. *History and Creativity in the Sephardi and Oriental Jewish Communities* (Hebrew). Jerusalem: Misgav Yerushalayim.

Alf Layla wa-Layla. n.d. (ed. Sa'īd Jawda al-Saḥḥār). Cairo: Dār Miṣr li-l-Ṭibā'a.

Al-Ali, Nadje Sadig. 1993. *Gender Writing/Writing Gender: The Representation of Women in a Selection of Modern Egyptian Literature*. Cairo: The American University in Cairo Press.

Allan, Michael. 2013. "Queer Couplings: Formations of Religion and Sexuality in 'Ala' al-Aswani's *'Imarat Ya'qubyan*." *International Journal of Middle East Studies* 45.2, pp. 253–69.

Allana, G. (ed.). 1973. *A Rosary of Islamic Readings*. Karachi and Rawalpindi: National Publishing House.

Allen, Roger (ed.). 1978. *In the Eye of the Beholder: Tales of Egyptian Life from the Writings of Yūsuf Idrīs*. Minneapolis and Chicago: Bibliotheca Islamica.

——. 1982. *The Arabic Novel: An Historical and Critical Introduction*. Syracuse: Syracuse University Press.

——. 1987. *Modern Arabic Literature*. New York: Frederick Ungar.

——. 1993. "The Impact of the Translated Text: The Case of Najīb Maḥfūẓ's Novels, with Special Emphasis on *The Trilogy*." *Edebiyât* 4, pp. 87–117.

——. 1993a. "Naguib Mahfouz and the Arabic Novel." In Michael Beard and Adnan Haydar (eds), *Naguib Mahfouz: From Regional Fame to Global Recognition*, pp. 28–36. Syracuse: Syracuse University Press.

——. 1994. "PROTA: The Project for the Translation of Arabic Literature." *Middle East Studies Association Bulletin* 28.2, pp. 165–8.

——. 1998. *The Arabic Literary Heritage: The Development of Its Genres and Criticism*. Cambridge: Cambridge University Press.

——. 1998a. "Autobiography and Memory: Maḥfūẓ's *Aṣda' al-Sīra al-Dhātiyya* " In Robin C. Ostle et al. (eds), *Writing the Self: Autobiographical Writing in Modern Arabic Literature*, pp. 207–16. London: Saqi Books.

——. 2000. *An Introduction to Arabic Literature*. Cambridge: Cambridge University Press.

——. 2006. "The Post-Classical Period: Parameters and Preliminaries." In Roger Allen and D. S. Richards (eds), *Arabic Literature in the Post-Classical Period*, pp. 1–21. Cambridge: Cambridge University Press.

——. 2007. "Rewriting Literary History: The Case of the Arabic Novel." *Journal of Arabic Literature* 38.3, pp. 247–60.

——. 2010 (ed.). *Essays in Arabic Literary Biography 1850–1950*. Wiesbaden: Harrassowitz Verlag.

——. 2011. "Rewriting Literary History: The Case of Moroccan Fiction in Arabic." *Journal of North African Studies* 16.3, pp. 311–24.

——. 2011a. "Najīb Maḥfūẓ's *Awlād Ḥāratinā*: A History and Interpretation." In Gail Ramsay and Stephan Guth (eds), *From New Values to New Aesthetics: Turning Points in Modern Arabic Literature (Proceedings of the 8th EURAMAL Conference, 11–14 June, 2008, Uppsala / Sweden). 1. From Modernism to the 1980s*, pp. 33–58. Wiesbaden: Harrassowitz Verlag.

——. and Michael Hillmann. 1989. "Arabic Literature in English Translation." *Literature East and West* 25, pp. 104–16.

——. and D. S. Richards (eds). 2006. *Arabic Literature in the Post-Classical Period*. Cambridge: Cambridge University Press.

——. and Robin Ostle (eds). 2015. *Studying Modern Arabic Literature: Mustafa Badawi, Scholar and Critic*. Edinburgh: Edinburgh University Press.

'Allūsh, Mūsā. 1981. *Dirāsāt fī al-Shi'r al-Sha'bī*. Jerusalem: Mu'assasat Ibn Rushd.

Almaiman, Salwa. 2014. "Le roman saoudien contemporain face à ses défis." *Arabian Humanities* 3. Available at: <https://cy.revues.org/2793> (last accessed 27 October 2016).

Altoma, Salih J. 1993. "The Reception of Najib Mahfuz in American Publications." *Yearbook of Comparative and General Literature* 41, pp. 160–79.

——. 1993a. *Modern Arabic Poetry in English Translation: A Bibliography*. Tangiers: King Fahd School of Translation.

——. 1996. "Contemporary Arabic Fiction in English Translation: A Chronological Survey: 1947–1996." *Yearbook of Comparative and General Literature* 44, pp. 137–53.
——. 1997. "Iraq's Modern Arabic Literature in English Translation: A Preliminary Bibliography." *Arab Studies Quarterly* 19.4, pp. 131–72.
——. 2000. "Arabic-Western Literary Relations in American Publications: A Selected Bibliography." *Yearbook of Comparative and General Literature* 48, pp. 221–62.
——. 2005. *Modern Arabic Literature in Translation: A Companion*. London: Saqi Books.
——. 2009. "Translating Contemporary Iraq's Arabic Literature: Ten Years of *Banipal*'s Record 1998–2008." *International Journal of Contemporary Iraqi Studies* 3.3, pp. 307–19.
——. 2010. *Iraq's Modern Arabic Literature: A Guide to English Translations Since 1950*. Lanham, MD: Scarecrow Press.
Alwan, Mohammed Bakir. 1970. *Ahmad Faris ash-Shidyaq and the West*. PhD thesis, Indiana University.
——. 1972. "A Bibliography of Modern Arabic Fiction in English Translation." *Middle East Journal* 26, pp. 195–200.
——. 1973. "A Bibliography of Modern Arabic Poetry in English Translation." *Middle East Journal* 27, pp. 373–81.
Amanṣūr, Muḥammad. n.d. "al-Riwāya al-Maghribiyya al-Mu'āṣira: Ḥafriyyāt fī al-Takawwun." *Maknasat—Revue de la Faculté des Lettres et des Sciences Humaines de Université Moulay Ismaïl* (Meknés), pp. 79–98.
Ambros, A. A. 1994. "Zur Inschrift von 'En 'Avda: Eine Mahnung zur Vorsicht." *Journal of Arabic Linguistics* 27, pp. 90–2.
al-'Āmilī, Muḥammad Bahā' al-Dīn. 1884. *Kitāb al-Kashkūl*. Cairo: Maktabat Muḥammad Afandī Muṣṭafā.
al-Amīn, 'Abd al-Wahhāb. 1936. "al-Ḥayāt al-Adabiyya fī Baghdād." *al-Risāla*, 9 March, pp. 381–3.
Amīn, Aḥmad. 1965. *Zu'amā' al-Iṣlāḥ fī al-'Aṣr al-Ḥadīth*. Cairo: Maktabat al-Nahḍa al-Miṣriyya.
Amin, Dina. 2008. "Censorship and Its Changing Taboos on the Egyptian Stage—From Politics and Religion to Sexual Frustration." *International Journal of Middle East Studies* 40.2, pp. 181–4.
Amin, Magda. 2000. "Stories, Stories, Stories: Rafik Schami's *Erzähler der Nacht*." *Alif—Journal of Comparative Literature* 20, pp. 211–33.
al-Amīnī, Muḥammad Hādī. 1964. *Rijāl al-Fikr wa-l-Adab fī al-Najaf Khilāla Alf 'Ām*. al-Najaf: Maṭba'at al-Ādāb.
'Āmir, 'Aṭiyya. 1967. *Lughat al-Masraḥ al-'Arabī*. Beirut: al-Maṭba'a al-Kāthūlīkiyya.
'Āmir, Ibrāhīm. 1970. "Najīb Maḥfūẓ Siyāsiyyan min Thawrat 1919 ilā Yūnyū 1967." *al-Hilāl*, February, pp. 26–37.
Amireh, Amal. 1996. "Publishing in the West: Problems and Prospects for Arab Women Writers." *AlJadid* (Los Angeles) 2.10, pp. 10–11.
——. and Lisa Suhair Majaj. 2000. *Going Global: The Transnational Reception of Third World Women Writers*. New York and London: Garland Publishing.
Amit-Kochavi, Hannah. 1996. "Israeli Arabic Literature in Hebrew Translation: Initiation, Dissemination and Reception." *The Translator* 2.1, pp. 27–44.
——. 1999. *Translations of Arabic Literature into Hebrew: Their Historical and Cultural Background and Their Reception by the Target Culture* (Hebrew). PhD thesis, Tel Aviv University.
——. 2000. "Hebrew Translations of Palestinian Literature—From Total Denial to Partial Recognition." *Études sur le texte et ses transformations* 13.1, pp. 53–80.
——. 2003. "Strangers and Enemies or Partners? Hebrew Translations of Palestinian Literature—Writers, Contents, and Texts" (Hebrew). *Jama'a* 10, pp. 39–68.
——. 2004. "Translations of Arabic Literature in the Literature Studies in Israeli Hebrew

Studies" (Hebrew). In Yosef Tobi (ed.), *Contacts between Arabic Literature and Jewish Literature in the Middle Ages and Modern Times* (Vol. 3) (Hebrew), pp. 190–210. Tel Aviv: Afikim.

——. 2006. "Bridging over the Conflict—The Ideology behind Translations of Arabic Literature into Hebrew (1896–2006)." *Trans: Internet-Zeitschrift für Kulturwissenschaften* 16. Available at: <http://www.inst.at/trans/16Nr/09_4/amit-kochavi16.htm> (last accessed 27 October 2016).

——. 2006a. "Israeli Jewish Nation Building and Hebrew Translations of Arabic Literature." In Yasir Suleiman and Ibrahim Muhawi (eds), *Literature and Nation in the Middle East*, pp. 100–9. Edinburgh: Edinburgh University Press.

'Ammār, Ibrāhīm. 1979. "al-Bu'd al-Qawmī li-l-Adab al-'Arabī." *al-Ādāb*, August–September, pp. 18–23.

Amo, Mercedes del. 2010. "La traducción al español de la literatura marroquí escrita en árabe (1940–2009)." *Miscelánea de Estudios Árabes y Hebraicos (Sección Árabe-Islam)* 59, pp. 239–57.

Amuni, O. K. 2005. "Arabic Language in Nigeria: An Indigenous Language and a National Heritage." *Research Journal RJIC* 1.6, pp. 108–22.

'Anān, Muḥammad 'Abd Allāh. 1937. "Kursī Khāṣṣ li-Dirāsat al-Adab al-Miṣrī al-Islāmī." *al-Risāla*, 15 February, pp. 249–50.

'Anānī, Muḥammad Zakariyyā. 1976. "Rifā'a al-Ṭahṭāwī wa-l-Adab: Tarjamat Télémaque." *al-Kātib* (Cairo) 189, pp. 8–25.

Anati, Nisreen M. 2012. "Arabic Young Adult Literature in English." *Arab World English Journal* 3.2, pp. 168–93.

And, Metin. 1963–4. *A History of Theatre and Popular Entertainment in Turkey*. Ankara: Forum Yayinlari.

Anderson, Amanda. 1998. "Cosmopolitanism, Universalism, and the Divided Legacies of Modernity." In Pheng Cheah and Bruce Robbins (eds), *Cosmopolitics: Thinking and Feeling Beyond the Nation*, pp. 265–89. Minneapolis: University of Minnesota Press.

Anderson, Benedict. 1991. *Imagined Communities: Reflections on the Origin and Spread of Nationalism*. London and New York: Verso.

Anderson, Jon. W. 2005. "Wiring Up: The Internet Difference for Muslim Networks." In Miriam Cooke and Bruce B. Lawrence (eds), *Muslim Networks from Hajj to Hip Hop*, pp. 252–63. Chapel Hill, NC: University of North Carolina Press.

Anderson, Margaret. (ed.). 1980. *Arabic Materials in English Translation*. Boston: G. K. Hall and Co.

Andrzejewski, B. W. 1974. "The Veneration of Sufi Saints and Its Impact on the Oral Literature of the Somali People and on Their Literature in Arabic." *African Language Studies* 15, pp. 15–53.

al-'Ānī, Yūsuf. 1999. *Shakhṣiyyāt wa-Dhikrayāt*. Beirut: al-Mu'assasa al-'Arabiyya li-l-Dirāsāt wa-l-Nashr.

Anishchenkova, Valerie. 2014. *Autobiographical Identities in Contemporary Arab Culture*. Edinburgh: Edinburgh University Press.

Ansell-Pearson, Keith et al. (eds). 1997. *Cultural Readings of Imperialism: Edward Said and the Gravity of History*. London: Lawrence and Wishart.

'Antara. 1905. *Dīwān*. Cairo: al-Maktaba al-Miṣriyya.

al-'Antīl, Fawzī. 1987. *al-Fulklūr Mā Huwa?* Beirut: Dār al-Masīra and Cairo: Madbūlī.

Antoon, Sinan. 2014. *The Poetics of the Obscene in Premodern Arabic Poetry: Ibn al-Ḥajjāj and Sukhf*. New York: Palgrave Macmillan.

Appiah, Kwame Anthony. 2005. *The Ethics of Identity*. Princeton: Princeton University Press.

——. 2006. *Cosmopolitanism: Ethics in a World of Strangers*. London: Penguin Books.

Appignanesi, Lisa and Sara Maitland (eds). 1990. *The Rushdie File*. Syracuse: Syracuse University Press.

Appleby, R. Scott (ed.). 1997. *Spokesmen for the Despised: Fundamentalist Leaders of the Middle East*. Chicago and London: University of Chicago Press.
Apter, Emily. 2013. *Against World Literature: On the Politics of Untranslatability*. London: Verso.
'Aql, Sa'īd. 1935. "Lebanese Poetry in French." *al-Mashriq* 33, July–September, pp. 381–93.
——. 1947 [1944]. *Qadmūs*. Beirut: Manshūrāt Dār al-Fikr.
al-'Aqqād, 'Abbās Maḥmūd. 1945. *Fī Baytī*. Cairo: Dār al-Ma'ārif.
——. and Ibrāhīm 'Abd al-Qādir al-Māzinī. n.d. [1921]. *al-Dīwān fī al-Adab wa-l-Naqd*. Cairo: al-Sha'b.
'Arāyidī, Na'īm. 1992. *Fatal Christening* (Hebrew). Tel Aviv: Bitan.
Arazi, A. 1997. "Shi'r (1. In Arabic)." In P. J. Bearman et al. (eds), *The Encyclopaedia of Islam*, New Edition, Vol. 9, pp. 448–62. Leiden: Brill.
——. and H. Ben-Shammay. 1995. "Risāla." In P. J. Bearman et al. (eds), *The Encyclopaedia of Islam*, New Edition, Vol. 8, pp. 532–9. Leiden: Brill.
Arberry, Arthur J. 1979 [1964]. *The Koran Interpreted*. Oxford: Oxford University Press.
Arebi, Saddeka. 1994. *Women and Words in Saudi Arabia: The Politics of Literary Discourse*. New York: Columbia University Press.
al-'Arīnī, 'Abd Allāh Ṣāliḥ. 1989. *al-Ittijāh al-Islāmī fī A'māl Najīb al-Kaylānī*. Riyadh: al-Ḥaras al-Waṭanī al-Sa'ūdī.
Arkoun, Mohammed. 2002. *The Unthought in Contemporary Islamic Thought*. London: Saqi Books and the Institute of Ismaili Studies.
Armbrust, Walter. 1992. "The National Vernacular: Folklore and Egyptian Popular Culture." *Michigan Quarterly Review* 31.2, pp. 525–42.
——. 1994–5. "Pre-1960s Egyptian Cinema and the Development of National Ideology." *Newsletter of the American Research Center in Egypt* 116, pp. 6–20.
——. 1996. *Mass Culture and Modernism in Egypt*. Cambridge: Cambridge University Press.
——. 2012. "A History of New Media in the Arab Middle East." *Journal for Cultural Research* 16.3, pp. 155–74.
——. 2013. "The Trickster in Egypt's January 25th Revolution." *Comparative Studies in Society and History* 55.4, pp. 834–64.
Arroues, Ophélie. 2011. "Formation de la littérature et dynamiques génériques dans la presse arabe du début du XXe siècle: al-Shabâb de Mahmûd Bayram al-Tûnisî." *IBLA: Revue de l'Institut des Belles Lettres Arabes* 207, pp. 31–51.
'Arsān, 'Alī 'Uqla. 1983. *al-Ẓawāhir al-Masraḥiyya 'inda al-'Arab*. Tripoli (Libya): al-Munsh'a al-'Āmma li-l-Nashr wa-l-Tawzī' wa-l-I'lān.
'Asāqla, 'Iṣām. 2011. *Binā' al-Shakhṣiyyāt fī Riwāyāt al-Khayāl al-'Ilmī fī al-Adab al-'Arabī*. Amman: Azmina li-l-Nashr wa-l-Tawzī'.
Asfour, John Mikhail (ed.). 1988. *When the Words Burn: An Anthology of Modern Arabic Poetry 1945–1987*. Dunvegan, Ontario: Cormorant Books.
Ashtiany, J. et al. 1990. *The Cambridge History of Arabic Literature: 'Abbasid Belles-Lettres*. Cambridge: Cambridge University Press.
Aṣlān, Ibrāhīm. 2003. *Khalwat al-Ghalabān*. Cairo: Dār al-Shurūq.
al-Aswānī, 'Alā'. 2002. *'Imārat Ya'qūbyān*. Cairo: Merit.
——. 2005. *The Yacoubian Building* (trans. Humphrey T. Davies). Cairo: The American University in Cairo Press.
'Aṭiyya, Aḥmad Muḥammad. 1977. *Ma'a Najīb Maḥfūẓ*. Beirut: Dār al-Jīl.
——. 1981. *al-Riwāya al-Siyāsiyya*. Cairo: Madbūlī.
——. 1982. *Ḥarb October fī al-Adab al-'Arabī al-Ḥadīth*. Cairo: Dār al-Ma'ārif.
——. 1992. *Humūm al-Mar'a al-'Arabiyya fī al-Qiṣṣa wa-l-Riwāya*. Cairo: al-Hay'a al-Miṣriyya al-'Āmma li-l-Kitāb.
Attwater, Donald. 1985. *Dictionary of Saints*. Harmondsworth: Penguin Books.

Austen, Jane. 1965 [1917]. *Northanger Abbey*. New York and Toronto: The New American Library.
Avino, Maria. 2001. "La traduzione letteraria dall'italiano in arabo, fino alla vigilia della seconda guerra mondiale." *Traduttore Nuovo* 56.1, pp. 53–66, 115.
Awad, A. A-R. Y. 1992. *Images of the West as Portrayed in the Political Cartoons of the United Kingdom-Based Arab Media*. PhD thesis, University of Bradford.
'Awaḍ, Lūwīs. 1963. *Dirāsāt fī al-Naqd wa-l-Adab*. Beirut: al-Maktab al-Tijārī.
——. 1966. *al-'Anqā' aw Ta'rīkh Ḥasan Muftāḥ*. Beirut: Dār al-Ṭalī'a.
——. 1988 [1947]. *Blūtūlānd wa-Qaṣā'id Ukhrā min Shi'r al-Khāṣṣa*. Cairo: al-Hay'a al-Miṣriyya al-'Āmma li-l-Kitāb.
——. 1991 [1965]. *Mudhakkirāt Ṭālib Ba'tha*. Cairo: al-Hay'a al-Miṣriyya al-'Āmma li-l-Kitāb.
'Awaḍ, Rītā. 1974. "'Awlād Ḥāratinā' Bayna al-Ru'yā wa-l-Ta'bīr." *al-Ādāb*, June, pp. 50–4.
'Awaḍ, Yūsuf Nūr. 1979. *Fann al-Maqāmāt Bayna al-Mashriq wa-l-Maghrib*. Beirut: Dār al-Qalam.
'Awwād, Mūrīs. 1983. *al-Anṭūlūjiyyā al-Lubnāniyye* [sic] *min al-Alf al-Tālit* [sic] *qabla al-Masīḥ li-Sanat 1982*. al-Dūrā: Khlīfī.
Ayalon, Ami. 1987. *Language and Change in the Arab Middle East*. New York and Oxford: Oxford University Press.
——. 1995. *The Press in the Arab Middle East*. New York and Oxford: Oxford University Press.
——. 1999. *Egypt's Quest for Cultural Orientation*. Tel Aviv: The Moshe Dayan Center for Middle Eastern and African Studies, Tel Aviv University.
——. 2004. *Reading Palestine: Printing and Literacy, 1900–1948*. Austin: University of Texas Press.
——. 2008. "Private Publishing in the *Nahḍa*." *International Journal of Middle East Studies* 40.4, pp. 561–77.
——. 2015. "New Practices: Arab Printing, Publishing and Mass Reading." In Liat Kozma et al. (eds), *A Global Middle East: Mobility, Materiality and Culture in the Modern Age, 1880–1940*, pp. 321–44. London and New York: I. B. Tauris.
——. 2016. *The Arabic Print Revolution: Cultural Production and Mass Readership*. Cambridge: Cambridge University Press.
Ayalon, Yaron. 2009. "Revisiting Ṭāhā Ḥusayn's *Fī al-Shi'r al-Jāhilī* and Its Sequel." *Welt des Islams* 49.1, pp. 98–121.
'Ayyād, Shukrī. 1970. "Ḥawla Waḥdat al-Thaqāfa al-'Arabiyya." *al-Majalla* (Cairo), February, pp. 2–3.
Ayyad, Shukry and Nancy Witherspoon. 1999. *Reflections and Deflections: A Study of the Contemporary Arab Mind Through Its Literary Creations*. Cairo: Prism Publications.
Ayyūb, Sa'īd. 1989. *Shayṭān al-Gharab: Salmān Rushdī al-Rajul al-Māriq*. Cairo: Dār al-I'tiṣām.
al-'Azab, Yusrī. 1971. *Fawāzīr Fallāḥiyya*. Cairo: n.pub.
——. 1981. *Azjāl Bayram al-Tunisī: Dirāsa Fanniyya*. Cairo: al-Hay'a al-Miṣriyya al-'Āmma li-l-Kitāb.
Azeriah, Ali. 1993. *Translated Children's Literature into Arabic: A Case Study of Translational Norms*. PhD thesis, State University of New York at Binghamton.
——. 2000. "The Role of Translation in Enhancing National Children's Literatures: A Case Study of Arabic Children's Literature." *Turjumān: Revue de Traduction et d'Interprétation* 9.1, pp. 11–29.
al-'Aẓm (al-Azm), Sadiq Jalal. 1981. "Orientalism and Orientalism in Reverse." *Khamsin* 8, pp. 5–26.
——. 1984. "Orientalism and Orientalism in Reverse." In Jon Rothschild (ed.), *Forbidden Agendas: Intolerance and Defiance in the Middle East*, pp. 349–76. London: Saqi Books.

——. 1988 [1969]. *Naqd al-Fikr al-Dīnī*. Beirut: Dār al-Ṭalī'a.
——. 1992. *Dhihniyyat al-Taḥrīm: Salmān Rushdī wa-Ḥaqīqat al-Adab*. London and Limassol: Riyāḍ al-Rayyis.
——. 1997. *Mā Ba'da Dhihniyyat al-Taḥrīm: Qirā'at al-Āyāt al-Shayṭāniyya, Radd wa-Ta'qīb*. Nicosia: Markaz al-Abḥāth wa-l-Dirāsāt al-Ishtirākiyya fī al-'Ālam al-'Arabī.
——. 2014. *On Fundamentalisms*. Berlin: Gerlach Press.
——. 2014a. *Islam—Submission and Disobedience*. Berlin: Gerlach Press.
——. 2014b. *Is Islam Secularizable? Challenging Political and Religious Taboos*. Berlin: Gerlach Press.
al-'Aẓma (al-Azmeh), 'Azīz. 1989. "The Satanic Flame." *New Statesman and Society* 20, pp. 16–17.
——. 1995. "Naṣr Ḥāmid Abū Zayd fīmā warā' al-Idāna wa-mā Qablahā." *Dirāsāt 'Arabiyya* 11–12, pp. 3–7.
——. 1995a. "Riwāya Kāfira." In *al-'Unf al-Uṣūlī: Muwājahāt al-Sayf wa-l-Qalam*, pp. 13–21. London and Beirut: Riyāḍ al-Rayyis.
——. 1995b. "Nationalism and the Arabs." *Arab Studies Quarterly* 17.1–2, pp. 1–17.
——. 1996. *Islams and Modernities*. London and New York: Verso.
Azouqa, Aida O. 2005. "Federico García Lorca and Ṣalāḥ 'Abd al-Ṣabūr as Composers of Modern Ballads: A Comparative Study." *Journal of Arabic Literature* 36.2, pp. 188–223.
al-'Azzāwī, Fāḍil. 1997. *al-Rūḥ al-Ḥayya: Jīl al-Sittīnāt fī al-'Irāq*. Damascus: Dār al-Madā li-l-Thaqāfa wa-l-Nashr.
Azzouna, Jalloul. 2008. "Inter-influences littéraires des poésies arabo-espagnole et romano-provençale au Moyen-Âge (1ère partie)." *Revue d'Études Andalouses* 39, pp. 7–28.
——. 2008a. "Inter-influences littéraires des poésies arabo-espagnole et romano-provençale au Moyen-Âge (2ème partie)." *Revue d'Études Andalouses* 40, pp. 13–29.
Badawī, 'Abd al-Ghanī. 1963. *Kāmil Kaylānī al-Rā'id al-'Arabī li-Adab al-Aṭfāl*. Cairo: al-Dār al-Qawmiyya.
Badawī, 'Abd al-Raḥmān. 1999. *Kāmil Kaylānī wa-Sīratuhu al-Dhātiyya*. Cairo: al-Hay'a al-Miṣriyya al-'Āmma li-l-Kitāb.
Badawi, M. M. 1975. *A Critical Introduction to Modern Arabic Poetry*. Cambridge: Cambridge University Press.
——. 1977. "To the Editor: Modern Arabic Poetry." *The Times Literary Supplement*, 7 January.
——. 1982. "Medieval Arabic Drama: Ibn Dāniyāl." *Journal of Arabic Literature* 13, pp. 83–107.
——. 1988. *Early Arabic Drama*. Cambridge: Cambridge University Press.
——. 1988a. *Modern Arabic Drama in Egypt*. Cambridge: Cambridge University Press.
——. (ed.). 1992. *Modern Arabic Literature*. Cambridge: Cambridge University Press.
——. 1993. *A Short History of Modern Arabic Literature*. Oxford: Clarendon Press.
——. 2000. "Perennial Themes in Modern Arabic Literature." In Derek Hopwood (ed.), *Arab Nation, Arab Nationalism*, pp. 129–53. Basingstoke: Macmillan Press.
Badawī, Muḥammad Muṣṭafā. 1984. "Mushkilat al-Ḥadātha wa-l-Taghyīr al-Ḥaḍārī fī al-Adab al-'Arabī al-Ḥadīth." *Fuṣūl* 4.3, pp. 98–106.
al-Badawī al-Mulaththam. 1963. *al-Bustānī wa-Ilyādhat Hūmīrūs*. Cairo: Dār al-Ma'ārif.
Badīr, Ḥilmī. 1982. *al-Mu'aththirāt al-Ajnabiyya fī al-Adab al-'Arabī al-Ḥadīth*. Cairo: Dār al-Ma'ārif.
——. 1986. *Athar al-Adab al-Sha'bī fī al-Adab al-Ḥadīth*. Cairo: Dār al-Ma'ārif.
——. 1991. *al-Shi'r al-Mutarjam wa-Ḥarakat al-Tajdīd fī al-Shi'r al-Ḥadīth*. Cairo: Dār al-Ma'ārif.
Badr, 'Abd al-Bāsiṭ (ed.). 1993. *Dalīl Maktabāt al-Adab al-Islāmī fī al-'Aṣr al-Ḥadīth*. Amman: Dār al-Bashīr.
Badr, 'Abd al-Muḥsin Ṭāhā. 1983. *Taṭawwur al-Riwāya al-'Arabiyya al-Ḥadītha fī Miṣr (1870–1938)*. Cairo: Dār al-Ma'ārif.

Badr, Liyāna. 1991. *'Ayn al-Mir'ā*. Casablanca: Dār Ṭūbqāl li-l-Nashr.

——. 1995. *The Eye of the Mirror* (trans. Samira Kawar). London: Garnet Publishing.

Badrān, Ḥusayn. 1972. *al-Thabt al-Biblūjrāfī li-l-A'māl al-Mutarjama 1956–1967*. Cairo: al-Hay'a al-Miṣriyya al-'Āmma li-l-Kitāb.

Badran, Margot. 1993. "More Than a Century of Feminism in Egypt." In Judith Tucker (ed.), *Arab Women: Old Boundaries, New Frontiers*, pp. 129–48. Bloomington: Indiana University Press.

——. 1995. *Feminists, Islam and Nation: Gender and the Making of Modern Egypt*. Princeton: Princeton University Press.

——. and Miriam Cooke. 1990. *Opening the Gates: A Century of Arab Feminist Writing*. Bloomington, IN: Indiana University Press.

Badrān, Muḥammad Abū al-Faḍl. 2001. *Adabiyyāt al-Karāma al-Ṣūfiyya: Dirāsa fī al-Shikl wa-l-Maḍmūn*. al-'Ayn, UAE: Markaz Zāyid li-l-Turāth wa-l-Ta'rīkh.

Baer, F. I. et al. (eds). 1938. *Magnes Anniversary Book* (Hebrew). Jerusalem: Hebrew University Press

Bagader, Abubaker et al. (eds). 1998. *Voices of Change: Short Stories by Saudi Arabian Women Writers*. London and Boulder, CO: Lynne Rienner Publishers.

al-Bagdadi, Nadia. 2008. "Registers of Arabic Literary History." *New Literary History* 39.3, pp. 437–61.

Bahī, 'Iṣām. 1994. *al-Khayāl al-'Ilmī fī Masraḥ Tawfīq al-Ḥakīm*. Cairo: al-Hay'a al-Miṣriyya al-'Āmma li-l-Kitāb.

al-Bahnasī, 'Afīf. 1997. *al-'Umrān al-Thaqāfī Bayna al-Turāth wa-l-Qawmiyya*. Cairo and Damascus: Dār al-Kitāb al-'Arabī.

Bahrani, Zainab. 2001. *Women of Babylon: Gender and Representation in Mesopotamia*. London and New York: Routledge.

Bailey, Clinton. 1991. *Bedouin Poetry from Sinai and the Negev*. Oxford: Clarendon Press.

Bakalla, Muhammad Hasan. 1980. *An Introduction to Arabic Language and Literature*. Taipei: European Languages Publications.

Baker, Mona (ed.). 2016. *Translating Dissent: Voices from and with the Egyptian Revolution*. New York and London: Routledge.

Bakkār, Yūsuf Ḥusayn. 1981. *Ittijāhāt al-Ghazal fī al-Qarn al-Thānī al-Hijrī*. Beirut: Dār al-Andalus.

Bakr, Salwā. 1991. *al-'Araba al-Dhahabiyya lā Taṣ'adu ilā al-Samā'*. Cairo: Dār Sīnā.

——. 1995. *The Golden Chariot* (trans. Dinah Manisty). London: Garnet Publishing.

al-Bakrī, Muḥammad Tawfīq. 1905. *Bayt al-Ṣiddīq*. Cairo: Maṭba'at al-Mu'ayyad.

——. 1907. *Ṣahārīj al-Lu'lu'*. Cairo: Maḥmūd Dajjāj al-Kutubī.

Albakry, Mohammed and Rebekah Maggor (eds). 2016. *Tahrir Tales: Plays from the Egyptian Revolution*. London: Seagull Books.

Balaa, Luma. 2013. "Misuse of Islam in El-Saadawi's *God Dies by the Nile* from a Socialist Feminist Perspective." *Hawwa: Journal of Women of the Middle East and the Islamic World* 11.2–3, pp. 187–211.

Ba'labakkī, Laylā. 1964 [1963]. *Safīnat Ḥanān ilā al-Qamar*. Beirut: al-Maktab al-Tijārī li-l-Ṭibā'a wa-l-Nashr.

al-Ba'labakkī, Munīr. 1972. "al-Kitāb al-'Arabī wa-Mushkilāt al-Nashr wa-l-Tawzī'." *al-Ādāb*, January, pp. 70–3.

Baldissera, E. 1995. "The Modern Short Story in the Sultanate of Oman." *Arabist: Budapest Studies in Arabic* 15–16, pp. 89–100.

Ball, Anna. 2012. *Palestinian Literature and Film in Postcolonial Feminist Perspective*. New York: Routledge.

Ballas, Shimon. 1980. *La littérature arabe et le conflict au proche-orient (1948–1973)*. Paris: Édition Anthropos.

——. 1992. *al-Adab al-'Arabī wa-l-Taḥdīth al-Fikrī*. Cologne: Manshūrāt al-Jamal.

——. and R. Snir (eds) 1998. *Studies in Canonical and Popular Arabic Literature*. Toronto: York Press.

Bamia, Aida Adib. 1992. "The North African Novel: Achievements and Prospects." *Mundus Arabicus* 5, pp. 61–88.

——. 2001. *The Graying of the Raven: Cultural and Sociopolitical Significance of Algerian Folk Poetry*. Cairo and New York: The American University in Cairo Press.

Bannūra, Jamāl. 1984. "'An Adab al-Sujūn." *al-Jadīd*, June–July, pp. 71–4.

al-Baqlī, Muḥammad Qindīl. 1962. *Ṣuwar min Adabinā al-Sha'bī aw al-Fulklūr al-Miṣrī*. Cairo: Maktabat al-Anglo al-Miṣriyya.

al-Baraddūnī, 'Abd Allāh. 1988. *Funūn al-Adab al-Sha'bī fī al-Yaman*. Beirut: Dār al-Ḥadātha.

Barakat, Halim. 1993. *The Arab World: Society, Culture, and State*. Berkeley: University of California Press.

——. 2000. "Explorations in Exile and Creativity: The Case of Arab-American Writers." In Kamal Abdel-Malek and Wael Hallaq (eds), *Tradition, Modernity, and Postmodernity in Arabic Literature: Essays in Honor of Professor Issa J. Boullata*, pp. 304–20. Leiden: Brill.

Barakāt, Hudā. 1990. *Ḥajar al-Ḍaḥk*. London: Riad El-Rayyes Books.

——. 1995. *The Stone of Laughter* (trans. Sophie Bennett). London: Garnet Publishing.

Baram, Amatzia. 1983. "Culture in the Service of *Waṭaniyya*: The Treatment of Mesopotamian-Inspired Art in Ba'thi Iraq." *Asian and African Studies* 17, pp. 265–313.

——. 1990. "Territorial Nationalism in the Middle East." *Middle Eastern Studies* 26.4, pp. 425–48.

——. 1994. "A Case of Imported Identity: The Modernizing of Secular Ruling Elites of Iraq and the Concept of Mesopotamian-Inspired Territorial Nationalism, 1922–1992." *Poetics Today* 15.2, pp. 279–319.

——. 2014. *Saddam Husayn and Islam, 1968–2003: Ba'thi Iraq from Secularism to Faith*. Washington, DC: Woodrow Wilson Center Press and Baltimore: The Johns Hopkins University Press.

Bardenstein, Carol. 2005. *Translation and Transformation in the Emergence of Modern Arabic Literature: The Indigenous Assertions of Muḥammad 'Uthmān Jalāl*. Wiesbaden: Harrassowitz Verlag.

al-Barghūthī, 'Abd al-Laṭīf. 1979. *al-Aghānī al-Sha'biyya fī Filasṭīn wa-l-Urdun*. Jerusalem: Maṭba'at al-Sharq al-'Arabiyya.

——. 1986. *Dīwān al-'Atābā al-Filasṭīnī*. Jerusalem and Birzeit: Mu'assasat al-Bayādir & Markaz al-Wathā'iq wa-l-Abḥāth fī Jāmi'at Bīr Zayt.

——. 1988. *Bayna al-Turāth al-Rasmī wa-l-Turāth al-Sha'bī*. Amman: Dār al-Karmil li-l-Nashr.

al-Bāridī, Muḥammad. 1997. "al-Sīra al-Dhātiyya fī al-Adab al-'Arabī al-Ḥadīth—Ḥudūd al-Jins wa-Ishkālātuhu." *Fuṣūl* 16.3, pp. 68–80.

——. 2005. *'Indamā Tatakallam al-Dhāt: al-Sīra al-Dhātiyya fī al-Adab al-'Arabī al-Ḥadīth*. Damascus: Manshūrāt Ittiḥād al-Kuttāb al-'Arab.

Barker, Martin. 1989. *Comics: Ideology, Power and the Critics*. Manchester: Manchester University Press.

al-Barnbālī, Ṭāhir. 1993. *Ṭifla Bitḥibbī Taḥta Saqf al-Rūḥ*. Cairo: al-Hay'a al-'Āmma li-Quṣūr al-Thaqāfa.

Baron, Beth Ann. 1988. *The Rise of a New Literary Culture: The Women's Press of Egypt 1892–1919*. PhD thesis, University of California, Los Angeles.

——. 1994. *Women's Awakening in Egypt: Culture, Society, and the Press*. New Haven and London: Yale University Press.

——. 1996. "A Field Matures: Recent Literature on Women in the Middle East." *Middle Eastern Studies* 32.3, pp. 172–86.

——. 1999. *al-Nahḍa al-Nisā'iyya fī Miṣr: al-Thaqāfa wa-l-Mujtama' wa-l-Ṣiḥāfa* (trans. Lamīs al-Naqqāsh). Cairo: al-Majlis al-A'lā li-l-Thaqāfa.

Baron, Salo Wittmayer. 1957. *A Social and Religious History of the Jews*. Philadelphia: The Jewish Publication Society of America.

Baroudi, Sami E. 2016. "The Islamic Realism of Sheikh Yusuf Qaradawi (1926–) and Sayyid Mohammad Hussein Fadlallah (1935–2010)." *British Journal of Middle Eastern Studies* 43.1, pp. 94–114.

Barqāwī, Aḥmad. 1995. "Asīr al-Wahm." In *al-'Unf al-Uṣūlī: Muwājahāt al-Sayf wa-l-Qalam*, pp. 81–114. London and Beirut: Riyāḍ al-Rayyis.

Barrāda, Muḥammad. 1996. *As'ilat al-Riwāya As'ilat al-Naqd*. Casablanca: al-Rābiṭa.

——. 2011. *al-Riwāya al-'Arabiyya wa-Rihān al-Tajdīd*. Cairo: al-Hay'a al-Miṣriyya al-'Āmma li-l-Kitāb.

al-Bārūdī, Maḥmūd Sāmī. 1954. *Dīwān*. Cairo: al-Maṭba'a al-Amīriyya.

——. 1993. *Maḥmūd Sāmī al-Bārūdī* (ed. Muḥammad 'Afīfī Maṭar). Beirut and Cairo: Dār al-Fatā al-'Arabī.

Baṣrī, Mīr. 1983. *A'lām al-Yahūd fī al-'Irāq al-Ḥadīth*. Jerusalem: Rābiṭat al-Jāmi'iyyīn al-Yahūd al-Nāziḥīn min al-'Irāq.

——. 1993. *A'lām al-Yahūd fī al-'Irāq al-Ḥadīth* (Vol. 2). Jerusalem: Rābiṭat al-Jāmi'iyyīn al-Yahūd al-Nāziḥīn min al-'Irāq.

——. 1994. *A'lām al-Adab fī al-'Irāq al-Ḥadīth*. London: Dār al-Ḥikma.

——. 1999. *A'lām al-Adab fī al-'Irāq al-Ḥadīth*. London: Dār al-Ḥikma.

Bassnett, Susan and André Lefevere (eds). 1990. *Translation, History and Culture*. London and New York: Pinter Publishers.

al-Bataineh, A. B. 1998. *The Modern Arabic Novel: A Literary and Linguistic Analysis of the Genre of Popular Fiction, with Special Reference to Translation from English*. PhD thesis, Heriot-Watt University.

Bauer, Thomas. 2003. "Vom Sinn der Zeit aus der Geschichte des arabischen Chronogramms." *Arabica* 50.4, pp. 501–31.

——. 2005. "Mamluk Literature: Misunderstandings and New Approaches." *Mamlūk Studies Review* 9.2, pp. 105–32.

——. 2006. "Die Badī'iyya des Nāṣīf al-Yāziǧī und das Problem der spätosmanischen arabischen Literatur. In A. Neuwirth and A. C. Islebe (eds), *Reflections on Reflections. Near Eastern Writers Reading Literature*, pp. 49–118. Wiesbaden: Reichert.

——. 2007. "In Search of 'Post-Classical Literature': A Review Article." *Mamlūk Studies Review* 11.2, pp. 137–67.

——. 2013. "'Ayna Hādhā min al-Mutanabbī!': Toward an Aesthetics of Mamluk Literature." *Mamlūk Studies Review* 17, pp. 5–22.

Bauman, Zygmunt. 2004. *Liquid Modernity*. Cambridge: Polity Press.

——. 2009. "Identity in the Globalizing World." In Anthony Elliott and Paul Du Gay (eds), *Identity in Question*, pp. 1–12. Los Angeles: Sage Publications.

Bawārdī, Bāsīlyūs Ḥannā. 1998. *Bayna al-Ṣaḥrā' wa-l-Baḥr: Baḥth fī Ta'thīr al-Qawmiyyatayn al-Lubnāniyya-al-Fīnīqiyya wa-l-Sūriyya 'alā al-Adab al-'Arabī al-Mu'āṣir*. MA thesis, University of Haifa.

——. 2000–1. "Adab al-Qawmiyya al-Lubnāniyya al-Fīnīqiyya: *al-Taṣwīnī*, Awwal Riwāya bi-l-Lugha al-Lubnāniyya ka-Namūdhaj Naṣṣī." *al-Karmil—Abḥāth fī al-Lugha wa-l-Adab* 21–2, pp. 7–79.

——. 2008. "First Steps in Writing Arabic Narrative Fiction: The Case of *Ḥadīqat al-Akhbār*." *Die Welt des Islams* 48, pp. 170–95.

Baybars, Ḍiyā' al-Dīn. 1970. "Talḥīn al-Qur'ān Bayna Ahl al-Fann wa-Rijāl al-Dīn." *al-Hilāl*, December, pp. 118–27.

Bayḍūn, 'Abbās. 1995. "Maḥmūd Darwīsh: Man Yaktub Ḥikāyatahu Yarith Arḍ al-Ḥikāya." *Mashārif* (Jerusalem and Haifa) 3, pp. 69–111.

al-Bayyātī, 'Abd al-Wahhāb. 1979. *Dīwān*. Beirut: Dār al-'Awda.

——. 1984. *Qamar Shīrāz*. Cairo: al-Hay'a al-Miṣriyya al-'Āmma li-l-Kitāb.
Beard, Michael and Adnan Haydar (eds). 1993. *Naguib Mahfouz: From Regional Fame to Global Recognition*. Syracuse: Syracuse University Press.
Beck, Lois and Nikki Keddie (eds). 1978. *Women in the Muslim World*. Cambridge, MA: Harvard University Press.
Beck, Ulrich and Natan Sznaider. 2006. "Unpacking Cosmopolitanism for the Social Sciences: A Research Agenda." *British Journal of Sociology* 57.1, pp. 1–23 (also published in a special issue of the *British Journal of Sociology*: "Shaping Sociology over 60 Years." 61 [2010], pp. 381–403).
Beeston, A. F. L. 1971. "The Genesis of the *Maqāmāt* Genre." *Journal of Arabic Literature* 2, pp. 1–12.
——. 1994. "Antecedents of Classical Arabic Verse." In Wolfhart Heinrichs and Greogr Schoeler (eds), *Festschrift Ewald Wagner zum 65 Geburtstag*, pp. 234–43. Beirut and Stuttgart: Franz Steiner Verlag.
Beinin, Joel. 1994. "Writing Class: Workers and Modern Egyptian Colloquial Poetry (*Zajal*)." *Poetics Today* 15.2, pp. 191–215.
Bellamy, J. A. 1990. "Arabic Verses from the First/Second Century: The Inscription of 'En 'Abdat." *Journal of Semitic Studies* 35.1, pp. 73–9.
Benarab, Abdelkader. 1995. *Les voix de l'exil*. Paris: L'Harmattan.
Bengio, Ofra. 1998. *Saddam's Word: Political Discourse in Iraq*. New York and Oxford: Oxford University Press.
——. 2002. "Saddam Husayn's Novel of Fear." *Middle East Quarterly* 9.1, pp. 9–18.
Benigni, Elisabetta. 2011. "Encounters between Arabic and Western Literatures: Emic Translations and the Etic Formation of Literary Canons." *Rivista degli Studi Orientali* 84.1–4, pp. 129–44.
Ben Jelloun, Tahar. 1987. *La nuit sacrée*. Paris: Éditions du Seuil.
——. 2006. "Mahfouz, the Middle Man." *The New York Times*, 3 September.
BenMas'ūd, Rashīda. 1994. *al-Mar'a wa-l-Kitāba: Su'āl al-Khuṣūṣiyya/Balāghat al-Ikhtilāf*. Casablanca: Ifrīqiyā al-Sharq.
Benn, Gottfried. 1997. *Qaṣā'id Mukhtāra* (trans. Khālid al-Ma'ālī). Cologne: Al-Kamel Verlag.
Bennett, Sophie. 1998. "A Life of One's Own?" In Robin C. Ostle et al. (eds), *Writing the Self: Autobiographical Writing in Modern Arabic Literature*, pp. 283–91. London: Saqi Books.
Ben-Shammai, H. 1993. *Hebrew and Arabic Studies in Honour of Joshua Blau Presented by Friends and Students on the Occasion of His Seventieth Birthday*. Jerusalem: Hebrew University, Institute of Asian and African Studies.
Ben-Yehuda, Nachman. 1995. *The Masada Myth: Collective Memory and Mythmaking in Israel*. Madison, WI: University of Wisconsin Press.
Berg, E. Nancy. 1996. *Exile from Exile: Israeli Writers from Iraq*. Albany: State University of New York Press.
Berkey, Jonathan P. 2001. *Popular Preaching and Religious Authority in the Medieval Islamic Near East*. Seattle and London: University of Washington Press.
Berman, Nina. 1998. "German and Middle Eastern Literary Traditions in a Novel by Salim Alafenisch: Thoughts on a Germanophone Beduin Author from the Negev." *German Quarterly* 71 (1998), pp. 271–83.
Bernard, Anna. 2013. *Rhetorics of Belonging: Nation, Narration, and Israel/Palestine*. Liverpool: Liverpool University Press.
Berque, Jacques. 1964. *The Arabs: Their History and Future* (trans. Jean Stewart). London: Faber and Faber.
——. 1969 [1960]. *Les arabes d'hier à demain*. Paris: Éditions du Seuil.
——. 1982. *al-'Arab min al-Ams ilā al-Ghad* (trans. 'Alī Sa'd). Beirut: Dār al-Kitāb al-Lubnānī & Maktabat al-Madrasa.

Beyerl, Jan. 1971. *The Style of the Modern Arabic Short Story*. Prague: Charles University.

Bhabha, Homi K. 1994. *The Location of Culture*. London and New York: Routledge.

al-Bīṭār, Nadīm. 1969. "Naḥwa 'Almana Inqilābiyya." *Mawāqif* 2, pp. 34–50.

Blachère, Régis. 1952. *Histoire de la littérature arabe*. Paris: Librairie Adrien—Maisonneuve.

——. 1984. *Ta'rīkh al-Adab al-'Arabī* (trans. Ibrāhīm al-Kaylānī). Damascus: Dār al-Fikr.

Blackshire-Belay, Carol Aisha (ed.). 1994. *The Germanic Mosaic: Cultural and Linguistic Diversity in Society*. New York: Greenwood.

Blanks, David R. 1997. *Images of the Other: Europe and the Muslim World Before 1700*. Cairo: The American University in Cairo Press.

Blau, Joshua. 1981. *The Emergence and Linguistic Background of Judaeo-Arabic: A Study of the Origins of Middle Arabic*. Jerusalem: Ben-Zvi Institute for the Study of Jewish Communities in the East.

Bohas, Georges and Djamel Eddine Kouloughli, 2001. "Toward a Systematic Corpus Analysis of Arabic Poetry." *Belgian Journal of Linguistics* 15, pp. 103–12.

Bois, M. 1992. "Arabic-Language Algerian Literature." *Research in African Literatures* 23.2, pp. 103–11.

Booth, Marilyn. 1987. "Women's Prison Memoirs in Egypt and Elsewhere: Prison, Gender, Praxis." *Middle East Report* 149, pp. 35–41.

——. 1990. *Bayram al-Tunisi's Egypt: Social Criticism and Narrative Strategies*. Exeter: Ithaca Press.

——. 1992. "Colloquial Arabic Poetry, Politics, and the Press in Modern Egypt." *International Journal of Middle East Studies* 24, pp. 419–40.

——. 1994. "Force and Transitivity: Bayram al-Tunisi and a Poetics of Anticolonialism." In Ferial J. Ghazoul and Barbara Harlow (eds), *The View from Within: Writers and Critics on Contemporary Arabic Literature*, pp. 149–76. Cairo: The American University in Cairo Press.

——. 2001. *May Her Likes Be Multiplied: Biography and Gender Politics in Egypt*. Berkeley: University of California Press.

——. 2009. "Exploding into the Seventies. Ahmad Fu'ad Nigm, Sheikh Imam, and the Aesthetics of a New Youth Politics." In Nicholas S. Hopkins (ed.), *Political and Social Protest in Egypt*, pp. 19–44. Cairo and New York: The American University in Cairo Press.

——. (ed.). 2010. *Harem Histories: Envisioning Places and Living Spaces*. Durham, NC: Duke University Press.

——. 2015. *Classes of Ladies of Cloistered Spaces: Writing Feminist History Through Biography in Fin-de-Siecle Egypt*. Edinburgh: Edinburgh University Press.

Bosworth, C. Edmund. 1996. "Arabic Influences in the Literature of Nineteenth and Early Twentieth Century Britain." In J. R. Smart (ed.), *Tradition and Modernity in Arabic Language and Literature*, pp. 155–64. Richmond: Curzon.

Boudot-Lamotte, Antoine. 1977. *Aḥmad Šawqī: L'homme et l'oeuvre*. Damascus: Institut Français de Damas.

Boullata, Issa J. (ed.). 1980. *Critical Perspectives on Modern Arabic Literature*. Washington, DC: Three Continents Press.

——. and Terri DeYoung (eds). 1997. *Tradition and Modernity in Arabic Literature*. Fayetteville, AR: University of Arkansas Press.

Boulus, Sargon. 1997. *Zeugen am Ufer* (trans. Khālid al-Ma'ālī and Stefan Weidner). Berlin: Das Arabische Buch.

Bouraoui, H. A. 1980. "Creative Project and Literary Projection in Francophone North Africa." In Issa J. Boullata (ed.), *Critical Perspectives on Modern Arabic Literature*, pp. 129–144. Washington, DC: Three Continents Press.

Bowen, Donna Lee and Evelyn A. Early (eds). 1993. *Everyday Life in the Muslim Middle East*. Bloomington and Indianapolis: Indiana University Press.

Boyd, Douglas A. 1999. *Broadcasting in the Arab World: A Survey of the Electronic Media in the Middle East*. Ames, IA: Iowa State University Press.

Bray, Julia. 2006. *Writing and Representations in Medieval Islam: Muslim Horizons*. New York and London: Routledge.

Brennan, Timothy. 1989. *Salman Rushdie and the Third World*. New York: St. Martin's Press.

Brenner, Rachel Feldhay. 1999. "'Hidden Transcripts' Made Public: Israeli Arab Fiction and Its Reception." *Critical Inquiry* 26, pp. 85–108.

——. 2003. *Inextricably Bonded: Israeli, Arab, and Jewish Writers Re-visioning Culture*. Madison, WI: University of Wisconsin Press.

Brīghash, Muḥammad Ḥasan. 1996. *Adab al-Aṭfāl Ahdāfuhu wa-Simātuhu*. Beirut: al-Risāla.

Brinner, William M. 1963. "The Significance of the Ḥarāfish and Their 'Sultan'? *Journal of the Economic and Social History of the Orient* 6.2, pp. 190–215.

Brockelmann, C. 1937–49. *Geschicte der Arabischen Litterature*. Leiden: Brill.

Brooks, Geraldine. 1995. *Nine Parts of Desire: The Hidden World of Islamic Women*. New York: Anchor Books.

Brugman, J. 1984. *An Introduction to the History of Modern Arabic Literature in Egypt*. Leiden: Brill.

Brumm, Ann-Marie. 1995. "Three Interviews." *Edebiyât* 6, pp. 81–98.

Bsīsū, Mu'īn. 1988. *al-A'māl al-Shi'riyya al-Kāmila*. Acre: Dār al-Aswār.

Buheiri, Marwan R. (ed.) 1981. *Intellectual Life in the Arab East, 1890–1939*. Beirut: The American University of Beirut.

Būmsahūlī, 'Abd al-'Azīz. 1998. *al-Shi'r wa-l-Ta'wīl: Qirā'a fī Shi'r Adūnīs*. Casablanca: Ifrīqiya al-Sharq.

al-Buraykī, Fāṭima. 2008. *al-Kitāba wa-l-Tiknūlūjiya*. Casablanca and Beirut: al-Markaz al-Thaqāfī al-'Arabī.

Burt, Clarissa. 1995. "Classical Motifs and Cultural Intertextuality in Contemporary Egyptian Poetry." *Critique*, pp. 91–9.

——. 1997. "The Good, the Bad and the Ugly: The Canonical Sieve and Poems from an Egyptian Avant Garde." *Journal of Arabic Literature* 28.1–2, pp. 141–78.

Bushrū'i, Suhayl Badī'. 1979. *Sirrī ma'a Allāh*. Beirut: Dār al-Āfāq al-Jadīda.

——. 1982. *James Joyce*. Beirut: Dār al-Āfāq al-Jadīda.

——. 1987. *Kahlil Gibran of Lebanon*. Gerrards Cross: Colin Smythe.

——. 2000. *al-Adab al-'Arabī bi-l-Inglīziyya*. Beirut: al-Mu'assasa al-'Arabiyya li-l-Dirāsāt wa-l-Nashr.

——. and James M. Malarkey (in collaboration with C. Bayan Bruss) (eds). 2012. *The Literary Heritage of the Arabs: An Anthology*. London: Saqi Books.

al-Bustānī, Buṭrus. 1859. *Khuṭba fī Ādāb al-'Arab*. Beirut: al-Maṭba'a al-Amīrkāniyya.

——. 1977. *Muḥīṭ al-Muḥīṭ*. Beirut: Maktabat Lubnān.

——. 1990. *al-Jam'iyya al-Sūriyya li-l-'Ulūm wa-l-Funūn 1847–1852*. Beirut: Dār al-Ḥamrā'.

al-Bustānī, Fu'ād Afrām (ed.). 1950. *al-Shaykh Nāṣīf al-Yāzijī: Muntakhabāt min Shi'rihi*. Beirut: al-Maṭba'a al-Kāthūlīkiyya.

al-Bustānī, Salīm. 1990. *Iftitāḥiyyāt Majallat al-Jinān al-Bayrūtiyya 1870–1884* (ed. Yūsuf Qazmā Khūrī). Beirut: Dār al-Ḥamrā'.

al-Bustānī, Sulaymān. 1904. *Ilyādhat Hūmīrūs*. Cairo: Dār al-Hilāl.

——. 1996. *Naẓariyyat al-Shi'r: Muqaddimat Tarjamat al-Ilyādha* (ed. Muḥammad Kāmil al-Khaṭīb). Damascus: Manshūrāt Wizārat al-Thaqāfa.

Cachia, Pierre. 1956. *Ṭāhā Ḥusayn: His Place in the Egyptian Literary Renaissance*. London: Luzac and Company.

——. 1967. "The Use of the Colloquial in Modern Arabic Literature." *Journal of the American Oriental Society* 87, pp. 12–22.

——. 1970. "The Dramatic Monologues of al-Maʿarrī." *Journal of Arabic Literature* 1, pp. 129–36.
——. 1975. "Social Values Reflected in Egyptian Popular Ballads." In Robin C. Ostle (ed.), *Studies in Modern Arabic Literature*, pp. 86–98. Warminster: Aris and Phillips.
——. 1977. "The Egyptian *Mawwāl*." *Journal of Arabic Literature* 8, pp. 77–103.
——. 1983. "An Uncommon Use of Nonsense Verse in Colloquial Arabic." *Journal of Arabic Literature* 14, pp. 60–6.
——. 1988. "From Sound to Echo in Late *Badīʿ* Literature." *Journal of the American Oriental Society* 108.2, pp. 219–25.
——. 1989. "The Development of a Modern Prose Style." *Bulletin of the School of Oriental and African Studies* 52.1, pp. 65–76.
——. 1990. *An Overview of Modern Arabic Literature*. Edinburgh: Edinburgh University Press.
——. 2008. "Arabic Literatures: 'Elite' and 'Folk' Junctions and Disjunctions". *Quaderni di Studi Arabi*, pp. 135–52.
Caiani, Fabio. 2007. *Contemporary Arab Fiction: Innovation from Rama to Yalu*. London: Routledge.
Camera d'Afflitto, Isabella. 1998. "Prison Narratives: Autobiography and Fiction." In Robin C. Ostle et al. (eds), *Writing the Self: Autobiographical Writing in Modern Arabic Literature*, pp. 148–56. London: Saqi Books.
——. 2001. "Letteratura araba contemporanea in Italia: un percorso personale." *Traduttore Nuovo* 56.1, pp. 11–16, 109–10.
Campbell, Ian. 2008. "Mapping Moroccan Literature: The Spatial Practices of Modernity in 'Abdelmajīd Ben Jallūn's *Fī al-Ṭufūla*." *Journal of Arabic Literature* 39.3, pp. 377–97.
——. 2013. *Labyrinths, Intellectuals and the Revolution: The Arabic-Language Moroccan Novel, 1957–72*. Leiden: Brill.
Campbell, Robert B. 1972. *The Arabic Journal Al-Mashriq: Its Beginnings and First Twenty-Five Years under the Editorship of Père Louis Cheikho*. PhD thesis, University of Michigan.
——. 1996. *Aʿlām al-Adab al-ʿArabī al-Muʿāṣir: Siyar wa-Siyar Dhātiyya*. Beirut: al-Maʿhad al-Almānī li-l-Abḥāth al-Sharqiyya.
Canter, H. V. 1930. "The Figure Adynaton in Greek and Latin Poetry." *American Journal of Philology* 51, pp. 32–41.
Caracciolo, Peter L. (ed.). 1988. *The Arabian Nights in English Literature: Studies in the Reception of the Thousand and One Nights into British Culture*. London: Macmillan Press.
Carr, E. H. 1965. *What is History?* Harmondsworth: Penguin Books.
Casanova, Pascale. 1999. *La République mondiale des lettres*. Paris: Éditions du Seuil.
——. 2002. *al-Jumhūriyya al-ʿĀlāmiyya li-l-Ādāb* (trans. Amal al-Ṣabbān). Cairo: al-Majlis al-Aʿlā li-l-Thaqāfa.
——. 2004. *The World Republic of Letters* (trans. M. B. DeBevoise). Cambridge, MA: Harvard University Press.
Caspi, Mishael Maswari and Julia Ann Blessing. 1993. "'O Bride Light of My Eyes': Bridal Songs of Arab Women in the Galilee." *Oral Tradition* 8.2, pp. 355–80.
Chalala, Elie. 1996. "'Apostasy' Charges Threaten Cairo University Professor's Marriage." *AlJadid* (Los Angeles) 2.10, p. 8.
——. 1999. "Marcel Khalife Faces Charge over Darwish Poem: Arab Intellectuals Rally to Defend Creative Freedom." *AlJadid* (Los Angeles) 28, pp. 7, 16.
Chatty, Dawn. 2006. *Nomadic Societies in the Middle East and North Africa: Entering the 21st Century*. Leiden: Brill.
Cheah, Pheng and Bruce Robbins (eds). 1998. *Cosmopolitics: Thinking and Feeling Beyond the Nation*. Minneapolis: University of Minnesota Press.

Cheikho (Shaykhū), Louis. 1924. *al-Ādāb al-ʿArabiyya fī al-Qarn al-Tāsiʿ ʿAshar: Min al-Sana 1800 ilā 1870*. Beirut: al-Maṭbaʿa al-Kāthūlīkiyya li-l-Ābāʾ al-Yasūʿiyyīn.

——. 1925. "Ḥuqūq al-Lugha al-ʿĀmmiyya bi-Izāʾ al-Lugha al-Faṣīḥa." *al-Mashriq* 23, pp. 161–71.

——. 1926. *al-Ādāb al-ʿArabiyya fī al-Qarn al-Tāsiʿ ʿAshar: Min al-Sana 1870 ilā 1900*. Beirut: Maṭbaʿat al-Ābāʾ al-Yasūʿiyyīn.

——. 1926a. *Taʾrīkh al-Ādāb al-ʿArabiyya fī al-Rubʿ al-Awwal min al-Qarn al-ʿIshrīn*. Beirut: Maṭbaʿat al-Ābāʾ al-Yasūʿiyyīn.

——. 1967. *Shuʿarāʾ al-Naṣrāniyya baʿda al-Islām*. Beirut: Dār al-Mashriq.

Chejne, Anwar G. 1969. *The Arabic Language: Its Role in History*. Minneapolis: University of Minnesota Press.

Chelkowsky, Peter. 1984. "Islam in Modern Drama and Theatre." *Die Welt des Islams* 23–4, pp. 45–69.

Classe, Olive (ed.). 2000. *Encyclopedia of Literary Translation into English*. London and Chicago: Fitzroy Dearborn Publishers.

Cleary, Joe. 2006. "The World Literary System: Atlas and Epitaph." *Field Day Review* 2, pp. 197–219.

Clerk, Jayana and Ruth Siegel (eds). 1995. *Modern Literatures of the Non-Western World: Where the Waters Are Born*. New York: HarperCollins College Publishers.

Cluny, Claude Michel. 1978. *Dictionnaire des nouveaux cinémas arabes*. Paris: Sindbad.

Clüver, Claus. 1986. "The Difference of Eight Decades: World Literature and the Demise of National Literatures." *Yearbook of Comparative and General Literature* 35, pp. 14–24.

——. 1988. "World Literature—Period or Type? In Response to Horst Steinmetz." *Yearbook of Comparative and General Literature* 37, pp. 134–9.

——. 1988a. "On Using Literary Constructs: In Response to Zoran Konstantinovic." *Yearbook of Comparative and General Literature* 37, pp. 143–4.

Cobham, Catherine. 1975. "Sex and Society in Yūsuf Idrīs: '*Qāʿ al-Madīna*.'" *Journal of Arabic Literature* 6, pp. 78–88.

Cohen, Dalia and Ruth Katz. 2006. *Palestinian Arab Music: A Maqām Tradition in Practice*. Chicago and London: University of Chicago Press.

Cohen, Esther and Robert Cohen. 1996. "Popular Culture and Elite Culture: An Illusory Contrast" (Hebrew). In Benjamin Z. Kedar (ed.), *Studies in the History of Popular Culture* (Hebrew), pp. 13–30. Jerusalem: The Zalman Shazar Center for Jewish History.

Cohen, Ralph. 1974. *New Directions in Literary History*. Baltimore: The Johns Hopkins University Press.

Cohen-Mor, Dalya. 2001. *A Matter of Fate: The Concept of Fate in the Arab World as Reflected in Modern Arabic Literature*. Oxford: Oxford University Press.

——. (ed.). 2005. *Arab Women Writers: An Anthology of Short Stories*. Albany: State University of New York Press.

Colin, G. S. 1971. "Ḥisāb al-Jummal." In P. J. Bearman et al. (eds), *The Encyclopaedia of Islam*, New Edition, Vol. 3, p. 468. Leiden: Brill.

Colla, Elliott. 2007. *Conflicted Antiquities: Egyptology, Egyptomania, Egyptian Modernity*. Durham, NC: Duke University Press.

——. 2009. "How *Zaynab* Became the First Arabic Novel." *History Compass* 7.1, pp. 214–25.

——. 2011. "Field Construction." *International Journal of Middle East Studies* 43.4, pp. 722–4.

Comendador, María Luz et al. 2000. "The Translation of Contemporary Arabic Literature into Spanish." *Yearbook of Comparative and General Literature* 48, pp. 115–25.

——. and Gonzalo Fernández-Parrilla. 2006. "Traducciones de literatura árabe al español 2001–2005." *Al-Andalus Magreb* 13, pp. 69–77.

Conant, Martha Pike. 1966 [1908]. *The Oriental Tale in England in the Eighteenth Century*. London: Frank Cass.

Connelly, Bridget. 1986. *Arab Folk Epic and Identity*. Berkeley: University of California Press.
Contini, Riccardo et al. (eds). 1993. *Semitica Serta Philologica Constantiono Tsereteli Dicata*. Turin: Silvio Zamorani Editore.
Cooke, Miriam. 1986. "Telling Their Lives: A Hundred Years of Arab Women's Writing." *World Literature Today* 60, pp. 212–16.
——. 1987. *Women Write War: The Centering of the Beirut Decentrists*. Oxford: Centre for Lebanese Studies.
——. 1987a. *War's Other Voices: Women Writers on the Lebanese Civil War*. Cambridge: Cambridge University Press.
——. 1993. *Gendering War Talk*. Princeton: Princeton University Press.
——. 1993a. "Men Constructed in the Mirror of Prostitution." In Michael Beard and Adnan Haydar (eds), *Naguib Mahfouz: From Regional Fame to Global Recognition*, pp. 106–25. Syracuse: Syracuse University Press.
——. 1994. "Zainab al-Ghazālī, Saint or Subversive?" *Die Welt des Islams* 34.1, pp. 1–20.
——. 1998. "*Ayyam min Hayati*: The Prison Memoirs of a Muslim Sister." In John C. Hawley (ed.), *Postcolonial Crescent: Islam's Impact on Contemporary Literature*, pp. 121–39. New York: Peter Lang.
——. 2001. *Women Claim Islam: Creating Islamic Feminism Through Literature*. New York and London: Routledge.
——. 2005. "Memoir: No Such Thing as Women's Literature." *Journal of Middle East Women's Studies* 1.2, pp. 25–54.
——. 2007. *Dissident Syria: Making Oppositional Arts Official*. Durham, NC: Duke University Press.
——. 2011. "The Cell Story: Syrian Prison Stories after Hafiz Asad." *Middle East Critique* 20.2, pp. 169–87.
——. 2014. *Tribal Modern: Branding New Nations in the Arab Gulf*. Berkeley: University of California Press.
——. and Roshmi Rustomji-Kerns (eds). 1994. *Blood into Ink: South Asian and Middle Eastern Women Write War*. Boulder, CO: Westview Press.
——. and Bruce B. Lawrence (eds). 2005. *Muslim Networks from Hajj to Hip Hop*. Chapel Hill, NC: University of North Carolina Press.
Cooperson, Michael. 2000. *Classical Arabic Biography: The Heirs of the Prophets in the Age of al-Ma'mun*. Cambridge: Cambridge University Press.
——. 2008. "'Ayyā. The Companion, Spy, Scoundrel in Premodern Arabic Popular Narratives." In Beatrice Gruendler (ed.), *Classical Arabic Humanities in Their Own Terms. Festschrift for Wolfhart Heinrichs on his 65th Birthday*, pp. 20–39. Brill: Leiden.
Corrao, Francesca Maria. 2001. "Tradurre poesia araba oggi." *Traduttore Nuovo* 56.1, pp. 17–21, 110–11.
Corriente, Federico. 1982. "The Metres of the *Muwaššaḥ*, an Andalusian Adaptation of *'Arūḍ* (A Bridging Hypothesis)." *Journal of Arabic Literature* 13, pp. 76–82.
——. 1986. "Again on the Metrical System of *Muwaššaḥ* and *Zajal*." *Journal of Arabic Literature* 17, pp. 34–49.
——. 2009. "On a Hopeless Last Stand for the Hypothesis of a Romance Origin of Andalusi Stanzaic Poetry: Homosexuality and Prostitution in the *Kharjas*." *Journal of Arabic Literature* 40.2, pp. 170–81.
Crane, R. S. 1967. *The Idea of the Humanities and Other Essays Critical and Historical*. Chicago: University of Chicago Press.
——. 1971. *Critical and Historical Principles of Literary History*. Chicago: University of Chicago Press.
Cuddon, J. A. 1986. *A Dictionary of Literary Terms*. Harmondsworth: Penguin Books.
Culhane, Hind Rassam. 1995. *East/West, an Ambiguous State of Being: The Construction and Representation of Egyptian Cultural Identity in Egyptian Film*. New York: Peter Lang.

Dabashi, Hamid. 2012. *The Arab Spring; The End of Postcolonialism*. London and New York: Zed Books.
——. 2012a. *The World of Persian Literary Humanism*. Cambridge, MA: Harvard University Press.
Dāghir, Iskandar. 1989. "Ḥiwār Sākhin ma'a al-Shā'ir al-Kabīr 'Abd al-Wahhāb al-Bayyātī: al-Nahr al-Dā'im al-Jarayān min al-Manba' ilā al-Baḥr." *al-Usbū' al-'Arabī*, 5 June, pp. 40–1.
Dāghir, Sharbal. 1995. "Adab 'Arabī Wāḥid am Ādāb 'Arabiyya Ḥadītha Mutanawwi'a." *al-Ḥayāt*, 2 April, p. 17.
——. 1996. "*Qālat al-Arḍ* li-Adūnīs: Ayy Zaman li-l-Qaṣīda." *al-Ḥayāt*, 7 September, p. 16.
al-Ḍa'īf, Rashīd. 2005. *Ma'bad Yanjaḥ fī Baghdād*. Beirut: Riyāḍ al-Rayyis.
——. 2007. *al-A'māl al-Shi'riyya*. Beirut: Riyāḍ al-Rayyis.
Dakhli, Leyla. 2013. "The *Mahjar* as Literary and Political Territory in the First Decades of the 20th Century: The Example of Amīn Rīḥānī (1876–1940)." In Dyala Hamzah (ed.), *The Making of the Arab Intellectual (1880–1960): Empire, Public Sphere and the Colonial Coordinates of Selfhood*, pp. 164–87. London: Routledge.
Damrosch, David. 2003. *What Is World Literature*? Princeton and Oxford: Princeton University Press.
——. 2009. *How To Read World Literature*. Chichester: Wiley-Blackwell
——. (ed.). 2009a. *Teaching World Literature*. New York: The Modern Language Association of America.
Daniel, Lucy. 2007. *The Little Black Book: Books. Over a Century of the Greatest Books, Writers, Characters, Passages and Events that Rocked the Literary World*. London: Cassell.
Daniels, Kate. 2005. "Turkish and Ottoman Motifs in Arabic Literature from the *Nahḍa* to the End of the Caliphate." *Eurasian Studies* 4.1, pp. 99–128.
Danielson, Virginia Louise. 1991. *Shaping Tradition in Arabic Song: The Career and Repertory of Umm Kulthūm*. PhD thesis, University of Illinois.
——. 1997. *The Voice of Egypt: Umm Kulthūm, Arabic Song, and Egyptian Society in the Twentieth Century*. Chicago and London: University of Chicago Press.
——. 1998. "Performance, Political Identity and Memory: Umm Kulthum and Gamal 'Abd al-Nasir." In Sherifa Zuhur (ed.), *Images of Enchantment: Visual and Performing Arts of the Middle East*, pp. 109–22. Cairo: The American University in Cairo Press.
Daoud, Mohamed et al. (eds). 2010. *Ecriture féminine: réception, discours et représentations*. Oran, Algeria: CRASC.
Daoud, Siham. 1995. "Interview with Emil Habibi." *Contemporary Theatre Review* 3.2, pp. 107–112.
Daoudi, Anissa. 2011. "Globalization, Computer-Mediated Communications and the Rise of e-Arabic." *Middle East Journal of Culture and Communication* 4.2, pp. 146–63.
Dārghawth, Rashād. 1963. *Fī al-'Ashāyā: Masraḥiyyāt wa-Qiṣaṣ wa-Aḥādīth li-l-Awlād*. Beirut: Dār al-Kutub.
——. 1994. *Ma'āthir al-Ṣaḥāba*. Beirut: Dār al-Nafā'is.
Darwīsh, 'Ādil and 'Imād 'Abd al-Rāziq. 1989. *al-Āyāt al-Shayṭāniyya Bayna al-Qalam wa-l-Sayf*. London: n.pub.
Darwīsh, Ḥanān and 'Azza Jawda. 1994. "Mādhā Yaqra' Aṭfāl Miṣr." *'Ālam al-Kitāb*, October, pp. 54–7.
Darwish, Mahmoud. 1995. *Memory for Forgetfulness* (trans. Ibrahim Muhawi). Berkeley: University of California Press.
Darwīsh, Maḥmūd. 1977. *al-A'rās*. Acre: Dār al-Aswār.
——. 1977a. *Dīwān*. Beirut: Dār al-'Awda.
——. 1987. *Dhākira li-l-Nisyān*. Acre: Dār al-Aswār.
——. 1987a. *Ward Aqall*. Acre: Dār al-Aswār.

——. 1988. *Dīwān*. Acre: Dār al-Aswār.
——. 2007. *Ḥayrat al-ʿĀʾid*. London: Riyāḍ al-Rayyis.
Darwish, Mustafa. 1998. *Dream Makers on the Nile: A Portrait of Egyptian Cinema*. Cairo: The American University in Cairo Press.
Darwīsh, Shālom. 1948. *Baʿḍ al-Nās*. Baghdad: Sharikat al-Tijāra wa-l-Ṭibāʿa al-Maḥdūda.
al-Dasūqī, ʿUmar. 1959. *Fī al-Adab al-Ḥadīth*. Cairo: Dār al-Fikr al-ʿArabī.
Dāʾūd, Anas. 1993. *Adab al-Aṭfāl: Fī al-Badʾ Kānat al-Unshūda*. Cairo: Dār al-Maʿārif.
Davidson, Cathy N. 2011. *Now You See It: How the Brain Science of Attention Will Transform the Way We Live, Work, and Learn*. New York: Viking.
Davis, Eric. 1983. *Challenging Colonialism: Bank Misr and Egyptian Industrialization, 1920–1941*. Princeton: Princeton University Press.
Davis, Ioan. 1990. *Writers in Prison*. Oxford: Basil Blackwell.
Daydāt, Aḥmad. 1990. *Shayṭāniyyat al-Āyāt al-Shayṭāniyya wa-Kayfa Khadaʿa Salmān Rushdī al-Gharb*. Cairo: Dār al-Faḍīla.
Ḍayf, Shawqī. n.d. *al-ʿAṣr al-Jāhilī*. Cairo: Dār al-Maʿārif.
——. 1987. *al-Maqāma*. Cairo: Dār al-Maʿārif.
De Angelis, Francesco. 2013. "Muṣṭafā Mušarrafah, a Pioneer of Narrative Techniques in his *Qanṭarah allaḏī Kafara*, the First Novel Entirely Written in Egyptian Dialect." *La Rivista de Arablit* 6, pp. 19–27.
Deeb, Muḥammad A. 1983. *'Unsī al-Ḥājj and the Poème en Prose in Modern Arabic Literature*. PhD thesis, University of Alberta.
Defoe, Daniel. 1906 [1719]. *Robinson Crusoe*. London: Dent and New York: Dutton.
Deguilhem, Randi and Manuela Marín. (eds) 2001. *Writing the Feminine: Women in Arab Sources*. London: I. B. Tauris.
Déjeux, Jean. 1973. *Littérature maghrébine de langue française*. Ottawa: Éditions Naaman.
De Larramendi et al. (eds). 1999. *Traducción, emigración y culturas*. Cuenca, Spain: Ediciones de la Universidad de Castilla-La Mancha.
De Vaux, B. Carra. 1934. "Taʾrīkh." In P. J. Bearman et al. (eds), *The Encyclopaedia of Islam*, First Edition, Vol. 4, p. 672. Leiden: Brill.
DeYoung, Terri. 1994. "*Muʿāraḍa* and Modern Arabic Poetry: Some Examples from the Work of Badr Shākir al-Sayyāb." *Edebiyât* 5.2, pp. 217–45.
——. 1998. *Placing the Poet: Badr Shakir al-Sayyab and Postcolonial Iraq*. Albany: State University of New York Press.
——. 2000. "T. S. Eliot and Modern Arabic Poetry." *Yearbook of Comparative and General Literature* 48, pp. 3–21.
——. and Mary St. Germain (eds). 2011. *Essays in Arabic Literary Biography 925–1350*. Wiesbaden: Harrassowitz Verlag.
D'haen, Theo et al. (eds). 2013. *World Literature: A Reader*. London and New York: Routledge.
al-Dhahabī, Muḥammad ibn Aḥmad. 1988. *Taʾrīkh al-Islām wa-Wafāyāt al-Mashāhīr wa-l-Aʿlām, Ḥawādith wa-Wafāyāt 141–160H* (ed. ʿUmar ʿAbd al-Salām Tadmurī). Beirut: Dār al-Kitāb al-ʿArabī.
Dhinī, Sihām. 2002. *Tharthara maʿa Najīb Maḥfūẓ*. Cairo: Dār Akhbār al-Yawm.
Dobrişan, Nicolae. 2004. "Extratextuality and the Translation of Fictional Work from Arabic into Romanian." *Romano-Arabica* 4, pp. 29–32.
Doufikar-Aerts, Faustina C. W. 2000. "The Marginal Voice of a Popular Romance: *Sīrat al-Iskandar wa-mā fīhā min al-ʿAjāyib wa-'l-Gharāyib*." In Robin C. Ostle (ed.), *Marginal Voices in Literature and Society: Individual and Society in the Mediterranean Muslim World*, pp. 13–23. Strasbourg: ESF.
Douglas, Allen and Fedwa Malti-Douglas. 1994. *Arab Comic Strips: Politics of an Emerging Mass Culture*. Bloomington and Indianapolis: Indiana University Press.
Duclos, Diane. 2012. "Cosmopolitanism and Iraqi Migration: Artists and Intellectuals from the 'Sixties and Seventies Generations' in Exile." In Jordi Tejel et al. (eds), *Writing*

the Modern History of Iraq: Historiographical and Political Challenges, pp. 391–401. Hackensack, NJ: World Scientific.
Du Gay, Paul. 2007. *Organizing Identity: Persons and Organizations "After Theory"*. Los Angeles: Sage Publications.
Duraković, Esad. 2000. "Frameworks and Presuppositions of Mahğar Literature." *Prilozi za Orijentalnu Filologiju* 50, pp. 265–96.
Dūs, Madīḥa and Humphrey Davies (eds). 2013. *al-'Āmmiyya al-Miṣriyya al-Maktūba*. Cairo: al-Hay'a al-Miṣriyya al-'Āmma li-l-Kitāb.
Duwāra, Fu'ād. 1963. "Ma'a Najīb Maḥfūẓ fī 'Īdihi al-Dhahabī." *al-Kātib* 22, January, pp. 4–24.
——. 1965. *'Asharatu Udabā' Yataḥaddathūna*. Cairo: Dār al-Hilāl.
Dziekan, Marek M. 2011. "Algerische Literatur im achtzehnten Jahrhundert." *Studia Orientalia* 111, pp. 39–57.
Early, Evelyn A. 1993. *Baladi Women of Cairo: Playing with Egg and a Stone*. London and Boulder, CO: Lynne Rienner Publishers.
Edzard, Lutz and Christian Szyska (eds). 1997. *Encounter of Words and Texts: Intercultural Studies in Honor of Stefan Wild on the Occasion of his 60th Birthday*. Hildesheim: Georg Olms Verlag.
Edzard, Lutz and Jan Retsö (eds). 2006. *Current Issues in the Analysis of Semitic Grammar and Lexicon II. Oslo-Göteborg Cooperation, 4–5 November 2005*. Wiesbaden: Harrassowitz Verlag.
Eichenbaum, Boris. 1965. "The Theory of the 'Formal Method.'" In Lee T. Lemon and Marion J. Reis (eds), *Russian Formalist Criticism*, pp. 99–139. Lincoln: University of Nebraska Press.
Eid, Mushira. 2002. *The World of Obituaries: Gender Across Culture and over Time*. Detroit: Wayne State University Press.
Einbinder, Susan. 1995. "The *Muwashshaḥ*-Like *Zajal*: A New Source for a Hebrew Poem." *Medieval Encounters* 1.2, pp. 252–70.
Eissa, Ashraf A. 2000. "*Majallat al-Jinān*: Arabic Narrative Discourse in the Making." *Quaderni di Studi Arabi* 18, pp. 41–9.
Eksell, Kerstin and Stephan Guth (eds). 2011. *Borders and Beyond: Crossings and Transitions in Modern Arabic Literature*. Wiesbaden: Harrassowitz Verlag.
Elad, Ami (ed.). 1993. *Writer, Culture, Text: Studies in Modern Arabic Literature*. Fredericton: York Press.
——. 1994. *The Village Novel in Modern Egyptian Literature*. Berlin: Klaus Schwartz Verlag.
——. 2007. *Voices of Exiles: A Study of al-Ṭayyib Ṣāliḥ and his Work*. Oxford: Oxford University Press.
El-Ariss, Tarek. 2010. "Hacking the Modern: Arabic Writing in the Virtual Age." *Comparative Literature Studies* 47.4, pp. 533–48.
——. 2012. "Fiction of Scandal." *Journal of Arabic Literature* 43.2–3, pp. 510–31.
——. 2013. *Trials of Arab Modernity: Literary Affects and the New Political*. New York: Fordham University Press.
——. 2013a. "Majnun Strikes Back: Crossing of Madness and Homosexuality in Contemporary Arabic Literature." *International Journal of Middle East Studies* 45.2, pp. 293–312.
——. 2015. "Let There Be *Nahdah*!" *The Cambridge Journal of Postcolonial Literary Inquiry* 2.2, pp. 260–6.
——. 2016. "Return of the Beast: From Pre-Islamic Ode to Contemporary Novel." *Journal of Arabic Literature* 47.1–2, pp. 62–90.
——. (ed.). [Forthcoming]. *The Arab Renaissance: A Bilingual Anthology of the* Nahda *(1800s–1900s)*. New York: Modern Language Association.
Elbaz, Robert. 1988. *The Changing Nature of the Self: A Critical Study of the Autobiographic Discourse*. London and Sydney: Croom Helm.

——. 1996. *Tahar ben Jelloun ou l'inassouvissement du désir narratif*. Paris: Éditions l'Harmattan.
El Beheiry, Kawsar Abdel Salam. 1980. *L'influence de la littérature française sur le roman arabe*. Sherbrooke: Éditions Naaman.
Elbousty, Moulay Youness. 2013. "Abu al-Qasim al-Shabbi's 'The Will to Live': Galvanising the Tunisian Revolution." *The Journal of North African Studies* 18.1, pp, 159–63.
El Cheikh, Nadia Maria et al. (eds). 2016. *One Hundred and Fifty*. Beirut: American University of Beirut.
El-Enany, Rasheed. 1989. "Poets and Rebels: Reflections of Lorca in Modern Arabic Poetry." *Third World Quarterly* 11.4, pp. 252–64.
——. 1993. *Naguib Mahfouz: The Pursuit of Meaning*. London and New York: Routledge.
——. 1998. "The Promethean Quest in Louis 'Awaḍ's *Memoires of an Overseas Student*." In Robin C. Ostle et al. (eds), *Writing the Self: Autobiographical Writing in Modern Arabic Literature*, pp. 61–71. London: Saqi Books.
——. 2014. "Translations of Naguib Mahfouz in English." In Robert Gleave (ed.), *Books and Bibliophiles: Studies in Honour of Paul Auchterlonie on the Bio-Bibliography of the Muslim World*, pp. 89–94. Cambridge: Gibb Memorial Trust.
El-Gabalawy, Saad (trans.). 1979. *Three Contemporary Egyptian Novels*. Fredericton: York Press.
El Hamamsy, Walid. 2010. "Epistolary Memory: Revisiting Traumas in Women's Writing." *Alif: Journal of Comparative Poetics* 30, pp. 150–75.
Elimelekh, Geula. 2012. "Freedom and Dissidence in the Arabic Prison Novels of 'Abd al-Raḥmān Munīf." *Die Welt des Islams* 52.2, pp. 166–82.
——. 2014. *Arabic Prison Literature: Resistance, Torture, Alienation, and Freedom*. Wiesbaden: Harrassowitz Verlag.
Elinson, Alexander E. 2009. "Opening the Circle: Storyteller and Audience in Moroccan Prison Literature." *Middle Eastern Literatures* 12.3, pp. 289–303.
Eliot, T. S. 1950. *Selected Essays*. New York: Harcourt.
——. 1969. *On Poetry and Poets*. London: Faber and Faber.
El Janabi, Abdul Kader. 1996. *Stance in the Desert: Surrealist Writings (1974–1986)*. Paris: Gilgamesh Publication.
——. 1999. *Le poèm arabe moderne*. Paris: Maisonneuve and Larose.
Elkad-Lehman, Ilana. 2008. "A Suitcase and a Fence: On *Dancing Arabs* and *Let It Be Morning* by Sayyid Qashshu'a." In Ilana Elkad-Lehman (ed.), *Israeli Identities: The Familiar and the Unknown* (Hebrew), pp. 119–54. Jerusalem: Carmel.
Elkhadem, Saad. 1985. *History of the Egyptian Novel: Its Rise and Early Beginnings*. Fredericton: York Press.
——. 2001. *On Egyptian Fiction: Five Essays*. Toronto: York Press.
Elliott, Anthony and Paul Du Gay (eds). 2009. *Identity in Question*. Los Angeles: Sage Publications.
Elmessiri, A. W. 1976. "Jahīn [sic], the Cunning Master." *Journal of Arabic Literature* 7, pp. 65–7.
Elmessiri, Nur and Abdelwahab Elmessiri (eds). 1996. *A Land of Stone and Thyme: An Anthology of Palestinian Short Stories*. London: Quartet Books.
El Moktâr Ould Bah, Mohamd. 1971. "Introduction à la poésie mauritanienne (1650–1900)." *Arabica* 18, pp. 1–48.
Elon, Amos. 1980. *Flight into Egypt* (Hebrew). Tel Aviv: Schocken.
El-Rouayheb, Khaled. 2005. "The Love of Boys in Arabic Poetry of the Early Ottoman Period, 1500–1800." *Middle Eastern Literatures* 8.1, pp. 3–22.
El Saadaoui, Naoual. 1984. *Douze femmes dans kanater* (trans. Magda Wassef). Paris: Des Femmes.

El Sa'adawi (El Saadawi), Nawal. 1983. *Woman at Point Zero* (trans. Sherif Hetata). London: Zed Books.

——. 1985. *God Dies by the Nile* (trans. Sherif Hetata). London: Zed Books.

——. 1986. *Memoirs from the Women's Prison* (trans. Marilyn Booth). London: Women's Press.

——. 1994. *The Innocence of the Devil* (trans. Sherif Hetata). Berkeley: University of California Press.

——. 1994a. *Memoirs from the Women's Prison* (trans. Marilyn Booth). Berkeley and Los Angeles: University of California Press.

——. 1995. *The Fall of the Imam* (trans. Sherif Hetata). London: Minerva.

El Sadda, Hoda. 1996. "Women's Writing in Egypt: Reflections on Salwa Bakr." In Deniz Kandiyoti (ed.), *Gendering the Middle East*, pp. 127–44. London and New York: I. B.Tauris.

——. 2010. "Arab Women Bloggers: The Emergence of Literary Counterpublics." *Middle East Journal of Culture and Communication* 3, pp. 312–32.

——. 2012. *Gender, Nation, and the Arabic Novel: Egypt, 1892–2008*. Edinburgh: Edinburgh University Press.

El-Shamy, Hasan M. (ed.). 1980. *Folktales of Egypt*. Chicago and London: University of Chicago Press.

——. 2005. "A Motif Index of *Alf Laylah wa Laylah*: Its Relevance to the Study of Culture, Society, the Individual, and Character Transmutation." *Journal of Arabic Literature* 36.3, pp. 235–68.

——. 2006. *A Motif Index of The Thousand and One Nights*. Bloomington: Indiana University Press.

El Sharkawi, B. 1992. *The Arab Press in London*. MA thesis, University of Salford.

Elster, Ernst. 1901. "Weltlitteratur und Litteraturvergleichung." *Archiv für das Studium der Neueren Sprachen und Literatur* 107, pp. 33–47.

——. 1986. "World Literature and Comparative Literature (1901)" (trans. Eric Metzler). *Yearbook of Comparative and General Literature* 35, pp. 7–13.

Enderwitz, Susanne. 1998. "From Curriculum Vitae to Self-Narration: Fiction in Arabic Autobiography." In Stefan Leder (ed.), *Story-Telling in the Framework of Non-Fictional Arabic Literature*, pp. 1–19. Wiesbaden: Harrassowitz Verlag.

——. 1999. "The Mission of the Palestinian Autobiographer." In Stephan Guth et al. (eds), *Conscious Voices: Concepts of Writing in the Middle East*, pp. 29–50. Beirut: Orient-Institut der DMG.

——. 2000. "Gibt es eine Arabische Autobiographie?" In Verena Klemm and Beatrice Gruendler (eds), *Understanding Near Eastern Literatures*, pp. 189–99. Wiesbaden: Reichert Verlag.

——. 2002. "Palestinian Autobiographies: A Source for Women's History." In Manuela Marín and Randi Deguilhem (eds), *Writing the Feminine: Women in Arab Sources*, pp. 49–72. London and New York: I. B. Tauris.

Engels, Odilo and Peter Schreiner (eds). 1993. *Die Begegung des Westens mit* dem Ostens. Sigmaringen, Germany: Jan Thorbecke Verlag.

Engineer, Asghar Ali (ed.). 2002. Islam in India: The Impact of Civilizations. New Delhi: Shipra Publications.

Epstein, Julia and Kristina Straub (eds). 1991. Body Guards: The Cultural Politics of Gender Ambiguity. New York and London: Routledge.

Erickson, John. 1998. Islam and Postcolonial Narrative. Cambridge: Cambridge University Press.

Erlich, Haggai. 1989. Students and Universities in 20th Century Egyptian Politics. London: Frank Cass.

——. 2014. Youth & Revolution in the Changing Middle East, 1908–2014. London and Boulder, CO: Lynne Rienner Publishers.

Erlich, Michel. 1986. La femme blessée: essai sur les mutilations sexuelles feminines. Paris: Éditions l'Harmattan.
Erlich, Victor. 1969. Russian Formalism: History, Doctrine. The Hague: Mouton.
Esposito, John L. 1992. The Islamic Threat: Myth or Reality? New York and Oxford: Oxford University Press.
——. (ed.). 1995. The Oxford Encyclopedia of the Modern Islamic World. New York: Oxford University Press.
——. 2000. "Islam and Secularism in the Twenty-First Century." In Azzam Tamimi and John L. Esposito (eds), Islam and Secularism in the Middle East, pp. 1–12. London: Hurst and Company.
Etman, Ahmed. 1993. "Round Table—Naguib Mahfouz and Arabic Literature: Problems of Translation." Graeco-Arabica 5, pp. 355–8.
Ettobi, Mustapha. 2006. "Cultural Representation in Literary Translation: Translators as Mediators/Creators." Journal of Arabic Literature 37.2, pp. 206–29.
Even-Zohar, Itamar. 1990. Polysystem Studies. Poetics Today 11.1. Tel Aviv: The Porter Institute for Poetics and Semiotics.
Fadhila, Drouche Fatima. 2011. "Society of Crisis in the Fictional Text: A Sociological Reading of Algerian Fiction." Contemporary Arab Affairs 4.3, pp. 301–21.
Fāḍil, Jihād. 1989. *Fatāfīt Shā'ir*. Cairo and Beirut: Dār al-Shurūq.
——. 1996. *al-Adab al-Ḥadīth fī Lubnān: Naẓra Mughāyira*. London and Beirut: Riyāḍ al-Rayyis.
Faḍl, Ṣalāḥ. 2002. *Taḥawwulāt al-Shi'riyya al-'Arabiyya*. Beirut: Dār al-Ādāb.
Faḍl Allāh, Muḥammad Ḥusayn. 1984. *Qaṣā'id li-l-Islām wa-l-Ḥayāt*. Beirut: al-Mu'assasa al-Jāmi'iyya li-l-Dirāsāt wa-l-Nashr.
——. 1985. *Yā Ẓilāl al-Islām*. Beirut: Dār al-Ta'āruf li-l-Maṭbū'āt.
——. 1990. *'Alā Shāṭi' al-Wujdān*. London: Riyāḍ al-Rayyis.
——. 1994. "Laysa min al-Ḍarūrī an Nuqaddisa al-Turāth Kayfamā Kāna." *al-Bilād* 173 (12 March), pp. 45–6.
——. 1995. "Hawā al-Sharq wa-Huwiyyat al-Islam." In *al-'Unf al-Uṣūlī: Muwājahāt al-Sayf wa-l-Qalam*, pp. 197–213. London and Beirut: Riyāḍ al-Rayyis.
Fahd, Toufic. 1993. "La traduction arabe de l'*Iliade*." *Graeco-Arabica* 5, pp. 259–66.
Fahmī, Māhir Ḥasan. 1982. *Muḥammad Tawfīq al-Bakrī*. Kuwait City: Dār al-Qalam.
Fahmy, Ziad. 2011. *Ordinary Egyptians: Creating the Modern Nation Through Popular Culture*. Stanford: Stanford University Press.
Fähndrich, Hartmut. 2000. "A Movement against a Structure: The Situation of Contemporary Arabic Literature in German-Speaking Countries Inside and Outside the Universities." *Awrāq: Estudios sobre el Mundo Arabe e Islámico Contemporáneo* 21, pp. 167–80.
——. 2000a. "Viewing 'The Orient' and Translating Its Literature in the Shadow of *The Arabian Nights*." *Yearbook of Comparative and General Literature* 48, pp. 95–106.
——. 2016. "Translating Contemporary Arabic Literature: A Pleasure with Many Obstacles." *CLINA: An Interdisciplinary Journal of Translation, Interpreting and Intercultural Communication* 2.1, pp. 13–28.
Fakhr al-Dīn, Yūsuf. 2007. *al-Zajal fī Bilād al-Shām ḥattā al-Qarn al-Khāmis 'Ashar*. MA thesis, University of Haifa.
——. 2010. *al-Zajal fī Bilād al-Shām*. Riyadh: Dār al-Hudā.
Fakhreddine, Huda J. 2015. *Metapoesis in the Arabic Tradition: From Modernists to Muḥdathūn*. Leiden: Brill.
Fanjul, Serafin. 1977. "The Erotic Popular *Mawwāl* in Egypt." *Journal of Arabic Literature* 8, pp. 104–22.
Fanon, Frantz. 1967. *Black Skin White Masks* (trans. Charles Lam Markmann). New York: Grove Press.

Fanous, Mohamad Wajih Subhi. 1980. *Aspects of the Lebanese Contribution to Modern Arabic Literary Criticism*. PhD thesis, Oxford University.

Fanus, Wajih. 1986. "Sulaymān al-Bustānī and Comparative Literary Studies in Arabic." *Journal of Arabic Literature* 17, pp. 105–19.

Faqir, Fadia (ed.). 1998. *In the House of Silence*. Reading: Garnet Publishing.

Farah, Madelain. 1984. *Marriage and Sexuality in Islam*. Salt Lake City: University of Utah Press.

Faraj, Murād. 1929. *al-Shuʿrāʾ al-Yahūd al-ʿArab*. Cairo: al-Maṭbaʿa al-Raḥmāniyya.

Faraj, Nabīl. 1971. "Yūsuf Idrīs Yataḥaddathu ʿan Tajribatihi al-Adabiyya." *al-Majalla* (Cairo), January, pp. 99–105.

——. 1993. *al-Maqāʿid al-Shāghira fī al-Thaqāfa al-ʿArabiyya*. Cairo: al-Hayʾa al-Miṣriyya al-ʿĀmma li-l-Kitāb.

AlFardi, Abdullah. 1989. *The Development of Commercial Advertising in Saudi Television from 1986–1988*. PhD thesis, University of North Texas.

Faris, David M. 2013. *Dissent and Revolution in a Digital Age: Social Media, Blogging and Activism in Egypt*. London: I. B. Tauris.

al-Fārisī, Muṣṭafā. 1972. "al-Bilād al-ʿArabiyya wa-Ḥuqūq al-Taʾlīf." *al-Ādāb*, January, pp. 77–80.

Farrāj, ʿAfīf. 1980. *al-Ḥurriyya fī Adab al-Marʾa*. Beirut: Muʾassasat al-Abḥāth al-ʿArabiyya.

Farrūkh, ʿUmar. 1961. *al-Qawmiyya al-Fuṣḥā*. Beirut: Dār al-ʿIlm li-l-Malāyīn.

Fāsha, Jamīl Mārī. 1976. *Dalīl al-Mudarris al-Maktabī*. Jerusalem: Ṣalāḥ al-Dīn.

al-Fāsī, Shams al-Dīn. 1989. *Āyāt Samāwiyya fī al-Radd ʿalā Kitāb Āyāt Shayṭāniyya*. Cairo: Dār Māyū al-Waṭaniyya li-l-Nashr.

al-Fattāl, ʿAlī. 1987. *Mullā ʿAbbūd al-Karkhī Rāʾid al-Shiʿr al-ʿĀmmī*. Baghdad: al-Maktaba al-ʿĀlamiyya.

Fāʿūr, Yāsīn. 1993. *al-Sukhriyya fī Adab Imīl Ḥabībī*. Sūsa, Tunis: Dār al-Maʿārif li-l-Ṭibāʿa wa-l-Nashr.

Fawzī, Maḥmūd. 1987. *Adab al-Aẓāfir al-Ṭawīla*. Cairo: Dār Nahḍat Miṣr li-l-Ṭibāʿa wa-l-Nashr.

——. 1988. *Najīb Maḥfūẓ: Zaʿīm al-Ḥarāfish*. Cairo: Dār al-Jīl.

——. 1988a. *Iḥsān ʿAbd al-Quddūs Bayna al-Ightiyāl al-Siyāsī wa-l-Shaghab al-Jinsī*. Cairo: Madbūlī.

Fay, Mary Ann (ed.). 2001. *Auto/Biography and the Construction of Identity and Community in the Middle East*. New York: Palgrave.

Fāyid, ʿAbd al-Laṭīf. 1995. "Qiṣṣat Abī Zayd." *Minbar al-Islām* 54.2, pp. 2–7.

al-Fayṣal, Samar Rūḥī. 1994. *al-Sijn al-Siyāsī fī al-Riwāya al-ʿArabiyya*. Tripoli (Lebanon): Jarrūs Press.

——. 1996. *Muʿjam al-Qāṣṣāt wa-l-Riwāʾiyyāt al-ʿArabiyyāt*. Tripoli (Lebanon): Jarrūs Press.

al-Faytūrī, Muḥammad. 1979. *Dīwān*. Beirut: Dār al-ʿAwda.

Fénelon, François de Salignac. 1934 [1699]. *Les aventures de Télémaque*. Paris: R. Hilsum.

Feodorov, Ioana. 2001. "Romanian Translations of Arabic Literature 1964–1994." *Romano-Arabica* 1, pp. 35–45.

Ferguson, Charles A. 1968 [1959]. "Myths about Arabic." In Joshua A. Fishman (ed.), *Readings in the Sociology of Language*, pp. 375–81. The Hague: Mouton.

Fernández-Parrilla, Gonzalo. 2013. "Translating Modern Arabic Literature into Spanish." *Middle Eastern Literatures* 16.1, pp. 88–101.

Fernea, Elizabeth Warnock (ed.). 1985. *Women and the Family in the Middle East*. Austin: University of Texas Press.

——. (ed.). 1995. *Children in the Muslim Middle East*. Austin: University of Texas Press.

——. 1998. *In Search of Islamic Feminism: One Woman's Global Journey*. New York and London: Doubleday.

——. and Basima Qattan Bezirgan (eds). 1977. *Middle Eastern Muslim Women Speak.* Austin and London: University of Texas Press.
Fierro, Maribel (ed.). 2014. *Orthodoxy and Heresy in Islam.* London: Routledge.
Filshtinsky, I. M. 1966. *Arabic Literature* (trans. Hilda Kasanina). Moscow: Nauka.
——. 1984. "Tradition and Canon in Medieval Arabic Poetry." *Rocznik Orientalistyczny* 43, pp. 65–70.
Finkelberg, Margalit and Guy G. Stroumsa (eds). 2003. *Homer, the Bible and Beyond: Literary and Religious Canons in the Ancient World.* Leiden: Brill.
Fischel, W. J. 1938. "'Resh-Galuta' (*Ra's al-Jālūt*) in Arabic Literature." In F. I. Baer et al. (eds), *Magnes Anniversary Book* (Hebrew), pp. 181–7. Jerusalem: Hebrew University Press.
Fishburn, Evelyn. 2004. "Traces of the *Thousand and One Nights* in Borges." *Middle Eastern Literatures* 7.2, pp. 213–22.
Fishelov, David. 2007. "Canonical and Popular Literature: On Prejudice, Garbage, Flowers and *Robinson Crusoe.*" In Yael Shapira et al. (eds), *Popular and Canonical: Literary Dialogues* (Hebrew), pp. 21–9. Tel Aviv: Resling.
Fishman, Joshua A. (ed.) 1968. *Readings in the Sociology of Language.* The Hague: Mouton.
Fitch, Brian T. 1982. *The Narcissistic Text: A Reading of Camus' Fiction.* Toronto: University of Toronto Press.
Foley, Sean. 2013. "When Life Imitates Art: The Arab Spring, the Middle East and the Modern World." *Alternatives: Turkish Journal of International Relations* 12.3, pp. 32–46.
Folorunsho, M. A. 1996. "Arabic Literary Activity among the Osogbo Muslims in Nigeria." *Journal of Muslim Minority Affairs* 16.2, pp. 287–93.
Fontaine, Jean. 1992. "Arabic-Language Tunisian Literature (1956–1990)." *Research in African Literatures* 23.2, pp. 183–93.
——. 1997. *Bibliographie de la littérature tunisienne contemporaine en arabe 1954–1996.* Tunis: IBLA.
——. 2010. "Roman tunisien 2009." *Revue de l'Institut des Belles Lettres Arabes* 205, pp. 117–44.
Foucault, Michel. 1966. *The Order of Things: An Archaeology of the Human Sciences.* Paris: Gallimard.
France, Peter (ed.). 2000. *The Oxford Guide to Literature in English Translation.* Oxford: Oxford University Press.
Fransīs, Īliyyā. 2000. *al-Shi'r al-'Arabī al-Mughannā: Dirāsa Taḥlīliyya li-Mūsīqā al-Shi'r.* Damascus: Qadmus.
Frolova, Olga. 1978. "Antifeodal'naya egipetskaya poėma 'Yasin i Bahiya' Nagiba Surura (An Anti-Feudal Poem 'Yāsin and Bahiya' of Nagīb Surūr)." *Palestinskiĭ Sbornik* 26.89, pp. 22–7.
——. 2004. "Nagib Mahfouz: Translations of his Works and Works about him Published in Russia." *Graeco-Arabica* 9–10, pp. 143–9.
Frosh, Stephen and Lisa Baraitser. 2009. "Goodbye to Identity?" In Anthony Elliott and Paul Du Gay (eds), *Identity in Question*, pp. 158–69. Los Angeles: Sage Publications.
Fry, C. George and James R. King (eds). 1974. *An Anthology of Middle Eastern Literature from the Twentieth Century.* Springfield, OH: n.pub.
Fudge, Bruce. 2016. "More Translators of *The Thousand and One Nights.*" *Journal of the American Oriental Society* 136.1 (January–March), pp. 135–46.
Furayḥa, Anīs. 1955. *Naḥwa 'Arabiyya Muyassara.* Beirut: Dār al-Thaqāfa.
——. 1988. *al-Nukta al-Lubnāniyya.* Beirut: Jarrūs Press.
al-Furayjāt, 'Ādil. 1994. *al-Shu'arā' al-Jāhiliyyūn al-Awā'il.* Beirut: Dār al-Mashriq.
Gabrieli, Francesco. 1967. *La letteratura arabe.* Florence: Sansoni and Milan: Accademia.
Gallagher, Nancy Elizabeth. 1994. *Approaches to the History of the Middle East: Interviews with Leading Middle East Historians.* Reading: Ithaca Press.
Gamal, Adel Suleiman. 1984. "Narrative Poetry in Classical Arabic Poetry." In A. H.

Green (ed.), *In Quest of an Islamic Humanism, Arabic and Islamic Studies in Memory of Mohamed al-Nowaihi*, pp. 25–38. Cairo: The American University in Cairo Press.
Gana, Nouri (ed.). 2013. *The Edinburgh Companion to the Arab Novel in English: The Politics of Anglo Arab and Arab American Literature and Culture*. Edinburgh: Edinburgh University Press.
Ganguly, Debjani. 2015. "Polysystems Redux: The Unfinished Business of World Literature." *The Cambridge Journal of Postcolonial Literary Inquiry* 2.2, pp. 272–81.
Gans, Herbert J. 1974. *Popular Culture and High Culture: An Analysis and Evaluation of Taste*. New York: Basic Books.
Gates, Henry Louis, Jr. 1992. *Loose Canons: Notes on the Culture Wars*. New York and Oxford: Oxford University Press.
Geer, Benjamin. 2009. "Prophets and Priests of the Nation: Naguib Mahfouz's Karnak Café and the 1967 Crisis in Egypt." *International Journal of Middle East Studies* 41.4, pp. 653–69.
Gelner, Ernest. 1983. *Nations and Nationalism*. Oxford: Blackwell.
Genette, Gérard. 1992. *The Architext: An Introduction* (trans. J. E. Lewin). Berkeley: University of California Press.
Gershoni, Israel and Meir Hatina (eds). 2008. *Narrating the Nile: Politics, Cultures, Identities*. London and Boulder, CO: Lynne Rienner Publishers.
al-Ghabbāshī, Shu'yb. 2002. *Ṣiḥāfat al-Aṭfāl fī al-Waṭan al-'Arabī*. Cairo: 'Ālam al-Kutub.
al-Ghadhdhāmī, 'Abd Allāh Muḥammad. 1987. *al-Ṣawt al-Qadīm al-Jadīd, Dirāsāt fī al-Judhūr al-'Arabiyya li-Mūsīqā al-Shi'r al-Ḥadīth*. Cairo: al-Hay'a al-Miṣriyya al-'Āmma li-l-Kitāb.
al-Ghamdi, Saleh Mued. 1989. *Autobiography in Classical Arabic Literature: An Ignored Literary Genre*. PhD thesis, Indiana University.
al-Ghāyātī, 'Alī. 1947 [1910]. *Waṭaniyyatī*. Cairo: Maṭba'at Minbar al-Sharq.
al-Ghayṭī, Muḥammad. 1993. *Thalāthat Alḥān min 'Uyūnik*. Cairo: al-Hay'a al-Miṣriyya al-'Āmma li-l-Kitāb.
al-Ghazālī, Abū Ḥāmid. 1956. *al-Munqidh min al-Ḍalāl* (ed. Jamīl Ṣalība and Kāmil 'Ayyād). Damascus: Maṭba'at al-Taraqqī.
al-Ghazālī, Zaynab. 1980. *Ayyām min Ḥayātī*. Cairo and Beirut: Dār al-Shurūq.
——. 1989. *al-Dā'iya Zaynab al-Ghazālī: Masīrat Jihād wa-Ḥadīth al-Dhikrayāt min Khilāli Kitābātihā*. Cairo: Dār al-I'tiṣām.
——. 1994. *Naẓarāt fī Kitāb Allāh* (ed. 'Abd Allāh al-Farmāwī). Cairo and Beirut: Dār al-Shurūq.
Ghazoul, Ferial J. 1994. "In Prison and on Prison." *Jusūr* 4, pp. 45–9.
——. 1996. *Nocturnal Poetics: The Arabian Nights in Comparative Context*. Cairo: The American University in Cairo Press.
——. 1998. "The Arabization of Othello." *Comparative Literature* 50.1, pp. 1–31.
——. 2009. "Literature and the Arts in Contemporary Iraqi Culture." *International Journal of Contemporary Iraqi Studies* 3.3, pp. 233–6.
——. and Barbara Harlow (eds). 1994. *The View from Within: Writers and Critics on Contemporary Arabic Literature*. Cairo: The American University in Cairo Press.
al-Ghīṭānī (Ghitany/al-Ghitani), Jamāl. 1974 [1971]. *al-Zaynī Barakāt*. Cairo: Madbūlī.
——. 1981 [1980]. *Khiṭaṭ al-Ghīṭānī*. Beirut: Dār al-Masīra.
——. 1985. *al-Zayni Barakat* (trans. Jean-François Fourcade). Paris: Éditions du Seuil.
——. 1986. "al-Turāth al-Ṣūfī wa-l-Judhūr." *al-Akhbār*, 28 May, p. 9.
——. 1986a. "al-Karāma al-Ṣūfiyya." *al-Akhbār*, 16 June, p. 9.
——. 1986b. "Turāthunā al-Qaṣaṣī—1." *al-Akhbār*, 16 July, p. 9.
——. 1986c. "Turāthunā al-Qaṣaṣī—3." *al-Akhbār*, 6 August, p. 9.
——.1988. *al-Zayni Barakat* (trans. Farouk Abdel Wahab). London: Penguin Books.
——. 2006. *al-Majālis al-Maḥfūẓiyya*. Cairo: Dār al-Shurūq.

Ghosh, Bishnupryia. 2000. "An Affair to Remember: Scripted Performances in the 'Nasreen Affair.'" In Amal Amireh and Lisa Suhair Majaj (eds), *Going Global: The Transnational Reception of Third World Women Writers*, pp. 39–83. New York and London: Garland Publishing.
Ghoussoub, Mai and Emma Sinclair-Webb (eds). 2000. *Imagined Masculinities: Male Identity and Culture in the Modern Middle East*. London: Saqi Books.
Ghulam-Sarwar, Yousof. 1994. *Dictionary of Traditional South-East Asian Theatre*. Kuala Lumpur: Oxford University Press.
Ghurayyib, Rūz. 1980. *Nasamāt fī al-Shiʿr al-Nisāʾī al-ʿArabī al-Muʿāṣir*. Beirut: al-Muʾassasa al-ʿArabiyya li-l-Dirāsāt wa-l-Nashr.
Gibb, Hamilton A. R. 1962. *Studies on the Civilization of Islam*. London: Routledge and Kegan.
——. 1963 [1926]. *Arabic Literature*. Oxford: Oxford University Press.
——. and Jacob M. Landau. 1968. *Arabische Literaturgeschicte*. Zurich and Stuttgart: Artemis Verlag.
——. and Jacob M. Landau. 1970. *Arabic Literature: An Introduction* (Hebrew). Tel Aviv: Am Oved.
Gibran, Khalil. 1918. *The Madman*. New York: Alfred A. Knopf.
——. 1920. *The Forerunner*. New York: Alfred A. Knopf.
——. 1924. *The Prophet*. New York: Alfred A. Knopf.
——. 1926. *Sand and Foam*. New York: Alfred A. Knopf.
——. 1928. *Jesus, the Son of Man*. New York: Alfred A. Knopf.
——. 1931. *The Earth Gods*. New York: Alfred A. Knopf.
——. 1932. *The Wanderer: His Parables and His Sayings*. New York: Alfred A. Knopf.
——. 1933. *The Garden of the Prophet*. New York: Alfred A. Knopf.
——. 1957. *The Broken Wings* (trans. A. R. Ferris). New York: Citadel Press.
——. 1973. *Lazarus and His Beloved: A One-Act* (ed. Khalil Gibran and Mary Gibran). Greenwich, CT: New York Philosophical Society.
——. 1982. *Dreams of Life* [*Lazarus and His Beloved* and *The Blind*] (ed. Khalil Gibran and Mary Gibran). Philadelphia: Westminster.
Giffen, Lois Anita. 1972. *Theory of Profane Love among the Arabs: The Development of the Genre*. London: University of London Press and New York: New York University Press.
——. 1996. *Naẓariyyat al-ʿIshq ʿinda al-ʿArab: Dirāsa Taʾrīkhiyya* (trans. Najm ʿAbd Allāh Muṣṭafā). Sūsa, Tunis: Dār al-Maʿarif li-l-Ṭibāʿa wa-l-Nashr.
Gifford, Denis. 1976. *Victorian Comics*. London: George Allen and Unwin.
Giladi, Avner. 1985. "Some Aspects of Social and National Contents in Egyptian Curricula and Textbooks." *Asian and African Studies* 19, pp. 157–86.
——. 1992. *Children of Islam: Concepts of Childhood in Medieval Muslim Society*. Basingstoke: Macmillan.
——. 1995. "Ṣaghīr." In P. J. Bearman et al. (eds), *The Encyclopaedia of Islam*, New Edition, Vol. 8, pp. 821–7. Leiden: Brill.
——. 1999. *Infants, Parents and Wet Nurses: Medieval Islamic Views on Breastfeeding and Their Social Implications*. Boston: Brill.
——. 2015. *Muslim Midwives: The Craft of Birthing in the Premodern Middle East*. New York: Cambridge University Press.
Gil Bardají, Anna. 2008. "Translation, Hegemony and Cultural Exchange: The Reception of Moroccan Literature in Spain." *Turjumān: Revue de Traduction et d'Interprétation* 17.1, pp. 57–63.
Giorgio, Pasqualina. 2001. "Narrativa araba contemporanea: alcune problematiche di traduzione." *Traduttore Nuovo* 56.1, pp. 23–8, 111–12.
Giovannucci, Perri. 2008. *Literature and Development in North Africa: The Modernizing Mission*. New York: Routledge.

Gleave, Robert (ed.). 2014. *Books and Bibliophiles: Studies in Honour of Paul Auchterlonie on the Bio-Bibliography of the Muslim World.* Cambridge: Gibb Memorial Trust.

Glowinski, Michael. 1969. "The Literary Genre and the Problems of Historical Poetics" (Hebrew). *Hasifrut* 2.1, pp. 14–25.

Gluzman, Michael. 2003. *The Politics of Canonicity: Lines of Resistance in Modernist Hebrew Poetry.* Stanford: Stanford University Press.

Göçek, Fatma Müge (ed.). 1998. *Political Cartoons in the Middle East.* Princeton: Markus Wiener Publishers.

——. and Shiva Balaghi. 1994. *Reconstructing Gender in the Middle East.* New York: Columbia University Press.

Goethe, Johann Wolfgang von. 1964. *Iphigenia fī Tauris* (trans. Muḥammad 'Abd al-Ḥalīm Karāra). Alexandria: Mansha'at al-Ma'ārif

——. 1966. *Nazwat al-'Āshiq wa-l-Shurakā'* (trans. Muṣṭafā Māhir). Cairo: al-Masraḥ al-'Ālamī.

——. 1967. *Tasso* (trans. 'Abd al-Ghaffār Makkāwī). Cairo: Dār al-Kātib al-'Arabī.

——. 1968. *Ālām Werther* (trans. Aḥmad Ḥasan al-Zayyāt). Beirut: Dār al-Kātib al-'Arabī.

——. 1978. *Ālām Werther* (trans. Lānā Abū Muṣliḥ). Beirut: al-Maktaba al-Ḥadītha li-l-Ṭibā'a wa-l-Nashr.

——. 1980. *al-Dīwān al-Sharqī li-l-Mu'allif al-Gharbī* (trans. 'Abd al-Raḥmān Badāwī). Beirut: al-Mu'assasa al-'Arabiyya li-l-Dirāsāt wa-l-Nashr.

——. 1980a. *al-Ansāb al-Mukhtāra* (trans. 'Abd al-Raḥmān Badāwī). Beirut: Dār al-Andalus.

——. 1999. *Mukhtārāt Shi'riyya wa-Nathriyya.* (trans. Abū al-'Īd Dūdū). Cologne: Manshūrāt al-Jamal.

——. 1999a. *Mukhtārāt Shi'riyya: Johann Wolfgang von Goethe fī al-Almāniyya wa-l-'Arabiyya* (trans. Fu'ād Rifqa). Beirut: Dār al-Andalus.

Goldziher, Ignac. 1966. *A Short History of Classical Arabic Literature* (trans. Joseph Desomogyi). Hildesheim: Georg Olms Verlag.

Golley, Nawar Al-Hassan. 2003. *Reading Arab Women's Autobiographies: Shahrazad Tells Her Story.* Austin: University of Texas Press.

Gombrich, E. H. 1969. *In Search of Cultural History.* Oxford: Clarendon Press.

Gonzalez-Quijano, Yves. 1998. "The Territory of Autobiography: Maḥmūd Darwīsh's *Memory for Forgetfulness.*" In Robin C. Ostle et al. (eds), *Writing the Self: Autobiographical Writing in Modern Arabic Literature,* pp. 183–91. London: Saqi Books.

——. 2000. "Pour une sociologie du fait littéraire dans le monde arabe: à propos de *The Limits of Freedom of Speech* par Mariana Stagh." *Arabic and Middle Eastern Literatures* 3.1, pp. 87–93.

Goodman, Dena. 1994. *The Republic of Letters: A Cultural History of the French Enlightenment.* Ithaca: Cornell University Press.

Goodman, Lenn Evan (ed.). 1972. *Ibn Tufayl's Hayy Ibn Yaqzan.* New York: Twayne Publishers.

——. 1983. "The Greek Impact on Arabic Literature." In A. F. L. Beeston et al. (eds), *Arabic Literature to the End of the Ummayad Period,* pp. 460–82. Cambridge: Cambridge University Press.

——. 1988. "The Sacred and the Secular: Rival Themes in Arabic Literature." Annual Lecture, The Irene Halmos Chair of Arabic Literature, Tel Aviv University, pp. 1–46.

Gordon, Haim. 1990. *Naguib Mahfouz's Egypt.* New York: Greenwood Press.

Gorton, T. J. 1974. "Arabic Influence on the Troubadours: Documents and Directions." *Journal of Arabic Literature* 5, pp. 11–16.

——. 1975. "The Metre of Ibn Quzmān: A 'Classical' Approach." *Journal of Arabic Literature* 6, pp. 1–29.

——. 1978. "*Zajal* and *Muwaššaḥ*: The Continuing Metrical Debate." *Journal of Arabic Literature* 9, pp. 32–40.

Gottesfeld, Dorit. 2011. "Harbingers of Feminism: A Fresh Look at the Works of Pioneering Palestinian Women Writers." *Journal of Levantine Studies* 1.2, pp. 75–101.

——. 2013. "'Mirrors of Alienation': West Bank Palestinian Women's Literature after Oslo." *Journal of Arabic and Islamic Studies* 13, pp. 22–40.

Gouhar, Saddik M. 2009. "Modernist Arabic Literature and the Clash of Civilizations Discourse." *Rupkatha Journal on Interdisciplinary Studies in Humanities* 1.1, pp. 43–57.

Graiouid, Said. 2008. "We Have not Buried the Simple Past: The Public Sphere and Post-Colonial Literature in Morocco." *Journal of African Cultural Studies* 20.2, pp. 145–58.

Gran, Peter. 1979. *Islamic Roots of Capitalism: Egypt, 1760–1840*. Austin : University of Texas Press.

——. 2016. "Arab Literary Exiles and Their Writing in Light of the Arab Spring." *Journal of Arabic Literature* 47.1–2, pp. 1–15.

Granqvist, Raoul and Jürgen Martini (eds). 1997. *Preserving the Landscape of Imagination: Children's Literature in Africa*. Amsterdam and Atlanta: Rodopi.

Grant, Damian. 1970. *Realism*. London: Methuen.

Green, A. H. (ed.). 1984. *In Quest of an Islamic Humanism, Arabic and Islamic Studies in Memory of Mohamed al-Nowaihi*. Cairo: The American University in Cairo Press.

Greenblatt, Stephen et al. (eds). 2009. *Cultural Mobility: A Manifesto*. Cambridge: Cambridge University Press.

Grippo, James R. 2006. "The Fool Sings a Hero's Song: Shaaban Abdel Rahim, Egyptian Shaabi, and the Video Clip Phenomenon." *Transnational Broadcasting Studies* 16. Available at: <http://tbsjournal.arabmediasociety.com/Grippo.html> (last accessed 28 October 2016)

Guillen, Claudio. 2015. *Literature as System: Essays Toward the Theory of Literary History*. Princeton: Princeton University Press

Günther, Sebastian. 1999. "Hostile Brothers in Transformation: An Archetypal Conflict in Classical and Modern Arabic Literature." In Angelika Neuwirth et al. (eds), *Myths, Historical Archetypes and Symbolic Figures in Arabic Literature*, pp. 309–36. Beirut: Orient-Institut der DMG.

——. and Stephan Milich (eds). 2016. *Representations and Visions of Homeland in Modern Arabic Literature*. Hildesheim: Georg Olms Verlag.

Gutas, Dimitri. 1998. "Tardjama (Translations from Greek and Syriac)." In P. J. Bearman et al. (eds), *The Encyclopaedia of Islam*, New Edition, Vol. 10, pp. 225–31. Leiden: Brill.

——. 1999. *Greek Thought, Arabic Culture: The Graeco-Arabic Translation Movement in Baghdad and Early 'Abbāsid Society (2nd–4th/8th–10th Centuries)*. London: Routledge.

——. 2000. *Greek Philosophers in the Arabic Tradition*. Aldershot: Ashgate.

Guth, Stephan et al. (eds). 1999. *Conscious Voices: Concepts of Writing in the Middle East*. Beirut: Orient-Institut der DMG.

——. 2003. "The Simultaneity of the Non-Simultaneous: The Global Dimensions of Middle Eastern Literature (esp. in the 19th Century)." In Christian Szyska and Friederike Pannewick (eds), *Crossings and Passages in Genre and Culture*, pp. 121–37. Wiesbaden: Reichert Verlag.

——. 2007. "Individuality Lost, Fun Gained: Some Recurrent Motifs in Late Twentieth-Century Arabic and Turkish Novels." *Journal of Arabic and Islamic Studies* 7, pp. 25–49.

——. 2011. "Literary Currents in Egypt since the Beginning/Mid-1960s." In Gail Ramsay and Stephan Guth (eds), *From New Values to New Aesthetics: Turning Points in Modern Arabic Literature (Proceedings of the 8th EURAMAL Conference, 11–14 June, 2008, Uppsala / Sweden). 1. From Modernism to the 1980s*, pp. 85–112. Wiesbaden: Harrassowitz Verlag.

——. and Gail Ramsay (eds). 2011. *From New Values to New Aesthetics: Turning Points in*

Modern Arabic Literature (Proceedings of the 8th EURAMAL Conference, 11–14 June, 2008, Uppsala / Sweden). 2. Postmodernism and Thereafter. Wiesbaden: Harrassowitz Verlag.

Guthrie, Shirley. 2001. *Arab Women in the Middle Ages: Private Lives and Public Roles*. London: Saqi Books.

Haase, Donald. 2004. "*The Arabian Nights*, Visual Culture, and Early German Cinema." *Fabula* 45.3–4, pp. 261–74.

Habib, Samar. 2007. *Female Homosexuality in the Middle East: Histories and Representations*. New York: Routledge.

Habibi, Émile. 1980. *L'Optissimiste: les circonstances étrangers de la disparition de Said Abou-An-Nahs* (trans. T. H.). Paris: Le Sycomore.

——. 1987. *Les aventures extraordinaires de Sa'ïd le Peptimiste* (trans. Jean-Patrick Guillaume). Paris: Gallimard.

Ḥabībī, Imīl. 1974. *al-Waqā'i' al-Gharība fi Ikhtifā' Sa'īd Abī al-Naḥs al-Mutashā'il*. Haifa: Dār al-Ittiḥād.

——. 1980. *Luka' ibn Luka'*. Nazareth: Manshūrāt Dār 30 Ādhār.

——. 1985. *Sudāsiyyat al-Ayyām al-Sitta; al-Waqā'i' al-Gharība fi Ikhtifā' Sa'īd Abī al-Naḥs al-Mutashā'il wa-Qiṣaṣ Ukhrā*. Haifa: Dār al-Ittiḥād.

Habiby, Emile. 1985. *The Secret Life of Saeed the Pessoptimist* (trans. Salma Khadra Jayyusi and Trevor Le Gassick). London: Zed Books.

Haddād, 'Abd al-Karīm. 2002. "Qaṣā'id li-Ghasl al-Dhākira wa-Tamjīd al-Qam' wa-l-Ḥurūb." *al-Mu'tamar* 314, pp. 2–8 August, p. 9.

al-Ḥaddād, Najīb. 1954. "Muqābala Bayna al-Shi'r al-'Arabī wa-l-Shi'r al-Ifranjī." In Muṣṭafā Luṭfī al-Manfalūṭī (ed.), *Mukhtārāt al-Manfalūṭī*, pp. 120–138. Cairo: Maṭba'at al-Sa'āda.

Haddad, Robert M. 1970. *Syrian Christians in Muslim Society: An Interpretation*. Princeton: Princeton University Press.

Hadeed, Khalid. 2013. "Homosexuality and Epistemic Closure in Modern Arabic Literature." *International Journal of Middle East Studies* 45.2, pp. 271–91.

al-Ḥadīdī, 'Alī. 1969. "al-Muqawwimāt al-Asāsiyya li-Adab al-Aṭfāl." *al-Majalla* (Cairo), November, pp. 49–53.

Haeri, Niloofar. 1996. *The Sociolinguistic Market of Cairo: Gender, Class, and Education*. London and New York: Kegan Paul.

Hafez, Kai (ed.). 2001. *Mass Media, Politics, and Society in the Middle East*. Cresskill, NJ: Hampton Press.

Hafez, Sabry. 1993. *The Genesis of Arabic Narrative Discourse: A Study in the Sociology of Modern Arabic Literature*. London: Saqi Books.

——. 2006. "The Master of the Arabic Novel." *Al-Ahram Weekly*, 7–13 September.

Ḥāfiẓ, Muḥammad Maḥmūd Sāmī. 1971. *Ta'rīkh al-Mūsīqā wa-l-Ghinā' al-'Arabī*. Cairo: al-Maṭba'a al-Fanniyya al-Ḥadītha.

Ḥāfiẓ, Ṣabrī. 1970. "al-Riwāya al-Miṣriyya mundhu Ẓuhūrihā 'Ām 1867 ilā 1969." *Majallat al-Kitāb al-'Arabī*, July, pp. 43–79.

Haikal, Mohammed Hussein. 1989. *Zainab* (trans. John Mohammed Grinsted). London: Darf.

Haist, Andrea. 2000. *Der Ägyptische Roman: Rezeption und Wertung von den Anfängen bis 1945*. Wiesbaden: Reichert Verlag.

al-Ḥājj, 'Azīz. 1983. *al-Ghazw al-Thaqāfī wa-Muqāwamatuhu*. Beirut: al-Mu'assasa al-'Arabiyya li-l-Dirāsāt wa-l-Nashr.

Hajjar, Nijmeh. 1993. "Immigrant Arabic Poets and Writers and the Modern Arab Renaissance." *Voices: The Quarterly Journal of the National Library of Australia* 3.2, pp. 44–50.

al-Ḥakīm, Tawfīq. 1933. *'Awdat al-Rūḥ*. Cairo: Maktabat al-Raghā'ib.

——. 1986. "al-Riwāya Aṣīla fī al-Turāth al-'Arabī." *al-Akhbār*, 6 August, p. 9.

——. 1990. *Return of the Spirit* (trans. William M. Hutchins).Washington, DC: Three Continents Press.

Halabi, Zeina G. 2017. *The Unmaking of the Arab Intellectual: Prophecy, Exile, and the Nation*. Edinburgh: Edinburgh University Press.

Ḥalāwa, Muḥammad al-Sayyid. 2002. *al-Adab al-Qaṣaṣī li-l-Ṭifl*. Alexandria: Mu'assasat Ḥūrus al-Dawliyya.

Halevi, Sharon and Fruma Zachs. 2007. "*Asma* (1873): The Early Arabic Novel as a Social Compass." *Studies in the Novel* 39.4, pp. 416–30.

Halim, Hala. 2014. *Alexandrian Cosmopolitanism: An Archive*. New York: Fordham University Press.

al-Ḥalīwī, Muḥammad. 1936. "al-Ḥayāt al-Adabiyya fī Tūnis." *al-Risāla*, 29 June, pp. 1062–4.

Hall, Stuart. 1996. "Introduction: Who Needs 'Identity'?" In Stuart Hall and Paul Du Gay (eds), *Questions of Cultural Identity*, pp. 1–17. London: Sage Publications.

——. and Paul Du Gay (eds). 1996. *Questions of Cultural Identity*. London: Sage Publications.

Hallaq, Boutros. 1998. "Autobiography and Polyphony." In Robin C. Ostle et al. (eds), *Writing the Self: Autobiographical Writing in Modern Arabic Literature*, pp. 192–206. London: Saqi Books.

Al-Halool, Musa. 2013. "Denys Johnson-Davies: The Translator Who Rushed in Where Angels Feared to Tread." *Arab Studies Quarterly* 35.1, pp. 39-53.

Ḥamāda, Ibrāhīm. 1963. *Khayāl al-Ẓill wa-Tamthīliyyāt Ibn Dāniyāl*. Cairo: al-Mu'assasa al-Miṣriyya al-'Āmma.

Ḥamāda, Muḥammad Māhir. 1992. *Riḥlat al-Kitāb al-'Arabī ilā Diyār al-Gharb Fikran wa-Māddatan*. Beirut: Mu'assasat al-Risāla.

al-Hamaḏāni. 1957. *Maqāmāt*. Paris: Librairie C. Klincksieck.

al-Hamadhānī, Abū al-Faḍl Badī' al-Zamān. AH 1298. *Maqāmāt Abī al-Faḍl Badī' al-Zamān al-Hamadhānī*. Constantinople: Maṭba'at al-Jawā'ib.

——. 1983. *Maqāmāt Badī' al-Zamān al-Hamadhānī wa-Sharḥuhā* (ed. Muḥammad 'Abduh). Beirut: al-Dār al-Muttaḥida li-l-Nashr.

——. 1993. *Maqāmāt Badī' al-Zamān al-Hamadhānī* (ed. 'Alī Bū Milḥim). Beirut: Dār wa-Maktabat al-Hilāl.

Ḥamdān, Mas'ūd. 1996. *The Theater Play as an Aesthetic Medium for Alternative Mass Communication: The Carnivalesque Satires of Durayd Laḥḥām and Muḥammad al-Māghūṭ* (Hebrew). MA thesis, University of Haifa.

——. 1998. *Artistic Genre as an Intuitive Perception of Reality and Aesthetic Reflection of Culture: Israel and the Arab World in the Mirror of Grotesque and Satiric Protest Theatres* (Hebrew). PhD thesis, University of Haifa.

——. 1999. "al-Istrātījiyya al-Marfa'iyya l-Fi'l al-Hijā' fī Masraḥ Durayd Laḥḥām wa-Muḥammad al-Māghūṭ." *al-Karmil—Abḥāth fī al-Lugha wa-l-Adab* 20, pp. 63–96.

——. 2005. *Poetics, Politics and Protest in Arab Theatre: The Bitter Cup and the Holy Rain*. Brighton: Sussex Academic Press.

Hamdouchi, Abdelilah. 2008. *The Final Bet* (trans. Jonathan Smolin). Cairo: The American University in Cairo Press.

Hämeen-Anttila, Jaakko. 1991. "A Note on the 'Ēn 'Avdat Inscription." *Studia Orientalia* 67, pp. 33–6.

——. 1994–5. "From East to West: The Transmission of Maqāmas and Other Narrative Material." *Orientalia Suecana* 43–4, pp. 105–13.

——. 2002. *Maqama—A History of a Genre*. Wiesbaden: Harrassowitz Verlag.

Hammond, Marle and Dana Sajdi (eds). 2008. *Transforming Loss into Beauty: Essays on Arabic Literature and Culture in Honor of Magda al-Nowaihi*. Cairo: The American University in Cairo Press.

Hamori, Andras. 1980. "Ilyādhat Hūmīrūs Bayna al-Ḥaqīqa wa-l-Taqlīd." In Sasson

Somekh (ed.), *Abḥāth fī al-Lugha wa-l-Uslūb*, pp. 15–22. Tel Aviv: Tel Aviv University Press.

Hamzah, Dyala (ed.). 2013. *The Making of the Arab Intellectual (1880–1960): Empire, Public Sphere and the Colonial Coordinates of Selfhood*. London: Routledge.

Ḥananī, Zāhir Jawhar. 2016. *Min Adab al-Asr: Shi'r al-Mu'taqalāt fī Filasṭīn*. Amman: Dār Dijla.

Handal, Nathalie (ed.). 2000. *The Poetry of Arab Women: A Contemporary Anthology*. New York and Northampton: Interlink Books.

——. 2012. *Poet in Andalucía*. Pittsburgh: University of Pittsburgh Press.

Hanley, Will. 2008. "Grieving Cosmopolitanism in Middle East Studies." *History Compass* 6.5, pp. 1346–67.

——. 2013. "Cosmopolitan Cursing in Late Nineteenth-Century Alexandria." In Derryl N. MacLean and Sikeena Karmali Ahmed (eds), *Cosmopolitanisms in Muslim Contexts: Perspectives from the Past*, pp. 92–104. Edinburgh: Edinburgh University Press.

Hanna, Nelly. 2003. *In Praise of Books: A Cultural History of Cairo's Middle Class, Sixteenth to the Eighteenth Century*. Syracuse: Syracuse University Press.

Hanna, Sameh F. 2009. "Othello in the Egyptian Vernacular: Negotiating the 'Doxic' in Drama Translation and Identity Formation." *Translator: Studies in Intercultural Communication* 15.1, pp. 157–78.

Hanoosh, Yasmeen. 2012. "Contempt: State Literati vs. Street Literati in Modern Iraq." *Journal of Arabic Literature* 43.2–3, pp. 372–408.

Ḥarb, 'Alī. 1995. "Ḥaql al-Alghām." In *al-'Unf al-Uṣūlī: Muwājahāt al-Sayf wa-l-Qalam*, pp. 219–54. London and Beirut: Riyāḍ al-Rayyis.

al-Ḥarīrī (al-Ḥarîri), al-Qāsim ibn 'Alī. 1969 [1867]. *The Assemblies of al-Ḥarîri* (Vol. 1) (trans. Thomas Chenery). Farnborough: Gregg International Publishers.

——. 1969 [1898]. *The Assemblies of al-Ḥarîri* (Vol. 2) (trans. F. Steingass). Farnborough: Gregg International Publishers.

——. 1971 [1850]. *Makamat* (trans. Theodore Preston). London: The Oriental Translation Fund.

——. 1985. *Maqāmāt al-Ḥarīrī*. Beirut: Dār Bayrūt.

Harris, Joseph and Karl Reichl (eds). 1997. *Prosimetrum: Cross-Cultural Perspectives on Narrative in Prose and Verse*. Cambridge, MA: D. S. Brewer.

Hartman, Michelle. 1998. *Subversions from the Borderlands: Readings of Intertextual Strategies in Contemporary Lebanese Women's Literature in Arabic and French*. PhD thesis, Oxford University.

——. 2002. *Jesus, Joseph and Job: Reading Rescriptings of Religious Figures in Lebanese Women's Fiction*. Wiesbaden: Reichert Verlag.

Hartmann, Martin. 1896. *Metrum und Rhytmus*. Giessen: J. Ricker.

Hary, Benjamin H. et al. (eds). 2000. *Judaism and Islam: Boundaries, Communication and Interaction: Essays in Honor of William M. Brinner*. Leiden and Boston: Brill.

al-Hasan, Hasan Y. A. 1984. *The Arabian Nights and Modern Arab Theatre*. PhD thesis, University of Exeter.

Ḥasan, Muḥammad Rushdī. 1974. *Athar al-Maqāma fī Nash'at al-Qiṣṣa al-Miṣriyya al-Ḥadītha*. Cairo: al-Hay'a al-Miṣriyya al-'Āmma li-l-Kitāb.

al-Hāshim, Jūzīf. 1960. *Sulaymān al-Bustānī wa-l-Ilyādha*. Beirut: Maktabat al-Madrasa wa-Dār al-Kitāb al-Lubnānī.

Al-Hassan, Nawar. 1994. *A Feminist Reading of Arab Women's Autobiographies*. PhD thesis, University of Nottingham.

Hassan, Waïl S. 2002. "Postcolonial Theory and Modern Arabic Literature: Horizons of Application." *Journal of Arabic Literature* 33.1, pp. 45–64.

——. 2003. *Tayeb Salih: Ideology and the Craft of Fiction*. Syracuse: Syracuse University Press.

——. 2011. *Immigrant Narratives: Orientalism and Cultural Translation in Arab American and Arab British Literature*. New York: Oxford University Press.

Hatem, Mervat F. 1998. "The Invisible American Half: Arab American Hybridity and Feminist Discourses in the 1990s." In Ella Shohat (ed.), *Talking Visions: Multicultural Feminism in a Transnational Age*, pp. 369–90. New York: New Museum of Contemporary Art and Cambridge, MA: The MIT Press.

Hatim, Basil. 1999. "Arabic Literature in Translation: Domestication Revisited." In Miguel Hernando De Larramendi et al. (eds), *Traducción, emigración y culturas*, pp. 185–203. Cuenca, Spain: Ediciones de la Universidad de Castilla-La Mancha.

Hatina, Meir. 2006. "Restoring a Lost Identity: Models of Education in Modern Islamic Thought." *British Journal of Middle Eastern Studies* 33, pp. 177–95.

——. 2007. *Identity Politics in the Middle East: Liberal Thought and Islamic Challenge in Egypt*. London: I. B. Tauris.

——. 2007a. "Where East Meets West: Sufism, Cultural Rapprochement and Politics." *International Journal of Middle East Studies* 39, pp. 389–409.

——. 2011. "Arab Liberal Discourse: Old Dilemmas, New Visions." *Middle East Critique* 20, pp. 3–20.

——. 2013. "Speaking Truth to Power: Liberal Discourse after 1967." *Historia* 30, pp. 33–59.

——. 2014. *Martyrdom in Modern Islam: Piety, Power and Politics*. Cambridge: Cambridge University Press.

al-Hawar, Munīr. 1994. "Ḥawla Kutub al-Aṭfāl." *Risālat al-Maktaba* (Amman) 29.4, pp. 50–4.

al-Ḥāwī, Īliyyā. 1980. *Ilyās Abū Shabaka Shā'ir al-Jaḥīm wa-l-Na'īm*. Beirut: Dār al-Kitāb al-Lubnānī.

Hawley, John C. (ed.). 1998. *Postcolonial Crescent: Islam's Impact on Contemporary Literature*. New York: Peter Lang.

Haydar, Adnan F. 2002. "*Al-Ḥidâ, al-Nabd, al-Ḥawrabah* and *al-Nawḥ* in Lebanese *Zajal* Poetry: A Study of Meter and Rhythm." *Edebiyât* 13.2, pp. 159–68.

Ḥaydar, Ḥaydar. 1983. *Walīma li-A'shāb al-Baḥr (Nashīd al-Mawt)*. Beirut: n.pub.

——. 1988. *Walīma li-A'shāb al-Baḥr (Nashīd al-Mawt)*. Beirut: Dār Amwāj.

——. 2000. *Walīma li-A'shāb al-Baḥr (Nashīd al-Mawt)*. Cairo: al-Hay'a al-'Āmma li-Quṣūr al-Thaqāfa.

Hayes, John R. (ed.). 1976. *The Genius of Arab Civilization: Source of Renaissance*. Oxford: Phaidon Press.

——. (ed.). 1990. *'Abqariyyat al-Ḥaḍāra al-'Arabiyya: Manba' al-Nahḍa al-Ūrubiyya* (trans. 'Abd al-Karīm Maḥfūẓ). Benghazi: al-Dār al-Jamāhīriyya li-l-Nashr wa-l-Tawzī' wa-l-I'lān.

Haykal, Bernard and Robyn Creswell. 2015. "Battle Lines: Want to Understand the Jihadist? Read Their Poetry." *The New Yorker*, 8 June.

Haykal, Muḥammad Ḥusayn. 1968 [1913]. *Zaynab*. Cairo: Maktabat al-Nahḍa.

——. 1965. *Thawrat al-Adab*. Cairo: Maktabat al-Nahḍa al-Miṣriyya.

Haywood, John A. 1971. *Modern Arabic Literature 1800–1970*. London: Lund Humphries.

al-Hazimi, Mansour I. et al. (eds). 2006. *Beyond the Dunes: An Anthology of Modern Saudi Literature*. London: I. B. Tauris.

Hazran, Yusri. 2013. "The Zajal: Popular Poetry and the Struggle over Lebanon's History." *Middle Eastern Literatures* 16.2, pp. 169–88.

Heath, P. 1984. "A Critical Review of Modern Scholarship on Sīrat Antar ibn Shaddād and the Popular Sīra." *Journal of Arabic Literature* 15, pp. 19–44.

Heinrichs, Wolfhart and Gregor Schoeler (eds). 1994. *Festschrift Ewald Wagner zum 65 Geburtstag*. Beirut and Stuttgart: Franz Steiner Verlag.

Hejaiej, Monia. 1996. *Behind Closed Doors: Women's Oral Narratives in Tunis*. London: Quartet Books.

Helgesson, Stefan. 2015. "Tayeb Salih, Sol Plaatje, and the Trajectories of World Literature." *The Cambridge Journal of Postcolonial Literary Inquiry* 2.2, pp. 253–60.
Hermes, Nizar F. 2012. *The [European] Other in Medieval Arabic Literature and Culture.* New York: Palgrave Macmillan.
Hever, Hannan. 1987. "Hebrew in an Israeli Arab Hand: Six Miniatures on Anton Shammas' *Arabesques.*" *Cultural Critique* 7, pp. 47–76.
——. 1989. "Israeli Literature's Achilles' Heel." *Tikkun* 4.5, pp. 30–2.
——. 1991. "Minority Discourse of a National Majority: Israeli Fiction of the Early Sixties." *Prooftexts* 11, pp. 129–47.
——. 2001. *Producing the Modern Hebrew Canon: Nation Building and Minority Discourse.* New York and London: New York University Press.
Higonnet, Margaret (ed.). 1994. *Borderwork: Feminist Engagements with Comparative Literature.* Ithaca: Cornell University Press.
Ḥijāzī, Aḥmad 'Abd al-Mu'ṭī. 1999. "Muḥāwala li-Fahm al-Shā'ir al-Ladhī Ya'tī wa-lā Ya'tī.'" *al-Sharq* (Shfaram) 29.3, pp. 91–6.
Hilāl, Muḥammad Ghunaymī. 1977. *al-Mawqif al-Adabī.* Beirut: Dār al-'Awda.
al-Ḥillī, Ṣafī al-Dīn. 1956. *al-Kitāb al-'Āṭil al-Ḥālī wa-l-Murakhkhaṣ al-Ghālī* (ed. Wilhelm Hoenerbach). Wiesbaden: Franz Steiner Verlag.
Hirsch, Lester M. (ed.). 1966. *Man and Space.* New York: Pitman Publishing Corporation.
——. (ed.). 1972. *al-Insān wa-l-Faḍā'* (trans. Ṣalāḥ Jalāl). Cairo: Maktabat al-Nahḍa al-Miṣriyya.
Hirschler, Konrad. 2006. *Medieval Arabic Historiography: Authors as Actors.* New York: Routledge.
——. 2012. *The Written Word in the Medieval Arabic Lands: A Social and Cultural History of Reading Practices.* Edinburgh: Edinburgh University Press.
——. and Sarah Savant. 2014. "Introduction—What is in a Period? Arabic Historiography and Periodization." *Der Islam* 91.1, pp. 6–19.
Hitti, Philip K. 1962. *Islam and the West: A Historical Cultural Survey.* Princeton: D. Van Nostrand.
Hobsbawm, Eric. 1992. *Nations and Nationalism since 1780: Programme, Myth, Reality.* Cambridge: Cambridge University Press.
——. and Terence Ranger (eds). 1992 [1983]. *The Invention of Tradition.* Cambridge: Cambridge University Press.
Hoffman, Valerie J. 1985. "An Islamic Activist: Zaynab al-Ghazali." In Elizabeth Warnock Fernea (ed.), *Women and the Family in the Middle East*, pp. 233–54. Austin: University of Texas Press.
Holes, Clive. 2004. *Modern Arabic: Structures, Functions, and Varieties.* Washington, DC: Georgetown University Press
——. and S. S. Abu Athera. 2009. *Poetry and Politics in Contemporary Bedouin Society.* Reading: Ithaca Press.
Holmberg, Bo. 2006. "Transculturating the Epic: The Arabic Awakening and the Translation of the *Iliad.*" In Margareta Petersson et al. (ed.), *Literary Interactions in the Modern World*, pp. 141–65. Berlin: De Gruyter.
Holt, Elizabeth M. 2009. "Narrative and the Reading Public in 1870s Beirut." *Journal of Arabic Literature* 40.1, pp. 37–70.
——. 2013. "'Bread or Freedom': The Congress for Cultural Freedom, the CIA, and the Arabic Literary Journal *Ḥiwār* (1962–67)." *Journal of Arabic Literature* 44.1, pp. 83–102.
——. 2016. "Narrating the Nahda: The Syrian Protestant College, *al-Muqtataf*, and the Rise of Jurji Zaydan." In Nadia Maria El Cheikh et al. (eds), *One Hundred and Fifty*, pp. 273–9. Beirut: American University of Beirut.
——. [Forthcoming]. *Novel Material: Speculating in Arabic from Beirut to Cairo, 1870–1907.* New York: Fordham University Press.

Homer. 1983. *The Iliad* (trans. E. V. Rieu). Harmondsworth: Penguin Books.

Hopkins, Nicholas S. (ed.). 2009. *Political and Social Protest in Egypt*. Cairo and New York: The American University in Cairo Press.

Hopwood, Derek. 1999. *Sexual Encounters in the Middle East: The British, the French, and the Arabs*. Reading: Ithaca Press.

——. (ed.). 2000. *Arab Nation, Arab Nationalism*. Basingstoke: Macmillan.

Horn, Pierre L. and Mary Beth Pringle (eds). 1984. *The Image of the Prostitute in Modern Literature*. New York: Frederick Ungar.

Hourani, Albert. 1986 [1962]. *Arabic Thought in the Liberal Age 1798–1939*. Cambridge: Cambridge University Press.

——. (ed.). 1991. *Islam in European Thought*. Cambridge: Cambridge University Press.

——. 1991a. "Sulaiman al-Bustani and the *Iliad*." In Albert Hourani (ed.), *Islam in European Thought*, pp. 174–87. Cambridge: Cambridge University Press.

Hout, Syrine. 2012. *Postwar Anglophone Lebanese Fiction: Home Matters in the Diaspora*. Edinburgh: Edinburgh University Press.

Hovannisian, Richard G. and Georges Sabagh (eds). 1997. *The Thousand and One Nights in Arabic Literature and Society*. Cambridge: Cambridge University Press.

Howarth, Herbert and Ibrahim Shukrallah. 1944. *Images from the Arab World: Fragments of Arab Literature Translated and Paraphrased with Variations and Comments*. London: The Pilot Press.

Huart, Clément. 1966. *A History of Arabic Literature*. Beirut: Khayats.

Hugo, Victor-Marie. 1937. *The Hunchback of Notre Dame*. Reading, PA: Spencer.

——. 1956. *Notre-Dame de Paris*. Paris: Librairie Greund.

——. 1959. *Aḥdab Notre Dame* (trans. ʿUmar ʿAbd al-ʿAzīz Amīn). Cairo: al-Dār al-Qawmiyya li-l-Ṭibāʿa wa-l-Nashr.

——. 1989. *Aḥdab Notre Dame* (trans. Ramaḍān Lāwand). Beirut: Dār al-ʿIlm li-l-Malāyīn.

al-Ḥumaydī, Abū ʿAbd Allāh. 1989. *Jadhwat al-Muqtabis fī Taʾrīkh ʿUlamāʾ al-Andalus* (ed. Ibrāhīm al-Abyārī). Cairo: Dār al-Kitāb al-Miṣrī and Beirut: Dār al-Kitāb al-Lubnānī.

Hunke, Sigrid. 1965. *Allahs Sonne über dem Abendland*. Frankfurt am Main and Hamburg: Fischer Bücherei.

——. 1979. *Shams al-ʿArab Tastaʿu ʿalā al-Gharb* (trans. Fārūq Bayḍūn and Kamāl Dasūqī). Beirut: al-Maktab al-Tijārī li-l-Ṭibāʿa wa-l-Tawzīʿ wa-l-Nashr.

Hunter, J. Paul. 1990. *Before Novels: The Cultural Contexts of Eighteenth-Century English Fiction*. New York and London: W. W. Norton.

Hunwick, John O. (ed.). 1995. *Arabic Literature of Africa* (Vol. 2): *The Writings of Central Sudanic Africa*. Leiden: Brill.

——. 1997. "The Arabic Literary Tradition of Nigeria." *Research in African Literatures* 28.3, pp. 210–23.

——. (ed.). 2003. *Arabic Literature of Africa* (Vol. 4): *The Writings of Western Sudanic Africa*. Leiden: Brill.

——. 2004. "West Africa and the Arabic Language." *Sudanic Africa: A Journal of Historical Sources* 15, pp. 133–44.

Huri, Yair. 2005. "'To Flee from All Languages': The Gap between Language and Experience in the Works of Modern Arab Poets." *Arab Studies Quarterly* 27.4, pp. 1–16.

——. 2006. *The Poetry of Saʿdi Yusuf*. Brighton: Sussex Academic Press.

Husain, Taha. 1976. *A Passage to France—The Third Volume of the Autobiography* (trans. Kenneth Cragg). Leiden: Brill.

Ḥusayn, Ḥamdī. 1993. "Fuʾād Ḥijāzī wa-l-Jāʾiza al-Tashjīʿiyya." *ʿĀlam al-Kitāb*, October, pp. 24–9.

Ḥusayn, Kamāl al-Dīn. 1993. *al-Turāth al-Shaʿbī fī al-Masraḥ al-Miṣrī*. Cairo: al-Dār al-Miṣriyya al-Lubnāniyya.

Ḥusayn, Ṭāhā. 1926. *Fī al-Shi'r al-Jāhilī*. Cairo: Dār al-Kutub.
——. 1927. *Fī al-Adab al-Jāhilī*. Cairo: Maṭba'at al-I'timād.
——. n.d. [1929]. *al-Ayyām* (Vol. 1). Cairo: Dār al-Ma'ārif.
——. 1945. "al-Adab al-'Arabī Bayna Amsihi wa-Ghadihi." *al-Kātib al-Miṣrī* I.1, October, pp. 4–27.
——. n.d. [1958]. *Alwān*. Cairo: Dār al-Ma'ārif.
——. 1964. *Ḥadīth al-Arbi'ā'*. Cairo: Dār al-Ma'ārif.
——. 1966 [1958]. *Min Adabinā al-Mu'āṣir*. Beirut: Dār al-Ādāb.
——. 1967 [1956]. *Naqd wa-Iṣlāḥ*. Beirut: Dār al-'Ilm li-l-Malāyīn.
——. n.d. [1973]. *al-Ayyām* (Vol. 3). Cairo: Dār al-Ma'ārif.
——. 2001 [1938]. *Mustaqbal al-Thaqāfa fī Miṣr*. Sūsa, Tunis: Dār al-Ma'ārif.
al-Ḥusaynī, Isḥāq Mūsā. 1966. *al-Adab wa-l-Qawmiyya al-'Arabiyya*. Cairo: Maṭba'at Lajnat al-Bayān al-'Arabī.
al-Ḥusnī, 'Abd al-Ḥayy. 1958. *al-Thaqāfa al-Islāmiyya fī al-Hind*. Damascus: Maṭbū'āt al-Majma' al-'Ilmī al-'Arabī.
al-Ḥuṣrī, Abū Khaldūn Sāṭi'. 1985. *Fī al-Lugha wa-l-Adab wa-'Alāqatihimā bi-l-Qawmiyya*. Beirut: Markaz Dirāsāt al-Waḥda al-'Arabiyya.
al-Hussein, R. H. 1989. *Nature and Death in the Poetry of al-Mala'ika, al-Shabbi, and Shukri, and Certain English Romantic Poets*. PhD thesis, University of St Andrews.
Hussein, Taha. 1954. *The Future of Culture in Egypt* (trans. S. Glazer). Washington, DC: American Council of Learned Societies.
Ibn al-Akfānī, Muḥammad ibn Ibrāhīm. 1998. *Kitāb Irshād al-Qāṣid ilā Asnā al-Maqāṣid* (ed. Maḥmūd Fākhūrī et al.). Beirut: Maktabat Lubnān.
Ibn Bassām, Abū al-Ḥasan 'Alī. 1979. *al-Dhākhīra fī Maḥāsin Ahl al-Jazīra* (ed. Iḥsān 'Abbās). Beirut: Dār al-Thaqāfa.
Ibn Jallūn, Muḥammad 'Abd al-Majīd. 1936. "al-Ḥayāt al-Adabiyya bi-l-Maghrib." *al-Risāla*, 4 May, pp. 743–4.
Ibn Kamāl Bāshā. 1994. *Rujū' al-Shaykh ilā Ṣibāhu*. Beirut?: Manshūrāt Samar. Available at: <http://kitabi01.blogspot.co.il/2016/01/download-pdf-book-Sheikh-return-to-his-boyhood-in-force-on-Beh.html> (last accessed 30 October 2016)
Ibn Khaldûn. 1967 [1958]. *The Muqaddimah: An Introduction to History* (trans. Franz Rosenthal). Princeton: Princeton University Press.
Ibn Khaldūn, 'Abd al-Raḥmān. 1979. *Muqaddimat Ibn Khaldūn*. Cairo: Dār Nahḍat Miṣr li-l-Ṭibā'a wa-l-Nashr.
Ibn Munqidh, Usāma. 1930. *Kitāb al-I'tibār* (ed. Philip Hitti). Princeton: Princeton University Press.
——. 1987. *Memoirs of an Arab-Syrian Gentleman and Warrior in the Period of the Crusades* (trans. Philip Hitti). London: I. B. Tauris.
Ibn al-Nadīm. 1970. *The Fihrist* (ed. and trans. Bayard Dodge). New York and London: Columbia University Press.
——. 1985. *al-Fihrist*. al-Dawha: Dār Qaṭrī ibn al-Fujā'a.
Ibn Qutayba, 'Abd Allāh ibn Muslim. 1928. *'Uyūn al-Akhbār*. Cairo: Maṭba'at Dār al-Kutub al-Miṣriyya.
Ibn Rashīq al-Qayrawānī. 1963. *al-'Umda* (ed. Muḥammad Muḥyī al-Dīn 'Abd al-Ḥamīd). Cairo: al-Maktaba al-Tijāriyya al-Kubrā.
Ibn Taghrībirdī, Jamāl al-Dīn. 1930. *al-Nujūm al-Zāhira fī Mulūk Miṣr wa-l-Qāhira*. Cairo: Maṭba'at Dār al-Kutub.
Ibn Ṭufayl. 1940. *Ḥayy ibn Yaqẓān* (ed. Jamīl Ṣalība and Kāmil 'Ayyād). Damascus: Maṭba'at al-Taraqqī.
Ibn Warraq. 2003. *Why I Am Not a Muslim*. Amherst, NY: Prometheus Books.
Ibn Zaydān, 'Abd al-Raḥmān. 1987. *As'ilat al-Masraḥ al-'Arabī*. Casablanca: Dār al-Thaqāfa.
Ibrāhīm, 'Abd Allāh. 1999. *al-Thaqāfa al-'Arabiyya wa-l-Marji'iyyāt al-Musta'āra:*

Tadākhul al-Ansāq wa-l-Mafāhīm wa-Rihānāt al-'Awlama. Casablanca: al-Markaz al-Thaqāfī al-'Arabī.
Ibrahim, 'Abdallah. 2006. "The Role of the Pre-Modern: The Generic Characteristics of the *Band*." In Roger Allen and D. S. Richards (eds), *Arabic Literature in the Post-Classical Period*, pp. 87–98. Cambridge: Cambridge University Press.
Ibrāhīm, Ḥāfiẓ. n.d. *Dīwān* (ed. Aḥmad Amīn et al.). Beirut: Dār al-'Awda.
Ibrāhīm, Riḍwān. 1965. "Sā'a ma'a al-Qaṣṣāṣ al-Miṣrī al-Duktūr Yūsuf Idrīs." *al-Adīb*, January, pp. 58–60.
al-Ibrāshī, 'Azīza. 1960. *Iṣlāḥ*. Cairo: Dār al-Fikr.
'Īd, Rajā'. 1986. *Falsafat al-Iltizām fī al-Naqd al-Adabī*. Alexandria: Munsha'at al-Ma'ārif.
——. 1993. *al-Madhhab al-Badī'ī fī al-Shi'r al-'Arabī*. Alexandria: Munsha'at al-Ma'ārif.
al-'Īd, Yumnā. 2005. *Fī Mafāhīm al-Naqd wa-Ḥarakat al-Thaqāfa al-'Arabiyya*. Beirut: Dār al-Fārābī.
al-Idlibī, Ulfat. 1992. *Naẓra fī Adabinā al-Sha'bī*. Damascus: Dār al-Shādī.
Idrīs, Aḥmad. 1998. *al-Adab al-'Arabī fī Shibh al-Qāra al-Hindiyya*. Cairo: 'Ayn li-l-Dirāsāt wa-l-Buḥūth al-Insāniyya wa-l-Ijtimā'iyya.
Idrīs, Yūsuf. n.d. [1965]. *Lughat al-Āy Āy*. Cairo: Maktabat Miṣr.
——. 1978. *The Cheapest Nights and Other Stories* (trans. Wadida Wassef). London: Heinemann.
——. 1984. *Rings of Burnished Brass* (trans. Catherine Cobham). Washington, DC: Three Continents Press.
——. 1987. *al-'Atab 'alā al-Naẓar*. Cairo: Markaz al-Ahrām li-l-Tarjama wa-l-Nashr.
——. 1992. *The Piper and Other Stories* (trans. Dalya Cohen-Mor). Potomac, MD: Sheba Press.
Idris, Youssef. 1988. *A Leader of Men/Abū al-Rijāl* (bilingual edition; trans. S. Elkhadem). Fredericton: York Press.
Idrissi, Alami. 2013. "Moroccan Nation-Building and the *Bildungsroman* in 'Abd al-Karīm Ghallāb's *Dafannā al-Māḍī* and *al-Mu'allim 'Alī*." *Middle Eastern Literatures* 16.1, pp. 60–75.
Ighbāriyya, Riḍā Aḥmad. 1997. *Masraḥ al-Ḥaraka al-Islāmiyya: Firqat al-I'tiṣām ka-Namūdhaj*. n.p.: n.pub.
Ilbert, Robert and Ilios Yannakakis (with Jacques Hassoun) (eds). 1997. *Alexandria 1860–1960: The Brief Life of a Cosmopolitan Community* (trans. Colin Clement). Alexandria: Harpocrates Publishing.
'Imāra, Muḥammad. 1979. *'Alī Mubārak: al-A'māl al-Kāmila*. Beirut: al-Mu'assasa al-'Arabiyya li-l-Dirāsāt wa-l-Nashr.
——. 1991. *Ma'ālim al-Minhaj al-Islāmī*. Beirut: Dār al-Shurūq.
Imru' al-Qays. 1964. *Dīwān*. Cairo: Dār al-Ma'ārif.
Ingrams, Doreen. 1983. *The Awakened: Women in Iraq*. London: Third World Centre for Research and Publishing.
Irele, F. Abiola (ed.). 2009. *The Cambridge Companion to African Novel*. Cambridge: Cambridge University Press.
Irwin, Robert. 1995. *The Arabian Nights: A Companion*. London: Penguin Books.
——. 2000. "Adonis in the Levant." *The Times Literary Supplement*, 1 September, pp. 14–15.
——. 2006. *For Lust of Knowing: The Orientalists and Their Enemies*. London: Penguin Books.
al-'Īsāwī, Bashīr. 2001. *al-Tarjama ilā al-'Arabiyya: Qaḍāyā wa-Ārā'*. Cairo: Dār al-Fikr al-'Arabī.
Iser, Wolfgang. 1989. *Prospecting: From Reader Response to Literary Anthropology*. Baltimore and London: The Johns Hopkins University Press.
al-Iṣfahānī, Abū Faraj. 1927. *Kitāb al-Aghānī*. Cairo: Maṭba'at Dār al-Kutub.

——. 1972. *Kitāb Adab al-Ghurabā'* (ed. Ṣalāḥ al-Dīn al-Munajjid). Beirut: Dār al-Kitāb al-Jadīd.

——. 1997. *Kitāb al-Aghānī*. Beirut: Dār Iḥyā' al-Turāth al-'Arabī.

——. 2000. *The Book of Strangers: Mediaeval Arabic Graffiti on the Theme of Nostalgia* (trans. Patricia Crone and Shmuel Moreh). Princeton: Markus Wiener Publishers.

Ishtiaque Ullah, Sahar. 2016. "Postclassical Poetics: The Role of the Amatory Prelude for the Medieval Islamic Republic of Letters." *The Cambridge Journal of Postcolonial Literary Inquiry* 3.2, pp. 203–25.

Ismā'īl, 'Izz al-Dīn. 1978. *al-Shi'r al-'Arabī al-Mu'āṣir: Qaḍāyāhu wa-Ẓawāhiruhu al-Fanniyya wa-l-Ma'nawiyya*. Cairo: Dār al-Fikr al-'Arabī.

——. (ed.). 1999. *al-Huwiyya al-Qawmiyya fī al-Adab al-'Arabī al-Mu'āṣir*. Cairo: Ma'had al-Buḥūth wa-l-Dirāsāt al-Arabiyya.

Ismā'īl, Sayyid 'Alī. 1997. *al-Raqāba wa-l-Masraḥ al-Marfūḍ 1923–1988*. Cairo: al-Hay'a al-Miṣriyya al-'Āmma li-l-Kitāb.

Issa, Ali. 2015. *Against All Odds: Voices of Popular Struggle in Iraq*. Washington, DC: Tadween Publishing.

Isstaif, Abdul-Nabi. 2002. "Forging a New Self, Embracing the Other: Modern Arabic Critical Theory and the West—Luwīs 'Awaḍ." *Middle Eastern Literatures* 5.2, pp. 161–80.

Jābir, Kawthar. 2006. *Tadākhul al-Anwā' fī al-Adab al-'Arabī al-Ḥadīth: Ṣalāḥ 'Abd al-Ṣabūr wa-Idwār al-Kharrāṭ Namūdhajan*. PhD thesis, University of Haifa.

al-Jābirī, Muḥammad 'Ābid. 1982. *al-Khiṭāb al-'Arabī al-Mu'āṣir: Dirāsa Taḥlīliyya Naqdiyya*. Beirut: Dār al-Ṭalī'a and Casablanca: al-Markaz al-Thaqāfī al-'Arabī.

——. 1993. "al-Thaqāfa al-'Arabiyya al-Yawm wa-Mas'alat 'al-Istiqlāl al-Thaqāfī.'" *al-Mustaqbal al-'Arabī*, August, pp. 4–14.

——. 1994. *al-Mas'ala al-Thaqāfiyya*. Beirut: Markaz Dirāsāt al-Waḥda al-'Arabiyya.

Jabrā, Ibrāhīm Jabrā. 1962? "al-Riwāya wa-l-Qiṣṣa al-Qaṣīra wa-l-Masraḥiyya wa-Dawruhā fī al-Mujtama' al-'Arabī." In Simon Jargy (ed.), *al-Adab al-'Arabī al-Mu'āṣir* (Proceedings of the Rome Conference on Contemporary Arabic Literature, 16–20 October 1961), pp. 215–25. n.p.: al-Aḍwā'.

——. 1987. *al-Bi'r al-Ūlā: Fuṣūl min Sīra Dhātiyya*. London: Riyāḍ al-Rayyis.

——. 1989. *Ta'ammulāt fī Bunyān Marmarī*. London: Riyāḍ al-Rayyis.

——. 1992. *Aqni'at al-Ḥaqīqa wa-Aqni'at al-Khayāl*. Beirut: al-Mu'assasa al-'Arabiyya li-l-Dirāsāt wa-l-Nashr.

al-Jabūrī, Jamīl. 1986. *Nūrī Thābit: Ḥabazbūz fī Tarīkh Siḥāfat al-Hazl wa-l-Kārīkātūr fī al-'Irāq*. Baghdad: Dār al-Shu'ūn al-Thaqāfiyya al-'Āmma Āfāq 'Arabiyya.

Jackman, Richard. 1992. "al-Tarjama wa-l-Haymana al-Thaqāfiyya: Ḥālat al-Tarjama al-Faransiyya/al-'Arabiyya." *Fuṣūl*, Summer, pp. 43–57.

Jacquemond, Richard. 2008. *Conscience of the Nation: Writers, State, and Society in Modern Egypt* (trans. David Tresilian). Cairo: The American University in Cairo Press.

Jad, A. B. 1983. *Form and Technique in the Egyptian Novel 1912–1971*. London: Ithaca Press.

al-Jada', Aḥmad 'Abd al-Laṭīf and Ḥusnī Adham Jarrār (eds). 1978–85. *Shu'arā' al-Da'wa al-Islāmiyya fī al-'Aṣr al-Ḥadīth* (9 Vols). Beirut: Mu'assasat al-Risāla.

Jafri, Naqi Husain (ed.). 2004. *Critical Theory: Perspectives from Asia*. New Delhi: Jamia Millia Islamia and Creative Books.

——. 2004a. "The Poetics and Politics of Troubadours: The Hispano-Arabic Connection." In Naqi Husain Jafri (ed.), *Critical Theory: Perspectives from Asia*, pp. 374–87. New Delhi: Jamia Millia Islamia and Creative Books.

al-Jāḥiẓ, Abū 'Uthmān. 1938. *al-Ḥayawān*. Cairo: al-Ḥalabī.

——. 1991. *Rasā'il* (ed. 'Alī Abū Milḥim). Beirut: Dār wa-Maktabat al-Hilāl.

Jakobson, Roman. 1971. "On Realism in Art." In Ladislav Matejka and Krystyna Pomorska (eds), *Readings in Russian Poetics: Formalist and Structuralist Views*, pp. 38–46. Cambridge, MA and London: The MIT Press.

——. 1986. *Semiotics, Linguistics, Poetics* (Hebrew) (ed. I. Even-Zohar and G. Toury). Tel Aviv: The Porter Institute for Poetics and Semiotics in Tel Aviv University.

——. and Petr Bogatyrev. 1971. "On the Boundary between Studies of Folklore and Literature." In Ladislav Matejka and Krystyna Pomorska (eds), *Readings in Russian Poetics: Formalist and Structuralist Views*, pp. 91–3. Cambridge, MA and London: The MIT Press.

al-Jamal, 'Abd al-Raḥmān Yūsuf Aḥmad. 1996. *al-Shi'r wa-l-Shu'arā' fī Ṣiqilliyya al-Islāmiyya*. Beirut: al-Ādāb.

Jameson, Fredric. 1972. *The Prison-House of Language: A Critical Account of Structuralism and Russian Formalism*. Princeton: Princeton University Press.

al-Jammāl, Fārūq. 2002. *Durayd Laḥḥām: Mishwār al-'Umr*. Beirut: Sharikat al-Maṭbū'āt li-l-Tawzī' wal-Nashr.

al-Janābī, 'Abd al-Qādir. 1994. *Risāla Maftūḥa ilā Adūnīs*. Paris: Manshūrāt Farādīs.

——. 1995. *Tarbiyat 'Abd al-Qādir al-Janābī*. Beirut: Dār al-Jadīd.

Janabi, Hatif. 1993. "Arabic Dramatic Thought: An Inside Thought." *Studia Arabistyczne i Islamistyczne* 1, pp. 55–61.

Jargy, Simon (ed.). 1962? *al-Adab al-'Arabī al-Mu'āṣir* (Proceedings of the Rome Conference on Contemporary Arabic Literature, 16–20 October). n.p.: al-Aḍwā'.

——. 1970. *La poésie populaire traditionnelle chantée au proche-orient arabe*. Paris: Mouton.

Jarrar, Maher. 2008. "*The Arabian Nights* and the Contemporary Arabic Novel." In Saree Makdisi and Felicity Nussbaum (eds), *The Arabian Nights in Historical Context between East and West*, pp. 297–315. Oxford: Oxford University Press.

Jarrār, Ma'mūn Farīz. 1984. *al-Ittijāh al-Islāmī fī al-Shi'r al-Filasṭīnī al-Ḥadīth*. Amman: Dār al-Bashīr.

Jason, H. 1996. "Indexing of Folk and Oral Literature in the Islam-Dominated Cultural Area." *Bulletin of the School of Oriental and African Studies* 59.1, pp. 102-116.

——. and El-Hasan Shamy. 2005. "Folktale Types of the Arab World." *Asian Folklore Studies* 64.2, pp. 299–303.

Jawani, Y. A. 1996. *Arab Political Thought on Arab Nationalism and Unity: The 1980s and the Dialectic of Old and New Paradigms*. PhD thesis, University of Kent.

al-Jawharī, Muḥammad. 2003. *Rushdī Ṣāliḥ wa-l-Fūlklūr al-Miṣrī*. Cairo: Jāmi'at al-Qāhira.

al-Jawharī, Muḥammad Maḥmūd. 1974. "al-Turāth al-Sha'bī Bayna al-Fūlklūr wa-'Ilm al-Ijtimā'." *Majallat al-Turāth wa-l-Mujtama'* 1, pp. 130–48.

Jayyusi, Salma Khadra. 1977. *Trends and Movements in Modern Arabic Poetry*. Leiden: Brill.

——. (ed.). 1988. *The Literature of Modern Arabia*. London and New York: Kegan Paul.

——. (ed.). 1992. *Anthology of Modern Palestinian Literature*. New York: Columbia University Press.

——. 1993. "The Arab Laureate and the Road to Nobel." In Michael Beard and Adnan Haydar (eds), *Naguib Mahfouz: From Regional Fame to Global Recognition*, pp. 10–20. Syracuse: Syracuse University Press.

——. (ed.). 1993a. *Islamic Spain*. Leiden: Brill.

——. 1996. "Tradition and Modernity in Arabic Poetry." In J. R. Smart (ed.), *Tradition and Modernity in Arabic Language and Literature*, pp. 27–48. Richmond: Curzon.

——. (ed.). 2003. *Short Arabic Plays: An Anthology*. New York: Interlink Books.

——. (ed.). 2005. *Modern Arabic Fiction: An Anthology*. New York: Columbia University Press.

——. 2008. "Response to Thomas Bauer." *Mamlūk Studies Review* 12.1, pp. 193–207.

——. (ed.). 2010. *Classical Arabic Stories: An Anthology*. New York: Columbia University Press.

al-Jazā'irī, Anīs. 1995. "Ḥadātha Salafiyya!?" In *al-'Unf al-Uṣūlī: Muwājahāt al-Sayf wa-l-Qalam*, pp. 23–38. London and Beirut: Riyāḍ al-Rayyis.
al-Jazā'irī, Ni'mat Allāh. 1994. *Zahr al-Rabī'*. Beirut: Dār al-Jinān.
al-Jazzār, Muḥammad Fikrī. 2002. *Mu'jam al-Wa'd: al-Naz'a al-Dhukūriyya fī al-Mu'jam al-'Arabī*. Cairo: Ītrāk li-l-Nashr wa-l-Tawzī'.
Jihad, Kadhim. 2000. "Sayyab, Lorca: une lecture croisée." *Revue d'Études Palestiniennes* 24, pp. 110–13.
Johnson-Davies, Denys. 1981 [1967]. *Modern Arabic Short Stories*. London: Heinemann.
——. 1994. "On Translating Arabic Literature." In Ferial J. Ghazoul and Barbara Harlow (eds), *The View from Within: Writers and Critics on Contemporary Arabic Literature*, pp. 272–82. Cairo: The American University in Cairo Press.
——. 2006. *Memories in Translation: A Life between the Lines of Arabic Literature*. Cairo: The American University in Cairo Press.
Jones, Alan. 1988. *Romance Kharjas in Andalusian Arabic Muwaššaḥ Poetry*. London: Ithaca Press.
——. (ed.). 1991. *Arabicus Felix—Luminosus Britannicus—Essays in Honour of A. F. L. Beeston on his Eightieth Birthday*. Reading: Ithaca Press.
——. 1992. *Early Arabic Poetry: Marāthī and Ṣu'lūk Poems*. Reading: Ithaca Press.
——. 2001. "The Real Satanic Verses?" *Arabist: Budapest Studies in Arabic* 23, pp. 125–33.
——. and Richard Hitchcock (eds). 1991. *Studies on the Muwaššaḥ and the Kharja*. Reading: Ithaca Press.
Joseph, Suad (ed.). 2000. *Gender and Citizenship in the Middle East*. Syracuse: Syracuse University Press.
——. and Susan Slyomovics (eds). 2001. *Women and Power in the Middle East*. Philadelphia: University of Pennsylvania Press.
Joyaux, Georges J. 1980. "Driss Chraïbi, Mohammed Dib, Kateb Yacine, and Indigenous North African Literature." In Issa J. Boullata (ed.), *Critical Perspectives on Modern Arabic Literature*, pp. 117–27. Washington, DC: Three Continents Press.
Jubrān, Jubrān Khalīl. n.d. [1912]. *al-Ajniḥa al-Mutakassira*. Beirut: n.pub.
——. 1981. *al-Majmū'a al-Kāmila li-Mu'allafāt Jubrān Khalīl Jubrān al-Mu'arraba 'an al-Inklīziyya*. Beirut: n.pub.
——. 1985. *al-Majmū'a al-Kāmila li-Mu'allafāt Jubrān Khalīl Jubrān al-'Arabiyya*. Beirut: n.pub.
Jubrān, Sulaymān. 1991. *Kitāb al-Fāryāq: Mabnāhu wa-Uslūbuhu wa-Sukhriyyatuhu*. Tel Aviv: Tel Aviv University Press.
Judt, Tony. 2010. *Ill Fares the Land*. New York: The Penguin Press.
Juḥā, Mīshāl Khalīl. 1999. *al-Shi'r al-'Arabī al-Ḥadīth min Aḥmad Shawqī ilā Maḥmūd Darwīsh*. Beirut: Dār al-'Awda & Dār al-Thaqāfa.
al-Jundī, Anwar. n.d. *Matā Ya'ūdu al-Adab al-Mu'aṣir ilā Aṣālatihi*. Cairo: Dār al-Anṣār.
——. 1963. *al-Lugha al-'Arabiyya Bayna Ḥumātihā wa-Khuṣūmihā*. Cairo: Maktabat al-Anglo al-Miṣriyya.
——. 1977. *al-Shu'ūbiyya fī al-Adab al-'Arabī al-Ḥadīth*. Cairo: Dār al-I'tiṣām.
——. 1977a. *Ṭāhā Ḥusayn: Ḥayātuhu wa-Fikruhu fī Mīzān al-Islām*. Cairo: Dār al-I'tiṣām
——. 1979. *Ukdhūbatān fī Ta'rīkh al-Adab al-Ḥadīth: Aḥmad Luṭfī al-Sayyid, Ṭāhā Ḥusayn*. Cairo: Dār al-Anṣār.
Juynboll, G. H. A. 1997. "Siḥāḳ." In P. J. Bearman et al. (eds), *The Encyclopaedia of Islam*, New Edition, Vol. 9, pp. 565–7. Leiden: Brill.
K., 'A. 1936. "al-Ḥayāt al-Adabiyya fī al-Maghrib al-Aqṣā." *al-Risāla*, 15 June, pp. 984–6.
Kabbani, Rana. 1986. *Europe's Myths of Orient: Devise and Rule*. London: Macmillan.
Kadalah, Mohammed. "The Impact of Arabic Literature on the Pre-Arab Spring Time Period." *International Journal of Arts and Sciences* 7.5, pp. 439–48.
Kadhim, Hussein N. 2004. *The Poetics of Anti-Colonialism in the Arabic Qaṣīda*. Leiden and Boston: Brill.

Kadi, Joanna (ed.). 1994. *Food for Our Grandmothers: Writing by Arab-American and Arab-Canadian Feminists*. Boston: South End Press.
Kahf, Mohja. 2000. "Braiding the Stories: Women's Eloquence in the Early Islamic Era." In Gisela Webb (ed.), *Windows of Faith: Muslim Women Scholar-Activists in North America*, pp. 147–71. Syracuse: Syracuse University Press.
——. 2001. "The Silences of Contemporary Syrian Literature." *World Literature Today* 75.2, pp. 225–36.
Kaḥḥāla, ʻUmar Riḍā. 1960. *Muʻjam al-Mu'allifīn*. Damascus: Maṭbaʻat al-Taraqqī.
Kahle, Paul (ed.). 1992. *Three Shadow Plays by Muhammad Ibn Daniyal*. Cambridge: Trustees of the E. J. W. Gibb Memorial.
al-Kakalī, ʻAbd al-Salām. 1992. *al-Zaman al-Riwā'ī: Jadaliyyat al-Māḍī wa-l-Ḥāḍir ʻinda Jamāl al-Ghīṭānī min Khilāli al-Zaynī Barakāt wa-Kitāb al-Tajalliyāt*. Cairo: Madbūlī.
Kallas, Elie. 2003. "Michel Ṭrād, In Memoriam." *Arabica* 50.4, pp. 447–63.
Kandiyoti, Deniz (ed.). 1996. *Gendering the Middle East*. London and New York: I. B.Tauris.
Karic, Enes. 2003. "The Arabic Cultural Influence on the Balkans: An Outline." *American Journal of Islamic Social Sciences* 20.1, pp. 107–120.
Karīm, Fawzī. 1992. "Thiyāb al-Imbarāṭūr: Maqāla fī al-Siyāq al-Shiʻrī al-Sā'id." *al-Laḥẓa al-Shiʻriyya* 1, Summer, pp. 68–80.
al-Karkhī, ʻAbbūd. 1956. *Dīwān*. Baghdād: Maṭbaʻat al-Maʻārif.
Kassab, Elizabeth Suzanne. 2010. *Contemporary Arab Thought: Cultural Critique in Comparative Perspective*. New York: Columbia University Press.
Kattānī, Yāsīn. 2000–1. "Qaṣṣ al-Ḥadātha: Dirāsa fī al-Tashkīl al-Fannī li-Riwāyat al-Kharrāṭ—*Turābuhā Zaʻfarān*." *al-Karmil—Abḥāth fī al-Lugha wa-l-Adab* 21–2, pp. 315–63.
Kaye, Alan S. 2008. "On the Use of the Aspects, Independent Personal Pronouns, Fillers, and Attention Grabbers in Algerian Arabic Oral Narratives." *Journal of Semitic Studies* 53.1, pp. 119–156.
al-Kaylānī, Najīb. 1963. *al-Islāmiyya wa-l-Madhāhib al-Adabiyya*. Tripoli (Libya): Maktabat al-Nūr.
——. 1981. *al-Islāmiyya wa-l-Madhāhib al-Adabiyya*. Beirut: Mu'assasat al-Risāla.
——. 1985. *Riḥlatī maʻa al-Adab al-Islāmī*. Beirut: Mu'assasat al-Risāla.
——. 1985a. *Āfāq al-Adab al-Islāmī*. Beirut: Mu'assasat al-Risāla.
——. 1986. *Adab al-Aṭfāl fī Ḍaw' al-Islām*. Beirut: Mu'assasat al-Risāla.
——. 1986a. *Ḥawla al-Masraḥ al-Islāmī*. Beirut: Mu'assasat al-Risāla.
Kayyal, Mahmoud. 2000. *Translational Norms in the Translations of Modern Hebrew Literature into Arabic between 1948–1990* (Hebrew). PhD thesis Tel Aviv University.
——. 2006. *Translation in the Shadow of Confrontation: Norms in the Translations of Modern Hebrew Literature into Arabic between 1948–1990* (Hebrew). Jerusalem: Magnes Press.
——. 2016. *Selected Issues in the Modern Intercultural Contacts between Arabic and Hebrew Cultures*. Leiden: Brill.
Kazzaz, Nissim. 1991. *The Jews in Iraq in the Twentieth Century* (Hebrew). Jerusalem: Ben-Zvi Institute.
Kazziha, Walid. 1981. "Another Reading into al-Husari's [sic] Concept of Arab Nationalism." In Marwan R. Buheiri (ed.), *Intellectual Life in the Arab East, 1890–1939*, pp. 154–64. Beirut: The American University of Beirut.
Kedar, Benjamin Z. (ed.). 1996. *Studies in the History of Popular Culture* (Hebrew). Jerusalem: The Zalman Shazar Center for Jewish History.
Keddie, Nikki R. and Beth Baron (eds). 1991. *Women in Middle Eastern History: Shifting Boundaries in Sex and Gender*. New Haven: Yale University Press.
Kendall, Elisabeth. 2003. "The Theoretical Roots of the Literary Avant-Garde in 1960s Egypt." *Edebiyât* 14.1–2, pp. 39–56.

——. 2006. *Literature, Journalism and the Avant-Garde Intersection in Egypt*. London: Routledge.
——. 2014. *Twenty-First Century Jihad: Law, Society and Military Action*. London: I. B. Tauris.
Kennedy, Philip F. 1991. "Thematic Relationships between the *Kharjas*, the Corpus of *Muwaššaḥāt* and Eastern Lyrical Poetry." In Alan Jones and Richard Hitchcock (eds), *Studies on the Muwaššaḥ and the Kharja*, pp. 68–87. Reading: Ithaca Press.
——. (ed.). 2005. *On the Fiction and Adab in Medieval Arabic Literature*. Wiesbaden: Harrassowitz Verlag.
Kepel, Gilles. 1984. *Le prophète et Pharaon: Les mouvements islamistes dans l'Égypte contemporaine*. Paris: La Découverte.
——. 1985. *The Prophet and Pharaoh: Muslim Extremism in Egypt* (trans. Jon Rothschild). London: Saqi Books.
Kermani, Navid. 1994. "Die Affäre Abu Zayd. Eine Kritik am Religiösen Diskurs und ihre Folgen." *Orient* 35, pp. 25–49.
Kermode, Frank. 1988. *History and Value*. Oxford: Clarendon Press.
Kernan, Alvin. 1990. *The Death of Literature*. New Haven: Yale University Press.
Khaḍr, Mahā Maẓlūm. 2001. *Binā' Riwāyat al-Khayāl al-'Ilmī fī al-Adab al-Miṣrī al-Mu'āṣir*. Cairo: Maṭba'at al-Offset al-Ḥadītha.
al-Khāl, Yūsuf. 1981. *al-Wilāda al-Tāniya* [sic]. Beirut: Dār al-Nahār li-l-Nashr.
Khalaf, Roseanne Saad. 2006. *Hikayat: Short Stories by Lebanese Women*. London and San Francisco: Telegram.
Khalafallah, Haifaa and A. Walmsley. 1983. "Sherif Hetata: How Free Is Egypt Today? An Egyptian Writer Describes the Insecurity and Fear in his Country." *Index on Censorship* 12.3, pp. 23–4.
Khaldi, Buthaynah. 2012. *Egypt Awakening in the Early Twentieth Century: Mayy Ziyadāh's Intellectual Circles*. New York: Palgrave Macmillan.
Khālid, Khālid Muḥammad. 1959. *Min Hunā Nabda'*. Tel Aviv: Sharikat al-Kitāb al-'Arabī.
Khalidi, Tarif (ed.). 2016. *An Anthology of Arabic Literature: From the Classical to the Modern*. Edinburgh: Edinburgh University Press.
Khalīl, 'Imād al-Dīn. 1987. *Madkhal ilā Naẓariyyat al-Adab al-Islāmī*. Beirut: Mu'assasat al-Risāla.
Khalil, Iman. 1994. "Narrative Strategies as Cultural Vehicles: Rafik Schami's Novel *Erzahler der Nacht*." In Carol Aisha Blackshire-Belay (ed.), *The Germanic Mosaic: Cultural and Linguistic Diversity in Society*, pp. 217–24. New York: Greenwood.
——. 1995. "Arab-German Literature." *World Literature Today* 69, pp. 521–7.
al-Khalīlī, 'Alī. 1977. *al-Turāth al-Filasṭīnī wa-l-Ṭabaqāt*. Jerusalem: Mu'assasat Ibn Rushd.
——. 1978. *Aghānī al-Aṭfāl fī Filasṭīn*. Jerusalem: Manshūrāt Ṣalāḥ al-Dīn.
——. 1979. *al-Baṭal al-Filasṭīnī fī al-Ḥikāya al-Sha'biyya*. Jerusalem: Mu'assasat Ibn Rushd.
Khalis, Abdus Salam. 1990. "The Islamic Concept of Literature." *Research Journal RJIC* (Sheikh Zayed Centre for Islamic and Arabic Studies, University of Peshawar) 1.1, pp. 54–7.
Khan, Maulana Wahiduddin. 1997. *Women between Islam and Western Societies*. New Delhi: al-Risala Books.
Khan, Zafarul-Islam. 1995. "Najib al-Kilani." *Muslim and Arab Perspectives* 7.2, pp. 178–9.
al-Khanīsī, 'Abd al-Ra'ūf. 1989. *Bayram al-Tūnisī Shā'ir al-Ālām wa-l-Āmāl*. Baghdad: Dār Thaqāfat al-Aṭfāl.
ALKharashi, Norah. 2016. "Modern Arabic Fiction in English: The Yacoubian Building; a Case in Point." *CLINA: An Interdisciplinary Journal of Translation, Interpreting and Intercultural Communication* 2.1, pp. 43–59.

al-Kharrāṭ, Idwār. 2005. *Mujāladat al-Mustaḥīl: Maqāti' min Sīra Dhātiyya li-l-Kitāba.* Cairo: Dār al-Bustānī li-l-Nashr wa-l-Tawzī'.
al-Khaṭīb, Muḥammad Kāmil (ed.). 1994. *Naẓariyyat al-Masraḥ (al-Qism al-Awwal: al-Maqālāt).* Damascus: Manshūrāt Wizārat al-Thaqāfa.
——. (ed.). 1994a. *Naẓariyyat al-Masraḥ (al-Qism al-Thānī: Muqaddimāt wa-Bayānāt).* Damascus: Manshūrāt Wizārat al-Thaqāfa.
——. 1995. *al-Riwāya wa-l-Yūtūbyā.* Damascus: Dār al-Madā li-l-Thaqāfa wa-l-Nashr.
——. (ed.). 1996. *Naẓariyyat al-Shi'r: Marḥalat Majallat Shi'r (al-Qism al-Awwal: al-Maqālāt).* Damascus: Manshūrāt Wizārat al-Thaqāfa.
——. (ed.). 1996a. *Naẓariyyat al-Shi'r: Marḥalat Majallat Shi'r (al-Qism al-Thānī: Maqālāt—Shahādāt—Muqaddimāt).* Damascus: Manshūrāt Wizārat al-Thaqāfa.
Khatibi, Abdelkebir. 1971. *La mémoire tatouée.* Paris: Denoel.
——. 1976. *Le lutteur de classe à la manière taoïste.* Paris: Sindbad.
al-Khaṭībī, 'Abd al-Kabīr. 1984. *al-Dhākira al-Mawshūma* (trans. Buṭrus al-Ḥallāq). Beirut: al-Mu'assasa al-'Arabiyya li-l-Dirāsāt wa-l-Nashr.
——. 1986. *al-Munāḍil al-Ṭabaqī 'alā al-Ṭarīqa al-Tāwiyya* (trans. Kāẓim Jihād). Casablanca: Dār Ṭūbqāl li-l-Nashr.
Khayyām, 'Umar. 1974. *Rubā'iyyāt* (trans. Muḥammad Rakhā). Cairo: al-Hay'a al-Miṣriyya al-'Āmma li-l-Kitāb.
——. 1977. *Rubā'iyyāt al-Khayyām* (trans. Aḥmad Rāmī). Beirut: Dār al-'Awda.
al-Khāzin, Wilyam and Nabīh al-Yān. 1970. *Kutub wa-Udabā'.* Beirut: al-Maktaba al-'Aṣriyya.
Khedr, Mona. 2012. "Ambivalences of Piety: Gendered Identities of Egyptian Women in Performance." *Performing Islam* 1.1, pp. 35–56.
Khouri, Mounah A. 1970. "Lewis 'Awaḍ: A Forgotten Pioneer of Arabic Literature." *Journal of Arabic Literature* 1, pp. 137–44.
——. 1971. *Poetry and the Making of Modern Egypt (1882–1922).* Leiden: Brill.
——. 1976. "Literature." In John R. Hayes (ed.), *The Genius of Arab Civilization: Source of Renaissance*, pp. 17–41. Oxford: Phaidon Press.
Khoury, Georges Raif. 2004. "Importance et rôle des traductions arabes au XIXe siècle comme moteur de la renaissance arabe moderne." In Naoum Abi-Rached (ed.), *Les problématiques de la traduction arabe, hier et aujourd'hui*, pp. 48–95. Strasbourg: Université Marc Bloch.
Khoury, Jeries. 2006. "Polysystems: A Theoretical Inquiry into Some General Concepts." *Journal of Arabic Literature* 37.1, pp. 1-20.
——. 2008. "Zarqā' al-Yamāma in the Modern Arabic Poetry: A Comparative Reading." *Journal of Semitic Studies* 53.2, pp. 311–28.
Khoury, Nuha N. N. 2010. "Where Are You From? Writing Home in Palestinian Children's Literature." *Third Text: Critical Perspectives on Contemporary Art & Culture* 24.6, pp. 697–718.
Al-Khozai, Mohamed A. 1984. *The Development of Early Arabic Drama (1847–1900).* London and New York: Longman.
al-Khūlī, Usāma Amīn (ed.). 1998. *al-'Arab wa-l-'Awlama.* Beirut: Markaz Dirāsāt al-Waḥda al-'Arabiyya.
Khulūsī, Ṣadā. 1991. *Toward a Theory of Arabic-English Translation with Special Reference to the Role of Arab Translators as Transmitters of Civilization.* PhD thesis, University of Exeter.
Khūrī, Ilyās. 1974. *Tajribat al-Baḥth 'an Ufq: Muqaddima li-Dirāsat al-Riwāya al-'Arabiyya ba'da al-Hazīma.* Beirut: Markaz al-Abḥāth fī Munaẓẓamat al-Taḥrīr al-Filasṭīniyya.
——. (ed.). 1981. *al-Masīḥiyyūn al-'Arab: Dirāsāt wa-Munāqashāt.* Beirut: Mu'assasat al-Abḥāth al-'Arabiyya.

Khūrī, Jiryis Na'īm. 1999. *al-Ughniyya al-Sha'biyya al-Filasṭīniyya fī al-Jalīl*. MA thesis, University of Haifa.

——. 1999a. "'Yā Ẓarīf al-Ṭūl': Ughniyya Sha'biyya Filasṭīniyya." *al-Karmil—Abḥāth fī al-Lugha wa-l-Adab* 20, pp. 97–128.

Khūrī, Munaḥ (ed.). 1966. *al-Shi'r Bayna Nuqqād Thalātha: T. S. Eliot, Archibald Macleish, I. A. Richards*. Beirut: Dār al-Thaqāfa.

——. 1990. "al-Adab." In John R. Hayes (ed.), *The Genius of Arab Civilization: Source of Renaissance*, pp. 31–75. Oxford: Phaidon Press.

Khūrshīd, Fārūq. 1991. *al-Judhūr al-Sha'biyya li-l-Masraḥ al-'Arabī*. Cairo: al-Hay'a al-Miṣriyya al-'Āmma li-l-Kitāb.

——. and Maḥmūd Dhihnī. 1980. *Fann Kitābat al-Sīra al-Sha'biyya*. Cairo: Manshūrāt Iqra'.

Kilito, Abdelfattah. 1983. *Les séances: récits et codes culturels chez Hamadhani et Hariri*. Paris: Sindbad.

——. 1993. *al-Maqāmāt: al-Sard wa-l-Ansāq al-Thaqāfiyya* (trans. 'Abd al-Kabīr al-Sharqāwī). Dār Tūbqāl li-l-Nashr.

——. 1999. *al-Ḥikāya wa-l-Ta'wīl: Dirāsāt fī al-Sard al-'Arabī*. Dār Tūbqāl li-l-Nashr.

——. 2001. *Lisān Ādam* (trans. 'Abd al-Kabīr al-Sharqāwī). Dār Tūbqāl li-l-Nashr.

——. 2002. *Lan Tatakallam Lughatī*. Beirut: Dār al-Ṭalī'a.

——. 2007. *al-Adab wa-l-Irtiyāb*. Dār Tūbqāl li-l-Nashr.

——. 2008. *Thou Shalt Not Speak My Language* (trans. Waïl S. Hassan). Syracuse: Syracuse University Press.

Kilpatrick, Hilary. 1974. *The Modern Egyptian Novel: A Study in Social Criticism*. London: Ithaca Press.

——. 1978. "The Contribution of Women to Modern Arabic Literature." *Azure* 2, pp. 7–9.

——. 1991. "Autobiography and Classical Arabic Literature." *Journal of Arabic Literature* 22.1, pp. 1–20.

——. 1996. "Primary Problems in Translating Contemporary Arabic Novels." *Edebiyât* 7, pp. 126–51.

——. 1998. "XXVI. Deutscher Orientalistentag, Leipzig, September 1995: Theoretical Approaches to Arabic Literature—New Perspectives and Projects." *Arabic and Middle Eastern Literatures* 1.1, pp. 113–16.

——. 2003. *Making the Great Book of Songs: Compilation and the Author's Craft in Abu l-Faraj al-Isbahani's Kitab al-Aghani*. London: RoutledgeCurzon.

——. 2004. "Brockelmann, Kaḥḥâla & Co: Reference Works on the Arabic Literature of Early Ottoman Syria." *Middle Eastern Literatures* 7.1, pp. 33–51.

Kirchner, Henner. 2001. "Internet in the Arab World: A Step toward 'Information Society?'" In Kai Hafez (ed.), *Mass Media, Politics, and Society in the Middle East*, pp. 137–58. Cresskill, NJ: Hampton Press.

Kishk, 'Abd al-Ḥamīd. 1986. *Qiṣṣat Ayyāmī: Mudhakkirāt al-Shaykh Kishk*. Cairo: Dār al-Mukhtār al-Islāmī.

Kishk, Muḥammad Jalāl. 1966. *al-Ghazw al-Fikrī*. Cairo: al-Dār al-Qawmiyya li-l-Ṭibā'a wa-l-Nashr.

——. 1989. *Awlād Ḥāratinā fīhā Qawlān*. Cairo: al-Zahrā' li-l-I'lām wa-l-Nashr.

Kishtainy, Khalid. 1982. *The Prostitute in Progressive Literature*. London: Allison and Busby.

——. 1985. *Arab Political Humour*. London: Quartet Books.

Kister, M. J. 1999. "'Exert Yourselves, O Banū Arfida!': Some Notes on Entertainment in the Islamic Tradition." *Jerusalem Studies in Arabic and Islam* 23, pp. 53–78.

Kitāb Mi'at Layla wa-Layla. 1979. (ed. Maḥmūd Ṭarshūna). Tunis: al-Dār al-'Arabiyya li-l-Kitāb.

Klein, L. S. (ed.). 1982. *Encyclopedia of World Literature in the 20th Century*. New York: Frederick Ungar.

Klemm, Verena and Beatrice Gruendler (eds). 2000. *Understanding Near Eastern Literatures.* Wiesbaden: Reichert Verlag.

Knio, Mona. 1994. *Toward a National Puppet Centre for the Lebanon.* PhD thesis, University of Leeds.

Knipp, C. 1974. "The *Arabian Nights* in England: Galland's Translation and Its Successors." *Journal of Arabic Literature* 5, pp. 44–54.

Konstantinovic, Zoran. 1988. "Response to Claus Clüver's 'The Difference of Eight Decades: World Literature and the Demise of National Literatures.'" *Yearbook of Comparative and General Literature* 37, pp. 141–42.

Kozma, Liat. 2011. *Policing Egyptian Women: Sex, Law, and Medicine in Khedival Egypt.* Syracuse: Syracuse University Press.

——. et al. (eds). 2015. *A Global Middle East: Mobility, Materiality and Culture in the Modern Age, 1880–1940.* London and New York: I. B. Tauris.

Krachkovskii, I. J. 1927. "Die Literatur der arabischen Emigranten in Amerika (1895-1915)." *Monde Oriental* 21, pp. 193–213.

——. 1989. *al-Riwāya al-Ta'rīkhiyya fī al-Adab al-'Arabī al-Ḥadīth wa-Dirāsāt Ukhrā* (trans. 'Abd al-Raḥīm al-'Aṭāwī). Rabat: Dār al-Kalām li-l-Nashr wa-l-Tawzī'.

Kraemer, J. L. 1984. "The Culture Bearers of Humanism in the Renaissance of Islam." Annual Lecture, The Irene Halmos Chair of Arabic Literature, Tel Aviv University, pp. 3–19.

Kramer, Martin. 1997. "The Oracle of Hizbullah: Sayyid Muhammad Husyan Fadlallah." In R. Scott Appleby (ed.), *Spokesmen for the Despised: Fundamentalist Leaders of the Middle East,* pp. 83–181. Chicago and London: University of Chicago Press.

——. 1998. *Fadlallah: The Compass of Hizbullah* (Hebrew). Tel Aviv: Dayan Centre.

Krishna Chaitanya. 1983. *A History of Arabic Literature.* New Delhi: Manohar.

Kritzeck, James (ed.). 1964. *Anthology of Islamic Literature.* New York: Holt, Rinehart and Winston.

——. 1970. *Modern Islamic Literature from 1800 to the Present.* New York: Mentor.

Kronholm, Tryggve. 1993. "Arab Culture—Reality or Fiction?" In Heikki Palva and Knut S. Vikør (eds), *Papers from the Second Nordic Conference on Middle Eastern Studies, Copenhagen 22–25, October 1992,* pp. 12–25. Copenhagen: Nordic Institute of Asian Studies.

Kropp, M. 1994. "A Puzzle of Old Arabic Tenses and Syntax: The Inscription of 'En 'Avdat." *Proceedings of the Seminar for Arabian Studies* 24, pp. 165–74.

Kruk, Remke. 2014. *The Warrior Women of Islam: Female Empowerment in Arabic Popular Literature.* London: I. B. Tauris.

Kurpershoek, P. Marcel. 1981. *The Stories of Yūsuf Idrīs: A Modern Egyptian Author.* Leiden: Brill.

——. 1994. *Oral Poetry and Narratives from Central Arabia: The Poetry of Dindān.* Leiden: Brill.

al-Kuttāb al-'Arab fī Amrīkā (special issue of *Mundus Arabicus*). 1981. Cambridge: Dār Mahjar li-l-Nashr wa-l-Tawzī'.

al-Lababīdī, Maḥmūd. 1943. "al-'Arab Bayna al-Falsafa al-Yūnāniyya wa-l-Adab al-Yūnānī." *al-Adīb,* May, pp. 29–35.

Lagrange, Frédéric. 2000. "Male Homosexuality in Modern Arabic Literature." In Mai Ghoussoub and Emma Sinclair-Webb (eds), *Imagined Masculinities: Male Identity and Culture in the Modern Middle East,* pp. 169–98. London: Saqi Books.

Lanasri, Ahmed. 1995. *La littérature algérienne de l'entre-deux-guerres: genèse et fonctionnement.* Paris: Publisud.

Landau, Jacob M. 1958. *Studies in the Arab Theatre and Cinema.* Philadelphia: University of Pennsylvania Press.

——. 1986. "Popular Arabic Plays, 1909." *Journal of Arabic Literature* 17, pp. 120–5.

——. 1995. "Pan-Arabism." In P. J. Bearman et al. (eds), *The Encyclopaedia of Islam*, New Edition, Vol. 8, pp. 245–50. Leiden: Brill.

Lane, E. W. 1859 [1839–41]. *The Arabian Nights' Entertainments*. London: John Murray.

——. 1954 [1908]. *Manners and Customs of the Modern Egyptians*. London: Dent and New York: Dutton.

——. 1968 [1865–74]. *Arabic–English Lexicon*. Beirut: Librairie du Liban.

Lang, Felix. 2016. *The Lebanese Post-Civil War Novel: Memory, Trauma, and Capital*. New York: Palgrave Macmillan.

Langner, Joachim. 2015. "Religion in Motion and the Essence of Islam: Manifestations of the Global in Muhammad 'Abduh's Response to Faraḥ Anṭūn." In Liat Kozma et al. (eds), *A Global Middle East: Mobility, Materiality and Culture in the Modern Age, 1880–1940*, pp. 356–63. London and New York: I. B. Tauris.

Larémont, Ricardo René (ed.). 2014. *Revolution, Revolt, and Reform in North Africa: The Arab Spring and Beyond*. New York: Routledge.

Larkin, Margaret. 2008. *Al-Mutanabbi: Voice of the 'Abbasid Poetic Ideal*. Oxford: Oneworld.

Laroui, Abdallah. 1976. *The Crisis of the Arab Intellectual: Traditionalism or Historicism?* (trans. Diarmid Cammell). Berkeley: University of California Press.

Larsen, David. 2009. "Precedence and Innovation in the Bilingual Nabataean Inscription at 'En 'Avdat." *Zeitschrift für Arabische Linguistik* 50, pp. 5–21.

LaTeef, Nelda. 1997. *Women of Lebanon*. Jefferson, NC and London: McFarland.

Lawall, Sarah. 1993. "Naguib Mahfouz and the Nobel Prize." In Michael Beard and Adnan Haydar (eds), *Naguib Mahfouz: From Regional Fame to Global Recognition*, pp. 21–7. Syracuse: Syracuse University Press.

Lazarus, Neil. 1997. "Transnationalism and the Alleged Death of the Nation-State." In Keith Ansell-Pearson et al. (eds), *Cultural Readings of Imperialism: Edward Said and the Gravity of History*, pp. 28–48. London: Lawrence and Wishart.

Leder, Stefan (ed.). 1998. *Story-Telling in the Framework of Non-Fictional Arabic Literature*. Wiesbaden: Harrassowitz Verlag.

Lefevere, André. 1990. "Translation: Its Genealogy in the West." In Susan Bassnett and André Lefevere (eds), *Translation, History and Culture*, pp. 14–28. London and New York: Pinter Publishers.

Le Gassick, Trevor. 1991. *Critical Perspectives on Naguib Mahfouz*. Washington, DC: Three Continents Press.

——. 1992. "The Arabic Novel in English Translation." *Mundus Arabicus* 5, pp. 47–60.

Lejeune, Philippe. 1975. *Le pacte autobiographique*. Paris: Éditions du Seuil.

——. 1982. "The Autobiographical Contact." In Tzvetan Todorov (ed.), *French Literary Theory Today: A Reader*, pp. 192–222. Cambridge: Cambridge University Press.

——. 1989. *On Autobiography*. Minneapolis: University of Minnesota Press.

——. 1994. *al-Sīra al-Dhātiyya: al-Mīthāq wa-l-Ta'rīkh al-Adabī*. Casablanca: al-Markaz al-Thaqāfī al-'Arabī.

Lemon, Lee T. and Marion J. Reis (eds). 1965. *Russian Formalist Criticism*. Lincoln, NE: University of Nebraska Press.

Lemu, Aisha B. 1993. *Laxity, Modernism and Extremism*. Herndon, VA and London: International Institute of Islamic Thought.

Lesmana, Maman. 2014. "Learning History from Novel: A Case Study in Arabic Literature." *Tawarikh: International Journal for Historical Studies* 6.1, pp. 83–92.

Levenson, Michael (ed.). 1999. *The Cambridge Companion to Modernism*. Cambridge: Cambridge University Press.

Levi, Tomer. 2012. *The Jews of Beirut: The Rise of a Levantine Community, 1860s–1930s*. New York: Peter Lang.

Levine, Lawrence. 1988. *Highbrow/Lowbrow: The Emergence of Cultural Hierarchy in America*. Cambridge, MA: Harvard University Press.

LeVine, Mark. 2015. "When Art Is the Weapon: Culture and Resistance Confronting Violence in the Post-Uprisings Arab World." *Relgions* 6, pp. 1277–313.
Levinson, Jerrold (ed.). 2003. *Aesthetics*. Oxford: Oxford University Press.
Lewis, Bernard. 1968. *The Middle East and the West*. London: Weidenfeld and Nicolson.
——. 1992. "Rethinking the Middle East." *Foreign Affairs* 71.4, pp. 99–119.
——. 1995. *Cultures in Conflict: Christians, Muslims, and Jews in the Age of Discovery*. New York and Oxford: Oxford University Press.
——. 2003. *What Went Wrong?: The Clash between Islam and Modernity in the Middle East*. New York: Perennial.
Lewis, Desiree. 2013. "Politics, Freedoms and Spirituality in Alaa Al Aswany's *Yacoubian Building*." *Journal for Islamic Studies* 33, pp. 101–26.
Lichtenstadter, Ilse. 1974. *Introduction to Classical Arabic Literature*. New York: Schocken.
Liebhaber, Samuel. 2011. "The Ḥumaynī Pulse Moves East: Yemeni Nationalism Meets Mahri Sung-Poetry." *British Journal of Middle Eastern Studies* 38.2, pp. 249–65.
Lindsey, Ursula. 2005. "*The Yacoubian Building*: A Drama of Novel Proportions." *Bidoun: Arts and Culture from the Middle East* 1.5, pp. 60–1.
Littmann, E. 1960. "Alf Layla wa-Layla." In P. J. Bearman et al. (eds), *The Encyclopaedia of Islam*, New Edition, Vol. 1, pp. 358–64. Leiden: Brill.
Litvin, Margaret. 2012. *Hamlet's Arab Journey: Shakespeare's Prince and Nasser's Ghost*. Princeton: Princeton University Press.
Long, Andrew C. 2014. *Reading Arabia: British Orientalism in the Age of Mass Publication, 1880–1930*. Syracuse: Syracuse University Press.
Lovejoy, Arthur Oncken. 1948. *Essays in the History of Ideas*. Baltimore: The Johns Hopkins University Press.
Lowry, Joseph E. and Devin J. Stewart (eds). 2009. *Essays in Arabic Literary Biography 1350–1850*. Wiesbaden: Harrassowitz Verlag.
Luffin, Xavier. 2004. "The Use of Arabic as a Written Language in Central Africa: The Case of the Uele Basin (Northern Congo) in the Late Nineteenth Century." *Sudanic Africa: A Journal of Historical Sources* 15, pp. 145–77.
Lu'lu'a, 'Abd al-Wāḥid. 1989. "Ṣūrat Jabrā fī Shabābihi, Shi'r bi-l-Inklīziyya." *al-Nāqid* 10, pp. 26–31.
——. 2002. *Madā'in al-Wahm: Shi'r al-Ḥadātha wa-l-Shatāt*. London: Riyāḍ al-Rayyis.
Lunt, Lora G. 1999. "Reclaiming the Past: Historical Novels by Contemporary Women Writers." *Revue de l'institut des belles lettres arabes* (Tunis) 184, pp. 135–58.
Lutz, Catherine A. and Lila Abu-Lughod (eds). 1990. *Language and the Politics of Emotion*. Cambridge: Cambridge University Press.
Lyall, Charles James (ed.). 1930. *Translation of Ancient Arabian Poetry*. London: Williams and Norgate.
Lyons, Malcolm Cameron. 1968. *The Poetic Vocabulary of Michel Trad: A Study in Lebanese Colloquial Poetry*. Beirut: al-Khal Brothers.
Maalouf, Amin. 1989. *Samarkand*. Paris: Jean-Claude Lattèrs.
——. 1993. *Le rocher de Tanois*. Paris: Grasset.
——. 1994. *Samarkand* (trans. R. Harris). London: Abacus.
——. 1995. *The Rock of Tanios* (trans. D. S. Blair). London: Abacus.
Al-Ma'arrī (al-Ma'arri), Abul Ala'. 1943. *Risalat Ul Ghufran—A Divine Comedy* (trans. G. Brackenbury). Cairo: Al-Maaref.
——. 1975. *Risālat al-Ghufrān* (ed. 'Alī Shalaq). Beirut: Dār al-Qalam.
——. 2016. *The Epistle of Forgiveness* (trans. Geert Jan van Gelder and Gregor Schoeler). New York: New York University Press.
Macaulay, Thomas Babington. 1972. *Selected Writings* (ed. J. Clive and T. Pinney). Chicago and London: University of Chicago Press.

MacDonald, Duncan Black. 1932. "A Bibliographical and Literary Study of the First Appearance of the *Arabian Nights* in Europe." *Library Quarterly* 2, pp. 387–420.
——. 1960 [1903]. *Muslim Theology, Jurisprudence and Constitutional Theory.* Lahore: The Premier Book House.
MacDonald, Margaret Read (ed.). 1999. *Traditional Storytelling Today.* London and Chicago: Fitzroy Dearborn.
Machado, Antonio. 1973. *Poesias completas.* Madrid: Espasa-Calpe.
Machut-Mendecka, Ewa. 1999. "The Individual and the Community in Arabic Literary Autobiography." *Arabica* 46.3–4, pp. 510–22.
——. 2008. "Literature—Untamed Element (A Proposal of a Typology of the Modern Arabic Prose)." *Studia Arabistyczne i Islamistyczne* 13, pp. 44–57.
Mack, Robert L. 2008. "Cultivating the Garden: Antoine Galland's *Arabian Nights* in the Traditions of English Literature." In Saree Makdisi and Felicity Nussbaum (eds), *The Arabian Nights in Historical Context between East and West*, pp. 51–81. Oxford: Oxford University Press.
MacLean, Derryl N. and Sikeena Karmali Ahmed (eds). 2013. *Cosmopolitanisms in Muslim Contexts: Perspectives from the Past.* Edinburgh: Edinburgh University Press.
al-Madanī, ʻIzz al-Dīn. 1973. "al-Adab wa-l-Ḥurriyya Mutarādifān." *al-Fikr* (Tunis), April, pp. 66–8.
Madkour, Ibrāhīm. 1962? "al-Adab al-ʻArabī Tujāh Mushkilatay al-Lugha wa-l-Ḥarf." In Simon Jargy (ed.), *al-Adab al-ʻArabī al-Muʻāṣir* (Proceedings of the Rome Conference on Contemporary Arabic Literature, 16–20 October), pp. 108–11. n.p.: al-Aḍwā'.
al-Māghūṭ, Muḥammad. 2002. *Ightiṣāb Kāna wa-Akhawātihā.* Damascus: Dār al-Balad.
——. 2005. *Sharq ʻAdan Gharb Allāh.* Damascus: Dār al-Madā.
al-Mahājarānī, ʻAṭā Allāh. 1993. *Mu'āmarat al-Āyāt al-Shayṭāniyya.* Beirut: Dār al-Wasīla.
Mahfouz, Naguib. 1966. *Midaq Alley, Cairo* (trans. Trevor Le Gassick). Beirut: Khayat Book and Publishing Company.
——. 1981. *Midaq Alley* (trans. Trevor Le Gassick). Washington, DC: Three Continents Press.
——. 1981a. *Children of Gebelawi* (trans. Philip Stewart). London: Heinemann.
——. 1991. *Palace of Desire* (The Cairo Trilogy II) (trans. W. M. Hutchines et al.). New York: Doubleday.
——. 1991a. *Fountain and Tomb (Hakayat Haretna)* (trans. Soad Sobhy et al.). Washington, DC: Three Continents Press.
——. 1992. *Sugar Street* (The Cairo Trilogy III) (trans. W. M. Hutchins and A. B. Samaan). Cairo: The American University in Cairo Press.
——. 1994. *Arabian Nights and Days* (trans. Denys Johnson-Davies). London: Doubleday.
——. 1997. *Echoes of an Autobiography* (trans. Denys Johnson-Davies). New York and London: Doubleday.
——. 2001. *Naguib Mahfouz at Sidi Gaber: Reflections of a Nobel Laureate 1994–2001* (ed. Mohamed Salmawy). Cairo and New York: The American University in Cairo Press.
——. 2001a. *Children of the Alley* (trans. Peter Theroux). Cairo: The American University in Cairo Press.
——. 2002. *Palace of Desire* (The Cairo Trilogy II) (trans. W. M. Hutchins et al.). Cairo: The American University in Cairo Press.
Maḥfūẓ, ʻIṣām. 1988 [1970]. *Carte Blanche.* Beirut: Dār al-Fikr al-ʻArabī.
——. 1988 [1971]. *al-Dīktātūr.* Beirut: Dār al-Fikr al-ʻArabī.
Maḥfūẓ, Najīb. n.d. [1947]. *Zuqāq al-Midaqq.* Cairo: Dār Miṣr.
——. n.d. [1957]. *Qaṣr al-Shawq.* Cairo: Dār Miṣr.
——. n.d. [1957a]. *al-Sukkariyya.* Cairo: Dār Miṣr.
——. 1967. *Awlād Ḥāratinā.* Beirut: Dār al-Ādāb.
——. 1968. "al-Adab, al-Ḥurriyya, al-Thawra." *Mawāqif* 1, October–November, pp. 85–6.
——. n.d. [1974]. *al-Karnak.* Cairo: Dār Miṣr.

——. n.d. [1975]. *Ḥikāyāt Ḥāratinā*. Cairo: Dār Miṣr.
——. n.d. [1982]. *Layālī Alf Layla*. Cairo: Maktabat Miṣr.
——. 1988. *Qashtamar*. Cairo: Maktabat Miṣr.
——. 1995. *Aṣda' al-Sīra al-Dhātiyya*. Cairo: Maktabat Miṣr.
——. 1996. *Ḥawla al-'Arab wa-l-'Urūba*. Cairo: al-Dār al-Miṣriyya al-Lubnāniyya.
——. 1999. *Ṣadā al-Nisyān*. Cairo: Maktabat Miṣr.
——. 2006. *Awlād Ḥāratinā*. Cairo: Dār al-Shurūq.
Māhir, Muṣṭafā (ed.). 1970. *Ṣafaḥāt Khālida min al-Adab al-Almānī: Min al-Bidāya Ḥattā al-'Aṣr al-Ḥaḍir*. Beirut: Dār Ṣādir.
——. (ed.). 1974. *Alwān min al-Adab al-Almānī al-Ḥadīth: al-Qiṣṣa, al-Shi'r, al-Maqāl*. Beirut: Dār Ṣādir.
al-Maḥlāwī, Ḥanafī. 1999. *Umm Kulthūm wa-Khamsūna Sanat Siyāsa*. Cairo: al-Dār al-Miṣriyya al-Lubnāniyya.
Mahmood, Saba. 2013. "Azazeel and the Politics of Historical Fiction in Egypt." *Comparative Literature* 65.3, pp. 265–84.
Mahmoudi, Abdelrashid. 1998. *Ṭāhā Ḥusayn's Education: From the Azhar to the Sorbonne*. Richmond: Curzon.
Maḥmūd, 'Alī 'Abd al-Ḥalīm. 1979. *al-Qiṣṣa al-'Arabiyya fī al-'Aṣr al-Jāhilī*. Cairo: Dār al-Ma'ārif.
Maḥmūd, Muṣṭafā. 1972. *Rajul Taḥta al-Ṣifr*. Beirut: Dār al-'Awda.
——. 1996. *Ziyāra li-l-Janna wa-l-Nār*. Cairo: Dār Akhbār al-Yawm.
Mājdūlīn, Sharaf al-Dīn. 2001. *Bayān Sharazād: al-Tashakkulāt al-Naw'iyya li-Ṣuwar al-Layālī*. Casablanca and Beirut: al-Markaz al-Thaqāfī al-'Arabī.
Majid, Anouar. 1998. "Islam and the Literature of Controversy." In John C. Hawley (ed.), *Postcolonial Crescent: Islam's Impact on Contemporary Literature*, pp. 84–92. New York: Peter Lang.
——. 2000. *Unveiling Traditions: Postcolonial Islam in a Polycentric World*. Durham, NC and London: Duke University Press.
Makar, Ragai N. 1998. *Modern Arabic Literature: A Bibliography*. Lanham, MD and London: Scarecrow Press.
Makarius, Raoul (ed.). 1964. *Anthologie de la littérature arabe contemporaine: Le roman et la nouvelle*. Paris: Éditions du Seuil.
Makdisi, George. 1981. *The Rise of Colleges: Institutions of Learning in Islam and the West*. Edinburgh: Edinburgh University Press.
——. 1990. *The Rise of Humanism in Classical Islam and the Christian West*. Edinburgh: Edinburgh University Press.
Makdisi, Saree and Felicity Nussbaum (eds). 2008. *The Arabian Nights in Historical Context between East and West*. Oxford: Oxford University Press.
Makhlūf, Īsā. 1998. "Li-Man Yaktubu al-Mu'allifūn al-'Arab." *al-Mulḥaq* (*al-Nahār*), 28 November, p. 9.
Makiya, Kanan. 1993. *Cruelty and the Silence: War, Tyranny, Uprising, and the Arab World*. New York and London: W. W. Norton.
Makkī, al-Ṭāhir Aḥmad. 1986. "Anghām lam Tusma' min Qabl." In Aḥmad Fu'ād Nigm (ed.), *Uyūn al-Kalām*, pp. 11–48. Cairo: Madbūlī.
al-Malā'ika, Nāzik. 1979. *Dīwān Nāzik al-Malā'ika*. Beirut: Dār al-'Awda.
——. 1983 [1962]. *Qaḍāyā al-Shi'r al-Mu'āṣir*. Beirut: Dār al-'Ilm li-l-Malāyīn.
Al Maleh, Layla (ed.). 2009. *Arab Voices in Diaspora: Critical Perspectives on Anglophone Arab Literature*. Amsterdam and New York: Rodopi.
Malti-Douglas, Fedwa. 1988. "Classical Arabic Crime Narratives: Thieves and Thievery in *Adab* Literature." *Journal of Arabic Literature* 19.2, pp. 108–27.
——. 1988a. "The Classical Arabic Detective." *Arabica* 35, pp. 59–91.
——. 1988b. *Blindness and Autobiography: Al-Ayyam of Taha Husayn*. Princeton: Princeton University Press.

——. 1991. *Woman's Body, Woman's Word: Gender and Discourse in Arabo-Islamic Writing*. Princeton: Princeton University Press.
——. 1994. "A Literature of Islamic Revival?: The Autobiography of Shaykh Kishk." In Şerif Mardin (ed.), *Cultural Transition in the Middle East*, pp. 116–29. Leiden: Brill.
——. 1994a. "Dangerous Crossings: Gender and Criticism in Arabic Literary Studies." In Margaret Higonnet (ed.), *Borderwork: Feminist Engagements with Comparative Literature*, pp. 224–9. Ithaca: Cornell University Press.
——. 1995. *Men, Women, and God(s)*. Berkeley: University of California Press.
——. 2000. "Postmoderning the Traditional in the Autobiography of Shaykh Kishk." In Zaki N. Abdel-Malek and Wael Hallaq (eds), *Tradition, Modernity, and Postmodernity in Arabic Literature: Essays in Honor of Professor Issa J. Boullata*, pp. 389–410. Leiden, Boston, and Cologne: Brill.
——. 2001. *Medicines of the Soul: Female Bodies and Sacred Geographies in a Transnational Islam*. Berkeley: University of California Press.
——. 2001a. *Power, Marginality, and the Body in Medieval Islam*. Aldershot: Ashgate.
Mamelouk, Douja. 2015. "New National Discourses: Tunisian Women Write the Revolution." *Alif: Journal of Comparative Poetics* 35, pp. 100–22.
Mandūr, Muḥammad. 1963 [1944]. *Fī al-Mīzān al-Jadīd*. Cairo: Maktabat Nahḍat Miṣr.
——. 1970. *A'lām al-Shi'r al-'Arabī al-Ḥadīth*. Beirut: al-Maktab al-Tijārī li-l-Ṭibā'a wa-l-Nashr wa-l-Tawzī'.
——. 1984. *al-Masraḥ al-Nathrī*. Cairo: Dār Nahḍat Miṣr li-l-Ṭab' wa-l-Nashr.
al-Manfalūṭī, Muṣṭafā Luṭfī. 1954 [1912]. *Mukhtārāt al-Manfalūṭī*. Cairo: Maṭba'at al-Sa'āda.
Manger, Leif. 1999. *Muslim Diversity: Local Islam in Global Contexts*. Richmond: Curzon.
Manisty, Dinah. 1998. "Negotiating the Space between Private and Public: Women's Autobiographical Writing in Egypt." In Robin C. Ostle et al. (eds), *Writing the Self: Autobiographical Writing in Modern Arabic Literature*, pp. 272–82. London: Saqi Books.
Mann, Thomas. 1970. *Buddenbrooks* (trans. H. T. Lowe-Porter). London: Secker and Warburg.
Mansiyyah, Munjiyyah 'Arafa. 1993. *Sulṭat al-Kalima 'inda Mufakkirī al-Iṣlāḥ—al-Ṭahṭāwī wa-Khayr al-Dīn*. Tunis: al-Dār al-Tūnisiyya li-l-Nashr.
——. 1997. *Adab al-Nahḍa wa-Izdiwājiyyat al-Khiṭāb ḥawla al-Mar'a*. Rabat: Manshūrāt Kulliyyat al-Ādāb wa-l-'Ulūm al-Insāniyya.
Mansour, Jacob (ed.). 1973. *Arabic and Islamic Studies* (Hebrew). Ramat Gan: Bar-Ilan University.
Manṣūr, Anīs. 1983. *Fī Ṣālūn al-'Aqqād Kānat Lanā Ayyām*. Cairo and Beirut: Dār al-Shurūq.
Manṣūr, 'Aṭāllāh. 1992. "Reach Thy Neighbor: Arabs Writing Hebrew." *Bulletin of the Israeli Academic Center in Cairo* 16 (May), pp. 63–6.
Manṣūr, Fawwāz (ed.). 1999. *Dirāsāt fī al-Ḥaḍāra al-Islāmiyya wa-l-'Arabiyya*. al-Ṭayba: n.pub.
Maoz, Nitza. 1998. *The Emergence of a System of Arabic Children's Literature in the Cultural Sphere of Palestine 1826–1918: The Socio-Cultural Shaping of Its Readership* (Hebrew). PhD thesis, Tel Aviv University.
al-Maqāliḥ, 'Abd al-'Azīz. 1978. *Shi'r al-'Āmmiyya fī al-Yaman*. Beirut: Dār al-'Awda.
Mardin, Şerif (ed.). 1994. *Cultural Transition in the Middle East*. Leiden: Brill.
Margolin, Uri. 1969. "The Problem of Periodization in Literary Studies" (Hebrew). *Hasifrut* 2.1, pp. 5–13.
Marín, Manuela and Randi Deguilhem (eds). 2002. *Writing the Feminine: Women in Arab Sources*. London and New York: I. B. Tauris.
al-Marrākushī, 'Abd al-Wāḥid. 1963. *al-Mu'jib fī Talkhīṣ Akhbār al-Maghrib* (ed. Muḥammad Sa'īd al-'Iryān). Cairo: Lajnat Iḥyā' al-Turāth al-Islāmī.

Martínez Lillo, Rosa-Isabel. 2011. "Mixtificación de al-Andalus en la literatura árabe actual." *Awraq: Revista de Análisis y Pensamiento sobre el Mundo Árabe e Islámico Contemporáneo* 3 (Nueva época), pp. 57–86.
Marzolph, Ulrich (ed.). 2006. *The Arabian Nights Reader*. Detroit: Wayne State University Press.
——. (ed.). 2007. *The Arabian Nights in Transnational Perspective*. Detroit: Wayne State University Press.
Masmoudi, Ikram. 2010. "Portraits of Iraqi Women: Between Testimony and Fiction." *International Journal of Contemporary Iraqi Studies* 4.1–2, pp. 59–71.
Matar, Nabil I. 1994. "Homosexuality in the Early Novels of Nageeb Mahfouz." *Journal of Homosexuality* 26.4, pp. 77–90.
Matejka, Ladislav and Krystyna Pomorska (eds). 1971. *Readings in Russian Poetics: Formalist and Structuralist Views*. Cambridge, MA and London: The MIT Press.
Maṭlūb, Aḥmad. 1968. *al-Naqd al-Adabī al-Ḥadīth fī al-'Iraq*. Baghdad: Ma'had al-Buḥūth wa-l-Dirāsāt al-'Arabiyya.
Mattock, J. N. 1984. "The Early History of the *Maqāma*." *Journal of Arabic Literature* 15, pp. 1–18.
Mavroudi, Maria. 2015. "Translations from Greek into Arabic and Latin during the Middle Ages: Searching for the Classical Tradition." *Speculum* 90.1 (January), pp. 28–59.
Mawāsī, Fārūq. 1995. *Ash'ār al-Dīwāniyyīn: Shi'r Madrasat al-Dīwān*. Jerusalem: Ministry of Education and Culture.
Maẓlūm, Muḥammad. 1996. "Fī al-Taṣnīf wa-l-Khārijīn Minhu wa-'Alayhi." *al-Kitāba al-Ukhrā* 12–13, pp. 136–43.
McCrum, Robert. 2010. *Globish: How the English Language Became the World's Language*. New York: W. W. Norton.
McKibben, Bill. 2007. *Deep Economy: The Wealth of Communities and the Durable Future*. New York: Times Books.
McManus, Anne-Marie. 2014. "The Contemporary Syrian Novel in Translation." *Arab Studies Journal* 22.1, pp. 322–33.
McNulty, F. H. 1981. "Mahjar Literature: An Annotated Bibliography of Literary Criticism and Biography in Western Languages." *Mundus Arabicus* 1, pp. 65–88.
Mehdid, M. 1993. *Tradition and Subversion: Gender and Post-Colonial Feminism: The Case of the Arab Region (with Particular Reference to Algeria)*. PhD thesis, University of Warwick.
Mehrez, Samia. 1985. *Bricolage as Hypertextuality*. PhD thesis, University of California, Los Angeles.
——. 1993. "Respected Sir." In Michael Beard and Adnan Haydar (eds), *Naguib Mahfouz: From Regional Fame to Global Recognition*, pp. 61–80. Syracuse: Syracuse University Press.
——. 1994. *Egyptian Writers between History and Fiction*. Cairo: The American University in Cairo Press.
——. 1994a. "Experimentation and the Institution: The Case of *Ida'a* and *Aswat*." In Ferial J. Ghazoul and Barbara Harlow (eds), *The View from Within: Writers and Critics on Contemporary Arabic Literature*, pp. 177–96. Cairo: The American University in Cairo Press.
——. 2008. *Egypt's Culture Wars: Politics and Practice*. London and New York: Routledge.
——. (ed.). 2010. *The Literary Atlas of Cairo: One Hundred Years on the Streets of the City*. Cairo: The American University in Cairo Press.
——. (ed.). 2011. *The Literary Life of Cairo: One Hundred Years in the Heart of the City*. Cairo: The American University in Cairo Press.
Mehta, Brinda J. 2007. *Rituals of Memory in Contemporary Arab Women's Writing*. Syracuse: Syracuse University Press.

Meijer, Roel (ed.). 1999. *Cosmopolitanism, Identity and Authenticity in the Middle East.* Richmond: Curzon.
——. 2002. *The Quest for Modernity: Secular Liberal and Left-Wing Political Thought in Egypt, 1945–1958.* London: RoutledgeCurzon.
Meisami, Julie Scott and Paul Starkey (eds). 1998. *Encyclopedia of Arabic Literature.* London and New York: Routledge.
Mejdell, Gunvor. 2006. "The Use of Colloquial in Modern Egyptian Literature—a Survey." In Lutz Edzard and Jan Retsö (eds), *Current Issues in the Analysis of Semitic Grammar and Lexicon II*, pp. 195–213. Wiesbaden: Harrassowitz Verlag.
Melucci, Alberto. 1997. "Identity and Difference in a Globalized World." In Pnina Werbner and Tariq Modood (eds), *Debating Cultural Hybridity: Multi-Cultural Identities and the Politics of Anti-Racism*, pp. 58–69. London and Atlantic Highlands, NJ: Zed Books.
Mendelson, David (ed.). 2001. *Francophonies.* Limoges: Presses Universitaires de Limoges.
Menocal, María Rosa. 1985. "Pride and Prejudice in Medieval Studies: European and Oriental." *Hispanic Review* 53, pp. 61–78.
——. 1987. *The Arabic Role in Medieval Literary History.* Philadelphia: University of Pennsylvania Press.
Meriwether, Margaret L. and Judith E. Tucker (eds). 1999. *A Social History of Women and Gender in the Modern Middle East.* Boulder, CO: Westview Press.
Messick, Brinkley Morris. 1993. *The Calligraphic State: Textual Domination and History in a Muslim Society.* Berkeley: University of California Press.
Mestyan, Adam. 2015. "Ignác Goldziher's Report on the Books Brought from the Orient for the Hungarian Academy of Sciences." *Journal of Semitic Studies* 60.2, pp. 443–80.
Metlitzki, Dorothee. 1977. *The Matter of Araby in Medieval England.* New Haven and London: Yale University Press.
Metwali, Mohamed Hanaa Abd El-Fattah. 1984. "The Role of *The Arabian Nights* in the Formation of the Arabic Theatre." *Rocznik Orientalistyczny* 43, pp. 101–8.
Meyer, Stefan G. 2001. *The Experimental Arabic Novel: Postcolonial Literary Modernism in the Levant.* Albany: State University of New York Press.
M'henni, Mansour (ed.). 1993. *Tahar Ben Jelloun: Stratégies d'Écriture.* Paris: Éditions L'Harmatten.
Michalak-Pikulska, Barbara. 1994. "Innovatory Trends in Modern Kuwaiti Short Story." *Studia Arabistyczne i Islamistyczne* 2, pp. 23–8.
——. 1998. "Bibliography of Contemporary Saudi Literature." *Studia Arabistyczne i Islamistyczne* 6, pp. 184–201.
——. 1999. "Gibran Khalil Gibran's Significance and Role in Arabic and World Literature and his Creative Reception in the World." *Folia Orientalia* 35, pp. 93–100.
——. 2001. "The Development of Cultural and Journalistic Activity in Oman." *Acta Asiatica Varsoviensia* 14, pp. 59–65.
——. 2008. "Diaspora—New Features of the Phenomenon and Its Cultural Impact: Case of Omani Poets." *Rocznik Orientalistyczny* 61.1, pp. 28–33.
——. 2009. "The Beginnings of Prose Writing in Bahrain." *Rocznik Orientalistyczny* 61.2, pp. 39–48.
——. 2011. "The Beginning of Modern Prose Writing in Oman." In Frederek Musall and Abdulbary al-Mudarris (eds), *Im Dialog bleiben: Sprache und Denken in den Kulturen des Vorderen Orients. Festschrift für Raif Georges Khoury*, pp. 281–91. Wiesbaden: Harrassowitz Verlag.
——. 2012. *Modern Literature of the United Arab Emirates.* Kraków: Jagiellonian University Press.
Micheau, Françoise. 2008. "Baghdad in the Abbasid Era: A Cosmopolitan and Multi-

Confessional Capital." In Salma K. Jayyusi (gen. ed.) and Renata Holod et al. (spec. eds), *The City in the Islamic World*, pp. 221–45. Leiden: Brill.
Miftah, Mohamed and Ahmed Bouhsane (eds). 1997. *Periodization: Tradition, Rupture and Process*. Rabat: Mohammed V University.
Miftāḥ, Muḥammad. 1999. *al-Mafāhīm Maʿālim: Naḥwa Ta'wīl Wāqiʿī*. Beirut and Casablanca: al-Markaz al-Thaqāfī al-ʿArabī.
——. and Aḥmad BūḤasan (eds). 1996. *Ashkāl al-Taḥqīb*. Rabat: Kulliyyat al-Ādāb wa-l-ʿUlūm al-Insāniyya.
Mikhail, Mona. 1979. *Images of Arab Women*. Washington, DC: Three Continents Press.
——. 1992. *Studies in the Short Fiction of Mahfouz and Idris*. New York: New York University Press.
——. 2004. *Seen and Heard: A Century of Arab Women in Literature and Culture*. Northampton, MA: Olive French Press.
Miles, Rosalind. 1988. *The Women's History of the World*. London: Michael Joseph.
Miller, Judith. 1996. *God Has Ninety-Nine Names: Reporting from a Militant Middle East*. New York: Simon and Schuster.
Milson, Menahem. 1998. *Najib Mahfuz: Philosopher Novelist of Cairo*. New York: St. Martin's Press.
Miquel, André. 1969. *La littérature arabe*. Paris: Presses universitaires de France.
al-Miṣrī, Ḥusayn Mujīb. 2001. *Fī al-Adab al-Shaʿbī al-Islāmī al-Muqārin*. Cairo: al-Dār al-Thaqāfiyya li-l-Nashr.
——. 2001a. *Ṣilāt Bayna al-ʿArab wa-l-Furs wa-l-Turk: Dirāsa Ta'rīkhiyya Adabiyya*. Cairo: al-Dār al-Thaqāfiyya li-l-Nashr.
——. 2003. *Bayna al-Adab al-ʿArabī wa-l-Turkī: Dirāsa fī al-Adab al-Islāmī al-Muqārin*. Cairo: al-Dār al-Thaqāfiyya li-l-Nashr.
Mitchell, G. D. 1979. *A New Dictionary of Sociology*. London: Routledge and Kegan Paul.
Mitra, Indrani. 2010. "'There Is No Sin in Our Love': Homoerotic Desire in the Stories of Two Muslim Women Writers." *Tulsa Studies in Women's Literature* 29.2, pp. 311–29.
al-Mizghannī, al-Munṣif. 1999. *ʿAbd al-Wahhāb al-Bayyātī fī Bayt al-Shiʿr*. Tunis: al-Sharika al-Tūnisiyya li-l-Nashr wa-Tanmiyat Funūn al-Rasm.
Moghissi, Haideh. 1999. *Feminism and Islamic Fundamentalism: The Limits of Postmodern Analysis*. London and New York: Zed Books.
Momigliano, Arnaldo. 1987. *On Pagans, Jews, and Christians*. Middletown, CT: Wesleyan University Press.
Monroe, James T. 1972. "Oral Composition in Pre-Islamic Poetry." *Journal of Arabic Literature* 3, pp. 1–53.
——. 1974. *Hispano-Arabic Poetry*. Berkeley: University of California Press.
——. 1993. "*Zajal* and *Muwashshaḥa*." In Salma Khadra Jayyusi (ed.), *Islamic Spain*, pp. 398–419. Leiden: Brill.
——. 2013. "Why Was Ibn Quzmān Not Awarded the Title of 'Abū Nuwās of the West'? ('Zajal 96', the Poet, and his Critics)." *Journal of Arabic Literature* 44.3, pp. 293–334.
Moosa, Matti. 1972. "Naqqāsh and the Rise of the Native Arab Theatre in Syria." *Journal of Arabic Literature* 3, pp. 106–17.
——. 1983. *The Origins of Modern Arabic Fiction*. Washington, DC: Three Continents Press.
Moreh, Shmuel. 1973. "The Neoclassical *Qaṣīda*: Modern Poets and Critics." In Gustave E. von Grunebaum (ed.), *Arabic Poetry: Theory and Development*, pp. 155–79. Wiesbaden: Harrassowitz Verlag.
——. 1976. *Modern Arabic Poetry 1800–1970*. Leiden: Brill.
——. 1979. "The Arabic Novel between Arabic and European Influences during the Nineteenth Century." In S. Pines et al. (eds), *Studia Orientalia Memoriae D. H. Baneth Dedicata*, pp. 367–94. Jerusalem: Magnes Press.

——. 1984. "Town and Country in Modern Arabic Poetry." *Asian and African Studies* 18, pp. 161–185.
——. 1986. *al-Shiʿr al-ʿArabī al-Ḥadīth 1800–1970, Taṭawwur Ashkālihi wa-Mawḍūʿātihi bi-Taʾthīr al-Adab al-Gharbī* (trans. Shafīʿ al-Sayyid and Saʿd Maṣlūḥ). Cairo: Dār al-Fikr al-ʿArabī.
——. 1987. "The Shadow Play (*Khayāl al-Ẓill*) in the Light of Arabic Literature." *Journal of Arabic Literature* 18, pp. 46–61.
——. 1988. *Studies in Modern Arabic Prose and Poetry*. Leiden: Brill.
——. 1992. *Live Theatre and Dramatic Literature in the Medieval Arabic World*. Edinburgh: Edinburgh University Press.
——. 1993. "Hebrew Words and Baghdadi Judaeo-Arabic Dialect in the Poetry of the Iraqi Poet Mullā ʿAbbūd al-Karkhī 1861–1946" (Hebrew). In H. Ben-Shammai (ed.), *Hebrew and Arabic Studies in Honour of Joshua Blau Presented by Friends and Students on the Occasion of his Seventieth Birthday*, pp. 351–73. Tel Aviv: Tel Aviv University, and Jerusalem: The Hebrew University.
——. 1998. "The Algerian Playwright Abraham Daninos and his Play *Nazāhat al-Mushtāq* (1847): Between *Fuṣḥā* and *ʿĀmmiyya*." In Shimon Ballas and Reuven Snir (eds), *Studies in Canonical and Popular Arabic Literature*, pp. 37–45. Toronto: York Press.
——. 1998a. *Tilka Ayyām al-Ṣibā*. Jerusalem: Rābiṭat al-Jāmiʿiyyīn al-Yahūd al-Nāziḥīn min al-ʿIrāq.
——. 2000. "Arabic Poetics from the Eighteenth to the Twentieth Centuries." In Binyamin Abrahamov (ed.), *Studies in Arabic and Islamic Culture* (Vol. 1), pp. vii–lxvii. Tel Aviv: Department of Arabic, Bar-Ilan University.
——. 2000a. "The Nineteenth-Century Jewish Abraham Daninos as a Bridge between Muslim and Jewish Theater." In Benjamin H. Hary et al. (eds), *Judaism and Islam: Boundaries, Communication and Interaction: Essays in Honor of William M. Brinner*. pp. 409–16. Leiden, Boston, and Cologne: Brill.
——. 2014. *Marvelous Chronicles: Biographies and Events* (*ʿAjāʾib al-Āthār fī ʾl-Tarājim wa-l-Akhbār*). Jerusalem: The Max Schloessinger Memorial Foundation, The Hebrew University of Jerusalem.
——. and Maḥmūd ʿAbbāsī. 1987. *Tarājim wa-Āthār fī al-Adab al-ʿArabī fī Isrāʾīl 1948–1986*. Shfaram: Dār al-Mashriq.
——. and Philip Sadgrove. 1996. *Jewish Contributions to Nineteenth-Century Arabic Theatre*. Oxford: Oxford University Press.
Mortensen, Inge Demant. 1992. "On the Development and Role of the *Taʿziyeh* Play in Popular Islam." In Bo Utas and Knut S. Vikør (eds), *Papers from the First Nordic Conference on Middle Eastern Studies, Uppsala 26–29 January 1989*, pp. 104–113. Bergen: Nordic Society for Middle Eastern Studies.
Mostyn, Trevor. 2001. *A History of Censorship in Islamic Societies*. London: Saqi Books.
Moukhlis, Salah. 2008. "The Forgotten Face of Postcoloniality: Moroccan Prison Narratives, Human Rights, and the Politics of Resistance." *Journal of Arabic Literature* 39.3, pp. 347–76.
al-Mousa, Nedal. 1998. "The Fortunes of Faust in Arabic Literature: A Comparative Study." *New Comparison: A Journal of Comparative and General Literary Studies* 26, pp. 103–17.
Moussa-Mahmoud, Fatma. 1973. *The Arabic Novel in Egypt 1914–1970*. Cairo: General Egyptian Book Organization.
——. 1976. "Arabic Novels in Translation." *Journal of Arabic Literature* 7, pp. 151–3.
——. 1996. "Changing Technique in Modern Arabic Poetry: A Reflection of Changing Values?" In J. R. Smart (ed.), *Tradition and Modernity in Arabic Language and Literature*, pp. 61–74. Richmond: Curzon.
Mowafy, Waheed Mohamed Awad. 1999. *Modern Arabic Literary Biography: A Study*

of Character Portrayal in the Works of Egyptian Biographers of the First Half of the Twentieth Century, with Special Reference to Literary Biography. PhD thesis, University of Leeds.

Mubārak, ʿAlī. 1882. *ʿAlam al-Dīn*. Alexandria: Maṭbaʿat Jarīdat al-Maḥrūsa.

Mubārak, Zakī. 1936. *al-Lugha wa-l-Dīn wa-l-Taqālīd fī Ḥayāt al-Istiqlāl*. Cairo: al-Ḥalabī.

Muḥammad, Muḥammad Sayyid. 1994. *al-Ghazw al-Thaqāfī wa-l-Mujtamaʿ al-ʿArabī al-Muʿāṣir*. Cairo: Dār al-Fikr al-ʿArabī.

Muḥammad, Ramaḍān Basṭāwīsī. 1993. "al-Qiṣṣa al-Imārātiyya Bayna Faḍā' al-Tajriba al-Ijtimāʿiyya wa-l-Muṭlaq al-Adabī." *al-Sharq al-Awsaṭ*, 17 March, p. 22.

Muhannā, ʿAbd. 1990. *Muʿjam al-Nisā' al-Shāʿirāt fī al-Jāhiliyya wa-l-Islām*. Beirut: Dār al-Kutub al-ʿIlmiyya.

Muhawi, Ibrahim and Sharif Kanaana. 1989. *Speak Bird, Speak Again: Palestinian Arab Folktales*. Berkeley: University of California Press.

Muhawwī, Ibrāhīm and Sharīf Kanāʿina. 2001. *Qūl Yā Ṭayr: Nuṣūṣ wa-Dirāsa fī al-Ḥikāya al-Shaʿbiyya al-Filasṭīniyya*. Beirut: Mu'assasat al-Dirāsāt al-Filasṭīniyya.

al-Muḥsin, Fāṭima. 1993. "Lahjat al-Rīf fī Mughāmaratihā al-Jamāliyya." *al-Ḥayāt*, 21 May, p. 20.

al-Muḥtasib, ʿAbd al-Majīd ʿAbd al-Salām. 1978. *Ṭāhā Ḥusayn Mufakkiran*. Beirut: Dār Iḥyā' al-Turāth al-ʿArabī.

Mujalī, ʿAbd al-Nāṣir. 2005. *Anṭulūjiyā al-Adab al-Saʿūdī al-Jadīd*. Beirut: al-Mu'assasa al-ʿArabiyya li-l-Dirāsāt wa-l-Nashr.

Muʿjam al-Bābaṭīn li-l-Shuʿarā' al-ʿArab al-Muʿāṣirīn. 1995. Kuwait City: Mu'assasat Jā'izat ʿAbd al-ʿAzīz Saʿūd al-Bābaṭīn li-l-Ibdāʿ al-Shiʿrī. Available at: <http://www.albabtainprize.org/Encyclopedia/MenuFile/index.htm> (last accessed 4 November 2016).

Muʿjam al-Bābaṭīn li-Shuʿarā' al-ʿArabiyya fī al-Qarnayn al-Tāsiʿ ʿAshar wa-l-ʿIshrīn. 2008. Kuwait City: Mu'assasat Jā'izat ʿAbd al-ʿAzīz Saʿūd al-Bābaṭīn li-l-Ibdāʿ al-Shiʿrī. Available at: <www.almoajam.org/main_page.html> (last accessed 2 November 2016).

al-Mukhkh, Jalāl. 1990. *Aḥmad Fu'ād Nigm min al-Thawra ilā al-Khayba*. Sūsa, Tunis: Dār al-Maʿārif.

Murshid, Muḥammad A. I. 1980. *The Modern Theatre in Egypt with Special Reference to Melodrama (1789–1956)*. PhD thesis, University of Exeter.

Mursī, Aḥmad ʿAlī. 1983. *al-Ughniyya al-Shaʿbiyya*. Cairo: Dār al-Maʿārif.

Murtāḍ, ʿAbd al-Malik. 1988. *Fann al-Maqāmāt fī al-Adab al-ʿArabī*. Tunis: al-Dār al-Tūnisiyya li-l-Nashr.

Mūsā, Salāma. 1945. *al-Balāgha al-ʿAṣriyya wa-l-Lugha al-ʿArabiyya*. Cairo: al-Maṭbaʿa al-ʿAṣriyya.

——. 1947. *al-Tathqīf al-Dhātī aw Kayfa Nurabbī Anfusanā*. Cairo: Maṭbaʿat Lajnat al-Ta'līf wa-l-Tarjama wa-l-Nashr.

——. 1962. *Mā Hiya al-Nahḍa*. Beirut: Manshūrāt Maktabat al-Maʿārif.

Mūsā, Shams al-Dīn. 1975. "Taqalluṣ Dawr al-Dawla wa-Hijrat al-Kuttāb." *al-Ṭalīʿa*, October, pp. 160–5.

Musall, Frederek and Abdulbary al-Mudarris (eds). 2011. *Im Dialog bleiben: Sprache und Denken in den Kulturen des Vorderen Orients. Festschrift für Raif Georges Khoury*. Wiesbaden: Harrassowitz Verlag.

al-Mūsawī, Muḥsin Jāsim. 1973. *al-Nafṭ al-ʿIrāqī: Dirāsa Wathā'iqiyya min Manḥ al-Imtiyāz ḥattā al-Ta'mīm*. Baghdad: Dār al-Ḥurriyya li-l-Ṭibāʿa.

——. 1973a. *al-Thawra al-Jadīda: Dirāsāt Taḥlīliyya fī al-Siyāsa wa-l-Iqtiṣād wa-l-Fikr*. Beirut: al-Mu'assasa al-ʿArabiyya li-l-Dirāsāt wa-l-Nashr.

——. 1986. *Alf Layla wa-Laylā fī Naẓariyyat al-Adab al-Inklīzī*. Beirut: Manshūrāt Markaz al-Inmā' al-Qawmī.

——. 1993. *al-Istishrāq fī al-Fikr al-'Arabī*. Beirut: al-Mu'assasa al-'Arabiyya li-l-Dirāsāt wa-l-Nashr.
——. 2000. *Mujtama' Alf Layla wa-Laylā*. Tunis: Markaz al-Nashr al-Jāmi'ī.
——. 2001. *al-Nukhba al-Fikriyya wa-l-Inshiqāq: Qirā'a fī Taḥawwulāt al-Ṣafwa al-'Ārifa fī al-Mujtama' al-'Arabī al-Ḥadīth*. Beirut: Dār al-Ādāb.
——. 2005. *al-Naẓariyya wa-l-Naqd al-Thaqāfī: al-Kitāba al-'Ārabiyya fī 'Ālam Muthaghyyir, Wāqi'uhā, Siyāqātuhā wa-Bunāhā al-Shu'ūriyya*. Beirut: al-Mu'assasa al-'Arabiyya li-l-Dirāsāt wa-l-Nashr.
——. 2016. *al-Dhākira al-Sha'biyya li-Mujtama'āt Alf Layla wa-Layla: al-Sard wa-Marja'iyyatuhu al-Ta'rīkhiyya wa-Āliyyatuhu*. Beirut: al-Markaz al-Thaqāfī al-'Arabī.
al-Musawi, Muhsin Jassim. 1981. *Scheherazade in England*. Washington, DC: Three Continents Press.
——. 2003. *The Postcolonial Arabic Novel: Debating Ambivalence*. Leiden: Brill.
——. 2006. "Pre-Modern Belletristic Prose." In Roger Allen and D. S. Richards (eds), *Arabic Literature in the Post-Classical Period*, pp. 101–33. Cambridge: Cambridge University Press.
——. 2006a. *Arabic Poetry: Trajectories of Modernity and Tradition*. London: Routledge.
——. 2006b. *Reading Iraq: Culture and Power in Conflict*. London: I. B. Tauris.
——. (ed.). 2009. *Arabic Literary Thresholds: Sites of Rhetorical Turn in Contemporary Scholarship*. Leiden: Brill.
——. 2009a. *Islam in the Street: The Dynamics of Arabic Literary Production*. Lanham, MD: Rowman & Littlefield.
——. 2009b. *The Islamic Context of the Thousand and One Nights*. New York: Columbia University Press.
——. 2013. "The Medieval Islamic Literary World-System: The Lexicographic Turn." *Mamlūk Studies Review* 17, pp. 43–71.
——. 2014. "The Republic of Letters: Arab Modernity? (Part1)." *The Cambridge Journal of Postcolonial Literary Inquiry* 1.2, pp. 265–80.
——. 2015. "The Republic of Letters: Arab Modernity? (Part 2)." *The Cambridge Journal of Postcolonial Literary Inquiry* 2.1, pp. 115–30.
——. 2015a. "The Medieval Islamic Republic of Letters as World Model." *The Cambridge Journal of Postcolonial Literary Inquiry* 2.2, pp. 281–6.
——. 2015b. *The Medieval Islamic Republic of Letters: Arabic Knowledge Construction*. Notre Dame, IN: University of Notre Dame Press.
Musharrafa, Muṣṭafā Muṣṭafā. 2012. *Qanṭara al-Ladhī Kafara*. Cairo: al-Hay'a al-Miṣriyya al-'Āmma li-l-Kitāb.
Mus'id, Aḥlām Wāsif. 2006. *Marāyā al-Ab wa-l-Sulṭa—Qirā'a Sūsyū-Thaqāfiyya fī al-Sīra al-Dhātiyya al-'Arabiyya al-Mu'āṣira*. Amman: Dār Azmina.
al-Muṣliḥ, Muḥammad. 1999. "Kitābat al-Shi'r Ta'bīr 'an al-Ḥālāt al-Muṣta'ṣiya fī al-Nafs al-Insāniyya" (interview with 'Abd al-Wahhāb al-Bayyātī). *al-Sharq* (Shfaram) 29.3, pp. 69–70.
Muṣṭafā, Aḥmad Amīn. 1991. *Fann al-Maqāma Bayna al-Badī' wa-l-Ḥarīrī wa-l-Suyūṭī*. n.p.: n.pub.
Mustafa, F. 1997. *Comparative Study of Modern and Classic Styles of Story-Telling in Arabic Literature*. MA thesis, University of Manchester.
al-Muṭī'ī, Lum'ā. 1993. "Thaqāfat Ṭifl al-Qarya (al-Wāqi' wa-l-Mustaqbal)." *'Ālam al-Kitāb*, October, pp. 12–17.
Myhill, John. 2006. *Language, Religion and National Identity in Europe and the Middle East*. Amsterdam and Philadelphia: John Benjamins Publishing Company.
al-Nābulsī, Shākir. 2001. *al-Fikr al-'Arabī fī al-Qarn al-'Ishrīn 1950–2000* (Vol. 1). Beirut: al-Mu'assasa al-'Arabiyya li-l-Dirāsāt wa-l-Nashr.
——. 2005. *al-Lībarāliyūn al-Judud—Jadal Fikrī*. Cologne: Manshūrāt al-Jamal.

——. 2013. *al-Jinsāniyya al-ʻArabiyya: al-Jins wa-l-Ḥaḍāra* (Vol. 1). Beirut: al-Mu'assasa al-ʻArabiyya li-l-Dirāsāt wa-l-Nashr.
——. 2013a. *al-Jinsāniyya al-ʻArabiyya: Mutʻat al-Wildān wa-Ḥubb al-Ghilmān* (Vol. 2). Beirut: al-Mu'assasa al-ʻArabiyya li-l-Dirāsāt wa-l-Nashr.
Naddaff, Sandra. 1991. *Arabesque: Narrative Structure and the Aesthetics in the 1001 Nights*. Evanston, IL: Northwestern University Press.
Nader, Laura. 1968. "A Note on Attitudes and the Use of Language." In Joshua Fishman (ed.), *Readings in the Sociology of Language*, pp. 276–81. The Hague: Mouton.
Nadwi, S. Ziaul Hasan. 2002. "India's Contribution to Arabic Literature." In Asghar Ali Engineer (ed.), *Islam in India: The Impact of Civilizations*, pp. 161–6. New Delhi: Shipra Publications.
Naff, Thomas. 1993. *Paths to the Middle East: Ten Scholars Look Back*. Albany: State University of New York Press.
al-Nafzāwī, Muḥammad ibn Muḥammad. 1983. *Shahādāt wa-Mukhtārāt min al-Rawḍ al-ʻĀṭir fī Nuzhat al-Khāṭir* (ed. Hānī al-Khayyir). Damascus: Maktabat Usāma.
——. 1990. *al-Rawḍ al-ʻĀṭir fī Nuzhat al-Khāṭir* (ed. Jamāl Jumʻa). London: Riyāḍ al-Rayyis.
Nahas, Michael. 1985. "A Translation of *Hayy b. Yaqzan* by the Elder Edward Pococke (1604–1691)." *Journal of Arabic Literature* 16, pp. 88–90.
al-Naḥawī, Khalīl. 1979. *Min al-Shiʻr al-Mūrītānī al-Muʻāṣir*. Damascus: Ittiḥād al-Kuttāb al-ʻArab.
al-Naḥḥās, Hāshim. 1986. *al-Huwiyya al-Qawmiyya fī al-Sīnamā al-ʻArabiyya*. Cairo: al-Hay'a al-Miṣriyya al-ʻĀmma li-l-Kitāb.
al-Nahrawānī, Abū al-Faraj al-Muʻāfā ibn Zakariyyā. 1987. *al-Jalīs al-Ṣāliḥ al-Kāfī wa-l-Anīs al-Nāṣiḥ al-Shāfī* (Vol. 3) (ed. Iḥsān ʻAbbās). Beirut: ʻĀlam al-Kutub.
Najīb, Aḥmad. 1982. *Fann al-Kitāba li-l-Aṭfāl*. Cairo: Dār al-Kātib al-ʻArabī.
——. 1995. *Dīwān Shiʻr li-l-Aṭfāl wa-l-Nāshi'īn*. Cairo: al-Hay'a al-Miṣriyya al-ʻĀmma li-l-Kitāb.
Najm, Muḥammad Yūsuf. 1956. *al-Masraḥiyya fī al-Adab al-ʻArabī al-Ḥadīth*. Beirut: Dār Bayrūt li-l-Ṭibāʻa wa-l-Nashr.
Nakhla, Rashīd. 1964. *Dīwān Rashīd Nakhla fī al-Zajal*. Beirut: Dār Maktabat al-Ḥayāt.
Naʻnaʻ, Ḥamīda. 1979. *al-Waṭan fī al-ʻAynayn*. Beirut: Dār al-Ādab.
——. 1995. *The Homeland* (trans. Martin Asser). London: Garnet Publishing.
al-Naqqāsh, Rajā'. 1992. *Thalāthūn ʻĀman maʻa al-Shiʻr wa-l-Shuʻarā'*. Kuwait City and Cairo: Dār Suʻād al-Ṣabāḥ.
——. 1998. *Najīb Maḥfūẓ: Ṣafaḥāt min Mudhakkirātihi wa-Aḍwā' Jadīda ʻalā Adabihi wa-Ḥayātihi*. Cairo: Markaz al-Ahrām li-l-Tarjama wa-l-Nashr.
——. 2006. *Fī Ḥubb Najīb Maḥfūẓ*. Cairo: Dār al-Shurūq.
Naqqāsh, Samīr. 1971. *al-Khaṭā'*. Jerusalem: Maṭbaʻat al-Maʻārif.
——. 1980. *Yawm Ḥabalat wa-Ajhaḍat al-Dunyā*. Jerusalem: Maṭbaʻat al-Sharq al-ʻArabiyya.
——. 1986. *Nzūla wa-Khayṭ al-Shayṭān*. Jerusalem: Rābiṭat al-Jāmiʻiyyīn al-Yahūd al-Nāziḥīn min al-ʻIrāq.
Nashashibi, Salwa Mikdadi. 1998. "Gender and Politics in Contemporary Art: Arab Women Empower the Image." In Sherifa Zuhur (ed.), *Images of Enchantment: Visual and Performing Arts of the Middle East*, pp. 165–82. Cairo: The American University in Cairo Press.
al-Nāshif, Zakī. 1989. "Shakespeare am al-Shaykh Zubayr." *al-Mawākib*, September–October, pp. 36–41.
Nasir, Sari J. 1976. *The Arabs and the English*. London: Longman.
Naṣr Allāh, Niḍāl. 2006. *Nizār Qabbāni wa-Qaṣā'id Kānat Mamnūʻa*. Damascus: al-Awā'il li-l-Nashr wa-l-Tawzīʻ.

al-Nassāj, Sayyid Ḥāmid. 1972. *Dalīl al-Qiṣṣa al-Miṣriyya al-Qaṣīra: Ṣuḥuf wa-Majmū'āt 1910–1961*. Cairo: al-Hay'a al-Miṣriyya al-'Āmma li-l-Kitāb.
Nassar, Hala Khamis and Najat Rahman (eds). 2008. *Mahmoud Darwish, Exile's Poet: Critical Essays*. Northampton, MA: Interlink Books.
Nassib, Sélim. 1994. *Oum*. Paris: Balland.
Navarrete, Ignacio. 1986. "A Polysystemic Approach to Literary Theory: In Response to Barry Jordan." *Yearbook of Comparative and General Literature* 35, pp. 122–6.
Nawfal, Muḥammad Maḥmūd Qāsim. 1983. *Ta'rīkh al-Mu'āraḍāt fī al-Shi'r al-'Arabī*. Beirut: Mu'assasat al-Risāla & Dār al-Furqān.
Nawfal, Nawfal Ni'mat Allāh. n.d. *Ṣannājat al-Ṭarab fī Taqaddumāt al-'Arab*. Beirut: Maṭba'at al-Amrīkān.
al-Nawwāb, Muẓaffar. 1996. *al-A'māl al-Shi'riyya al-Kāmila*. London: Dār Qanbar.
al-Nayhūm, al-Ṣādiq. 1991. *al-Islām fī al-Asr*. London and Limassol: Riyāḍ al-Rayyis.
——. 1994. *Islām Ḍidd al-Islām*. London and Beirut: Riyāḍ al-Rayyis.
Negev, Avraham. 1986. "Obodas the God." *Israel Exploration Journal* 36.1–2, pp. 56–60.
Nelson, Cynthia. 1998. "Feminist Expression as Self-Identity and Cultural Critique: The Discourse of Doria Shafik." In John C. Hawley (ed.), *Postcolonial Crescent: Islam's Impact on Contemporary Literature*, pp. 95–120. New York: Peter Lang.
Nemah, H. 1974. "Andalusian *Maqāmāt*." *Journal of Arabic Literature* 5, pp. 83–92.
Netton, Ian Richard. 1992. *A Popular Dictionary of Islam*. London: Humanities Press International.
——. 1996. *Text and Trauma: An East–West Primer*. Richmond: Curzon.
Neuwirth, Angelika. 1998. "Jabrā Ibrāhīm Jabrā's Autobiography *al-Bi'r al-Ūlā*, and his Concept of a Celebration of Life." In Robin C. Ostle et al. (eds), *Writing the Self: Autobiographical Writing in Modern Arabic Literature*, pp. 115–27. London: Saqi Books.
——. et al. (eds). 1999. *Myths, Historical Archetypes and Symbolic Figures in Arabic Literature*. Beirut: Orient-Institut der DMG.
——. and Andreas Christian Islebe (eds). 2006. *Reflections on Reflections: Near Eastern Writers Reading Literature*. Wiesbaden: Reichert Verlag.
——. et al. (eds). 2006a. *Poetry's Voice: Society's Norms: Forms of Interaction between Middle Eastern Writers and Their Societies*. Wiesbaden: Reichert Verlag.
——. et al. (eds). 2010. *Arabic Literature: Postmodern Perspectives*. London: Saqi Books.
Nicholson, Reynold A. 1969 [1907]. *A Literary History of the Arabs*. Cambridge: Cambridge University Press.
Nieten, Ulrike-Rebekka. 2006. "Arabic Poetry and the Songs of the Troubadours: A Cross-Cultural Approach." In Angelika Neuwirth and Andreas Christian Islebe (eds), *Reflections on Reflections: Near Eastern Writers Reading Literature*, pp. 253–61. Wiesbaden: Reichert Verlag.
Nieuwkerk, Karin van. 1995. *"A Trade Like Any Other": Female Singers and Dancers in Egypt*. Austin: University of Texas Press.
——. 1998. "Changing Images and Shifting Identities: Female Performers in Egypt." In Sherifa Zuhur (ed.), *Images of Enchantment: Visual and Performing Arts of the Middle East*, pp. 21–35. Cairo: The American University in Cairo Press.
——. 2002. "Shifting Narratives on Marginality: Female Entertainers in Twentieth-Century Egypt." In Eugene Rogan (ed.), *Outside In: On the Margins of the Modern Middle East*, pp. 231–51. London and New York: I. B. Tauris.
——. 2011. *Muslim Rap, Halal Soaps and Revolutionary Theater: Artistic Developments in the Muslim World*. Austin: University of Texas Press.
Nigm (Najm), Aḥmad Fu'ād (ed.). 1986. *'Uyūn al-Kalām*. Cairo: Madbūlī.
——. 1991. *Qaṣā'id min Warā' al-Shams*. Ramallah and al-Bireh: al-Yarmūk.
——. 1993. *al-Fājūmī, Ta'rīkh Ḥayāt Muwāṭin Shāyil fī Qalbihi Waṭan*. Cairo: Dār Sphinx.

Nijland, C. 1993. "Al-Râbiṭa al-Qalamiyya: An Arabic Literary Circle in New York." *Bibliotheca Orientalis* 50.3–4, pp. 329–41.
Nirenberg, David. 2008. "Islam and the West: Two Dialectical Fantasies." *Journal of Religion in Europe* 1.1, pp. 3–33.
——. 2013. *Anti-Judaism: The Western Tradition*. New York: W. W. Norton.
——. 2014. *Neighboring Faiths: Christianity, Islam, and Judaism in the Middle Ages and Today*. Chicago and London: University of Chicago Press.
Niyāzī, Ṣalāḥ. 1999. *al-Ightirāb wa-l-Baṭal al-Qawmī*. Beirut: Mu'assasat al-Intishār al-'Arabī.
Noja, Sergio. 1993. "A Further Discussion of the Arabic Sentence of the 1st Century AD and Its Poetical Form." In Riccardo Contini et al. (eds), *Semitica Serta Philologica Constantiono Tsereteli Dicata*, pp. 183–8. Turin: Silvio Zamorani Editore.
Noorani, Yaseen. 2010. "Iraqi Modernism and the Representation of Femininity: Badr Shakir al-Sayyab and Abd al-Wahhab al-Bayati. *International Journal of Contemporary Iraqi Studies* 4.1–2, pp. 101–19.
——. 2016. "Estrangement and Selfhood in the Classical Concept of *Waṭan*." *Journal of Arabic Literature* 47.1–2, pp. 16–42.
Norin, Luc and Édouard Tarabay (eds). 1967. *Anthologie de la littérature arabe contemporaine: La poésie*. Paris: Éditions du Seuil.
Novitz, David. 2003. "Aesthetics of Popular Art." In Jerrold Levinson (ed.), *Aesthetics*, pp. 733–47. Oxford: Oxford University Press.
al-Nsour, Tayseer. 2012. "Challenges Facing Arab Women Writers." *European Journal of Social Sciences* 30.4, pp. 625–7.
Nu'ayma, Mīkhā'īl. 1964 [1923]. *al-Ghirbāl*. Beirut: Dār Ṣādir and Dār Bayrūt.
——. 1989 [1917]. *al-Ābā' wa-l-Banūn*. Beirut: Mu'assasat Nawfal.
al-Nu'aymī, Salwā. 2001. *Shāraktu fī al-Khadī'a*. Damascus: Sharikat Qadmus li-l-Nashr wa-l-Tawzī'.
Nuṣayr, 'Āyida. 1992. "Qanāt al-Tarjama Bayna al-Thaqāfatayn al-'Arabiyya wa-l-Faransiyya fī Qarnayn." *'Ālam al-Kitāb*, pp. 43–7.
al-Nuwayhī, Muḥammad. 1971 [1964]. *Qaḍiyyat al-Shi'r al-Jadīd*. Cairo: Maktabat al-Khānjī and Dār al-Fikr.
Nykl, A. R. 1946. *Hispano-Arabic Poetry and Its Relations with the Old Provençal Troubadours*. Baltimore: J. H. Furst Company.
Obadyā, Ibrāhīm. 1999. *Fī Dunyā al-Maqāmāt wa-l-Ghinā' al-Sha'bī al-'Irāqī*. Shfaram: Dār al-Mashriq.
Odeh, Nadja. 1998. "Coded Emotions: The Description of Nature in Arab Women's Autobiographies." In Robin C. Ostle et al. (eds), *Writing the Self: Autobiographical Writing in Modern Arabic Literature*, pp. 263–71. London: Saqi Books.
O'Fahey, R. S. (ed.). 1994. *Arabic Literature of Africa* (Vol. 1): *The Writings of Eastern Sudanic Africa to c. 1900*. Leiden: Brill.
——. (ed.). 2003. *Arabic Literature of Africa* (Vol. 3): *The Writings of the Muslim Peoples of Northeastern Africa*. Leiden: Brill.
Oleksy, Alicja. 2002. "The Secret Doors: Uncovering the History of Arab Women Writers." *Studia Arabistyczne i Islamistyczne* 10, pp. 74–80.
Oliverius, Jaroslav. 2000. "Bemerkungen zu zwei autobiographischen Werken von Luwīs 'Awaḍ." *Asian and African Studies* (Bratislava) 9.1, pp. 16–23.
Omri, Mohamed-Saleh. 1998. "'Gulf Laughter Break': Cartoons in Tunisia during the Gulf Conflict." In Fatma Müge Göçek (ed.), *Political Cartoons in the Middle East*, pp. 133–54. Princeton: Markus Wiener Publishers.
——. 2000. "*Adab* in the Seventeenth Century: Narrative and Parody in al-Shirbīnī's *Hazz al-Quḥūf*." *Edebiyât* 11.2, pp. 169–96.
——. 2002. "Maghrebi Literatures in Britain: Research, Translation, Circulation." *Revue d'Histoire Maghrébine / Al-Majalla al-Tārīkhīya al-Maghāribīya* 29, pp. 189–96.

——. 2007. "Introduction" (for Special Issue: "The Novelization of Islamic Literatures: The Intersections of Western, Arabic, Persian, Urdu, and Turkish Traditions." *Comparative Critical Studies* 4.3, pp. 317–28.
——. 2011. "Notes on the Traffic between Theory and Arabic Literature." *International Journal of Middle East Studies* 43.4, pp. 731–3.
Orlando, Valérie K. 2010. "Feminine Spaces and Places in the Dark Recesses of Morocco's Past: The Prison Testimonials in Poetry and Prose of Saïda Menebhi and Fatna el Bouih." *Journal of North African Studies* 15.3, pp. 273–88.
Ormsby, E. L. 1982. "Modern Arabic Literature in North Africa: An Annotated Bibliography of Works in European Languages." *Mundus Arabicus* 2, pp. 65–85.
Orsini, Francesca. 2015. "Whose Amnesia? Literary Modernity in Multilingual South Asia." *The Cambridge Journal of Postcolonial Literary Inquiry* 2.2, pp. 266–72.
Ostle, Robin C. 1971. "Khalīl Muṭrān: The Precursor of Lyrical Poetry in Modern Arabic." *Journal of Arabic Literature* 2, pp. 116–26.
——. (ed.). 1975. *Studies in Modern Arabic Literature*. Warminster: Aris and Phillips.
——. (ed.). 1991. *Modern Literature in the Near and Middle East 1850–1970*. London and New York: Routledge.
——. 1991a. "Romantic Poetry and the Tradition: The Case of Ibrāhīm Nāgī." In Alan Jones (ed.), *Arabicus Felix—Luminosus Britannicus—Essays in Honour of A. F. L. Beeston on his Eightieth Birthday*, pp. 202–12. Reading: Ithaca Press.
——. 1997. "The Printing Press and the Renaissance of Modern Arabic Literature." *Culture and History* 16, pp. 145–57.
——. (ed.). 2000. *Marginal Voices in Literature and Society: Individual and Society in the Mediterranean Muslim World*. Strasbourg: ESF.
——. 2008. *Sensibilities of the Islamic Mediterranean: Self-Expression in a Muslim Culture from Post-Classical Times to the Present Day*. London: I. B. Tauris.
——. et al. (eds). 1998. *Writing the Self: Autobiographical Writing in Modern Arabic Literature*. London: Saqi Books.
Ouyang, Wen-Chin. 1997. *Literary Criticism in Medieval Arabic-Islamic Culture: The Making of a Tradition*. Edinburgh: Edinburgh University Press.
——. 2007. "Fictive Mode, 'Journey to the West', and Transformation of Space: 'Ali Mubarak's Discourses of Modernization." *Comparative Critical Studies: The Journal of the British Comparative Literature Association* 4.3, pp. 331–58.
Pach, S. E. Yacoub Artin (trans.). 1968. *Contes populaires inédis de la vallée du Nil*. Paris: Maisonneuve and Larose.
Palgrave, Turner Francis. 1906 [1861]. *The Golden Treasury*. London: Dent and New York: Dutton.
Palva, Heikki and Knut S. Vikør (eds). 1993. *Papers from the Second Nordic Conference on Middle Eastern Studies, Copenhagen 22–25, October 1992*. Copenhagen: Nordic Institute of Asian Studies.
Pannewick, Friederike. 2009. "Performativity and Mobility: Middle Eastern Traditions on the Move." In Stephen Greenblatt et al. (eds), *Cultural Mobility: A Manifesto*, pp. 215–49. Cambridge: Cambridge University Press.
——. and Georges Khalil (eds). 2015. *Commitment and Beyond: Locating the Political in Arabic Literature since the 1940s*. Wiesbaden: Reichert Verlag.
Pappé, Ilan. 2005. *The Modern Middle East*. London and New York: Routledge.
Parmenter, Barbara M. 1994. *Giving Voice to Stones: Place and Identity in Palestinian Literature*. Austin: University of Texas Press.
Patel, Abdulrazzak. 2013. *The Arab Nahḍah: The Making of the Intellectual and Humanist Movement*. Edinburgh: Edinburgh University Press.
Peled, Mattityahu. 1979. "Creative Translation." *Journal of Arabic Literature* 10, pp. 128–50.
——. 1983. *Religion, My Own: The Literary Works of Najīb Maḥfūẓ*. New Brunswick, NJ and London: Transaction Books.

——. 1986. "Nodding the Necks: A Literary Study of Shirbīnī's Hazz al-Quḥūf." *Die Welt des Islams* 26, pp. 57–75.
——. 1998. "Prison Literature." In Shimon Ballas and Reuven Snir (eds), *Studies in Canonical and Popular Arabic Literature*, pp. 69–76. Toronto: York Press.
——. and Shimon Shamir (eds). 1978. *Egyptian Intellectuals on National Priorities* (Hebrew). Jerusalem: The Hebrew University.
Peleg, Ilan (ed.). 1993. *Patterns of Censorship Around the World*. Boulder, CO: Westview Press.
Pellat, Charles. 1960. "Ḥikāya." In P. J. Bearman et al. (eds), *The Encyclopaedia of Islam*, New Edition, Vol. 3, pp. 367–72. Leiden: Brill.
——. 1986. "Ḳiṣṣa." In P.J. Bearman et al. (eds), *The Encyclopaedia of Islam*, New Edition, Vol. 5, pp. 185–7. Leiden: Brill.
——. 1986a. "Liwāṭ." In P. J. Bearman et al. (eds), *The Encyclopaedia of Islam*, New Edition, Vol. 5, pp. 776–9. Leiden: Brill.
——. 1991. "Maḳāma." In P. J. Bearman et al. (eds), *The Encyclopaedia of Islam*, New Edition, Vol. 6, pp. 107–15. Leiden: Brill.
——. 1992. "Liwāṭ." In Arno Schmitt and Jehoeda Sofer (eds), *Sexuality and Eroticism among Males in Moslem Societies*, pp. 151–67. New York: Harrington Park Press.
Pepe, Teresa. 2012. "Improper Narratives: Egyptian Personal Blogs and the Arabic Notion of Adab." *LEA—Lingue e Letterature d'Oriente e d'Occidente* 1, pp. 547–62.
——. 2015. "When Writers Activate Readers: How the Autofictional Blog Transforms Arabic Literature." *Journal of Arabic and Islamic Studies* 15, pp. 73–1.
Pérès, Henri. 1937. "Le roman, le conte et la nouvelle dans littérature arabe modern." *Annales de l'Institut d'Études Orientales* 3, pp. 266–337.
Perriman M'rabet, Inaam. 2003. "The Movement of Ideas Through Translation: A Case Study of Maghrebi Literature." *Arab Historical Review for Ottoman Studies/Al-Majalla al-Tārīkhīya al-'Arabīya li-l-Dirāsāt al-'Uthmānīya*, pp. 151–7.
Petersson, Margareta et al. (eds). 2006. *Literary Interactions in the Modern World*. Berlin: De Gruyter.
Pettersson, Anders. 1990. *A Theory of Literary Discourse*. Lund: Lund University Press.
Philipp, Thomas. 1979. *Ǧurǧī Zaidan: His Life and Thought*. Beirut and Wiesbaden: Orient-Institut der DMG.
——. 1993. "The Autobiography in Modern Arab Literature and Culture." *Poetics Today* 14.3, pp. 573–604.
——. 2014. *Jurji Zaidan and the Foundations of Arab Nationalism: A Study*. Syracuse: Syracuse University Press.
Phillips, Christina. 2008. "An Attempt to Apply Gérard Genette's Model of Hypertextuality to Najīb Maḥfūẓ's *Malḥamat al-Ḥarāfīsh*." *Middle Eastern Literatures* 11.3, pp. 283–300.
Pinault, David. 1992. *Story-Telling Techniques in the Arabian Nights*. Leiden: Brill.
Pines, S. et al. (eds). 1979. *Studia Orientalia Memoriae D. H. Baneth Dedicata*. Jerusalem: Magnes Press.
Podeh, Elie. 2011. *The Politics of National Celebrations in the Arab Middle East*. Cambridge: Cambridge University Press.
Polka, Sagi. 2000. *Between Liberalism and Fundamentalism: The Political Thought of Mainstream Islam (Wasatiyya) in Contemporary Egypt* (Hebrew). PhD thesis, Bar-Ilan University.
Popp, Richard Alan. 2001. "Al-Rābiṭah al-Qalamīyah, 1916." *Journal of Arabic Literature* 32.1, pp. 30–52.
Preminger, Alex (ed.). 1974. *Princeton Encyclopedia of Poetics and Poetry*. Princeton: Princeton University Press.
Procházka, Stephan. 2009. "Women's Wedding Songs from Adana: Forty Quatrains in Cilician Arabic." *Estudios de Dialectología Norteafricana y Andalusí* 13, pp. 235–55.
Qabbish, Aḥmad. 1971. *Ta'rīkh al-Shi'r al-'Arabī al-Ḥadīth*. Damascus: n.pub.

——. 1981. *Majma' al-Ḥikam wa-l-Amthāl fī al-Shi'r al-'Arabī*. Beirut: Dār al-Jīl.
al-Qadhdhāfī, Mu'ammar. 1995. *al-Qarya al-Qarya al-Arḍ al-Arḍ wa-Intiḥār Rā'id al-Faḍā' wa-Qiṣaṣ Ukhrā*. London and Beirut: Riyāḍ al-Rayyis.
al-Qāḍī, Īmān. 1992. *al-Riwāya al-Niswiyya fī Bilād al-Sha'm: al-Simāt al-Nafsiyya wa-l-Fanniyya 1950–1985*. Damascus: al-Ahālī li-l-Ṭibā'a wa-l-Nashr.
al-Qāḍī, Muḥammad. 1993. "al-Ẓāhir wa-l-Bāṭin fī Kitāb *al-Ayyām*: Baḥth fī al-Tab'īr." In *Mā'wiyyt Ṭāhā Ḥusayn: Waqā'i' Nadwat Bayt al-Ḥikma bi-Qarṭāj 27 wa–28 June 1990*. al-Majma' al-Tunisī li-l-'Ulūm wa-l-Ādāb wa-l-Funūn, Bayt al-Ḥikma, pp. 207–32.
al-Qāḍī, Wadād. 1981. "East and West in 'Ali Mubarak's *'Alamuddin*." In Marwan R. Buheiri (ed.), *Intellectual Life in the Arab East, 1890–1939*, pp. 21–37. Beirut: The American University of Beirut.
——. 2009. "In the Footsteps of Arabic Biographical Literature: A Journey, Unfinished, in the Company of Knowledge." *Journal of Near Eastern Studies* 68.4, pp. 241–51.
al-Qa'īd, Yūsuf. 1994. *Laban al-'Uṣfūr*. Cairo: Dār al-Hilāl.
al-Qalamāwī, Suhayr. 1966. *Alf Layla wa-Layla*. Cairo: Dār al-Ma'ārif.
al-Qaraḍāwī, Yūsuf. 1985. *Nafaḥāt wa-Lafaḥāt* (ed. Ḥusnī Adham Jarrār). Amman: Dār al-Ḍiyā' li-l-Nashr wa-l-Tawzī'.
——. 1994. *al-Thaqāfa al-'Arabiyya al-Islāmiyya Bayna al-Aṣāla wa-l-Mu'āṣra*. Cairo: Maktabat Wahba.
——. 2003. *Man Jadd lam Yajid*. London: Dār al-Ḥikma.
Qāsim, Aḥmad Shawqī. 1980. *al-Masraḥ al-Islāmī Rawāfiduhu wa-Manāhijuhu*. Cairo: Dār al-Fikr al-'Arabī.
Qāsim, Maḥmūd. 1993. *al-Khayāl al-'Ilmī fī Adab al-Qarn al-'Ishrīn*. Cairo: al-Hay'a al-Miṣriyya al-'Āmma li-l-Kitāb.
——. 1993a. "Hal Intahā 'Aṣr al-Qirā'a." *al-Shurūq*, 21 July, pp. 40–3.
——. 1996. *al-Adab al-'Arabī al-Maktūb bi-l-Faransiyya*. Cairo: al-Hay'a al-Miṣriyya al-'Āmma li-l-Kitāb.
——. 2002. *Dalīl al-Aflām fī al-Qarn al-'Ishrīn fī Miṣr wa-l-'Ālam al-'Arabī*. Cairo: Maktabat Madbūlī.
Qāsim, Muḥammad Khalīl. 1968. *al-Shamandūra*. Cairo: Dār al-Kātib li-l-Ṭibā'a wa-l-Nashr.
al-Qāsim, Samīḥ. 1970. *Qaraqāsh*. Haifa: Dār al-Ittiḥād.
——. 1970a. *Qaraqāsh*. Beirut: Dār al-'Awda.
——. 1977. *Ilā al-Jaḥīm Ayyuhā al-Laylak*. Jerusalem: Manshūrāt Ṣalāḥ al-Dīn.
——. 1980. *al-Ṣūra al-Akhīra fī al-Albūm*. Beirut: Dār Ibn Khaldūn.
——. 1986. *Persona Non Grata*. Dālyat al-Karmil: al-'Imād.
——. 1991. *al-Masraḥ wa-l-Ḥikāya*. Kfar Qara': Dār al-Hudā.
Alqassime, S. K. 1996. *Education Policy and National Development in the UAE*. PhD thesis, University of Manchester.
al-Qassūs, Jiryis. 1936. "al-Ḥayāt al-Adabiyya fī Sharq al-Urdun." *al-Risāla*, 25 May, pp. 865–7.
al-Qā'ūd, Ḥilmī Maḥmūd. 1996. *al-Wāqi'iyya al-Islāmiyya fī Riwāyāt Najīb al-Kaylānī*. Amman: Dār al-Bashīr.
al-Qazwīnī, Zakariyyā ibn Muḥammad. 1960. *Āthār al-Bilād wa-Akhbār al-'Ibād*. Beirut: Dār Ṣādir & Dār Bayrūt.
al-Qishṭīnī, Khālid. 2001. *Mā Qīla wa-Mā Yaqūlu*. London: Dār al-Ḥikma.
Quṭb, Muḥammad. 1963? [1960]. *Minhaj al-Fann al-Islāmī*. Cairo: Dār al-Aqlām.
——. et al. 1988 [1976]. *al-Thaqāfa al-Islāmiyya*. Jidda: Markaz al-Nashr al-'Ilmī, Jāmi'at al-Malik 'Abd al-'Azīz.
Quṭb, Sayyid. 1965. *Khaṣā'iṣ al-Taṣawwur al-Islāmī wa-Muqawwimātuhu*. Cairo: Dār Iḥyā' al-Kutub al-'Arabiyya.
Qutbuddin, Tahera. 2007. "Arabic in India: A Survey and Classification of Its Uses, Compared with Persian." *Journal of the American Oriental Society* 127.3, pp. 315–38.

Rābiṭat al-ʿĀlam al-Islāmī fī Khamsatin wa-ʿIshrīn ʿĀman. 1987. Mecca: Rābiṭat al-ʿĀlam al-Islāmī.
Rābiṭat al-ʿĀlam al-Islāmī, al-Dalīl al-Iʿlāmī. 1989. Mecca: Rābiṭat al-ʿĀlam al-Islāmī.
Racy, A. J. 2003. *Making Music in the Arab World: The Culture and Artistry of Ṭarab*. Cambridge: Cambridge University Press.
Radwan, Noha. 2004. "Two Masters of Egyptian *ʿĀmmiyya* Poetry." *Journal of Arabic Literature* 35.2, pp. 221–43.
——. 2011. "Palestine in Egyptian Colloquial Poetry." *Journal of Palestine Studies* 40.4, pp. 61–77.
al-Rāfiʿī, Muṣṭafā Ṣādiq. 1960. *Waḥy al-Qalam*. Beirut: Dār al-Kitāb al-ʿArabī.
——. 2000. *Taḥta Rāyat al-Qur'ān*. Beirut: Dār al-Kutub al-ʿIlmiyya.
Rāghib, Nabīl. 1981. *Dalīl al-Nāqid al-Adabī*. Cairo: Maktabat Gharīb.
al-Rāʿī, ʿAlī. 1991. *al-Riwāya al-ʿArabiyya fī al-Waṭan al-ʿArabī*. Beirut: Dār al-Mustaqbal al-ʿArabī.
Rā'if, Aḥmad. 1987. *al-Buʿd al-Khāmis*. Cairo: al-Zahrā' li-l-Iʿlām al-ʿArabī.
Rainey, Lawrence. 1999. "The Cultural Economy of Modernism." In Michael Levenson (ed.), *The Cambridge Companion to Modernism*, pp. 33–69. Cambridge: Cambridge University Press.
Rajab, Ṭāriq (ed.). 1995. *Mutābaʿāt Naqdiyya fī Adab Samīḥ al-Qāsim*. Haifa: al-Wādī li-l-Ṭibāʿa wa-l-Nashr.
Raji, Moshood Gbola Adeniyi. 1986. *A Modern Trend in Nigerian Arabic Literature: The Contribution of ʿUmar Ibrāhīm*. PhD thesis, University of London.
Ramadan, Yasmine. 2012. "The Emergence of the Sixties Generation in Egypt and the Anxiety over Categorization." *Journal of Arabic Literature* 43.2–3, pp. 409–30.
Rāmī, Aḥmad. n.d. *Dīwān*. Beirut: Dār al-ʿAwda.
al-Ramlī, Līnīn. 1992. *Saʿdūn al-Majnūn*. Kuwait City: Dār Suʿād al-Ṣabāḥ.
Ramsay, Gail. 2002–3. "Styles of Expression in Women's Literature in the Gulf." *Orientalia Suecana* 51–2, pp. 371–90.
——. 2006. "Global Heroes and Local Characters in Short Stories from the United Arab Emirates and the Sultanate of Oman." *Middle Eastern Literatures* 9.2, pp. 211–16.
——. and Stephan Guth (eds). 2011. *From New Values to New Aesthetics: Turning Points in Modern Arabic Literature (Proceedings of the 8th EURAMAL Conference, 11–14 June, Uppsala / Sweden). 1. From Modernism to the 1980s*. Wiesbaden: Harrassowitz Verlag.
Rastegar, Kamran. 2005. "The Changing Value of *Alf Laylah wa Laylah* for Nineteenth-Century Arabic, Persian, and English Readerships." *Journal of Arabic Literature* 36.3, pp. 269–87.
——. 2007. *Literary Modernity between the Middle East and Europe: Textual Transactions in Nineteenth-Century Arabic, English and Persian Literatures*. London: Routledge.
——. 2013. "Authoring the Nahda" (Introduction to special issue). *Middle Eastern Literatures* 16.3, pp. 227–31.
Ra'ūf, Jīhān Ṣafwat. 1982. *Shelly fī al-Adab al-ʿArabī fī Miṣr*. Cairo: Dār al-Maʿārif.
Rausch, Margaret. 2006. "Nightingales Across the Winds of Time: Medieval Arabic Poetry and Modern Moroccan Women Wedding Singers." In Angelika Neuwirth and Andreas Christian Islebe (eds), *Reflections on Reflections: Near Eastern Writers Reading Literature*, pp. 291–304. Wiesbaden: Reichert Verlag.
Raven, John. 2010. "Using Digital Storytelling to Build a Sense of National Identity amongst Emirati Students." *Education, Business and Society: Contemporary Middle Eastern Issues* 3.3, pp. 201–17.
al-Rāwī, Muḥammad (ed.). 1982. *Udabā' al-Jīl Yataḥaddathūna*. Suez: Maṭbūʿāt al-Kalima al-Jadīda.
Rayhanova, Baian. 2004. "The Past and Present in the Modern Arabic Novel." *Zeitschrift der Deutschen Morgenländischen Gesellschaft* 154.1, pp. 71-84.
al-Rayyis, Riyāḍ Najīb. 1996. *Aktubu Ilaykum bi-Ghaḍab*. London: Riyāḍ al-Rayyis.

Razzūq, Faraj Razzūq. 1970. *Ilyās Abū Shabaka wa-Shi'ruhu*. Beirut: Dār al-Kitāb al-Lubnānī.

Redfield, Robert and Milton Singer. 1969. "The Cultural Role of Cities." In Richard Sennett (ed.), *Classical Essays in the Culture of Cities*, pp. 206–33. New York: Appleton-Century-Crofts.

Reeves, Minou. 2000. *Muhammad in Europe*. New York: New York University Press.

Regaïeg, Najiba. 2010. "Pour une poétique du féminin au Maghreb." In Mohamed Daoud et al. (eds), *Ecriture féminine: réception, discours et représentations*, pp. 21–33. Oran, Algeria: CRASC.

Reichmuth, Stefan. 2002. "Arabic Literature and Islamic Scholarship in the 17th/18th Century: Topics and Biographies." *Die Welt des Islams* 42.3, pp. 281–8.

Rejwan, Nissim. 1998. *Arabs Face the Modern World: Religious, Cultural, and Political Responses to the West*. Gainesville, FL: University Press of Florida.

Reynolds, Dwight Fletcher. 1995. *Heroic Poets, Poetic Heroes: The Ethnography of Performance in an Arabic Oral Epic Tradition*. Ithaca and London: Cornell University Press.

——. 1997. "Shā'ir (E. The Folk Poet in Arab Society)." In P. J. Bearman et al. (eds), *The Encyclopaedia of Islam*, New Edition, Vol. 9, pp. 233–6. Leiden: Brill.

——. (ed.). 2001. *Interpreting the Self: Autobiography in the Arabic Literary Tradition*. Berkeley: University of California Press.

——. (ed.). 2005. "Symbolic Narratives of Self: Dreams in Medieval Arabic Autobiographies." In Philip F. Kennedy (ed.), *On the Fiction and Adab in Medieval Arabic Literature*, pp. 261–84. Wiesbaden: Harrassowitz Verlag.

——. 2007. *Arab Folklore: A Handbook*. Westport, CT: Greenwood Press.

——. (ed.). 2015. *The Cambridge Companion to Modern Arab Culture*. Cambridge: Cambridge University Press.

Ricci, Ronit. 2011. *Islam Translated: Literature, Conversion, and the Arabic Cosmopolis of South and Southeast Asia*. Chicago: University of Chicago Press.

Richards, D. S. 1991. "The *Maqāmāt* of al-Hamadhānī: General Remarks and a Consideration of the Manuscripts." *Journal of Arabic Literature* 22.2, pp. 89–99.

Riedel, Dagmar Anne. 1998. "Medieval Arabic Literature between History and Psychology: Gustave von Grunebaum's Approach to Literary Criticism within the Western Orientalist Tradition." *Arabist: Budapest Studies in Arabic* 19–20, pp. 111–22.

Ritt-Benmimoun, Veronika. 2009. "Bedouin Women's Poetry in Southern Tunisia." *Estudios de Dialectología Norteafricana y Andalusí* 13, pp. 217–33.

Roded, Ruth. 1994. *Women in Islamic Biographical Collections: From Ibn Sa'd to Who's Who*. London and Boulder, CO: Lynne Rienner Publishers.

——. 1999. *Women in Islam and the Middle East: A Reader*. London and New York: I. B. Tauris.

Rodenbeck, John. 1997. "Cervantes and Islam: Attitudes towards Islam and Islamic Culture in Don Quixote." In David R. Blanks (ed.), *Cairo Papers in Social Science: Images of the Other: Europe and the Muslim World Before 1700*, pp. 55–72. Cairo: The American University in Cairo Press.

Rogan, Eugene (ed.). 2002. *Outside In: On the Margins of the Modern Middle East*. London and New York: I. B. Tauris.

Rooke, Tetz. 1997. *In My Childhood: A Study of Arabic Autobiography*. Stockholm: Almquist and Wiksell International.

——. 2011. "The Emergence of the Arabic Bestseller: Arabic Fiction and World Literature." In Stephan Guth and Gail Ramsay (eds), *From New Values to New Aesthetics: Turning Points in Modern Arabic Literature (Proceedings of the 8th EURAMAL Conference, 11–14 June, 2008, Uppsala / Sweden). 2. Postmodernism and Thereafter*, pp. 201–13. Wiesbaden: Harrassowitz Verlag.

Rosenbaum, Gabriel M. 2010. "'I Want to Write in the Colloquial': An Example of the Language of Contemporary Egyptian Prose." *Folia Orientalia* 47.1, pp. 71–97.

Rosenthal, Franz. 1979. "Literature." In Joseph Schacht and C. E. Bosworth (eds), *The Legacy of Islam*, pp. 321–49. Oxford: Oxford University Press.

——. 1979a. "Fiction and Reality: Sources for the Role of Sex in Medieval Muslim Society." In al-Sayyid-Marsot (ed.), *Society and the Sexes in Medieval Islam*, pp. 3–22. Malibu: Undena Publications.

Rothschild, Jon (ed.). 1984. *Forbidden Agendas: Intolerance and Defiance in the Middle East*. London: Saqi Books.

Rowson, Everett K. 1991. "The Categorization of Gender and Sexual Irregularity in Medieval Arabic Vice Lists." In Julia Epstein and Kristina Straub (eds), *Body Guards: The Cultural Politics of Gender Ambiguity*, pp. 50–79. New York and London: Routledge.

——. 1991a. "The Effeminates of Early Medina." *Journal of the American Oriental Society* 111.4, pp. 671–93.

Roy, Olivier. 2004. *Globalized Islam: The Search for a New Ummah*. New York: Columbia University Press.

Rugh, William A. 1979. *The Arab Press: News Media and Political Process in the Arab World*. Syracuse: Syracuse University Press.

Ruocco, Monica. 2000. "A Survey of Translations and Studies on Arabic Literature Published in Italy (1987–1997)." *Arabic and Middle Eastern Literatures* 3.1, pp. 63–73.

——. 2001. "La traduzione della terminologia teatrale in lingua araba." *Traduttore Nuovo* 56.1, pp. 29–37, 112.

——. 2014. "La géographie du nouveau roman saoudien selon Yūsuf al-Muḥaymīd." *Arabian Humanities* 3. Available at: <https://cy.revues.org/2740> (last accessed 3 November 2016).

Rushdie, Salman. 1988. *The Satanic Verses*. London: Viking.

Russell, Sharon A. 1998. *Guide to African Cinema*. Westport, CT: Greenwood Press.

Ruthven, Malise. 1990. *A Satanic Affair: Salman Rushdie and the Rage of Islam*. London: Chatto and Windus.

Saad el Din, Mursi and John Cromer. 1991. *Under Egypt's Spell: The Influence of Egypt on Writers in English from the 18th Century*. London: Bellew Publishing.

Sabra, Martina. 2010. "The Poem of the Day Direct to Your Smartphone? Modern Arabic Literature on the Worldwide Web." *Fikrun wa Fann* 93, pp. 32–5.

Ṣabrī, Muḥammad (ed.). 1979. *al-Shawqiyyāt al-Majhūla*. Beirut: Dār al-Masīra.

Sacks, Jeffrey. 2015. *Iterations of Loss: Mutilation and Aesthetic Form, al-Shidyaq to Darwish*. New York: Fordham University Press.

Sa'd, Fārūq. 1962. *Min Waḥy Alf Layla wa-Layla*. Beirut: al-Maktaba al-Ahliyya.

Sadan, Joseph. 1997–8. "al-'Ibra al-Adabiyya wa-l-Akhlāqiyya fī Qiṣṣat 'Qitāl al-Qiṭṭ wa-l-Fa'r', Nashr al-Naṣṣ wa-Mulāḥaẓāt Awwaliyya." *al-Karmil—Abḥāth fī al-Lugha wa-l-Adab* 18–19, pp. 179–97.

——. 1998. "Hārūn al-Rashīd and the Brewer: Preliminary Remarks on the *Adab* of the Elite versus *Ḥikāyāt*. The Continuation of Some of the Traditional Literary Models, from the 'Classical' Arabic Heritage, up to the Time of the Emergence of Modern Forms." In Shimon Ballas and Reuven Snir (eds), *Studies in Canonical and Popular Arabic Literature*, pp. 1–22. Toronto: York Press.

——. 1999. "'Awdat 'Alā' al-Dīn wa-Miṣbāḥuhu ilā Judhūrihimā: Naẓra Jadīda fī al-Mafāhīm al-Rāsikha wa-l-Abḥāth al-Mutrākima Ḥawla Majmū'at 'Alf Layla wa-Layla' wa-Naẓā'irihā. al-Musāhama al-'Arabiyya-al-Faransiyya fī Balwarat Ba'ḍ al-Ḥikāyāt." *al-Karmil—Abḥāth fī al-Lugha wa-l-Adab* 20, pp. 149–88.

——. 2001. "L'Orient pittoresque et Aladin retrouvé." In David Mendelson (ed.), *Francophonies*, pp. 169–84. Limoges: Presses Universitaires de Limoges.

——. 2011. "The Arabian Nights and the Jews." In Frederek Musall and Abdulbary al-Mudarris (eds), *Im Dialog bleiben: Sprache und Denken in den Kulturen des Vorderen*

Orients. Festschrift für Raif Georges Khoury, pp. 236–48. Wiesbaden: Harrassowitz Verlag.
Sadān, Yūsuf. 1983. *al-Adab al-'Arabī al-Hāzil wa-Nawādir al-Huzalā'*. Tel Aviv: Tel Aviv University and Acre: Maktabat al-Sarūjī.
——. 1988. "Risāla fī al-Damāma li-Muḥammad ibn Ḥamza al-Kūzalḥiṣārī al-Aydīnī wa-Mā Sabaqhā min Mawāqif al-Udabā' min al-'Āhāt wa-l-Qubḥ." *al-Karmil—Abḥāth fī al-Lugha wa-l-Adab* 9, pp. 7–33.
al-Sādāt, Jīhān. 1992. *Athar al-Naqd al-Inglīzī fī al-Nuqqād al-Rūmānsiyyīn fī Miṣr*. Cairo: Dār al-Ma'ārif.
al-Sa'dāwī, Nawāl. 1978 [1974]. *Mawt al-Rajul al-Waḥīd 'alā al-Arḍ*. Beirut: Dār al-Ādāb.
——. 1979. *Imra'a 'inda Nuqṭat al-Ṣifr*. Beirut: Dār al-Ādāb.
——. 1982. *al-Insān: Ithnay 'Ashara* [sic] *Imra'a fī Zinzāna Wāḥida*. Cairo: Madbūlī.
——. 1984. *Mudhakkirāt fī Sijn al-Nisā'*. Cairo: Dār al-Mustaqbal al-'Arabī.
——. 1987. *Suqūṭ al-Imām*. Cairo: Dār al-Mustaqbal al-'Arabī.
——. 1992. *Jannāt wa-Iblīs*. Beirut: Dār al-Ādāb.
Sadek, Mohamed. 1994. Letter to the Editor: Response to "A Note on the Study of Homosexuality in the Arab/Islamic Civilization." *Arab Studies Journal* 2, p. 65.
Sadgrove, P. C. 1996. *The Egyptian Theatre in the Nineteenth Century (1799–1882)*. Reading: Ithaca Press.
——. (ed.). 2004. *History of Printing and Publishing in the Languages and Countries of the Middle East*. Oxford: Oxford University Press.
al-Sa'dī, Abū Zayyān. 1989. *Fī al-Adab al-Tūnisī al-Mu'āṣir*. Sūsa, Tunis: Dār al-Ma'ārif.
Sadoul, Georges (ed.). 1966. *The Cinema in the Arab Countries*. Beirut: Interarab Centre of Cinema and Television.
Sagaster, Börte et al. (eds). 2016. *Crime Fiction in and Around the Eastern Mediterranean*. Wiesbaden: Harrassowitz Verlag.
Ṣāghiyya, Ḥāzim. 1999. *Wadā' al-'Urūba*. London: Dār al-Sāqī.
al-Saḥḥār, Sa'īd Jawda. 1999. *Mawsū'at A'lām al-Fikr al-'Arabī*. Cairo: Maktabat Miṣr.
Sā'ī, Aḥmad Bassām. 1985. *al-Wāqi'iyya al-Islāmiyya fī al-Adab wa-l-Naqd*. Jidda: Dār al-Manāra lil-Nashr.
Said, Edward W. 1976. "Under Western Eyes." *The Times Literary Supplement*, 10 December, pp. 1559–60.
——. 1985 [1978]. *Orientalism*. London: Penguin Books.
——. 1990. "Embargoed Literature." *The Nation*, 17 September.
——. 1994. *Culture and Imperialism*. London: Vintage.
——. 1994a. *The Politics of Dispossession: The Struggle for Palestinian Self-Determination, 1969–1994*. New York: Pantheon Books.
Sa'īd, Nafūsa Zakariyyā. 1980. *Ta'rīkh al-Da'wa ilā al-'Āmmiyya wa-Āthāruhā fī Miṣr*. Cairo: Dār al-Ma'ārif.
Sakkut, Hamdy. 1971. *The Egyptian Novel and Its Main Trends 1913–1953*. Cairo: The American University in Cairo Press.
Ṣalāḥ, Rā'id. 2006. *Zaghārīd al-Sujūn*. Acre: Dār al-Aswār.
Ṣalāḥ al-Dīn, Muḥammad. 1998. *al-Dīn wa-l-'Aqīda fī al-Sīnamā al-Miṣriyya*. Cairo: Maktabat Madbūlī.
Salāma, Ziyād Aḥmad. 1998. *Ma'a Ṭāhā Ḥusayn fī al-Shi'r al-Jāhilī*. Amman and Beirut: Dār al-Bayāriq.
al-Salāwī, Muḥammad Adīb. 1986. *al-Shi'r al-Maghribī: Muqāraba Ta'rīkhiyya 1830–1960*. Casablanca: Ifrīqiya al-Sharq.
al-Saleh, Asaad. 2015. *Voices of the Arab Spring: Personal Stories from the Arab Revolutions*. New York: Columbia University Press.
Salem, Alma. 2001. "Teoria e pratica della traduzione in arabo della letteratura per l'infanzia." *Traduttore Nuovo* 56.1, pp. 75–82, 116–17.
Salem, Elise. 2000–1. "The Dynamics of Canon Formation: Arabic Literature in

'Translation.'" *Al-Abhath: Journal of the Faculty of Arts and Sciences of the American University of Beirut* 48–9, pp. 85–98.

——. 2003. *Constructing Lebanon: A Century of Literary Narratives*. Gainesville, FL: University Press of Florida.

Salhi, Zahia Smail (ed.). 2013. *Gender and Violence in Islamic Societies: Patriarchy, Islamism and Politics in the Middle East and North Africa*. London: I. B. Tauris.

al-Ṣāliḥ, 'Alī 'Alī (ed.). 2004. *al-Tahālīl: Aghānī Tanwīm al-Aṭfāl fī Filasṭīn*. Haifa: Maktabat Kull Shay'.

Ṣāliḥ, Fakhrī (ed.). 1995. *al-Mu'aththirāt al-Ajnabiyya fī al-Shi'r al-'Arabī al-Mu'āṣir*. Beirut: al-Mu'assasa al-'Arabiyya li-l-Dirāsāt wa-l-Nashr.

Ṣāliḥ, Rushdī (ed.). 1982. *Bayram al-Tūnisī: Bayram wa-l-'Arab wa-l-'Ālam*. Cairo: al-Hay'a al-Miṣriyya al-'Āmma li-l-Kitāb.

Sālim, Kamāl Laṭīf. 1986. *Nāẓim al-Ghazālī: Safīr al-Ughniyya al-'Irāqiyya*. Baghdad: Manshūrāt Maktabat al-Ishtirākī.

Samad, Yunas. 1991. "Book Burning and Race Relations: Political Mobilisation of Bradford Muslims." *New Community* 18.4, pp. 507–19.

Samarīn, Rajā. 1990. *Shi'r al-Mar'a al-'Arabiyya al-Mu'āṣir*. Beirut: Dār al-Ḥadātha.

al-Sāmarrā'ī, Ibrāhīm. 1980. *Lughat al-Masraḥ Bayna Jīlayn*. Beirut: al-Mu'assasa al-Jāmi'iyya li-l-Dirāsāt wa-l-Nashr.

al-Samman, Hanadi. 2008. "Out of the Closet: Representation of Homosexuals and Lesbians in Modern Arabic Literature." *Journal of Arabic Literature* 39.2, pp. 270–310.

——. 2015. *Anxiety of Erasure: Trauma, Authorship, and the Diaspora in Arab Womens Writings*. Syracuse: Syracuse University Press.

——. and Tarek El-Ariss. 2013. "Queer Affects: Introduction." *International Journal of Middle East Studies* 45, pp. 205-209.

al-Sammān, Nabīl. 1989. *Hamazāt Shayṭāniyya wa-Salmān Rushdī*. Amman: Jam'iyyat A'māl al-Maṭābi' al-Ta'āwuniyya.

Sanaullah, Muhammad. 2010. "Symbolic Islamo-European Encounter in Prosody: *Muwashshaḥāt, Azjāl* and the Catalan Troubadours." *Islamic Studies* 49.3, pp. 357–400.

Ṣanāwī, Sa'dī. 1994. *Madkhal ilā 'Ilm Ijtimā' al-Adab*. Beirut: Dār al-Fikr al-'Arabī.

Sandel, Michael J. 2009. *Justice: What's the Right Thing To Do?* London: Penguin Books.

Sanni, Amidu. 1995. "Oriental Pearls from Southern Nigeria—Arabic-Islamic Scholarship in Yorubaland: A Case Study in Acculturation." *Islamic Studies* 34.4, pp. 427–50.

Sardar, Ziauddin and Merryl Wyn Davies. 1990. *Distorted Imagination: Lessons from the Rushdie Affair*. London: Grey Seal and Kuala Lumpur: Berita.

al-Sārīsī, 'Umar 'Abd al-Raḥmān. 1996. *Maqālāt fī al-Adab al-Islāmī*. Amman: Dār al-Furqān.

Ṣarrāf, Aḥmad Ḥāmid. 1960. *'Umar al-Khayyām*. Baghdād: Maṭba'at al-Ma'ārif.

Sa'ūd, Ṣā'ib. 1991. *al-Radd 'alā al-Murtadd Salmān Rushdī Shayṭān al-Ṣahāyina*. Tripoli (Lebanon): Jarrūs Press.

Sawā'ī, Muḥammad. 1999. *Azmat al-Muṣṭalaḥ al-'Arabī fī al-Qarn al-Tāsi' 'Ashar*. Beirut: Dār al-Gharb al-Islāmī.

Ṣawāyā, Mīkhā'īl. 1960. *Sulaymān al-Bustānī Rā'id al-Baḥth al-Adabī wa-l-Naqd al-Ḥadīth*. Beirut: Manshūrāt Dār al-Sharq al-Jadīd.

al-Ṣāwī, Muḥammad. 1990. *Sīnimā Yūsuf Shāhīn: Riḥla Aydiyūlūjiyya*. Alexandria: Dār al-Maṭbū'āt al-Jadīda.

Sayf, Muḥammad. 1986. *Ṣalāḥ Jāhīn wa-'Ālamuhu al-Shi'rī*. Cairo: Madbūlī.

al-Sayyāb, Badr Shākir. 1971. *Dīwān*. Beirut: Dār al-'Awda.

al-Sayyid, Sharīfa. 1999. Interview with 'Abd al-Wahhāb al-Bayyātī. *Barīd al-Janūb*, 21 February, pp. 14–15.

al-Sayyid-Marsot, Afaf Lutfi (ed.). 1979. *Society and the Sexes in Medieval Islam*. Malibu, CA: Undena Publications.

Sazzad, Rehnuma. 2013. "'Life Would Be a Meaningless Game and a Bad Joke' without

Freedom: Naguib Mahfouz as an Oppositional Writer." *Middle East Journal of Culture and Communication* 6.2, pp. 194–212.
Schacht, Joseph and C. E. Bosworth (eds). 1979. *The Legacy of Islam*. Oxford: Oxford University Press.
Schami, Rafik. 1987. *Erzähler der Nacht*. Weinheim and Basel: Beltz.
——. 1989. *Eine Hand Voller Sterne*. Weinheim and Basel: Beltz.
——. 1993. *Damascus Nights* (trans. Philip Boehm). New York: Farrar, Straus and Giroux.
——. 1995. *Reise zwischen Nacht und Morgen*. Munich: Carl Hanser Verlag.
——. 1996. *A Hand Full of Stars* (Hebrew) (trans. Daphna Amit). Tel Aviv: Schocken.
——. 2004. *Die dunkle Seite der Liebe*. Munich: Carl Hanser Verlag.
——. 2009. *The Dark Side of Love* (trans. Anthea Bell). Northampton: Interlink Books.
——. 2010. *The Calligrapher's Secret* (trans. Anthea Bell). London: Arabia.
Schildgen, Brenda Deen et al. (eds). 2006. *Other Renaissances: A New Approach to World Literature*. New York: Palgrave Macmillan.
Schimmel, Annemarie. 1982. *As Through a Veil: Mystical Poetry in Islam*. New York: Columbia University Press.
Schmitt, Arno. 2001–2. "*Liwāṭ* in *Fiqh*: Männliche Homosexualität?" *Journal of Arabic and Islamic Studies* 4, pp. 49–110.
——. and Jehoeda Sofer (eds). 1992. *Sexuality and Eroticism among Males in Moslem Societies*. New York: Harrington Park Press.
Schoeler, Gregor. 2009. *The Genesis of Literature in Islam: From the Aural to the Read* (trans. Shawkat Toorawa). Edinburgh: Edinburgh University Press.
Sebeok, Thomas A. (ed.). 1986. *Encyclopedic Dictionary of Semiotics*. Berlin: Mouton.
Seigneurie, Ken (ed.). 2003. *Crisis and Memory: The Representation of Space in Modern Levantine Narrative*. Wiesbaden: Reichert Verlag.
——. 2012. "Discourses of the 2011 Arab Revolutions." *Journal of Arabic Literature* 43.2–3, pp. 484–509.
Selim, Samah. 2003. "The Narrative Craft: Realism and Fiction in the Arabic Canon." *Edebiyât* 14.1–2, pp. 109–28.
——. 2004. "The *Nahdah*, Popular Fiction and the Politics of Translation." *MIT Electronic Journal of Middle East Studies* 4.2, pp. 71–89.
——. 2004a. *The Novel and the Rural Imaginary in Egypt, 1880–1985*. London: RoutledgeCurzon.
——. 2006. "The People's Entertainment: Translation, Popular Fiction, and the Nahdah in Egypt." In Brenda Deen Schildgen et al. (eds), *Other Renaissances: A New Approach to World Literature*, pp. 35–58. New York: Palgrave Macmillan.
——. 2010. "Fiction and Colonial Identities: Arsène Lupin in Arabic." *Middle Eastern Literatures* 13.2, pp. 191–210.
——. 2011. "Theory and Arabic Literature in the United States." *International Journal of Middle East Studies* 43.4, pp. 722–4.
——. 2011a. "Toward a New Literary History." *International Journal of Middle East Studies* 43.4, pp. 734–6.
Semaan, Khalil I. 1980. *Islam and the Medieval West*. Albany: State University of New York Press.
Semah, David. 1974. *Four Egyptian Literary Critics*. Leiden: Brill.
——. 1988. "Jawla fī Baḥr al-Basīṭ." *al-Karmil—Abḥāth fī al-Lugha wa-l-Adab* 9, pp. 49–73.
——. 1990. "al-ʿArūḍ fī al-Shiʿr Ghayr al-Muʿrab." *al-Karmil—Abḥāth fī al-Lugha wa-l-Adab* 11, pp. 93–127.
——. 1991. "Dirāsa fī al-Shiʿr al-ʿĀmmī al-Miṣrī." *al-Karmil—Abḥāth fī al-Lugha wa-l-Adab* 12, pp. 153–61.
——. 1991a. "On the Metre of Bedouin Poetry." *Asian and African Studies* 25, pp. 187–200.

——. 1992. "al-Shiʿr al-ʿĀmmī al-Lubnānī wa-l-Filasṭīnī wa-Mushkilat al-Awzān." *al-Karmil—Abḥāth fī al-Lugha wa-l-Adab* 13, pp. 95–143.
——. 1995. *Karmiliyyāt: Dirāsāt fī Ashkāl al-Shiʿr al-ʿArabī wa-Awzānihi*. Nazareth: Wizārat al-Maʿārif wa-l-Thaqāfa.
Sennett, Richard (ed.). 1969. *Classical Essays in the Culture of Cities*. New York: Appleton-Century-Crofts.
Sfeir, George N. 1998. "Basic Freedoms in Fractured Legal Culture: Egypt and the Case of Nasr Hamid Abu Zayd." *Middle East Journal* 52.3, pp. 402–14.
Shaʿbān, Buthayna. 1993. "al-Riwāya al-Nisāʾiyya al-ʿArabiyya." *Mawāqif* 70–1, pp. 211–34.
——. 1999. *100 ʿĀm min al-Riwāya al-Nisāʾiyya al-ʿArabiyya (1899–1999)*. Beirut: Dār al-Ādāb.
Shabkashī, ʿAbd al-Majīd. 1936. "al-Ḥayāt al-Adabiyya fī al-Ḥijāz." *al-Risāla*, 13 April, pp. 586–7.
Shablūl, Aḥmad Faḍl. 1998. *Adab al-Aṭfāl fī al-Waṭan al-ʿArabī*. Alexandria: Dār al-Wafāʾ li-Dunyā al-Ṭibāʿa wa-l-Nashr.
——. 1999. *Taknūlūjiyā Adab al-Aṭfāl*. Alexandria: Dār al-Wafāʾ li-Dunyā al-Ṭibāʿa wa-l-Nashr.
Shafer, Boyd C. 1955. *Nationalism*. New York: Harvest.
Shafik, Viola. 1998. *Arab Cinema: History and Cultural Identity*. Cairo: The American University in Cairo Press.
——. 2007. *Popular Egyptian Cinema: Gender, Class and Nation*. Cairo: The American University in Cairo Press.
Shaheen, Mohammed. 2001. "Tayeb Salih: There Is a Much Wider Potential Readership for Arabic Literature Than Publishers Are Prepared to Admit." *Banipal* 10.11, pp. 82–5.
Shahīd, Irfan. 1984. *Byzantum and the Arabs in the Fourth Century*. Washington, DC: Dumbarton Oaks Research Library and Collection.
——. 2000. "Gibran and the American Literary Canon: The Problem of *The Prophet*." In Kamal Abdel-Malek and Wael Hallaq (eds), *Tradition, Modernity, and Postmodernity in Arabic Literature: Essays in Honor of Professor Issa J. Boullata*, pp. 321–34. Leiden: Brill.
al-Shāhir, ʿAbd Allāh. 1997. *Muẓaffar al-Nawwāb: Malāmiḥ wa-Mumayyizāt*. Damascus: n.pub.
Shākir, Tahānī ʿAbd al-Fattāḥ. 2002. *al-Sīra al-Dhātiyya fī al-Adab al-ʿArabī: Fadwā Ṭūqān wa-Jabrā Ibrāhīm Jabrā wa-Iḥsān ʿAbbās Namūdhajan*. Beirut: al-Muʾassasa al-ʿArabiyya li-l-Dirāsāt wa-l-Nashr.
Shalabī, Najwā. 1990. "Āfāq Jadīda fī Maʿriḍ Būlūnyā al-Dawlī li-Kutub al-Aṭfāl." *Ibdāʿ*, May, pp. 146–50.
Shaʿlān, Ibrāhīm Aḥmad. 1993. *al-Nawādir al-Shaʿbiyya al-Miṣriyya: Dirāsa Taʾrīkhiyya Ijtimāʿiyya*. Cairo: Madbūlī.
al-Shamʿa, Khaldūn. 1989. "Ḥawla al-Narjasiyya al-Quṭriyya." *al-Dustūr* (London), 5 June, p. 78.
Shāmī, Rafīq. 1997. *Yad Milʾuhā al-Nujūm* (trans. [from English] Marsel Sagiv). Tel Aviv: Schocken.
Shamma, Tarek. 2005. "The Exotic Dimension of Foreignizing Strategies: Burton's Translation of the *Arabian Nights*." *Translator: Studies in Intercultural Communication* 11.1, pp. 51–67.
——. 2016. "Arabic Literature in Translation: Politics and Poetics." *CLINA: An Interdisciplinary Journal of Translation, Interpreting and Intercultural Communication* 2.1, pp. 7–11.
Shammās, Anton. 1979. *No Man's Land* (Hebrew). Tel Aviv: Hakibutz Hameuḥad.
——. 1986. *Arabesques* (Hebrew). Tel Aviv: Am Oved.
——. 1988. *Arabesques* (trans. Vivian Eden). London: Viking.

——. 1992. Introduction to a Special Issue on the Middle East, *Michigan Quarterly Review* 31.4 (Fall), pp. 453–6.
Shammās, Mūrīs. 2003. *'Azza, Ḥafīdat Nefertiti*. Shfaram: Dār al-Mashriq.
Shapira, Yael et al. (eds). 2007. *Popular and Canonical: Literary Dialogues* (Hebrew). Tel Aviv: Resling.
al-Shaqīfī, Sāmī. 1936. "al-Ḥayāt al-Adabiyya fī Lubnān." *al-Risāla*, 6 April, pp. 540–1.
Sharabi (Sharābī), Hisham. 1970. *Arab Intellectuals and the West: The Formative Years, 1875–1914*. Baltimore: The Johns Hopkins University Press.
——. 1988. *Neopatriarchy: A Theory of Distorted Change in Arab Society*. New York: Oxford University Press.
——. 1993. "al-Muthaqqafūn al-'Arab wa-l-Gharb fī Nihāyat al-Qarn al-'Ishrīn." *al-Mustaqbal*, September, pp. 29–35.
——. 2008. *Embers and Ashes: Memoirs of an Arab Intellectual* (trans. Issa J. Boullata). Northampton, MA: Olive Branch Press.
Sharaf, 'Abd al-'Azīz. 1992. *Adab al-Sīra al-Dhātiyya*. Cairo: al-Sharika al-Miṣriyya al-'Ālamiyya li-l-Nashr—Longman and Maktabat Lubnān.
Sharāra, Waḍḍāḥ. 1995. "Ḥarb 'alā al-Riwāya." In *al-'Unf al-Uṣūlī: Muwājahāt al-Sayf wa-l-Qalam*, pp. 59–80. London and Beirut: Riyāḍ al-Rayyis.
Sharfuddin, Mohammed. 1994. *Islam and Romantic Orientalism*. London: I. B. Tauris.
Sharīf, Nihād. 1981. *al-Ladhī Taḥaddā al-I'ṣār*. Cairo: al-Hay'a al-Miṣriyya al-'Āmma li-l-Kitāb.
——. 1989. *al-Shay'*. Cairo: al-Hay'a al-Miṣriyya al-'Āmma li-l-Kitāb.
Sharkey, Heather. 2004. "Christian Missionaries and Colloquial Arabic Printing." In P. C. Sadgrove (ed.), *History of Printing and Publishing in the Languages and Countries of the Middle East*, pp. 131–49. Oxford: Oxford University Press.
al-Sharqawī, 'Abd al-Raḥmān. 1968 [1953]. *al-Arḍ*. Cairo: Dār al-Kātib al-'Arabī li-l-Ṭibā'a wa-l-Nashr.
al-Sharqawi, Abdel Rahman. 1990 [1962]. *Egyptian Earth* (trans. D. Stewart). Austin: University of Texas Press.
al-Shārūnī, Yūsuf. 1980. "al-Khayāl al-'Ilmī fī al-Adab al-'Arabī." *'Ālam al-Fikr*, October–December, pp. 243–76.
——. 1990. *Fī al-Adab al-'Ummānī al-Ḥadīth*. London: Riyāḍ al-Rayyis.
——. 1990a. *A'lām min 'Ummān*. London: Riyāḍ al-Rayyis.
Shavit, Yaacov. 1996. "Supplying a Missing System: Between Official and Unofficial Popular Culture in the Hebrew National Culture in Eretz-Israel" (Hebrew). In Benjamin Z. Kedar (ed.), *Studies in the History of Popular Culture* (Hebrew), pp. 327–45. Jerusalem: The Zalman Shazar Center for Jewish History.
Shaw, George Bernard. 1954. *Back to Methuselah*. Harmondsworth: Penguin Books.
Shawqī, Aḥmad. n.d. *al-Shawqiyyāt*. Cairo: n.pub.
——. 1982. *Dīwān al-Nahḍa*. Beirut: Dār al-'Ilm li-l-Malāyīn.
——. 1984. *Dīwān Shawqī li-l-Aṭfāl*. Cairo: Dār al-Ma'ārif.
al-Shayyāl, Jamāl al-Dīn. 1950. *Ta'rīkh al-Tarjama fī Miṣr fī 'Ahd al-Ḥamla al-Faransiyya*. Cairo: Dār al-Fikr al-'Arabī.
——. 1951. *Ta'rīkh al-Tarjama wa-l-Ḥaraka al-Thaqāfiyya fī Miṣr fī 'Aṣr Muḥammad 'Alī*. Cairo: Dār al-Fikr al-'Arabī.
Shechter, Relli (ed.). 2003. *Transitions in Domestic Consumption and Family Life in the Modern Middle East: Houses in Motion*. Basingstoke: Palgrave Macmillan.
——. 2004. "From Journalism to Promotion of Goods: Why and How Did Press Publishers Establish Advertising Agencies in Egypt, 1890–1939?" In P. C. Sadgrove (ed.), *History of Printing and Publishing in the Languages and Countries of the Middle East*, pp. 179–90. Oxford: Oxford University Press.
——. 2006. *Smoking, Culture and Economy in the Middle East: The Egyptian Tobacco Market 1850–2000*. London: I. B. Tauris.

al-Sheddi, Baker. 1997. *The Roots of Arabic Theatre*. PhD thesis, University of Durham.

Sheehi, Stephen. 2004. *Foundations of Modern Arab Identity*. Gainesville, FL: University Press of Florida.

——. 2012. "Toward a Critical Theory of *al-Nahḍah*: Epistemology, Ideology and Capital." *Journal of Arabic Literature* 43.2-3, pp. 269–98.

Sheetrit, Ariel M. 2012. "The Poetics of the Poet's Autobiography: Voicings and Mutings in Fadwā Ṭūqān's Narrative Journey." *Journal of Arabic Literature* 43.1, pp. 102–31.

Sheffy, Raqefet. 1996. "The Image of 'The Popular' as Manipulation by Elite Culture: The Late 18th-Century German 'Trivialroman' as a Literary Problem" (Hebrew). In Benjamin Z. Kedar (ed.), *Studies in the History of Popular Culture* (Hebrew), pp. 225–43. Jerusalem: The Zalman Shazar Center for Jewish History.

Shenberg, Galia. 1998. "Diglossia and Bilingualism: Storytelling by Druze Women" (Hebrew). *'Iyyun ve-Mehkar be-Hachsharat Morim* (Gordon College, Haifa) 21, pp. 21-29.

Shepard, William E. 2014. "Satanic Verses and the Death of God: Salmān Rushdie and Najīb Maḥfūẓ." In Maribel Fierro (ed.), *Orthodoxy and Heresy in Islam*, pp. 55–73. London: Routledge.

al-Shidyāq, Aḥmad Fāris. 1855. *al-Sāq 'alā al-Sāq fī mā Huwa al-Fāryāq*. Paris: Benjamin Duprat.

——. 2014. *Leg Over Leg or The Turtle in the Tree: Concerning the Fāryāq, What Manner of Creature Might He Be* (ed. and trans. Humphrey Davies). New York and London: New York University Press.

Shihāb, Usāma Yūsuf. 1985. *Naḥwa Adab Islāmī Mu'āṣir*. Amman: Dār al-Bashīr.

Shiḥāta, Ḥasan. 1991. *Adab al-Ṭifl al-'Arabī*. Cairo: al-Dār al-Miṣriyya al-Lubnāniyya.

——. 1994. *Adab al-Ṭifl al-'Arabī* (2nd ed.). Cairo: al-Dār al-Miṣriyya al-Lubnāniyya.

——. 1996. *Qirā'āt li-l-Aṭfāl*. Cairo: al-Dār al-Miṣriyya al-Lubnāniyya.

Shiḥāta, Muḥammad. 1993. "al-Ibdā' al-Grāfikī wa-Mut'at al-Qirā'a fī Kutub al-Aṭfāl." *'Ālam al-Kitāb*, October, pp. 18–23.

Shiloah, Amnon. 1995. *Music in the World of Islam: A Socio-Cultural Study*. Aldershot: Scolar Press.

al-Shirbīnī, Yūsuf. 2005. *Kitab Hazz al-Quhūf bi-Sharḥ Qaṣīd Abī Shādūf* (*Brains Confounded by the Ode of Abū Shādūf Expounded*) (Vol. 1) (ed. Humphrey Davies). Dudley, MA: Peeters.

——. 2007. *Yusuf al-Shirbini's Brains Confounded by the Ode of Abū Shādūf Expounded* (*Kitab Hazz al-Quhūf bi-Sharḥ Qaṣīd Abī Shādūf*) (Vol. 2) (trans. Humphrey Davies). Dudley, MA: Peeters.

Shitrit-Sasson, Sharon. 2015. *Between the Wild Thorns and the Sunflower: Personal Identity and National Identity in the Writings of the Palestinian Female Authors Fadwā Ṭūqān and Saḥar Khalīfa* (Hebrew). Tel Aviv: Resling.

Shklovsky, Victor. 1965. "Art as Technique." In Lee T. Lemon and Marion J. Reis (eds), *Russian Formalist Criticism*, pp. 3–24. Lincoln, NE: University of Nebraska Press.

Shohat, Ella (ed.). 1998. *Talking Visions: Multicultural Feminism in a Transnational Age*. New York: New Museum of Contemporary Art and Cambridge, MA: The MIT Press.

Shohet, Nir. 1982. *The Story of an Exile—A Short History of the Jews of Iraq* (ed. and trans. Abraham Zilkha). Tel Aviv: The Association for the Promotion of Research, Literature and Art.

Shoshan, Boaz. 1993. *Popular Culture in Medieval Cairo*. Cambridge: Cambridge University Press.

Shraybom-Shivtiel, Shlomit. 1995. "The Role of the Colloquial in the Renaissance of Standard Arabic." *Israel Oriental Studies* 15, pp. 207–15.

——. 2005. *The Renaissance of the Arabic Language and the Idea of Nationalism in Egypt* (Hebrew). Jerusalem: Magnes Press.

Shuiskii, Sergei A. 1982. "Some Observations on Modern Arabic Autobiography." *Journal of Arabic Literature* 13, pp. 111–23.

Shukrī, Ghālī. 1972. "al-Mufakkir Rāqiṣan 'alā Birmīl min al-Bārūd." *al-Ṭalī'a*, July, pp. 176–9.

——. 1978 [1968]. *Shi'runā al-Ḥadīth... Ilā Ayna?* Beirut: Dār al-Āfāq al-Jadīda.

——. 1989. *Burj Bābil: al-Naqd wa-l-Ḥadātha al-Sharīda*. London: Riyāḍ al-Rayyis.

——. 1991. *Azmat al-Jins fī al-Qiṣṣa al-'Arabiyya*. Beirut and Cairo: Dār al-Shurūq.

——. 1992. *Aqni'at al-Irhāb: al-Baḥth 'an 'Almāniyya Jadīda*. Cairo: al-Hay'a al-Miṣriyya al-'Āmma li-l-Kitāb.

——. 1993. "Dhākirat al-Umma." *al-Ahrām*, 9 June, p. 14.

——. 1994. "Bal Thaqāfa Wāḥida wa-Thaqāfāt Muta'addida." *al-Ahrām*, 30 March, p. 11.

——. 1994a. *al-Khurūj 'alā al-Naṣṣ: Taḥaddiyāt al-Thaqāfa wa-l-Dīmuqrāṭiyya*. Cairo: Sīnā li-l-Nashr.

Shūmān, Muḥammad Zīnū. 1994. "Amīn Ma'lūf wa-l-Kūmīdyā al-Ilāhiyya." *al-Bilād*, 26 March, p. 41.

Shuraydi, Hasan. 2014. *The Raven and the Falcon: Youth versus Old Age in Medieval Arabic Literature*. Leiden and Boston: Brill.

Shusterman, Richard. 1992. *Pragmatist Aesthetics: Living Beauty, Rethinking Art*. Oxford: Blackwell.

——. 1993. "Don't Believe the Hype: Animadversions on the Critique of Popular Art." *Poetics Today* 14.1, pp. 101–22.

——. 1993a. "Too Legit To Quit? Popular Art and Legitimation." *Iyyun: The Jerusalem Philosophical Quarterly* 42, pp. 215–24.

——. 2000. *Performing Live: Aesthetic Alternatives for the Ends of Art*. Ithaca: Cornell University Press.

al-Sibā'ī, Yūsuf. 1952. *al-Saqqā Māt*. Cairo: al-Khānijī.

Siddiq, Muhammad. 1992. "Partial Theory: A Review of Sasson Somekh's *Genre and Language in Modern Arabic Literature*." *al-'Arabiyya* 25, pp. 97–105.

——. 2007. *Arab Culture and the Novel: Gender, Identity, and Agency in Egyptian Fiction*. London and New York: Routledge.

Silverberg, Robert. 1983. *The Nebula Awards Stories Eighteen*. San Diego: Science Fiction Writers of America.

——. (ed.). 1986. *Qiṣaṣ min al-Khayāl al-'Ilmī* (trans. Fatḥī 'Abd al-Fattāḥ). Cairo: Maktabat Gharīb.

Singer, Milton. 1972. *When a Great Tradition Modernizes: An Anthropological Approach to Indian Civilization*. New York: Praeger Publishers.

Sinno, Nadine. 2011. "From Confinement to Creativity: Women's Reconfiguration of the Prison and Mental Asylum in Salwa Bakr's *The Golden Chariot* and Fadia Faqir's *Pillars of Salt*." *Journal of Arabic Literature* 42.1, pp. 67–94.

Slyomovics, Susan. 1986. "Arabic Folk Literature and Political Expression." *Arab Studies Quarterly* 8, pp. 178–85.

——. 1987. *The Merchant of Art: An Egyptian Hilali Oral Epic Poet in Performance*. Berkeley: University of California Press.

——. 1991. "'To Put One's Fingers in the Bleeding Wound': Palestinian Theatre under Israeli Censorship." *The Drama Review* 35.2, pp. 18–38.

——. 1992. "Algeria Caricatures the Gulf War." *Public Culture* 4.2, pp. 93–9.

——. 1993. "Cartoon Commentary: Algerian and Moroccan Caricatures from the Gulf War." *Middle East Report* 23.1, pp. 21–4.

——. 1994. "Performing *A Thousand and One Nights* in Egypt." *Oral Tradition* 9.2, pp. 390–419.

——. 2001. "Sex, Lies, and Television: Algerian and Moroccan Caricatures of the Gulf War." In Suad Joseph and Susan Slyomovics (eds), *Women and Power in the Middle East*, pp. 72–98. Philadelphia: University of Pennsylvania Press.

——. 2014. "Algerian Women's Būqālah Poetry: Oral Literature, Cultural Politics, and Anti-Colonial Resistance." *Journal of Arabic Literature* 45.2–3, pp. 145–68.

Smart, J. R. (ed.). 1996. *Tradition and Modernity in Arabic Language and Literature*. Richmond: Curzon.

Smolin, Jonathan. 2007. *Moroccan Noir: The Genesis of the Arabic Police Procedural*. PhD thesis, Harvard University.

Snir, Reuven. 1984. "Sufi Elements in Modern Arabic Poetry and the Role of the Egyptian Poet Ṣalāḥ 'Abd al-Ṣabūr." *Bulletin of the Israeli Academic Center in Cairo* 5, pp. 12–13.

——. 1985. "Ṣūfiyya bi-lā Taṣawwuf Islāmī: Qirā'a Jadīda fī Qaṣīdat Ṣalāḥ 'Abd al-Ṣabūr 'al-Ilāh al-Ṣaghīr.'" *al-Karmil—Abḥāth fī al-Lugha wa-l-Adab* 6, pp. 129–46.

——. 1986. *Sufi Elements in Modern Arabic Poetry 1940–1980* (Hebrew). PhD thesis, The Hebrew University of Jerusalem.

——. 1986a. *Anthology of Ascetic, Mystic and Metaphysical Arabic Poetry from the 8th Century to Our Days*. Jerusalem: Academon.

——. 1988. "Cultural Changes as Reflected in Literature: The Beginning of the Arabic Short Story by Jewish Authors in Iraq" (Hebrew). *Pe'amim* 36, pp. 108–29.

——. 1989. "The Arab–Israeli Conflict as Reflected in the Writing of Najīb Maḥfūẓ." *Abr-Nahrain* 27, pp. 120–53.

——. 1989a. "Human Existence according to Kafka and Ṣalāḥ 'Abd al-Ṣabūr." *Jusūr* 5, pp. 31–43.

——. 1990. "'A Wound Out of his Wounds': Palestinian Arabic Literature in Israel" (Hebrew). *Alpayim* 2, pp. 244–68.

——. 1991. "'We Were Like Those Who Dream': Iraqi-Jewish Writers in Israel in the 1950s." *Prooftexts* 11, pp. 153–73.

——. 1991a. "Figliastri pieni d'amore: Scrittori arabi in lingua ebraica." *La Rassegna Mensile di Israel* 57.1–2, pp. 245–53.

——. 1991b. "Achilles' Heel or Narcissus' Reflection?" (Hebrew). *Alpayim* 4, pp. 202–5.

——. 1992. "'al-Zayt fī al-Miṣbāḥ Lan Yajiffa': Jadaliyyat al-Burj al-'Ājī'/al-Manāra fī Mir'āt al-Shi'r al-Multazim." *al-Karmil—Abḥāth fī al-Lugha wa-l-Adab* 13, pp. 7–54.

——. 1992a. "Neo-Sufism in the Writing of the Egyptian Poet Salah 'Abd As-Sabur." *Sufi: A Journal of Sufism* 13, pp. 24–6.

——. 1992b. "Step-Sons and Lovers" (Hebrew). *Moznaim*, May, pp. 6–9.

——. 1992c. "Arabic Literature in Syria between Distinctiveness and Unity" (Hebrew). *Moznaim*, December, pp. 61–4.

——. 1993. "al-'Anāṣir al-Masraḥiyya fī al-Turāth al-Sha'bī al-'Arabī al-Qadīm" (review article of Moreh 1992). *al-Karmil—Abḥāth fī al-Lugha wa-l-Adab* 14, pp. 149–70.

——. 1993a. "The Inscription of 'En 'Abdat: An Early Evolutionary Stage of Ancient Arabic Poetry." *Abr Nahrain* 31, pp. 110–25.

——. 1993b. "The Poetic Creative Process according to Ṣalāḥ 'Abd al-Ṣabūr." In Ami Elad (ed.), *Writer, Culture, Text: Studies in Modern Arabic Literature*, pp. 74–88. Fredericton: York Press.

——. 1993c. "'Limādhā Tunfā al-Kalimāt?': al-Shā'ir wa-Ṣakhratuhu fī Mir'āt al-Shi'r al-Multazim." *al-Karmil—Abḥāth fī al-Lugha wa-l-Adab* 14, pp. 49–93.

——. 1993d. "Original and Translation on the Contact Line" (Hebrew). In Sasson Somekh (ed.), *Translation as a Challenge: Papers on Translation of Arabic Literature into Hebrew* (Hebrew), pp. 21–39. Tel Aviv: Tel Aviv University Press.

——. 1993e. "al-Adīb Muharrijan: Mulāḥazāt Ḥawla Dawr al-Adīb al-Filasṭīnī fī al-Ḥalba al-Thaqāfiyya al-Isrā'īliyya." *Mawāqif* (Haifa and Nazereth), March–April, pp. 52–61.

——. 1993f. "al-Tanāfur al-Ma'rifī fī Thaqāfat al-Aghlabiyya Izā' Thaqāfat al-Aqalliyya fī Isrā'īl." *Filasṭīn al-Thawra*, 16 May, pp. 28–9.

——. 1993g. "The Beginnings of Political Palestinian Theatre: *Qaraqāsh* by Samīḥ al-Qāsim" (Hebrew). *HaMizrah HeHadash* 35, pp. 129–47.

——. 1994. "Adab, Ta'rīkh, wa-Ta'rīkh al-Adab." *al-Karmil—Abḥāth fī al-Lugha wa-l-Adab* 15, pp. 61–85.
——. 1994a. "The 'World Upsidedown' in Modern Arabic Literature: New Literary Renditions of an Antique Religious Topos." *Edebiyât* 5.1, pp. 51–75.
——. 1994b. "'Under the Patronage of Muḥammad': Islamic Motifs in the Poetry of Jewish Writers from Iraq" (Hebrew). In Tamar Alexander et al. (eds), *History and Creativity in the Sephardi and Oriental Jewish Communities* (Hebrew), pp. 161–93. Jerusalem: Misgav Yerushalayim.
——. 1994c. "Arabic Literature in the Twentieth Century: An Historical Dynamic Functional Model" (Hebrew). *HaMizrah HeHadash* 36, pp. 49–80.
——. 1994d. "A Study of *Elegy for al-Ḥallāj* by Adūnīs." *Journal of Arabic Literature* 25.2, pp. 245–56.
——. 1994e. "The Arabic Literature of Babylonian Jewry." *The Scribe* 62, September, p. 23.
——. 1994f. Review Essay of Kazzaz 1991, *The Jewish Quarterly Review* 34.4, pp. 487–93.
——. 1994–5. "Mysticism and Poetry in Arabic Literature." *Orientalia Suecana* 43–4, pp. 165–75.
——. 1995. "'Hebrew as the Language of Grace': Arab-Palestinian Writers in Hebrew." *Prooftexts* 15, pp. 163–83.
——. 1995a. "Palestinian Theatre: Historical Development and Contemporary Distinctive Identity." *Contemporary Theatre Review* 3.2, pp. 29–73.
——. 1995b. "The Image of the Jew in Modern Arabic Culture" (Hebrew). *Moznaim*, January 1995, pp. 32–4.
——. 1995c. "Arabic Literature of Iraqi Jews: The Dynamics of the Jewish Cultural System and the Relationship with the Arabic Cultural System" (Hebrew). *Miqqedem Umiyyam* 6, pp. 255–88.
——. 1995d. "Jewish–Muslim Relations in the Literature and Periodicals of Iraqi Jewry" (Hebrew). *Pe'amim* 63, pp. 5–40.
——. 1995e. "Bawākīr al-Masraḥ al-Siyāsī al-Filasṭīnī: Samīḥ al-Qāsim wa-Masraḥiyyat *Qaraqāsh*." In Ṭāriq Rajab (ed.), *Mutāba'āt Naqdiyya fī Adab Samīḥ al-Qāsim*, pp. 63–103. Haifa: al-Wādī li-l-Ṭibā'a wa-l-Nashr.
——. 1995f. "Neo-Sufism in Modern Arabic Poetry." *Sufi: A Journal of Sufism* 27, pp. 23–7.
——. 1996. "'Armed with Roses and Sweet Basil: The Emergence of Feminist Culture in the Arab World" (Hebrew). *Motar: Journal of the Yolanada and David Katz Faculty of the Arts, Tel Aviv University* 4, pp. 65–72.
——. 1996a. "Palestinian Theatre as a Junction of Cultures: The Case of Samīḥ al-Qāsim's *Qaraqāsh*." *Journal of Theatre and Drama* 2, pp. 101–20.
——. 1996b. "The Arabic Literary System in Syria in the Modern Period" (Hebrew). *HaMizrah HeHadash* 38, pp. 165–82.
——. 1997. "'And I Hallucinate in No-Man's Land': Arab-Palestinian Writers in Hebrew" (Hebrew). *Hebrew Linguistics* 41–2, pp. 141–53.
——. 1997a. "Zionism as Reflected in Arabic and Hebrew Belles Lettres of Iraqi Jewry" (Hebrew). *Pe'amim* 73, pp. 128–46.
——. 1997–8. "'Gharīqan fī al-Nūr': Qirā'a fī Qaṣīdat 'Nār al-Shi'r' by 'Abd al-Wahhāb al-Bayyātī." *al-Karmil—Studies in Arabic Language and Literature* 18–19, pp. 199–230.
——. 1998. "Synchronic and Diachronic Dynamics in Modern Arabic Literature." In Shimon Ballas and Reuven Snir (eds), *Studies in Canonical and Popular Arabic Literature*, pp. 87–121. Toronto: York Press.
——. 1998a. "Intersecting Circles between Hebrew and Arabic Literature" (Hebrew). In Yosef Tobi (ed.), *Contacts between Arabic Literature and Jewish Literature in the Middle Ages and Modern Times* (Vol. 1) (Hebrew), pp. 177–210. Tel Aviv: Afikim.

——. 1998b. "The Palestinian al-Ḥakawati Theater: A Brief History." *Arab Studies Journal* 6.2–7.1, pp. 57–71.
——. 1999. "Virginia Woolf in Arabic Literature: Translations, Influence, and Reception." *Virginia Woolf Miscellany* 54, pp. 6–7.
——. 2000. "The Emergence of Science Fiction in Arabic Literature." *Der Islam* 77.2, pp. 263–85.
——. 2000a. "Modern Arabic Literature and the West: Self-Image, Interference, and Reception." *Yearbook of Comparative and General Literature* 48, pp. 53–71.
——. 2000b. "'Al-Andalus Arising from Damascus': Al-Andalus in Modern Arabic Poetry." *Hispanic Issues* 21, pp. 263–93.
——. 2000c. "Between Reality and Utopia: Images of Arab Leaders in Modern Arabic Literature" (Hebrew). *HaMizrah HeHadash* 41, pp. 171–88.
——. 2001. *Modern Arabic Literature: A Functional Dynamic Historical Model.* Toronto: York Press.
——. 2001a. "'Postcards in the Morning': Palestinians Writing in Hebrew." *Hebrew Studies* 42, pp. 197–224.
——. 2002. *Rak'atān fī al-'Ishq: Dirāsa fī Shi'r 'Abd al-Wahhāb al-Bayyātī.* Beirut: Dār al-Sāqī.
——. 2002a. "'My Heart Beats with Love of the Arabs': Iraqi Jews Writing in Arabic in the Twentieth Century." *Journal of Modern Jewish Studies* 1.2, pp. 182–203.
——. 2002b. "Science Fiction in Arabic Literature: Translation, Adaptation, Original Writing and Canonization," *Arabic Language & Literature* (Seoul) 2, pp. 209–29.
——. 2004. "'Forget Baghdad!': The Clash of Literary Narratives among Iraqi Jews in Israel." *Orientalia Suecana* 53, pp. 143–63.
——. 2004–5. "'Will Homer Be Born after Us?': Intertextuality and Myth in Maḥmūd Darwīsh's Poetry in the 1980s." *al-Karmil—Studies in Arabic Language and Literature* 25–6, pp. 17–85 (English part).
——. 2005. "Arabic Literature by Iraqi Jews in the Twentieth Century: The Case of Ishaq Bar-Moshe (1927–2003)." *Middle Eastern Studies* 41.1, pp. 7–29.
——. 2005a. *Arabness, Jewishness, Zionism: A Struggle of Identities in the Literature of Iraqi Jews* (Hebrew). Jerusalem: Ben-Zvi Institute.
——. 2005b. "The Emergence of Palestinian Professional Theatre after 1967: al-Balālīn Self-Reference Play *al-'Atma* (The Darkness)." *Theatre Survey* 46.1, pp. 5–29.
——. 2005c. *Palestinian Theatre.* Wiesbaden: Reichert Verlag.
——. 2005d. "Jews as Arabs: The State of the Art" (Hebrew). *Ruaḥ Mizraḥit* 2, pp. 9–17.
——. 2005e. "'We Are Arabs before We Are Jews': The Emergence and Demise of Arab-Jewish Culture in Modern Times." *EJOS—Electronic Journal of Oriental Studies* 8, pp. 1–47.
——. 2005f. "'When the Time Stopped': Ishaq Bar-Moshe as Arab-Jewish Writer in Israel." *Jewish Social Studies* 11.2, pp. 102–35.
——. 2006. *Religion, Mysticism and Modern Arabic Literature.* Wiesbaden: Harrassowitz Verlag.
——. 2006a. "Arabic in the Service of Regeneration of Jews: The Participation of Jews in Arabic Press and Journalism in the 19th and 20th Centuries." *Acta Orientalia* (Budapest) 59, pp. 283–323.
——. 2006b. "Arabness, Egyptianess, Zionism, and Cosmopolitanism: The Arabic Cultural and Journalistic Activities of Egyptian Jews in the 19th and 20th Centuries." *Orientalia Suecana* 55, pp. 133–64.
——. 2006c. "'Arabs of the Mosaic Faith': Chronicle of a Cultural Extinction Foretold." *Die Welt des Islams* 46.1, pp. 43–60.
——. 2006d. "'A Carbon Copy of Ibn al-Balad'?: The Participation of Egyptian Jews in Modern Arab Culture." *Archiv Orientální* 74, pp. 37–64.
——. 2006e. "'Arabs of the Mosaic Faith': Jewish Writers in Modern Iraq and the Clash of

Narratives after Their Immigration to Israel." In Andreas Pflitsch and Barbara Winckler (eds), *Poetry's Voice—Society's Norms: Forms of Interaction between Middle Eastern Writers and Their Societies*, pp. 147–71. Wiesbaden: Reichert.
——. 2006f. "From al-Samaw'al to Ibn al-Samaw'al: Modern Arab-Jewish Culture, Its Historical Background and Current Demise." *Acta Orientalia* (Oslo) 67, pp. 19–79.
——. 2006g. "'*Anā min al-Yahūd*': The Demise of Arab-Jewish Culture in the Twentieth Century." *Archiv Orientální* 74, pp. 387–424.
——. 2006h. "'Till Spring Comes': Arabic and Hebrew Literary Debates among Iraqi-Jews in Israel (1950–2000)." *Shofar—An Interdisciplinary Journal of Jewish Studies* 24.2, pp. 92–123.
——. 2006i. "Jewishness, Arabness and Egyptianness: The Participation of Egyptian Jews in Arabic Press and Journalism during the Nineteenth and Twentieth Centuries." *Australian Journal of Jewish Studies* 20, pp. 199–238.
——. 2006j. "'Do Not They and I Share a Common Source?': Modern Arab-Jewish Culture." *Journal of Oriental and African Studies* (Athens) 15, pp. 37–82.
——. 2006k. "'Religion is for God, the Fatherland is for Everyone': Arab-Jewish Writers in Modern Iraq and the Clash of Narratives after Their Immigration to Israel." *Journal of the American Oriental Society* 126.3, pp. 379–99.
——. 2006l. "My Childhood Blossomed on the Waters of the Tigris": The Arabic Literature of Iraqi Jews in the 20th Century." *Bulletin of the Royal Institute for Inter-Faith Studies* (Amman) 8.1–8.2, pp. 29–68.
——. 2007. "'Mosaic Arabs' between Total and Conditioned Arabization: The Participation of Jews in Arabic Press and Journalism in Muslim Societies during the Nineteenth and Twentieth Centuries." *Journal of Muslim Minority Affairs* 27.2, pp. 261–95.
——. 2007a. "Arabic Journalism as a Vehicle for Enlightenment: Iraqi Jews in the Arabic Press during the Nineteenth and Twentieth Centuries." *Journal of Modern Jewish Studies* 6.3, pp. 219–37.
——. 2007b. "'The Tail above the Head': Literary Representations of 'Abd al-Nāṣir's Regime as a World Upside Down." *Quaderni di Studi Arabi* n.s. 2, pp. 181–208.
——. 2008. "Other Barbarians Will Come": Intertextuality, Meta-Poetry, and Meta-Myth in Maḥmūd Darwīsh's Poetry." In Hala Khamis Nassar and Najat Rahman (eds), *Mahmoud Darwish, Exile's Poet: Critical Essays*, pp. 123–66. Northampton, MA: Interlink Books.
——. 2009. "The Arab Jews: Language, Poetry, and Singularity." *Art and Thought* 9, pp. 40–7.
——. 2010–11. "Baghdad, Yesterday: On History, Identity, and Poetry" (Hebrew). *Pe'amim* 125–7, pp. 97–156.
——. 2011. "Arabisch." *Enzyklopädie jüdischer Geschichte und Kultur*, Vol. 1, pp. 127–34.
——. 2011–12. "Between Arabness and Zionism: Iraqi-Jewish Writers in Arabic in the 20th Century." *al-Karmil—Studies in Arabic Language and Literature* 32–3, pp. 28–73 (English part).
——. 2012. *Adonis—Index of the Acts of the Wind* (Hebrew). Tel Aviv: Keshev.
——. 2012a. "Who Needs Arab-Jewish Identity? Fragmented Consciousness, 'Inessential Solidarity', and the 'Coming Community' (Part 1)." *Journal of Modern Jewish Studies* 11.2, pp. 169–89.
——. 2013. *Baghdad—The City in Verse*. Cambridge, MA: Harvard University Press.
——. 2013a. "Double Exclusion and the Search for Inessential Solidarities: The Experience of Iraqi Jews as Heralding a New Concept of Identity and Belonging." In David Tal (ed.), *Israeli Identity between Orient and Occident*, pp. 140–60. London and New York: Routledge.
——. 2015. *Mahmud Darwish—Fifty Years of Poetry* (Hebrew). Tel Aviv: Keshev.
——. 2015a. "Who Needs Arab-Jewish Identity? Fragmented Consciousness, 'Inessential

Solidarity', and the 'Coming Community' (Part 2)." *Journal of Modern Jewish Studies* 14.2, pp. 299–314.
——. 2015b. *Who Needs Arab-Jewish Identity? Interpellation, Exclusion, and Inessential Solidarities*. Leiden: Brill.
Solaiman, M. 1999. "Al-Barudi and the Neo-Classical School in Modern Arabic Poetry." *Dhaka University Studies* 56.2, pp. 185–96.
Somekh, Sasson. 1973. "Arabic Literature and Hebrew Translation" (Hebrew). In Jacob Mansour (ed.), *Arabic and Islamic Studies* (Hebrew), pp. 141–52. Ramat Gan: Bar-Ilan University.
——. 1973a. *The Changing Rhythm*. Leiden: Brill.
——. 1980. (ed.) *Abḥāth fī al-Lugha wa-l-Uslūb*. Tel Aviv: Tel Aviv University Press.
——. 1982. "Bidāyāt al-Tarjama al-Adabiyya fī al-Qarn al-Tāsi' 'Ashar wa-Mushkilat al-Uslūb al-Qaṣaṣī." *al-Karmil—Abḥāth fī al-Lugha wa-l-Adab* 3, pp. 45–59.
——. 1984. *Lughat al-Qiṣṣa fī Adab Yūsuf Idrīs*. Tel Aviv: Tel Aviv University Press and Acre: Maktabat al-Sarūjī.
——. 1988. "al-Tashābuk al-Lughawī fi 'Yāsīn wa-Bahiyya.'" *al-Karmil—Abḥāth fī al-Lugha wa-l-Adab* 9, pp. 35–47.
——. 1989. "Modern Arabic Poetry and Its Medieval Palimpsest: Two Types of Intertextuality." *Edebiyât* 3.1, pp. 105–17.
——. 1991. *Genre and Language in Modern Arabic Literature*. Wiesbaden: Harrassowitz Verlag.
——. 1992. "The Neoclassical Arab Poets." In M. M. Badawi (ed.), *Modern Arabic Literature*, pp. 36–81, 491–4. Cambridge: Cambridge University Press.
——. (ed.). 1993. *Translation as a Challenge: Papers on Translation of Arabic Literature into Hebrew* (Hebrew). Tel Aviv: Tel Aviv University Press.
——. 1993a. "Colloquialized *Fuṣḥā* in Modern Arabic Prose Fiction." *Jerusalem Studies in Arabic and Islam* 16, pp. 176–94.
——. 2008. *Call it Dreaming: Memoirs 1951–2000* (Hebrew). Tel Aviv: Ha-Kibbutz Ha-Me'uḥad.
Sorour, Wafaa. 2006. "(Counter-)memories and National History in Modern Arabic Feminist Literature." *Trans: Internet-Zeitschrift für Kulturwissenschaften* 16. Available at: <http://www.inst.at/trans/16Nr/03_3/sorour_report16.htm> (last accessed 3 November 2016).
Southern, R. W. 1962. *Western Views of Islam in the Middle Ages*. Cambridge, MA: Harvard University Press.
Sowayan, Saad Abdullah. 1985. *Nabati Poetry: The Oral Poetry of Arabia*. Berkeley and Los Angeles: University of California Press.
——. 1992. *The Arabian Oral Historical Narrative: An Ethnographic and Linguistic Analysis*. Wiesbaden: Harrassowitz Verlag.
Sperl, Stefan and Christopher Shackle (eds). 1996. *Qasida Poetry in Islamic Africa and Asia: Classical Traditions and Modern Meanings*. Leiden: Brill.
——. (eds). 1996a. *Qasida Poetry in Islamic Africa and Asia: Eulogy's Bounty, Meaning's Abundance and Anthology*. Leiden: Brill.
Stagh, Marina. 1992. "A Critical Review of a Contemporary Work on the Literary History of Egypt." In Bo Utas and Knut S. Vikør (eds), *Papers from the First Nordic Conference on Middle Eastern Studies, Uppsala 26–29 January 1989*, pp. 63–72. Bergen: Nordic Society for Middle Eastern Studies.
——. 1993. *The Limits of Freedom of Speech: Prose Literature and Prose Writers in Egypt under Nasser and Sadat*. Stockholm: Almqvist and Wiksell International.
——. 1999. "The Translation of Arabic Literature into Swedish." *Cuadernos (Escuela de Traductores de Toledo)* 2, pp. 41–6.
——. 2000. "The Translation of Arabic Literature into Swedish." *Yearbook of Comparative and General Literature* 48, pp. 107–14.

Stapleton, Michael. 1985. *The Cambridge Guide to English Literature*. Cambridge: Cambridge University Press.

Starkey, Paul. 2006. *Modern Arabic Literature*. Edinburgh: Edinburgh University Press.

——. and Janet Starkey (eds). 1998. *Travellers in Egypt*. London and New York: I. B. Tauris.

Starr, Deborah. 2008. *Remembering Cosmopolitan Egypt: Culture, Society and Empire*. London: Routledge.

Stauth, Georg and Sami Zubaida (eds). 1987. *Mass Culture, Popular Culture, and Social Life in the Middle East*. Frankfurt: Campus Verlag.

Steiner, Peter. 1984. *Russian Formalism: A Metapoetics*. Ithaca and London: Cornell University Press.

Steinmetz, Horst. 1988. "Response to Claus Clüver's 'The Difference of Eight Decades: World Literature and the Demise of National Literatures.'" *Yearbook of Comparative and General Literature* 37, pp. 131–3.

Stephan, Rita. 2006. "Arab Women Writing Their Sexuality." *Hawwa: Journal of Women of the Middle East and the Islamic World* 4.2–3, pp. 159–80.

Stern, Samuel Miklos. 1974. *Hispano-Arabic Poetry*. Oxford: Clarendon Press.

Sterne, Laurence. 1964 [1760–7]. *Tristram Shandy*. London: Dent, and New York: Dutton.

Stetkevych, Jaroslav. 1969. "Arabism and Arabic Literature: Self-View of a Profession." *Journal of Near Eastern Studies* 28.3, pp. 145–56.

——. 2016. *The Hunt in Arabic Poetry: From Heroic to Lyric to Metapoetic*. Notre Dame, IN: University of Notre Dame Press.

Stetkevych, Suzanne Pinckney. 1993. *The Mute Immortals Speak: Pre-Islamic Poetry and the Poetics of Ritual*. Ithaca and London: Cornell University Press.

——. (ed.). 2009. *Early Islamic Poetry and Poetics*. Farnham and Burlington: Ashgate.

Stewart, Devin. 2006. "The Maqāma." In Roger Allen and D. S. Richards (eds), *Arabic Literature in the Post-Classical Period*, pp. 143–58. Cambridge: Cambridge University Press.

Stewart, Philip J. 1963. *Awlad Haretna: Its Value as Literature and the Public Reaction*. MLitt thesis, Oxford University.

——. 1991. "An Arabic Nobodaddy: The Gebelawi of Naguib Mahfouz." In Alan Jones (ed.), *Arabicus Felix—Luminosus Britannicus—Essays in Honour of A. F. L. Beeston on his Eightieth Birthday*, pp. 213–20. Reading: Ithaca Press.

——. 2001. "*Awlād Ḥāratinā*: A Tale of Two Texts." *Arabic and Middle Eastern Literatures* 4.4, pp. 37–42.

Stoll, Georg. 1998. "Immigrant Muslim Writers in Germany." In John C. Hawley (ed.), *Postcolonial Crescent: Islam's Impact on Contemporary Literature*, pp. 266–83. New York: Peter Lang.

al-Sudeary, Mashael A. 2013. "Reception of the Anglo-Arab Novel in the Euro-American Literary World." *Cross-Cultural Communication* 9.4, pp. 1–7.

Sulaiman, J. Y. 1991. *Victorian Travellers' Attitudes to the Arab World*. PhD thesis, Bangor University.

Sulaiman, Khalid A. 1984. *Palestine and Modern Arab Poetry*. London: Zed Books.

Sulaymān, Nabīl. 1995. "Ilā al-Jaḥīm Ayyuhā al-Laylak." In Ṭāriq Rajab (ed.), *Mutāba'āt Naqdiyya fī Adab Samīḥ al-Qāsim*, pp. 104–33. Haifa: al-Wādī li-l-Ṭibā'a wa-l-Nashr.

Suleiman, Yasir. 2003. *The Arabic Language and National Identity*. Edinburgh: Edinburgh University Press.

——. 2004. *A War of Words: Language and Conflict in the Middle East*. Cambridge: Cambridge University Press.

——. and Ibrahim Muhawi (eds). 2006. *Literature and Nation in the Middle East*. Edinburgh: Edinburgh University Press.

Surūr, Najīb. n.d. [1965]. *Yāsīn wa-Bahiyya*. Cairo: Madbūlī.

——. n.d. [1972?]. *Qūlū li-'Ayn al-Shams*. Cairo: Madbūlī.
——. 1980 [1968]. *Āh Yā Layl Yā Qamar*. Cairo: Madbūlī.
Suvorov, M. 2012. "Representation of National Folklore and Classical Historical Narratives in Modern Yemeni Prose." *Manuscripta Orientalia: International Journal for Oriental Manuscript Research* 18.2, pp. 24–30.
Suwayd, Maḥmūd. 1995. "Ḥiwār Shāmil ma'a al-'Allāma al-Sayyid Muḥammad Ḥusayn Faḍl Allāh Ḥawla Nash'atihi al-Fikriyya wa-Mawāqifihi min al-Qaḍāyā al-Bāriza al-Latī Tushghilu al-Waṭan al-'Arabī wa-l-'Ālam al-Islāmī." *Majallat al-Dirāsāt al-Filisṭiniyya* 23, pp. 93–121.
Suwaylim, Aḥmad. 1987. *Aṭfālunā fī 'Uyūn al-Shu'arā'*. Cairo: Dār al-Ma'ārif.
Suyoufie, Fadia. 2008. "The Appropriation of Tradition in Selected Works of Contemporary Arab Women Writers." *Journal of Arabic Literature* 39.2, pp. 216–49.
al-Suyūṭī, Jalāl al-Dīn. n.d. *al-Muzhir fī 'Ulūm al-Lugha wa-Anwā'ihā*. Cairo: Dār Iḥyā' al-Kutub al-'Arabiyya.
——. 1990. *Isbāl al-Kisā' 'alā 'Awrāt al-Nisā'* (ed. Khālid 'Abd al-Karīm Jum'a and 'Abd al-Qādir Aḥmad 'Abd al-Qādir). Kuwait City: Dār al-'Urūba li-l-Nashr wa-l-Tawzī'.
Szombathy, Zoltan. 2007. "Freedom of Expression and Censorship in Medieval Arabic Literature." *Journal of Arabic and Islamic Studies* 7, pp. 1–24.
Szyska, Christian. 1995. "On Utopian Writings in Nasserist Prison and Laicist Turkey." *Die Welt des Islams* 35.1, pp. 95–125.
——. 1997. "Rewriting the European Canon: 'Alī Aḥmad Bākathīr's 'New Faust.'" In Lutz Edzard and Christian Szyska (eds), *Encounter of Words and Texts: Intercultural Studies in Honor of Stefan Wild on the Occasion of his 60th Birthday*, pp. 131–45. Hildesheim: Georg Olms Verlag.
——. 1997–8. "Ḥawla al-Kitāba al-Ṭūbāwiyya fī Sujūn Jamāl 'Abd al-Nāṣir." *al-Karmil—Abḥāth fī al-Lugha wa-l-Adab* 18–19, pp. 115–42.
——. 1999. "Najīb al-Kīlānī on his Career, or How to Become the Ideal Muslim Author." In Stephan Guth et al. (eds), *Conscious Voices: Concepts of Writing in the Middle East: Proceedings of the Berne Symposium, July 1997*, pp. 221–35. Beirut: Orient-Institut der DMG.
——. 1999a. "'Illā al-Ladhīna Āmanū wa-'Amilū al-Ṣāliḥāt wa-Dhakarū Allāh Kathīran': Ḥawla Mafhūm 'al-Adab al-Multazim' 'inda Udabā' al-Ḥarakāt al-Islāmiyya." *al-Karmil—Abḥāth fī al-Lugha wa-l-Adab* 20, pp. 33–62.
——. and Friederike Pannewick (eds). 2003. *Crossings and Passages in Genre and Culture*. Wiesbaden: Reichert Verlag.
al-Ṭabarī, Abū Ja'far. 1961. *Ta'rīkh al-Ṭabarī* (ed. Muḥammad Abū al-Faḍl Ibrāhīm). Cairo: Dār al-Ma'ārif.
Tageldin, Shaden M. 2011. "The Returns of Theory." *International Journal of Middle East Studies* 43.4, pp. 728–30.
——. 2012. "Proxidistant Reading: Toward a Critical Pedagogy of the *Nahḍah* in U.S. Comparative Literary Studies." *Journal of Arabic Literature* 43.2–3, pp. 227–68.
Taha, Ibrahim. 2000. "Text-Genre Interrelations: A Topographical Chart of Generic Activity." *Semiotica* 132.1–2, pp. 101–19.
——. 2002. *The Palestinian Novel: A Communication Study*. London: RoutledgeCurzon.
——. 2008. "'Swimming against the Current': Toward an Arab Feminist Poetic Strategy." *Orientalia Suecana* 56, pp. 193–222.
——. 2009. *Arabic Minimalist Story: Genre, Politics and Poetics in the Self-Colonial Era*. Wiesbaden: Reichert Verlag.
al-Ṭaḥāwī, Mīrāl. 2010. "La evolución de lo prohibido en la literatura árabe femenina." *Culturas: Revista de Análisis y Debate sobre Oriente Próximo y el Mediterráneo* 7, pp. 151–61.
Ṭāhir, Bahā'. 2006. *Fī Madīḥ al-Riwāya*. Amman: Azmina li-l-Nashr wa-l-Tawzī'.

——. 2007. *Wāḥat al-Ghurūb*. Beirut: Dār al-Ādāb.
Tājir, Jāk. 1945? *Ḥarakat al-Tarjama bi-Miṣr Khilāla al-Qarn al-Tāsiʿ ʿAshar*. Cairo: Dār al-Maʿārif.
Tal, David (ed.). 2013. *Israeli Identity between Orient and Occident*. London and New York: Routledge.
Ṭalfāḥ, Khayr Allāh. 1976. "al-Taʿrīb Awwalan." *al-Thawra* (Baghdad), 8 August, p. 4.
Talib, Adam et al. (eds). 2014. *The Rude, the Bad and the Bawdy: Essays in Honour of Professor Geert Jan van Gelder*. Cambridge: Gibb Memorial Trust.
al-Ṭālib, ʿUmar Muḥammad. 1987. *Malāmiḥ al-Masraḥiyya al-ʿArabiyya al-Islāmiyya*. al-Maghrib: Dār al-Āfāq al-Jadīda.
al-Tami, Ahmad Salih. 1988. *The Poetic Theories of the Leading Poet-Critics of Arabic New Poetry*. PhD thesis, Indiana University.
al-Tami, Ahmed. 1993. "Arabic 'Free Verse': The Problem of Terminology." *Journal of Arabic Literature* 24.2, pp. 185–98.
Tamimi, Azzam. 2000. "The Origins of Arab Secularism." In Azzam Tamimi and John L. Esposito (eds), *Islam and Secularism in the Middle East*, pp. 13–28. London: Hurst and Company.
——. and John L. Esposito (eds). 2000. *Islam and Secularism in the Middle East*. London: Hurst and Company.
al-Ṭannāḥī, Maḥmūd Muḥammad. 1996. *al-Kitāb al-Maṭbūʿ bi-Miṣr fī al-Qarn al-Tāsiʿ ʿAshar*. Cairo: al-Hilāl.
al-Ṭanṭāwī, ʿAlī. 1936. "al-Ḥayāt al-Adabiyya fī Dimashq." *al-Risāla*, 10 February, pp. 214–16.
Ṭarrāzī, Philip de. 1913. *Taʾrīkh al-Ṣiḥāfa al-ʿArabiyya*. Beirut: al-Maṭbaʿa al-Adabiyya.
Tauzin, A. 1989. "A haute voix: poésie féminine contemporaine en Mauritanie." *Revue du Monde Musulman et de la Méditerranée* 54, pp. 178–87.
Tawfiq, M. A. 1980. *ʿAli Ahmad Bakathir: A Study of Islamic Commitment in Modern Arabic Literature*. PhD thesis, University of Manchester.
al-Ṭawīl, Tawfīq. 1990. *al-Ḥaḍāra al-Islāmiyya wa-l-Ḥaḍāra al-Ūrubiyya*. Cairo: Maktabat al-Turāth l-Islāmī.
Teesing, Hubert Paul Hans. 1948. *Das Problem der Perioden in der Literaturgeschicte*. Groningen: J. B. Wolters.
Ten Bos, René. 2005. "Giorgio Agamben and the Community without Identity." *Sociological Review* 53.1, pp. 16–29.
Testen, D. 1996. "On the Arabic of the 'En Avdat Inscription." *Journal of Near Eastern Studies* 55.4, pp. 281–92.
The Arab World, A Catalogue of Doctoral Dissertations, 1938–1984. University Microfilms International, February 1985.
Theroux, Peter. 2001–2. "Children of the Alley: A Translator's Tale." *Massachusetts Review: A Quarterly of Literature, the Arts, and Public Affairs* 42.4, pp. 666–71.
Tibawi, Abd al-Latif. 1974. *Arabic and Islamic Themes: Historical, Educational and Literary Studies*. London: Luzac and Company.
al-Tīfāshī, Shihāb al-Dīn Aḥmad. 1992. *Nuzhat al-Albāb fīmā lā Yūjad fī Kitāb* (ed. Jamāl Jumʿa). London: Riyāḍ al-Rayyis.
Tijani, Olatunbosun Ishaq. 2008. "Gendering the Iraq–Kuwait Conflict: Literary Representations of Kuwaiti Women's Resilience and Resistance." *Journal of Arabic Literature* 39.2, pp. 250–69.
Tobi, Yosef. 1995. "The Reaction of Rav Saʿadia Gaon to Arabic Poetry and Poetics." *Hebrew Studies* 36, pp. 35–53.
——. (ed.). 1998. *Contacts between Arabic Literature and Jewish Literature in the Middle Ages and Modern Times* (Vol. 1) (Hebrew). Tel Aviv: Afikim.
——. (ed.). 2004. *Contacts between Arabic Literature and Jewish Literature in the Middle Ages and Modern Times* (Vol. 3) (Hebrew). Tel Aviv: Afikim.

Todorov, Tzvetan (ed.). 1982. *French Literary Theory Today: A Reader* (trans. R. Carter). Cambridge: Cambridge University Press.

Tomiche, Nada (ed.). 1969. *Le théâtre arabe*. Paris: Unesco.

——. 1982. "L'oeuvre de Ṣun' Allāh Ibrāhīm ou la 'littérature des prisons' (*adab al-suğūn*)." *Annales Islamologiques* 18, pp. 255–71.

——. 1993. *La littérature arabe contemporaine*. Paris: Éditions Maisonneuve et Larose.

Tottoli, Roberto. 2002. *Biblical Prophets in the Qur'ān and Muslim Literature*. Richmond: Curzon.

Trudewind, Stephan. 2000. "al-Adab al-'Arabī al-Mu'āṣir al-Mutarjam ilā al-Almāniyya." *Fikr wa-Fann* 72, pp. 49–51.

Tuchman, Gaye and Nina E. Fortin. 1989. *Edging Women Out: Victorian Novelists, Publishers and Social Change*. New Haven and London: Yale University Press.

Tucker, Judith E. 1993. *Arab Women: Old Boundaries, New Frontiers*. Bloomington and Indianapolis: Indiana University Press.

——. 2008. *Women, Family and Gender in Islamic Law*. Cambridge: Cambridge University Press.

al-Tūnisī, Bayram. 1976. *al-Maqāmāt*. Cairo: al-Hay'a al-Miṣriyya al-'Āmma li-l-Kitāb.

——. 1976–86. *al-A'māl al-Kāmila* (ed. Rushdī Ṣāliḥ). Cairo: al-Hay'a al-Miṣriyya al-'Āmma li-l-Kitāb.

——. 1986. *al-Sayyid wa-Marātuh fī Bārīs*. Cairo: al-Hay'a al-Miṣriyya al-'Āmma li-l-Kitāb.

——. 1987. *Dīwān Bayram al-Tūnisī*. Cairo: Dār Miṣr.

——. 2001. *Mudhakkirātī*. Tunis: Dār al-Janūb li-l-Nashr.

Ṭūqān (Tuqan), Fadwā. 1985. *Riḥla Ṣa'ba, Riḥla Jabaliyya*. Acre: Dār al-Aswār.

——. 1990. *A Mountainous Journey* (trans. O. Kenny; poetry by Naomi Shihab Nye; ed. Salma Khadra Jayyusi). St. Paul, MN: Graywolf Books.

——. 1994. *al-Riḥla al-Aṣ'ab*. Nāblus: Dār al-Shurūq.

Ṭūqān, Ibrāhīm. 1975. *Dīwān Ibrāhīm*. Beirut: Dār al-Quds.

Ṭūqān, Qadrī Ḥāfiẓ. 1936. "al-Thaqāfa wa-l-Intāj al-'Ilmī fī Filasṭīn." *al-Risāla*, 14 December, pp. 2047–8.

Turgenev, Ivan Sergeevich. 1951 [1917]. *A House of Gentlefolk* (trans. Constance Garnett). New York: The Macmillan Company.

Turkiyya, Salīm. 1999. *Kāna Ṣarḥan min Khayāl* (trans. Bassām Ḥajjār). Beirut: al-Masār.

Ullah, Najib. 1963. *Islamic Literature*. New York: Washington Square Press.

'Umar, Ḥazīn. 2000. *al-Mughtarib Ghālī Shukrī*. Cairo: al-Hay'a al-Miṣriyya al-'Āmma li-l-Kitāb.

Underhill, Evelyn. 1961. *Mysticism*. New York: Dutton.

al-'Unf al-Uṣūlī: Muwājahāt al-Sayf wa-l-Qalam. 1995. London and Beirut: Riyāḍ al-Rayyis. London and Beirut: Riyāḍ al-Rayyis.

al-'Urayyiḍ, Ibrāhīm. 1958. *Min al-Shi'r al-Ḥadīth 1900–1950*. Beirut: Dār al-'Ilm li-l-Malāyin.

Usman, Muhammad Tukur. 2009. "Maghreb Influence on the Arabic Literary Tradition of Northern Nigeria." *Maghreb Review* 34.2–3, pp. 207–26.

al-Usṭā, Ādil. 1999. *Muẓaffar al-Nawwāb wa-Ḥuḍūruhu fī Filasṭīn*. n.p.: n.pub.

Utas, Bo and Knut S. Vikør (eds). 1992. *Papers from the First Nordic Conference on Middle Eastern Studies, Uppsala 26–29 January 1989*. Bergen: Nordic Society for Middle Eastern Studies.

Valassopoulos, Anastasia. 2003. "The Legacy of Orientalism in Middle Eastern Feminism." *Thamyris / Intersecting* 10, pp. 183–99.

——. 2007. *Contemporary Arab Women Writers: Cultural Expression in Context*. London and New York: Routledge.

Van Gelder, Geert Jan. 1996. "Najib Haddad's Essay on the Comparison of Arabic and

European Poetry." In J. R. Smart (ed.), *Tradition and Modernity in Arabic Language and Literature*, pp. 144–52. Richmond: Curzon.
——. (ed.). 2013. *Classical Arabic Literature: A Library of Arabic Literature Anthology*. New York: New York University Press.
van Leeuwen, Richard. 2016. "European Translations of the Thousand and One Nights and their Reception: Orientalist Falsification or Literary Fascination?" *CLINA: An Interdisciplinary Journal of Translation, Interpreting and Intercultural Communication* 2.1, pp. 29–41.
Vatikiotis, P. J. 1991. "Vanishing Cultural Bridges between East and West." *Asian and African Studies* 25, pp. 179–85.
Versteegh, Kees et al. (eds). 2006. *Encyclopedia of Arabic Language and Literature*. Leiden and Boston: Brill.
——. 2014. *The Arabic Language*. Edinburgh: Edinburgh University Press.
Vial, Ch. 1986. "Ḳiṣṣa." In P. J. Bearman et al. (eds), *The Encyclopaedia of Islam*, New Edition, Vol. 5, pp. 187–93. Leiden: Brill.
Voltaire, François-Marie Arouet. 1959 [1759]. *Candide ou l'optimisme*. Paris: Librairie Nizet.
Von Grunebaum, Gustave E. 1953. *Medieval Islam*. Chicago: University of Chicago Press.
——. 1967. "Literature in the Context of Islamic Civilization." *Oriens* 20, pp. 1–14.
——. (ed.). 1973. *Arabic Poetry: Theory and Development*. Wiesbaden: Harrassowitz Verlag.
Wādī, Ṭāhā. 1981. "al-Baḥth 'an Qaḍiyya fī Sīrat Aḥmad Rāmī wa-Shi'rihi." *Fuṣūl* 1.4, pp. 227–33.
——. 1996. *al-Riwāya al-Siyāsiyya*. Cairo: Dār al-Nashr li-l-Jāmi'āt al-Miṣriyya.
——. 2001. *al-Qiṣṣa Dīwān al-'Arab: Qaḍāyā wa-Namādhij*. Cairo: al-Sharika al-Miṣriyya al-'Ālamiyya li-l-Nahsr—Longman.
Wagner, Mark S. 2004. "Changing Visions of the Tribesman in Yemeni Vernacular Literature." *Al-Masar / Al-Masār* 5.3, pp. 3–30.
Waḥdat al-Thaqāfa al-'Arabiyya: Abḥāth Nadwat 'Ammān (10–12 Kānūn al-Awwal 1993). 1995. Amman: Manshūrāt al-Ittiḥād al-'Āmm li-l-Udabā' wa-l-Kuttāb al-'Arab.
Walther, Wiebke. 1987. *Tausand und eine Nacht*. Munich and Zurich: Artemis Verlag.
Wannūs, Sa'd Allāh. 1989. *al-Fīl Yā Malik al-Zamān wa-Mughāmarat Ra's al-Mamlūk Jābir*. Beirut: Dār al-Ādāb.
al-Wardī, 'Alī. 1957. *Usṭūrat al-Adab al-Rafī'*. Baghdad: Maṭba'at al-Rābiṭa.
——. 2001 [1951]. *Shkhṣiyyat al-Fard al-'Irāqī: Baḥth fī Nafsiyyat al-Sha'b al-'Irāqī 'alā Ḍaw' 'Ilm al-Ijtimā' al-Ḥadīth*. London: Manshūrāt Dār Laylā.
Wasserstein, David J. 1991. "The Language Situation in al-Andalus." In Alan Jones and Richard Hitchcock (eds), *Studies on the Muwaššaḥ and the Kharja*, pp. 1–15. Reading: Ithaca Press.
Wasserstrom, Steven M. 1995. *Between Muslim and Jew: The Problem of Symbiosis under Early Islam*. Princeton: Princeton University Press.
Watson, Helen. 1992. *Women in the City of the Dead*. London: Hurst and Company.
Watt, W. Montgomery. 1963. *The Faith and Practice of al-Ghazali*. London: George Allen and Unwin.
——. 1972. *The Influence of Islam on Medieval Europe*. Edinburgh: Edinburgh University Press.
Waugh, Earle H. 1989. *The Munshidīn* [sic] *of Egypt: Their World and Their Song*. Columbia, SC: University of South Carolina Press.
Wāzin, 'Abduh. 1993. *Ḥadīqat al-Ḥawāss*. Beirut: Dār al-Jadīd.
——. 2006. *Maḥmūd Darwīsh: al-Gharīb Yaqa'u 'alā Nafsihi*. Beirut: Riyāḍ al-Rayyis.
Webb, Gisela. 2000. *Windows of Faith: Muslim Women Scholar-Activists in North America*. Syracuse: Syracuse University Press.

Webb, Peter. 2016. *Imagining the Arabs: Arab Identity and the Rise of Islam*. Edinburgh: Edinburgh University Press.

Wehr, Hans. 1976. *A Dictionary of Modern Written Arabic*. Ithaca: Spoken Language Services.

Weidner, Stefan. 2012. "Exile that Enriches: The Cultural Achievements of Iranian and Arab Authors in Germany." *Fikrun wa Fann* 97, pp. 68–74.

Wellek, René. 1941. "Periods and Movements in Literary History." In *English Institute Annual 1940*, pp. 73–93. New York: Columbia University Press.

——. 1966. *The Rise of English Literary History*. New York: McGraw-Hill.

——. and Austin Warren. 1963. *Theory of Literature*. London: Jonathan Cape.

Werbner, Pnina and Tariq Modood (eds). 1997. *Debating Cultural Hybridity: Multicultural Identities and the Politics of Anti-Racism*. London and Atlantic Highlands, NJ: Zed Books.

Werner, Karin. 2001. "'Coming Close to God' Through the Media: A Phenomenology of the Media Practices of Islamist Women in Egypt." In Kai Hafez (ed.), *Mass Media, Politics, and Society in the Middle East*, pp. 199–216. Cresskill, NJ: Hampton Press.

Westerlund, David and Ingvar Svanberg (eds). 1999. *Islam Outside the Arab World*. New York: St. Martin's Press.

Wiet, Gaston. 1966. *Introduction a la littérature arabe*. Paris: Éditions Maisonneuve et Larose.

Wild, Stefan. 1996. "Islamic Enlightenment and the Paradox of Averroes." *Die Welt des Islams* 36.3, pp. 379–90.

——. 1999. "A Tale of Two Redemptions: A Comparative Analysis of Ṭāhā Ḥusayn's *The Days* and Muḥammad Shukrī's *For Bread Alone*." In Angelika Neuwirth et al. (eds), *Myths, Historical Archetypes and Symbolic Figures in Arabic Literature*, pp. 349–61. Beirut: Orient-Institut der DMG.

Wilpert, Gero von. 1964. *Sachwörterbuch der Literatur*. Stuttgart: Kröner Verlag.

Winkler, Stefan. 2001. "Distribution of Ideas: Book Production and Publishing in Egypt, Lebanon, and the Middle East." In Kai Hafez (ed.), *Mass Media, Politics, and Society in the Middle East*, pp. 159–73. Cresskill, NJ: Hampton Press.

Winter, Michael. 2000. "Beyond the Slogans: Islamic Fundamentalists' Historical and Religious Arguments." In Binyamin Abrahamov (ed.), *Studies in Arabic and Islamic Culture* (Vol. 1), pp. lxix–lxxix. Tel Aviv: Department of Arabic, Bar-Ilan University.

Woidich, Manfred and Jacob M. Landau. 1993. *Arabishes Volkstheater in Kairo im Jahre 1909*. Beirut and Stuttgart: Franz Steiner Verlag.

Wright, J. W. and Everett K. Rowson (eds). 1997. *Homoeroticism in Classical Arabic Literature*. New York: Columbia University Press.

Yāghī, ʿAbd al-Raḥmān. 1969. *Ra'y Fī al-Maqāmāt*. Beirut: al-Maktab al-Tijārī li-l-Ṭibāʿa wa-l-Nashr wa-l-Tawzīʿ.

——. 1980. *Fī al-Juhūd al-Masraḥiyya al-Ighrīqiyya al-Ūrūbiyya al-ʿArabiyya (min al-Naqqāsh ilā al-Ḥakīm)*. Beirut: al-Mu'assasa al-ʿArabiyya li-l-Dirāsāt wa-l-Nashr.

Yaḥyā, Rāfiʿ. 2001. *Ta'thīr Alf Layla wa-Layla ʿalā Adab al-Aṭfāl al-ʿArabī*. Haifa: al-Kulliyya al-ʿArabiyya li-l-Tarbiya fī Isrā'īl, Markaz Adab al-Aṭfāl.

Yaḥyāwī, Rashīd. 2015. *al-Kalām ʿalā al-Kalām fī al-Turāth: Madākhil li-Maqāṣid al-Taʿrīb wa-l-Tadyīn*. Amman: Dār Kunūz al-Maʿrifa.

Yamanaka, Yuriko and Tetsuo Nishio (eds). 2006. *The Arabian Nights and Orientalism: Perspectives from East & West*. London and New York: I. B. Tauris.

Yannakakis, Ilios. 1997. "The Death of Cosmopolitanism." In Robert Ilbert and Ilios Yannakakis (eds), *Alexandria 1860–1960: The Brief Life of a Cosmopolitan Community* (trans. Colin Clement), pp. 190–4. Alexandria: Harpocrates Publishing.

Yaqub, Nadia G. 2007. *Pens, Swords, and the Springs of Art: The Oral Poetry Dueling of Palestinian Weddings in the Galilee*. Boston: Brill.

Yāqūt. 1991. *Mu'jam al-Udabā'*. Beirut: Dār al-Kutub al-'Ilmiyya.

Yawākīm, Fāris. 2013. *Ḥikāyāt al-Aghānī: Riḥlat al-Qaṣīda min al-Dīwān ilā al-Ughniyya*. London: Riyāḍ al-Rayyis.

al-Yāzijī, Ibrāhīm. 1983. *al-'Iqd*. Beirut: Dār Mārūn 'Abbūd.

al-Yāzijī, Nāṣīf. 1904. *Dīwān*. Beirut: al-Maṭba'a al-Sharqiyya.

——. 1958. *Majma' al-Baḥrayn*. Beirut: Dār Ṣādir.

Young, George. 1927. *Egypt*. London: Ernest Benn.

Yousef, Tawfiq. 2000. "The Reception and Translation of American Literature in the Arab World." *Yearbook of Comparative and General Literature* 48, pp. 73–86.

——. 2000a. "The Reception of Willian Faulkner in the Arab World." *Yearbook of Comparative and General Literature* 48, pp. 87–93.

al-Yousfi, Muhammad Lutfi. 2006. "Poetic Creativity in the Sixteenth to Eighteenth Centuries." In Roger Allen and D. S. Richards (eds), *Arabic Literature in the Post-Classical Period*, pp. 60–73. Cambridge: Cambridge University Press.

Yūnus, 'Abd al-Ḥamīd. 1973. *Difā' 'an al-Fūlklūr*. Cairo: al-Hay'a al-Miṣriyya al-'Āmma li-l-Kitāb.

Yūsuf, 'Abd al-Qādir. 1999. "Naqd li-Riwāyat 'al-Āyāt al-Shayṭāniyya' li-Salmān Rushdī." In Fawwāz Manṣūr (ed.), *Dirāsāt fī al-Ḥaḍāra al-Islāmiyya wa-l-'Arabiyya*, pp. 9–25. al-Ṭayba: n.pub.

Yūsuf, 'Abd al-Tawwāb. 1983. "Kutub al-Aṭfāl fī al-Duwal al-Nāmiya, Dirāsa Istiṭlā'iyya." *Kitābāt* (Manāma) 19, pp. 99–143.

——. 1987. *al-Harāwī Rā'id Masraḥ al-Ṭifl al-'Arabī*. Cairo: Dār al-Kitāb al-Miṣrī.

——. 1988. *Dīwān Kāmil Kaylānī li-l-Aṭfāl*. Cairo: Hay'at al-Kitāb.

——. 1992. *al-Ṭifl al-'Arabī wa-l-Adab al-Sh'abī*. Cairo: al-Dār al-Miṣriyya al-Lubnāniyya.

——. 1999. *Tajribatī fī al-Kitāba li-l-Aṭfāl*. Cairo: al-Hay'a al-Miṣriyya al-'Āmma li-l-Kitāb.

Al-Yusuf, Ahmed Abdullah. 1989. *Commercial Advertising in Saudi Arabia: A Content Analysis*. MA thesis, The Florida State University.

——. 1994. *Attitudes and Perceptions about Television Advertising among Women in Saudi Arabia*. PhD thesis, The Florida State University.

Yūsuf, Sa'dī. 1989. *Sa'dī Yūsuf* (ed. Firyāl Jabūrī Ghazūl). Beirut and Cairo: Dār al-Fatā al-'Arabī.

Yusuf, S. M. 1967. "Arabic Language and Literature in the Indo-Pakistan Subcontinent." *Iqbal* 16.1, pp. 54–66.

Zachs, Fruma. 2005. *The Making of Syrian Identity: Intellectuals and Merchants in Nineteenth-Century Beirut*. Leiden: Brill.

——. 2011. "Subversive Voices of Daughters of the *Nahḍa*: Alice al-Bustani and *Riwayat Sa'iba* (1891)." *Hawwa: Journal of Women of the Middle East and the Islamic World* 9.3, pp. 332–57.

——. and Bāsīlyūs Ḥannā Bawārdī. [forthcoming]. "Changing Arabic Esthetic Taste: Pre-Detective, Detective and Adventure Narratives: The Forgotten Works of Nasīb al-Mash'alānī in the Journal *al-Ḍiya'*."

——. and Sharon Halevi. 2009. "From *Difā' al-Nisā'* to *Mas'alat al-Nisā'* in Greater Syria: Readers and Writers Debate Women and Their Rights, 1858–1900." *International Journal of Middle East Studies* 41.4, pp. 615–33.

——. and Sharon Halevi. 2015. *Gendering Culture in Greater Syria: Intellectuals and Ideology in the Late Ottoman Period*. London and New York: I. B. Tauris.

Zack, Elisabeth. 2001. "The Use of Colloquial Arabic in Prose Literature: *Laban il-'Aṣfūr* by Yūsuf al-Qa'īd." *Quaderni di Studi Arabi* 19, pp. 193–219.

al-Zahāwī, Jamīl Ṣidqī. 1972. *Dīwān*. Beirut: Dār al-'Awda.

Zāhir, 'Abd al-Hādī. 1999–2000. *Ṣilat al-Muwashshaḥāt wa-l-Azjāl bi-Shi'r al-Trūbādūr*. Cairo: Maktabat al-Ādāb.

Zajda, Joseph. 2009. "Nation-Building, Identity and Citizenship Education: Introduction."

In Joseph Zajda (ed.), *Nation-Building, Identity and Citizenship Education*, pp. 1–11. Dordrecht: Springer.
——. et al. (eds). 2009a. *Nation-Building, Identity and Citizenship Education*. Dordrecht: Springer.
Zakī, ʻAbd al-Ḥamīd Tawfīq. 1992. *al-Sayyid Darwīsh fī ʻĪd Mīlādihi al-Miʼawī*. Cairo: Dār al-Maʻārif.
Zakī, Fikriyya. 1934. "al-ʻĀmil al-Iqtiṣādī fī al-Adab." *al-Risāla*, 20 August, p. 1374.
Zalaṭ, Aḥmad. 1994. *Adab al-Ṭufūla Bayna Kāmil al-Kaylānī and Muḥammad al-Harāwī*. Cairo: Dār al-Maʻārif.
Zartman, William (ed.). 2015. *Arab Spring: Negotiating in the Shadow of the Intifadat*. Athens: University of Georgia Press.
Zaydān, Joseph. 1986. *Maṣādir al-Adab al-Nisāʼī fī al-ʻĀlam al-ʻArabī al-Ḥadīth*. Jidda: al-Nādī al-Adabī al-Thaqāfī.
Zaydān, Jurjī. 1902. *al-Ḥajjāj ibn Yūsuf*. Cairo: Dār al-Hilāl.
Zaydān, Muḥammad Ḥusayn. 1973. "al-ʻUrūba Arḍ wa-Turāth wa-Maṣīr." *al-Fikr* (Tunis), April, pp. 121–6.
Zaydān, Yūsuf. 1992. "al-Qiṣṣa ʻinda al-Ṣūfiyya." *al-Hilāl*, May, pp. 48–55.
Zayyād, Tawfiq. n.d. *Dīwān*. Beirut: Dār al-ʻAwda.
al-Zayyāt, Aḥmad Ḥasan. n.d. *Taʼrīkh al-Adab al-ʻArabī*. Cairo: Maktabat Nahḍat Miṣr.
——. 1996. *Taʼrīkh al-Adab al-ʻArabī li-l-Madāris al-Thānawiyya wa-l-ʻUlyā*. Beirut: Dār al-Maʻrifa
al-Zayyāt, Laṭīfa (ed.). 1994. *Kull Hādhā al-Ṣawt al-Jamīl*. Cairo: Nūr, Dār al-Marʼa al-ʻArabiyya li-l-Nashr.
Zeidan, Joseph T. 1995. *Arab Women Novelists: The Formative Years and Beyond*. Albany: State University of New York Press.
——. 1997. "Modern Arab Theater: The Journey Back." In Issa J. Boullata and Terri DeYoung (eds), *Tradition and Modernity in Arabic Literature*, pp. 173–91. Fayetteville, AR: University of Arkansas Press.
Zeidel, Ronen. 2011. "The Iraqi Novel and the Kurds." *Review of Middle East Studies* 45.1, pp. 19–34.
——. 2011a. "The Shīʻa in Iraqi Novels." *Die Welt des Islams* 51.3–4, pp. 327–57.
Zipin, Amnon. 1980. *Bibliography of Modern Hebrew Literature in Arabic Translation, 1948–1979*. Tel Aviv: The Institute for the Translation of Hebrew Literature.
al-Ziriklī, Khayr al-Dīn. 1984. *al-Aʻlām*. Beirut: Dār al-ʻIlm li-l-Malāyīn.
Zirinski, Roni. 1999. *Ad-Hoc Arabism: A Semiotic-Historic Analysis of Saudi Advertising* (Hebrew). MA thesis, University of Haifa.
——. 2005. *Ad-Hoc Arabism: Advertising, Culture, and Technology in Saudi Arabia*. New York: Peter Lang.
Ziyāda, Aḥmad. 1996. *Ṣalāḥ Jāhīn 1930–1986*. Cairo: Dār al-Amīn.
Zoepf, Katherine. 2005. "Bestseller in Mideast: Barbie with a Prayer Mat." *The New York Times*, 22 September.
——. 2016. *Excellent Daughters: The Secret Lives of Young Women Who Are Transforming the Arab World*. London: Penguin Books.
Zubaida, Sami. 1999. "Cosmopolitanism and the Middle East." In Roel Meijer (ed.), *Cosmopolitanism, Identity and Authenticity in the Middle East*, pp. 15–33. Richmond: Curzon.
——. 2002. "Entertainers in Baghdad: 1900–50." In Eugene Rogan (ed.), *Outside In: On the Margins of the Modern Middle East*, pp. 212–30. London and New York: I. B. Tauris.
——. 2002a. "The Fragments Imagine the Nation: The Case of Iraq." *International Journal of Middle East Studies* 34.2, pp. 205–15.
al-Zubaidi, A. M. K. 1970. "The Dīwān School." *Journal of Arabic Literature* 1, pp. 36–48.

——. 1974. “The Apollo School’s Early Experiments in ‘Free Verse.’” *Journal of Arabic Literature* 5, pp. 17–43.
Zuhur, Sherifa (ed.). 1998. *Images of Enchantment: Visual and Performing Arts of the Middle East*. Cairo: The American University in Cairo Press.
——. 1998a. “Asmahan: Arab Musical Performance and Musicianship under the Myth.” In Sherifa Zuhur (ed.), *Images of Enchantment: Visual and Performing Arts of the Middle East*, pp. 81–107. Cairo: The American University in Cairo Press.
——. 2000. *Asmahan’s Secrets: Woman, War, and Song*. Austin: University of Texas Press.
Zwettler, Michael N. 1978. *The Oral Tradition of Classical Arabic Poetry: Its Character and Implications*. Columbus, OH: The Ohio State University Press.

Index

Note: The definite article *al* is not taken into consideration in the alphabetical order. It appears in this form throughout the entire book before solar and lunar letters. The following terms and their derivatives do not appear in the Index as independent entries or appear only partly: Arab, Arabic, Egypt, Iraq, Islam, language, literature, poetry, popular, reading, system, text.

al-Ābā' wa-l-Banūn (play), 231n
'Abbās, Aḥmad, 38
'Abbās, Ḥasan Maḥmūd, 189
'Abbās, Iḥsān, 189n, 224
'Abbāsīd, Abbasid, Abbasids, 18, 24, 25n, 26, 147, 178n, 179n, 194, 195, 251
'Abbūd, Sumayya, 88
'Abd al-Hādī, Khālid (Khalid Abdel-Hadi [nicknamed Kali]), 12n
'Abd al-Muṭṭalib, Muḥammad, 195
'Abd al-Nāṣir, Gamāl, 72, 76, 84, 88, 104n, 118–19, 138n, 248
'Abd al-Qādir, Fārūq, 99n
'Abd al-Quddūs, Iḥsān, 41–2, 118–19
'Abd al-Raḥīm, Sha'bān, 78
'Abd al-Raḥmān, 'Umar, 142–3
'Abd al-Rāziq, 'Alī, 120n
'Abd al-Ṣabūr, Ṣalāḥ, 44n, 95n, 201n, 236–7
'Abd al-Salām, Fātiḥ, 37n
'Abd al-Tawwāb, Ramaḍān, 171n
'Abduh, Muḥammad, 117n
'Abd al-Wahhāb, Muḥammad, 77, 130
Abel, 127–8
Abī Zayd, Fu'ād, 264n
al-Abnūdī, 'Abd al-Raḥmān, 30n, 72, 75, 76
abolitionism, 228
Abraham (prophet), 134–6
abstraction and simplification, 23
absurd, absurdity, 9, 98
Abū 'Alyawī, Ḥasan Maḥmūd, 54n
Abū Buthayna, Muḥammad 'Abd al-Mun'im, 73
Abu Dhabi, 36n, 63–4, 225
Abū Dīb, Kamāl (Kamal Abu-Deeb), 102, 152
Abū Fāshā, Ṭāhir, 95n
Abū al-Futūḥ, Sayyid Ḥāfiẓ, 141
Abū Ḥadīd, Muḥammad Farīd, 187n, 213
Abū Ḥannā, Ḥannā, 87n
Abū Māḍī, Īliyyā, 130
Abū Nuwās (al-Ḥasan ibn Hānī al-Ḥakamī), 117–18, 147n
"Abū al-Rijāl" (short story), 12n
Abū al-Sa'd, 'Abd al-Ra'ūf, 61n
Abū Shabaka, Ilyās, 25n, 80n, 89n
Abū Shādī, Aḥmad Zakī, 198
Abū Tammām (Ḥabīb ibn Aws), 192–3
Abū al-Wafā, Maḥmūd, 56
Abū Zayd, Naṣr Ḥāmid, 121
academic, academics 4, 60, 61, 66, 107, 111, 252, 260, 272
  academic freedom, 122
  academic periodicals, 14, 17n
  see also universities
ACLA (American Comparative Literature Association), 148, 185n, 194
Acre ('Akkā, 'Akko), 134, 156, 157
al-Ādāb (journal), 32, 45, 51, 103, 120n, 129n, 164, 165, 189n, 206n
adab, ādāb, adīb, 21, 55n, 95n, 109, 186–7, 233, 245–6
  al-adab al-'ālī, 21; *see also* canonical literature
  adab al-'āmma, al-adab al-'āmmī, 21, 69, 71, 246, 249; *see also* non-canonical literature
  adab/adabiyyāt al-aṭfāl, 55n; *see also* child, children
  adab al-aṭrāf, 21; *see also* non-canonical literature
  adab fāḥish, 67n, 96; *see also* sex literature
  adab al-faqāqī', 21; *see also* canonical literature
  al-adab al-faṣīḥ, 21, 71; *see also* canonical literature
  adab al-fi'āt al-dunyā, 21; *see also* non-canonical literature

adab, ādāb, adīb (*cont.*)
al-adab ghayr al-mu'taraf bihi, 21; *see also* non-canonical literature
al-adab ghayr al-rasmī, 21; *see also* non-canonical literature
adab al-hāmish, al-adab al-hāmishī, 21; *see also* non-canonical literature
adab ibāḥī, 67n, 96; *see also* sex literature
al-adab al-Imārātī, 167
adab Islāmī, 49–50; *see also* Islamist literature
adab al-ithāra al-jinsiyya, 67, 91n, 96; *see also* sex literature
al-adab al-jamāhīrī, 21; *see also* non-canonical literature
adab al-jins, 67n, 96; *see also* sex literature
adab khalā'ī, 96; *see also* sex literature
al-adab al-khāṣṣ, 21; *see also* canonical literature
adab al-khāṣṣa, 21, 37n; *see also* canonical literature
al-adab al-klāsīkī, 21n; *see also* classicism
adab makshūf, 67n, 79, 96; *see also* sex literature
adab al-markaz, 21; *see also* canonical literature
adab mā warā' al-rasmī, 21; *see also* non-canonical literature
al-adab al-Mūrītānī, 167n
adab al-nukhba, 21; *see also* canonical literature
al-adab al-Qaṭarī, 167n
adab al-qurrā' al-muthaqqafīn, 21; *see also* canonical literature
al-adab al-rafī', 21; *see also* canonical literature
al-adab al-rakhīṣ, 21, 91; *see also* non-canonical literature
al-adab al-rāqī, 21; *see also* canonical literature
al-adab al-rasmī, 21, 71; *see also* canonical literature
adab al-riḥla, 109n, 235; *see also* travel literature
adab al-ṣafwa, 21; *see also* canonical literature
al-adab al-sā'id, 21; *see also* canonical literature
al-adab al-sha'bī, 21, 67n; *see also* non-canonical literature
al-adab al-shādhdh 'an al-mustawā al-maqbūl, 21; *see also* non-canonical literature
al-adab al-shā'i', 21; *see also* non-canonical literature
adab al-sujūn, 48n; *see also* prison literature
al-adab al-sulṭānī, 21 *see also* canonical literature
adab tawjīhī, 56; *see also* didactic, didacticism
al-adab al-'Ummānī, 167n
adab al-ummiyyīn, 21; *see also* non-canonical literature
Adab wa-Naqd (journal), 75
Ādām, Muḥammad, 185n
adaptation (in literature), 33n, 56n, 57, 60, 65, 82, 89n, 95n, 180, 227, 232
adāt, 217n; *see also* evaluation, merit, value, worth
ADC (American-Arab Anti-Discrimination Committee), 130
aḍdād, taḍadd, 239
Aden, 179
adjustment (in literature), 230
adolescents (literature for), 41
adoption (in literature), 203, 211, 230
Adūnīs, Adonis ('Alī Aḥmad Sa'īd), 31n, 104n, 105n, 110, 115, 130n, 131, 132–8, 143n, 144, 170, 185, 187–8, 196, 202–3, 225, 226n, 260–1
adventure stories, 10, 57, 88
Adventures of Tarzan, 88
advertisements (commercial), 55n, 83n, 84n, 95n, 103n
adynata, adynaton, 37n
aesthetics, aestheticians, aesthetic/non-aesthetic 11n, 13, 20, 23, 34, 36, 53n, 66, 81, 87, 136, 191, 192, 194, 195, 201, 211, 245, 250n, 263n
aesthetic constraint, 66
aesthetic criteria, 9n, 18
aesthetic inquiry, 17
aesthetic legitimacy, legitimation, 4, 8n, 9, 14–19, 248
aesthetic potential, 17
aesthetic preference, 30, 39
aesthetic quality, 13
aesthetic requirements, 17
aesthetic self-respect, 15
aesthetic text, 23
aesthetic validity, 17
aesthetic value, 75, 80n
philosophical aesthetics, 17
Āfāq 'Ārabiyya (journal), 253
Afrāḥ al-Qubba (novel), 77n
Africa, African 6, 110n, 151n, 153
African-Americans, 262n
African literature, 173n
Central Sudanic Africa, 154
Eastern Sudanic Africa, 154
Northeastern Africa, 154
Saharan, Sub-Saharan Africa, 154
Western Sudanic Africa, 154
see also North Africa
Agamben, Giorgio, 270–1
Aḥādīth ma'a Allāh (=*Aḥādīth ma'a Nafsī*), 120n
al-Aḥājī wa-l-Nawādir wa-l-Fukāhāt, 75n
Aḥmad, Makram Muḥammad, 125
Aḥmad, Zakariyyā, 75n, 78
Ahmad, Zubaid (Zubayd), 153
Āh Yā Layl Yā Qamar (play), 99n
AIDS, 9
'Ajā'ib al-Āthar fī al-Tarājim wa-l-Akhbār (book), 156n
al-'Ajamī, Muḥammad, 125–6
al-Ajniḥa al-Mutakassira (novel), 113

al-akādīmiyyūn al-sha'biyyūn, 22n
ākhar, ukhrā, 75, 203n; *see also* European "Other"
Alafenisch, Salīm, 115
'Alam al-Dīn (travel book), 22n
'Ālam al-Kitāb (journal), 74–5
"al-'Alawiyya al-Ūlā" (poem), 195
Albanian, 55n
ALECSO (Arab League Educational, Cultural and Scientific Organization), 164–5
Alexander the Great, 90n, 225
Alexandria, 134, 214, 220
  Alexandria's Royal Library, 134
  as a cosmopolitan city, 242–3, 267–8
alfāẓ mafātīḥ, 65n; *see also* key terms
Alf Layla wa-Layla, 18n, 81, 90–7, 110n, 111n, 112n, 207, 263
  adaptations of, 56n, 95n
  and children's literature, 85n, 95, 97
  and popular culture, 90–1, 111n, 207
  canonization of, 81, 92–3, 96
  changing appreciation, 18, 81, 92–4
  "cheap arousing" of, 91n, 92, 94
  "harmful" influence of, 90–4
  influence and impact on world literature, 97
  language of, 90
  popularity of, 91
  reading and reception of, 93n, 94, 263
  research and scholarship of, 91n
  sexual themes in, 91n, 92, 94, 96
  status in Europe, 81, 93–4
  translations into other languages, 92–4
Algeria, Algerian, 62n, 113n, 124n, 167, 169n, 170n, 179, 220
'Alī, Muḥammad (artist), 72n
'Alī, Muḥammad (Pasha), 92n
'Alī, Muḥammad Abū al-Anwar Muḥammad, 22n
al-'Alī, Nājī, 76
alienation, alienated, estrangement, 16, 33, 76
al-'Ālim, Maḥmūd Amīn, 48n
allegory, allegorical 138
  allegorical novel 138
Allen, Roger, xi, 1, 9n, 102, 178n, 191, 211n, 215n, 240, 251
'almāniyya, 'ilmāniyya, 46n; *see also* secularism
Āl Shamshūn, 84n; *see also The Simpsons*
Altoma, Salih J., 261–2
al-Amarānī, Ḥasan, 49
ambiguity, ambiguous, 95, 136, 202, 269; *see also* clarity, obscurity
America, American, 11n, 14, 18, 19, 50n, 53n, 64, 84, 88n, 111n, 128, 141, 143n, 149, 253, 261, 262
  African-Americans, 262n
  American-Arab, Arab-American, 112n, 122n, 130
  American-Arab Anti-Discrimination Committee (ADC), 130
  American Association of Teachers of Arabic (AATA), 108n
  American authors, 64
  American Comparative Literature Association (ACLA), 148, 185n
  American-Jewish, 50n
  American literature, 13n, 63n, 64, 161
  American pop culture, 62n
  American readers, 9, 10, 263
  American reception of Arabic literature, 63n, 111n, 262–3
  American spirit, 64
  French-American, 44n
  Latin America, 160n, 264
  North America, 149, 152
  North American universities, 14
  South America, 149
Amichai, Yehuda, 227n
al-Amīn, 'Abd al-Wahhāb, 104n
Amīn, Aḥmad, 254n
Amīn, Samīr, 103n
Amīn, 'Umar 'Abd al-'Azīz, 88
al-Amīnī, Muḥammad Hādī, 53–4
Amīr Shi'r al-Ṭufūla, 56; *see also* al-Harāwī, Maḥmūd
Amīr al-Shu'arā', 147; *see also* Shawqī, Aḥmad
Amīr al-Shu'arā' (TV program), 36
amīr al-zajal al-Lubnānī, 80
Amman, 54, 186n, 253
'Ammār, Kamāl, 30n
'āmmiyya 29–33, 35, 36–40, 45, 54n, 65–70, 73n, 75n, 79–80, 85–7, 90, 98, 155, 156, 166n, 171–2, 193, 220, 221, 273; *see also* colloquial; dialect; vernacular
Amnesty International Secretariat 123n
'Amru (al-Mu'ayyad's nephew), 243
amusement (literature), 92, 96
Anā Aḥyā (novel), 118
'Anān, 'Abd Allāh, 170n
ancien régime, 72n, 192
al-Andalus, Andalusia, Andalusi, Andalusian, 135, 150, 187, 205n, 247
Anderson, Benedict, 249
anonymity, anonymous, 22n, 121n, 271
al-'Anqā' aw Ta'rīkh Ḥasan Muftāḥ (novel), 36n
anthology, anthologizing, 24, 46, 55n, 82, 87n, 91, 132n, 152, 168n, 192–3, 277
  multinational anthologies, 261
anthropologist, anthropological, 21n, 70n, 81n, 160
anti-Jewish, 118
anti-Zionist, 30
Antoon, Sinan, 128n
Aphrodite, 214
Apollo group, 198, 199n
apology, apologists, apologetic, 17, 18, 69, 256
apparatuses
  conceptual apparatuses, 64
  cultural apparatuses, 165
apprenticeship novel, 190
'Aql, Sa'īd, 45, 65n, 80, 162n, 172, 231n
'aqliyyat al-haymana, 115n

al-ʿAqqād, ʿAbbās Maḥmūd, 22n, 41, 132, 159, 198, 200, 212n, 217
ʿaks, 158n
Arabian Nights, 91, 94, 95n, 96n, 111n, 207n; *see also Alf Layla wa-Layla*
Arabian Peninsula, 151–2
Arabic
  and Qur'ān, 55n, 155n, 170–1, 172–3, 233
  and teaching, 108n, 261–2
  Arabizi, 62n
  study in the West, 141, 262
  see also ʿāmmiyya; *fuṣḥā*; language
Arabism, 133, 166n, 185, 232
  pan-Arabism, 29n, 165, 174
Arabization
  Arabization and Abridgment, 64
  Arabization of sciences, 171n
Arabized Jews, 135n
Arab League, 59, 164, 169
Arab-Muslim civilization, 120, 190s
Arab Spring, 64, 105, 276
al-ʿArabiyya lā tatanaṣṣaru, 148n
ʿArāyidī, Naʿīm, 116, 226n
archetype, archetypal, 44
  archetypal conflict, 127n
ʿArīḍa, Nasīb, 199
al-ʿArīs, Ibrāhīm, 73, 162
Arkān al-Islām (video cassette), 56n
Arkoun, Mohammed, 121n
Armbrust, Walter, 15n, 105n, 179n
Armenian, 148
ʿArsān, ʿAlī ʿUqla, 170
Arsène Lupin, 88, 89n
art, arts, artist, artistic, 3, 16, 17, 19, 20, 24, 31, 33–4, 36, 41, 58, 64, 68, 71, 72n, 85, 92, 95, 124, 129, 130, 155, 161, 162, 170n, 176, 187–8, 204, 214, 216, 217, 218n, 231, 266, 276
  art and Islam, 46, 50–4
  art and pleasure, 11n, 17, 86
  artistic creativity, 125
  artistic discourse, 52, 144
  artistic expression, 144, 233
  artistic recognition, 17
  autonomous Art, 31n
  fine arts, 51, 170n
  high/popular art, 19, 23n
  Islamic/Islamist art, 46, 50–4
  music and arts, 66n, 95
  philosophy of art, 15
  popular art, 9, 15, 17
  video art, 107
ʿaruḍ, 158n; *see also* meter, prosody
al-Asad, Ḥāfiẓ, 140
asātidhat al-adab al-rasmī, 71
Ashkāl Ukhrā (an entry in *ʿĀlam al-Kitāb*), 75
al-Ashqar, Yūsuf Ḥabashī, 174
Ashraf, Syed Ali, 144
ashrāṭ al-sāʿa, 13n
al-ʿAshrī, Jalāl, 99n
Aṣlān, Ibrāhīm, 38n
Asmahān, 77
Assimilation, 89n, 254, 256
Assyrian 204n
al-Aswānī, ʿAlā', 13n
Aṣwāt (journal), 41n, 203n, 275
ʿatābā, 69
al-ʿAtab ʿalā al-Naẓar (short stories collection), 12n
Atatürk, Mustafa Kemal, 261
atheist, atheists, 52, 271
  atheist mode of writing, 52
Athens, 25n
ʿāṭil, ʿawāṭil, ʿawāṭil al-ʿawāṭil, 15n, 158n
ʿAṭiyya, Aḥmad Muḥammad, 104n
aṭlāl, 157, 198
Atlantic, 151n
Atlantic Ocean, 182, 235
al-Aṭrash, Amal *see* Asmahān
al-Aṭrash, Farīd, 77
audience, 16, 40, 50, 57, 83n, 109, 114, 179n, 197, 221n, 226n, 262
audio cassette, 15n, 56n, 57–8, 87, 107, 222
Austen, Jane, 215–16
Austerlitz, 132
Austria (Emperor of), 158
authentic, authenticity, 146, 147, 212
  authentic representation, 30, 31n
autobiographical, autobiography, 20, 46, 52n, 102n, 132n, 135, 159, 189–90, 191, 209n, 215n, 216
  Arabic autobiographical works 189
  definition of autobiography, 63n
automatic
  automatic stock, 3, 177, 209
  automatism of perception, 200
  automatization/de-automatization, 3, 176–7, 181, 200, 208, 210
  autonomous/heteronomous, 28
avant-garde
  avant-garde journals, 131n
  avant-garde poets, 185
Averroës *see* Ibn Rushd
ʿAwaḍ, Ilyās, 205n
ʿAwaḍ, Luwīs, 36n, 111n, 120n, 206n, 262
ʿAwdat al-Rūḥ (novel), 104n
Awlād ʿAlī, 70n
Awlād Ḥāratinā (novel), 138–9, 142–3, 217n
  and *The Satanic Verses*, 138–9, 145n
ʿAyyād, Shukrī, 163
al-Ayyām (autobiography), 93n, 159, 209n, 253n
ayyām al-ʿArab, 206n
Ayyām min Ḥayātī (autobiography), 54n
Ayyūb, Rashīd, 199
al-ʿAzab, Yusrī, 73–4, 75
al-Azdī, Abū al-Muṭahhar, 220
al-Azhar, 47, 119, 120n, 122, 125
al-ʿAẓm, Ṣādiq Jalāl, 126, 132n, 144
al-ʿAẓma (al-Azmeh), ʿAzīz, 121, 145–6, 165
al-Azrī, Ḥamīd, 142

'Azza, Ḥafīdat Nefertiti (autobiography), 135n
al-'Azzāwī, Fāḍil, 41n

al-Bābaṭīn
  al-Bābaṭīn Central Library, 35n
  Mu'assasat Jā'izat 'Abd al-'Azīz Sa'ūd al-Bābaṭīn li-l-Ibdā' al-Shi'rī, 36
  Mu'jam al-Bābaṭīn li-Shu'arā' al-'Arabiyya (encyclopedic dictionary), 20n
  Mu'jam al-Bābaṭīn li-l-Shu'arā' al-'Arab al-Mu'āṣirīn (encyclopedic dictionary), 19–20, 35
Back to Methuselah (play), 142n
Badawi, Muhammad Mustafa, 11n, 178–81, 191
badī', 158n; *see also* rhetorical
Badr, 'Abd al-Bāsiṭ, 54n
Badr, Liyāna, 102n, 143n
Baghdad, 42n, 61n, 66n, 85, 168, 245, 253
  as center of Arab culture, 150, 154, 242–4
  as pluralistic, multi-confessional city, 243
  Baghdad destruction (by Hulagu), 44, 246, 248, 261–2
  Baghdad—The City in Verse (book), 274n
Bahai, 150
al-Bahnasī, 'Afīf, 184n
Bahrain, Bahraini, 167, 192, 264n
Bākathīr, 'Alī Aḥmad, 47n, 51n, 114
Bakr, Salwā, 102n
al-Bakrī, Muḥammad Tawfīq, 131–2
Bakriyya Sufi Brotherhood, 132
Ba'labakkī, Laylā, 118
al-Ba'labakkī, Munīr, 63, 88
Balba', 'Azza, 72n
Ballas, Shimon (Sham'ūn Ballāṣ), 83n
Baluchi, 55n
Bamia, Aida Adib, 169n
al-Banāt wa-l-Ṣayf (novel), 118–19
band, 71n
Bangladesh, 121n, 153n
Banipal (journal), 14, 33n
Bank Miṣr, 197
Banū Hilāl, 76n, 81n, 207, 248n
al-Baraddūnī, 'Abd Allāh, 22n
Baraitser, Lisa, 266
Barakāt, Hudā, 101n
barbarians, 235
  "barbaric culture," 262
Barbie (doll), 53n
  "Barbie culture," 53n
al-Barghūthī, 'Abd al-Laṭīf, 94n, 172–3
al-Barjawī, Sa'īd, 118
al-Barnbālī, Ṭāhir, 73n
Barrāda, Muḥammad (Mohammed Berrada), 113, 143n
al-Bārūdī, 'Abd al-Fattāḥ, 73, 194n
al-Bārūdī, Maḥmūd Sāmī, 60n, 104n, 132n, 196
Bashīr, Anṭūnyūs, 112n
Bashīr, al-Tījānī Yūsuf, 198
Basra, 243
  as freethinking city, 243
Bastille, 85, 86
baṭal, abṭāl, buṭūla, 38, 66, 187n; *see also* hero
Bauer, Thomas, 21n, 184n, 249, 250n
Bauman, Zygmunt, 265, 270
Baybars, 207, 248n
Bayle, Pierre, 237
Bayt al-Ṣiddīq (book), 132n
al-Bayyātī, 'Abd al-Wahhāb, 42–3, 125, 162, 166, 177n, 185n
Bazīgh, Shawqī, 129
al-Bazzāz, 'Aī (Ali Albazzaz), 116
BDS (Boycott, Divest, Sanction), 274n
Beck, Ulrich, 269
Becker, Wolfgang, 114n
Beckford, William, 93
Bedouin, 70n, 81n, 115
  Arab-Bedouin character, 182
  Awlād 'Alī (Egypt), 70n
  "Bedouin poet," 196
Beijerland, 48
Beirut, 41n, 60, 63, 64, 65, 88, 113, 118, 119, 124n, 126, 128, 129, 130, 150, 154, 211, 213n, 220, 264n
  Beirut International Book Fair, 12n
Beldi, 81n
Belgium, 116, 162n
belles letters, belletristic, 27n, 62n, 68n, 150, 153, 190n, 245, 246, 259
Bengali, 55n
Benin, 154n
Ben Jelloun, Tahar (al-Ṭāhir ibn Jallūn), 113, 140n, 143n, 224
Berber, 55n, 152
Berlin, 18n
Bhabha, Homi K., 146
Bible, biblical, 126
bid'a, 49
Bi-Dūn / Bidoun (journal), 11n
Bīkār, Ḥusayn, 55n
Bilād al-Sūdān 154
Bildungsroman, 190
bilingual, bilingualism, 58, 83
  bilingual editions, 58, 61n, 65
  bilingual magazine, 115n
  bilingual writers, 112n, 116, 226n
Bilkrāmī (Bilgrāmī), Ghulām 'Alī Āzād, 147
binary, binarism, 23, 244
  binary analytical methods, 269
  binary structure, 239
Bin Laden, Osama, 104n, 124n
biography, biographical, 11n, 20, 28n, 37, 46, 58, 64, 100, 156, 199n
  biographical dictionaries, 153
  see also autobiography; *tarjamāt*
bird, 76, 127
  as a symbol of femininity, 168
Birzeit
  Birzeit University, 54n, 67n

black
black slave, 169n
black/white, 239
Blackmore, R. D., 65
blank verse, 132
blasphemy (accusations)
against 'Abd al-'Azīz al-Maqāliḥ, 137n
against Adūnīs, 137
against Mārsīl Khalīfa, 126–30
against Muḥammad 'Abd al-Wahhāb, 130
against Muḥammad Iqbāl, 137
against Najīb Maḥfūẓ, 138–47
against Nawāl al-Sa'dāwī, 123
against Salman Rushdie, 138–47
Blūtūlānd wa-Qaṣā'id Ukhrā (poetry collection) 37n
Bois de Boulogne, 132
book, books
adab books, 189n; *see also adab, ādāb, adīb*
Beirut International Book Fair, 12n
book fairs, 11
Book of Psalms, 233n
books about books, 256
bookstores, 87, 118
censorship of books, 117, 120n; *see also* censorship
covers (of books), 30
fairs for children's literature, 59
Frankfurt Book Fair, 147
throwing of books into the Tigris, 248
Borges, Jorge Luis, 97n, 257
borrowing (in literature), 27, 117, 176, 178–9, 230, 238
from the West, 232
Bourdieu, Pierre, 238
bourgeois, bourgeoisie
bourgeoise monopolies of poetry, 46
classlessness of the bourgeoisie, 270
petty bourgeoisie, 270–1
Box of Wonders, Magic Box, 218–19
as semi-theatrical phenomenon, 218–19
Braudel, Fernand, 238
Brennan, Timothy, 137
Britain, British, 33, 141, 165, 179, 180, 245, 263, 269
British Parliament, 27
Brockelmann, Carl, 149n
Brontë, Charlotte, 63, 65
Brooke-Rose, Christine, 257
Brown, Dan, 119
Bsīsū, Mu'īn, 219n
Buck, Pearl, 63
Buddenbrooks (novel), 215n
Buddhism, Buddhist, 271
al-Bu'd al-Khāmis (play), 50n, 82n
al-Buḥturī, al-Walīd ibn 'Ubayd, 18
Būluṣ, Sarkūn, 45
Bunyan, John, 251
Burlesque, 210n
Burt, Clarisa, 8n, 203n
Burton, Richard, 94, 263
al-Bustānī, Buṭrus, 109, 188n, 233–4
al-Bustānī, Fu'ād Afrām, 158
al-Bustānī, Salīm, 92, 103, 158, 212, 218n
al-Bustānī, Sulaymān, 25–6
Byzantine, 184

Cain, 127, 128n
Cairo, Cairene, 37n, 38, 52, 58, 59, 60, 63, 65, 67, 73, 84, 99n, 110, 121, 123, 141, 143, 148, 150, 154, 163, 164, 197, 211n
the republic of letters' capital, 241–6
calendar (Christian, Hijri) 158
caliph, caliphate, 69n, 148n, 195, 243, 247
calligraphic state, 257
Cambridge, 36n, 144
Cambridge History of Arabic Literature (book series), 11
Cameroon, 154
Campbell, Robert B., 20, 189n
Canaanite, 133
Candide (book), 210n
Cannes Film Festival, 129n
canon, canons, canonical, canonized
"blanket" canonization, 41n
canonical center, 40–1, 54, 65, 81, 82n, 83, 89, 96, 99, 132, 144, 149, 150, 151, 154–6, 158, 163, 172, 204, 205–6, 220–1, 246, 247, 249, 273, 218, 246, 249, 273
canonical establishment, 58n, 74
canonical literature, 2, 11, 21, 22, 29–30, 35–65, 89–99, 106–7, 110n, 132, 155–6, 188, 194, 195, 198–9, 204–7, 212
canonicity, 2, 4, 22, 28, 29, 30, 33, 38, 66, 68, 273
canonization, 4, 28, 30, 33, 40, 41n, 66, 74, 90, 93, 96, 99, 172, 203–4, 208, 210, 211–12, 242, 273
canonized literature, 2–4, 14, 21–3, 29–30, 33, 71, 81–2, 85, 229; *see also* canonical literature
non-canonical literature, 15n, 21, 29, 35, 37, 41, 61n, 65–99, 106, 184, 188, 205n, 207, 246–8, 273
non-canonized literature, 2–4, 21–3, 29, 33, 79, 229; *see also* non-canonical literature
capital, capitalist, capitalism, 102n, 103, 133, 249
accumulated cultural capital, 6, 241, 242, 246, 253, 254, 256
Cairo as a cultural capital, 130, 241
global capitalism, 271
symbolic capital, 238, 255, 258
caricatures, 30, 172
carnival, carnivalesque, 222n
Carter, Jimmy, 72n
cartoons, cartoonists, 76, 78, 85
Casanova, Pascale, 7, 237–60
Catalan, 110n
category, categories, categorization, 8, 19, 23,

46, 64, 74, 78n, 152, 178n, 181n, 194, 210n, 211n, 213n, 229, 230, 239
catharsis, 50
Catholic, 118n, 162n
CDs, 58
celebrations (weddings, circumcisions), 79n, 97n
national celebrations, 162n
censorship, 68n, 118, 119, 120–1, 147, 247n, 275
banning of books, 117
elite censorship, 247n
General Security Censorship Bureau (Lebanon), 128
morality-based censorship, 118
party censorship, 121n
self-censorship, 121n
sexual taboos, 147
state censorship, 120n
theoretical dimensions of censorship, 121n
center, centers
canonical center, 40–1, 54, 65, 81, 82n, 83, 89, 96, 99, 132, 144, 149, 150, 151, 154–6, 158, 163, 172, 204, 205–6, 220–1, 246, 247, 249, 273
global centers, 24n
Center for Human Rights Legal Aid (CHRLA), 122
Chad, 154
Chahine, Youssef *see* Shāhīn, Yūsuf
Chandler, Raymond, 88
change/continuity, 6, 177, 181, 182, 183, 192
Chanson Douce (novel), 113
characters (in literature and drama), 12n, 13n, 31n, 33, 38–9, 50, 53n, 68n, 84, 144, 220, 221, 224, 227
Arab-Bedouin character, 182
main/subsidiary characters, 68n
chauvinism, 163
Chedid, Andrée, 113
Chef de Bureau, 159, 259n
Cheikho (Shaykhū), Louis, 71n, 97, 179n, 212
child, children (culture, literature, theater), 2, 4, 12, 19, 35, 53n, 54n, 55–62, 64, 65n, 66, 68, 81n, 84–7, 95, 97, 99n, 193, 208n, 227, 229
children's comics, 47n, 68, 84–5
children's drawings, 59n
children's games and songs, 61n
"prince of children's poetry," 56
public libraries for children, 55
Children of Gebelawi, 138n; *see also Awlād Ḥāratinā*
Children of Our Alley, 138, 147, 217; *see also Awlād Ḥāratinā*
China, Chinese, 91n, 108, 264
chivalry, 186, 235
Chraïbi, Driss, 113
Christ, Christian, Christianity, 10, 41, 90, 110, 115, 119, 126, 129, 131, 134, 137n, 141, 148–9, 158, 160n, 198–9, 210n, 220, 231, 233, 243, 271
Christian saints, 41n
Christian translators, 26
Christie, Agatha, 88
Christmas Songs, 87n
cinema, films, 15n, 50n, 65n, 79n, 95, 97, 114n, 129n, 170n, 261, 262n
adapting literary works to cinema, 42n
cinema and *khayāl al-ẓill*, 218n
Egyptian films, 80, 118n, 155n
Islamist cinema, 50n
movie industry, 106
producers and directors, 50n, 114n
citizen, citizenship, 122, 125, 152, 238, 270n, 271
civilization, 162, 164, 190, 191, 233, 236, 248
Arab/ Islamic civilization, 12n, 25n, 116, 120, 141, 145, 164, 191, 195, 243, 245, 255
European civilization, 236
Western civilization, 10, 11, 109n, 187, 233, 235, 272
civil rights, 122
clarity, 136; *see also* ambiguity; obscurity
class, classes, 46, 71, 94, 96, 102, 218n, 232, 270
"classlessness of the bourgeoisie," 271
elite, upper class, 55n, 217n
lower-class masses, 70, 79n
middle-class, 87
classicism, classic, classical, classicist (sources, texts), 5, 14, 15n, 18, 21n, 27, 36, 48n, 58, 63, 71, 75n, 76, 81n, 83, 92, 96, 97, 103, 110, 115, 116, 117, 127n, 132, 134, 136, 147, 152, 163, 170, 173, 176, 178, 179n, 181, 182, 183, 184, 185, 186, 189, 191, 193, 194, 195, 199, 206, 208, 218, 219, 200, 222, 244, 245, 247, 254, 255, 256, 264
classicist bias, 190
classics, 58, 63, 65, 193, 232
neoclassical, 31, 131, 158, 180, 196n, 197, 198, 206n
post-classical, 6, 156, 230, 238, 240, 241, 242, 246, 248, 249, 250, 254, 257n, 260n
classification, 75, 160, 183, 254
Cleary, Joe, 240n, 242, 258–9
clichés (about Islam), 147n, 261
coexistence, 244
colloquial, colloquialism, 14, 31n, 33, 38, 39, 71, 202, 273
colloquial poetry, 69, 70n, 78, 246, 248, 249
see also ʿāmmiyya; dialect; vernacular
Cologne, 115, 131, 138
colonial, colonialist, colonization, Colonialism, 114, 185n, 188, 228, 259
colonial identities, 89n
"colonial linguistic projects," 66n
colonial politics, 228
see also post-colonial
comics, 84
for children, 47n, 68, 84–5
Majīd (comics), 84
Samīr (comics), 84

commemoration, 156, 158, 247n
and *ḥisāb al-jummal*, 156, 158
commentary, commentaries, commentators, commentarial, 34, 249, 255, 256–7
commentarial surplus, 254
commerce, commercial, commercialism, 16, 27, 40, 55n, 59, 60, 78, 83, 226
intellectual commerce, 241
commitment, 36, 48, 51, 75, 259; *see also iltizām*
common, 166
common people, 17, 29, 247
commonwealth, 45, 170n
Islamic commonwealth of nations, 170n
communication, communicative, 3, 4, 11, 50, 89, 106, 108, 155, 173, 184, 245, 270, 271
communicative space (*literaturayj byt*), 100
Internet communication, 105, 106, 173, 266
mass communication, 50, 155, 106n
poetry-as-communication, 16
communist, communism, 133
Lebanese Communist Party, 128n
community, communities, 2, 8, 9, 22, 23, 55n, 147, 149n, 150, 184, 229, 252, 270, 271, 272
cosmopolitan community, 267
comparative literature, 148, 149n, 161, 185n, 189, 191, 219
compendium, compendia, 242, 247, 254, 256, 257
composing, composers 69n, 77n, 78, 126; *see also* music
computer (technology, games), 50n
Conant, Martha Pike, 93n
concealment (in literature), 238–9
Condé Nast International, 83n
confession
multi-confessional, 243
connotation, 238
Constantinople, 131
constellation of knowledge, 259
constraints (aesthetic/non-aesthetic), 66, 150
extrasystemic constraints, 90
consumption (literary), 1, 5, 17, 22, 60, 96, 102, 270
content, 3, 87, 91, 108, 121n, 139n, 142, 146, 156, 186, 197, 226, 249, 269
content/form, 183
content on Internet, 108
context, ix, 23, 56, 91n, 125, 131, 196, 237, 246, 248n, 258, 273
communicative context, 3
context-dependent functional category
cultural context, 4, 13n, 148
historical context, 176, 228
politico-economic context, 109
sexual context, 135n
social, sociocultural context, 3, 178n
continuity/change, 6, 177, 181, 182, 183, 192
contrafactum, 196; *see also muʿāraḍa*
conventions, conventional, 66n, 71, 79n, 181, 195, 196, 198, 199, 200, 251, 267n
conventional poets, 168
conventional prosody, 144n, 199
conversion (transformation) (in literature), 72
Cooke, Miriam, 68n
Cooperson, Michael, 26n
Copt, Coptic, 139
Coptic Pope, 149n
corpuses (of texts), 8n, 30n, 61n, 90, 189n, 195, 246–9, 254, 273
cosmopolis, cosmopolitan, cosmopolitanism, 173–4, 238, 241–4, 267–71
Alexandrian cosmopolitanism, 242, 267–8
Arabic cosmopolis, 25n
cosmopolitan community, 267
cosmopolitan intermediaries, 242
cosmopolitan republic, 238
cosmopolitan spirit, 267
cosmopolitan turn, 243, 267–71
death of cosmopolitanism, 267–8
moral cosmopolitanism, 270n
countryside, 70, 209n, 223n
poets of the countryside, 70
"spirit of the countryside," 223n
see also rīf, aryāf; town/country
creation, creative, creativity (in culture), 1n, 5n, 15, 20n, 36, 53n, 56, 68n, 86, 95, 100, 102, 107, 100n, 113n, 124, 125, 129, 149, 161, 164, 167n, 176, 182, 184, 186, 189n, 211, 218, 222, 257, 249–50, 266, 276, 277
creative ability (*ibdāʿ*), 188
cri de coeur, 109, 231n
criterion, criteria (for canonicity), 17, 20, 29, 38, 45, 217
aesthetic criteria, 8n, 18
criticism, critique, critics, critical (literary), 4, 11, 13, 15n, 17, 18, 20, 21, 22, 24, 25n, 26n, 28n, 31, 32, 34, 38, 39, 40, 41n, 45, 47, 48n, 50n, 51, 52, 54, 60, 66, 71, 73, 75, 79, 83, 87, 93, 99, 100, 103, 104n, 107, 109, 110, 112, 113, 120n, 124n, 133n, 136, 141n, 144, 152, 161, 163, 169, 170, 180, 181, 185n, 186, 188n, 189n, 195, 196, 199, 201, 202, 205n, 207n, 220, 224, 225, 231, 232, 236, 238, 242, 252, 253, 254, 257, 258, 262, 263, 264, 268, 274; *see also naqd*
antiessentialist critique, 265
social/political criticism, 84, 102, 210
crossword, sudoku, 158, 170
Crusades, 141, 187
culture, cultural, 5, 12, 13n, 15, 19, 22, 23, 27, 42n, 45, 46–7, 55, 58, 59, 61, 63, 65, 69, 70, 71, 77n, 85, 95, 97, 102, 104–5, 106, 107, 116, 121, 131, 133, 134, 146, 148, 150, 155, 160, 162, 164–5, 189, 190, 211, 216, 218, 219, 233, 237, 252, 272
Arab-American culture, 112n
Arab-German culture, 114–15
Arab-Jewish culture, 274n
"barbaric culture," 262
Barbie culture, 53n

cross-cultural interaction, 64, 110
cultural capital, 6, 130, 238, 241, 242, 246, 253, 254, 256, 258
cultural heritage, 2, 14, 16, 22, 83n, 89n, 131, 132, 133, 134n, 145n, 146, 149, 154n, 164n, 168, 169, 170n, 190n, 219n, 233, 244, 251
cultural identities, 32n, 53n, 89n, 113, 116–17, 133, 145, 149n, 155n, 163n, 164, 169n, 170, 247, 274
cultural invasion, 52, 62, 83
cultural relativism, 24, 146
cultural systems, 28, 89, 100, 149
cultural territorialism, 160–74
cultural value, quality, 8, 16
cultural violence, 125
culture populaire, 2
definitions (of culture), 11n, 70n
Egyptian culture, 29n, 30n, 37n, 80, 138n, 151n
electronic culture, 60
feminist culture, 90
German culture, 114
global, globalized culture, 5, 32n, 174
Greek culture, 24–5
high/highbrow culture, 11, 16, 17, 18
Israeli culture, 226n
Jewish culture, 150
mass culture, 15, 84, 165
material culture, 66n
Ministry of Culture (Egypt), 73–4, 124, 143–4
Ministry of Culture and Information (Iraq), 66n
multicultural policy, 243–4
peasant culture, 219, 254
popular culture, 14, 15n, 17n
sociocultural context, distinctions, 2, 3, 15, 16, 21, 22n, 72, 103, 159, 184
Supreme Council for Culture *see al-Majlis al-A'lā li-l-Thaqāfa*
Western culture, 81, 84, 94, 108, 109, 184, 187, 193, 194, 231–2, 263
curriculum, curricula (for schools), 38, 55n
Cyprus, 124n

Dabashi, Hamid, 259
Dabka, 219
al-Ḍaʻīf (Daïf), Rashīd, 69n, 224, 225
d'Alembert, Jean Le Rond, 260
Dalīla (Delilah), 92, 150
Dalīl Maktabāt al-Adab al-Islāmī (book), 54n
Dalʻūnā, 219
Damascus, 117, 157, 168, 201, 219n
al-Dāmūn (prison), 49n
dance, dancers, 66n, 219
Daninos, Abraham, 220
Dante, Alighieri, 187, 188
Dara (doll), 53n
Dārghawth, Rashād, 56
Dār al-Ḥarb, 210n
Dār al-Islām, 210n
Dark Ages, 128, 129; *see also* Middle Ages
Darwīsh, Maḥmūd, 76, 97n, 126, 143n, 225, 226n
Darwīsh, Sayyid, 71n, 73n
Darwīsh, Shālom, 209n
Dā'ūd, Anas, 61
Dāʻūq, Bashīr, 126
Davidson, Cathy, x
al-daʻwa ilā al-ʻāmmiyya, 171n
Ḍayf, Aḥmad, 162n
Day of Judgment, 13n
death/rebirth, 137n
death sentence, 122, 125, 138–9, 142
de-automatization/de-familiarization, 3, 176–7, 181, 200, 208, 210
de Balzac, Honoré, 214, 224
decadence, 108, 177n, 232, 248, 251, 252; *see also* decline; *inḥiṭāṭ*; stagnation
de Cervantes, Miguel, 65, 187
decline, 32n, 79, 114, 172, 247, 268
of Arabs' self-esteem, 232, 233, 237, 254n
of Arab culture in the post-classical period, 248, 251, 255; *see also* decadence; *inḥiṭāṭ*; stagnation
decolonization, 250, 255
dedications (in literary works), 15n, 30, 48, 80, 113, 120, 130, 253n
Defoe, Daniel, 65, 90, 188–9
de Montaigne, Michel, 256, 257
descriptive, 19, 100, 228, 229
de Staël, Madame, 214
detective stories, novels, 10, 13, 18, 67, 82–3, 87–8
deviation, deviant, 39n, 57, 187, 188, 250, 255
deviations in metrics, 199, 201
sexual deviation, 94
DeYoung, Terri, 180–1
dhākira
dhākira jamāʻiyya, 95
al-Dhākira al-Mawshūma (novel), 160n
dhākirat al-umma, 107
see also memory, memories
Dhihnī, Maḥmūd, 15n
Dhihniyyat al-Taḥrīm (book), 144
Mā Baʻda Dhihniyyat al-Taḥrīm (book), 144n
dhikr (rituals), 47n, 247
dhuyūl, 256
diachronic, diachrony, 4–5, 230
diachronic correlativity, 273
diachronic intersystemic development, 100–74
diachronic value, 229, 273
generic and diachronic cross-section, 175–227
diacritical points, 156–7
dialect, 29, 30, 31, 33n, 35, 36, 37n, 65, 67n, 71, 89n, 106n, 159, 171, 172–3, 201, 256n
dialectal poetry, 69
dialect literature, 68
see also ʻāmmiyya; colloquial; vernacular
dialogue, dialogic, 84n, 110, 115n, 208, 213, 215, 219, 221, 241
dialogic space, 259

dialogue, dialogic (*cont.*)
dialogue in fiction, 14, 29, 31, 33, 36, 38–9, 67, 68
meta-fictional dialogue, 216
diaspora, 126, 146, 149
dichotomy, dichotomies
canonical/non-canonical, 15n
domestic/foreign, x, 269
fuṣḥā/*ʿāmmiyya*, 33
good/bad (in literature), 22, 225n
great tradition/little tradition, 21n
iqlīmiyya/ *waḥda*, 164
maḥalliyya/*qawmiyya*, 164
office/home, x
private/public, x, 185n, 238
work/play, x
Dickens, Charles, 63, 65
dictator, dictatorship, 84, 105, 146, 171n
diction (poetic), 132, 254
dictionary, dictionaries
biographical dictionary, 153
encyclopedic dictionary, 19–20, 35–6
*see also mu*ʿ*jam*; *qāmūs*
didactic, didacticism, 56, 61, 62
didactic committed literature, 56
didactic historical novels, 212
didactic romance, 90n
Diderot, Denis, 260
Die Serapionsbrüder (collection of stories), 215
digital
digital humanities, 148
digital texts, 266
diglossia, 155, 246
al-Dindān (ʿAbd Allāh ibn Muḥammad ibn Ḥazayyim), 81
discourse, 22, 54, 111, 125, 135, 166, 210, 230, 265
European, 253, 254
Islamist, 52, 56, 123n, 144, 146
journalistic discourse, 210
liberal, xn, 119n, 121n
literary, 3, 144
metadiscourse, 256
metalinguistic, 65n
modernist, 146
narrative, 92n, 207–8, 211
poetical, 30, 200
postcolonial, orientalist, 139, 248
Preliminary Discourse, 6, 238, 253, 260
religious, 134, 144
scholarly, 51n
secular, secularist, 53, 145
totalizing, 102
dismissive attitude (toward popular literature), 13, 205n
dissertations (doctoral), 14, 153
dissimulation (in literature), 238–9
distinctive, distinction, distinctiveness, 18, 19n, 28, 31, 46, 50, 65, 149, 163, 164n, 170, 173, 183, 201, 229, 241, 249
devalorizing, 23n
ethnographic, 165
high/popular art, 23n
distribution (of literature), 46n, 63
diversion (assets, wealth, capital, resources), 254–5
diversity/unity, 164–5
al-Dīwān fī al-Adab wa-l-Naqd (book), 159, 198n
al-Dīwān group, 198
Djebar, Assia, 113
Djiboutian, 169
dolls (as symbols of culture), 9, 53n
domestic/public sphere, 102
Donald Duck, 84
Don Quixote (novel), 65, 187
Douglas, Allen, 84
Doyle, Conan
drama, dramatists, 9, 10, 29, 30, 40, 46, 50, 65n, 98–9, 115n, 152, 161, 179, 186, 218–22, 223, 227
dramatic adaptation, 227
dramatic characters, 221
dramatic monologues, 218n
monodrama, 226n
semi-dramatic, 218
social drama, 30–1, 68
verse, versified drama, 99
see also masraḥ; theater
dress code, 53n
drugs, 30n, 90n
Druze, 153, 160n
Dualist, 243
du Bellay, Joachim, 255
Dumas, Alexandre, 65
Dünges, Petra, 61n
Dunqul, Amal, 97
Dutch, 116
Dylan, Bob, 19, 126

Eagleton, Terry, 5, 241
East, Eastern, 20, 68n, 93, 94, 109, 110, 115n, 133n, 145, 154, 155n, 164, 166, 174, 182, 187–8, 191, 198, 205n, 219, 223, 232n, 236; *see also* Middle East; Orientalism; "reversed Orientalism"; West
Easternization of the West, 187–8
East Jordan, 168
Ebers, George, 114, 213n
economic, economics, 4, 5, 11n, 28, 62n, 109, 152, 188n, 197n, 267, 270, 272
economic systems, 102–3
economy-world system, 238
Western economic capitalism, 103
edifice (literary, canonical), 9n, 238
edition, editions, 9, 20n, 30, 31n, 37n, 58, 60n, 65, 69n, 82n, 83n, 87, 91n, 96n, 113, 116, 117, 118, 120n, 124n, 136n, 193n, 200, 203n, 223, 235
bilingual editions, 58, 61n, 65

electronic edition, 20
pirate edition, 136n
education, educational, 17, 23n, 56, 58, 59n, 61, 62n, 107, 162, 183, 188n, 195, 252, 253, 260
educational shows, plays, music, 56
education of children, 55n, 58, 59n, 62n
education of princes, 55n
Ministry of Education (Egypt), 38
Ministry of Education (Gaza), 168n
Ministry of Education (Ramallah), 168n
"Minute on Indian Education," 190n
effeminate, 12n; *see also* gay; homosexual
Eisenhower, Dwight D., 217
El-Ariss, Tarek, 255
Elbaz, Robert, 113n
electronic media, 5, 36, 52, 60, 74, 77, 101, 106, 107, 162, 210, 221
Dubai-based Arabic MBC, 84n
Egyptian National Radio, 78
electronic culture, 60
electronic edition, 20
mass media, 15n, 50, 78, 106n, 155
satellite channels, 78, 84n, 106n, 155, 276
social media, 125, 274–8
transistor radio, 77n
see also journalism; radio; television
elegy, 8n, 25n, 44n, 135, 166; *see also marthiya, rithā'*
Eliot, T. S., 24, 33–4, 202
elite, elitist, elitism, 18, 21–2, 29n, 40n, 45, 62n, 91, 96, 126, 158n, 247, 254, 256, 267, 268, 276
cosmopolitan elite, 268n
critical elite, 21
elite poetry, 15–16, 249
elite prose, 249
Elkhadem, Saad, 87, 88
Elster, Ernst, 161n
embellishments (rhetorical), 156n, 159
empire, 243, 256
Ottoman Empire, 108, 131, 232, 267
'En 'Abdat (inscription), 204
encyclopedia, encyclopedic, 19, 35, 167, 240, 243, 260
England, 18, 68n, 90n, 165, 215
English, Englishness, 12n, 14, 33, 34, 58, 60, 62, 63, 65, 81–2, 83n, 87, 90, 92, 93n, 94, 101n, 111n, 112, 114, 138n, 151, 152–3, 161, 171n, 179n, 189, 193, 199, 202, 206n, 207n, 208n, 213n, 221n, 251, 263, 268
Arab authors in English, 112, 264
English as *lingua franca*, 267
Inglizi, 62n
Enlightenment, 238
European Enlightenment, 252, 253–4
see also Nahḍa
entertainment, 10, 68n, 77n, 212
demi-monde of, 90
in Islamic tradition, 219n
popular, 18
semi-theatrical, 247
EOHR (Egyptian Organization for Human Rights), 122, 125n
epics, epic poetry, 25, 207, 247, 248n
epic trilogy, 99n; *see also thulāthiyya malḥamiyya*
epigonic, 195
episteme, epistemology, epistemological, 8n, 180
equations, 69
adab and belles letters, 246
'āmmiyya and non-canonized literature, 33, 68, 273
fuṣḥā and canonized literature, 33, 68, 273
Latin and Arabic, 238
secularism, humanism, and modernism, 259, 260
erotic, 67, 68n, 139n
erotic literature, 67
homoerotic texts, 13n
establishment (literary), 11, 21, 22, 28, 38, 53, 59, 72, 73, 74, 76, 132, 146, 152, 153; *see also* canonical center
ethnos, ethnic, ethnicity, ethnographic, 81, 150, 152, 165, 243, 265, 268
etymology, 239
eunuch poets, 42
euphemistic, 22
Euphrates, 204n
Eurocentric, Eurocentrism, 261
Eurocentric biases, 148
Europe, European, 10, 27, 34, 45n, 90, 92, 93–4, 95n, 108, 109–10, 111n, 121, 147, 169, 171n, 177n, 179, 183, 185n, 186–7, 190n, 191, 207n, 210n, 214, 216, 220, 232–3, 235, 236, 241, 244, 245, 246, 248, 250, 252, 253, 254–5, 257, 260, 262–3, 267
European languages, ix, 92
European reception of Arabic literature, 262–3
Old Europe, 241
seductive Europe, 252, 255
see also West, Western
evaluation (of literature and art), evaluative, 9n, 15n, 21n, 22, 273
evaluative judgments, 19, 20, 24n, 229n
evaluative mantra, 269n
see also merit, value, worth
exclusive, exclusion, 15n, 28, 40, 214, 216, 226, 249
of Arab culture, 263
see also inclusion/exclusion
exilarch, 243
exile, 54n, 67n, 85, 241
exiled poets, 203
existentialist alienation, 16
exotic, exotics, 215
and *Alf Layla wa-Layla*, 263
experiment, experimental, 37, 104, 186, 199–200, 215n, 225, 277
experimental encounter, 112
experimental writing, 30, 102, 105
literary experiments, 186

extra-literary, non-literary (systems, contexts), 100, 103, 116, 176, 229, 261, 273
extroversion/introversion, 250n

fables, 92, 219n
Facebook, 274–8
Facebook poet, 278
Facebook texts, 275
Fāḍil, Jihād, 45, 133, 170, 172
Fāḍil, Suhayl, 115; *see also* Schami, Rafik
Faḍl, Ṣalāḥ, 120n
Faḍl Allāh, Muḥammad Ḥusayn, 41n, 47n, 68n, 132n, 145
Fahmī, 'Alī, 29n
Fā'iq, Ṣalāḥ, 276
Fakhreddine, Huda J., 178n
fanatical, fanaticism, 110, 143n, 145, 171n
fann, funūn, fannān, fannī, 15, 20, 36, 39n, 51, 67n, 77n, 83n, 187n, 188, 220n, 260n
fann al-niswān, 218n
fantasy (and science fiction), 81n
Farādīs (journal), 131n, 138n, 203
Faraj, Murād, 134–5
al-faraj ba'da al-shidda, 206n
farce, 219, 221
Farḥāt, Muḥammad 'Alī, 223n
Farīd, Muḥammad, 70
al-Fārisī, Sa'īda Khāṭir, 147
al-Fāris: Majallat al-Rajul al-'Aṣrī (magazine), 83n
fascism, 145, 146, 171n
fatwā, 125
against Maḥfūẓ, 142–3
against Rushdie, 139
Faust (play), 114, 116n
fawāzīr, 86
Fawda (Foda), Faraj, 122, 125
Fayrūz, 18, 78, 87n
Fayyāḍ, Ashraf, 125
Feghali, Jeanette; *see* Ṣabāḥ
fellahin, 76
feminist, feminism, femininity, 25n, 102n, 103, 123n, 265
culture, 90
Islamic feminism, 102n
literature, 101n, 102n
magazine, 83n
oppression (of women), 67n, 123
post-feminism, 270
studies, 102n
symbol of femininity, 168n
writings, 105n, 122, 276
Fénelon, François de Salignac, 90n
Ferguson, Charles, 173
Fezzan, 154
Fī al-Adab al-Jāhilī (book), 120
Fī al-'Ashāyā (children's book), 56
fiction, fictional, fictionality, fictionalized, 81n, 206–18, 224–5
dialogue in, 14, 29, 31, 33, 36, 38, 67n, 68, 208n, 213–16
fictional techniques, 215n
metafictional, 187
popular, 81
science fiction, 81–2
al-Fihrist al-'Aṣriyya li-l-Waṭan al-'Arabī (book), 74
Fikr wa-Fann (journal), 111n, 114n
films *see* cinema
Filshtinsky, I. M., 184
fine arts, 51
firāsa, 213
al-Firdaws (journal), 47n
Firqat al-Mukhtabar al-Masraḥī al-Sūrī, 219n
First World War, World War I, 87, 161, 269n
Fī al-Shi'r al-Jāhilī (book), 119–20
fitna, 198
Flanders, 162n
Flemish, 162n
fluid, fluidity (of identity), 266, 268
folklore, folkloristic, 17n, 66n, 76n, 90, 168n, 186, 219
folktales, folkloristic tales, 92, 168n
heritage, 14n, 169
music, 66n, 79n, 205n
songs, 70
see also canon; stratification; *zajal*
Fontaine, Jean, 167n
form, forms (literary), 3, 15, 20, 31n, 46, 47, 48n, 55n, 69, 71n, 75, 76, 80, 82, 86, 87, 89, 97, 102, 105, 156, 161, 176, 177n, 183, 185n, 186, 193, 194, 195, 197, 198, 199, 200–6, 212, 228, 229, 249
Formalism, Formalists, 2, 3, 100
Foucault, Michel, 256–7
fragmented, fragmentation 106, 133n, 170, 171n, 206n, 224, 246, 265, 269, 271
framework, frameworks, 23, 33, 90, 94, 116, 117, 132, 137, 146, 147, 148, 149, 150, 176, 193, 196, 197, 199, 205, 229, 230
theoretical framework, ix, 2, 4, 5, 7, 9, 19, 237, 265, 269, 273–4
France, French, 7, 23n, 44, 62n, 63, 67, 87–8, 90n, 92, 97, 103, 11n, 113, 131, 132, 141, 160, 161, 162n, 165, 168, 170n, 171n, 179, 180, 187n, 202, 207, 211, 214, 215, 216, 217, 221, 237, 238, 239n, 245, 246n, 255, 264, 267, 268
Arabs authors in French, 112–14, 231n, 264
French as *lingua franca*, 268
Franks, Frankish, 234–5; *see also Ifranj, Ifranjī*
free verse, 48n, 177n, 193, 199–205, 275; *see also shi'r ḥurr*
freedom, 11n, 105, 188, 200, 242, 251, 257, 259, 272
academic freedom, 122
freedom of speech, expression, 120n, 121n, 125, 128, 129n, 130
fringes (of society, literary system), 79, 93, 247; *see also hāmish, hawāmish*; margins
Frosh, Stephen, 266

fukāha, fukāhāt, 75n, 212
ḥusn al-fukāha, 159
al-Fukāha wa-l-Ītinās fī Mujūn Abī Nuwās (book), 118
Fulk ibn Fulk (Fulk, King of Jerusalem), 234–5
Fulla (doll), 53n
function, functional, functionalist, 3, 4, 18, 20, 23, 24, 26, 27, 28, 30, 33, 68, 72, 100, 107, 136, 177, 181, 194n, 210, 212, 222n, 229, 242, 252, 272, 273
functional dynamic historical model, 4, 33, 229
functional interrelationships, 4, 89
non-static function, 4, 33
poetic function, 3, 177
pre-functionalist, 28
fundamentalist, fundamentalism, 121, 129, 145, 152, 261
fundamentalist madness, 243
Furayḥa (Frayha, Freiha), Anīs, 66
furūsiyya, 234
fuṣḥā, 15n, 29–33, 35, 36–40, 45, 54n, 56, 65–6, 67n, 68–71, 75, 76, 77, 79, 80n, 85n, 86, 88, 90, 98, 155, 156, 171, 172–3, 193, 194, 195, 220, 221, 273
fuṣḥā sha'biyya, 65n
see also Arabic; language

Gajarati, 55n
Galilei, Galileo, 121
Galland, Antoine, 93n
Gates, Henrey Louis, 28
gay, 9, 12, 84n; *see also* effeminate; homosexual
gay magazine, 12n
gay rights, 13n
gender, gendering, 5, 101–2, 149n, 152
gender and feminist literature, 113–14
interaction with literature, 102
generation, 24, 41, 57, 64, 66n, 71, 158, 177, 181, 182, 203, 212, 232, 238, 249, 265, 268, 271, 274
Internet generation, 268
nineties poets, 8n
sixties generation, 181n; *see also jīl al-sittīnāt*
genre, generic, 3, 5, 8, 10, 11, 13, 14, 15n, 18, 21, 25, 29, 30, 35, 39, 40, 46, 48, 49, 50–1, 55n, 63, 66n, 75, 81–3, 84, 88, 89, 90n, 95, 97, 98, 99, 109n, 144n, 146, 152, 153, 156n, 175–227, 230, 247, 248, 251, 254, 263n, 272, 275
generic interrelationships, 222–7
genre theory, 5, 175
mixture of genres, 254
non-literary genres, 8
oral genres, 69n
Genette, Gérard, 250n
German, Germany, 10, 61n, 63, 67n, 92, 97, 111n, 114–15, 118, 141, 147, 161, 165, 171, 213, 215, 235, 264
Arab-German cultural dialogue, 115n
Arab-German literature, 115n
Arab writers in German, 114–15
Arabic-German magazine, 115n
German cinema and literature, 97
German influence in the Middle East, 114
German-Jewish, 13n
German Orientalism, 114n
German scholarship, 114n
German translations of Arabic works, 115
Ghānim, Shukrī, 264n
gharb, maghrib, 20, 95n, 140, 144, 145, 157n, 164, 187, 205n, 231; *see also* West
gharīb, 98, 132
ghawghā', 71
al-Ghāyātī, 'Alī, 70
al-Ghayṭī, Muḥammad, 74
ghazal, 157, 194
al-Ghazālī, Abū Ḥāmid, 189n
al-Ghazālī, Nāẓim, 78
al-Ghazālī, Zaynab, 54n
Ghāzī, Aḥmad, 74
ghazw thaqāfī, 24n, 52, 62, 83n
Ghazzūl, Firyāl Jabūrī, 60n
ghinnāwas, 70n; *see also ughniyya, aghānin*
al-Ghirbāl (book), 109, 231
al-Ghīṭānī, Jamāl, 143n, 210
Gibb, Hamilton, 183, 191–2
Gibran, Kahlil, 89n, 112n, 113; *see also* Jubrān, Jubrān Khalīl
global, globalization, 32n, 59, 173–4, 243, 265, 267–71
global capitalism, 271
global centers, 24n
global cities, 269
globalized culture, 174, 268
globalized Middle East, 268
global literary space, 5, 241
global transformation of modernity, 269
global village, 268
Globish, 268
glocalization, 269
glorification, 70, 125, 132, 234
Gnostic, 243
Goethe, Johann Wolfgang von, 114, 115–16, 141
Goethean tragedy, 114
golden age, 87, 91, 191n, 192, 196
Goldziher, Ignác, 174, 181, 215
report for the Hungarian Academy of Sciences, 174, 215
Gombrich, E. H., 176
good/bad (in literature), 22, 225n
Good Bye, Lenin! (film), 114n
Goodman, Dena, 7, 237
graffiti, 69n
grammar (Arabic), 25, 233n, 249
Granada, 44n
"that crime in Granada," 44n
graphics (in literature), 59
Great Tradition/Little Tradition, 21n

Greek, Greece, 25–7, 31, 147, 148, 182, 183, 184, 192
Greek culture, 24–7
Greek descent, 147
Greek literary models, 24–5
Greek literature, 25–7, 182, 183, 184
translation from Greek, 24–7
Greenwich meridian, 242
Guantánamo Bay (prison), 88n
Guernica (painting), 107
Gulf, 151n, 152, 173n
Gulf War, 85n
Persian Gulf, 180, 182
Gulliver's Travels (satire), 57–8
Gutenberg Museum Mainz, 61n

Ḥabībī, Imīl, 104n, 143n, 210, 219n, 227, 263n
habitus, 13
ḥadātha, 185n; *see also* modernism
Ḥaddād, Fu'ād, 73, 75
al-Ḥaddād, Najīb, 108n
Ḥaddād, Nuhād, 18, 78; *see also* Fayrūz
Ḥadīqat al-Akhbār (newspaper), 27, 211
Ḥadīqat al-Ḥawāss (poetic texts), 119
Ḥadīth 'Īsā ibn Hishām (book), 187
Ḥadīth (Prophetic traditions), 125
Haeri, Niloofar, 173n
Ḥāfiẓ, 'Abd al-Ḥalīm, 78
Ḥāfiẓ, Sabrī (Sabry Hafez), 207n
Haggard, Rider, 214
Haifa, 14, 54n, 189n
Haifa Municipal Theater, 226n
al-Hajeri, Saud, 107n
al-Ḥajj, 47n
al-Ḥajjāj ibn Yūsuf al-Thaqafī (historical novel), 212
Ḥajjār, Bassām, 88
ḥakawātī, 218, 219n, 222; *see also* storytellers
al-Ḥakīm, Tawfīq, 37n, 82n, 104n, 120n, 144, 217, 218n, 221n, 263n
Hale, Sondra, 123n
Ḥalīb al-Thīrān (collection of short stories), 37n
"Hal Kāna Ḥubban?" (poem), 200
Hall, Stuart, 265
"hallucinatory" literature, 90n
al-Hamadhānī, Badī' al-Zamān, 117, 157, 210n
ḥamās, 92
Hamas, 168n
al-Ḥamāsa (anthology), 192–3
Ḥamdī, Muḥammad, 55n
Hamdouchi, Abdelilah, 83n
hāmish, hawāmish, 21
hawāmish bashariyya, 37
see also fringes; margins
Ḥammād 'Ajrad, 243
Handal, Nathalie, 44n
Hanley, Will, 267n, 268
Hansel and Gretel (fairy tale), 57
Ḥarāfish, 29–30
Malḥamat al-Ḥarāfish (novel), 250
ḥarakat al-tarjama, 90; *see also* translation
al-Harāwī, Maḥmūd, 56
al-Ḥarīrī, Abū Muḥammad al-Qāsim ibn 'Alī, 42, 129, 131, 157
al-Ḥarīrī, Rafīq, 129
Harry Potter, 88n
Hašek, Jaroslav, 210n
Hassan, Waïl S., 26n
"Ḥassān al-Hind," 147
Hausa, 55
Havermann, Hermann, 108
Ḥawāmida, Mūsā, 128n
ḥawāshin, 256
Ḥāwī, Khalīl, 144
al-Hay'a al-Miṣriyya al-'Āmma li-l-Kitāb, 58n, 60n
al-Ḥayāt (newspaper), 105n, 188n
al-ḥayāt al-adabiyya, 151n, 168n, 246n
Ḥaydar, Ḥaydar, 124
al-Ḥaydarī, Buland, 107
Haykal, Muḥammad Ḥussayn, 211, 216n, 263n
Haywood, John A., 13–14, 191
Ḥayy ibn Yaqẓān (book), 189–90, 190n
Hebrew, 27n, 99, 162, 226, 264
Hebrew literature, 28, 63, 104
Hebrew literature and Zionism, 104
Hebrew words in Arabic poetry, 36
Palestinian writes in Hebrew, 116, 160n, 227n
translations from Hebrew literature, 11n, 118
hegemony, hegemonic, hegemonistic, 50, 103, 198n
hegemonic global centers, 24n
Hemingway, Ernest, 63
hemistich (in poetry), 156–7
heretic, 130n, 137, 243; *see also* blasphemy; *mulḥid*; *zindīq*
heritage, 2, 14, 16, 22, 39n, 40, 48, 67, 83, 86, 89n, 95n, 97n, 131n, 132, 133, 134n, 140, 143n, 145n, 146, 149, 154n, 164, 168, 179n, 190n, 193, 233, 264, 270, 277
Abu Dhabi Authority for Culture and Heritage, 36n, 63
Arabic literary heritage, 40, 149, 170n, 178n, 185, 186n, 207n, 233, 244, 277
Arab-Muslim heritage, 131n, 203n, 251, 255
folkloristic heritage, 14n, 169
Lebanese heritage written in French, 264n
Palestinian theatrical heritage, 219n
hero, heroine, heroism, 74, 84, 169n, 214, 216, 219n, 250n, 270n
hierarchy, hierarchies, 46, 176, 244
hierarchies of value, 19, 24n
highbrow/lowbrow, 11, 12, 13, 14, 15, 21, 90; *see also* canon, canons, canonical, canonized
hijā', 198
Ḥijāz, 150, 168n
Ḥijāzī, Aḥmad 'Abd al-Mu'ṭī, 201n
Ḥijāzī, Aḥmad Ibrāhīm, 76
Ḥijāzī, Fu'ād, 58
al-Hijra, 47n

ḥikāya, *ḥikāyāt*, 37, 91n, 219, 220
ḥikāya laṭīfa, 109n, 235
Ḥikāyat Abī al-Qāsim al-Baghdādī (book), 220
Ḥikāyāt Ḥāratinā (novel), 209
Ḥikāyat Zahra (novel), 119
al-Hilāl (journal), 73n, 163
al-Ḥillī, Ṣafī al-Dīn, 15n
Hindus, 271
Ḥīra, 204
ḥisāb al-jummal, 156–8
Ḥisba, 123–4
Hispano-Arabic, 179n
history, historic, historical, historians, 18, 24, 26, 31, 34, 44, 47, 55n, 58, 64, 65, 76, 86, 89, 93, 102n, 121, 137, 142n, 146, 152, 153, 160, 162, 166, 167n, 169n, 175, 212, 213, 224, 236, 240, 245, 255n, 257, 261, 267, 268, 271
combative history, 16
historical chronicles, 210, 244
historical hero, 84
historical novels, 10, 69n, 114, 212–13
historical periods, 81n, 179
historical plays, 40, 221
historical poetics, 2, 3, 180, 181
historic, historical present (tense), 208n, 228n
historical relativism, 24, 146
historical romances, 10, 91
historicization, 119n
historicizing the Qur'ān, 137
historiography, 24, 268
history and value, 228
literary history, 1, 3, 8n, 11, 49, 101n, 131, 148, 150, 152, 153, 163, 175–81, 183, 185n, 192, 204n, 208n, 211n, 274
transhistorical, 228
Ḥitāta, Sharīf (Sherif Hatata), 123
Ḥizb Allāh, 42n, 50n, 51n, 68n, 145
Hobsbawm, Eric, 160, 161, 162n
Hoffmann, E. T. A., 215 n
Holland, 48, 165
Hollywood, 50n, 262n
Homer, Homeric, 25, 137n
homo-erotic themes, 13n
homogenization, homogenized, 165
homosexual, homosexuality, 10, 12, 13n, 68n
homosexuality in Islam, 12n
see also effeminate; gay
Huart, Clément, 170n
Hugo, Victor, 63, 65, 227
Hulagu, 43–4, 248
humanism, humanist
Arab classical humanism, 255
humanism and modernism, 259
humanism in Islam, 23n
Latinist humanism, 255
scholar/humanist, 117n
secularism, humanism, and modernism, 259, 260
humanitarian, 42
humanities, 148, 269
digital humanities, 148
human rights, 122, 124, 270
Human Rights Watch, 129n, 130
al-Ḥumaydī, Muḥammad Jāsim, 67n
humor, humoristic, 22, 30, 36n, 70, 168n, 212, 254
political humor, 13
Hungarian Academy of Sciences, 174, 215
hunt, 177n
hunt poems, 177n, 194
witch hunt, 129
Hunwick, J. O., 153
Ḥusayn, Muḥammad al-Kahḍr, 119n
Ḥusayn, Muṣṭafā, 55n
Ḥusayn, Ṣaddām, 42n, 70, 84, 104n, 253n
Ḥusayn, Ṭāhā, 26, 28, 31, 32n, 93n, 94n, 101, 116, 119–21, 133n, 144, 159, 170n, 182–3, 191, 201, 209n, 217, 253, 256, 259n, 260
al-Ḥusnī, ʻAbd al-Ḥayy, 153
Ḥusnī, Suʻād, 118n
al-Ḥuṣrī, Sāṭiʻ, 163, 170
Hussein, Taha *see* Ḥusayn, Ṭāhā
hymns, 47n, 124
hypertextuality, 250

iʻādat tarkīb, 172
ibdāʻ, 20n, 85, 95, 187–8, 196n, 277; *see also* creation
Ibdāʻ (journal), 74
ibn ʻAbd al-Qaddūs, Ṣāliḥ, 243
ibn Abd al-Wahhab, Muhammad, 179
ibn Abī Ṭālib, ʻAlī, 48n, 195
ibn Aḥmad, al-Khalīl, 144n, 201, 243
ibn al-ʻAjjāj, Ru'ba, 131
ibn al-Akfānī, Muḥammad ibn Ibrāhīm, 245n
Ibn Bassām al-Andalusī, 205n
ibn Burd, Bashshār, 147n, 243
ibn Fahd, Fayṣal, 30n
Ibn Ḥazm, 205n
ibn Isḥāq, Ḥunayn, 25n
Ibn Kamāl Bāshā (Aḥmad ibn Sulaymān), 96n
Ibn Khaldūn, 98n, 191
ibn Muḥammad, al-Nāshī Abū al-ʻAbbās ʻAbd Allāh, 98n
ibn Muḥammad al-Ḥimyarī, al-Sayyid, 243
ibn Mujāshiʻ, Sufyān, 243
ibn Munqidh, Usāma, 31n, 189n, 234–5
ibn al-Muthannā, Khalaf, 243
Ibn al-Nadīm, 91, 218n, 219n
Ibn Naẓīr, 243
Ibn Quzmān, 69n
Ibn al-Rūmī, 146n
Ibn Rushd, 121
Ibn Rushd Fund for Freedom of Thought, 66
ibn Sahl, Ibrāhīm, 135
ibn Saʻīd, Qābūs (the Sultan), 169
Ibn Ṣayqal al-Jazarī, 157n
ibn Sinān al-Ḥarrānī, Rawḥ, 243
ibn Ṭalāl, al-Walīd, 56

ibn Tamīm, 'Alī, 64
ibn Thābit, Ḥassān, 147
ibn Ṭufayl, Abū Bakr, 189
ibn Wahb, Ma'bad, 69n
Ibn Warraq, 139n
ibn Yazīd, al-Walīd (the Caliph), 69n
ibn Yūsuf, al-Ḥajjāj, 212
Ibrāhīm, Ḥāfiẓ, 132n, 196, 198
Ibrāhīm, Ṣun' Allāh, 143n, 223n
Ibrāhīm Pasha, 156–7
Ibrāhīm (prophet), 134–6
al-Ibrāshī, 'Azīza, 49n
iconic, 84n
iconoclasm (poetic), 185
'Īd, 'Abd al-Razzāq, 124n
'Īd, Rajā', 25n
Iḍā'a (journal), 203n
identity, identification, 106, 116, 133, 139n, 145, 149, 155, 183, 187, 226, 247, 265–71
  and globalization, 32n, 265, 267, 270
  colonial identities, 89n
  community identity, 267, 270, 271
  cultural identity, 53n, 113, 163n, 164, 265
  deconstruction of identity, 266, 271
  fake identities, 266
  fixed identity, 269–70
  Islamic identity, identification, 32n, 53n
  national identity, 169n
  territorial identity, 66, 169n, 170, 174
ideology, ideological, 48n, 70, 83n, 84, 116, 123, 136n, 152, 172, 180, 221, 236, 255
  cultural and ideological invasion, 62; *see also ghazw thaqāfī*
  false ideology, 228n
  literature and ideology, 49
al-Idlibī, Ulfat, 91n
Idrīs, Samāḥ, 129n
Idrīs, Suhayl, 32, 45
Idrīs, Yūsuf, 12n, 39, 41, 207n, 212n, 263n
Ifranj, Ifranjī, 108n, 187n, 234–5
al-Ightirāb al-Adabī (journal), 151n
Ikhlāṣī, Walīd, 88n
al-Ikhwān al-Muslimūn, 51, 143
Ikhwān al-Ṣafā' (encyclopedic work), 240, 243
iktifā' dhātī, 163; *see also* self-sufficient
Iliad (epic poem), 25–6, 137n, 204
  Iliad of the Arabs, 25n; *see also Sīrat 'Antara*
illustrations, illustrators, 58, 59n, 60
  for children's books, 55
  illustrated books, 55
'ilm, 'ulūm, 'ālim, 46, 171, 233, 245, 260
  'ilm al-naḥw, 158n, 196n, 233n
  'ilm al-ṣarf, 158n, 196n, 233n
iltizām, 51; *see also* commitment
image, images, imagery, 16, 84n, 94, 95, 97n, 130n, 134, 141, 180, 201, 236, 244, 247, 267
  Arabs' self-image, 27, 108, 109, 232–7, 254, 272
  image of the Arabs, 94
  negative image of Islam, 57
imagination, 3, 76, 153, 187, 195, 214, 244, 266
Imām, 'Īsā *see* Shaykh Imām
'Imāra, Muḥammad, 109n, 171
'Imārat Ya'qūbyān (novel), 13n
imitation, 31n, 39n, 82n, 136, 195, 213n, 238, 256, 260n
  blind imitation, 177n
Imperialism, imperial, imperialistic 42n, 114n, 188, 255n, 259, 269n
Implicitness, 238
Impressionistic, 230
Imprimerie Catholique, 118n
Imru' al-Qays, 204n
'Ināyat, Rājī, 81n, 82n
inclusion/exclusion, 19, 24, 28, 36, 40, 75, 214, 216, 248, 263
  inclusiveness, 273
  see also exclusive, exclusion
independence, 46, 68, 164, 179, 184
Independence Day (movie), 50n
Index Islamicus (classified bibliography), ix
India, Indian, 10, 13n, 25, 49, 91n, 129, 147, 153, 190n, 264n
individual, individuality, 133, 177, 181, 271
  extra-individual, 15n
  hyper-individualists, 270
  individual dignity, 11n
  individuality (in periodization), 177, 181
indoctrination, 162
Indonesian, 110n
Indo-Pakistan, 153
inferiority (of Arab culture), 49, 187
influence (in culture), 22, 24, 32, 34, 47n, 51, 60, 69, 91, 94, 95, 97, 102, 103n, 104, 105, 106, 107, 109–10, 112n, 113n, 114, 144, 148, 154, 159, 164, 174, 183, 185, 195, 199, 205n, 209n, 210n, 213n, 215n, 221, 226, 230, 232, 265, 266, 270
  of Arabs on the West, 110, 189–90
  of electronic media, 60, 106, 107, 221, 266
  of Greek culture, 24
  Western influence, 16, 61n, 63, 186, 220
Inglizi, 62n
inḥiṭāṭ, 108, 232; *see also* decadence; decline; stagnation
innovation, innovative, innovators, 3, 5, 23n, 24, 64, 160, 175, 177, 181, 183, 185, 195, 196n, 201, 208, 210, 241, 242
Inquisition, 129
al-Insān: Ithnay 'Ashar (sic!) *Imra'a fī Zinzāna Wāḥida* (play), 49n
inscriptions, 204n
  'En 'Abdat inscription, 204
inspiration, 7, 86, 95, 97n, 114n, 115n, 123, 162, 193n, 215n, 230
interactions, interrelationships, 3, 4, 5, 28, 35n, 89, 96–7, 99, 100–2, 104n, 110–11, 114, 116, 131, 148, 150, 155–6, 159–60, 164, 166n, 174, 175, 188–9, 193, 207n, 216, 222, 227, 229–33, 254n, 266, 272

interference, 24, 27, 81, 89, 112, 114, 208, 210, 216
translation as a channel for interference, 24, 263
International Book Center (Troy), 57, 63, 65, 87n, 88
Internet, ix–x, 49, 60, 77, 78, 80, 87, 106–8, 123, 155, 173, 187n, 189n, 222, 225, 265–8, 271, 273–8
ADABIYAT, 108n
ARABIC-L, 107n
Arabic Lit Scholars, 185n, 195
Baidu, 108
blogs, blogging, x, 189n, 266
Facebook, 274–8
Google, 108
homepages, 107
interactive literature, x
Internet generation, 268
Internet technologies, ix–x, 49, 106–8, 173, 222, 265, 267, 273–5
Internet usage statistics, 265
mailing lists, 107n
MSN, 108
online literary texts, 107, 266, 275, 276
search engines, 108
social media, 125, 274–8
techno-writing, x
websites, 60, 61n, 64, 83n, 107, 125n, 131n
World Wide Web, 107
www.elaph.com, 131n
Yahoo, 108
interpretation, 22, 31n, 54, 89n, 124n, 127n, 128n, 138n, 161n, 175, 237, 240, 257, 267, 269
infinity of Interpretation, 256
interpreting interpretations, 256
intertextuality, intertextual, 227, 255
ironic mode, 136, 224
linear mode, 134
Intifāḍa, 78, 128n
invasion
American invasion of Iraq, 78
cultural and ideological *see ghazw thaqāfī*
invention, invented, 228, 229, 250, 265
invented traditions, 23n, 160–2
officially invented, 15n
inventory, inventories (literary, translated texts), 4, 33, 35, 60, 65, 67–8, 84, 87, 97
potential inventories, texts, ix, 2, 9, 229, 246
inversion (literary), 176
Iqbāl, Muḥammad, 51, 137, 180n
iqlīmiyya, 162n, 164; *see also* territorial nationalism
na'ra iqlīmiyya, 163
Iran, Iranian, 48, 52–3, 133n, 139, 142n, 146n, 147–8
Iranian revolutionary songs, 128
see also Persian
al-Īrānī, Mu'ayyad Ibrāhīm, 150n
Ireland, Irish, 52, 192, 225
irony, ironic, ironical, 16, 114, 159, 224, 254
ironic mode of intertextuality, 136, 224
ironic *mu'āraḍa*, 197n
ironic poetic allusion, 130n
linear mode of intertextuality, 134
al-'Iryān, Muḥammd Sa'īd, 55n
'Īsā, Norman, 226n
'Īsā, Ṣalāḥ, 16, 30n, 76–7
Iser, Wolfgang, 106–7
al-Iṣfahānī, Abū Faraj, 69n
Iṣlāḥ (novel), 49n
Islāmānī, 46n, 133n, 144
Islamica, 260
Islamist, 82, 83n, 116n, 122–4, 130n, 133n, 138, 142, 144–6, 171
Islamist literature, 29, 40, 46–56; *see also adab Islāmī*
Islamist realism, 52; *see also wāqi'iyya Islāmiyya*
Islamist theater, 50–1; *see also masraḥ Islāmī*
al-Islāmiyya wa-l-Madhāhib al-Adabiyya (book), 52
Islamization, 121n, 150
al-Islām wa-Uṣūl al-Ḥukm (book), 120n
Ismā'īl, 'Izz al-Dīn, 201, 202
Ismā'īl (the Khedive), 158
Israel, Israeli, 48n, 49n, 74, 78, 83n, 115n, 118, 125, 150n, 161, 165n, 171n, 226n, 227n, 264n, 274n
Arab–Israeli conflict, 104
bilingual Israeli Palestinian authors, 116, 226n
Israeli nationalism, 161
Israeli prisons, 49n
Istanbul, 64, 114n, 148
Istikhdām al-Ḥayāt (novel), 125
istishrāq, 95n, 133, 140, 253; *see also* Orientalism
Istishrāq (journal), 253
Italy, 63, 111n, 125n, 141, 179, 187n, 220
ivory tower, 30n

Jabal 'Āmil, 54n
al-Jabartī, 'Abd al-Raḥmān, 156n
al-Jābirī, Majdī, 97n
al-Jābirī, Muḥammad 'Ābid (Mohammed Abed al-Jabri), 104n, 155n
Jabrā, Jabrā Ibrāhīm, 110n, 112n, 187n
Jacob (prophet), 127
al-Jada', Aḥmad 'Abd al-Laṭīf, 46n
Jaffa
Arab-Hebrew Theater in Jaffa, 226n
Jāhilī, Jāhiliyya (Jahiliyyah), 119–20, 133, 136, 276; *see also* pre-Islamic
Jāhīn, Ṣalāḥ, 72
al-Jāḥiẓ, 26, 210
Jakobson, Roman, 3, 31n
Jalāl, Muḥammad 'Abd al-Mun'im, 88
Jalāl, Muḥammad 'Uthmān, 56
Jameson, Fredric, 90, 176

jamhara (verb and noun), 239; *see also jumhūr, jumhūriyya*
Jam'iyyat Aṣdiqā' Mūsīqā al-Sayyid Darwīsh, 73n
Jam'iyyat Shu'rā' al-Sha'b, 70
jam' wa-tafrīq, 239n
al-Janābī, 'Abd al-Qādir (Abdul Kader El Janabi), 112n, 131n, 138n, 154, 203
al-Janābī, Hātif, 276
Jannāt wa-Iblīs (novel), 13n, 123
Japan, 187n, 264
Jarash festival, 128n
al-Jārim, 'Alī, 196, 213
al-Jarīma al-Ghāmiḍa (novel), 83n
Jarrār, Ḥusnī Adham, 46n
Jāsim, 'Azīz al-Sayyid, 253n
Javanese, 55
al-Jawāhirī, Muḥammad Mahdī, 196
Jawdat, Ṣāliḥ, 79
al-Jayyūsī (Jayyusi), Salmā al-Khadrā', 151–3, 168, 196n, 240n
Jesuit, 97, 118n, 212
Jesus, Christ, 10, 112n
Jeune Afrique (journal), 113
Jew, Jewish, Judaism, 10, 13n, 27n, 50n, 78, 83n, 88n, 93n, 118, 120n, 128n, 130n, 134–5, 139n, 141, 142, 148, 149n, 150, 161, 209n, 221, 226n, 243, 244n, 274n
Jibrīl, Muḥammad, 32
Jibrīl (Gibreel, Gabriel), 139n, 144
al-Jihād (group), 142
jīl al-sittīnāt, 181n, 203n
al-Jinān (journal), 92, 103, 158, 212, 218n
jinās, 159
jināyat al-siyāsa wa-l-ṣiḥāfa 'alā al-adab, 104n
jinsāniyya 13n; *see also* sex, sexuality
Johnson, Samuel, 93
Johnson-Davies, Denys, 33, 36n
jokes, joke books, 75n, 84n, 91, 159
Jordan, 12n, 53n, 54n, 62n, 120n, 128n, 152, 166, 168, 173n, 179
Joseph (prophet), 127, 130
journalism, journalists, press, 11, 27, 32n, 38, 41n, 84n, 90, 121n, 124, 129, 149, 159, 210, 220, 226n, 239n, 260, 264
  censorship of the press, 121n
  gutter press, 165
  journalistic discourse, 210
  pioneering Arab free journalism, 220
Journal of Arabic Literature (journal), 14, 252
Joyce, James, 186
al-Jubbūrī (Jubouri), Amal, 115n
Jubrān, Jubrān Khalīl, 112n, 113, 199, 264n
Judt, Tony, 269n
al-Juhanī, Dīnā (Deena Aljuhani Abdulaziz), 83n
jumhūr, jumhūriyya, 239–40, 252; *see also* republic of letters
jurisprudence, 257
Jurnāl al-Khidīw (newspaper), 92n
justifications (aesthetic and poetic), 17, 30, 37, 38, 39, 68, 136, 169, 238, 248
Jyllands-Posten (Muhammad's cartoons), 78

Kabbani, Rana, 94
Kafr Qara', 57
kalām 'alā kalām, 268
Kalima (project of translations), 63–4
Kamāl, Ṣafwat, 67, 99n
Kāmil, Muṣṭafā, 52
Kanā'ina, Sharīf, 168n
Karbalā' (Battle), 247n
Kārīkātīr (journal), 30
Karīm, Fawzī, 138n, 203n
Karīm, Muḥammad, 211n
al-Karkhī, Mullā 'Abbūd, 79n, 80
al-Karmil—Abḥāth fī al-Lugha wa-l-Adab (journal), 14
al-Karnak (novel), 49n
al-Kātiba (journal), 151n
Kātib al-Miṣrī (journal), 182
al-Kawnī (al-Koni), Ibrāhīm, 236
Kaylānī, Kāmil, 55–6, 94n, 95n
al-Kaylānī, Najīb, 52
al-Kāẓimī, 'Abd al-Muḥsin, 196n
Keddie, Nikki, 102n
Kennedy, Robert F., 270n
Kermode, Frank, 34, 172, 194, 228
khabab (meter), 202
al-Khādim, Sa'd, 59n
"khaki poems," 70
al-Khāl, Yūsuf, 68n
khalā'a, 96; *see also* sex literature
Khālid, Khālid Muḥammad, 120n
Khalīfa, Mārsīl (Marcel Khalife), 126–30, 147
Khalīfa, Saḥar, 276
al-Khalīlī, 'Alī, 67n
al-Khanīsī, 'Abd al-Ra'ūf, 85–7
Kharīdat Lubnān (novel), 212
Khārijī, 243
al-Kharrāṭ, Idwār (Edward), 28n, 124, 263n
Khaṣā'iṣ al-Taṣawwur al-Islāmī (book), 51
khāṣṣ, khāṣṣa, 33, 37n
al-Khaṭīb, Ḥusām, 45n, 95n, 96n
al-Khaṭībī, 'Abd al-Kabīr (Abdelkebir Khatibi), 113, 160n
al-Khāṭirī, Marwān, 106n
khayāl, 198, 219
  khayāl 'ilmī, 81; *see also* science fiction
  khayāl al-ẓill, 218, 219, 247n; *see also* shadow theater
khayfā' (qaṣīda), 158n
Khayyām, Omar, 79n, 129n
Khayyat, Yasmine, 185n
khiṭāb, 54; *see also* discourse
al-Khū'ī, Abū al-Qāsim, 48n
al-Khūlī, Amīn, 162n
al-Khūlī, Muḥammad Badawī, 80n
Khumaynī, Āyatullāh Rūḥullah (Ruhollah Khomeini), 139, 143

khurāfa, khurāfāt, 92, 219n
Khūrī, Ilyās, 89n, 144n, 149n, 207n, 224n
al-Khūrī, Khalīl, 144, 211
Khūrī, Munaḥ (Mounah), 112
al-Khūrī, Rashīd Salīm, 141
Khūrshīd, Fārūq, 15n
Khuṭba fī Ādāb al-'Arab (lecture), 109, 233–4
Khuṭwa 'alā Ṭarīq al-Ta'ṣīl (book), 49
Kilito, Abdelfattah, 26n, 250, 255
Kilpatrick, Hilary, 102n
Kirkuk
  Jamā'at Kirkūk, 203n
Kishk, 'Abd al-Ḥamīd, 54n
Kishk, Muḥammad Jalāl, 116n
kiṣṣa, 186; *see also qiṣṣa*
Kitāb al-Aghānī (book), 69n
kitāba ukhrā, 21n; *see also* non-canonical literature
al-Kitāba al-Ukhrā (magzine), 21n, 29, 67n, 203n
Kitab Hazz al-Quhūf bi-Sharḥ Qaṣīd Abī Shādūf (book), 254, 257
Kitāb al-I'tibār (book), 31n, 189n, 234–5
Kitāb Mi'at Layla wa-Layla (book), 91n
"know yourself!," 236
Koran, Koranic *see* Qur'ān, Qur'ānic
Krachkovskii, I. J., 114, 148n
Kritzeck, James, 55n, 89n, 96n, 190n
"al-Kūlīrā" (poem), 200
Kulliyyat al-Qiddīs Yūsuf, 212n
Kurds, Kurdish, 55n, 147, 148, 152
Kuwait, Kuwaiti, Kuwaitian, 20n, 35n, 59n, 75, 167, 179
al-Kuzbarī, Salmā Luṭfī al-Ḥaffār, 22n

Laban al-'Uṣfūr (novel), 37–8
Labnanat al-'ālam, 162n
Labor Party (Egypt), 124
Laḥḥām, Durayd, 222
lahja, 173
  lahja shāmiyya, 69n
laḥn, 15n
  laḥn al-qawl, 238
al-Laḥẓa al-Shi'riyya (journal), 138n, 151n, 203n
Lajja (novel), 121n
Lamartine, Alphonse de, 141
Lāmiyat al-'Arab (poem), 208
Lammens, Henri, 212
Lane, E. W., 112n
language
  and Arabism, 133, 166n
  and mysticism, 162n
  and realism, 31
  language purists, 62n
  metaphorical and poetic language, 3, 30, 199
  sacred, holy language, 123, 155n, 214
  standard national languages, 161, 238, 250
  subjective language, 16
  see also 'āmmiyya; Arabic; *fuṣḥā*
La nuit sacrée (novel), 113
al-Lāt, 139n
Latin, Latinist, 65n, 66n, 110n, 166n, 169, 171n, 184, 187n, 249
  equation Latin/Arabic, 238
  Latin America, 264
  Latin and national languages, 238
  Latin characters, script, 65n
  Latin literatures, 182
  Latinist humanism, 255
L'Avare (play), 220
Layālī Alf Layla (novel), 95n
Laylā (beloved), 198
Laylak (magazine), 83n
Laylat al-Qadr, 140
Lebanon, Lebanese, 18, 25n, 27, 42n, 45, 51, 54n, 56, 57, 62n, 63, 65, 66n, 68n, 69, 78, 80, 82, 83, 88, 89n, 95n, 103, 112n, 113, 114n, 118–19, 121n, 124n, 126–30, 142, 143n, 144n, 145, 152, 158, 161, 162n, 167, 168, 170, 172, 179, 206n, 207n, 212, 221n, 223n, 224, 231, 264
  Lebanese Communist Party, 128n
  Lebanonization of the world, 162n
Leblanc, Maurice, 88
legitimate/illegitimate, 2, 21, 22
legitimation, legitimatization, 4, 9
  aesthetic legitimation, legitimatization, 4, 9, 14, 15n, 16
  popular literature and legitimation, 14–19
leisure, 266
Lejeune, Philippe, 190
Lermontov, Mikhail, 231
Le rocher de Tanois (novel), 113
Les aventures de Télémaque (novel), 90n
lesbian, lesbianism, 12n, 13n
Les Mille et une nuits, 94; *see also Alf Layla wa-Layla*
Lewis, Bernard, 160n, 165n, 235
lexicon, lexical, 29, 37n, 181, 242
  lexical transmission, appropriation, and transference, 249
  philological-lexicographic revolution, 250
LGBT (lesbian, Gay, Bisexual, and Transgender), 12
liberal, liberalism, 117–22, 126, 131n, 166, 243
  liberal discourse, x, 119n, 121n
  Liberal Manifesto, 166n
liberty, liberties, 41n, 101, 129n, 201
library, libraries, 54n, 57n, 59, 60, 64, 87, 107, 153n, 168n, 190n, 241, 248
  Alexandria's Royal Library, 134
  al-Bābaṭīn Central Library, 35n
  public libraries for children, 55
Libya, Libyan, 104, 179, 236
Lichtenstadter, Ilse, 191
li-kull maqām maqāl, 276
linear, 182
  linear mode of the intertextuality, 146
lingua franca, 267–8
  English, 267
  French, 268

lingual, linguist, linguistic, linguistics, 5, 31, 38, 62n, 65, 81, 106, 108n, 131n, 133, 150, 155, 162, 183, 242, 249, 264
colonial linguistic projects, 66n
lingual systems, 156
linguistic acrobatics, 157
linguistic competence, 265n
linguistic education, 195
"linguistic Iron Curtain," 261
linguistic monopoly, 272n
linguistic perfection, 20, 36
metalinguistic discourse, 65n
sociolinguistic interviews, 173n
literacy/illiteracy, illiterate, 10, 59–60
littérature engage, 52n; *see also* commitment; *iltizām*
liturgy
Christian liturgy, 90n
Liwā' al-Islām (journal), 47, 50n
loans (literary), 24, 110
localism *see maḥalliyya*
London, 110n, 117, 151
Lorca, Federico García, 44n
lost paradise, 191n, 268
Loti, Pierre, 214
Louis XIV, 255
love (mystical, profane), 13n, 33n, 25n, 47, 53, 70, 71n, 73, 86, 125, 155
love poetry, 12, 132, 200
love songs, 78
love stories, 10, 57, 67, 82, 83, 87, 91
see also mystic, mystical, mysticism; Sufi, Sufism
Lubnān (newspaper), 66n
Lucknow, 49
al-lughā al-libnāniye, 172
lughz, alghāz, 158n; *see also* riddle; *uḥjiyya*
lullabies, 87n; *see also* nursery rhymes; *tahālīl*
lyric, lyrical, lyrics
lyrical recordings of the Qur'ān, 128
lyrics of songs, 19, 77n, 126, 193
lyric poems, 70n
Romance lyrics, 110n

al-Ma'ālī, Khālid, 115
ma'ārik al-'āmmiyya wa-l-fuṣḥā, 171n
al-Ma'arrī, Abū al-'Alā', 208–9, 210n, 218n
Ma'āthir al-Ṣaḥāba (children's book), 56
Macaulay, T. B., 190n
Machado, Antonio, 44n
al-Madanī, 'Izz al-Dīn, 172
Madārāt (*Orbits*), 105n, 188n
māḍī (tense), 208n
madīḥ, midḥa, 157, 198, 225
madness
and poetry, 250–1
and mysticism, 251n
fundamentalist madness, 243
Madrid, 43–4
Maghrib, Maghreb, 154n
al-Māghūṭ, Muḥammad, 18, 45, 222
maḥaliyya, 164
Maḥfūẓ, 'Iṣām, 65n
Maḥfūẓ, Najīb, 12n, 32, 49n, 51n, 60, 67n, 77n, 82n, 87, 93n, 95n, 103n, 111n, 125, 138–44, 147, 177n, 186, 192, 197n, 208n, 209, 213–18, 224, 226, 25n, 261, 262
Mahjar, Mahjari, 121, 130, 149, 199n, 231
Mahound (=Muḥammad the Prophet), 139
maḥṣūl, 217n; *see also* evaluation, merit, value, worth
al-Majalla (journal), 163–4
Majallat al-Azhar (journal), 47
Majallat al-Ṭifl al-Muslim (magazine), 47n
Majallat al-Turāth al-Sha'bī (journal), 66n
Majīd (comics), 84
al-Majlis al-A'lā li-l-Thaqāfa, 72, 73, 201
Majma' al-Baḥrayn (book of *maqāmāt*), 157
majority/minority, 23n, 145, 239
plebian majority, 268n
majūsī see Zoroastrian
makāma, 186, 206n; *see also maqāma*
Makdisi, George, 245
al-Malā'ika, Nāzik, 193n, 199–200, 203n
Malay, 55n
Mali, 154
Malti-Douglas, Fedwa, 22n, 83n, 84
Ma'lūf, Amīn (Amin Maalouf), 113, 143n, 114n
Mamlūk, Mamluk, 29n, 91n, 184n, 179n, 250n
al-Manāṣira, 'Izz al-Dīn, 97n
Manāt, 139n
mandates (in the Middle East), 179
Mandūr, Muḥammad, 31, 40, 107, 220n
al-Manfalūṭī, Muṣṭafā Luṭfī, 22n, 132n, 214
manifestation/actualization, 10n, 28, 72, 79n, 105, 128n, 265
manifesto, 138
Liberal Manifesto, 166n
Mann, Thomas, 215n
m'anna, 69
Mannā', 'Abd Allāh, 171n
mannerism, 11n
al-Mansur (the Caliph), 243
Manṣūr, 'Alī, 203n
Manṣūr, Anīs, 30n
al-Maqāliḥ, 'Abd al-'Azīz, 32n, 137n
maqām, 69n
maqāma, maqāmāt, 30n, 42, 75, 117, 156, 157, 186, 205n, 206, 210, 219–20
al-Maqāma al-Maghribiyya, 157n
al-Maqāma al-Marāghiyya, 157n
al-Maqāma al-Qahqariyya, 157n
al-Maqāma al-Raqṭā', 157 n
margins, marginal, marginalized, marginality, marginalization, 22n, 23n, 29n, 30n, 46, 79, 90, 96, 102, 104, 117, 151, 155, 168n, 188, 190n, 195, 199, 200, 202, 203n, 204, 205, 211, 214, 215, 216, 223, 225, 239, 246n, 261, 262
human marginalia, 37

literary marginalia, 29
see also fringes; *hāmish, hawāmish*
Markaz Tawzī' al-Kitāb al-Islāmī, 46n
al-Markaz al-Wathā'iqī li-Turāth Ahl al-Bayt, 48
market, marketing, marketers, marketplace, 4, 17, 50n, 63, 83n, 108, 247, 261n
Arabic Internet market, 108
Arabic translation market, 64
Arab science market, 234
market of symbols, 162n
market-oriented reasoning, 270
market triumphalism, 270
markets as spaces for popular performances, 247
non-market norms, 270
Maronite, 126
al-Marrākushī, 'Abd al-Wāḥid, 205n
marthiya, 8, 135; *see also* elegy; *rithā'*
Mary (mother of Jesus), 186
Marx, Karl, 141
Marxism, Marxist, 102–3, 133, 228
Marzolph, Ulrich, 91n
Maṣālḥa, Salmān, 227n
ma'sāt shi'riyya, 99n, 264n
masculine, 12n
al-Mashriq (journal), 212
Mash'ūr, Yārā (Yara Mashour), 83n
Mashyakhat al-Mashā'ikh, 132
masraḥ, maṣraḥiyya, 73n, 144
masraḥ Islāmī, 50, 56
maṣraḥiyya 'āmmiyya, 40
maṣraḥiyya shi'riyya, 99
Masraḥ al-Jayb, 99n
see also drama, theater
mass, masses, 41, 50, 53, 70, 76, 82, 102n, 107, 138, 164, 234, 256
mass communication, 50
mass culture, 15, 84, 165
mass media, 15n, 50, 78, 106n, 155
masterpieces, 18, 31, 63, 79, 89n, 93, 96, 191, 231
Maṭar, Muḥammad 'Afīfī, 60n, 177n
al-Ma'thūrāt al-Sha'biyya (journal), 66n
al-Ma'aṭṭ, Yāsīn Ṣāliḥānī, 95n
Mauretanian, 167n, 169
mawālid, 219
Mawāqif (journal), 101n, 105n, 131n, 203
Mawāsī, Fārūq, 36
Mawlid al-Nabī, 47n
al-mawqif, 131n
al-Mawsim (journal), 48
mawwāl, mawāwīl, 69, 248n
mawāwīl siyāsiyya, 70n
al-Maydān (weekly), 123
al-Māzinī, Ibrāhīm 'Abd al-Qādir, 159, 196n, 198, 217
McKibben, Bill, 270
meaning (in literature), 4, 15, 23, 26, 31, 33, 99, 100, 188n, 227, 228, 229, 239, 245, 255, 270n
Mecca, 46n, 47n, 119
media, ix, 15, 73, 129, 149, 222, 277
mass media, 15n, 50, 78, 106n, 155
multimedia, 106
popular media, 262
social media, 125, 274–8
see also electronic media; journalism; radio; television
medieval, 5, 68n, 154, 164, 208, 244, 248
medieval Arabic culture, 12n, 21n, 29n, 55, 109n, 121n, 147, 155, 176, 182, 184, 186, 190, 192, 210, 219n, 220, 223, 235, 236
Medieval Islamic Republic of Letters, 6–7, 14, 52, 237–61
medieval linguistic monopoly, 272n
medieval Muslim world
medieval Spain, 69
Medina, 47n
Mediterranean, 267
Megally, Hanny, 130
meliorism, melioristic, 17
Melucci, Alberto, 266
memory, memories, 33, 48, 70, 75, 87, 88n, 97n, 113, 120n, 248, 253n, 266
collective memory, 2, 22, 95
memoirs, 16, 30n, 36n, 48n, 49n, 54n, 76, 93n, 268
memorial processions, 247n
memory of the nation (*dhākirat al-umma*), 107
mentality, 92, 234, 267
mentality of domination, 115n
proscribing mentality, 144
merit, 71, 75, 246, 252, 259
aesthetic merit, 15n, 17, 191, 261
see also evaluation, value, worth
Mesopotamian, 162
Messick, Brinkley, 257
metadiscourse, 256
metafictional, 187, 212, 213, 216
metalinguistic, 65n
meta-literary, 98
metaphor, 33, 48n, 94, 138n, 177n, 199, 206, 223n, 233, 241
metaphysics, metaphysical, 225, 265
post-Cartesian western metaphysics, 265
meta-poetic, metapoesis, 98, 178n
meter, 26, 36, 194, 196, 201, 202, 204, 206, 216; *see also 'aruḍ*, prosody
metropolis, metropolitan
labyrinths of metropolis, 266
metropolitan-peripheral demarcation, 244
Mexico, 121
Mickey Mouse, 84
Midad (Midād)—Deutsch–Arabisches Literaturforum, 115n
Middle Ages, 110n, 129, 150, 155, 180, 184, 191, 237, 252, 254n, 255
Middle East, Middle Eastern, 11n, 15n, 52, 53n, 58, 64, 83n, 102n, 105, 106n, 114, 121, 126, 130, 147–8, 151, 160, 161, 179, 220n, 222, 242, 262, 264, 265, 268; *see also* East

migration, immigration, 83n, 116, 146, 220, 221, 241, 266, 267, 268, 271
immigrant writers, 114n
Mihyār, 147n
Miles, Rosalind, 123n, 190n, 264
Miller, Judith, 143n
Mimesis, 31n
Minbar al-Islām (journal), 47
Minhaj al-Fann al-Islāmī (book), 51
"Minute on Indian Education," 190n
Mirrors for Princes, 55n
Miṣrī Fallāḥ, 211
al-Mīthūlūjyā al-Tamūziyya, al-Rāfidayniyya, 172n
Mizna (journal), 112n
mobility, 183
mobility in Middle Eastern traditions, 220n
modernity, modernist, modernism, 10–11, 29, 97, 120, 138, 146, 151, 159, 160, 177, 178, 181, 196n, 203n, 211n, 216, 245, 255, 258, 259, 267, 268, 269
Arab modernity, 6, 149n, 250n, 251, 255, 272n
"modernists," 237, 239, 249, 251–61
modernization, 11n, 200, 220
secularism, humanism, and modernism, 259, 260
Molière, 85–6
Mongols, 248
Monks, 212n
monographs, 153, 252n
monologue, 38
dramatic monologues, 218n
monopoly, 46, 247
linguistic monopoly, 272n
literary monopoly, 272
Monroe, James T., 69n, 205n
monster stories, novels, 10, 67
moral, morals, morality, 32n, 47n, 53n, 55n, 56, 67n, 68n, 92, 94, 96n, 117, 118, 125, 143n, 152n, 236, 243, 270n
Moreh, Shmuel, 135n
Morocco, Moroccan, 48n, 49, 104, 113, 121n, 143n, 160n, 167, 168n, 173n, 179, 277
morphology, 37n, 233n
mother tongue, 162n, 227n
motto, 169n, 227n
al-Muʿallaqāt, 15n
al-Muʿallim, Muḥammad, 60n
muʿāraḍa, 196, 197n
ironic *muʿāraḍa*, 197n
al-muʾassasa al-thaqāfiyya al-rasmiyya, 30; *see also* canonical center; establishment
Mubārak, ʿAlī, 109, 235
Mubārak, Ḥusnī, 78, 120n, 122
al-Mubārak, Muḥammad, 52
Mubārak, Suzanne, 59
muḍāriʿ (tense), 208
Mudhakkirāt fī Sijn al-Nisāʾ (memoirs), 49n
Mudhakkirāt Ṭālib Baʿtha (memoirs), 36n
Mufrad bi-Ṣīghat Jamʿ (poetry collection), 137n
mufti, 123, 130, 142, 143
al-Muhājir (*The Emigrant*) (film), 129
Muḥammad (the Prophet), 48, 56, 57, 124, 139n, 155n
Muhammad's cartoons, 78
Muḥammad's wives, 139n
Muḥarram, Aḥmad, 196
muḥāṣara, 73
Muhawwī, Ibrāhīm, 168
muʿjam, 20, 31–2, 35; *see also* dictionary
muʿjama (*qaṣīda*), 158n
mujūn, 118
mukhannathūn, 12n
mukharrib, 137
mulammaʿa (*qaṣīda*), 158n
mulḥid, 137; *see also* blasphemy; heretic; *zindīq*
multicultural environment, 243–4
multimedia, 106
munājāt, munājayāt, 120n
Munaẓẓamat al-Iʿlām al-ʿArabī, 48
Munīf, ʿAbd al-Raḥmān, 148n
al-Munqidh min al-Ḍalāl (book), 189n
munshidūn (Sufi), 47n
Muntaṣir, Ṣalāḥ, 12n
muntijūn, 225
Muqaddima (by Ibn Khaldūn) (book), 98n
Muqaddima fī Fiqh al-Lugha al-ʿArabiyya (book), 120n
Murād, Salīma, 78
Murrār, Muṣṭafā, 57
Mūsā, Salāma, 27n, 103, 253
Musāmarāt al-Jayb (magazine), 260n
al-Mūsawī (al-Musawi), Muḥsin Jāsim, 6–7, 52, 95, 149n, 237–61
museums, 40n, 61n
Musharrafa, Muṣṭafā Muṣṭafā, 37n
music, musical, musicians, 15n, 19, 20, 25, 36, 44n, 56, 58, 66n, 69n, 73n, 74, 75, 77, 78n, 79n, 80, 95, 106, 126, 128n, 130, 202, 205n, 222, 261
musical perfection, 20, 36
music and poetry, 202
poems set to music, 74, 77, 130
vocal compositions, 77
youth music, 79
Muslim Brotherhood *see* al-Ikhwān al-Muslimūn
Muṣṭafā, Najm ʿAbd Allāh, 21n
mustahlikūn, 225
Mustaqbal al-Thaqāfa fī Miṣr (book), 133n
al-mustawā al-jamālī wa-l-fannī, 20, 36
Musul, 247
mutakallim al-naṣārā, 243
mutʾakhkhir, 159
al-Mutanabbī, Abū al-Ṭayyib, 182
Muṭrān, Khalīl, 132n, 198
muwashshaḥ, muwashshaḥāt, 110n, 204–5, 247
al-Muwayliḥī, Muḥammad, 187
MY.Kali (magazine), 12n
mystery novel, 87

mystic, mystical, mysticism 162n
mysticism and madness, 251n
see also Sufi, Sufism
myth, mythical, mythological, 18, 94, 128n, 160, 185n
Mesopotamian mythology, 162
mythological hero, 84
nationalist mythology, 162n

nabaṭī, 69, 204n
al-Nābulusī (al-Nābulsī), ʻAbd al-Ghanī, 157
al-Nābulusī (al-Nābulsī), Shākir, 13n, 120n, 166
Nādī Madrasat al-Muʻallimīn al-ʻUlyā, 197
Naffāʻ, Fu'ād Ghibriyāl, 264n
al-Nafzāwī, Muḥammad ibn Muḥammad, 45n, 67n, 95n, 96, 117
al-Nahār (newspaper), 113
Nahḍa, 148n, 149, 158, 171n, 177n, 178, 187n, 188n, 196n, 213n, 248, 253n, 255, 260n; *see also* renaissance; revival
al-Naḥlāwī, Shākir, 157
al-Najaf, 47n, 53
Nājī, Aḥmad, 125
Nājī, Ibrāhīm, 198n
Najīb, Aḥmad, 58
Najīb, Ḥāfiẓ, 82n
Najm (Nigm), Aḥmad Fu'ād, 16, 30n, 70, 72, 75, 76
Nakhla, Rashīd, 80
name, names, xn, 13n, 73, 98n, 105, 118n, 122, 127, 139n, 141, 187, 188, 190n, 211, 219, 264
nicknames, 12n, 56, 81n, 126, 147, 196, 243
Naʻnaʻ, Ḥamīda, 101n
Napoleon Bonaparte, 184, 185n, 220n
naqd, 73n, 119n, 126, 144, 149, 198n; *see also* criticism
Naqd al-Fikr al-Dīnī (book), 126
al-Nāqid (journal), 145n, 151n
al-Naqqāsh, Mārūn, 220
al-Naqqāsh, Rajā', 73n
al-Naqqāsh, Salīm, 220
Naqqāsh, Samīr, 13n, 88n, 93n, 135n
Nar, Ali, 82n
narjasiyya quṭriyya, 169; *see also* territorial nationalism
narrator, narration, narrative, 29, 37–8, 39n, 47n, 48n, 54, 80, 81, 89, 92n, 99n, 109, 130, 145n, 146n, 169, 180, 190n, 206–18, 223, 224, 235, 255
counter-narrative, 250
oral narrative, 11n
self-conscious narration, 106
al-Nār wa-l-Kalimāt (poetry collection), 42
al-Nās fī Bilādī (poetry collection), 95n
Nashrat al-Īdāʻ (Legal Deposit Bulletin), 60n
nasib, 198
al-Nāṣirī, Nāṣīf, 277
al-Nāṣiriyya, 252
naskh (abrogation), 139n
Nasreen, Taslima, 121n
Nasser, Nasserist, 133n, 138n; *see also* ʻAbd al-Nāṣir, Gamāl
nathr, 193, 202, 203n, 205
nathr ākhar, 293n; *see also* prose poem
see also prose
nation, national, nationalist, nationality, nationalism, 5, 9, 10, 22n, 32, 37n, 40, 42, 45, 53, 60, 61, 62, 64, 66, 67, 70, 72n, 78, 80, 86, 87, 104, 107, 126, 133, 141, 142, 148, 151, 154n, 160–74, 180, 182, 190, 192, 197, 212, 222, 224, 232, 236, 238, 241, 249, 250, 255, 258, 261, 265, 267, 268, 271
anti-nationalist teleology, 268
bi-national families, 269
national character, 161
nationalistic songs, 126
nation-building, 15n, 33, 50, 104,166n, 173, 221
nation-state, 14n, 40, 160–3, 174, 252, 253, 254, 268, 269
territorial nationalism, 40, 80n, 160–74
transnationalism, 269
native, nativism, 146
native speakers, 58, 65n, 173, 190n, 226n, 273
Nawfal, Nawfal Niʻmat Allāh, 92
al-Nawwāb, Muẓaffar, 70, 77n, 80, 97n
al-Nayhūm, al-Ṣādiq, 123n, 129
Nazareth, 83n
naẓariyya, tanẓir, tanẓirāt, 162n, 172
naẓariyyat al-iqlīmiyya, 162n
see also theory
Nefertiti, 135n
Negev, 204
Neo-Arabic, 183
Neo-Arabic literature, 183
neoclassical, neoclassicist, neoclassicism, 31, 131, 158, 193, 194–8, 206n
neo-Sufi, neo-Sufism, 150
New York, 143n, 150, 198
New York Times Book Review (newspaper), 9, 264
Nicholson, Reynold A., 204
Niger, 154
Nigeria, Nigerian 154, 167
nihilistic, nihilism, 144, 228, 271
Nile, 78, 86, 123, 151
nineties' poets, 8n, 203n
Niqābat al-Ashrāf, 132
niẓām nabrī, 202
Nobel Prize, 19, 111n, 138n, 142, 192, 217, 261, 262
non-canonical, non-canonized *see* canon
Nordic, 165
norms (cultural, literary), 28, 31, 39, 72, 90, 131n, 176, 178, 181, 188, 194, 201, 205, 206, 208, 218, 235, 270
sacred norms, 206
theatrical norms, 222
traditional norms, 198
translational norms, 65n, 90

North Africa, 83n, 130, 170n, 173n, 247
Northanger Abbey (novel), 215–16
nostalgia, 69n, 269
grieving nostalgia, 268
novel
historical novels, 10, 69n, 114, 212–13
novelization of Islamic literatures, 224n
picaresque novel, 186n, 210n
serial novels, 212, 215n
see also prose, fiction
Nuʿayma, Mīkhāʾīl, 109, 112n, 141, 199, 231
Nūr, Muḥammad, 119
nursery rhymes, 87, 89n; *see also* lullabies; *tahālīl*
al-Nuṣūṣ al-Muḥarrama (poetry collection), 117–18
al-Nuwayhī, Muḥammad, 202
Nwayyir (Nuwayyir), ʿAlī, 277–8
Nzūla wa-Khayṭ al-Shayṭān (novel), 135n

objective/subjective, 230
obscurity, 15–16, 136, 202; *see also* ambiguity; clarity
Odyssey (epic poem), 25, 204
O'Fahey, R. S., 153
official
official *Dīwān*, 41n, 79
official literature, 71
officially invented, 15n
"official scholars," 22n
official site, 53n
official texts, 22, 223
official translations, 138n
see also canonical literature; *rasmī*
oil, 152
Iraqi oil, 252n
oil companies, 252n
Oman, Omani, 147, 167, 169
One Thousand and One Nights see *Alf Layla wa-Layla*
oppression, 67n, 86, 123
oral, orality, 66n, 69, 136, 204n
Jāhilī orality, 136
oral genres, 69n, 219
oral narratives, 11n, 81
oral poetry, 69, 81
oral tradition, 67n, 219
orator/audience, 197
oratorical poetry, 197
Orient, Oriental, Orientalized, 26n, 93–4, 147n, 190n, 207n, 215
Orientalism, Orientalists, 102n, 114, 120, 133, 139, 140, 141, 151n, 170n, 190, 195, 218, 248, 251, 253, 255
Orientalism (book), 265
ornamentations (verbal, literary), 270, 245
ornate stylization, 194
orthography, 37n
Othello (play)
European "Other," 235n
translated into Arabic, 89n
Ottoman, 110, 148n
Ottoman Empire, 108, 131, 232, 254, 267, 268
Ottoman Sultanate, 261
oud, 126; *see also ʿūd, aʿwād*
Oxford, Oxonian, 191, 203

pagan, pagans
pagan elements in poetry, 25–6
Pakistan, Pakistani, 129, 153, 243n
Palestine, Palestinian, 36, 42n, 44n, 48n, 53n, 54n, 57, 61, 62n, 66n, 67n, 69, 70, 73, 75, 76, 80n, 87n, 89n, 97, 99, 104, 110n, 112n, 115, 116, 121n, 125, 126–30, 143, 151, 152, 161, 167, 168n, 172, 173, 179, 197n, 219n, 226n, 227, 263, 264n, 275, 276
Palestinian Occupied Territories, 48n, 128n, 221
Palgrave, Turner Francis, 192–3
Palindromes, 158
Pan-Arab, Pan-Arabism, 29n, 165, 166n, 174
Panjabi, 55
paradigm, paradigmatic, 250
nation-state paradigm, 269
paradigmatic position, 229, 273
paradigm of political changes/cultural life, 248, 251
paradigm of world literature, 24n
Paradise, 155n, 191n, 208, 268
paraenetic literature, 25n
Paris, 31n, 36n, 73, 84, 86, 110, 138n, 151, 203, 241, 246
capital of the world republic of letters, 242, 244–6, 258
Parisian salons, 238
Parks, Tim, 272n
parody, 176, 200n, 210n, 257
particularist, particularism, 162, 165, 168, 169
particularistic territorial identity, 66, 167
Pashto, 55n
Pastiche, 210n
patriotic, patriotism, 161, 162, 207
patriotic poems, 70
Syrian patriotism, 212
Patristic, 183
patronizing (attitude to Arabic literature), 190, 261
patterns (of culture), 28, 106, 114, 188, 193
paytanic (Hebrew) school, 27n
pedagogy, 60
Arabic translation pedagogy, 64
critical pedagogy of the *Nahḍa*, 149
peep-show, 218–19
Pellat, Charles, 168–9
performers, performance, performativity, 58, 77, 92, 220, 221, 222, 247
performative self, 265
period, 5, 8, 12, 13n, 18, 19, 23, 33, 44, 74, 76, 81, 93, 104, 107, 141, 158, 159, 164, 175–91, 194–5, 196n, 200, 201n, 204, 205, 211, 222,

228–9, 237, 238, 240–3, 246, 247, 248–57, 260–1, 267, 273
Abbasid period, 24, 26–7, 147
Age of Conflicting Ideologies, 180
Age of Romanticism and Nationalism, 180
Age of Superfluity, 258n
Age of Translations and Adaptations, 180
interwar period, 199
Neoclassicism, 180
post-classical period, 156, 238n, 242, 246, 248–50, 256
pre-Islamic period, Jāhiliyya 147, 276
Umayyad period, 69n
see also periodization
periodicals, journals, magazines, 10, 11, 14, 17n, 30, 36n, 38n, 48, 49, 55n, 56, 59, 62, 66n, 67n, 69, 71n, 72, 74, 82, 83, 103, 107, 131n, 151n, 163, 167n, 203, 212, 241, 277; *see also* journalism
periodization, 5, 175, 176–81, 228, 240–1; *see also* period
periphery, peripheries, peripheral, 89, 151n, 184, 242, 244, 273
Persia, Persian 25, 48, 52, 54, 55, 79n, 93n, 96n, 108n, 110n, 128, 147, 148, 153n, 224, 243, 244, 264
Persian Gulf, 180, 182
see also Iran, Iranian
persona, 130n
Peter and the Wolf (children's story), 58
Peter Pan (children's story), 57
Pharaoh, 114
Philippines, 276
philological, philology, 120, 195
philological-lexicographic revolution, 250
philosophy, philosopher, philosophical, 5, 25, 93, 104, 119, 121, 141, 188, 189, 208, 265
philosophical aesthetics, 17
philosophy of art, 15
Phoenician, 162
Phoenix, 36n
phonographs, records, recordings, 58, 77, 78, 128
phraseological, 29
picaresque
European picaresque novel, 186n, 210
Picasso, Pablo, 107
pilgrimage, 234
Muslim *Ḥajj*, 47n, 123
platform poetry, 197
play, playwright, 14, 40, 49, 50n, 52, 54n, 56, 58, 61, 112, 142, 185, 218–22, 227, 231n; *see also* drama, theater
pleasure, satisfaction (in arts), 11n, 15, 17, 86, 125, 137, 220, 270
pluralism, pluralized, pluralistic, 170, 243
Pococke, Elder Edward, 189n
poetic, poetics, 8, 20n, 25, 28, 30, 33, 36, 46, 68n, 69n, 79, 80n, 89n, 97, 100, 112, 125, 130n, 133, 136, 137, 156n, 157, 158, 168, 176, 185, 193, 194–206, 213, 224, 241, 247, 249, 250, 251, 255, 259, 264, 275, 276
historical poetics, 2–3, 180–1
meta-poetic, 98, 178n
poetic experience, 37, 172, 202–3
poetic function, 3, 15, 177
poetic idols, 41n, 198n
poetic license, 146
poetic prose, 132
poetic sensibility, 159
poetics of Jāhilī orality, 136
poetry, poems, poets
and madness, 250–1
epic poetry, 25, 264
eunuch poets, 42
hunt poems, 177n, 194
"khaki poems," 70
obscene poems, 79n
poems set to music, 74, 77, 130
poetry-as-communication, 16
poetry-as-medium, 16
poetry-as-message, 16
poetry of occasions, 197
trope-laden poetry, 134, 156
Poets', Essayists', and Novelists' Club (PEN), 121n
politics, political, politicization, depoliticization, 5, 9, 11, 22, 27, 30, 41, 47, 48, 70, 76, 84–5, 102, 109, 124, 128–9, 138, 146, 152–3, 160, 165–9, 181, 184, 192, 209–11, 213n, 228, 236, 238, 241–4, 248, 251, 257, 259, 265, 269–71
literature and politics, 103–5
political clips, 78
political humor, 13
political novel, 104
politics of location, 265
polyglot, 242
polymath, 257
pornography 119; *see also* sex literature
post-Cartesian, 265
post-classical, postclassical, 5n, 6, 156, 230, 238n, 240, 241, 242, 246, 248, 249, 250, 256, 257n, 260n
postcolonial, 18, 95–6, 139n, 149n
postcolonial theory and Arabic literature, 96n
post-feminism, 270
postmodernist, postmodernism, 138, 175, 186n, 213n, 250, 251n, 265, 270
post-structuralism, 270
potential
potential movement, 105
potential texts, inventories, ix, 2, 9, 24, 229, 246
poverty, 32
"the poverty of satisfaction," 270n
pragmatic (context), 3
preference (aesthetic), 30, 39, 224n, 275
pre-Islamic, 119, 123, 133, 147, 150, 179n, 194, 195, 204; *see also* Jāhilī, Jāhiliyya

prejudice
  against Arabs, 226n, 261
pre-romantic, 198–9
press *see* journalism
prestige
  literary prestige, 242, 244
primitive, primitivism, 204–5
primordial, 162n
prison, imprisonment, jails, 38, 48, 60–1, 80, 88, 118, 125, 128, 130, 143, 253
  prison literature, 48n
  theatrical presentations of prisoners, 48n
private/public, x, 185n, 238
prizes, awards (literary), 22, 55n, 59, 65, 72, 74
  al-Bābṭīn's Prize for Poetic Creation, 20n, 36
  Booker Prize, 225
  Egyptian state prize for literature, 15n
  International Prize for Arabic Fiction, 225
  King Fayṣal International Prize, 22n
  Lajnat Jawā'iz al-Dawla al-Tashjī'iyya, 74
  Nobel Prize for Literature, 19, 111n, 138n, 142, 192, 217, 261, 262
  Prix de Maison de la Presse, 113
  Prix Goncourt, 113
  Sheikh Zayed Book Award, 251
  State Prize for Children's Literature, 58
Prokofiev, Sergei, 58
pronunciation, 86
  "European pronunciation" (*lukna ūrūbiyya*), 185n
propaganda
  anti-Islamic propaganda, 139n
  Jewish propaganda, 50n
  propaganda for *'āmmiyya*, 171n
Prophet, Prophetic, prophet, 47n, 48, 56, 57, 89n, 112n, 113n, 124, 127, 130, 132, 137, 139n, 147, 155, 194, 197, 219
  Prophetic praise poems, 194
prose, 26, 41, 59, 67–8, 72n, 97, 120n, 131, 134n, 135n, 156, 184n, 185n, 190n, 206–18, 222–3, 226, 241, 245, 248–9, 275
  poetic prose, 132
  popular prose, 67, 81, 249
  prose committee, 201n
  prose masterpieces, 63
  prose poem, 193, 201n, 202, 203, 205–6
  see also fiction, novel, short story
prosecution, prosecutor, 118, 119, 126, 128, 130
prosody, prosodic, 26, 71, 110n, 144n, 199, 201, 202, 206
  accentual/quantitative measures, 202
  basīṭ, 201n
  bayt, abyāt, 159, 187n, 196n
  canons of prosody, 201
  foot, feet, 199
  khabab, 202
  niẓām nabrī, 202
  non-classical metrics, 71n
  prosodic conventions, 71
  rajaz, 202
  taf'īla, 199
  traditional meters, 201
  verse, verses (poetry), 48n, 59, 73n, 77n, 81n, 86, 97, 98, 99, 132, 134–6, 156–9, 177n, 193, 197, 199–205, 208n, 212, 216, 243, 248, 274n, 275, 276
  see also 'aruḍ, meter
prostitutes, prostitution (in literature), 67n, 68n
protagonist (in literary works), 12n, 39, 98, 104, 183
protectorate (French), 180
prototype, 44, 53
  for an Islamic republic of letters, 240, 243
Proust, Marcel, 186
proverbs, 43n, 132, 159
pseudo-correction, 86
pseudonym, pen name, 106, 115, 211, 243
psychology, psychological, 26n, 28n, 64, 100, 162n, 264
psychoanalysis, 265, 270
publishers, publishing houses, printing, 22, 30, 54n, 57, 59, 63, 88, 102n, 117, 119, 121n, 124n, 224, 231, 241, 242, 253, 262, 263n
  Al-Kamel Verlag (*Manshūrāt al-Jamal*), 115
  Dār al-Bashīr, 54n
  Dār al-Biḥār, 65
  Dār al-Fatā al-'Arabī, 60
  Dār al-Hilāl, 65, 88
  Dār al-Hudā, 57
  Dār al-Jadīd, 136n
  Dār al-Kitāb, 57
  Dār al-Ma'ārif, 55, 57, 95n, 120n
  Dār al-Nafā'is, 83
  Dār Rātib, 82
  Dār al-Shurūq, 60, 81n
  Dār al-Ṭalī'a, 126
  Maktabat Miṣr, 57
  Maktabat Usāma, 117
  Manshūrāt 'Uwaydāt, 63
  al-Markaz al-'Arabī li-l-Nashr, 57, 88
  Mu'assasat al-Risāla, 66
  Riyāḍ al-Rayyis, 117
puppets, puppeteer, 222
  puppet shadow theater, 247
Pushkin, Alexander, 231

al-Qabbānī, Abū Khalīl Aḥmad, 221
Qabbānī, Muḥammad Rāshid, 130
Qabbānī, Nizār, 41–5, 107
al-Qadhdhāfī, Mu'ammar, 104n
al-Qāhira (journal), 45n
al-Qa'īd, Yūsuf, 36–8
al-Qā'ida (Al-Qaeda), 104n
al-Qalamāwī, Suhayr, 94n
Qālat al-Arḍ (poetry collection), 136n
Qālū 'an al-Islām: Rasā'il ilā Salmān Rushdī (book), 141
Qamar Shīrāz (poetry collection), 136n
al-Qamḥāwī, 'Izzat, 73n

qāmūs, 37; *see also* dictionary
Qanṭara al-Ladhī Kafara (novel), 37n
al-Qaraḍāwī, Yūsuf, 47n, 48n
Qaraqāsh (verse drama), 99
Qarrādī, 69
Qaṣā'id Ūlā (poetry collection), 135
Qashshū'a, Sayyid (Sayed Kashua), 226n
qaṣīda, 46, 47n, 48n, 80n, 97n, 110n, 144n, 149, 156, 172, 193, 194, 197, 198, 200, 202, 203, 204, 205, 206, 275
  'āṭil, 15n
  'awāṭil, 158n
  'awāṭil al-'awāṭil, 158n
  khayfā', 158n
  mu'jama, 158n
  mulamma'a, 158n
  pre-*qaṣīda* period, 204–5
  qaṣīdat al-'āmmiyya, 172, 80n
  qaṣīdat nathr, 193, 202, 203, 205; *see also* *nathr*; prose poem
  raqṭā', 158n
  see also poetry
Qāsim, 'Abd al-Karīm, 84
Qāsim, Maḥmūd, 58
Qāsim, Muḥammad Khalīl, 48
Qāsim, Samīḥ, 44, 99, 226
Qaṣr al-Shawq (novel), 33, 197, 213
qāṣṣ, quṣṣāṣ, 219n; *see also* storytellers
Qatar, 53, 84, 125, 167n
Qā'ūd, Fu'ād, 206n
Qa'wār, Jamāl, 89n
qawm, qawmiyya, 164, 172n, 198
  thaqāfa qawmiyya, 163
  see also nation; territorial nationalism; *waṭan*
al-Qayrawānī, Ibn Rashīq, 98, 222–3, 224
al-Qazwīnī, Zakariyyā ibn Muḥammad, 235
Qirā'a li-Judrān Zinzāna (poetry collection), 48
Qishṭa, Hishām, 29–30
qiṣṣa, qiṣaṣ, qaṣṣ, 38, 39, 47n, 54n, 57, 213n, 215, 217, 224
  qiṣaṣ al-anbiyā', 206n
  qiṣaṣ būlīsiyya, 82
  see also short story; story, stories
Qiṣṣat Ayyāmī: Mudhakkirāt al-Shaykh Kishk (memoirs), 54n
al-Quds al-'Arabī (newspaper), 48, 151n
Qumm, 48
Qur'ān (Koran), Qur'ānic (Koranic), 15n, 54n, 55n, 116, 119, 122, 124, 125, 126, 127, 128, 130, 134–53, 155, 170–3, 186, 217, 233, 243
  lyrical recordings of the Qur'ān, 128
  Qur'ān and music, 126, 128
  Qur'ānic themes, 51
  riwāyat al-gharānīq, 139n
  sura, suras, 127, 186, 217n
  verse, verses (Qur'ān), 123n, 126, 127, 128, 130, 134–6, 138–42, 146–7, 171, 243
al-Quṭayṭāt al-'Izāz (children's book), 55n
Quṭb, Muḥammad, 55n
Quṭb, Sayyid, 51

Rabat, 104n
Rābiṭat al-Adab al-Islāmī al-'Ālamiyya, 49
Rābiṭat al-'Ālam al-Islāmī, 46n
al-Rābiṭa al-Qalamiyya, 198, 199n
Rābiṭat al-Zajjālīn, 73
race, racism, 94, 133, 171n, 259, 268
  race and identity, 133
  racial manipulation, 259
  tribal racism, 259
radio, 58, 72n, 77, 106, 107
  circulation of transistor radio, 77n
  Egyptian National Radio, 78
  radio and poetry, 106
  satellite radio, 78
  Yemen TV and Radio Corporation, 32n
  see also electronic media
rāfiḍī, 243; *see also* Shiite
al-Rāfi'ī, Muṣṭafā Ṣādiq, 119n, 155n
Raḥbānī, 'Āṣī, 80
Raḥbānī, Elias, 87n
Raḥbānī, Manṣūr, 80
Raḥbānī, Ziyād, 129
al-Rā'ī, 'Alī, 223–4
Rā'id Masraḥ al-Ṭifl al-'Arabī *see* al-Harāwī, Maḥmūd
Rā'if, Aḥmad, 50, 82n
Ra'īs al-Dīwān al-Sulṭānī, 159, 259n
Rajab, Adham, 103n, 218n
rajaz (meter), 202
rakāka, rakīk 40, 159, 196n
Rakhā, Muḥammad, 79–80n
Rakwat 'Arab (musical album), 126
Ramadan, Ramaḍān, 77n, 84, 219
Ramallah, 168n
Rāmī, Aḥmad, 79, 129n
al-Ramla (prison), 49n
al-Ramlī, Linīn (Lenin), 115
Ramses, 84
ramz, 156n; *see also* *ḥisāb al-jummal*
Rapunzel (fairy tale), 57
raqṭā' (*maqāma*), 157n
raqṭā' (*qaṣīda*), 158n
rasmī, 21, 30, 71
  al-rasmiyyūn al-akādīmiyyīn, 22n
  see also official
Rastanāwī, Ḥamza, 276
rational, rationale, rationalism, rationalization, 42n, 94, 120, 148n, 192n, 248
  rationalization of the Qur'ān, 119n
al-Rawḍ al-'Āṭir (book), 45n, 67n, 96, 117
al-Rayūwī, Fāṭima al-Zahrā' (Fatima al-Zohra al-Rghioui), 277
al-Rayyis, Riyāḍ Najīb, 146n
readers, readership, reading public, 1, 10, 14, 27, 29, 31, 32n, 33, 41, 44n, 45, 48n, 49, 57, 65, 75, 82n, 83n, 87, 93n, 96n, 101, 102, 103, 106, 159, 195, 197, 215, 218n, 225, 226, 242, 253n, 262, 263, 273, 276
realism, 31, 51, 202
  Islamist realism *see* *wāqi'iyya Islāmiyya*

realism (*cont.*)
magical realism, 262
socialist realism, 52
reality, 10, 19, 31, 121, 149n, 156, 160, 187, 214, 216, 224, 244, 266, 267n, 269
reality television poetry competition, 36n
representation of reality, 30, 31, 93
rebirth *see* death/rebirth
reception, receptor (of literature), 32, 63n
modes of reception, 16, 23n
reception of *Alf Layla wa-Layla*
reception of Arabic literature, 91n, 94, 11n, 113n, 117, 262n, 263
see also reading, readership
reconstruction, 172
records, recordings, phonographs, 58, 77, 78, 128
reformer, reformist, 11n, 117, 131n
refugees, 10, 13n
region, regional, 5, 9n, 80, 81n, 83n, 125, 148, 151n, 153, 154, 161, 162n, 165, 168n, 182, 185n, 241, 242, 246n, 252, 267
regional literature, 9n
regional pride, 173
regional school/theory, 162n
regression, regressive, 259
"architects of regression," 252, 255
relativism (literary, cultural, historical), 24, 31n, 146
religion, religious, 5, 25, 27, 45–8, 55, 56, 57, 64, 68n, 90, 91, 109, 116–50, 155n, 162n, 170, 179, 188, 219, 235, 238, 243, 254, 261, 264
Greek religion, 25–6
multi-religious society, 126
religion and identity, 149n, 155n, 170
religion and literature, 116–50
"Religion of the Common People," 41n
religious discourse, 54, 56, 134, 144–6
religious fanaticism, 143n, 145, 171n
religious minorities, 243
religious poems, 47, 48n, 78
religious symbols, 89n
religious tolerance, 57, 137, 244
traditional religious fetters, 146–7
renaissance, 155, 169, 177, 178
Arab, 68n, 149, 179, 184, 187, 188n, 194, 220, 223, 248, 261
European, 110n, 233, 260
see also Nahḍa; revival
renovation, 177, 181, 192–3, 204, 205, 208, 210; *see also* periodization
repertoire, repertory (literary), 24, 26, 27, 78, 79, 185n, 272
repetitions, repetitive usage, 3, 177, 180, 199, 200
representations (literary), 11, 30, 31n, 101n, 138n, 211, 262
representative, 28, 38, 41, 73, 131, 132, 185, 215n, 261, 275
republic of letters (république des letters), 5, 6–7, 52, 149n, 237–61, 272n
according to D. Goodman, 7, 249–50
according to M. J. al-Musawi, 6–7, 237–61
according to P. Casanova, 7, 249–59
spaces (temporal, territorial) of the republic, 240–1
terminology, 237–40
resistance, 128, 258
politics of resistance, 48n
"reversed Orientalism," 133; *see also* Orientalism
revival, 88, 120, 142n, 157n, 176, 177n, 183, 197n; *see also Nahḍa*; renaissance
revolt, 37–8, 105
revolt against the father, 188
revolution, revolutionary, x, 29n, 42, 53, 72n, 77n, 102n, 105n, 138, 186
1919 Revolution, 104n
1952 Revolution, 76n, 104n
Islamic revolution in Iran, 128, 133n, 139
Paris revolutionaries, 31n
philological-lexicographic revolution, 250
revolutionary Arab poet, 225
revolutionary vernacularizing thrust, 249–50
technology revolution, 106n, 107
rhetorical, rhetoric, rhetorician, 156, 197, 238–9, 246–7, 249, 256–7, 258n
rhetorical embellishments, 159
rhetorical prose style, 131
rhetorical triumphalism, 194
rhetorical tropes, 195
rhyme, rhyming, 57, 81n
nursery rhymes, 87, 89n, 98, 132, 158, 194, 196, 204, 221; *see also* lullabies; *tahālīl*
Ricci, Ronit, 250n
riddle, riddles 75n, 87, 158n; *see also lughz*; *uḥjiyya*
Riders to the Sea (play), 52
rīf, aryāf, 70, 82, 209, 253n
al-rūḥ al-rīfiyya, 223n
shu'arā' al-aryāf, 70
see also countryside; town/country
al-Rifā'ī, Jalāl, 76
Rif'at, Alīfa, 263n
al-Riḥānī, Amīn, 112n, 149n
Rijāl al-Fikr wa-l-Adab fī al-Najaf (biographical dictionary), 53–4
risāla (genre), 206–7
al-Risāla (journal), 103, 151, 163, 168, 170, 246n
al Risālah (television channel), 56–7
Risālat al-Ghufrān (book), 208–9
rithā', 48; *see also* elegy; *marthiya*
rituals, 47n, 123, 247
dhikr, 47n, 247
mourning rituals, 247
riwāya, riwāyāt, 144, 212n, 224, 225, 276
Riwāya bi-l-'Āmmiyya al-Miṣriyya, 37
Riwāyat al-Bakhīl (play), 220
riwāyāt būlīsiyya, 82–3
"*al-riwāya dīwān al-'arab al-jadīd*," 223
"*al-riwāya mir'āt al-sha'b*," 223
riwāya nisā'iyya, niswiyya see feminist literature

Riwāyat Dal wa-Taymān (novel), 114
riwāyat al-gharānīq, 139n
Riwāyāt al-Jayb, 87
"Riwāya Kāfira," 145
Riwāyat al-Shaqīqatayn (novel), 212
riwāya shi'riyya, 98, 104
riwāya siyāsiyya see political novel
Zaman al-Riwāya (special volume of *Fuṣūl*), 223n
see also fiction; novel
Riyadh, 151
Robinson Crusoe (novel), 18n, 57, 65, 90n, 188–9
Rome, 110
romance, romances, 90n, 92, 110, 184, 187n
historical romance, 10, 91
philosophical romance, 93
romance stories, 211
romantic, romanticism, 83, 94, 132, 180, 193, 198–9, 268
Romanian, 111n
Romans, 31
Rosenthal, Franz, 91, 93, 98n
Rubā'iyyāt al-Khayyām (poetic quatrains), 79n, 129n
Rujū' al-Shaykh ilā Ṣibāhu (book), 96n
rūmansiyyāt, 82–3
al-Ruṣāfī, Ma'rūf, 196
Rushdie, Salman, 123n, 138–47
Russia, Russian, 2, 3, 58, 63, 111, 114, 171n, 232, 264
Rūz al-Yūsuf (magazine), 41n

Ṣa'b, Wilyam, 32n, 80n
Ṣabāḥ (singer), 78
ṣābi'ī, 243
Ṣabrī, Ismā'īl, 132n, 196
Sadan, Joseph (Yūsuf), 21n, 91n
al-Sādāt, Anwar, 72n
al-Sa'dāwī (El Sa'adawi, El Saadaoui), Nawāl, 13n, 49n, 68n, 122–4
Sa'dūn al-Majnūn (play), 114n
Safinat Ḥanān ilā al-Qamar (short stories collection), 118
Ṣafwān, Muṣṭafā, 89n
Sahara, 153–4
Ṣahārīj al-Lu'lu' (book), 131
al-Saḥḥār, 'Abd al-Ḥamīd Jawda, 51n
Sa'īd, 'Alī Aḥmad *see* Adūnīs
Said, Edward W., 114n, 133n, 180, 190n, 261n, 264
saints
birthdays of saints, 219
canonization of Christian saints, 41n
al-Sakkūt, Ḥamdī Sayyid Aḥmad, 22n
Saladin, 132, 144
Salām, Rif'at, 80n, 106n
salāma lughawiyya, 20, 36
salāma mūsīqiyya, 20, 36
Salamāwī, Muḥammad, 124
Ṣāliḥ, Fakhrī, 185n
Ṣāliḥ, Rushdī, 76n
Ṣāliḥ, al-Ṭayyib, 207n, 263n
salons (cultural, literary), 4
Parisian salons, 238
Samad, Yunus, 146
Samarkand (novel), 113
Samīr (comics), 84
Samīr (journal), 62
al-Sammān, Nabīl, 140–1
ṣan'a, ṣinā'a, 15n, 43, 192
ṣan'at al-shi'r, 98
Sand, George, 214
Sandel, Michael J., 270n
Ṣān al-Dīn, Muḥammad 'Abd al-Raḥmān, 47n
Ṣannājat al-Ṭarab (book), 92
Sanskrit, 190n
Ṣanū',Ya'qūb (Jacob Sanua), 221
al-Sāq 'alā al-Sāq (book), 210n
Sara, Sārra, Sarah (doll), 53n
Sarajevo, 48n
Sarḥan, Haitham, 62n
al-Sarūjī, Abū Zayd, 42–4
Satan, Satans, Satanic 123, 139n; *see also The Satanic Verses*
satellite channels, 78, 106n, 155
MBC satellite channel, 84n
satire, satirical
carnivalesque satires, 222n
satire on elitism, 254
satirical plays, 221–2
Sa'ūd, Ṣā'ib, 140
Saudi, Saudi Arabia, 30n, 42n, 50, 54, 56, 83n, 84n, 103n, 108, 125, 137, 143n, 152, 167, 171
Sa'ūdī, Ilhām, 57n
Sawāfī (search engine), 108
al-Sayyāb, Badr Shākir, 47n, 115n, 162, 197n, 199–200
Sayyidatī (magazine), 83n, 84n, 103n
al-Sayyid wa-Marātu fi Bārīs (novel), 36n
Schami, Rafik, 115
Schéhadé, Georges, 113
Scheherazade, 95–6
scholarship (of Arabic literature), x, 1–7, 11, 14n, 22, 25n, 46n, 54, 61, 63–4, 66, 68n, 69, 81, 101, 104, 106, 114n, 131, 141–2, 153–4, 161, 141–2, 182–94, 198–99, 202–3, 218–19, 230–1, 237–78
school, schools, 23n, 53n, 57, 61, 148, 153, 161, 165, 166n, 227, 267
al-Naḥḥāsīn School, 197n
school curricula, 38, 55
science fiction, 10, 11, 13, 29, 81
Scott, Walter, 213n
script, 66n, 84, 107, 108
diacritical points, 156–7
Latin characters, 65n, 66n
sculpture, 95
Second World War, World War II, 87, 180

secular, secularized, secularism, 16, 29, 37n, 46, 48n, 51n, 120, 121, 124n, 131, 133n, 149n, 160n, 219, 243n, 259, 260
secular canonical center, 144
secularism, humanism, and modernism, 259, 260
secularist discourse, 53, 133n, 145
Seekport, 108
self
self-censorship, 121n; *see also* censorship
self-conscious narration, 106
self-esteem, 232–3
self-image (cultural), 27, 108, 232–4, 237, 272
self-reflexive, 178n
self-regarding, 16
self-respect (aesthetic), 15
self-sufficient, self-sufficiency, 26, 163
semiotics, semiotic, 4, 28
semiotic–historic examination, 83n, 103n
semi-theatrical, 12n, 218–19, 247
Senegal, 154n
sensations, sensationalism, 41
sensibility (poetic), 16, 159, 250
series (literary), 57–8, 60, 63–5, 81–9, 120n, 153
Adventures of Tarzan, 88
Aghrab min al-Khayāl, 81n
Arab Women Writers, 101n
Butterfly Series, 58
Écritures Arabes, 112n
Faḍḥ al-Sā'id, 138
Iqra' wa-Lawwin, 57
Ishrāqāt Adabiyya, 74
Kitābāt Ukhrā, 203
Ladybird Series, 57, 58
al-Maktaba al-'Ālamiyya li-l-Fityān wa-l-Fatāyāt, 64
al-Maktaba al-Ṣaghīra, 57n
Makabat al-Aṭfāl, 55
Mughāmarāt Ḥawla al-'Ālam, 58n
Mughāmarāt Ṭarāzān, 88
Rawā'i' al-Adab wa-l-Fikr, 63
Riwāyāt al-Jayb, 87
Shu'arā' al-Da'wa al-Islāmiyya, 46n
al-Silsila al-Būlīsiyya, 88
al-Silsila al-Fanniyya al-Muṣawwara, 77n
Silsilat al-Mashāhīr, 85
Silsilat al-Riwāyāt al-Būlīsiyya, 83
Silsilat Rūmansiyyāt Nātālī, 83
Silsilat al-Shi'r wa-l-Shu'arā', 60
Silsilat Turāth, 264
Silsilat al-'Uṣba al-Khafiyya, 83
serious/light (literature), 19n, 229
sex, sexuality, 11, 12, 41, 67, 68n, 94, 117, 118, 119, 123, 125, 135, 168
Arab sexuality, 13n
explicit sexual language, 168n
repressed sexuality, 94
sex episodes, 42n, 56n, 91n
sex literature, 96
sexual disturbances, 118
sexual fantasies, 94n
sexual perversion, 94
sexual satisfaction, 9
sexual taboos, 147
see also homosexual; lesbian
al-Sha'b (newspaper), 124
shabābī, 78n
al-Shābbī, Abū al-Qāsim, 198
sha'bī, 21, 66, 67, 71, 78
Sha'bola *see* 'Abd al-Raḥīm, Sha'bān
shadow theater, 56n, 218, 219, 222, 247n
Shafer, Boyd C., 161
shaghab jinsī, 118
al-Shahāwī, Aḥmad, 125
shahīd, shaheed, 139n
Shāhīn, Yūsuf, 129
shā'ir (storyteller), 218; *see also* storytellers
shā'ir, shu'arā' (poet), 20, 85, 159, 172, 187n, 200, 222, 260, 277; *see also* poetry
Shakespeare, William, 18, 65, 85, 89n, 187
Shākir, Īhāb, 60n
Shakkūr, George, 206n
al-Sham'a, Khaldūn, 169, 186n
al-Shamandūra (novel), 48n
Shammās, Anton, 116, 148n, 226n, 227n, 263
Shammās, Maurice (Abū Farīd), 135
al-Shanfarā, 208
Sharābī, Hishām, 103
Sharāra, Waḍḍāḥ, 142
Sha'rāwī, Muḥammad Mutawallī, 120n
sharī'a, 46, 55n, 257
Sharīf, Nihād, 82, 190n
sharq, mashriq, 20, 77n, 145, 157, 164, 187–8, 198; *see also* East
al-Sharqawī, 'Abd al-Raḥmān, 169n
al-Sharq al-Awsaṭ (newspaper), 151n
Shā'ūl, Paul, 129
Shaw, George Bernard, 141, 142n
Shawqī, Aḥmad, 41n, 56, 60n, 79, 114, 132, 134, 136, 147, 196, 197, 235
al-Shawqiyyāt al-Majhūla (poetry collection), 41n, 79n
al-Shaykh, Ḥanān, 119, 143n
Shaykh Imām, 72n, 74n, 75, 76n, 77n
al-Shaykh Zubayr, 187; *see also* Shakespeare, William
Sheehi, Stephen P., 128
Sheikh Abdel Rahman, 143n; *see also* 'Abd al-Raḥmān, 'Umar
Shelley, Mary, 64
Shelley, Percy Bysshe, 90n
Shibl, Mālik, 113n
al-Shidyāq, Aḥmad Fāris, 210n
Shifrat da Vinci (novel), 119
Shihāb, 'Abd al-Raḥmān, 129–30
Shiite, 47n, 48, 54n, 68n, 145, 243
Higher Shiite Council (Lebanon), 128
Shinūda (Shenouda) the Third (Coptic Pope), 149n

shi'r, shi'rī, shi'riyya, 20, 26, 37, 47, 54n, 60, 80n, 98, 105, 108n, 115n, 119, 120n, 125, 138n, 144, 151n, 172, 185n, 187, 192, 195, 196n, 198, 200, 202, 277
amīr shi'r al-ṭufūla, 56
malḥama shi'riyya, 264n
ma'sāt shi'riyya, 99n
maṣraḥiyya shi'riyya, 99
riwāya shi'riyya, 98
shi'r 'āmmī, shi'r al-'āmmiyya, 69, 71; *see also* vernacular (poetry); *zajal*
al-shi'r dīwān al-'Arab, 222, 223
al-shi'r al-faṣīḥ, 71
shi'r ḥurr, 48n, 193, 199; *see also* free verse
shi'r khiṭābī, 197
shi'r minbarī, 197
shi'r munāsabāt, 197
shi'r mursal see blank verse
shi'riyyat al-kitāba, 136
shi'riyyat al-shafawiyya al-jāhiliyya, 136
Shi'r (journal [Beirut]), 68n, 203
al-Shi'r (journal [Cairo]), 74
"al-Shi'r" (poem), 198
al-Shirbīnī, Yūsuf, 254, 257
Shklovsky (Shklovskij), Victor, 2–3, 90
Shlashwīq (Schleswig), 235
short story, 12, 28, 39, 46, 48n, 51, 61, 64, 68, 82, 111n, 118, 152, 167, 186, 206–9, 216–18, 223, 227; *see also* fiction; prose; *qiṣṣa*; story
shrūqī, 69
Shu'arā' al-Da'wa al-Islāmiyya (series of books), 46n
Shukrī, 'Abd al-Raḥmān, 143, 198
Shukrī, Ghālī, 22n, 48n, 71, 103, 107, 109, 138, 141, 181, 205n, 232
Shukrī Bāshā, 159, 259n
Shūmān, Mas'ūd, 15
Shumayyil, Shiblī, 141
Shuqayr, Shākir, 158
shurūḥ, 256–7
shu'ūbī, shu'ūbiyya, 45n, 170
al-Sibā'ī, Yūsuf, 38–9
Sicily, 153, 187
siege, 73
ṣīgha nihā'iyya, 136
siḥāq, musāḥaqa see lesbian, lesbianism
Siḥr: Majallat al-Tajaddud wa-l-Fann wa-l-'Ā'ila (magazine), 83n
Sijill al-Thaqāfa al-Rafī'a, 163
Siksak (Sikseck), Ayman, 227n
Simenon, Georges, 88
simile, 132, 206
al-Sinbāṭī, Riyāḍ, 75
sincerity (in literature), 180, 201
Sindi, 55
Sindibād (magazine), 95n
al-Sindibād, 92
al-Sindibād al-Baḥrī (children's book), 56n
singing, singers, songs, 16, 18, 19, 41n, 42, 43, 47n, 56n, 58, 61n, 62, 65n, 69n, 70, 71, 72n, 74n, 75, 76, 77n, 78, 79n, 85, 86, 87, 89n, 97n, 110n, 126–30, 131n, 129n, 165, 169n, 204, 219, 220, 235
Christmas Songs, 87n
folk songs, 70, 87
Iranian revolutionary songs, 128
lyrics of songs, 19, 77n, 126, 193
nationalistic songs, 126
peasant songs, 89n
singing of the Qur'ān, 128, 130
songs in *'āmmiyya*, 65n, 70, 75, 79
singularity, 271
singularity without identity, 271
sīra, siyar, 15n, 20, 90n, 189n, 207, 215
sīra sha'biyya, 15n
Sīrat al-Amīra Dhāt al-Himma, 248n
Sīrat 'Antara, 25n, 90n, 92, 169, 207
Sīrat Banī Hilāl, al-Sīra al-Hilāliyya, 76n, 81n, 207, 248n
Sīrat al-Iskandar, 90n
Sīrat Sayf ibn Dhī Yazan, 248n
Sīrat al-Ẓāhir Baybars, 107, 128n, 207, 248n
Siyar al-Anbiyā', 207
Sirḥān, Samīr, 58n
Sisyphic agony, 16
Sīwa, 225
siyāsat al-batr, 184n
slang, 62
Slavonic, 184
"slough of despond," 251
social, socialist, socialism, 10, 17, 28, 50, 59, 70–2, 100, 106, 123, 133n, 243, 257, 267–70
Nasserist socialism, 133n
social comedy, 221
social criticism, 84
social drama, 30–1, 40, 68
social engineering, 33, 160–1
social media, 125, 274–8
social networks, x, 238
social songs, 86
socialist feminist perspective, 123n
socialist realism, 52
sociocultural, 2, 3, 15, 16, 21, 22n, 103, 159, 184
Socrates, 236
Somali, 55, 167
Soueif, Ahdaf, 263n
Soviet, 141
space, spaces
between text, author, and reader, 4–5
communicative space, 100
cosmopolitan space, 242; *see also* cosmopolis, cosmopolitan
democratization of space, 247
dynamic space of negotiation, 272
geopolitical space, 241
imaginative space, 94
literary space, 4–5, 94, 100, 154n, 241, 249–50, 259, 272
metaphorical space, 241–6

space, spaces (*cont.*)
outer space, 81
space of theory, 172, 238
temporal spaces, 240–1
territorial space, 241–6
urban spaces, 247
Spain, Spanish, 69, 150, 179, 205; *see also* Andalus, Andalusi
sphere, spheres, 6, 51n, 62n, 102, 177, 179, 205, 238, 241, 270
spirit, spiritual, spirituality, 5, 28, 40n, 42, 53, 70, 76, 87, 104, 110, 129, 133, 140, 145, 183, 201, 202, 215, 231, 252, 265, 272, 278
American spirit, 64
cosmopolitan spirit, 267
spirit of the countryside, 223n
spiritual leader, 42n, 68n, 139, 145
Spiro, Socrates, 171n
spontaneous, spontaneity, 45, 180, 276
sport (stories), 10, 64
spy literature, 10, 11, 67
stage, 50n, 99, 221, 222, 247
professional stages, 40, 221
stage directions, 30, 221
stage performance, 221
see also drama; theater
stagnation (in culture and literature), 19n, 185n, 248; *see also* decadence; decline; *inḥiṭāṭ*
standards, standardization, standardized, 15, 18, 21, 23, 28, 31n, 66, 161, 170, 171, 181, 238, 240n
aesthetic standards, 250n
standard-bearer, 23n, 37n
standardization of the *qaṣīda*, 204
standard literary Arabic, 38–9; *see also fuṣḥā*
Starkey, Paul, 108n
status (of text, genre), 13n, 15n, 22, 30, 36–7, 39, 40, 46, 68, 73n, 74, 76, 79–80, 90n, 93, 94, 109, 114, 119, 138n, 151, 152, 155, 168n, 171n, 172, 188, 211–16, 222, 226, 229, 231, 233, 237, 246n, 248, 254
canonical/non-canonical status, 12n, 18, 30, 37, 72, 79, 91, 96, 199, 205
stereotypy, stereotypicity, stereotyping, 3, 177, 200, 210
Stern, Samuel Miklos, 110
Sterne, Laurence, 210n
Stetkevych, Jaroslav, 177n
Stetkevych, Suzanne P., 194, 238
Stewart, Philip J., 138n, 142n
story, stories
adventure stories, 10, 57, 88
animal stories, 57
detective stories, 10, 13, 67, 82, 83, 87, 88
love stories, 10, 67, 82, 83, 87, 91
Qur'ānic stories, 186
romance stories, 211
scientific stories, 57
translated stories, 48n, 55, 62, 87, 88
see also fiction; prose; *qiṣṣa*; short story
storytellers, tellers, 81n, 91, 218–19, 222
itinerant storytellers, 219n
Stowe, Harriet Beecher, 63
stratification (socio-cultural), 2, 21, 22n, 28, 29n, 273
stream of consciousness, 97n
"street" (culture), 247–8
strophic poetry, 71n, 110n, 199, 204, 205
style, stylistic, stylization, 3, 27, 39, 53n, 55n, 69, 76, 79n, 92, 106, 117, 120, 131, 132, 140, 155, 159, 163, 180, 186, 195, 205n, 208–11, 254, 260n, 277
classical style, 208
ornate stylization, 194
poetic style, 196
subjective, subjectivity, subjectivities, 16, 224, 230, 265, 269
Sudan, Sudanese, 129, 154, 167, 198
Suez, 80
Suez Canal, 218
Suez War, 45
Sufi, Sufism, 97n, 110, 117, 132, 25–1
Neo-Sufi, 150
Sufi brotherhood, 132
Sufi experience, 251n
Sufi heritage, 185
Sufi *munshidūn*, 47n
Sufi networks, 242
Sufi orders, 250
Sufi terminology, 250
see also mystic, mystical, mysticism
ṣufrī see Khārijī
Sulaymā (beloved), 198
Sulaymān, Īmān Qāsim, 57
Sulaymān, Muḥammad, 41n
al-Sulaymānī, Laylā (Leïla Slimani), 113
Sumarian, 133
ṣundūq al-dunyā, *ṣundūq al-ʿajab*, 218–19; *see also* peep-show
Sunnī, Sunnis, 130, 243
superficial, 11n, 15, 45, 107, 201
superfluous, superfluity, 181, 256, 257
age of superfluity, 258n
superior, superiority, 19n, 22, 108, 109, 157, 224, 236, 255, 275
Suqūṭ al-Imām (book), 122–3
sūra, *sūras*, 139, 243
Sūrat Yūsuf, 127
surreal, surrealist, surrealism, 97n, 203n
Surūr, Najīb, 98–9
Swahili, 55, 110
Sweden, Swedish, 19, 111, 121n
Syllogisms, 181
symbol, symbolic, symbolist, symbolism, 28, 53n, 95, 105, 110n, 131, 140, 141, 160, 249
market of symbols, 162n
religious symbols, 89n
symbol of femininity, 168n
symbolic capital, 238, 255n
symbolist poetry, 80n

synchrony, synchronic, 23
synchronic cross-section, 4, 35–99, 100, 229, 230, 273
synchronic value, 229, 273
Synge, J. M., 52
syntax, syntactical, 29, 37n
Syria, Syrian, Syriac, 12, 18, 22, 25, 31n, 41, 53, 65, 67, 69, 70, 88, 94, 102, 106n, 107, 110, 115, 121n, 124, 131, 136, 140, 143n, 148–9, 152, 161, 167–71, 179, 183, 212, 213n, 220, 221, 248, 274, 276
Sznaider, Natan, 269
Szyska, Christian, 52n

ṭab'a muqarṣana, 136n
taboos, 12, 41
sexual taboos, 147
Tadjik, 55
taf'īla, 199; *see also 'aruḍ*, meter; prosody
tafkīk see deconstruction
Tagore, Rabindranath, 51
Ṭāhā, 'Alī Maḥmūd, 198
tahālīl, 87n; *see also* lullabies; nursery rhymes
Ṭāhir, Bahā', 83n, 165, 225
al-Ṭahṭāwī, 'Abduh Ismā'īl, 47n
al-Ṭahṭāwī, Rifā'a Rāfi', 56
Tāj, Nabīl, 60n
al-Tajammu' al-Waṭanī al-Taqddumī al-Waḥdawī, 76
tale, tales, 87, 92, 96, 138, 184, 189, 209, 210n, 220
fairy tales, 57
folktale, folkloristic tales, 81n, 97n, 168n
Oriental tales, 93
tales of chivalry, 186
al-Ṭalī'a (journal), 103, 223
tamaddun, 11
tamaddun dākhilī, 11
tamaddun khārijī, 11
Tamil, 55
Ṭanṭāwī, Ḥusayn, 72
Ṭanṭāwī, Muḥammad Sayyid, 143
Taoist, 160n
taqnīn al-'āmmiyya, 172
Ṭarāzān (Tarzan), 88
ṭard, 158n
target literature, 24, 26, 109, 272; *see also* translation
ta'rīb, 232
ta'rīb al-'ulūm, 171n
ta'rīb wa-talkhīṣ, 64
ta'rīḍ, 238
ta'rīkh, tawārīkh, 156n; *see also ḥisāb al-jummal*
ṭarīqa, 132
taṣnīf, 232
taste (in art), 18, 107, 158, 211, 273
aesthetic literary taste, 211
popular taste, 45
tasteless, tastelessness, 4, 18, 215
ta'thīr wa-ta'atthur, 189n; *see also* influence
Tātūr, Dārīn (Dareen Tatour), 125
al-Tawḥīd (journal), 48
tawriya, 159
barā'at al-tawriya, 159
teaching, teachers, 49, 56, 139n, 165, 171n, 191, 197, 235, 245
American Association of Teachers of Arabic, 108n
Arabic language teaching, 108n
classroom instruction, 263n
status of teachers, 197n
Teesing, Hubert Paul Hans, 181
Tehran, 50n, 52, 53n, 148
television, 15n, 36n, 40, 42n, 58, 60, 77, 78, 95, 165, 219, 221
Channel 2 television (Israel), 226
reality television poetry competition, 36n
satellite television channels, 106n
see also electronic media
Telugu, 55
ten Bos, René, 271
terms, terminology, 2, 6, 11, 15, 19n, 21–3, 29n, 46n, 48n, 49, 55n, 62n, 67, 69, 70n, 83n, 104, 108, 131n, 160, 163, 169, 177, 179, 180, 181, 193n, 194n, 198–9, 202, 211, 215n, 227, 230, 232, 235, 237–40, 242, 244, 245–6, 247, 250, 254, 255, 257, 258, 259, 269, 270
generic term, 69
key terms, 65n
Sufi terminology, 250
territory, territorial, territorialism, 5, 6, 17, 150–5, 161, 241–2, 247
territorial narcissism (*narjasiyya quṭriyya*), 169
territorial nationalism, 40, 66, 67n, 80, 151, 160–74
terror, terrorist, terrorism, 53n, 125, 143, 171
11 September 2001 attacks, 56
intellectual terrorism, 122
text, textual (semiotically), 4
online literary texts, 266
primal Text, 256–7
print/ digital texts, 266
sovereignty of an original text, 256
textbooks, 52, 62n
thanawī 243; *see also* dualist
thaqāfa, thaqāfāt, 24n, 164, 236
al-Thaqāfa al-Islāmiyya (book), 52
thaqāfa qawmiyya, 163
thaqāfāt ghāziya, 83; *see also ghazw thaqāfī*
thaqāfa waṭaniyya, 163
The Brethren of Purity see *Ikhwān al-Ṣafā'*
The da Vinci Code (novel), 119
The Golden Treasury (anthology), 192–3
The Good Soldier Švejk (play), 210n
The Hunchback of Notre Dame (novel), 65, 227
The Perfumed Garden, 67n, 96, 117; *see also al-Rawḍ al-'Āṭir*
The Prophet (book), 89n, 112n, 113n
The Satanic Verses (novel), 135n, 138–47
The Simpsons (sitcom), 84n

The Sunday Times Books (newspaper), 11
theater, theatrical, 5, 18, 27, 48n, 50–1, 56, 61, 80, 95, 97, 99, 120, 144, 186, 188, 194, 218–22, 223, 227
audience, spectators, 16, 40, 50, 57, 83n, 109, 114, 179n, 197, 221n, 226n, 262
comedy, 221, 226
farce, 219, 221
Islamic/Islamist theater, 50–1
language in theater, 221
performance, 92, 221, 222, 247
playwrights, 185, 219n, 221
professional theater, 221
semi-theatrical, 12n, 247
Southeast Asian theater, 97
troupes, 221n
see also drama; *masraḥ*
theme, themes, thematic, 6, 10, 13n, 51, 59, 67n, 68, 69, 109, 132, 142n, 162, 169, 180, 185n, 192, 196, 204, 206, 236, 247
ancient themes, 169
Greek themes, 27n
national themes, 70
Qur'ānic themes, 51
religious themes, 47, 150
sexual themes, 91n, 92, 94, 96
thematic allusions, 169
theory, theoretical, 71, 99n, 149, 172, 190, 209, 274
genre theory, 5, 175
literary theory, 28n
Marxist theory, 102, 103n
postcolonial theory, 96
regional theory, 162n
space of theory, 172, 238
theory/praxis, 185n
world-systems theory, 238
Theroux, Peter, 138n
Third World, 45
thrillers, 10, 50n, 67, 84
thulāthiyya malḥamiyya see epic trilogy
ṭibāq, 159
al-Tīfāshī, Shihāb al-Dīn Aḥmad, 67n
Tigris, 248
titillation, 41
title, titles, subtitles (literary), 12n, 21n, 37n, 84n, 139n
titles (publications), 63, 101n
Togo, 154n
Tolstoy, Leo Nikolayevich, 141
tonal system, 202
tongue, 155, 245
mother tongue, 162, 227
sacred tongue, 123, 155n, 214
vulgar tongues, 249
see also 'āmmiyya; Arabic; *fuṣḥā*; language
totalitarian, totalitarianism, 16, 161
town/country, 223n; *see also rīf, aryāf*
Ṭrād, Michel, 80, 172
tradition, traditional, 36, 47n, 53n, 55n, 62n, 66n, 67n, 69, 71n, 77, 91, 97, 108n, 110, 112, 122, 128n, 132, 136n, 137n, 138, 139n, 146, 149n, 150, 156, 176, 183, 185, 194, 199, 212, 213, 219, 220, 222, 224n, 242, 246, 252, 256, 257, 260, 261, 267
anti-traditionalist teleology, 268
great tradition/little tradition, 21n
invented traditions, 160–1
literary tradition, 46, 148, 153, 154, 177n, 184, 186, 195, 198, 200, 205n, 206, 211, 216, 275
Orientalist tradition, 26n
traditional culture, 170, 182n
tragedy, 45, 48n, 99n, 114, 247n, 264
transformation, 72, 133n, 136, 176, 230, 246, 249, 265, 269
Transjordan, 152, 179
translation, 4, 9, 12, 19, 24–7, 32–3, 35, 46, 51, 48n, 54–8, 62–5, 79, 81–4, 87–96, 109–19, 128, 138n, 151–5, 180, 188–90, 193, 195, 207–16, 220, 221, 227, 229, 231–2, 238–9, 241, 242, 263, 266, 272, 275
into English, 111n
into French, 111n
into German, 111n
into Hebrew, 111n
into Italian, 111n
into Romanian, 111n
into Russian, 111n
into Spanish, 111n
into Swedish, 111n
target literature, 24, 26, 109, 272
translation market, 64
translational norms, 65n, 90
transliteration, xii, 279n
travel literature, 54n, 57–8, 109n, 131–2, 241, 244
tribe, tribes, 171, 222
tribal racism, 259
tribal sheikhs, 225
trilogy, 99, 197, 215, 217; *see also* epic trilogy
Tristram Shandy (novel), 210n
trivial, triviality (in literature), 2, 19n, 184n
trop, trops, 134, 156, 185n, 195, 241
troubadours, 110n
Troy, 43–4
Troy (Michigan), 57, 63, 65, 87n, 88n
al-Tūnī, Ḥilmī, 60n
Tunis, Tunisia, Tunisian, 29n, 61n, 85n, 86, 125–6, 152, 167, 170, 172, 179, 198, 253
al-Tūnisī, Bayram, 36, 72, 73, 74, 75, 78, 80n, 85–7, 206
Ṭūqān, Fadwā, 168n, 226n
Ṭūqān, Ibrāhīm, 197n
al-Ṭūr (prison), 48n
turāth, 39n, 40, 48, 66n, 95n, 133, 134n, 145, 147n, 164, 172, 203n, 260n, 264n, 277; *see also* heritage
Turgenev, Ivan Sergeyevich, 231–2
Turkey, Turks, Turkish, 25, 49, 50n, 52, 54, 55n,

von Grunebaum, Gustave E., 26n, 110
vulgar, vulgarity (literature), 32, 140
  expressions, 12n
  stories, 56
  tongues, 249

Wādī, Ṭāhā, 224
Wāḥat al-Ghurūb (novel), 225
al-Waḥsh, Nabīh, 123
Wajdī, Muḥammad Farīd, 119n
Walīma li-A'shāb al-Baḥr (novel), 124
Wannūs, Sa'd Allāh, 219n
wāqi'iyya Islāmiyya, 52
war, wars, 70, 166, 171n, 259, 267
  1967 War, 76, 227
  First World War, World War I, 87, 161, 269n
  Gulf War, 85n
  interwar period, 180, 199
  Lebanon War (1982), 126
  October War (1973), 104n
  religious wars, 238
  Second World War, World War II, 87, 180
  Suez War, 45
al-Warda al-Bayḍā' (film), 65n, 79n
Ward Aqall (poetry collection), 126–7
al-Wardī, 'Alī, 15n
Warren, Austin, 181
waṣāyā, 55n
Waṣāyā fī 'Ishq al-Nisā' (poetry collection), 125
waṭan, waṭaniyya, waṭanī, 37, 86, 140, 162, 172, 187n, 200
  thaqāfa waṭaniyya, 163
  see also nation; *qawm*; territorial nationalism
Wāzin, 'Abduh, 119
Weidner, Stefan, 115n, 147n
Wellek, René, 181
West, Western, 14–15, 16, 17n, 20, 31, 45n, 52, 53n, 56, 57, 61n, 63, 82, 84, 89, 91, 93, 94, 96, 97, 99, 102n, 103, 108–16, 138, 141, 180, 211, 216, 230–7, 260–4, 272
  Western civilization, 10n, 11, 233, 235, 272
  Western culture, 11n, 53n, 81, 84, 94, 103, 108, 109, 184, 187, 193, 194, 231, 232, 263, 272
  Western scholarship, 54n, 55n, 60, 64, 66, 71n, 81, 101, 107, 151, 155, 161, 167, 180–94, 218, 252, 265, 274n
  Westernization, 11, 50n, 109, 114
  see also East; Europe
Wild, Stefan, 118n
Willcocks, William, 171n
William Tell (story), 57
Willmore, John Selden, 171n
Wilson, Edmund, 11n
Wodehouse, P. G., 10
world literature, 6, 24n, 93, 94n, 106, 113n, 148, 161n, 167, 238, 240, 242, 258, 261, 272
worth, 61, 71n, 74, 152, 190n, 229
  aesthetic worthlessness, 18
  see also evaluation, merit, value

Yāghī, 'Abd al-Raḥmān, 188n
Yannakakis, Ilios, 267–8
Yāsīn, Kātib (Kateb Yacine), 113, 170n
Yāsīn wa-Bahiyya (play), 98–9
al-Yāzijī, Ibrāhīm, 132n
al-Yāzijī, Nāṣīf, 134–6, 148n, 156–8
Yemen, Yemenite, 22n, 32n, 137n, 173n, 257
Yoruba, Yorubaland, 154n
Young, George, 192
Yūnus, 'Abd al-Ḥamīd, 15n
Yūnus, Ibtihāl Kamāl, 121
Yūsuf, 'Abd al-Tawwāb, 60n, 94n
al-Yūsuf, Fāṭima (Rūz), 41n
Yūsuf, Rashād, 47n
Yūsuf, Sa'dī, 60n, 225n

al-Zabūr, 233
al-Zahāwī, Jamīl Ṣidqī, 196, 223
Zaḥla, 172
zajal, azjāl, 30, 32n, 41n, 69–81, 85n, 86, 97n, 110n, 172, 205n, 206n, 247, 248n; *see also shi'r 'āmmī*; vernacular (poetry)
Zakhyā, 'Abd Allāh, 128
Zakī, Aḥmad, 232
Zalaṭ, Aḥmad, 61
Zarqā' al-Yamāma, 97n
Za'rūr, Mnashshī, 130n
Zaydān, Jurjī, 114, 141, 147n, 212–13, 253
Zaynab (novel), 211
Zayyād, Tawfīq, 48n
al-Zayyāt, Aḥmad Ḥasan, 25n, 90n, 251–61
Zévaco, Michel, 214
zindīq, 243; *see also* blasphemy; heretic; *mulḥid*
Zionist, Zionism, anti-Zionist, 30, 42, 104, 140
Ziyāda, Mayy, 22
Zomorodian, Ahmad, 139
Zoroastrian, 243
Zu'aytir, 'Ādil 'Umar, 210n
Zubayda (Zubaida), Sāmī, 268n
Zughayyib, Henri, 89n
Zuhur, Sherifa, 123n
Zuqāq al-Midaqq (novel), 12n, 67n

EU representative:
Easy Access System Europe
Mustamäe tee 50, 10621 Tallinn, Estonia
Gpsr.requests@easproject.com

www.ingramcontent.com/pod-product-compliance
Lightning Source LLC
Chambersburg PA
CBHW052054300426
44117CB00013B/2124
9781474441254